CRIMINAL JUSTICE
A Public Policy Approach

CRIMINAL JUSTICE
A Public Policy Approach

JAMES P. LEVINE

Brooklyn College
of the City University of New York

MICHAEL C. MUSHENO

Center of Criminal Justice
Arizona State University

DENNIS J. PALUMBO

University of Kansas

 HARCOURT BRACE JOVANOVICH, INC.

New York San Diego Chicago San Francisco Atlanta
London Sydney Toronto

ISBN: 0-15-516094-X

Library of Congress Catalog Card Number: 79-65389

Printed in the United States of America

Picture credits appear on page 591.

To

Della, Joan, Sachiko

PREFACE

The ideas behind this text originated on a train bound from New York City to Washington, D.C., in January 1974, when the authors began what was to become a long-term collaboration on various criminal justice projects. We were then acting as consultants to a research institute that was studying the impact of a relatively new form of handling criminal cases called "diversion." An understanding of why the three of us agreed to take on this consulting responsibility (and others that followed) provides a key to the approach that we subsequently developed in this text to explain how the criminal justice system works. We were seeking professional recognition, intellectual challenge, and money; it is our contention that a similar set of self-interests motivates criminal justice institutions and officials—for better or for worse. As time passed, our own self-interest led us to the theory of self-interest that we use to analyze diversion as well as many other criminal justice practices and policies discussed in this book.

After this initial theoretical work, we undertook two field studies, one for the New York City Police Department and one for the New York City Housing Authority, both of which enriched our perspective on criminal justice. The first was a study of crime in the New York garment district, an area of Manhattan where a large percentage of the clothes sold in this country is produced. As we interviewed manufacturers, union leaders, insurance agents, and others, we began to recognize that the costs of reducing crimes against business were more than the losses generated by the crimes (which are generally passed on to the consumer in higher prices). Schemes for reducing theft by employees might generate the wrath of unions, and truckers engaged in extortion would not react too kindly to attempts to check them. For most manufacturers, it seemed better to tolerate a certain level of crime in the industry than to try to fight it. Our study thus enlightened us about the wide range of interests affected by crime, indicated how crime-reduction proposals have varying impacts on these interests, and highlighted the importance of self-interest politics in dealing with crime.

The garment district investigation also substantiated the usefulness of our self-interest theory in explaining the behavior of officials. Too often the police seemed more concerned about "street crimes" that occurred in the area than about tangling with complex white-collar crimes or the largely clandestine infiltration of organized crime. Going after prostitutes and purse-snatchers can generate arrests that capture public attention and make the police look effective.

Our second study was an evaluation of a security program in a large New York City public housing project. High-crime areas such as lobbies were outfitted with cameras that beamed pictures into the television sets of all the residents in the buildings. Interviews with residents that we conducted before and after the equipment was installed indicated that this attempt at deterring crime was a failure.

This study taught us several lessons about criminal justice. First, it underscored the importance of careful measurement of outcomes in the assessment of crime policy. No matter how plausible any crime-prevention approach sounds, its ultimate virtue depends on its demonstrated effectiveness. What is good in theory may be terrible in practice.

Second, we learned that criminals are a wily and persistent lot who are fairly adept at guarding their own self-interests. They were apparently able to outsmart the system: equipment was vandalized, which put the whole program out of commission for periods of time, and locations for crime outside camera range were discovered. What this suggested is that crime policy must be multifaceted to be effective and that simple measures designed to crack down on criminals are likely to go awry.

Finally, we were alerted to the decisive role of implementation if criminal justice policies are to be successful. From its outset, the security project was plagued with bureaucratic unresponsiveness that kept its potential from ever being realized. Contractors were lax in making repairs; housing officials failed to instruct residents about security procedures and took no steps to encourage greater use of the equipment; personnel assigned to view central monitors were haphazard in their performance; police on the premises balked at efforts to improve telephone communications with residents. This bungling and shirking of obligations attests to the importance of organizational follow-through in transforming mere policies into operational crime-prevention strategies.

We have since collaborated on a number of other research projects, and over the years each of us separately has been involved in criminal justice research, consulting work, and administration in a variety of capacities. In this book we have tried to provide an integrated understanding of the criminal justice process by blending theory, fact, and the intuitive knowledge we have gained from rubbing shoulders with real-world problems and practices.

An empirical spirit pervades the text. Legalistic analysis is kept to a minimum, because we believe that the study of legal procedures and formal rules in itself tells us little about how the criminal justice system really works. Instead we have used the findings of social scientists, who have systematically observed the actual behavior of officials, criminals, victims, and social groups to discover how laws on the books affect the norms and practices of everyday life. We have also included the accounts of insiders, reports of recent events, and some fictional dramatizations, in places where they illuminate themes more convincingly than do the frequently bland and lifeless statistics amassed in quantitative studies. We have drawn on our diverse experiences of Indianapolis; Lawrence, Kansas; Minneapolis; New York City; Phoenix; and a rural section of upstate New York, where we have lived at various times, to inform our description of the American criminal justice system. Thus we have unabashedly gleaned our materials from a host of objective and not-so-objective sources, which helps demonstrate the wisdom of Supreme Court Justice Oliver Wendell Holmes's classic statement "The life of the law has not been logic but experience."

The conceptual framework that ties together all the information in the text reflects our background as political scientists. Much of the analysis assumes that decision making in criminal justice is the result of conflicts of interest and clashes of values. Various processes are used to resolve this discord, such as bargaining, compromise, persuasion, manipulation, deception, and the use of force. Choices of goals and selection of concrete policies are primarily the result of a rough-and-tumble political process.

The subtitle of this book is *A Public Policy Approach.* In our opinion, it is not enough merely to understand what government officials do and what accounts for their actions; it is also necessary to be sensitive to the consequences of their behavior. Therefore, our focus is not just on the inputs of decision making but on its outcomes—the impact of policies on people, groups, and the values they hold. One part of the text is devoted to an examination of four specific policies that have been commonly attempted to cope with crime, and another section describes procedures for evaluating any policy scientifically. While this kind of critical analysis cannot in itself remedy the many imperfections in our criminal justice system, it perhaps can prevent a repetition of some of the blunders of the past, reduce some squandering of scarce resources, and curtail the adoption of proposals that are futile or self-defeating. While we as authors can only suggest modest positive reforms, we believe that the experimental, questioning approach to public policy that we advocate is the best hope for improvement in the field of criminal justice.

Each of us brought certain areas of expertise to the writing of the text. Within these areas we each wrote five chapters, revised them extensively, and eventually combined our efforts to produce the final version. Levine had primary responsibility for Chapters 1, 6, 7, 9, and 13; Musheno for Chapters 2, 5, 11, 12, and 15; and Palumbo for Chapters 3, 4, 8, 10, and 14. At every stage of the process, interaction between us was intense and continual. This was truly a collaborative effort, and therefore we list our names alphabetically.

In writing the book, we benefited enormously from the careful reviews of early drafts by a number of eminent criminal justice authorities in political science, sociology, and law. We appreciate the constructive spirit with which the critiques were offered. We would like to thank all these reviewers, especially Don Gibbons, Portland State University; James Eisenstein, Pennsylvania State University; Joel Grossman, University of Wisconsin; Dorothy Guyot, Rutgers University; Gordon Hawkins, University of Chicago Law School; Samuel Krislov, University of Minnesota; Norval Morris, University of Chicago Law School; Tom Murton, formerly of the University of Minnesota; Stuart Nagel, University of Illinois; Raymond Nimmer, Bates School of Law, University of Houston; David Perry, University of Texas; Albert Reiss, Yale University; Wesley Skogan, Northwestern University; and Franklin Zimring, University of Chicago Law School.

Joanne Daniels, our editor at Harcourt Brace Jovanovich, encouraged us to undertake the book, efficiently handled the myriad of technical matters that arose, and provided unwavering moral support. Lee Shenkman and Elaine Romano did a superb job of editing the manuscript—improving the quality of the writing, detecting errors, and forcing us to clarify our thinking, We also wish to thank the staff of Harcourt Brace Jovanovich for their cooperation and assistance.

Over the course of our careers, many people have contributed to the development of our thinking and supported our work. As we wrote this book and engaged in the research that preceded it, the three of us have received invaluable help from students, secretaries, colleagues, government officials, and a host of other unsung individuals. We thank them all.

James P. Levine
Michael C. Musheno
Dennis J. Palumbo

CONTENTS

CHAPTER THREE

Criminals: What Makes Them Tick? 68

CHAPTER FOUR

The Making of Criminal Justice Policy 116

P A R T   T W O   **The Agencies of the Criminal Justice Establishment 155**

CHAPTER   SEVEN

Decision Making by Courts: The Speculative Nature of Adjudication   242

CHAPTER EIGHT

CHAPTER NINE

CHAPTER TEN

Rehabilitation: The Orthodox Cure
for Criminal Behavior 400

CHAPTER ELEVEN

Decriminalization and Legalization: Shrinking the Scope
of Criminal Codes 430

CHAPTER TWELVE

Diversion of the Accused: Community-Based
Conflict Resolution, Counseling, and Treatment **462**

P A R T   F O U R   **Assessing and Improving Criminal Justice Policy 489**

PART ONE

ANALYZING CRIME AND CRIMINAL JUSTICE

Criminal justice matters have overwhelmed Americans. Newspapers are filled with stories of crime; election campaigns often focus on it; and it is a major concern to average Americans throughout the nation. The dramatic escalation in public expenditures for law enforcement at local, state, and federal levels reflects this concern. The prominence of the crime problem in American society is an undebatable fact of life.

Only a few years ago undergraduate courses in criminal justice were almost unknown while today entire departments and curricula are devoted to the topic. A whole field of research has blossomed, reflected in the outpouring of books and periodicals devoted exclusively to crime and justice. Occupations that traditionally involved relatively little formal instruction, such as that of police officer, are being steadily professionalized; and entirely new careers that require technical expertise, such as court administrator, are being developed. Criminal justice is becoming a scholarly field with its own vocabulary, standardized practices, and research methodology.

These developments have had two contradictory effects. On the one hand, our knowledge about criminal justice has been enhanced as every facet of law and crime is studied and restudied in meticulous detail. This has resulted in the debunking of much folklore about law and crime. But on the other hand new myths and half-truths have appeared; and some have gained widespread acceptance. So, although both the public and professionals have become saturated with information, fact and fiction are often difficult to distinguish. The dynamics of criminal justice remain shrouded in mystery.

This confusion has hindered attempts to improve the law enforcement process. First, all of the rhetoric and publicity about crime have raised public expectations so high that modest reforms and partial solutions are dismissed as unsatisfactory. Part I shows that there are very real limits to what can be accomplished and stresses the importance of examining the practical and political feasibility of policies that are advocated.

Second, our failure to comprehend the intricacies of the criminal justice system has caused our efforts to be misdirected. In order to increase opportunities for containing crime while simultaneously respecting other values such as due process and justice, we must stop looking at law enforcement as simply a pitched battle between the forces of good and evil. Rather, we must recognize that self-interests govern the worlds of the criminal, the victim, the official—as well as the larger society affected by all of them. The fundamental theme of Part I is that the criminal justice process entails continuous conflicts and compromises among many different competing values and interests. In both the adoption and implementation of policies, choices of ends and means must be made—and the influence of political factors on such decisions is inescapable.

An understanding of these dynamics is essential if our growing knowledge about criminal justice is to be put into practice. Learning about the motivation and interests of those involved with crime can not only explain why certain practices persist but it can help reveal what is necessary to make criminal justice decision makers responsive to new information and ideas. Improvement in the field of criminal justice requires both sophistication about strategies and goals and a sensitivity to the political and social environments in which policies are applied.

The overall purpose of Part I, then, is to provide a perspective for analyzing criminal justice that enables us to distinguish myths about how the system is supposed to operate from the reality of its actual functioning. Certain fallacies about the law are exposed: Legal rules alone do *not* determine how police and courts behave; the public interest is *not* the only concern of lawmakers; the law is almost invariably a political instrument used to benefit some at the expense of others. Misconceptions about crime and criminals are similarly corrected: Crime "waves" are *not* a new phenomenon but have recurred regularly in the past; the criminal population does *not* share some common character defect or psychological perversion but is made up of rather ordinary people who through prior background or present circumstance become entangled in particular kinds of criminal pursuits; what is considered criminal behavior is *not* determined exclusively (or even primarily) by legal codes but is, in fact, a complex social-judgment process in which prevailing moral sentiments are brought to bear.

In place of these mistaken notions a conceptual framework is created based on certain basic human characteristics, organizational behavior, and social forces, as well as the political process as a whole. The result is what we call a "public policy approach"—an emphasis on what government can accomplish in the field of criminal justice based on a knowledge of the system's inner workings and external milieu. The major ingredient in this analysis is political choice.

Chapter 1 articulates an interest theory of criminal justice motivation that is utilized throughout the book. Public policy choices and the evolution of routine practices are shown to result from the interplay of self-serving motives and conflicting public goals. A variety of personal ambitions such as career satisfaction and the drive for power dictates certain kinds of behavior and influences which goals take priority in defining the public interest. Certain sacrifices and exchanges must be made in choosing among competing goals such as crime prevention and due process, and more often than not the resolution of the clash of individual, institutional, and special interests determines the final outcome.

The nature of crime and the way it is perceived are the topics of Chapter 2. In pursuit of their own self-interests politicians, bureaucrats, the media, and the academic community often misrepresent the crime problem or give only one side of it. They exaggerate the extent of crime, oversimplify its causes, and propose unrealistic solutions. In fact, experts disagree about the true dimensions of the crime peril or how best to cope with it. The complexities of crime create formidable obstacles to its elimination and make significant reduction of it an elusive goal.

Chapter 3 takes a close look at criminals. What becomes clear is that they represent a broad spectrum of humanity and that no single theory can explain what channels them into illegal activities. In many respects they are like law-abiding people in their pursuit of self-interest, except that they go beyond certain accepted constraints in advancing their own cause. In order to deal with criminals effectively and to muster the resources necessary to reduce crime, we must understand how criminals perceive themselves and how society views them.

Finally, Chapter 4 examines the formulation and implementation of policy in criminal justice, which together are shown to be a patchwork of often uncoordinated and sometimes inexplicable decisions made by a wide assortment of personnel. But while the activities of officialdom are highly discretionary, they are not random. What appears to be irrationality is normally the operation of a complex set of political and bureaucratic imperatives. Policy making is almost inevitably a process of "muddling through"—the balancing of multiple demands, interests, and priorities. While criminal justice leadership can play an important role in defining and redefining policy, the influence of political elites, public opinion, interest groups, and organizational structures is crucial in determining what initiatives are taken and which ones are carried out. Because so many people and agencies are involved in the establishment of policy, the status quo is quite resistant to change.

From 1953 to 1969 Earl Warren served as chief justice of the United States Supreme Court. In this position he led the Court as it made its far-reaching decisions in favor of human rights—ending segregation in public schools, providing the right to counsel in criminal cases for poor defendants, banning prayers in the schoolroom, and requiring fair apportionment of legislatures. Many praised the Court's decisions during this era while others raged bitterly against them, but virtually everyone admits that Warren was one of the most forceful chief justices in American history.

How did Warren gain his post? The answer is simple— through a lifetime spent in partisan politics, during which time he ran for public office eight times.[1] For two decades he was the most important Republican in the state of California; he held every major office in that state, including the gover-

CHAPTER ONE

CONFLICTING PRIORITIES
Private Motives and Public Interests in Criminal Justice

norship for 11 years. He ran as the Republican vice-presidential candidate in 1948 and came close to obtaining that party's nomination for the presidency in 1952. When Dwight Eisenhower was chosen the party's candidate instead, Warren, a firm believer in party loyalty, campaigned all over the country and helped Eisenhower win a landslide victory. Eisenhower soon rewarded Warren with the chief justiceship—one of the most coveted positions a president can bestow.

And where did Warren get his start? By shrewd and delicate maneuvering, he managed to advance from deputy in the Alameda County (Oakland) prosecutor's office to district attorney, a position that had fallen vacant due to a resignation. Thereafter, he conducted his affairs in office with one thing always in mind: "Get elected."[2] He aggressively exposed massive corruption in Oakland, sending many public officials and private citizens to jail. He challenged the entrenched vice peddlers—bootleggers, drug pushers, and gamblers. No target was immune—from Republican party bosses, to figures in organized crime, to the pillars of high society involved in graft.

To the public he appeared as a heroic crusader, a courageous knight on a white horse, attacking the bastions of sin, greed, and entrenched power. For the ambitious Warren, the fight paid off: three times he was returned to the district attorney's office by ever-increasing margins. His 13-year tenure as district attorney proved to be a victory for law enforcement in Oakland and an invaluable political staging ground for Warren. An aspiring politician's personal self-interest and the public's interest in vigilant law enforcement and honest government went hand in hand.

Far-removed from the world of California politics, in the Arkansas prison system, self-interest was equally important for many years—but with grievously different consequences. In most prisons control of prisoners is the main priority of wardens and guards.[3] Inmates grossly outnumber prison officials, so the latter are always faced with the difficult job of obtaining obedience to the highly op-

7

pressive rules of prison life. Violence, rebellion, and unlawful behavior are persistent threats to prison order. Unruly prisoners can pose an acute physical danger to guards. Forcing people to live a regimented, dreary, and often brutal life for long periods of time is no mean task.

This becomes evident to the public when riots break out, guards are taken hostage, and inmates temporarily take over. But smaller, less newsworthy "incidents" are a daily phenomenon of prison life—smuggling of narcotics, possession of home-made weapons, sabotage of work routines, and disruption of mess halls. Prison officials are in a constant struggle, sometimes of a life-and-death nature, to keep their captive populations under control.

To cope with this problem, officials in two Arkansas prisons in the past resorted to gruesome methods of punishment in order to keep recalcitrant prisoners in line and to intimidate others who might contemplate resisting authority. At Tucker Prison, troublemakers were punished with a contraption called the "Tucker telephone," which was still in use as recently as 1968. The device consisted of an old-fashioned crank telephone that was connected to two dry-cell batteries. Wires from this apparatus were connected to the big toe and penis of an offending inmate, who had been stripped naked and strapped to a table. Turning the crank would send excruciating electric shocks through the prisoner's testicles, causing some of them to "go out of their mind."[4] Fear of such gruesome treatment kept most prisoners totally obedient—no matter how arbitrary the commands they were given.

A sister institution in Arkansas, Cummins Prison, went even further to keep inmates in line. It was revealed in 1968 that prisoners had been routinely murdered as punishment for offenses and then buried in a remote cow pasture. Three skeletons were unearthed during excavations ordered by a reform-minded prison superintendent, and the total number of killings is estimated to be over 100.[5]

The use of such barbaric tactics no doubt helped officials keep order. Few prisoners would dare to risk the wrath of officials who used such ghastly sanctions. But the self-interest of wardens and guards in maintaining order took a terrible toll in human lives and suffering. Basic notions of fairness, justice, and human decency were disregarded in order to make the job of officials safer and easier.

The two episodes just described, Warren's use of the prosecutor's office in his rise to political power and the Arkansas prison officials' inhuman-control methods, illustrate a fundamental theme of this book: *The behavior of criminal justice officials and the policies they pursue are often dictated by self-serving motivations.* Sometimes the consequences of this phenomenon are positive, as when a young, politically unknown prosecutor establishes his reputation and advances his career by ferreting out crime. At other times the impact of self-interest can undermine important social ideals, as the indefensible Arkansas prison experience demonstrates. But for better or worse, the pursuit of self-interest is an inherent part of human nature; it significantly influences the behavior of public officials as much as it affects everyone else. Personal goals and priorities are the key to understanding and improving the criminal justice system.

Self-Interest in Criminal Justice: A Theory of Motivation

Self-interest is a complex concept. Basically it refers to the wide-ranging set of personal aspirations that motivate much human behavior. We say that people act in their self-interest when they are concerned primarily with advantages to themselves rather than the needs of other people or the good of the society. It is a notion aptly expressed in the title of the best-selling book *Looking Out for Number One*, a phrase that means paying attention to one's own needs and desires and directing one's efforts to satisfying them.[6]

Self-interest obviously motivates criminals. Although the causes of crime are many (as Chapter 3 will explain), the quest for economic gain certainly accounts for a great deal of lawbreaking. When the famed outlaw Willie Sutton was asked why he robbed banks, he supposedly answered, "Because that's where the money is." What is amusing about this response is its straightforward honesty; it is a simple explanation that rings true. People will often violate the law if they decide probable gains outweigh the risk; they will steal and even kill to get what they want—regardless of the havoc they may wreak on the lives of others.

A similar kind of self-centeredness explains much *non*criminal behavior, including many of the actions of law enforcers; in short, the cops and robbers have much in common regarding ultimate aims. While moral norms and fear of sanctions do inhibit may public servants from using illegal or improper means to accomplish their own ends, their behavior can often best be understood by searching for personal motives that have little to do with the broader functions of their jobs.

One reason why personal motives are sometimes overlooked is that they may result in good works being done. Thus some prominent (often high-priced) lawyers who defend unfairly persecuted clients with tremendous vigor may be doing so mainly for the lucrative fee they are earning. But the net result is every bit as desirable as if they had acted selflessly: Due process is honored and the right to a fair trial is protected.

Sometimes underlying motives are concealed from public view because they are camouflaged by persuasive rationalizations. Such might be the case when police officers justify not wearing name tags because they and their families might be harassed by individuals they arrest. In reality, the reason for refusing to wear name tags may be to make it difficult for citizens to report improper police behavior.

Thus, in this book we adopt the orientation of Anthony Downs, who writes in his treatise on bureaucracy: "We assume that every official acts at least partly in his own interest, and some officials are motivated solely by their own self-interest."[7] This viewpoint is supported by a great volume of empirical research on the criminal justice system that demystifies the legal process and recognizes that those involved are flesh-and-blood individuals with their own lives to consider. Rationality, or goal-directed behavior, is now more often associated with individuals in criminal justice agencies than with the agencies themselves. A picture is emerging wherein "the idealized perspective of the *rational organization* pursuing its single set of goals is replaced by a perspective of the set of *rational individuals* who comprise the system, in this case the prosecutor, defense counsel, police, defendant, clerks, etc. pursuing their various individual goals."[8]

Although this kind of conceptualization has only recently been applied to criminal justice, it is by no means original. Over the centuries the analyses of many political philosophers have assumed the primacy of self-interest.

Indeed, the works of Englishman Thomas Hobbes (1588–1679), who has been called the founder of the scientific approach to the study of politics, state that the instinct for self-preservation lies behind all human activities. Life, according to Hobbes, is an endless pursuit of the means for survival, a constant struggle for self-protection. And because the security obtained is always destructible in a moment, the quest for power to provide for future security is insatiable. In a famous passage, Hobbes makes the point baldly:

> I put for a general inclination of all mankind, a perpetual and restless desire of power after power, that ceaseth only in death. And the cause of this, is not always that a man hopes for a more intensive delight than he has already obtained to; or that he cannot be content with a more moderate power; but because he cannot assure the power and means to live well, which he hath present, without the acquisition of more.[9]

Perhaps this outlook sounds cynical, but the framers of the American Constitution (who were political theorists in their own right) constructed the American political system on just such a premise about human nature. The intellectual justification of the Constitution is found in *The Federalist*, a set of essays written by James Madison, Alexander Hamilton, and John Jay, who were the architects of its basic provisions.[10] According to Madison, who borrowed many of his ideas from philosopher John Locke, one of the inevitable results of freedom is that people would pursue their own selfish desires; therefore, political institutions have to be created to contain and reconcile them. In *The Federalist*, No. 10 and No. 48, Madison explicitly argues that concepts such as the separation of powers, federalism, and checks and balances are designed to combat the pernicious effects of "factions"—groups of people acting in concert to benefit themselves at the expense of others.[11]

Another philosopher, Jeremy Bentham, a strong advocate of political liberalism and one of the earliest criminologists, based his thinking on axioms about self-interest as well. *All* decisions in life, in his view, are based on hedonism—the desire to obtain personal happiness, defined as the attainment of pleasure and the avoidance of pain. Where the satisfaction of these drives interferes with the happiness of others, laws are passed imposing painful punishments that outweigh the joys of engaging in such socially harmful behavior. Following in the footsteps of Hobbes, Locke, and Madison, Bentham argues that both moral philosophy and legal rules are attempts to cope with the essentially hedonistic nature of man. Like Hobbes, Bentham is unequivocal:

> Nature has placed mankind under the governance of two sovereign masters, *Pleasure* and *Pain*. To them . . . we refer all our decisions, every resolve that we make in life. The man who affects to have withdrawn himself from their despotic sway does not know what he is talking about. To seek pleasure and to shun pain is his sole aim, even at the moment when he is denying himself the greatest enjoyment or courting penalties the most severe.[12]

This is an extreme statement that reduces *all* activities to the quest for pleasure. It probably oversimplifies human motivation by totally excluding the possibility of altruism—unselfish concern for the welfare of others. In this book, we do not go as far as Bentham, and we acknowledge that criminal justice officials sometimes do act simply to help others. We can point to examples of police officers who risk their lives to apprehend violent criminals; defense lawyers who work overtime to prepare a sound case for their clients, knowing full well they will never get full compensation; jurors who endure days of deliberation in stuffy rooms to arrive at proper verdicts; and probation officers who use their own money to help those on parole stay out of trouble. Human motivation is surely a mixture of selfishness and selflessness.

However, even though self-interest does not explain everything, it does enable us to understand a great deal of behavior in the criminal justice system. Self-interest theory does what theory is supposed to do—it makes sense out of what otherwise would be a hodgepodge of assorted facts and integrates a wide variety of empirical findings in a plausible way.[13] In other words the self-interest theory of motivation goes a long way in explaining the various phenomena discussed in this book—how crime is perceived and analyzed (Chapter 2), what motivates criminals (Chapter 3), how policies are formulated and implemented (Chapter 4), how criminal justice institutions work (Part II), and what is the impact of public policy intended to thwart crime (Part III). Self-interest also plays a critical role in the improvement of criminal justice, the topic of Part IV. In short, self-interest is the keystone of this book.

THE COMPLEXITY OF SELF-INTEREST

The modern approach to self-interest, which we adopt, departs from that of the earlier theorists by recognizing a multiplicity of individual drives, goals, and values.[14] While people usually act in ways that suit themselves, no single motivation—be it money, power, sex, or pleasure—is the wellspring of all behavior. People's wants differ, and their preferences vary. This is easily seen with regard to consumer tastes: Some like Chevrolets while others are attracted to Fords; ice cream parlors that offer 31 flavors have a clear advantage over competitors that provide a more limited choice.

But such variation is true in a more profound way. While the entire human race shares certain basic drives—the desire for food and water, for example—people differ enormously in the value they place on various goals. Some are bent on making a fortune; others are consumed with obtaining satisfying personal relationships; and still others are driven by creative urges.

Thus, we reject the notion that materialism motivates most behavior in America, as was suggested by Russian dissident Aleksandr Solzhenitsyn in his noted 1978 commencement address at Harvard University.[15] True enough, acquisitiveness is pervasive, and the desire for more money is often paramount. But the reality of self-interest is much more complex, and it is necessary to recognize multiple personal goals in order to understand the behavior of the criminal justice system. Although a comprehensive list is impossible to draw up, the six motives discussed below seem operative in the world of criminal justice.

ECONOMIC GAIN The pursuit of greater wealth is an important consideration for many people—in and out of criminal justice. This motivation is blatant when we observe phenomena such as police corruption or the decision-making process of bail bondsmen who decide whether to provide the cash to free defendants from jail prior to trial. But sometimes the influence of this concern is more subtle, as when private defense lawyers determine how hard they will work for clients based on what the clients can afford.

What limits the overall significance of this motive, however, is that many criminal justice participants—such as police, judges, or corrections personnel—are on fixed salaries and have little opportunity for legally obtaining extra money on the basis of job performance. Most pay increases are the result of collective bargaining or simple longevity on the job; merit increases are almost nonexistent. Acquiring higher, better-paying positions often depends on the successful completion of civil service examinations or political intrigue. Thus, since remuneration is normally not contingent on job performance, it is rather irrelevant in day-to-day behavior.

SELF-ACTUALIZATION Psychologist Abraham Maslow has articulated the concept of self-actualization, which refers to the desire for self-fulfillment and the development of one's innate capabilities to the fullest.[16] People want to engage in activities that are intrinsically satisfying—pursuits that are enjoyable, challenging, or meaningful in themselves.

When applied to the job context, this means trying to conduct oneself in a professional or craftsmanlike manner. For example, there are occasions when police derive satisfaction out of resolving a family quarrel effectively or calming angry crowds in a peaceful way. Likewise, some judges take pride in reaching legally sound decisions by laboriously poring over and digesting past precedents. For some, doing one's job well is sufficient reward in itself.

However, many in the American work force, including a good number of those employed in criminal justice, are "alienated" from work—discontented with the nature of their jobs.[17] Thus, the interviews with the police conducted by Arthur Niederhoffer, a retired police officer who became a sociologist, show that many become quite embittered within a couple of years of joining the force, because they are engulfed by feelings of futility about doing their jobs.[18] Assistant district attorneys and public defenders, too, are often frustrated for they rarely engage in the excitement of trials, spending most of their time instead in routine hearings, tedious office work, and repetitive plea bargaining. In other words, there is often little opportunity for self-actualization in criminal justice work, so other motives take precedence.

COMFORT   If it is not often possible to use the criminal justice system for more wealth or for self-actualization, it is usually feasible to conduct oneself in a way that provides on-the-job comfort. There are officials who strive to make their work safe, convenient, and relatively undemanding. For police and prison guards, safety is a major concern. This motive was clear-cut when Cleveland police went on strike in July 1978 rather than obey an order that they begin one-person patrols of housing projects with high crime rates. Officers candidly admitted that they balked at these assignments because they thought they were too dangerous.[19]

The comfort motive is more frequently operative in activities and decisions designed to make the job more pleasant. A good example is the resistance of the New York City police officers' union to using one-person squad cars even though a Police Foundation study of their use in San Diego showed them to be "more efficient, safer, and at least as effective."[20] Police probably relish the companionship of other officers to interrupt the hours of boredom that routine patrol entails.

When carried to the extreme, the attempt to achieve job comfort can lead to boondoggling—making the job easier by shirking obligations and avoiding obnoxious chores. Police can respond slowly to calls about crimes in progress; defense lawyers can question prospective jurors hastily; judges can adjourn early in the day; prison guards can turn their backs on fights among inmates. Sometimes routinization converts otherwise demanding tasks into mindless mechanical ones, as when court personnel engage in assembly-line processing of defendants at early hearings.

The devotion to comfort and the boondoggling mentality may in part be the outgrowth of a general turn inward. Americans today belong to the "me generation." Commentator Tom Wolfe has argued that the 1970s witnessed an increased emphasis in this country on personal self-development.[21] While this is just another synonym for self-actualization, the new twist according to Wolfe is that many people turned to their private lives to seek satisfaction and began to perceive their work as simply a means to achieve that end. People pursue satisfaction in a myriad of ways—through sports, music, "do-it-yourself" hobbies, religion, and psychotherapy, for example. Thus, jobs are seen more and more simply as providing the wherewithal to pursue these extra-vocational pastimes.

What is essential to our understanding of criminal justice is that many officials may believe that energetic performance of their jobs yields neither economic gains nor personal satisfaction. Under these circumstances the concern about job comfort and convenience may become preeminent.

POWER   Another self-interest motive is power—control over other people's lives. Many people seek career advancement, not so much out of a desire for more money but because they want to dominate politically or have social impact. This seems to be the aim of many prosecutors who use the publicity of their office to advance themselves politically.

At the outset of this chapter, we speculated that Earl Warren was so motivated when he was a district attorney in California. There is even better evidence of this ambition in James ("Big Jim") Thompson, the Republican governor of Illinois. As a federal prosecutor, he made a name for himself by convicting 259 public officials of corruption, including an ex-governor turned federal judge (Otto Kerner), 6 Chicago aldermen, a city clerk, 57 police officers, and Mayor Richard Daley's press secretary—in short, some of the most powerful Democrats in the state.[22] Thereafter, he won the governorship in 1976 with a landslide victory. From his earliest years his political aspirations were well known, and he himself signed his high-school yearbook, "Jim Thompson, President of the U.S., 1984–1992."[23] While we can hardly pin down Thompson's motivations with certainty from that lone incident, the power and responsibility of higher office do seem to tempt many ambitious officials and affect their behavior.

FAME   Related to the craving for power is the motive of fame—the desire to be widely respected and acclaimed. This spirit was well stated by Vince Lom-

WHY JUDGES RESIST SENTENCING REFORMS: THE POWER MOTIVE

It is at least a viable hypothesis that the judiciary perceives sentencing accountability as an intrusion, a modification of authority that would appreciably reduce its sacred tradition and life style. A significant manifestation of the power and identity of the office and its incumbents is to be found in sentence imposition and the associated judicial degrees of freedom surrounding that function. . . .

The pivotal conflict throughout the entire criminal justice system in relation to reform hinges upon the extent and types of opportunities that different personnel have for employing personal, private, unencumbered, unsupervised discretion—i.e., acting with independence and autonomy—and the importance to them of the exercise of such unregulated, unmonitored, unevaluated, free decision-making in the performance of their work and as an integrally satisfying part of it. A safe hypothesis here would seem to be that judges are no different from the police, correctional custodial staff, probation officers, social workers, or aftercare counsellors (or even the reformists and intellectuals who vigorously advance the case for sentencing accountability) in jealously guarding their occupational prerogatives—and all the more so the scarcer such pleasures and prerogatives are.

Gerald Robin, "Judicial Resistance to Sentencing Accountability," *Crime and Delinquency*, July 1975, pp. 210–11 (italics in original).

bardi, coach of the great Green Bay Packer football teams of the 1960s, who once said: "Winning isn't everything; it's the only thing."

In a study of business executives, Michael Macoby discerned this motivation as rampant in the modern corporation. The "gamesman," as Macoby termed this type of individual, is characterized as follows:

> He is cooperative but competitive, detached and playful but compulsively driven to succeed; a team player but a would-be superstar. . . . He is energized to compete not because he wants to build an empire, not for riches, but rather for fame, glory, the exhilaration of running his team and of gaining victories. His main goal is to be known as a winner, and his deepest fear is to be labeled a loser.[24]

Certainly some lawyers are gamesmen in the sense that the pride of winning is a crucial end in itself. Martin Erdmann, an independently wealthy attorney who is considered one of the top criminal defense lawyers in the country, frankly admits this drive in himself. Erdmann scoffs when people call him dedicated: "That's just plain nonsense. The one word that does *not* describe me is dedicated. I reserve that word for people who do something that requires sacrifice. I don't sacrifice anything. The only reason I'm good is because I have an ego. I like to win."[25]

PEER APPROVAL   Most people like to feel that they are accepted by those with whom they associate; they desire a feeling of belongingness. At the same time, they want to avoid being criticized or (worse) ostracized by those around them. The striving for social acceptance can play a significant role in criminal justice as officials seek the approval of their co-workers.

Thus, police solidarity is a well-documented phenomenon.[26] In general terms, police recruits learn early to adopt the rather conservative values that permeate most police departments. More specifically, there is often an unwritten "buddy code" to which most officers subscribe; according to this code, they will never reveal another officer's misbehavior, even if they disapprove of it.

This code was acknowledged by two police officers while testifying at a police department trial in New York City. The officers admitted that they had first refused to inform their superiors that another officer had "planted" a weapon on the victim he shot in order to make that act look like justified self-defense. Said one officer, "I didn't want other police officers to think I would tell on another police officer."[27]

The intense loyalty of police officers to each other may stem from their extraordinary need to rely on one another in times of crisis when their lives may be endangered. However, even where such mutual dependence is lacking, people often cherish the esteem of others with whom they are interacting. This surely is a factor in some jury deliberations when dissenters quickly discard their opinions about guilt or innocence and yield to the will of the majority.[28] Being an outcast can be very uncomfortable.

Acceptance by colleagues is for most people a valued end, and conformity to group norms may be one result. Certainly currying the favor of job acquaintances is a common occurrence. Clan instinct seems to be part of human nature.

Thus, self-interest has many faces and many guises. Different people seek different things; a consuming lust for power no more characterizes humanity than does an insatiable greed. But what most people, including criminal justice officials, have in common is concern for their own well being, however each may define it. They use their jobs, in good measure, to help themselves.

ORGANIZATIONAL SELF-INTEREST

Self-interest is a motivating force for more than just individuals. Larger social units have their own interests apart from the concerns of the individuals composing them. Thus, it makes sense to speak of organizational self-interest, community self-interest, and national self-interest. The criminal justice system is run by many different public organizations and is affected by numerous private organizations. Police departments and the press corps are more than the sum total of the people working for them.

Some theorists do argue the contrary—that it is improper to conceptualize organizations as analytically distinct structures with specific goals and interests. In a classic work on organization theory, Chester Bernard contends that "the individual is always the basic strategic factor in organizations" and that understanding how organizations behave can only be based on an examination of how organizations are used by their members to fulfill their own individual purposes.[29] Whether, ultimately, all organizational goals can be reduced to such individual interests need not be resolved here. Nonetheless, for some purposes it is fruitful to analyze organizations as distinct entities with their own purposes.

Organizational self-interests, then, are the collective intentions of the membership to obtain some goal that is mutually beneficial to virtually everyone in the organization. External goals (sometimes called *transitive goals*) are commonly held commitments to bring about some change in the environment in order to accomplish some function. Internal goals (also called *reflexive goals*) are members' joint concerns about protecting the organization itself—an interest in sustaining the institution that members need for the nurturing of their personal self-interests.[30] In the criminal justice system organizations address themselves to fulfilling both kinds of goals.

EXTERNAL GOALS These are the specific tasks that various institutions are charged with performing. Police departments attempt to quell street disorders and apprehend felons. The prosecutor's office seeks high conviction rates and steady movement of cases. Prisons are interested in punishing, controlling, and to some extent rehabilitating inmates.

These government organizations are concerned with such goals because of external pressures and expectations. Not only must they, within some very broad limits, satisfy the public whose taxes support them but they must deal with the demands of other organizations with which they interact. Courts, for example, must do *something* with the many defendants channeled to them by police; some way must be found to process them expeditiously.

Private organizations, too, have external goals that affect criminal justice. The media want to make money—to sell newspapers or attract viewers; they handle crime stories with this interest in mind. Conservative taxpayer groups strive to keep government spending down, so they may lobby against expensive crime prevention programs. The point is that these firms and associations do have external missions to accomplish, and they conduct themselves accordingly.

INTERNAL GOALS On the other hand, there are also aims and purposes that are oriented strictly to the needs of the organization. For individuals affiliated with organizations, their own welfare is intimately linked with the fate of the institution to which they belong. The crime reporter's job may depend on how much profit his or her newspaper is making. There is a convergence between individual self-interest and organizational self-interest.

Consequently, one of the highest priorities of organizations is often survival. For example, when drug therapy programs endure long after they have been shown to be ineffectual, this may reflect the desire and ability of the organization to sustain itself rather than the fulfillment of any legitimate public purpose. Just as chambers of commerce in declining small towns often persist even when the business section of the community is disintegrating, so too do criminal justice organizations resist extinction even though their continuation is no longer justified.

Another internal goal is expansion. To gain the greater prestige and power associated with large size, many organizations try to augment their staffs, budgets, and responsibilities—even though big organizations are often more difficult to manage, more impersonal, and less responsive to their clientele. Often a cardinal rule for agencies of government, such as police departments, and subagencies, such as vice squads, is to ask for more funds than the previous year, regardless of whether the additional resources are needed for their assigned tasks. Expansionist tendencies are well illustrated by the growth of the Bureau of Customs from a minor federal agency charged with collecting tariffs to a major one that polices illegal trade in pornography, drugs, and other contraband from abroad.

A third internal goal of organizations is territoriality. They are very eager to protect themselves from the attempts of other organizations to intrude into their domain of responsibilities. Thus, fire marshals and arson units of police departments will sometimes vie with each other for control over investigations of suspicious fires. Similarly, in order to dominate the field of corrections, prison officials occasionally resist efforts to transfer inmates to community-based corrections centers that are not under their authority, even though the latter may be more effective means of rehabilitating convicts. This tendency of organizations to guard their own "turf" can stymy attempts to allocate criminal justice functions rationally to the most appropriate agency and to coordinate the efforts of various institutions.

SELF-INTEREST AND PUBLIC POLICY

The fact that people work from self-interest can have positive as well as negative consequences. People's persistent attention to satisfying their own ambitions can result in socially beneficial outcomes as well as harmful ones. The morality of actions depends on whether the effects of such actions benefit the broader public, not on the nature of the motivation that inspired them. Self-interested judges who honor due process because they do not want their decisions reversed by appellate courts are preferable to altruistic judges who disregard defendants' rights (and their own professional reputation) because they are passionately committed to "law and order." The purest motives can produce awful results.

Self-interest often produces good policy and effective job performance in the criminal justice system. Not long after New York police captured "Son of Sam," the killer who stalked the streets of the city for over a year and murdered 6 women selected at random, 25 officers who engaged in tireless efforts trying to solve the case were promoted to higher-paying positions.[31] One year later, New York police had another horrible crime on their hands: a group of teen-agers with baseball bats viciously clubbed a group of Central Park strollers and joggers, fracturing the skulls of five men, including former Olympic skating champion Dick Button. Within hours, a team of 30 detectives began the process of arduously and endlessly talking to people in the neighborhoods near the park—an inquiry that ultimately led them to an apartment containing blood-stained baseball bats and to the eventual arrest of several suspects who lived and visited there.[32] Some of the officers who acted so diligently in this case may have had promotions on their mind, hoping to reap the same dividends as their counterparts in the "Son of Sam" case. But this motivation (if it existed) in no way detracts from the valuable service rendered—the capture of violent criminals.

A study of parole officers in Illinois illuminates how self-interest can work in the opposite way—undermining desirable public policy objectives.[33] Parole officers have the job of supervising and counseling parolees, those who have been allowed to leave prison before the expiration of their term. However, many of these parole officers are very concerned about maintaining their own professional reputations. Often they will "sacrifice" the lives of wayward parolees, giving up on them and seeing that they return to prison, simply to enhance their reputation for being tough. At other times they will overlook serious parole violations, such as carrying weapons, to protect themselves from looking like failures as counselors. The purposes of a parole agency, to help convicts readjust to outside life and to protect society from those who are returning to their criminal ways, are corrupted by the predominance of self-interested behavior.

Thus, self-interest can lead to both good and bad results. To evaluate the practices of individuals and organizations in the criminal justice system, we must examine their broader social impacts. We must develop some notions of what is "good" and what is "bad." In short, we must define the public interest in criminal justice: the goals of the society.

The Public Interest in Criminal Justice

In May 1971 in Washington, D.C., the police dealt with the last massive demonstration against the Vietnam war in a most unorthodox way. Fearing chaos in the nation's capital, they began arresting anyone in the streets where disruption of traffic and blocking of access to buildings were taking place. The dragnet sweeps resulted in the arrest of 13,400 people during a four-day period—a national record. Normal arrest procedures were suspended; no names were written down, no specific crimes were indicated, no arresting officers were listed. The police followed the orders of Police Chief Jeremy Wilson: "Just bring them in and lock them up."[34] While some of those arrested were in fact violating the law, most were peacefully demonstrating, and a good number were totally uninvolved but happened to be in the wrong place at the wrong time.

The policy was effective in preserving order in the city: No violence took place, traffic proceeded normally, and by 9:00 A.M. the main streets were clear of protesters. President Nixon hailed the police actions, saying, "I think Jeremy Wilson and the police did a magnificent job."[35] Two years later a federal judge disagreed, and, taking notice of the fact that only 6 percent of those arrested were ever convicted of anything, he scathingly criticized law enforcement and ordered that those subjected to the indiscriminate arrests be given monetary damages for their ordeal.[36] Who was right—Nixon or the judge? Were the mass arrests proper under the circumstances?

In April 1974, San Francisco experienced its twelfth slaying in a year by the so-called Zebra killer, a name derived from the fact that the assailant was a black man who randomly selected white people as victims. To cope with this dire situation, police officials established "Operation Zebra," which permitted officers to stop, question, and search anyone who even vaguely resembled the description of the killer. Any black male with a mustache who was between the ages of 20 and 30 and whose height was between 5 feet 8 inches and 6 feet was subject to such treatment, even if he were doing nothing wrong and even if he were in no way implicated in the crimes. In one week alone 1,000 blacks were stopped under this program, including 6 who were ordered out of a theater by police officers prowling with flashlights and subjected to a search in the lobby (which turned out to be fruitless).

Mayor Joseph Alioto defended this practice, claiming that "extraordinary situations call for extraordinary measures."[37] On the other hand, a representative of the American Civil Liberties Union decried it as a "racist outrage."[38] Ultimately, a federal judge issued an injunction stopping the operation, long before the criminal was finally caught. Should Operation Zebra have been started and should the judge have halted it?

In July 1977 New York City experienced a blackout during which tens of thousands of people took to the darkened streets and went on a looting and burning rampage that cost 1,576 businesses about $135 million and devastated some slum neighborhoods that were already severely blighted. The police arrested 3,841 people, and Mayor Abraham Beame demanded stern treatment for those who took advantage of the city when it was so vulnerable. Due to insufficient facilities and the inability of officials to cope with such a chaotic emergency situation, many arrested persons were held without court hearings for hours and even days in overcrowded city jails, stifling courthouse detention pens, and bulging police lock-ups.[39]

In order to protect innocent people from unjustified detention and to give innocent and guilty alike a chance to defend themselves, the law requires a "prompt" hearing before a judge (within 72 hours of arrest). Some condemned the delays in the looting cases as gross violations of civil rights, while others, angered by the destruction caused by the looters, said that those arrested deserved everything they got—and more. Should the people who were denied a speedy hearing have been freed, and should their cases have been dismissed?

Answering the above questions and assessing the practices involved are difficult tasks. The reason is that various social ideals are at stake—racial justice, individual rights, effective law enforcement, and public order. The public interest to be served by criminal justice policies is comprised of many goals that cannot often be achieved simultaneously. Moreover, there is a great deal of controversy about the priority of the various goals: Which are most important and which most expendable?

There is simply no clear-cut way of defining the public interest—with regard to criminal justice or any other affairs of state. Some argue that the very idea of a public interest is faulty because there are too many "publics" having too many diverse "interests."[40] Society, according to this perspective, has no goals because it is too abstract and too diffuse. The "public good" is undefinable, and those who presume to know what it is are just espousing their own values and interests. Poet Carl Sandburg has made the point well:*

> Who shall speak for the people?
> Who has the answer?
> Where is the sure interpreter?
> Who knows what to say?
>
> . . .
>
> Who shall speak for the people?
> Who knows the works from A to Z so he can say
> "I know what the people want?"
>
> . . .
>
> The people is a myth, an abstraction.[41]

Sandburg and all the other critics of the concept of the public interest may be right. Nevertheless, there do seem to be certain broad, enduring policy ob-

*From Carl Sandburg, *The People, Yes* (1936). Reprinted by permission of Harcourt Brace Jovanovich, Inc.

jectives in the field of criminal justice that many within society consider desirable even though complete consensus is impossible. Although there is much debate about their relative importance, the goals of crime prevention, public tranquillity, justice, due process, efficiency, and accountability seem indisputably within the public interest. Those goals are the ultimate outcomes that we want our institutions and policies to achieve. But as a discussion of such goals will show, each is inherently complex and none is easy to define.

CRIME PREVENTION

The continuing role of crime as a major political issue and the regularly expressed fears of ordinary people attest to the importance of prevention. The concept of "crime," however, is very broad; it includes many kinds of wrongdoing from price fixing to murder. Due to the limited resources and capabilities of the criminal justice system, certain crimes must be targeted for concentrated attack while others are relegated to a lower place on the list of priorities. Some of the major battles in politics are over deciding which crimes warrant maximum attention and which can be dismissed. For example, Richard Nixon called the Watergate episode a "third-rate burglary" not worthy of much fuss, but the majority of the nation and most members of Congress eventually disagreed, which resulted in Nixon's resignation from office.

The ranking of crimes according to seriousness varies among individuals and groups and over eras. While most people think violations of "no smoking" rules are rather trivial acts, those suffering from emphysema and other lung diseases may react quite differently. To many white people, violation of civil rights laws may be petty matters, but to blacks who experience the woes of racial discrimination, they are major offenses to be dealt with sternly. The middle class may find shoplifting and employee pilferage disturbing, but many poor people perceive it as a legitimate means of coping with low-paying jobs and unemployment. Most older people, who were raised in a more restrictive atmosphere, abhor pornography peddlers, while today's youths are more indifferent. And the nation has changed its attitude toward marijuana possession in recent years, resulting in formal decriminalization in some places and lax enforcement in other areas. Clearly, there is no fixed standard to measure the wrongfulness of different crimes.

Nevertheless, there does seem to be a consensus among most Americans that physical attacks and threats to personal property constitute the worst crime problems. The physical, economic, and psychological losses occasioned by homicides, robberies, rapes, assaults, and burglaries are direct, highly visible, and often irreversible. The fear that such crimes generate causes people to curtail normal activities like walking the streets at night and to move away from neighborhoods. Other crimes may cause more damage objectively; drunk drivers cause more deaths than murderers, swindlers steal more than burglars, and tax evaders deprive the government of billions of dollars in revenues. But so-called street crimes are the ones that weigh on people's minds and wrack their nerves, so it is these that are the focus of national concern.

Where consensus ends is in resolving which communities have the greatest crime problem. While crime rates in the slums and ghettoes of the inner city are the highest in the nation, outlying areas and suburbs have experienced sharper increases in recent years, resulting in a cry for more protection. Thus Harlem, a black ghetto in New York, has 40 times the robberies of Bensonhurst, an all-white neighborhood in Brooklyn; but Bensonhurst has experienced robbery increases of 400 percent, while Harlem's rate has remained constant.[42] Determining which of these communities warrants more intense law enforcement is a political issue that is not easily resolved.

Regardless of the resolution, making all communities safe is surely a high priority of public policy. Freedom from personal attack and security of one's personal possessions are goals to which almost everyone subscribes—from the derelicts clutching their bottles of cheap wine to millionaires worried about intrusions into their mansions. Reducing the risk of crime against our homes, our property, and ourselves is a goal about which much consensus exists.

PUBLIC TRANQUILLITY

Let us imagine the following situation. A young woman takes her two preschool children to a neighborhood park. When she arrives she finds it occupied by several alcoholics who are drinking wine on the park benches; she is approached by scruffy-looking vagrants who are begging for money, and she is confronted by loud-mouthed teen-age boys smoking marijuana around the swings. While it is unlikely that she will be criminally assaulted, the woman is highly upset by this state of affairs and wants something done about it.

She is seeking *public tranquillity*—a peaceful environment in which to live her life and raise her family. Her right to enjoy the park is being denied in two ways: She is exposed to a series of unpleasant irritants, and she is made to feel afraid. This highlights the twofold nature of public tranquillity: Objectively, it is the right to be free of unnerving provocations and nuisances; subjectively, it is freedom from fear.

PUBLIC ORDER   People want their communities to be orderly, pleasant, and relatively homogeneous. This is the objective dimension of public tranquillity so important in urban areas. Cities tend to permit more kinds of social deviance that can be offensive to the majority of their citizens than nonurban areas.

Many people are offended by unorthodox life styles—young people who engage in raucous parties on street corners or panhandlers who wander around train stations looking for handouts. Also, some scorn types of behavior considered immoral—the wide-open operation of pornographic movie theaters or the use of drugs in public. One purpose of the criminal justice system is "social sani-

Achieving public tranquillity

tation,"[43] decreasing the visibility of such deviants and maintaining the identity of the community.

Another side to public order is conflict management. Diversity within cities creates the potential for all kinds of disputes. Furthermore, minor feuds occur even in harmonious communities: Parties to traffic accidents get angry with one another; people imbibing at taverns get into fights; young people blasting stereos disturb neighborhood residents. One purpose of the criminal justice system is to moderate these tensions and keep hostilities from escalating. Indeed, we shall see in Chapter 5 that peacekeeping is one of the primary missions of the police.

As important as this goal is, if it is pursued too zealously, the right of people to be different may be impaired. There is a fine line between obnoxious conduct that intrudes into other people's lives and harmless behavior that merely defies common standards of propriety. Thus, neighbors may be annoyed when teen-agers "hang out" on the streets and use vulgar language, but it is arguable that they have a right to do so if they do not interfere with passers-by. Likewise, demonstrators passing out political fliers often disturb people who disagree with their views, and the discarded sheets of paper can cause a mess, but to prohibit such activities would invade the constitutional right of freedom of speech. Too much emphasis on public peace can lead to social repression and an insistence on mass conformity.

FREEDOM FROM FEAR   Although the objective probability of being victimized by crime is rather small for most people except those living in the inner city, anxiety about crime runs high even in relatively safe areas. This has many untoward consequences: It causes people to desert public places such as parks, making them more dangerous in reality; it hastens the flight of the more affluent from cities, compounding our urban problems; and it simply adds to the stresses of people's daily lives. Therefore, some have suggested that a major law enforcement priority should be to provide reassurance and to calm people's fears. The aim is to change subjective perceptions of crime rather than to deal with the objective reality of crime.

Various policies may produce this effect. Charles Bahn has proposed that uniformed police be deployed where population density is greatest to maximize the number of people partaking of the calming influence of having police in the vicinity.[44] Similarly, most police departments, as standard procedure, add extra officers temporarily in areas where a serious crime has taken place, even though the criminal is unlikely to strike again in the same location.

Political leaders can engender public tranquillity by decreasing the stridency of their rhetoric about crime. Police officials can record and interpret crime statistics in a manner that deflates instead of exaggerates crime rates. Prosecutors can charge single defendants with many different crimes to make it appear as if more crimes have been solved. Calming frightened citizens is the goal of such efforts—not crime prevention.

There are several objections to this approach. It can entail deceptive and dishonest actions by officials. It may lead people to a false sense of security, which may cause them to let up on their guard in protecting themselves. And in the long run it cannot work if crime continues to escalate, because people are one way or another going to learn about the real crime peril confronting them.

JUSTICE

If people have committed crimes, we as a society expect that they should be treated in accordance with certain accepted moral principles of right and wrong. The commitment to "justice for all" in the American Pledge of Allegiance expresses a strong and enduring human value. What, then, is justice?

One way of answering this question is to ask why former President Ford's popularity rating plummeted by an unprecedented 20 percent in the public opinion polls in the week following his pardon of Richard Nixon, his predecessor, for Nixon's involvement in the conspiracy to cover up White House participation in the burglary of Democratic party headquarters in the Watergate Hotel. While some may have been disturbed by the prematurity of the action, which occurred prior to any indictment or trial, or by the fact that Ford seemed to be reneging on a commitment he made to the Congress when his appointment to the vice-presidency was being considered, it was probably two other factors that most appalled people. First, Nixon's associates, who may have been no more culpable than he, were being prosecuted while he emerged unscathed; to many, this was gross inequality. Second, the principle that criminals should pay for their crimes appeared to be violated: Not only was Nixon going unpunished for obstruction of justice but he was actually being rewarded by receipt of a large lifetime pension and other government subsidies. Thus, two central precepts in our ideas of justice were violated by the pardon: equality and retribution.

EQUALITY   When Jimmy Carter delivered his speech accepting the presidential nomination of the Democratic party in July 1976, he received sustained applause for the following line: "I see no reason why big-shot criminals should go free and the poor ones go to jail."[45] While this was no doubt partially an allusion to the politically advantageous (for Democrats) Watergate affair, his audience was clearly responding to an underlying natural sentiment that is part of the American ideology—equality before the law.

Many Americans are rankled when a criminal's wealth or power seems to determine punishment rather than the nature of the crime itself. Because equal treatment of the same kinds of offenders is inherent in most definitions of justice, the relatively light sentences handed to people like the millionaire Bernard Bergman, who was convicted of misusing public funds in his sordid nursing homes, cause much resentment. Why should Bergman get a four-month jail sentence for swindling millions of dollars in Medicaid funds while the elderly patients in his nursing homes continue to live in abominable conditions?

It was this concern about inequality that caused the Supreme Court to invalidate several death penalty statutes in 1972.[46] Not only was capital punishment imposed very rarely but extraneous factors such as the race and income of those convicted seemed to determine whether they lived or died. Thus, of the 455 people executed for rape in this country between 1930 and 1973, 89 percent were black—prima facie evidence of racial discrimination.[47] Justice William Douglas's concurring opinion in *Furman* v. *Georgia* succinctly explains the injustice of this situation:

> A law that stated that anyone making more than $50,000 would be exempt from the death penalty would plainly fall, as would a law that in terms said that Blacks, those who never went beyond the fifth grade in school, or those who made less than $3,000 a year, or those who were unpopular or unstable should be the only people executed. A law which in the overall view reaches that result in practice has no more sanctity than a law which in terms provides the same.[48]

RETRIBUTION   Apart from any possible future impact on crime, most people have an intuitive feeling that there should be punishment proportionate to the seriousness of the crime and the blameworthiness of the criminal. This idea has recently been called the principle of "commensurate desert": people should pay for their wrongs in accordance with the damage they inflicted.[49] This idea has strong religious and historical roots. The Bible states the notion forthrightly:

When one man strikes another and kills him he shall be put to death. Whoever strikes a beast and kills it shall make restitution, life for life. When one man injures and disfigures his fellow-countryman, it shall be done to him as he has done; fracture for fracture, eye for eye, tooth for tooth; the injury and disfigurement that he has inflicted upon another shall in turn be inflicted upon him.[50]

The need for vengeance remains deeply ingrained in the human psyche, and most of us can point to times when we wanted to "get even" with those who wronged us. Many popular songs express this longing; for example, "I will have sweet, sweet, sweet, bitter revenge" was a hit country-and-western song.

Even more poignant are the real-life words of Joanne Lomino, an 18-year-old woman paralyzed from the waist down by one of "Son of Sam's" bullets. Said the young woman after the suspect was caught: "After all the things he did to me, to all of us, he should be punished—he should be punished in a way that he would suffer a lot, and then he should die."[51]

We sympathize with such words, because it somehow seems morally right that a wrongdoer be punished—for the simple reason that he or she deserves it. Many would agree with the observation of Justice Potter Stewart: "The instinct for retribution is part of the nature of man, and channeling that instinct in the administration of justice serves an important purpose."[52]

However, all civilized societies set certain limits on the kinds of punishment and the degree of suffering that can be inflicted on criminals. Most people accept the legitimacy of fines and imprisonment in appropriate cases, and a clear majority of Americans approve of the death penalty. But fewer would be in favor of torture, and it is very doubtful that many would countenance sentencing offenders to long years of hard labor followed by death—a penalty allegedly prescribed for counterrevolutionaries during the political upheavals in China in the 1960s.

Where to draw the line is a troublesome question, one that the courts have had to tackle in determining what constitutes cruel and unusual punishment, which is prohibited by the Eighth Amendment. While the Supreme Court has sanctioned the use of capital punishment for murder,[53] it has ruled that it is excessive when applied to rapists.[54] And a district court in New York State ruled that life imprisonment for small sales of cocaine is so disproportionate to the gravity of the offense that it is impermissible.[55]

Concern about overreaction to criminals reflects a social ambivalence about retribution. It has long been recognized that violent responses to crime may legitimize and foster the use of violence in general. For this reason psychiatrist Karl Menninger, in his book *The Crime of Punishment*, urges that *all* punitive measures against criminals be replaced with therapeutic approaches.[56]

MERCY   There is another reason why we balk at automatically inflicting specified punishments against serious criminals, as the stern law of retribution would dictate. To assess blame, the circumstances of the crime must be taken into account. A famous nineteenth-century British murder case, *Queen* v. *Dudley and Stephens*, illustrates this point.[57]

The defendants in that case were indicted for the murder of a 17-year-old boy; the crime was committed in a lifeboat boarded by four people after a shipwreck on the high seas 1,600 miles from land. After eight days without food and six days without water, the boy was killed and his body eaten in four days by the remaining three men. The boy was sick and near death when his throat was slashed—too weak and helpless to resist. Four days later a passing ship rescued the survivors, who were brought back to England and tried for murder. At the trial the prosecution admitted that everyone would have died of starvation had the boy not been consumed. The court convicted them of premeditated murder, a capital crime, but the Queen reduced the sentence to six months' imprisonment.

Why was there such light treatment in this case of willful murder? Because we often temper retribution with mercy when there are mitigating circumstances leading to the criminal act. In the shipwreck case we can well understand the compulsion to survive, and we ask, Which of us could have resisted the torment of starvation and the terror of death? Although the felt need to commit crimes provides no legal defense, justice seems to demand that we take motives into account in determining punishment. As compelling as the idea of standardized, mandatory sentences is as a means of achieving "equal justice under law," the moral imperative of leniency in some cases causes us to resist imposing such a policy (or to find ways around it, like reducing charges in certain cases). Indeed, when a person is totally incapable of controlling his or her behavior due to insanity, the law itself absolves the person of any responsibility for the crimes.

What makes this facet of justice so slippery, however, is that if we dig deeply enough we can almost always find aspects of a criminal's situation or background that induced the errant behavior. The complex environments that shape our lives and that are beyond our control often make even the most heinous crimes seem understandable. The desperation of the stranded seafarers is obvious to all, but the pressures on the "ordinary" criminal may be every bit as irresistible.

Most people abhorred the armed takeover of three District of Columbia buildings, containing 149 hostages, by Hanafi Muslims in March 1977 that led to the murder of one man and the wounding of others. But our judgment may be qualified by knowing that the leader of the group, Hamaas Abdul Khaalis, was harboring bitter resentment about the 1973 murder of five of *his* small children in their beds by members of the rival Black Muslim religious sect whom Khaalis wanted brought before him for judgment. As awful as Khaalis's crime was, understanding the anguish and rage he was living with for four years may engender some sympathy for him.[58]

Lesser criminals, too, often have compelling excuses for what they did. How harsh should we be on the welfare mother who steals milk because she is

---

JUSTICE IN AN UNJUST WORLD

The law, in its majestic equality, forbids the rich as well as the poor to sleep under bridges, to beg in the streets, and to steal bread.

Anatole France, *Le Lys Rouge* (1894).

unable to feed her hungry infant? Is the waiter who barely makes a living wage justified in concealing tips from his income tax? What about the negligent driver who accidentally runs down a pedestrian while speeding his injured child to a hospital? Or the narcotics peddler who himself is addicted to heroin? Our culture believes in the values of mercy and compassion and hence in "individualized justice," but it sharply disagrees when these values should be applied.

DUE PROCESS

In May 1973 Herbert and Evelyn Giglotto were abruptly awakened by intruders entering their apartment in the quiet, middle-class town of Collinsville, Illinois, a suburb of St. Louis. Acting without search warrants, federal drug enforcement agents kicked down the couple's front door, charged into the bedroom where the Giglottos were sleeping, and began tearing the house apart. Bookshelves were overturned, clothes were scattered in closets, a television was toppled, and a Polaroid camera was smashed. The agents used abusive language and handcuffed Mr. Giglotto with his hands behind his back while his terrified wife looked on, dressed in her negligee. They then threw Giglotto face down on his bed, held a pistol to his head, and demanded to know where the illegal drugs were hidden. Said one agent to Giglotto, "Where's it at? You s.o.b., you move and you're dead."[59]

The search continued for half an hour; then the agents found some personal papers that identified the couple. It turned out that the agents had invaded the wrong house; the Giglottos were totally innocent of any connection with narcotics peddling; and the whole episode was a horrible mistake. A local attorney summed up the community's shocked reactions: "I declare it frightens people to death. The thousand-year Reich [i.e., Germany under Nazi rule] they've read about. But they don't expect it here. No sir, not in Madison County."[60]

This outrage conveys people's indignation about procedures that are . . . outrageous. It is the same horror that most Americans feel when reading about trials in countries run by dictators where people are summarily arrested, imprisoned, and even executed. Indeed, Aleksandr Solzhenitsyn became a national hero for describing vividly in *The Gulag Archipelago* how Soviet authorities under Stalin had dealt with millions of political opponents in such fashion,[61] and more recently the world was shocked by similar actions of Idi Amin, the now-deposed leader of Uganda, Chile's military government, and the revolutionaries controlling Iran after the downfall of the Shah.

The notion of detaining and punishing people without a reasonable process for determining guilt or innocence is antagonistic to the basic American creed. It is this ideal, that individuals who are accused of crimes be dealt with fairly by authorities, that is central to the concept of due process of law. Many of the constitutional guarantees stated in the Bill of Rights—the right to counsel, the right to confront one's accusers, the right to a jury trial—are intended to ensure that there are procedures designed to protect the individual from biased judgments and unfair treatment. Because safeguarding the innocent is as important, if not

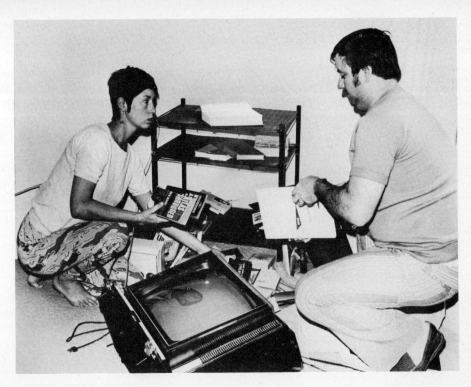

Collinsville, Illinois: A horrible mistake

more so, than convicting the guilty, we have developed through our courts and legislatures a range of legal procedures and civil rights to protect the individual from wrongful arrest, conviction, and punishment.

But the idea of due process goes beyond protecting those accused of crime. It entails restraints on government power, thus assuring everyone the right to carry on their private lives without unwarranted intrusions by authorities. To this end, we actually prefer to let some guilty persons go free rather than allow officials to use unlimited measures to catch and convict them. Thus, a federal judge in Los Angeles dismissed all charges against Daniel Ellsberg—who had without question unlawfully given the classified history of the Vietnam war (the *Pentagon Papers*) to the press—when it was revealed that White House officials had burglarized the office of Ellsberg's psychiatrist in search of incriminating information about Ellsberg. More generally, the "exclusionary rule" announced by the Supreme Court in *Mapp* v. *Ohio* forbids the use of illegally seized evidence against a defendant in state and local courts in order to deter police from such wrongdoing.[62] Indeed, many of the specific restrictions we place on officials, such as requiring them to get search warrants in most cases before entering private homes and insisting that police have valid grounds for accosting and interrogating people on the street, are intended to protect all of us from unjustified interference with our basic freedoms.

While the precious nature of individual rights is deeply rooted in American ideology and specific guarantees against government abuses of power are enun-

CONSTITUTIONAL PROTECTION OF DUE PROCESS: ROCHIN V. CALIFORNIA

Having "some information that [Rochin, the appellant] was selling narcotics," three deputy sheriffs of the County of Los Angeles [went to] the two-story dwelling house in which Rochin lived with his mother, common-law wife, brothers and sisters. Finding the outside door open, they entered and then forced open the door to Rochin's room on the second floor. Inside they found [Rochin] sitting partly dressed on the side of the bed, upon which his wife was lying. On a "night stand" beside the bed the deputies spied two capsules. When asked "Whose stuff is this?" Rochin seized the capsules and put them in his mouth. A struggle ensued, in the course of which the three officers "jumped upon him" and [unsuccessfully] attempted to extract the capsules. [Rochin] was handcuffed and taken to the hospital. At the direction of one of the officers a doctor forced an emetic solution through a tube into Rochin's stomach against his will. This "stomach pumping" produced vomiting. In the vomited matter were found two capsules which proved to contain morphine. [Rochin was convicted of possessing morphine] and sentenced to sixty days' imprisonment. The chief evidence against him was the two capsules. . . .

The proceedings by which this conviction was obtained do more than offend some fastidious squeamishness or private sentimentalism about combatting crime energetically. This is conduct that shocks the conscience. Illegally breaking into the privacy of the [appellant], the struggle to open his mouth and remove what was there, the forcible extraction of his stomach's contents—this course of proceeding by agents of government is bound to offend even hardened sensibilities. They are methods too close to the rack and the screw to permit of constitutional differentiation.

It has long since ceased to be true that due process of law is heedless of the means by which otherwise relevant and credible evidence is obtained. . . . [There is a] general requirement that States in their prosecutions respect certain decencies of civilized conduct. Due process of law, as a historic and generative principle, precludes defining, and thereby confining, these standards of conduct more precisely than to say that convictions cannot be brought about by methods that offend a "sense of justice."

Rochin v. California, 342 U.S. 165 (1952).

ciated in the Constitution, controversy persists over how far to extend these rights and how to apply them to specific cases. In a landmark case decided in 1937, *Palko* v. *Connecticut*, the Supreme Court ruled that only those deprivations that violate "fundamental principles of liberty and justice" are incorporated into the due process clause of the Fourteenth Amendment, which limits the actions of states.[63] Moreover, in that very case the Court, speaking through Justice Benjamin Cardozo (one of the most liberal judges of that era), said that the Fifth Amendment protection against double jeopardy (being tried twice for the same crime) was *not* "implicit in the concept of ordered liberty." Therefore, the state of Connecticut could constitutionally try Palko for first-degree murder *after* a jury had already found him guilty of only the lesser crime of second-degree murder. The prosecution had a right, according to the Supreme Court, to seek a new trial to correct errors made in the first trial, such as the exclusion of certain evidence and improper instructions given to the jury by the judge on the difference between first- and second-degree murder.

Palko's case ended with his execution for the crime of first-degree murder, but debate about the definition of the fundamental rights involved has continued. In the 1950s and 1960s when Earl Warren was Chief Justice, the Supreme Court incorporated most of the provisions of the Bill of Rights into the Fourteenth Amendment, so that state authorities now have almost the same obligations to the accused as the federal government. Thus, the Sixth Amendment right to counsel, the Fifth Amendment protection against self-incrimination, and the Fourth Amendment prohibition of unreasonable searches and seizures now restrict state and local law enforcement authorities as well. The *Palko* decision itself was overruled in 1969, when Justice Marshall proclaimed that the double jeopardy prohibition "represents a fundamental ideal in our Constitutional heritage"—a judgment which came 27 years too late for the hapless Mr. Palko.[64]

But this constitutional trend has still left many issues unresolved. Defining the specific meaning of due process protections and their applicability to concrete situations has posed enduring dilemmas. Drawing the fine line between proper and improper government conduct in pursuing criminals involves complex and subjective judgments in which opposing values must be weighed. Whether or not a person has been fairly treated cannot be decided by referring to rigid formulas. This idea was well put by Justice Felix Frankfurter: "Due process is not a mechanical instrument. It is not a yardstick. It is a process."[65]

The process of deciding how far to extend basic rights involves judges, legislators, police, and the entire society. Officials more or less reflect community opinions, especially with regard to emotionally charged issues like crime. Thus the liberalism of the Warren Court has given way to the "law and order" perspective of the Burger Court, a majority of whose members are conservative justices, five appointed by conservative presidents (Nixon and Ford). But as we discuss a few specific due process problems, it should become evident that many dilemmas remain in applying basic constitutional norms to everyday situations and that the meaning of due process is continuously being redefined.

MIRANDA WARNINGS While a defendant's own admission of guilt is, in some ways, the best evidence against that person, it is well known that under pressure people will admit to deeds they did not do. To prevent this from happening, the framers of the Constitution included in the Fifth Amendment the privilege against self-incrimination, meaning that people cannot be forced to testify against themselves.

What constitutes force, however, has been a troubling issue in recent years. In the important case of *Miranda* v. *Arizona* a closely divided Supreme Court ruled that merely keeping a person in custody after an arrest is an inherently intimidating experience.[66] Therefore, prior to any interrogation suspects must be advised by police of four rights: (1) the right to remain silent; (2) the right to know that anything that they say can be used against them; (3) the right to have a lawyer present during questioning; and (4) the right to be provided with a lawyer if they cannot afford one. These have come to be known as "Miranda warnings."

By insisting that coercion against defendants be eliminated, the courts have no doubt allowed some guilty parties to go free, just as Miranda's rape conviction was overturned even though two victims correctly picked him out of a police line-up and the evidence did implicate him. Such cases pose a profound dilemma: Can we make fact-finding procedures so rigorous that it becomes almost impossible to convict anyone? Wary of this possibility, the Supreme Court—in allowing the incriminating testimony of a witness discovered through a defendant's statement made without Miranda warnings—observed that "the law does not require that a defendant receive a perfect trial, only a fair one."[67] But this brings us right back to the central and plaguing question of due process: What is fair?

THE RIGHT TO PRIVACY Just as controversy abounds in deciding what constitutes fairness, there are also arguments about the meaning of another facet of due process—the right to privacy. The belief that a man's home is his castle has strong roots in Anglo-American history, perhaps best expressed centuries ago in a famous speech by William Pitt, a British statesman:

> The poorest man may in his cottage bid defiance to all the force of the Crown. It may be frail; its roof may shake; the wind may blow through it; the storms may enter it, the rain may enter,—but the King of England cannot enter; all his forces dare not cross the threshold of the ruined tenement.[68]

Once again, however, it is easy to establish the general principle and difficult to apply it. All kinds of questions emerge. What evidence must a judge have to issue a search warrant? Are the allegations of police informants enough? How far can police search after making a valid arrest—a person's clothes? the car? the glove compartment of the car? the bedroom? the whole house? Under what conditions can wiretapping be used—in national security investigations? against suspected terrorists? to fight organized crime? Can investigators secure bank records, such as photocopied canceled checks, without the permission of depositors? Must those who voluntarily consent to be searched first be told of their right to refuse?

In answering these questions, lawmakers and courts have had to weigh the need for effective law enforcement tactics against losses of individual privacy that may result. The wiretapping decisions indicate that the courts have steered a middle course—approving electronic surveillance in principle,[69] but striking down particular procedures that fail to provide judicial safeguards against indiscriminate use.[70] But despite these restrictions, the use of wiretapping has continued, with approximately 431,370 conversations admittedly recorded by federal and state authorities in 1976.[71] Most of these conversations prove to be innocuous, but some put dangerous criminals in prison. Some targets of wiretaps pose threats to society, while others have done nothing worse than express unorthodox views or espouse unpopular causes (like Martin Luther King, Jr., whose phone was tapped for many years by the F.B.I.). As early as 1928 Justice Oliver Wendell Holmes condemned wiretapping as a "dirty business."[72] But the tendency in this country is to grant police the power they need (or think they need) to match wits with criminals. And while Manhattan District Attorney Frank Hogan called wiretapping "the single most important tool for investigating organized crime,"[73] Professor Herman Schwartz claims it "is a rending of the fabric of trust in a society without which free speech and association are not possible."[74] In deciding which view is correct, whether police surveillance is worse than the crime problem it is supposed to remedy, a choice of priorities must be made.

EFFICIENCY

Efficiency is something we expect from all government agencies delivering services. We want them to utilize scarce resources effectively. The fact that politicians are able to win votes by promising to reduce government waste and protect the taxpayer's dollar attests to the importance of this goal. The public interest in keeping taxes down was well demonstrated by the overwhelming success in 1978 of Proposition 13 in California, the public referendum that required an enormous reduction in local property taxes and foreshadowed serious cutbacks in government services.

PRODUCTIVITY One major facet of efficiency is productivity—obtaining high output at low cost. One advantage of plea bargaining is, in fact, that many convictions are secured through minimal expenditures. Likewise, the widespread use of probation as an alternative to prison may be a more productive means of rehabilitation; for example, it costs about $15,000 a year to incarcerate convicts, while allowing them their freedom with court supervision of their conduct costs about one-tenth as much.

One of the major aims of criminal justice administrators and government leaders is to increase productivity throughout the system—to keep police from waiting aimlessly to testify in court, to assign jurors to cases with a minimum of delay, to process court papers swiftly, to deliver jailed defendants to their trials on schedule. An obstacle to accomplishing this is that many officials are incompetent, either unskilled for assigned tasks or lacking sufficient dedication to the job.

PROFESSIONALISM In order to increase efficiency, proposals are constantly being made to improve the performance of law enforcement personnel by recruiting trained personnel or upgrading those presently on the job. Professionalism is the carrying out of one's duties through the use of special skills and expertise. Examples of specific policies intended to encourage this are the Missouri plan for selecting judges on the basis of merit (see Chapter 7) and "lateral entry" for the police to allow computer experts and the like to enter police work without having to serve first as patrol officers.

REDUCING CORRUPTION Another barrier to efficiency is corruption, the conscious undermining of crime prevention goals by personnel who receive bribes to overlook crime. Since there are so many private people and businesses eager to protect themselves and their lucrative illegal enterprises, police, prosecutors, judges, and even prison officials are tempted continuously by those willing to pay high prices to escape punishment for their crimes. Many criminal justice policies are intended to increase the honesty of officials by increasing the risk of apprehension for graft. Use of special prosecutors operating independently of the district attorney's office and internal investigating divisions in police departments are intended to suppress and ferret out corruption.

OPPORTUNITY COSTS   A final dimension of efficiency is opportunity costs, the untried alternatives that might have been selected had not present programs been adopted instead. Adopting certain programs results in the loss of other opportunities that might have been better.

Thus, a study by the General Accounting Office of the Congress showed that the F.B.I. secures prosecution in only 9 percent of all cases because it spends so much time investigating minor cases, and it recommended that the agency concentrate on a small number of important cases rather than opting for a high quantity of investigations.[75] Similarly, a recent critical analysis of prostitution enforcement by the New York City Police Department points out that most women are fined an average of $194 for prostitution, but the cost of making and disposing of such arrests is about $2,000.[76] In assessing the efficacy of any law enforcement program, we must always ask if the funds could have been spent better on something else.

The same question should also be raised with regard to our total investment in law enforcement—about $17 billion for all levels of government in 1975. Might we get a better return on our tax dollars if we expanded other government services that are easier to provide (e.g., public works jobs or mass transit) rather than spend so much pursuing the elusive and largely unattainable goals of criminal justice? Some social problems are better solved by government programs than others, and consideration must be given to what we are forfeiting by concentrating so much of our resources on law enforcement.

ACCOUNTABILITY

In a democracy we expect government policies and procedures to be under popular control—"of the people, by the people, for the people." By accountability we mean that the society generally should have a major role in criminal justice decision making. There are three dimensions of accountability: democratic selection of officials, government responsiveness to public opinion, and popular participation in government.

DEMOCRATIC SELECTION OF OFFICIALS   Elections have been a primary mode of picking judges and district attorneys in this country, but the rather tight control that political parties exercise over nominations and the issueless nature of campaigns for these offices make it questionable whether ordinary people have much choice in elections. In fact it may be that appointment of top law enforcement officials by the president, governors, and mayors gives citizens more control, for these politicians are sensitive to public sentiment and sometimes must have their selections reviewed in public hearings. Perhaps least subject to popular choice are rank-and-file workers (police, probation officers, etc.) selected by civil service examinations. Because these street-level bureaucrats are the officials of criminal justice agencies that most people encounter, some community groups have called for increased involvement in the selection and retention of rank-and-file workers.

THE INFLUENCE OF PUBLIC OPINION   Law enforcement is such a salient and visible political issue that the determination of priorities and methods in criminal justice is often dictated by public opinion. Public sentiment is one reason for renewed advocacy of the death penalty by politicians. For example, former Mayor Abraham Beame of New York had previously opposed it, but he advocated it in his unsuccessful reelection campaign in 1977. And Governors Jerry Brown of California and Hugh Carey of New York, who vetoed bills restoring capital punishment, have received much criticism for flouting the will of the public.

A clear example of how public feelings influence policy was the change in direction of the Department of Justice when Richard Nixon replaced Lyndon Johnson as president. In reaction to the conservative mandate Nixon received at the polls in 1968, Attorney General John Mitchell slashed the manpower of the Civil Rights Division, which deals with illegal racial discrimination, and shifted attention to drug violators and disruptive political demonstrators.[77] This action was no doubt partly a response to public concern about the growing "drug culture" and to public anger over the excesses of militant dissenters.

POPULAR PARTICIPATION   There are many ways in which the public plays a direct role in criminal justice decision making. The most obvious is public participation on grand juries, which decide whether to indict people for felonies, and petit juries, which decide guilt or innocence. In some cities, civilian review boards weigh allegations of police brutality. Perhaps most significant is the testimony in court of eyewitnesses. In Chapter 15 we discuss ways that citizens might become more directly involved in crime prevention.

As is the case concerning other criminal justice goals, too much accountability can be a bad thing. We pride ourselves in having a "government of laws, not men"; this means that crime standards and procedures should remain fixed, rather than change in response to every political wind. Thus, the lynch mobs of the frontier and the old South gave the majority absolute and immediate control over criminal justice, but concerns like due process were all but ignored. The passionate reactions of the public to crime may be an unhealthy influence on criminal justice processes if they are not kept within bounds. Too much public influence can threaten the independence of the judiciary that we so prize.

Public Policy and the Choice of Goals

All of the aims discussed in this chapter have convincing justifications. Unfortunately, it is impossible to implement all of them at the same time. A common cliché is clearly applicable in criminal justice: "You can't have your cake and eat it too."

First, the goals themselves are incompatible. Due process has rightly been called by Professor Herbert Packer an "obstacle course" to conviction, in conflict with the goals of crime prevention and efficiency.[78] Public tranquillity requires visible law enforcement activities, which may be exactly the opposite of what is needed to curb certain kinds of crime. The price of accomplishing one goal is often sacrifice of another.

Moreover, different dimensions of the same goal sometimes conflict with one another. Securing the truth, an essential element of due process, may be best accomplished by such methods as eavesdropping, infiltration, and the use of truth serums, all of which are gross invasions of privacy, another element of due process. And it is difficult for *individualized* justice and *equal* justice to coexist. For example, to allow former Attorney General Mitchell to serve his prison sentence for his Watergate crimes in a minimum security prison with air-conditioned barracks and to grant him five months of furlough from prison to receive medical treatment may have been a fitting act of compassion,[79] but many other less prominent and less powerful prisoners do not get similar sympathy. In other words, the very concepts of due process and justice have internal contradictions.

A related problem is the means-ends complication in criminal justice. Various programs under consideration by policy makers are often directed at achieving different goals. To determine which is better, we must clarify specific goals to be served and decide which is most important. A dialogue in *Alice in Wonderland* brings this out. In the midst of her confused wandering, Alice asks the Cheshire Cat which way she ought to go. The cat says that depends on where she wants to get.

> "I don't much care—" said Alice.
> "Then it doesn't matter which way you go," said the Cat.

The point is that assessing which direction is wisest requires us to choose our destination. A persistent police quandary illustrates the fact that means and ends are inseparable. Police departments continuously question their method of deploying personnel: What is the best way to allocate a given number of police to various kinds of units on the force? Is it better policy to put more officers in cruising squad cars, on foot patrol, or in undercover units composed of plainclothes officers, sometimes disguised as decoys who mingle inconspicuously with the public?

The answer, as Table 1-1 suggests, is confused by the fact that multiple goals are at stake. All of the above police methods are useful in varying degrees, depending on how these goals are ordered. A strategy necessary to prevent

TABLE 1-1
Estimated Relative Utility
of Alternative Police Deployment Methods[1]

| | Public Interest Goals | | |
Deployment Methods	Public Tranquillity	Deterring Street Crime	Accountability
Cruising squad cars	1	2	3
Foot patrol officers	2	3	1
Undercover units	3	1	2

[1] The utilities are all estimated on the basis of a general knowledge of how the various units function. Other rank orderings of the contribution of different methods to the various goals could also be defended. The correctness of the rank ordering is not crucial to the point being made in the text.

street crime may be different from one needed to provide public tranquillity. Each of the methods listed in Table 1-1 may be quite use*ful* in accomplishing one or more of the enumerated goals and virtually use*less* in achieving others.

Foot patrol can increase accountability because the police deal more directly with the public and learn about their attitudes toward law enforcement; but because officers on foot have low mobility and minimal surveillance capabilities, they may have a limited impact on deterring street crime. Cruising squad cars contribute to public tranquillity because of their visibility to the general public; but their effectiveness in stopping street crimes is questionable because they usually arrive after the damage is done. Therefore, before the correct means can be rationally selected, we must first decide which goals are preferable.

How do people choose among conflicting priorities? Individuals often decide according to how their *self*-interests are related to broader public interest goals. A middle-class homeowner faced with the prospect of increased property taxes may opt for efficiency. The beleagured inner-city merchant who has been repeatedly robbed may want to reduce crime regardless of cost and government waste of resources. The poor person who is more apt to be arrested than the affluent may be more concerned about due process. Thus, in some ways the public interest is really nothing more than individual and group self-interests writ large.

In figuring out the public interest in criminal justice, we make political choices, or trade-offs, among different priorities. One of the major purposes of the political process is to resolve conflicts and decide which version of the public interest is to become the basis of public policy.

Decisions about goals are not made abstractly: Legislatures do not pass resolutions rating the relative importance of crime prevention, due process, and the like. Rather, goals become meaningful only in the context of specific policy alternatives and concrete institutional practices.[81] The weight to be given to conflicting priorities is determined when we decide the merits of particular criminal justice actions. Our choice of means determines how much we value certain ends.

As we analyze the institutions of criminal justice in Part II, we shall see that the weighing of various goals is made on a day-to-day basis by tens of thousands of unknown functionaries—from patrol officers on the beat to prison guards to appellate court judges. Whether to arrest lawbreakers, what to charge them with, whether to acquit or convict, and how to sentence them all entail preferences about the ultimate purposes of the system.

Likewise, both the theory and practice of the four important criminal justice policies described in Part III have varying impacts on public interest goals. In choosing among deterrence, rehabilitation, decriminalization, and diversion, policy makers implicitly judge the value of the different goals. In formulating and implementing criminal justice policies, we are not only asking "What works?" but more profoundly "What do we want to achieve?"

In short, the public interest is constantly being defined and redefined. The balance among its various facets is always shifting. As is true in any area of public policy, the choice of ideals in criminal justice is the result of an unpredictable, ever-changing, and very intricate political process.

Conclusion

We have contended that the motivating force of self-interest provides the soundest explanation of how the criminal justice system functions. This is a theory; like all theories it may oversimplify or distort reality, or it may be dead wrong. It is impossible to actually probe people's thoughts to find out *why* they are doing things—sometimes they do not know themselves. However, much criminal justice decision making that otherwise seems perplexing or absurd often makes sense if we take account of the personal concerns and aspirations of the decision makers. The idea of self-interest seems to unravel many mysteries.

Criminal justice officials are no better or worse than others inside and outside government. That police, lawyers, and judges often put themselves first simply reflects the normal human instinct for self-preservation and self-improvement. In coping with their jobs, police must deal with physical dangers, prosecutors must respond to voter expectations, and defense lawyers must adapt to the monetary realities of legal practice. How they act is determined largely by the threats and uncertainties of their environment.

Reformers must be aware of self-interest in framing new policies. We cannot expect criminal justice personnel to act in ways that harm them. The accomplishment of socially desirable goals requires meshing the self-interests of officials with the broader public interest. If it is advantageous for police and others to fight crime, seek justice, or respect due process, they will do so. But it is unreasonable to expect all but small numbers of heroes and martyrs to act in ways that are self-destructive. The key to better practices in the criminal justice system is providing incentives for people to change their behavior, an idea to which we will return in our final chapter on the future of criminal justice.

There are other obstacles to reform, including conflicts among the goals themselves. Confusion exists about what is desirable; public expectations are varied, inconsistent, and in flux. Consequently, the policy-making process is normally one of political compromise and trade—a little of *A* to get a little of *X*, a bit of *B* to obtain a bit of *Y*. Criminologist Jack Gibbs makes this point well: "Commentators often fail to recognize the criminal justice system for what it is—a mishmash, complete with conflicting goals and even conflicting means to the same goal. So the miracle is that the system functions at all."[82]

This conclusion need not make us unduly pessimistic. Achieving something is better than achieving nothing at all. Stopping ten murders saves ten lives—even if it is a "drop in the bucket" of all crime. Preventing one innocent person from being convicted is a victory for justice, although much injustice may remain.

However, our sights must be kept relatively low, lest we strive for the impossible. The incongruities between goals will never be resolved, and self-interests will never be synchronized fully with social ideals. The harsh reality of conflicting priorities sets an upper limit on the capabilities of the criminal justice system.

SUMMARY

We outline a theory of motivation behind criminal justice decision making based on the concept of self-interest, which can have both positive and negative aspects. Individuals within the criminal justice system have many personal goals that often explain how they act; they seek money, self-actualization, comfort, power, fame, and peer approval. The organizations of which they are part have external goals that are the tasks they are required to achieve; in addition, they have internal, self-protective goals—survival and expansion, for example.

The public interest in criminal justice is a confusing and conflicting set of socially desirable goals sought by wide sectors of the population. Six important goals are crime prevention, public tranquillity, justice, due process, efficiency, and accountability. In formulating and implementing public policy, we make choices about how these goals are to be ranked. This is an ongoing political process that invariably involves negotiation and compromise.

FOOTNOTES

[1] The facts about Earl Warren's career are taken from Leo Katcher, *Earl Warren: A Political Biography* (New York: McGraw-Hill, 1967).

[2] Ibid., p. 5.

[3] Gresham Sykes, *The Society of Captives: A Study of a Maximum Security Prison* (Princeton, N.J.: Princeton University Press, 1958).

[4] Tom Murton with Joe Hymans, *Accomplices to the Crime* (New York: Grove Press, 1969), p. 7.

[5] "Arkansas: The Telltale Skeletons," *Newsweek*, February 12, 1968, pp. 42–43.

[6] Robert Ringer, *Looking Out for Number One* (New York: Fawcett, 1978).

[7] Anthony Downs, *Inside Bureaucracy* (Boston: Little, Brown, 1967), p. 83.

[8] Malcolm Feeley, "Two Models of the Criminal Justice System: An Organizational Perspective," *Law and Society Review*, 7 (Spring 1973), 413 (italics in original).

[9] Thomas Hobbes, *Leviathan*, chap. 11, quoted in George Sabine. *A History of Political Theory*, 3rd ed. (New York: Holt, Rinehart & Winston, 1961), p. 463.

[10] Alexander Hamilton, James Madison, John Jay, *The Federalist Papers* (New York: New American Library, 1961), p. 463.

[11] Ibid., pp. 77–84, 308–13.

[12] Jeremy Bentham, *Theory of Legislation*, quoted in W. T. Jones, *Masters of Political Thought*, vol. II (Boston: Houghton Mifflin, 1959), 369.

[13] This is also the view of Abraham Kaplan, *The Conduct of Inquiry* (San Francisco: Chandler Publishing, 1964); and Hans Zetterberg, *On Theory and Verification in Sociology*, 3rd ed. (Totowa, N.J.: Bedminster Press, 1965).

[14] Representative of the modern approach are Abraham Maslow, *Motivation and Personality*, 2nd ed. (New York: Harper & Row, 1970); and William Mitchell, "The Shape of Political Theory to Come: From Political Sociology to Political Economy," in *Politics and the Social Sciences*, ed. Seymour Lipset (New York: Oxford University Press, 1969), pp. 101–36.

[15] Israel Shenker, "Solzhenitsyn, in Harvard Speech, Terms West Weak and Cowardly," *New York Times*, June 9, 1978, p. 8.

[16] Maslow, op. cit., pp. 46–47, 149–81.

[17] Judson Gooding, *The Job Revolution* (New York: Walker, 1972).

[18] Arthur Niederhoffer, *Behind the Shield: The Police in Urban Society* (New York: Doubleday, 1969).

[19] *New York Post*, July 14, 1978, p. 1.

[20] The study was quoted by Michael Rosenbaum and Carl Pelleck, in "PBA Defiant on 1-Cop Cars," *New York Post*, June 21, 1977, p. 3.

[21] Tom Wolfe, "The 'Me' Decade and the Third Great Awakening," *New York Magazine*, August 23, 1976, pp. 26–40.

[22] The record of prosecution is reported in *Time*, October 18, 1976, p. 40.

[23] "Illinois's Big Jim vs. Big Mike," *Newsweek*, October 11, 1976, p. 32.

[24] Michael Macoby, *The Gamesmen* (New York: Simon & Schuster, 1977), p. 100.

[25] Quoted in James Mills, "I Have Nothing to Do with Justice," *Before the Law: An Introduction to the Legal Process* eds. John Bonsignore et al. (Boston: Houghton Mifflin, 1974), p. 312.

[26] Jerome Skolnick, *Justice Without Trial* (New York: Wiley, 1966), pp. 52–62.

[27] Quoted in Edith Asbury, "2 Tell of a Cover-Up in Killing by Officer," *New York Times*, March 15, 1977, p. 41.

[28] Harry Kalven and Hans Zeisel, *The American Jury* (Boston: Little, Brown, 1966), p. 489.

[29] Chester Bernard, *The Functions of the Executive* (Cambridge, Mass.: Harvard University Press, 1938), p. 139.

[30] For a detailed discussion of organizational goals, see Lawrence Mohr, "The Concept of Organizational Goal," *American Political Science Review* 67 (1973), 470–81.

[31] Leonard Buder, "25 Win Promotions in 'Son of Sam' Case," *New York Times*, August 20, 1977, p. 10.

[32] *New York Times*, July 14, 1978, p. B3.

[33] Richard McCleary, "How Structural Variables Constrain the Parole Officer's Use of Discretionary Powers," *Social Problems* 23 (December 1975), 209–25.

[34] Quoted in "The Biggest Bust," *Newsweek*, May 17, 1971, p. 25D.

[35] Ibid., p. 26.

[36] "Paying Off May Day," *Time*, April 30, 1973, p. 66.

[37] Quoted in "The Zebra Killers," *Newsweek*, April 29, 1974, p. 27.

[38] Ibid.

[39] See Peter Kihss, "Theft Damage Cost in Blackout Put at $135 Million Out of Total Business Loss in 'Hundreds of Millions,'" *New York Times*, July 22, 1977, p. A12; and Tom Goldstein, "Some Suspects in Looting Still Awaiting Day in Court," *New York Times*, July 19, 1977, p. 26.

[40] See, for example, Glendon Schubert, *The Public Interest* (Glencoe, Ill: The Free Press, 1960), chap. 4.

[41] Carl Sandburg, *The People, Yes*, quoted in Schubert, ibid., pp. 7, 79, 136.

[42] These data are based on reported crime figures taken from a study done by the *New York Times* and the New York City Rand Institute, and published in David Burnham, "A Wide Disparity Is Found in Crime Throughout City," *New York Times*, February 14, 1972, pp. 1, 16; and David Burnham, "Police Efficiency Constant All Over City, Study Finds," *New York Times*, February 15, 1972, pp. 1, 22.

[43] The concept of "social sanitation" is taken from John Galtung, "The Social Functions of a Prison," in *Prison Within Society*, ed. Lawrence Hazalrigg (Garden City, N.Y.: Doubleday, 1968).

[44] Charles Bahn, "The Reassurance Factor in Police Patrol," *Criminology* 12 (November 1974), 338–45.

[45] Quoted in the *New York Times*, July 16, 1976, p. A10.

[46] In Furman v. Georgia, 408 U.S. 238 (1972).

[47] Statistic is from Federal Bureau of Investigations, *Sourcebook of Criminal Justice Statistics—1975* (Washington, D.C.: U.S. Government Printing Office).

[48] Furman v. Georgia.

[49] Andrew von Hirsch, *Doing Justice: The Choice of Punishments* (New York: Hill & Wang, 1976), chap. 8.

[50] Lev. 24: 17–22.

[51] Quoted in the *New York Times*, August 12, 1977, p. 10.

[52] Furman v. Georgia.

[53] Gregg v. Georgia, 428 U.S. 153 (1976).

[54] Coker v. Georgia, 433 U.S. 584 (1977).

[55] *New York Times*, August 8, 1977, p. 1.

[56] Karl Menninger, *The Crime of Punishment* (New York: Viking Press, 1968).

[57] Queen v. Dudley and Stephens, 14 W.B.D. 273 (1884).

[58] *New York Times*, July 3, 1977, p. 18.

[59] Quoted in "Law Enforcement: The Collinsville Reich," *Newsweek*, May 14, 1973, p. 45.

[60] Quoted in ibid.

[61] Aleksandr Solzhenitsyn, *The Gulag Archipelago, 1918–1956: An Experiment in Literary Investigations* (New York: Harper & Row, 1974).

[62] Mapp v. Ohio, 367 U.S. 643 (1961).

[63] Palko v. Connecticut, 302 U.S. 319 (1937).

[64] Benton v. Maryland, 395 U.S. 784 (1969).

[65] Joint Anti-Fascist Refugee Committee v. McGrath, 341 U.S. 123 (1951).

[66] Miranda v. Arizona, 384 U.S. 436 (1966).

[67] Michigan v. Tucker, 417 U.S. 433 (1974).

[68] Quoted in C. Herman Pritchett, *The American Constitution*, 3rd ed. (New York: McGraw-Hill, 1977), p. 427.

[69] Katz v. United States, 389 U.S. 347 (1967).

[70] Berger v. New York, 388 U.S. 41 (1967): United States v. United States District Court, 407 U.S. 297 (1972).

[71] Herman Schwartz, *Taps, Bugs, and Fooling the People* (New York: Field Foundation, 1977), p. 17.

[72] Olmstead v. United States, 277 U.S. 438 (1928).

[73] Quoted in Schwartz, op. cit., p. 27.

[74] Ibid., p. 6.

[75] Paul Houston, "GAO Studies FBI's Least Wanted List," *New York Post*, September 30, 1976, p. 68.

[76] Reported in *New York Daily News*, July 18, 1977, p. 14.

[77] Richard Harris, *Justice* (New York: Avon Books, 1970).

[78] Herbert Packer, *The Limits of the Criminal Sanction* (Stanford, Calif.: Stanford University Press, 1968).

[79] Reported in the *New York Times*, July 21, 1978, p. A10.

[80] Lewis Carroll, *The Annotated Alice* (New York: Bramhill House, 1960), p. 88.

[81] Charles Schultze, *The Politics and Economics of Public Spending* (Washington, D.C.: Brookings Institution, 1968), pp. 38–39.

[82] Jack Gibbs, *Crime, Punishment, and Deterrence* (New York: Elsevier, 1975), p. 23.

BIBLIOGRAPHY

DeWolf, L. Harold. *Crime and Justice in America*. New York: Harper & Row, 1975.

Downs, Anthony. *Inside Bureaucracy*. Boston: Little, Brown, 1967.

Feeley, Malcolm. "Two Models of the Criminal Justice System: An Organizational Perspective." *Law and Society Review* 7 (Spring 1973), 407–26.

Fleming, Macklin. *The Price of Perfect Justice*. New York: Basic Books, 1974.

Macoby, Michael. *The Gamesmen*. New York: Simon & Schuster, 1977.

Maslow, Abraham. *Motivation and Personality*. 2nd ed. New York: Harper & Row, 1970.

Mohn, Lawrence. "The Concept of Organizational Goal." *American Political Science Review* 67 (1973), 470–81.

Packer, Herbert. *The Limits of the Criminal Sanction*. Stanford, Calif.: Stanford University Press, 1968.

Pritchett, C. Herman. *The American Constitution*. 3rd ed. New York: McGraw-Hill, 1977, chaps. 18, 25, and 26.

Schubert, Glendon. *The Public Interest*. Glencoe, Ill.: The Free Press, 1960.

Von Hirsch, Andrew. *Doing Justice: The Choice of Punishments*. New York: Hill & Wang, 1976.

Wilson, James. *Political Organizations*. New York: Basic Books, 1973, chaps. 2, 3.

In the late 1800s, some newspaper editors started a drive to glorify the Jesse James gang, depicting them as a Robin Hood-like band of chivalrous men emerging to fight the injustices heaped on those who had supported the Confederate side in the Civil War:

> Their fame has become national, aye, world-wide. Ever since the war closed, and left them outlawed, they have borne themselves like men who have only to die, and have determined to do it without flinching. For the last two or three years the whole country has rung with their daring and hardihood.[1]

Through a series of short stories and newspaper accounts,[2] a segment of the media soon made Jesse James a folklore hero:

CHAPTER TWO

PERCEIVING CRIME

Jesse, along with his brother Frank, return from Confederate guerrilla service in the Civil War only to find their home state of Missouri overrun with carpetbaggers and other Yankee oppressors. The story line states that these opportunists and Yankee persecutors attack Jesse's father, jail his mother, and savagely beat him, with the law serving the cause of the vindictive Unionists. To secure justice, Jesse James must live outside the law. He rights the wrongs inflicted by the economic aristocracy by preying upon the banking and railroad industries and by living a life devoted to opposing the established system.[3]

Historians have pieced together a very different picture of Jesse James, beginning with his activities during the Civil War. He joined Quantrill's raiders, a group that used the cause of the Confederacy as a cover to plunder, murder, and rape. As a member of this loosely organized band of marauders, Jesse James engaged in a range of criminal activities, including the massacre at Lawrence, Kansas, where approximately 200 civilians were "gunned down or burned alive."[4] Following the war, he formed his own gang and embarked on a criminal career that revolved around robbery and murder.

Why did a segment of the media create such myths about the Jesse James gang? More broadly, what motivates the media and other popular sources of information to present misleading pictures of America's crime problem to the public? A central purpose of this chapter is to answer these questions and to reveal contemporary misperceptions fostered by the media and politicians concerning the nature and extent of crime in America. Many crime myths, or portrayals of crime that are only partly true, form lasting impressions on the public and ultimately influence our society's response to crime problems.

43

Sources of Perceptions

What prompted Missouri newspapers to make Jesse James a folk hero? According to historians it was because Missouri and other western states were devastated during the Civil War by the fighting between the Union occupation army and Confederate guerrillas.[5] After the war newspaper editors, sympathetic to the Confederate side and closely tied to economic interests in the West, glorified the James gang as heroic southern diehards who would never rob from other southerners.[6]

The eastern press hotly disputed these stories. Nevertheless, they were well received in the emerging West, where hatred toward eastern-controlled banks and railroads ran high. Therefore, bandit stories in the press became tools to manipulate public opinion in what was actually the beginning of a long economic rivalry "between the established East and the upstart West."[7]

As we will see in Chapter 4, politicians and the media play critical roles in shaping today's governmental strategies for attacking crime. At the same time, these groups have their own motives for promoting misperceptions about crime and the criminal justice system. Some politicians use crime issues as a way to acquire popular support at election time. Newspaper publishers and editors have found that certain crime themes boost circulation at a time when many newspapers are in serious financial trouble and in intense competition with television news programs.

Also, with the decline in popularity of cowboy-and-Indian television shows and movies, many film companies and producers have discovered that crime themes and dramatizations of police work produce both home-viewing and box-office successes. Thus, for the news media and the entertainment business, crime often provides significant financial gains.

NEWS MEDIA

Today newspapers and television news programs give extraordinary attention to the crime problem in many cities. Media owners have found that crime stories can add to their economic benefits.

Some newspapers like the *New York Daily News* have been winning circulation battles with competitors by giving front-page coverage to violent crimes like murder and rape. On February 5, 1973, the *Daily News* reported in a six-inch banner headline, "Missing Coed Found Slain: Westchester Girl Killed with Bra."[8] On the same day, the *New York Times* covered the same story with a one-inch headline in the back of the paper entitled, "Body of Coed Found Near Boston."[9] While these two competing newspapers differed in their crime coverage during the late 1950s and early 1960s,[10] a 1975 study has shown that the *New York Times* currently is stressing crime stories at a rate similar to its chief rival.[11]

Exaggerated coverage of such unusual violent crimes by the three major

HOW THE MEDIA CREATED A CRIME WAVE

Through their interactions and reliance on official sources, news organizations both invoke and reproduce prevailing concepts of "serious crime." . . . In late 1976, New York City experienced a major crime wave. The city's three daily newspapers and five local television stations reported a surge of violence against elderly people. The crime wave lasted approximately seven weeks, eventually receiving national television and newspaper coverage.

One consequence of this was the public definition of a new type of crime. "Crimes against the elderly" became a typical crime with typical victims, offenders, and circumstances.

It is doubtful that there really was a crime wave or any unusual surge of violence against elderly people. No one really knows, least of all the journalists who reported the crime wave. The police statistics from the N.Y.P.D. do not show a crime wave. In fact, for one type of crime, homicide, the police showed a nineteen percent *drop* over the previous year's rate of elderly people murdered. This is significant because the news media began their reporting with coverage of several gruesome murders. (Twenty-eight percent of the stories reported by the three media organizations I surveyed were stories about homicides. In contrast, the police reported that homicides made up less than one percent of crimes against the elderly in 1976).

Mark Fishman, "Crime Wave as Ideology," *Social Problems*, June 1978, pp. 531–32.

newspapers in New York City reached a peak during the reign of "Son of Sam," or the .44-caliber killer, in 1976 and 1977. Some observers criticized this sensationalism:

> By transforming a person who has killed or wounded 13 people into a seemingly omnipotent monster stalking the city, the press has created the kind of public and official hysteria that may cause the death of innocent suspects and will make a fair trial of an accused killer nearly impossible.[12]

However, playing up such crimes does sell newspapers. Newsstands reported greater sales than any period since the assassination of President John F. Kennedy in 1963. The *Daily News* added over 400,000 copies to its daily run, and the *New York Post* sold more than 1 million copies—400,000 more than usual—on the day they spread "CAUGHT" (in red letters) across their front page.[13]

Even more alarming than newspapers playing up crime is that citizens and governmental officials apparently gauge the nature and extent of crime in their town or city largely on the basis of news coverage, rather than on official crime statistics.[14] Such dependence would be reasonable if newspaper reporters presented a balanced picture of crime in their communities. However, as reported by researcher E. Terrence Jones, newspapers as an overall source of accurate information about crime are quite unreliable. In his study, he compared crime statistics with the nature of crime coverage in the newspapers of St. Louis, Missouri, and found three kinds of distortions: (1) Crime increases and decreases from year to year bore no relationship to the amount of yearly attention newspapers gave to crime coverage. (2) Papers overstress crimes occurring in white, middle-class areas of the city; (3) Violent crimes and crimes against persons (e.g., rape) received far more attention (30 to 90 times more) than more typical property crimes (e.g., burglaries).[15] Thus, the news media are an undependable source for determining how much, where, and what kinds of crime exist in our communities. More reliable sources for acquiring answers to such questions are discussed in Chapter 13.

While the news media often distort crime, they occasionally provide the public with in-depth coverage of important crime topics. For example, the *Arizona Republic*, the major daily newspaper for the Phoenix metropolitan area, ran a lengthy series in 1977 that closely monitored the state legislature's deliberations over a new criminal code.[16]

In 1977 the University of California at San Diego developed a newspaper course on criminal justice issues that was funded through a grant from the National Endowment for the Humanities.[17] Written by some of the nation's most prominent criminal justice experts, a series of 15 newspaper articles appeared in newspapers throughout the nation in the fall of 1977. These weekly articles were published in conjunction with a course offered for credit at over 200 colleges and universities, which enabled interested students and citizens to explore more deeply the topics raised in the articles.

Such responsible journalism can play an important role in reversing public myths surrounding America's crime problem. Chapter 3 shows how ingrained societal myths about certain classes of criminal acts play a role in shaping the severity of our response to criminal behavior.

THE ENTERTAINMENT INDUSTRY

The television networks devote a tremendous amount of air time to crime stories and law enforcement programing. For example, during the 1976–1977 television season, police programs consumed nearly 20 of the 65 hours of prime-time television. How realistic are these many depictions of criminal behavior and police work?

By viewing a week of prime-time network programing in 1972 and comparing these findings with official crime statistics, a professor of communications, Joseph Dominick, identified a number of distortions and omissions resulting from TV entertainment shows.[18] He summarized the misperceptions as follows:

> (1) Television overrepresents violent crimes directed at individuals. Real-world crime is usually non-violent and directed at property; (2) television criminals bear little resemblance to their real life counterparts. Blacks, young people, and lower-class individuals are underrepresented in the TV criminal world; (3) television crime does not pay. TV criminals are almost always apprehended. In real life, the legal system is not nearly so efficient; (4) the less visual elements of the legal system are seldom seen on television. Most of the events from the suspect's capture until his trial are ignored; (5) non-whites are underrepresented as murder victims; and (6) violent crimes between family members are underrepresented.[19]

In 1977 political scientist Alan Arcuri surveyed a large number of police officers in New Jersey in order to find out how accurately they feel police programs depict their work. The officers were asked to rank 13 shows according to their degree of realism. "Adam 12" and "Dragnet" were considered among the most realistic; they generally present the routines of policing, the potential for human error, and the dimensions of professionalism. Such shows as "McMillan and Wife" and "Mod Squad" were dismissed as sheer fantasies or jokes.[20]

The police officers were also asked to identify the fictional elements these programs commonly present to viewing audiences. In all of the programs that were studied, they found myths about crime.[21] They felt that police shows dramatize police work as much more exciting than it is; in addition, the shows portray the cop as a superman who always nabs his quarry. The following responses to the survey by police officers summarize their concern about potential public misperceptions that emerge from these television dramatizations:

> [1] The public gets the impression that you can take fingerprints off water. They're under the impression that every criminal leaves a clue; [2] the public thinks all the goddam crimes should be solved within a half an hour, even with commercials; [3] the public must think what fun it is to be a cop . . . work undercover and solve big crimes. . . . The "big crimes" are more often a complaint about a neighbor's dog pissing on a favorite bush.[22]

Other researchers have shown that television crime stories also greatly mislead the public about due process guarantees. In a three-year study of prime-time shows, one researcher found that police conducted illegal searches and failed to inform individuals of their constitutional rights in a majority of scenes depicting such incidents.[23] The authors of a 1977 *Saturday Review* article came to similar conclusions in their one-week analysis of 15 randomly selected prime-time police programs. They found 43 scenes of probable lawless police activity, including 20 "clear constitutional violations."[24]

At least one expert has concluded that these television distortions do have an effect on citizen perceptions of police work. In 1973 the superintendent of the Chicago Police Department conducted interviews with 500 citizens who reported dissatisfaction with police service. His findings tended to confirm law enforcement agencies' apprehensions regarding the entertainment media's conveyance of policing myths:

> Perhaps because of the influence of movies and television programs, where police investigations are brought to a swift and neat conclusion, citizens expect each and every crime to be concluded. . . . Further evidence of the influence entertainment programs generate was found in the vocabulary citizens chose to rate the quality of police service. Many of the returned survey cards contained such police jargon as . . . "beat man okay, but patrol sergeant discourteous."[25]

While researchers have established that criminal justice myths are routinely generated by the entertainment industry, more research is needed. The extent to which society responds to America's crime problems based on these myths must still be determined.

POLITICIANS

National and local politicians often use the crime problem as a vote-getting device and present themselves as able to solve all crime problems. The use of crime as a campaign issue was especially apparent during the late 1960s and early 1970s, when Richard Nixon used a "law and order" theme to boost his own presidential candidacy in 1968 as well as to campaign for like-minded congressional candidates to support his programs.[26] Under this law and order banner, crime was linked to terrorism, drug use, obscenity, and student protests when the president said that he was working to stem a rising rate of lawlessness that was "sweeping" the country.[27] For example, while visiting Albuquerque, New Mexico, in 1970, President Nixon stressed this campaign theme:

> I said I would appoint a stronger Attorney General. I said I would appoint stronger judges. I said I would ask for stronger laws. I have tried to do all of these things.
> We need to strengthen the peace forces as against the criminal forces in the United States of America. . . . We need men in the United States Senate . . . who will support the President when he asks for stronger laws, men who will vote

to approve those judges, who are going to take that strong stand for respect for law and for enforcing the law. . . .

The wave of crime is not going to be that wave of the future for these young people of America."[28]

The ramifications of Watergate and the failure of the Nixon and Ford presidencies to stem crime blunted this issue for the 1976 presidential race, but state and local politicians from both major political parties still play on crime as a campaign issue. In a 1977 mayoral primary in New York City, all of the major candidates hotly debated the issue of capital punishment, even though the mayor has no authority to impose the death penalty.

Marc Adams, a newspaper reporter for the *Arizona Republic*, labeled the tactics behind the state legislature's debate over a tough new criminal code as the "villain-hero" method:

Essentially, the legislators feel compelled to adhere to the popular notion that all crime occurs basically the same way—violently by the crazed molester, the assailant poised behind the bush for the attack. . . . These the legislator identifies as "villains."

The legislator then overcompensates by glossing the new criminal laws with overboard and tough sounding language and creates impressive penalties to fit, in hopes that he or she will be identified as "hero" come election day.[29]

In interviewing a legislative leader in the Arizona House of Representatives, Adams was told that a "go get crime" strategy sounds good at election time and that it's nearly "impossible to explain the nuances of crime to the public."[30] In the final chapter of this book, we argue that despite the creation of crime myths by media and politicians, citizens can, and must, be exposed to both the nuances of crime and the intricacies of the agencies that together comprise the criminal justice system.

Types of Misperceptions

As a result of the self-interest of politicians, the news media, and the entertainment industry, many misperceptions about the agencies of the criminal justice system and crime in our society are presented to the public. What follows is a closer analysis of three misperceptions that cloud our society's ability to respond realistically to critical crime problems.

WHO IS THE CRIMINAL?

"Bloodthirsty Madman Stalks New York City Streets"[31] typified the headlines splashed across the front pages of newspapers throughout the country in 1977. National and local news programs gave considerable air time to describing the movements of New York City's .44-caliber killer, who stalked attractive dark-haired women in the middle-class communities of Brooklyn, Queens, and the Bronx.

This example of crime coverage is representative of the role the news media, television programs, and movies currently play in distorting citizens' perceptions of criminals in America.[32] Most people have a cops-and-robbers image of crime that usually pits a deranged, yet cunning, killer against an overworked, but tenacious, team of police detectives.

Citizens come to view the universe of crime as stranger-to-stranger attacks by street predators who seriously injure or kill decent people. This media- and politician-generated picture imprints a physical mug shot of the "typical" criminal in the minds of people, who believe they can spot one in a crowd as easily as they can a clown in a circus.

As with David Berkowitz, the .44-caliber killer, neighbors are shocked when they learn that the quiet gentleman next door who holds down a responsible job in the community is a mass murderer. These expressions of disbelief symbolize the gap between images of criminals and the reality of criminal behavior.

Sociologist John Conklin argues that citizens' perceptions of criminals as "outsiders," or people from communities other than their own, reduce certain anxieties.[33] Residents of communities are able to dissociate themselves from offenders and feel less threatened while around their homes. In middle-class communities such perceptions allow citizens to stereotype criminals so as to reinforce existing racial and ethnic prejudices. As Conklin notes, "When crime is associated with the lower class or with a racial or ethnic minority, fear of crime can contribute to segregation of that group in housing and education."[34]

However, Conklin's research reveals that most serious crimes are committed by local residents instead of outsiders.[35] Other experts have studied a particular serious crime, murder, and found that (1) most murders in the United States are committed by young adults; (2) nearly all murders are *intra*racial; (3) victims and killers usually know each other and are often related; (4) murder rates are higher in the South and North Central region than in the Northeast; and (5) despite the higher murder rate in large cities, most urban murders occur in very isolated sections of the metropolis.[36] Further, in his comprehensive analysis of murder, Donald Lunde presents a description of a "common kind of murder" and shows the typical conditions associated with murder:

> a father and grown son [are] drinking to excess on holiday or a Saturday night. Other relatives are often present as well. A quarrel erupts and father or son grabs a gun, and someone is killed. . . . The next day, when sober, the killer may have no memory of the events of the preceding night, having experienced alcoholic amnesia.[37]

This description is quite different from the public image of the murderer as someone stalking the city's streets ready to kill if theft victims resist.

Murder is only one indicator of the crime problem. Many citizens break the law. Most crimes that occur are misdemeanors, often involving no assailant-victim relationship. As described in Chapters 3 and 11, nearly all citizens have committed some crime on one or more occasions. If you have gone to a park and consumed liquor out of an open container, cheated on your income taxes, lived with a member of the opposite sex without having taken marriage vows, or experimented with an illicit drug like marijuana, then you are considered a law-breaker in many states.

However, are these serious criminal acts? In Chapter 3, we look at a number of ways to determine both the breadth and seriousness of criminal activity. Making such determinations is necessary in order to understand both the limitations of governmental efforts to reduce some crimes and the potential of specific policies for ameliorating certain crime problems. Evaluating the seriousness of crime is also important in determining law enforcement priorities.

WHO IS THE VICTIM?

We must also acquire a realistic understanding of victims of crime. Popular sources of information about crime often provide citizens with an inaccurate picture of their chances of becoming victims. Thus, for predatory street crime, many elderly people have a heightened fear of crime well beyond the likelihood of their ever being victims.[38] Excessive fear of crime can greatly lower the quality of life for senior citizens, often forcing them off the streets and out of parks that are quite safe.

For other citizens popular images of crime create a false sense of security. Citizens moving to the suburbs often build homes that are difficult to secure against household crimes like burglary. An underestimation of one's likelihood of being a victim can lead to crime-prevention laziness in which commonsense safeguards, such as locking one's car at night, are ignored.

Such misperceptions have caused police departments to develop programs for alerting city residents to the types of crimes they are likely to experience and how they might lower their chances of victimization.[39] Researchers have developed a variety of methods for tracking crimes according to victim characteristics. Surveys of victims pinpointing trends in street crimes and household crimes have been carried out in 26 cities.[40] (These surveys and many other methods of collecting crime statistics are fully explored in Chapter 13.) The 1974–1975 victimization survey findings for Newark, New Jersey, and Dallas, Texas, illustrate how racial and income characteristics influence one's probabilities of being a victim.

In both Dallas and Newark, minorities are more likely than whites to be victims of violent street crimes, such as rape, robbery, or assault.[41] Also, the lower one's family income, the more likely an individual will become the victim of a crime. For example, in Dallas individuals whose family income is between $3,000 and $7,499 experience 56.6 crimes of violence for every 1,000 residents;

but those whose family income is between $15,000 and $24,999 are victimized at a rate of only 39.3 per 1,000 residents.[42]

For household crimes like burglary, minorities are again more often victims than whites in both cities.[43] However, individuals living in households with incomes of $25,000 or higher are more likely to be burglarized in both Dallas and Newark than those from lower income strata. Nonetheless, in both cities, the burglary rate for low-income people ($3,000–$7,499) is parallel to the burglary level for middle-income homes ($15,000–$24,999).[44]

Poor people do suffer from high rates of both street crimes and household crimes. It is difficult to determine the most likely victims of white-collar crimes such as fraud, embezzlement, illegal price fixing, and tax evasion. But the poor are probably significant victims again.

Various studies suggest that the economic losses from white-collar crime are of much greater dimensions than violent crimes or street thefts and burglaries.[45] But such crime has much less visible impact because its costs are passed on to consumers indirectly through higher prices, interest rates, and taxes. This deferral of costs hurts the poor more than others because they spend a higher proportion of their income on consumer goods, they buy more things on credit, and they bear the brunt of a regressive tax structure. Thus, as with most social problems, the hardships produced by crime are disproportionately borne by the poor.

Still, citizens from all income levels can be victimized by some crimes. Therefore, it is important for a community's law enforcement agency to use available crime data to provide neighborhoods with specific information on the crimes they are most likely to experience. The dissemination of crime information could be the first step toward increasing citizen self-help efforts. Citizen "crime proofing" as one strategy for lowering the rate of property and street crimes will be discussed in the concluding chapter on the future of crime policy.

CRIME SOLUTIONS

In this section we look briefly at two examples of popular solutions to crime problems that lack considerable plausibility when subjected to critical analysis. Politicians, news media people, and criminal justice personnel frequently support local solutions to criminal activity that are actually much larger in scope. For example, these individuals promote community crackdowns on local drug dealers as solutions to drug trafficking. As we will see below, such tactics ignore certain international and economic realities about drug peddling.

Movies and TV dramas often emphasize "get tough" police tactics (e.g., *Dirty Harry* with Clint Eastwood), but they also frequently show citizens protecting themselves from street crimes with guns. And Westerns have long stressed the theme of law-abiding citizens arming themselves to ward off bands of thieves who threaten the essential stability of their community.

More recently, films have dramatized similar vigilante tactics to fight muggers, rapists, and burglars in central cities. In *Death Wish*, for example, the distraught Charles Bronson reacts to the rape-murder of his wife and daughter by acquiring a handgun and roaming the darkened alleys and parks of New York City posing as a likely target for a mugger. When approached by a street predator, Bronson metes out justice directly by murdering these criminals with his collector's handgun. He becomes a hero in the local newspapers; when discovered by the police, he is simply forced to leave town.

HANDGUN REALITIES What are the more likely effects of citizens' reliance on handguns for self-protection? In reality, these weapons usually end up being used to injure or murder a family member or close acquaintance rather than being unleashed on a potential street criminal.[46]

As shown in Figure 2-1, handguns were associated with over 50 percent of the murders reported in 1975. For the most part, these handgun murders were *not* the result of either predatory street crimes or shootouts between criminals and defense-minded citizens. America's stockpiling of handguns for generations has reached "the point where the likelihood of personal disaster from possession of guns far exceeds the likelihood of protection."[47] This "domestic mini-arms race," sparked most recently to retard household crimes like burglaries, increases the probability of murder among acquaintances, friends, and family members, while doing little to retard burglars.[48] After all, most burglars are successful because they choose to enter a home when no one is there. Thus, while many murders that result from temporary anger and fatal accidents caused by

FIGURE 2-1

Murder by Type of Weapon Used, 1975

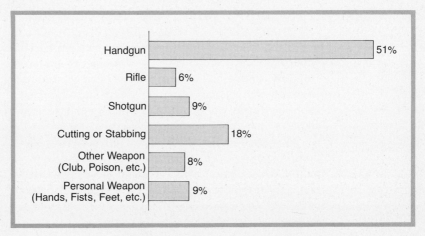

* Due to rounding, does not add to 100 percent.
SOURCE: U.S. Department of Justice, *Crime in the United States—1975* (Washington, D.C.: U.S. Government Printing Office, 1975), p. 17.

The easy availability of handguns at a truck stop in Tennessee

gun mishaps would not occur if there were fewer guns in circulation, the burglary rate would be relatively unaffected.

INTERNATIONAL AND ECONOMIC ROADBLOCKS TO CRIME CONTROL Unlike Europe, our strategic geographic location has traditionally provided us an opportunity to treat domestic social problems and foreign affairs as very different. Domestic problems like crime have been viewed as local in nature. Recently, however, writers and researchers have linked our crime problem and means of controlling it to worldwide phenomena evolving from the impact of technology and economics on a shrinking planet.

Researchers have looked to Latin America not only to document the relationship between illicit heroin trafficking and crime but also to illustrate how multinational corporations can blunt strict domestic restrictions on the production and distribution of popular "uppers and downers."[49] For example, John Pekkanen, in his book on the American drug industry, has described how one drug manufacturer, having lost a battle to fight off strict domestic restrictions on its amphetamines, shifted production of the drug to a Mexico City subsidiary.[50] Operation Blackjack, conducted by the Bureau of Narcotics and Dangerous

Drugs (now the Drug Enforcement Agency), revealed that the Mexican-produced drug was shipped to eight border drugstores, which served as bases for reaching the American black market. The investigation eventually led to the nonrenewal of the firm's export license for this particular drug, but Pekkanen views the episode as an example of the lack of social conscience among the drug industry's multinational corporations. This example shows that controlling some illegal drugs is dependent on the actions of both governments and private companies largely outside the control of local American law enforcement agencies.

This example of the drug industry's operations can also be viewed as a reflection of America's "criminogenic" nature.[51] Our society's economic system, capitalism, openly encourages gaining the competitive edge, even if it means less than legal activity. Watergate revealed both how political competition can lead to criminal activity (burglary of the rival party's offices); "Koreagate," the Korean influence-buying scandal, showed how corporations and foreign governments corrupt the political process in order to enhance their self-interests.[52] As with the following illegal campaign contribution case, the profits gained from such activity usually far outweigh the criminal consequences, even when a business is caught subverting the public interest:

> Late in President Nixon's first term, ten important dairymen visited the White House. The reason for their tour was business; the dairy business. The dairy industry had labored for some time to persuade the President to okay a hike in the federal price support for milk. Until this huddle, the President had steadfastly refused. Shortly after their visit, however, the Secretary of Agriculture announced a support increase which, according to some estimates, would add approximately $600,000,000 to dairymen bank accounts. Not too long after that, about $300,000 was "contributed" by various dairy organizations to the Republican Party for use in the 1972 elections.
>
> What was the upshot of this souring of the electoral process? A few underlings went to jail. Several top dairy executives were fined. And something in the neighborhood of a half-billion dollars was earned by dairymen—at the expense of every American milk drinker. It was a wise investment.[53]

Policy makers are beginning to perceive the need to develop policies that recognize financial incentive as a method of combating our crime problems. For example, the House of Representatives Select Committee on Narcotics suggested to the Carter Administration that "the United States should buy and destroy up to $36 million worth of narcotics from Southeast Asia's opium warlords." While rejecting preemptive buying as a useful strategy based on their discussions with government officials in Burma and Thailand, the Administration acknowledged that insurgent army leaders in northern Burma control the trafficking of 40 percent of the worldwide supply of illicit opium.[54] Thus, there is a growing recognition that crime policies have become entangled with an assortment of economic and foreign policy issues.

CONCLUSION

As will be shown in the following chapters, knowing the actual dimensions of crimes and even improving the public's awareness of unworkable remedies will do little to end crime. It is unrealistic to believe, as is often asserted by politicians in the heat of a campaign, that this country's crime problem can be solved or eliminated.

The potential for lowering the incidence of certain crimes, a realistic goal, requires that crime-fighting agencies change some of their operations and that self-help measures be established by law-abiding citizens to make it more difficult for criminals to carry out their acts. Moreover, policy makers, crime-fighting agencies, and citizens will need to accept the fact that there will always be some level of crime in contemporary America. Recognizing our limitations is especially difficult because many Americans have acquired simplistic misperceptions about the nature of crime and solutions to it.

A Temporal Perspective: Is Crime Gaining Momentum?

We also think about crime from a temporal perspective. A central concern of this perception of crime is whether or not it is getting worse. One of the reasons that we cannot provide an absolute answer to this question is that temporal perspectives on crime require us to designate a time from the past to compare with present conditions.

HISTORICAL PERSPECTIVES

If we take a broad historical perspective, we would most likely view the crime problem of the late 1960s through the 1970s as serious, but equaled by earlier periods of broad social unrest. While we lack reliable crime statistics for the 1800s, we do know from historical accounts that crimes were of grave concern to established residents during the era of massive European immigration. For example, James Richardson, in his historical analysis of New York's police force, paints a picture of crime between 1845 and 1855 very similar to current reports linking the explosion of street crime to youthful offenders:

> The children of the foreign born, suspended between two cultures and often learning the ways of the city more quickly than their parents, provided the raw materials for the dangerous classes. About two-thirds were girls between the ages of eight and sixteen who were forced to steal by inebriate parents. Professional thieves used these children in Fagin-like fashion because magistrates hesitated to punish them. Most of the girls were prostitutes as well as thieves. . . . The boys, more likely to arouse suspicion than the girls, tended to concentrate on thieving around the piers.[55]

Zane Miller, in his historical study of Cleveland's political system in the 1800s, labels the period from 1884 to 1894 the "decade of disorder."[56] In 1884 "police had made 12 arrests for malicious shooting, 29 for malicious cutting, 47 for cutting with intent to wound, 284 for shooting with intent to kill, 92 for murder and manslaughter, and 948 for carrying a concealed weapon. There were a total of 56,784 arrests."[57]

Also, riots that produce significant jumps in crime rates are hardly unique to contemporary America. Psychologist Sheldon Levy conducted a 150-year study of political violence in the United States by analyzing newspaper accounts. He found that the 1960s represent a violent period similar to several previous eras, including the depression of the 1930s. In fact, riots during the depression produced a much higher rate of deaths and personal injuries than contemporary disruptions.[58]

Riots surrounding war and foreign affairs issues are also common occurrences in American history. For example, the great New York City draft riot of July 1863 dwarfs all contemporary racial and antiwar riots. A military draft was imposed two days prior to the riots and included a clause saying that one could be excluded by paying a $300 fee to the government. Poor Irish immigrants, who could not afford to pay, lashed out against property and blacks to vent their frustrations and fears over going to war. With as many as 50,000 rioters battling police, militia, and federal troops for five straight days, a recent chronicler of the event set the death toll at around 1,300 and damage at over $5 million (which has not been adjusted for over 100 years of dollar inflation).[59]

Due to changes in crime-reporting practices, no long-term data on trends is fully reliable (see Chapter 13). However, most scholars agree that the century of arrest data for Chicago (see Figure 2-2) roughly mirrors national crime trends.[60] Three periods in which crime reached peak levels were the late 1800s, the Prohibition era, and the late 1960s through the 1970s. We are coming to realize that crime rises and falls; it is not *always* on the rise.

THE CONTEMPORARY PERSPECTIVE

Looking at crime from a short-term perspective, scholars and police alike see crime on the rise. Today, experts usually rely on a uniform compilation of statistics called the Uniform Crime Reports, which are described more fully in Chapter 13. Starting with 1933, these reports show short-term trends for the following offenses: criminal homicide, forcible rape, robbery, aggravated assault, burglary, larceny-theft, and motor vehicle theft.[61]

Based on these statistics violent street crimes in particular have risen in the 1960s and 1970s. Many street crimes today are characterized by the use or the threat of force and, on occasion, by viciousness. In his study of criminal violence Charles Silberman, a former journalist and more recently a Rockefeller Foundation researcher, refers to street criminals who "kill, maim, and injure without reason or remorse."[62] Some experts view the recent surge in assaults and other

FIGURE 2-2

Chicago: Total Arrests per
1,000 Population, 1868–1970

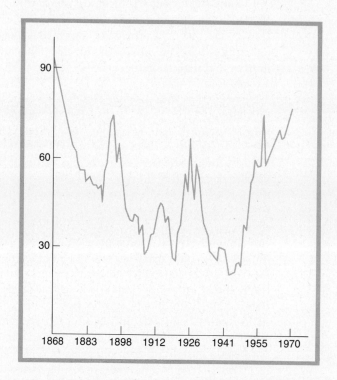

SOURCE: This figure is reprinted from "The Best of Times, the Worst of Times: Trends in Crime in Four Societies" by Ted Robert Gurr in *The Politics of Crime and Conflict: A Comparative History of Four Cities*, Ted Robert Gurr et al., editors, © 1977, p. 647 by permission of the Publisher, Sage Publications, Inc. (Beverly Hills/London) and the author. The figure is based on data from Wesley G. Skogan, *Chicago Since 1840: A Time-Series Data Handbook* (Urbana, Ill.: Institute of Government and Public Affairs, University of Illinois, 1975).

street crimes as a function of the current population bulge of crime-prone individuals between the ages of 15 and 24. This age group represents a population "untamed in the ways of society" and is therefore more likely to commit crimes.[63] These experts point to the baby boom following the Second World War and continuing into the 1950s as the reason for the unusually large proportion of young people, many of whom live in urban areas.

Some experts assert that street crimes will significantly decrease only when the crime-prone population shrinks, as is predicted for the 1980s. When the Justice Department reported a 6 percent nationwide decrease in serious crimes from 1976 to 1977, some people speculated that this one-year shift was attributable to "a decline in the number of young people of crime-committing age."[64]

Others, including the political scientist James Q. Wilson, argue that our society could reduce violent street crimes if we would be more willing to incarcerate youthful offenders. He believes that such a policy would enable society to pass through this high crime era with the least harm to potential victims.[65]

CONCLUSION

Factors other than the actual surge in numbers of a crime-prone population can inflate or deflate crime trend data. Due to increased media attention, the emergence of concerned citizens' groups, or the creation of new government agencies, certain criminal offenses may seem to increase dramatically. Such is the case for crimes related to child abuse, for example. While the hiding of such crimes continues to be a serious problem, especially in middle-class communities, several states have initiated programs that have resulted in increased reports of child abuse.[66] The same effect can occur when insurance companies expand or contract the scope of their theft and personal injury policies.

Technological changes in methods of monitoring crime may also radically alter our temporal framework and thereby generate considerable attention. For example, Florida established a centralized reporting system for child abuse based on a statewide, toll-free hotline.[67] As a result, this new telephone system flooded the relevant civil and criminal justice agencies with cases that required investigation. Therefore, changing technologies can create "statistical crime waves" that are reported as actual increases in crime.

Of course, the crime picture does change with time. While youth crime has always been a serious problem throughout American history, we can detect aspects of criminal behavior that do reflect contemporary changes. For example, available crime data reveal that the 1960s and 1970s represented a period when violent street crimes significantly increased. In Chapter 13 we shall study crime data in greater detail, focusing especially on the utility and reliability of various methods for collecting such data.

Intellectual Perspectives

We have analyzed several elements that play a central role in shaping individuals' perceptions of the crime problem, but we have yet to present an explanation of the nature of crime or how the crime problem should be studied in our society. Experts attempt to define crime—explain its root causes—and to determine whether efforts to cope with crime are effective both on the basis of the facts they gather and evaluate as well as through the normative values they acquire from their respective intellectual affiliations. To fully illustrate the differences among these intellectual perspectives, we will explore the variety of ways experts study a basic crime topic—public drunkenness.

CRIMINOLOGISTS

Criminologists have traditionally searched for the root causes of criminal or deviant behavior. Therefore, many criminologists interested in public drunkenness have concentrated their studies on the backgrounds and social habits of street inebriates or skid-row drunks. They are interested in determining the societal pressures that cause certain individuals to end up in the skid-row areas of our major cities.

Recognizing that most individuals exposed to harsh social conditions remain law-abiding and productive members of society, Edwin Sutherland, a noted criminologist, created a "theory of differential association" that emphasizes societal pressures that play on an individual's learning processes. Crime is learned or passed on "through interaction with carriers of criminal culture."[68] Those individuals exposed largely to lawbreaking attitudes will eventually commit criminal acts. Conversely, people exposed mostly to law-abiding cues from potential carriers (e.g., family, peers) during their formative years are unlikely candidates for demonstrating criminal behavior.

Many criminologists interested in skid-row inebriates and other street people have followed Sutherland's lead by investigating the peer relationships among individuals who come to regard the streets as their homes. Through participant observation and riding along with police officers in areas where street inebriates are concentrated, criminologists have searched for the root causes of such deviancy by studying peer relations among inebriates and also by exploring the role that the police play as "helping" agents: settling disputes among members of this subculture and arresting skid-row drunks when they lack money for either flophouses or liquor.[69]

Criminologists Richard Cloward and Lloyd Ohlin studied another group of street people—delinquent gangs—also looking for the root causes of their criminal behavior.[70] They found that strong peer pressures emerge from delinquent subcultures—gangs that require recruits to commit criminal acts. As a result of such pressures, members build up negative feelings toward parents, schoolteachers, and police officers.[71] In place of the values of traditional reference groups, gang members substitute one of three sets of delinquent values: (1) "criminal values," which encourage members to organize mostly to reap material gains through extortion and theft; (2) "violence values," which confer status for the use or threat of violence; or (3) "drug values," which emphasize gaining "kicks" or "highs."[72]

CONFLICT CRIMINOLOGY Conflict criminologists try to explain crime as a by-product of capitalism and class bias.[73] Therefore, in trying to explain why labels like "tramp" and "vagrant" appear in criminal codes, these criminologists point to the links between economic elites and those who make the laws. Economic and political elites are seen as manipulating criminal labels in order to exercise social control over elements in society who might pose a threat to capitalism or the political and economic elites in a community.

Returning to our example of public drunkenness, individuals accused of drinking in public were also frequently arrested under vagrancy and tramping laws throughout the nineteenth and early twentieth centuries. For example, New York State's nineteenth-century tramp law stated that "all vagrants living without labor or visible means of support, who stroll over the countryside without lawful occupation shall be held to be tramps."[74]

In his analysis of this law, criminologist Sidney Harring showed that economic elites prodded the state legislature to formulate the tramp act and that wealthy businessmen had sufficient influence with the police to assure enforcement of this law.[75] According to Harring, the tramp laws were enacted and enforced by elites to keep the unemployed dispersed and under state control during a severe economic depression.

SUMMARY   Both traditional criminologists and conflict criminologists are interested in explaining crime. They arrive at different causal explanations in part because they investigate very different crimes. Traditional criminologists frequently concentrate on offenses like assault or theft, prohibited acts that pose an obvious threat to the safety or property of law-abiding citizens. Therefore, these criminologists search for certain social factors that cause individuals to follow criminal careers.

Alternatively, conflict criminologists look at criminal laws, like those against vagrancy and public drunkenness, which differentiate law-abiding individuals from lawbreakers on the basis of an individual's circumstances. Only unemployed people can be tramps or vagrants. Therefore, for conflict criminologists, explaining crime requires an investigation of the social forces that shape and enforce laws. Within this framework, crime emerges as a by-product of capitalism and class bias.

LEGAL EXPERTS

While criminologists are interested in explaining crime, the major concern of legal scholars is with defining crime—that is, in saying what *is* and what *is not* a crime. They attempt to determine what is the proper scope of the criminal law. Legal scholars, too, have their schools of thought, each of which offers differing norms for defining proper scope and content of the criminal law.

NATURAL LAW   Few, if any, scholars today hold to the tenets of natural law as a proper foundation for American criminal lawmaking. Under natural law morality and law are viewed as the same. From this perspective law defines the rights and obligations of human beings in a moral sense; therefore, law is unchanging because the moral obligations of individuals transcend time and place.[76]

Given the explicit separation of church and state in our Constitution, the moral behavior of individuals is mostly left to religious groups, which list the moral obligations of individuals. There are, of course, many acts that are violations of both criminal law and moral law—taking the life of another human being, for example.

Still, criminal laws exist in many states that attempt to enforce traditional moral precepts. Advocates of natural law, for example, would insist on the retention of public drunkenness statutes because excessive drinking reveals a moral weakness in individuals that must be curtailed. The many laws that regulate sexual behavior—such as adultery, fornication, and illicit cohabitation statutes—provide additional examples of the overlap of criminal and moral laws. In their collaborative study the legal scholar Norval Morris and criminologist Gordon Hawkins argue that these laws extend the criminal label to millions of citizens: "Indeed, it is as if the sex offense laws were designed to provide an enormous legislative chastity belt encompassing the whole population and proscribing everything but solitary and joyless masturbation and 'normal coitus' inside wedlock."[77]

As we will see in Chapter 11, decriminalization and legalization are public policies designed to reduce the scope of criminal statutes based on the norms of natural law.

ANALYTICAL JURISPRUDENCE   Many legal scholars proclaim analytical jurisprudence as the proper framework for defining the scope of criminal law. A law school education stresses that the gathering and rational analysis of authoritative legal material, like our Constitution, determine the nature and scope of the criminal law. Case laws, legal decisions proclaimed by judges, are often influenced by the doctrine of *stare decisis*—the principle that judges are bound by precedent. Their decisions are based on the careful analysis of previous court decisions.

In the 1960s a number of judges ruled that public drunkenness statutes fail to conform to certain legal principles associated with the criminal law. For example, in *Easter* v. *District of Columbia* a federal district court judge ruled in 1966 that a chronic alcoholic cannot be arrested for public drunkenness in Washington, D.C., because his drinking is an illness rather than a voluntary and willful act.[78] This ruling was an affirmation of the English common law concept of *mens rea*, which requires that criminal laws address only those acts in which intent clearly exists.[79]

SOCIOLOGICAL JURISPRUDENCE   Judicial and legislative decision makers openly weigh other sources of information besides legal material. Therefore, they are considerably more than just human components of a "great logic machine."[80]

Legal experts who define crime according to the principles of natural law and those who argue that the meaning of criminal law is derived from logic are linked by at least one common thread. Both present perceptions of criminal laws that are defined in a vacuum free of societal intrusions. On the other hand, advocates of sociological jurisprudence see criminal law defined in response to societal realities; conversely, they see criminal law as one instrument for bringing about social change.

We can see the role that social realities play in defining crime by briefly looking at the Supreme Court's decision in *Powell* v. *Texas.*[81] In that case, the Court acknowledged that invoking the criminal process for public drunkenness was inappropriate, but the justices still upheld a public-drunkenness law because they saw no institutions outside of the criminal justice system available for treating chronic skid-row inebriates. Therefore, they implied that alternative facilities were needed for helping chronic inebriates before the criminal justice system could give up this responsibility. Advocates of sociological jurisprudence can point to this example to show that criminal laws are pragmatically formulated to reflect certain social realities.

POLICY ANALYSIS

Differing from both legal scholars, who are mostly interested in defining crime, and criminologists, who search for the causes of criminal behavior, policy analysts are interested in distinguishing what government can and cannot do about crime. Representing a variety of social science disciplines (e.g., political science, economics, psychology), policy analysts attempt to determine how well governmental policies that are designed to cope with crime actually work.[82] Political scientists, like ourselves, analyze government crime-fighting efforts from a political perspective, looking at the politics of making and carrying out these policies.

Assuming that politics involves the resolution of struggles to maximize benefits for oneself, one's group, or one's organization, we want to know the effect that politically derived policies actually have on our society's attempt to cope with crime. For example, does decriminalization of public drunkenness rather than the traditional criminal processing of public inebriates better meet intended public interest goals? We investigate this question in Chapter 11, which focuses on policies developed to cope with so-called victimless crimes. Because one of our central interests is to determine the effectiveness of government policies in meeting public interest goals, we label our specific orientation for studying such strategies a "policy impact approach."[83]

The policy-making activity that often gets the most public attention is the creation and readjustment of criminal codes. These codes are legislative definitions of criminal behavior and prescriptions of punishment for different categories of criminal behavior.

We are interested in studying the impact of changes in criminal codes, and our definition of crime reflects that interest. Crime is any act that lawmakers designate as "court-punishable behavior."[84] We view lawmaking as essentially a political process. Legislative designations of criminal behavior sometimes emerge and change as a means to resolve political struggles among individuals, groups, and public service agencies (e.g., police agencies) rather than to eliminate threatening crime problems. This, too, is illustrated in Chapter 11, which traces the political struggle that shaped the criminalization of marijuana use in the early 1900s; we show that a new federal law enforcement agency used this issue to expand its resources.

While a policy analysis perspective is emphasized throughout the remainder of the book, the ideas emerging from this vantage point do not represent fundamental truths. Few, if any, basic truths have been established concerning the proper definition of crime, its root causes, or how it can be reduced. Therefore, our approach should be viewed as only one of several imperfect ways of studying crime.

SUMMARY

A number of popular images of crime have been promoted by the media, politicians, and the entertainment industry that cloud many citizens' understanding of who is the criminal, who is the victim, and how crime is solved. In addition, many misperceptions surround these popular portraits of crime. In this chapter we provide two perspectives for assessing the seriousness of this country's crime problem today. From a broad historical perspective the current crime problem is similar to that of some previous eras; on the other hand, a shorter, more limited perspective shows a significant rise in crime—although there are some important qualifications to this short-term perspective.

Also examined were three intellectual perspectives on crime: the criminologists' search for the causes of criminal behavior; the legal experts' exploration of the definition of crime; and the policy analysts' interest in the effectiveness of government policies designed to cope with crime. The remaining chapters use a policy analysis framework for studying crime and the criminal justice system in the United States.

FOOTNOTES

[1] *Kansas City Times*, May 5, 1875, p. 1.
[2] See, for example, James Dacus, *Illustrated Lives and Adventures of Frank and Jesse James and the Younger Brothers, the Noted Western Outlaws* (St. Louis, Mo.: N. D. Thompson, 1882).
[3] James Inciardi, Alan Block, and Lyle Hallowell, *Histori-*

cal Approaches to Crime (Beverly Hills, Calif.: Sage Publications, 1977), p. 66.
[4] Ibid.
[5] W. A. Settle, *Jesse James Was His Name* (Columbia, Mo.: University of Missouri Press, 1966).
[6] Inciardi, Block, and Hallowell, op. cit., p. 52.
[7] Ibid.

8 *Daily News*, February 5, 1973, p. 1.

9 *New York Times*, February 5, 1973 p. 26.

10 Rita Bachmuth, S. M. Miller, and Linda Rosen, "Juvenile Delinquency in the Daily Press," *Alpha Kappa Delta* 30 (Spring 1960), 4.

11 John C. Meyer, "Newspaper Reporting of Crime and Justice: Analysis of an Assumed Difference," *Journalism Quarterly* 52 (Winter 1975), 731–34.

12 Jack Egan, "Sensational Coverage of Son of Sam Story Alarms Press Critics," *Arizona Republic*, August 14, 1977, p. A4.

13 Ibid.

14 G. Ray Funkhouser, "The Issues of the Sixties: An Exploratory Study in the Dynamics of Public Opinion," *Public Opinion Quarterly* 37 (1973), 67; and Richard Quinney, *The Social Reality of Crime* (Boston: Little, Brown, 1970), p. 282.

15 E. Terrence Jones, "The Press as Metropolitan Monitor," *Journalism Quarterly* 53 (Summer 1976), 239–44.

16 Marc Adams, *Villains and Heroes* (Phoenix, Ariz.: The Arizona Republic, 1978). This is a compilation of articles appearing in print from December 4 through December 11, 1977 in the *Arizona Republic*.

17 Jerome Skolnick et al., eds., *Crime and Justice in America:* (Del Mar, Calif: Publisher's Inc., 1977).

18 Joseph R. Dominick, "Crime and Law Enforcement on Prime-Time Television," *Public Opinion Quarterly* 37 (Summer 1973), 241–49.

19 Ibid., 249.

20 Alan Arcuri, "You Can't Take Fingerprints Off Water: Police Officers' Views Toward Cop Television Shows," *Human Relations* 30, no. 3 (1977), 237–47.

21 Ibid., 242.

22 Ibid., 243.

23 A. Tedesco, "TV Policemen Become More Lawless," *Intellect* 102 (November 1974), 80–84.

24 S. Arons and K. Katsch, "How Cops Flout the Law," *Saturday Review*, March 19, 1977, pp. 11–19.

25 G. J. M. Rochford, "Determining Police Effectiveness," *F.B.I. Law Enforcement Bulletin*, 43 (October 1974), 17.

26 James Q. Wilson, *Thinking about Crime* (New York: Basic Books, 1975), pp. 64–80.

27 U.S. president. "Remarks in Grand Forks, North Dakota," *Public Papers of the Presidents of the U.S.: Richard Nixon* (1970), by the National Archives and Records Service (Washington, D.C.: U.S. Government Printing Office, 1971), pp. 888–89.

28 Ibid., pp. 1044–45.

29 Adams, op. cit., p. 4.

30 Ibid.

31 *Arizona Republic*, July 3, 1977, p. C1.

32 National Advisory Commission on Civil Disorders, *Report* (New York: E. P. Dutton, 1968), pp. 362–88. An empirical analysis of crime reporting by the press is presented by John C. Meyer, Jr., "Reporting Crime and Justice in the Press," *Criminology* 14 (August 1976), 277–78.

33 John E. Conklin, *The Impact of Crime* (New York: Macmillan, 1975), pp. 30–42.

34 Ibid., p. 34.

35 Ibid., p. 31.

36 Donald T. Lunde, *Murder and Madness* (San Francisco, Calif.: San Francisco Book, 1976).

37 Ibid., p. 32.

38 F. L. Cook and T. D. Cook, "Evaluating the Rhetoric of Crisis: A Case Study of Victimization of the Elderly," *Social Science Review* 50 (December 1976), 632–46; Frank Clemente and Michael Kleiman, "Fear of Crime among the Aged," *The Gerontologist* 16 (1976), 207–208; Frank Furstenburg, "Public Reaction to Crime in the Streets," *The American Scholar* 40 (Autumn 1971), 38–43.

39 Paul Cirel et al., *Community Crime Prevention* (Washington, D.C.: U.S. Government Printing Office, 1977).

40 See, for example, U.S. Department of Justice, *Criminal Victimization Surveys in Eight Cities: A Comparison of 1971/72 and 1974/75 Findings* (Washington, D.C.: U.S. Government Printing Office, 1976).

41 Ibid., pp. 64–65, 96–97.

42 Ibid.

43 Ibid., pp. 68–69, 100–101.

44 Ibid.

45 President's Commission on Law Enforcement and Administration of Justice, *Task Force Report: Crime and Its Impact* (Washington, D.C.: U.S. Government Printing Office, 1967), pp. 42–53.

46 See, for example, James Wright and Linda Marston, "The Ownership of the Means of Destruction," *Social Problems* 22 (October 1975), 93–107.

47 Lunde, op. cit., p. 29.

48 Ibid.

49 David E. Smith and Donald R. Wesson, eds., *Uppers and Downers* (Englewood Cliffs, N.J.: Prentice-Hall, 1973).

50 John Pekkanen, *The American Connection: Profiteering and Politicking in the "Ethical" Drug Industry* (Chicago: Follett Publishing, 1973).

51 Don G. Gibbons, *Society, Crime and Criminal Careers* (Englewood Cliffs, N.J.: Prentice-Hall, 1968).

52 Stephen Barber, "Koreagate Gets to the Boil," *Far Eastern Economic Review* 96 (November 4, 1977), 40.

53 Theodore Becker, *American Government: Past, Present, Future* (Boston: Allyn & Bacon, 1976), 378–79.

54 *Arizona Republic*, July 13, 1977, p. A10.

55 James F. Richardson, *The New York Police: Colonial Times to 1901* (New York: Oxford University Press, 1970), pp. 51–52.

56 Zane L. Miller, *Boss Cox's Cincinnati* (New York: Oxford University Press, 1968), p. 57.

57 Ibid., p. 59.

58 Sheldon G. Levy, "A 150-Year Study of Political Violence in the United States," in *The History of Violence in America*, eds. Hugh Graham and Ted Gurr (New York: Praeger, 1969), pp. 84–100.

59 Robin Brooks, "Domestic Violence and America's Wars: An Historical Interpretation," in ibid., pp. 529–50.

60 Ted Robert Gurr, Peter Grabosky, and Richard Hula,

The Politics of Crime and Conflict (Beverly Hills, Calif.: Sage Publications, 1977), p. 646.

[61] See, for example, U.S. Federal Bureau of Investigation, *Uniform Crime Reports for the United States—1975* (Washington, D.C.: U.S. Government Printing Office, 1975), pp. 1–7.

[62] Charles E. Silberman, *Criminal Violence, Criminal Justice* (New York: Random House, 1978), p. 5.

[63] Fred Graham, "A Contemporary History of American Crime," in *The History of Violence in America, op. cit.*, 503–504.

[64] John Herbers, "Decline in Crime Rate is Reported; May Aid Renewal of Central Cities," *New York Times*, June 25, 1978, p. 1.

[65] James Q. Wilson, "Lock 'Em Up," in *Crime and Justice in America, op. cit.*, (Del Mar, Calif.: Publisher's, Inc., 1977), pp. 8–16.

[66] Arnold Schuchter, *Child Abuse Intervention* (Washington, D.C.: U.S. Government Printing Office, 1976), p. 12.

[67] Ibid.

[68] Edwin Sutherland's work is summarized in Don C. Gibbons, *Society, Crime and Criminal Careers* (Englewood Cliffs, N.J.: Prentice-Hall, 1973), 7–80.

[69] Egon Bittner, "The Police in Skid Row: A Study of Peace Keeping," *American Sociological Review* 72 (October 1967), 701–706.

[70] Richard Cloward and Lloyd Ohlin, *Delinquency and Opportunity* (Glencoe, Ill.: The Free Press, 1960).

[71] Ibid., p. 21.

[72] Ibid., p. 20.

[73] See, for example, Steven Spitzer, "Toward a Marxian Theory of Deviance," *Social Problems* 22 (June 1975), 638–51.

[74] Reported in Sidney Harring "Class Conflict and the Suppression of Tramps in Buffalo, 1892–1894," *Law and Society Review* 11 (Summer 1977), 909.

[75] Ibid.

[76] See Eduard Ziegenhagen, "The Reconceptualization of Legal Systems and Processes," in *The Politics of Local Justice*, eds. James R. Klonoski and Robert I. Mendelsohn (Boston: Little, Brown, 1970), pp. 26–35.

[77] Norval Morris and Gordon Hawkins, *The Honest Politician's Guide to Crime Control* (Chicago: University of Chicago Press, 1969), p. 15.

[78] Easter v. District of Columbia, 361 F.2d 50 (D.C. Cir. 1966).

[79] See David Aaronson, C. Thomas Dienes, and Michael Musheno, "Changing the Public Drunkenness Laws: The Impact of Decriminalization," *Law and Society Review* (Spring 1978), 407–408.

[80] Michael Barkun, ed., *Law and the Social System* (New York: Leber-Atherton, 1973), p. 2.

[81] Powell v. Texas, 392 U.S. 514 (1968).

[82] See, for example, Stuart S. Nagel, ed., *Modeling the Criminal Justice System* (Beverly Hills, Calif.: Sage Publications, 1977).

[83] Michael Musheno, Dennis Palumbo, and James Levine, "Evaluating Alternatives to Criminal Justice: A Policy Impact Model," *Crime and Delinquency* 22 (July 1976), 265–83.

[84] Daniel Glaser, *Crime in a Changing Society* (New York: Holt, Rinehart & Winston, 1978), p. 5.

BIBLIOGRAPHY

Arcuri, Alan. "You Can't Take Fingerprints Off Water: Police Officers' Views Toward Cop Television Shows." *Human Relations* 30, no. 3 (1977), 237–47.

Clemente, Frank, and Kleiman, Michael. "Fear of Crime among the Aged." *The Gerontologist* 16 (1976), 207–208.

Conklin, John E. *The Impact of Crime*. New York: Macmillan, 1975.

Dominick, Joseph R. "Crime and Law Enforcement on Prime-Time Television." *Public Opinion Quarterly* 37 (Summer 1973), 241–49.

Glaser, Daniel. *Crime in a Changing Society*. New York: Holt, Rinehart & Winston, 1978.

Gordon, David. "Capitalism, Class and Crime in America." *Crime and Delinquency* 19 (April 1973), 163–86.

Graham, Hugh, and Gurr, Ted, eds., *The History of Violence in America*. New York: Praeger, 1969.

Gurr, Ted; Grabosky, Peter; and Hula, Richard. *The Politics of Crime and Conflict*. Beverly Hills, Calif.: Sage Publications, 1977.

Inciardi, James; Block, Alan; and Hallowell, Lyle. *Historical Approaches to Crime*. Beverly Hills, Calif.: Sage Publications, 1977.

Lunde, Donald. *Murder and Madness*. San Francisco, Calif.: San Francisco Book, 1976.

Meyer, John C. "Newspaper Reporting of Crime and Justice: Analysis of an Assumed Difference." *Journalism Quarterly* 52 (Winter 1975), 731–34.

Morris, Norval, and Hawkins, Gordon. *The Honest Politician's Guide to Crime Control*. Chicago: University of Chicago Press, 1969.

Musheno, Michael; Palumbo, Dennis; and Levine, James. "Evaluating Alternatives in Criminal

Justice: A Policy Impact Model." *Crime and Delinquency* 22 (July 1976), 265–83.

Pekkanen, John. *The American Connection: Profiteering and Politicking in the Ethical Drug Industry.* Chicago: Follett Publishing, 1973.

Radzinowicz, Leon, and King, Joan. *The Growth of Crime: The International Experience.* New York: Basic Books, 1977.

Richardson, James F. *The New York Police: Colonial Times to 1901.* New York: Oxford University Press, 1970.

Wilson, James Q. *Thinking about Crime.* New York: Basic Books, 1975.

Criminals are an amazingly varied lot. They engage in a wide range of illegal activities, from passing bad checks to wanton and brutal murder. Some of them do not believe that they are criminals, even though the public may feel they are. In contrast, some think of themselves as criminals, although the public believes that the crimes they commit are relatively harmless and even justified. Many commit only one serious crime and then lead law-abiding lives, but some are persistent offenders. The following examples illustrate this wide range of criminal activity.

On a hot summer weekend in a large American city, 15 people were murdered. Among the victims was Manuel Bernard, 44, who was shot by Rosado Migdal, 43, during an argument at a social club. Police said Migdal, a

CHAPTER THREE

CRIMINALS
What Makes Them Tick?

Puerto Rican, became enraged when the victim told him he looked Mexican.[1]

A. Carl Kotchian, former president of Lockheed Aircraft Corporation, authorized secret payments of $12 million to various Japanese business and government officials, including the prime minister, in order to land contracts for the sale of Lockheed's Tri-Star planes to All-Nippon Airlines. When asked why he agreed to the secret payments, Kotchian responded:

What businessman who is dealing with commercial and trade matters could decline a request for certain amounts of money when that money would enable him to get the contract? For someone like myself, who had been struggling against plots and severe competition for over two months, it was almost impossible to dismiss this opportunity.[2]

A number of 16- and 17-year-old boys were sitting around a city concrete basketball court smoking pot and drinking beer. Several were playing one-on-one basketball when a young man pulled up in a stolen car and asked the others if they wanted to go for a ride. Just as several of them walked up to the car and got in, the police appeared and arrested a number of them for possession of a stolen car and marijuana, and public intoxication.

In the Yazoo land scandals that occurred shortly after the American Revolution, a number of prominent citizens of the states of Connecticut and Massachusetts, as well as United States senators, congressmen, and a Supreme Court justice, bought 35 million acres of land at one-and-a-half cents an acre. The participants in the scheme had bribed the Georgia state legislature to enable them to buy the land. They were defended against the charge of graft by attorneys Alexander Hamilton and Robert G. Harper and won the case on appeal before the United States Supreme Court in the historic case of *Fletcher* v. *Peck* in 1810. Although many of the speculators participated in corrupting the Georgia state legislature, the Supreme Court declared them "innocent purchasers" and agreed they should be reimbursed for the losses they incurred when the fraud was uncovered. The individuals involved included senators Robert Morris of Pennsylvania and James Gunn of Georgia, prominent citizens Samual Sewall, James Sullivan, Samuel Dexter, and Associate Justice James Wilson of the Supreme Court. The accused went on to enjoy greater political and economic success than those who first called attention to and condemned their action.[3]

On April 27, 1926, at 8:40 P.M., William H. McSwiggin, a highly regarded deputy of the Illinois attorney's office, was one of three men killed by machine gun bullets in front of the saloon at 5613 West Roosevelt Road in the town of Cicero, just west of the Chicago city limits. His slain companions, Doherty and Duffy, were known gangsters. Public excitement and indignation were high. The newspapers asked what an assistant state's attorney was doing in the company of known gangsters and why he was killed in gangland style. Al Capone was interviewed and asked if he had killed McSwiggin; he replied:

Of course, I didn't kill him. Why should I? I liked the kid. Only the day before he got killed he was up to my place and when he went home I gave him a bottle of scotch for his old man. I paid McSwiggin and I paid him plenty, and I got what I was paying for.[4]

After conducting hearings before five grand juries in order to find out who murdered McSwiggin, the state's prosecutor dropped the case, saying, "I know who killed McSwiggin, but I want to know it legally and be able to present it conclusively."[5]

"A MAN OF SPLENDID ABILITIES"

Congressman Randolph described one of the congressmen involved in the Yazoo land scandal as "a man of splendid abilities, but utterly corrupt. He shines and stinks like a rotten mackerel by moonlight."

Larry Berg, Harlan Hahn, and John Schonidhouser, *Corruption in the American Political System*, (1976), p. 15.

Which of these five sketches depict serious crimes? If you answered the murders of Manuel Bernard and State's attorney McSwiggin, you are in agreement with the public, as expressed by the press. Most people condemn violence, especially a senseless killing such as that of Bernard. But there was not much public indignation over the Lockheed payoffs or the Yazoo land fraud. In fact, many people would not call the Lockheed payoffs a crime at all. They believe it is a necessary business practice—a little unethical, perhaps, but not seriously wrong. Many would argue that Kotchian would have lost the contract if he had not made the payoffs, and American business would have been hurt. The Yazoo land fraud is similar to what the nineteenth-century Tammany Hall political boss George Washington Plunkett called "honest graft." Plunkett believed that a smart public official who sees a chance to make a lot of money by taking advantage of his position is no different than the business person who uses inside tips to buy a large number of shares on the stock market. He held that the practice is not wrong as long as the public is not harmed in the process. "I've seen my opportunities and I took them," Plunkett said.[6]

Amazingly enough, only one of the individuals involved in the five incidents usually sees himself as a criminal. The others do not have a criminal self-image. Murderers, such as the one in the first example, are often guilt-ridden over their act, but they do not really believe themselves criminals. The president of Lockheed described in the second example wrote an article defending his action. Nowhere in this article did he indicate he did anything wrong, and in several places he emphasized that he violated no laws, for there was no legislation covering business payoffs in international trade at the time. The young men smoking pot and drinking beer certainly did not think of themselves as criminals, since many urban teen-agers engage in this pastime. The officials in the Yazoo land fraud did not conceive of themselves as criminals, either. Their actions were hardly worse then the behavior of many elected officials at the time, including some of our most revered political heros. It is the organized criminal, such as Al Capone, who generally has a criminal self-image—although Al Capone is reported to have said: "Public service is my motto. I've always regarded it as a public benefaction if people were given decent liquor and square games."[7] But the public service that Capone provided was criminal, and Capone undoubtedly knew it.

"To close on an upbeat note, I'm happy to report we received twenty-two percent more in kickbacks than we paid out in bribes."

Drawing by Dana Fradon; © 1976 The New Yorker Magazine, Inc.

Both the public and criminals themselves reveal a remarkable ambivalence about what constitutes serious crime. In the popular image, however, violence and murder tend to be condemned, although there are exceptions. For example, murder committed by an enraged husband or wife who discovers a spouse in bed with another person is not treated too harshly in American law. But, in general, the public condemns violence because, as Harvard political scientist James Q. Wilson has noted, one of the prime requisites of a civilized society is to be able to move about freely in public without fear of physical assault.[8] And this tends to be true of most countries at most times in history. Both individual and group violence are universally condemned; political scientist Ted Gurr notes: "An enduring feature of the legal codes of virtually all Western society is a set of statutes authorizing officials to control such collective actions as riotous behavior, unlawful assembly, and acts of mutiny, rebellion, and sedition."[9] Violent crimes are considered in most societies to be reprehensible. They are usually severely punished.

Understanding how society reacts to criminal behavior is important for two reasons. First, the definition of what constitutes criminal behavior depends upon the society, the time, and the place where it occurs. There is no such thing as crime in an absolute sense. Definitions of crime differ greatly from culture to culture and at different times in history. In ancient Egypt, for example, killing a cat was a criminal offense. In the Soviet Union today selling something for monetary profit is a crime. It is also true that theories about the causes of criminal behavior reflect cultural views. No objective theory about criminal behavior exists simply because what is criminal is socially determined.[10] Second, society largely determines which laws will be enforced most vigorously. As we shall see later in this chapter, society's and the criminal's own perception about what constitutes criminal behavior are two forces that shape what public policy can and cannot do to reduce crime. First, however, let us turn to some leading theories about crime.

Causal Versus Policy-Relevant Theories of Crime

In a 1975 speech before a meeting of county prosecutors, Mathew P. Boylan, director of the New Jersey Division of Criminal Justice, said that "deterrence has little impact upon the irrational and amoral behavior of the children of disorganized family structures now present in increasing numbers in the United States."[11] Street crime, Boylan continued, can be attributed to family disintegration, a condition that is beyond the control of the police. He therefore recommended that higher priority be given to catching white-collar criminals and that efforts be made to dispel the illusion that police can prevent street crime.

Boylan's theory of crime is unorthodox for a member of the criminal justice system. The police as well as other law enforcement personnel are more likely to subscribe to the "rotten egg" theory of criminal behavior—the belief that crime is committed by bad or psychopathic individuals. The rotten egg theory points to biological factors as the principal cause of crime, whereas Boylan stresses sociological factors. These are two of the main types of explanations of what causes crime, but, as we shall see next, there are many others as well.

BIOLOGICAL THEORIES

The rotten egg theory that the public holds about criminal behavior is a direct descendant of biological theories. Such theories hold that some people are "born criminals—a view that was enormously popular in many "B" movies of the 1940s and 1950s.

Cesare Lombroso (1835–1909) is generally credited with originating the notion that criminal behavior is due to natural biological factors. Criminals, he believed, could be identified by their skulls and facial bones. Lombroso classified criminals into four categories: (1) born criminals, (2) insane criminals, (3) criminals by passion, and (4) occasional criminals. In earlier writings he stated that the majority of criminals were in the first category, but he later reduced the proportion of offenders that he ascribed to biology. Little empirical evidence existed to support Lombroso's theory, and it was finally refuted in 1913 when a British scientist examined the skulls of convicts, soldiers, university students, and hospital patients and found no significant statistical differences among them.

Despite these findings, others continued to rely on biological explanations. William Sheldon carried Lombroso's work further and developed a classification of all people, noncriminals as well as criminals, into three body types with their respective personalities. These are: (1) endomorphic (round and soft body), who have relaxed and extroverted personalities; (2) mesomorphic (muscular), who are aggressive and extroverted; and (3) ectomorphic (thin, fragile), who are anxious and introverted.[12] Sheldon believed that the second—muscular individuals—were most likely to be criminals.

Although there was little scientific evidence to support them, biological theories were the basis of correctional policies for a long period. In Illinois prisons in 1933, for example, the law required a psychiatric examination of all prisoners, and over 75 percent received the diagnosis "constitutional psychopathic inferior," implying that they were immoral by heredity.[13] In addition, chronic offenders were sterilized under the assumption that they would pass on defective genes to their children. The United States Supreme Court, in *Skinner v. Oklahoma,* finally declared this practice unconstitutional in 1942.

The search to link biological factors and criminal behavior continues today. Some research suggests that criminals are deficient in the hormone epinephrine. Individuals lacking this hormone are likely to be slower in avoiding shocks administered whenever they make errors in solving puzzles. The test results led some to hypothesize that persistent criminals are slow to learn to avoid punishment, and this deficiency, some believe, explains their persistence in crime.[14]

Another form of biological theory is the argument that I.Q. is a major factor in criminal behavior and that intelligence is inherited. The I.Q. theory started in the late nineteenth century, when intelligence tests were used to identify "defective delinquents." The first I.Q. tests were administered almost entirely to incarcerated populations. However, the evidence for a link between I.Q. and criminality is weak. In fact, white-collar and professional criminals have high intelligence quotients. In addition, debate rages about the validity of I.Q. tests themselves, particularly about the cultural bias in such tests.

On balance, most biological theories have little empirical support. While biology may explain some kinds of criminal behavior, it is but one small factor.

PSYCHOLOGICAL THEORIES

Psychological theories are based on the assumption that most criminal offenders are emotionally sick rather than genetically defective. This is a more optimistic view, since it is presumably easier to correct emotional ills than it is to change genetics.

Recently, research has begun to focus upon personality characteristics in order to try to relate these to criminal behavior. Such characteristics include feelings of hostility, isolation, and trust. The Jesness Inventory, for example, measures, among other things, attitude toward authority, family orientation, and emotional maturity. Its use in the California correctional system showed that delinquents tend to have a hostile attitude toward authority, are more suspicious and distrustful, are less emotionally mature, and have greater feelings of isolation than nondelinquents.

One of the more frequently used personality scales for analyzing criminal behavior is the Minnesota Multiphasic Personality Inventory (M.M.P.I.). It consists of hundreds of questions relating to an individual's moral, family, social, sexual, religious, and political attitudes, as well as to delusions, phobias, and sadistic tendencies. A number of studies have used the M.M.P.I.'s personality guidelines as a basis. A 1974 study, for example, found that narcotics offenders and burglars could be identified on the M.M.P.I. scale.[15] Other studies using the M.M.P.I. come to the same conclusion. A 1974 study by Glenn Wilson and Alastair MacLean of the University of London's Institute of Psychiatry found that criminals tend to be more psychotic, extroverted, and neurotic than noncriminals.[16] And a study by Vdai P. Singh of the University of Bhagalpur in India found that recidivists (those who are arrested for a crime more than once) hold a more unfavorable attitude toward authority, and tend to be more neurotic than nonrecidivists.[17]

The general concept of "psychopathy" was developed in psychiatry to designate a person who is impulsive, unable to learn from experience, unable to love, irresponsible, and lacking emotions. There are some criminals who seem to fit this profile, such as the professional killer. However, the theory received considerable criticism, and the American Psychiatric Association in 1952 replaced the term "psychopath" with "sociopath." A sociopath is one who has developed negative and hostile attitudes toward society and its laws.

In general, psychological theories can be criticized on the grounds that they confuse cause and effect. For example, hostile attitudes toward authority can be seen as an *effect* of the way troubled youth have been treated by their parents and other authority figures rather than as a *cause* of delinquent behavior. When criminal justice authorities consider hostility, distrust, and feelings of isolation as causes of crime, they may actually be setting up a self-fulfilling prophesy. The process can occur in the following way. An angry young man, full of hostility, gets himself into trouble. He is arrested and sent to a "correctional treatment" facility. He is labeled as a delinquent. As a result, he becomes even more hostile and angry. When he is released, he is singled out by police and other officials, who keep him under close surveillance because he is considered a high risk. He is thus more likely to be caught for violating a law, and the vicious cycle of criminality begins anew.

Thus, the essential difficulty with psychological theories is that they define all criminal behavior as being the result of characteristics of the individual rather than society. Of course, it may be true that some kinds of criminal behavior are rooted in an individual's personality. But it is also true that society contributes to many types of criminal behavior. Psychological theories, therefore, afford only partial explanations and must be coupled with sociological theories in order to account for a wide enough range of criminal behavior.

SOCIAL-PSYCHOLOGICAL THEORIES

Sociopsychological theories tend to emphasize motivation. A rational person will commit a crime only if he or she is not penalized for doing so. According to these theories "natural instincts" lead to crime unless they are controlled. A social-psychological understanding of human behavior requires that we know the meanings that the individual gives to committing a crime. Many criminals are able to justify their illegal acts in their own minds. They may have a gambling or drug problem that requires large amounts of money. Their illegal acts to obtain money are justified in their minds. Embezzlers, for example, usually believe they are just "borrowing" the money temporarily. The point is that we can better understand, and perhaps also control, this form of criminal behavior if we know what meaning the behavior has for the person engaged in it.

Civilization is bought at the cost of repression, according to Sigmund Freud, the father of modern psychology. Individuals have a "natural drive" to commit crime if they feel they can get away with it and thus must be controlled. Events such as the New York City blackout in 1977, when people went on a rampage and looted numerous businesses, tend to support the theory that, unless checked, people will engage in criminal behavior. During the blackout, people felt they had nothing to lose by stealing, since they could not be caught. Millions of dollars of food, clothing, and appliances were stolen. But examples to contradict this notion can be found as well. There have been times when entire communities have not engaged in looting when the police have been out on strike. And, even in cases where looting has occured on a large scale, such as during the

New York City blackout, only a small minority in the community actually engaged in looting. Thus, the basic assumption of the theories appears to work only for some individuals and, perhaps, only for certain kinds of crimes. For example, most murders are committed in the heat of passion, and murderers do not seem to consider the costs of their actions. The theory of rational motivation does not work for most murders. But some kinds of criminals do appear to consider the costs versus the benefits of their actions. For example, a New York City Rand Corporation study found that subway robberies did decrease when police were assigned to the subways. The study concluded that offenders "do in fact try to estimate the risks of criminal activity and are deterred if they perceive an increased threat of apprehension."[18] We shall return to this point in Chapter 9.

SOCIOLOGICAL THEORIES

French sociologist Émile Durkheim believed that a certain amount of crime is normal and healthy in any society. Repressing criminality completely is not desirable, Durkheim wrote, for that would create a situation that is inimical to innovation and social change.[19] However, crime becomes dysfunctional for society when it rises above certain levels.[20] Sociological theories provide several different explanations of why crime becomes excessive. One views crime as an alternative that is seized upon because legitimate channels of social mobility are blocked. Thus, Italians, Jews, and the Irish turned to organized crime during prohibition when they found that legitimate channels were closed to them due to discrimination.

Another sociological explanation emphasizes social disorganization as a cause of crime. According to this theory, industrialization and urbanization lead to alienation and anomie. These occur when individuals move from a rural to an urban existence and primary groups, such as the family and neighborhood, where people know each other intimately, break down, thereby removing an important source of socialization and stability. As the structure of people's lives collapses, deviant behavior increases, including alcoholism, illegitimacy, suicide, crime, and delinquency.[21]

A third sociological explanation is that crime is due to poverty and unemployment. But the relationship between economic conditions and crime is complex. The crime rate is not strongly related to unemployment nor to depressions. In fact, wealthier countries such as the United States have a higher rate of crime than poorer countries. And the crime rate in the United States increased at a rapid rate during the 1960s, when personal income was also increasing. Thus if there is any relationship between poverty and crime, it is a very indirect one. Most poor people are law abiding. Thus, poverty is not a sufficient condition for one to turn to crime, for when a sufficient condition exists, crime will occur. Also, many well-off people commit crimes. Thus, poverty is not a necessary condition for crime, for a necessary condition is one that must always be present when crime occurs. Poverty, therefore, cannot be a cause of crime. Poor people are more likely to commit violent rather than white-collar crime. And they are more likely to end in jail, but this is because they are discriminated against, not because they commit more of the total amount of crime that occurs.

Contemporary sociological theories are usually based upon statistical analyses that relate certain sociological facts—broken homes, poverty, and minority group status—to violent crime. The correlations themselves, however, do not explain why violent crimes are more prevalent under these circumstances. Thus, some sociologists have combined societal factors with a theory about the influence of "subcultures." According to this theory, children who grow up in broken homes and ghetto environments learn criminal behavior in their peer culture. For example, acts of murder are most frequent among those who have grown up in a subculture of violence and who have been subjected to a number of disorganizing social influences such as broken and culturally deprived families over an extended period of time. These individuals tend to look upon others as potential assailants, and their violence is perceived by themselves as an act of self-defense—get the other guy before he gets you.[22]

Culture conflict is the one theme that sociological theories of crime causation have in common. According to these theories, some groups do not accept the legal norms of society. They develop different standards of what is appropriate behavior, and these standards conflict with those of the dominant culture.[23] According to sociologist Walter Miller, the lower-class person learns values such as toughness, smartness, love of danger, belief in fate, and a desire for autonomy. Many lower-class individuals are raised in a household headed by a woman, and this raises the probability of becoming a delinquent.[24] According to criminologists Marvin Wolfgang and Fred Ferracuti, violence is encouraged among certain ethnic groups under certain conditions—to defend manliness, to survive, to defend against insults.[25] Family conditions, coupled with situational factors, are thus the most frequently cited explanations of violent behavior by sociologists today.

Some researchers have challenged the subcultural thesis. In one survey of Milwaukee lower-class males, the researcher found that nonfighters were more likely to be well liked by others than those who engaged in fist fights. If fist-fighters have little social support, their conduct does not reflect group culture.[26] Moreover, many subcultural norms are not in opposition to the norms of the larger society. While violence is more prevalent among members of the lower class, the use of force is not valued more highly by the lower than the middle and upper classes.

Alcoholism, lack of parental control, domination, neglect, jealousy, and being brought up in a foster home are all considered precipitating factors in criminal behavior. When a particular situation arises, such as gang conflict or encouragement by peers, an individual raised in such circumstances is likely to engage in criminal behavior.

But, of course, no direct relationship can be shown. Not all individuals brought up under these conditions and facing the same situational factors engage in crime; in addition, some individuals who have been brought up in stable middle-class environments have become criminals, as was the case with a Texas safe robber who drifted into crime after becoming detached from familiar ties— he found that he liked robbing safes.[27] Since the majority of individuals brought up in poor home environments are law abiding, being poor cannot be *the* cause of crime. Many people do not turn to violence and crime despite terrible living conditions.

Sociological theories are weakened even further when we consider crime in other countries. Tokyo, Japan, for example, has crowded, densely populated, poor areas in which people face the same conditions of neglect, alienation, lack of parental control, and frustration as similarly situated Americans. Yet, Japanese police do not carry guns, and crimes of violence are relatively rare in Tokyo.

The failure of various sociological theories to explain a wide range of criminal behavior has led some investigators to search for multiple-cause theories. Sociologist Don Gibbons has combined three kinds of causes. His theory is that there are certain "root causes" of crime, such as rapid social change, anomie, and economic dislocation. Then, there are intervening variables, such as family experience and differential association (i.e., subcultural "teaching" of criminal behavior).[28] Finally, there are the precipitating factors, such as personality and situational opportunities that, when combined, cause some individuals to become criminals.[29]

In summary, most existing theories of crime are deficient because they do not explain a wide enough range of criminal behavior. Biological theories have very little empirical support. Psychological theories do not take into account social aspects of criminal behavior. Social psychological theories rely too heavily on rational motives. And sociological theories do not adequately explain white-collar crime. Some investigators therefore conclude that what is needed is a different theory for each type of crime—that is, crime-specific theories.

CRIME-SPECIFIC THEORIES

In all probability, no one theory will be able to explain all types of crime because criminals are too varied and complex. Thus, the most recent research aims to explain different kinds of crime with different theories, the underlying assumption being that each major type of crime has common characteristics. Murder, for example, must be explained by a different theory than embezzlement.

The success of such an approach depends upon the development of a typology that brings into each category all of the crimes that have a common basis. Some existing typologies are based upon the distinction between violent and nonviolent crimes. Others, however, focus upon crime careers—or the patterns and crimes in which individuals specialize.

A number of typologies of crime careers have been offered. Criminologists Marshall Clinard and Richard Quinney have distinguished eight types of crimes based upon the criminal career of the offender, the extent to which the behavior has group support, the correspondence between criminal and legitimate behavior, and society's reaction to the criminal. The eight types of crimes they develop on these criteria are:

1. Violent personal crimes (acts in which physical injury is inflicted, such as murder)
2. Occasional property crimes (the opposite of professional crimes; offenses are committed infrequently)
3. Occupational crimes (all crimes that occur in the course of occupational activity)
4. Political crimes (illegal activities that occur in the course of protest or attempts to change an existing government)
5. Public-order crimes (those that upset public order, such as drunkenness, prostitution, and disorderly conduct)
6. Conventional crimes (mostly property crimes that are part of the way of life of the offender)
7. Organized crimes (business enterprises organized for the purpose of making economic gain through illegal activity)
8. Professional crimes (crimes by highly skilled criminals—people who run confidence games, pickpockets, and counterfeiters)[30]

A second major typology is that of Don Gibbons. His is built around the types of criminals. The following is a shortened version of his typology:

1. Property criminals (professional thieves who engage in a variety of nonviolent and complex forms of property crime)
2. Naive check forgers (amateur thieves who pass bad checks)
3. White-collar criminals (employees who steal for the benefit of the employer)
4. Embezzlers (persons in a position of trust stealing *from* employers)
5. Murderers and assaulters
6. Sexual deviants (includes different types of rapists as well as child molesters, exhibitionists, and voyeurs)
7. Organized criminals (organized societies engaged in extortion, loan sharking, narcotics, prostitution, etc.)[31]

The above two typologies do not themselves constitute theories about criminal behavior. To develop a theory it would be necessary to determine what the common underlying characteristics of each category are, how individuals in these categories perceive themselves, and how they become involved in the particular crimes. A good theory enables us to make predictions about how much crime of various types we can expect and what conditions will produce it. Crime-specific theories are not well enough developed to enable us to make such predictions. Thus, while they offer promise, they cannot yet be useful to explain crime.

Public Policy and Criminal Behavior

Because criminals are so varied, it is not likely that they can be explained by a single theory. Crime-specific theories are a much better way of approaching the subject. After all, what do the embezzler, prostitute, con man, murderer, and marijuana smoker have in common other than the fact that they all break a law? In addition, as noted previously, we are not interested here primarily in the root causes of crime in general but in those aspects of criminal behavior that may be changed, reduced, or redirected by public policy. The pertinent question is, "Can government do anything about the criminal behavior in question?" In this regard we agree with James Q. Wilson, who has written:

> Ultimate causes cannot be the object of policy efforts precisely because, being ultimate, they cannot be changed. For example, criminologists have shown beyond doubt that men commit more crimes than women and younger men more (or certain *kinds*) than older ones. It is a theoretically important and correct observation. Yet, it means little for policy makers concerned with crime prevention, since men cannot be changed into women or made to skip over the adolescent years.[32]

Sociologist Daniel Glaser writes that as a guide for public policy, it is useful to classify crimes by those features that most closely affect their measurement and control. An important aspect of this task is whether or not the individual against whom a crime is directed *feels* victimized.[33] One who does not feel victimized is unlikely to ask the government to step in to do something. Thus, Glaser proposes that crimes be classified as predatory (involving victims) and nonpredatory (involving no victims). The nonpredatory crimes can be further subdivided into whether they are criminal only when they have a complaining audience (e.g., disorderly conduct), or whether it is because of what is sold, purchased, used, or possessed (e.g., prostitution).

The three dimensions that we find most useful in analyzing criminal justice policy are (1) the motivation of the criminal (Was economic gain involved? Was the person rational?); (2) the perception the general public has of the criminal (Is the crime a serious one? Should government try to do anything about it?); and (3) the object of the crime (Was it against a person or property?).

The type of policy to reduce or control crime that should be adopted—whether it be deterrence, rehabilitation, decriminalization, diversion, or some other policy—depends upon the extent to which these three dimensions are involved. Deterrence, for example, may not work if the offender does not rationally calculate the benefits and costs incurred from committing a crime. We cannot expect to deter a particular criminal by imposing harsher penalities if the criminal is totally and irrationally unconcerned with the risk of being caught and the penalty that the crime carries. In the remainder of this chapter, we shall describe a number of major types of criminals and look at each in light of the three dimensions mentioned above. The discussion will center on three questions.

First, *how do criminals view their own behavior?* A different kind of public policy must be followed for those who see themselves as criminals as opposed to those who do not. Criminologists in the past have paid very little, attention to the self-image of criminals, and this is a major shortcoming of most analyses of criminal justice. Peter Letkemann, one of the few writers to look at criminals through their own eyes, writes, "When we can recognize the criminal's perspective, we will not so readily impose conventional and possibly misleading categories on the behavior under study."[34] It is important to recognize criminals' own perspective because if offenders do not have a criminal self-image, then they are not likely to be affected by policies aimed at controlling criminal behavior. Embezzlers are a good example; since they do not have a criminal self-image, they are not likely to be detected by complicated controls or deterred by the threat of punishment.[35]

The second important question is, *how serious is society's reaction to the particular criminal activity?* We include in the term "society" community leaders, public opinion, opinion makers such as the media, and public officials. Society, of course, is not a unified body with but one opinion. Community leaders, for example, may believe that a particular crime is very serious (e.g., gambling and prostitution), while other elements of the society may not consider these very grave. Community leaders may well have greater influence than the general public in determining the seriousness of various crimes, at least in so far as seriousness is measured by the degree of a penalty attached to a crime (see Chapter 4 for the impact of community leaders on criminal justice policy). Public opinion plays some role in determining the seriousness of crimes. For example, a large part of the "law and order" policy of the early 1970s reflected the public's fear of crime. But criminal justice officials—police, prosecuting attorneys, and judges—are public officials, and they too have a great impact on criminal justice policy.

If society believes that certain acts are not particularly serious, then public policy cannot do much to reduce that kind of crime. At the very least, policy makers must realize that some parts of society will not support efforts to suppress a particular activity. For example, apparently most Americans do not feel that the president of the Lockheed Corporation engaged in criminal behavior when he paid off Japanese business and government officials because the public attention it received was short-lived. Given this attitude, it is unlikely that administrators will rigorously enforce laws aimed at this type of crime, or that the courts will mete out heavy punishment for such offenses.

The importance of society's attitude becomes especially apparent when it directly affects a public official. For example, one judge in Madison, Wisconsin, released a young man accused of raping a girl and said that provocative dress and permissive attitudes have encouraged young men to rape. The judge was defeated in a recall election in 1978 because Madison, Wisconsin, is a liberal community where feminist groups are well organized, as the judge discovered. But the example shows how important it is to take society's views, or those of particular segments of society, into consideration when criminal justice policy is being considered.

The third question our discussion will raise is, *what is the object of the crime—a person or property?* As we will see in Chapter 11, many crimes that are heavily prosecuted include no loss of property or harm to individuals. These crimes might better be handled through decriminalization or other policies. Such policies may be especially desired for so-called victimless crimes, in which the individual does not view himself or herself as a criminal and society is not unified in seeing the crime as serious. Despite our society's feeling that property crimes are less serious than crimes involving physical harm, we will see below that certain kinds of property-related crime may be more easy to reduce than the most prevalent forms of violent crimes.

Crime-specific theories, we have said, offer better policy guidance than broad-gauged biological, sociological, or psychological theories. But there is not enough knowledge available yet to enable us to group together a number of different crimes into a single category so that all of the crimes that fall into this category can be treated similarly by public policy. Even a single crime such as homicide covers acts as diverse as an unintentional accident and a brutal slaying; society's reaction to the former is lenient but harsh to the latter. The legal definition of crimes against the person is similarly broad, covering everything from simple assault (a slap or shove) to murder (intentional killing). And the range of property crimes includes theft (taking someone else's property), burglary (breaking into a building or dwelling unit to commit a felony), fraud (misrepresentation to obtain property), and robbery (taking money or other goods by force).

The Many Varieties of Criminal Behavior

VIOLENT CRIMINALS

A husband accuses his wife of giving money to another man, and while she is making breakfast, he attacks her with an orange-juice bottle, then a heavy pot, and finally a chair. Having a kitchen knife in hand, she stabs him during the fight. He is pronounced dead on arrival at the hospital.

This incident illustrates the irrational, amateur aspect of most violent crimes. In the public's view, most murderers, assaulters, and rapists are fiends with pathological personalities. However, the individuals who commit these crimes do not think of themselves as criminals. They kill or attack one another in a fit of passion, usually after drinking, and are remorseful when it is all over. And, contrary to the popular belief, most do not repeat their violent acts after being released from prison.

These generalizations hold true for most violent crimes. The public abhors such crimes but at the same time seems to be fascinated by them, and crime coverage in newspapers, on television, and in the movies concentrates on crimes of violence and passion. Violent crimes include murder, assault, robbery, rape, child beating, and kidnapping. Physical attacks that are not fatal are called assaults. Assault is a felony when it results in serious injury or when there is evidence that death or great harm was intended. While assault is legally distinct from homicide (defined below), the statistical evidence suggests that they have the same cause, and thus we shall discuss them both in this section.

The rash of violence that began in the 1960s greatly alarmed the American public; the assassination of a president and other leading political figures, urban riots, bizarre killings, skyjackings and terrorism, and muggings and robberies helped create an image of a society gone beserk. But then the terrorism and robberies and assassinations declined in the late 1970s, and the public's concern with crime also declined. Economics—inflation, taxes, and unemployment—replaced it as the number one issue. But violent crimes still remain an important concern of the American public, even though they comprise only about 10 percent of the crimes known to the police (see Table 3-1).

MURDERERS AND ASSAULTERS   Murder is the most sensational of violent crimes. Human beings are extremely versatile in the many ways they are able to kill their fellow beings. A short discussion of the legal categories will help us give some order to this category.

Elmer Wayne Henley: Mass murderer

TABLE 3-1
Index of Crime, United States, 1968–1977

Population[1]	Crime Index Total	Violent Crime[2]	Property Crime[2]	Murder and Non-negligent Man-slaughter	Forcible Rape	Robbery	Aggra-vated Assault	Burglary	Larceny-Theft	Motor Vehicle Theft
Number of offenses:										
1968—199,399,000	6,720,200	595,010	6,125,200	13,800	31,670	262,840	286,700	1,858,900	3,482,700	783,600
1969—201,385,000	7,410,900	661,870	6,749,000	14,760	37,170	298,850	311,090	1,981,900	3,888,600	878,500
1970—203,235,298	8,098,000	738,820	7,359,200	16,000	37,990	349,860	334,970	2,205,000	4,225,800	928,400
1971—206,212,000	8,588,200	816,500	7,771,700	17,780	42,260	387,700	368,700	2,399,300	4,424,200	948,200
1972—208,230,000	8,248,800	834,900	7,413,900	18,670	46,850	376,290	393,090	2,375,500	4,151,200	887,200
1973—209,851,000	8,718,100	875,910	7,842,200	19,640	51,400	384,220	420,650	2,565,500	4,347,900	928,800
1974—211,392,000	10,253,400	974,720	9,278,700	20,710	55,400	442,400	456,210	3,039,200	5,262,500	977,100
1975—213,124,000	11,256,600	1,026,280	10,230,300	20,510	56,090	464,970	484,710	3,252,100	5,977,700	1,000,500
1976—214,659,000	11,304,800	986,580	10,318,200	18,780	56,730	420,210	490,850	3,089,800	6,270,800	957,600
1977—216,332,000	10,935,800	1,009,500	9,926,300	19,120	63,020	404,850	522,510	3,052,200	5,905,700	968,400
Rate per 100,000 inhabitants:[3]										
1968	3,370.2	298.4	3,071.8	6.9	15.9	131.8	143.8	932.3	1,746.6	393.0
1969	3,680.0	328.7	3,351.3	7.3	18.5	148.4	154.5	984.1	1,930.9	436.2
1970	3,984.5	363.5	3,621.0	7.9	18.7	172.1	164.8	1,084.9	2,079.3	456.8
1971	4,164.7	396.0	3,768.8	8.6	20.5	188.0	178.8	1,163.5	2,145.5	459.8
1972	3,961.4	401.0	3,560.4	9.0	22.5	180.7	188.8	1,140.8	1,993.6	426.1
1973	4,154.4	417.4	3,737.0	9.4	24.5	183.1	200.5	1,222.5	2,071.9	442.6
1974	4,850.4	461.1	4,389.3	9.8	26.2	209.3	215.8	1,437.7	2,489.5	462.2
1975	5,281.7	481.5	4,800.2	9.6	26.3	218.2	227.4	1,525.9	2,804.8	469.4
1976	5,266.4	459.6	4,806.8	8.8	26.4	195.8	228.7	1,439.4	2,921.3	446.1
1977	5,055.1	466.6	4,588.4	8.8	29.1	187.1	241.5	1,410.9	2,729.9	447.6

[1] Populations are Bureau of the Census provisional estimates as of July 1, except April 1, 1970, census.
[2] Violent crime is offenses of murder, forcible rape, robbery, and aggravated assault. Property crime is offenses of burglary, larceny-theft, and motor vehicle theft.
[3] Crime rates calculated prior to rounding number of offenses.
SOURCE: U.S. Department of Justice, *Crime in the United States—1977* (Washington, D.C.: U.S. Government Printing Office, 1978), p. 37.

There are three types of homicides—justifiable, culpable, and negligent. A good example of justifiable homicide is the police officer who kills a fleeing criminal. Culpable homicide is where there is an intent to kill. Culpable homicide can be subdivided into two categories—first- and second-degree murder. These rest upon degrees of premeditation or malice aforethought. Premeditation means planning to kill. Malice aforethought means simple presence of intent to kill at the time of the act. First-degree murder requires both premeditation and malice aforethought. Second-degree murder—also called reckless homicide—occurs when there is no premeditation but death results from a reckless act. Negligent homicide, also called manslaughter, is unintended and unwitting homicide.

In order for one to be guilty of culpable homicide, the person's mental state must be considered. The classic case of *Commonwealth* v. *Pierce* readily illustrates the problems involved in determining the offender's state of mind. In that case the physician who was attending Mary A. Bemis prescribed that her flannel shirt, drawers, and stockings should be saturated with kerosene oil every three hours. Even though the patient and her husband complained that this made her suffer, the physician directed that the treatment continue. This was done for two full days; later, when the clothing was removed, it was discovered that her skin was blistered and burned by the kerosene. She died a week later.

Was the physician guilty of first- or second-degree murder, or only of manslaughter? It depends upon whether he intended to kill Mary Bemis and had planned to do so. The prosecution tried to prove that a reasonable man in Dr. Pierce's position would have known of the risk he was taking, and, therefore, he was grossly negligent. The defendant asked the jury to adhere to the following rule: If the defendant made the prescription with the honest purpose of curing the deceased, he is not guilty of the offense, no matter how ignorant he may have been of the quality of the remedy. But the judge instructed the jury that it was not necessary to show evil intent. If the defendant caused the death by gross and reckless negligence, he is guilty of culpable homicide, no matter what he intended. The jury, however, decided that he was guilty only of manslaughter. They found that the kerosene oil was applied as a result of foolhardy presumption. But they also found there was no intent to kill Mrs. Bemis (malice aforethought) nor calm reflection before going through with it (premeditation).[36] In some jurisdictions, this would be no crime at all.

Under most state laws any death that results from another dangerous felony (robbery, rape, burglary, kidnapping) is also a homicide, even if the death is accidental. For example, if three men collaborate in a robbery and one accidentally shoots the victim, or if the police fire at them and kill an innocent bystander, all three can be charged with murder. The F.B.I. reports that one-third of all homicides in 1976 were the consequence of other felonies rather than a straightforward slaying.

When we consider the different types of murderers, we find an amazing variety. According to psychiatrist Manfred Guttmacher, there are normal, sociopathic, alcoholic, avenging, schizophrenic, temporarily psychotic, psychotic, sadistic, hysteric, and mentally defective murderers.[37]

Murders happen most often on weekends, with 66 percent of homicides occurring between Friday and Sunday, and 32 percent on Saturday between the hours of 8 P.M. and 2 A.M. Two-thirds of all murders occur in predominantly black, overcrowded, physically deteriorated slums. One study found that 73 percent of the victims and 75 percent of the offenders were black males.[38] The black male murder rate is 41.7 per 100,000 people, as compared to 3.4 for the general population—12 times as high. In fact, murder is the leading cause of death for black males between the ages of 15 and 33.

Close friends are involved in 28 percent of murder cases, family relatives in 25 percent.[39] F.B.I. statistics show that 22 percent of murders in 1971 were within kinship groups, and in one-half of these, murderer and victim were married to each other. In 45 percent of 1975 homicides, the victim and offender were not kin, but they were acquaintances, former friends, or lovers. While alcohol is involved in about two-thirds of murders, a large number are precipitated by the victim, who frequently strikes the first blow. Stabbing is higher among victim-precipitated homicides than among nonvictim-precipitated homicides.

The murder of Magnolia McBride is a classic illustration of the way most American murders occur. On December 9, 1973, Randell McBride, a 44-year-old auto worker, shot and killed his 42-year-old wife. It was homicide number 700 for the city of Detroit for that year, a city that had become known as "Murder Capital, U.S.A." McBride cooly pleaded guilty to second-degree

Homicide as a consequence of another felony

murder at his arraignment two days later. He was released on his own recognizance and returned home.

McBride was born in Mississippi, the son of a poor farmer; he went through sixth grade, worked in a sawmill, and for a time owned a small café in the northwest Mississippi hamlet of Eupora. Although he had no criminal record, he had a reputation for being high-strung and quick-tempered. His wife, Magnolia, had worked in an auto supply firm until she hurt her back lifting bucket seats and could no longer work. They lived with Magnolia's sisters after they were married, and this was a source of considerable tension and dissatisfaction for Randell, who felt the sisters were trying to dominate him. For several weeks prior to the murder he had been sick, mostly from frustration and tension. On Sunday, December 9, he had several arguments with his wife. The final one was when he asked her to prepare dinner and she refused. He said she hit him, he hit back. Then she threw a flower pot at him. The 210-pound Mrs. McBride then pushed 128-pound McBride down the stairs, whereupon he got his .25-caliber gun and shot her. "I just lost my temper," McBride said. "I was sorry right after it happened, but it had to happen."[40]

The murder rate has declined in the past 100 years. It was twice as high in the nineteenth as in the early twentieth century.[41] Murder tends to be higher in poverty areas in all countries, and is higher in Latin American countries, where "machismo" is emphasized. (Machismo is the "manly" ideal of toughness and physical strength and stresses honor and quick reaction to insult.) However, ethnicity is not a cause of homicide for homicide rates earlier in the century were higher among young Poles and Italians than the general population. This homicide rate has declined as these groups have moved out of poverty. In recent years blacks have a high homicide rate.[42]

Although the homicide rate has declined in the past century, there was an increase in murders in the late 1960s and 1970s in American cities. The homicide rate in 1955 was 4.8 per 100,000 persons. In 1965 it was 5.1. And by 1975 it was 9.6. There are a number of possible reasons for this increase. First, the migration of Chicanos, Puerto Ricans, and blacks to the northern cities and the subsequent poverty and overcrowding produced a transient and volatile social situation in which a number of groups at the bottom of the socioeconomic ladder were pitted against each other. In addition, since 1960, the homicide rate has been highest in larger cities, and there has been a drop in the average age of those arrested for homicide, from about 30 prior to 1965 to 26.4 in the mid-1970s. The greatest growth in the homicide rate has been among 15- through 19-year-olds.[43] This, coupled with a baby boom, which added to the number of people in the 18 to 26 year old group, and with a growing ease of obtaining small handguns, explains a large part of the increase in homicide in the late 1960s and 1970s. Ease of obtaining handguns is certainly one factor in the increase in homicide, as indicated by the fact that a greater percentage of homicides is committed by handguns in the South, where it is easier to get such guns, than in the North (73 percent as against 46 percent). However, it should be emphasized that having a handgun is only one factor in homicide, and not the most important.

The flammable socioeconomic situation in most cities is very likely the more important of the two reasons.

Aggravated assault is very much like murder. The principal difference is one of degree: Murder is assault carried to its logical ending. While there were 19,000 murders reported in 1978, there were some 490,000 crimes of aggravated assault. Murder and assault are similar in many respects. The same time, condition, and motives of occurrence are present. There are two major kinds of assault: One—the most frequent kind—is due to the tensions and disorder that are the result of living in a crowded, dirty, and desultory environment such as a slum. The second is psychological; particular types of socialization experiences produce individuals with atypically hostile psychological orientations.[44] This type of violent offenders is usually raised in a more rigid family environment and has stricter, more dominating fathers than the first type. They are not only poorly socialized, but insensitive to social influences, and frequently volatile in disposition. They often show records of juvenile misconduct involving unprovoked attacks on their peers and, on occasion, animals. Indeed, acts of extreme cruelty to animals and others are characteristic of such offenders. They exhibit a chip on the shoulder, believe themselves tough and manly, and generally are defined as hopeless criminals and kept in custody for long periods of time. In prison, where they are a small group, they are known as "hard guys," or "gorillas," and are generally avoided.[45] But they make up only a small minority of all murderers and assaulters.

The pattern of incidents makes it apparent that the majority of homicides and assaults cannot be deterred by more effective police action or by capital punishment. Both of these measures are meant to convince a rational person that it does not pay to commit murder or assault. But the murderer and assaulter are usually not rational. A 1977 study conducted by the Institute of Law and Social Research of the University of Minnesota found that capital punishment does not deter homicides. The researcher hypothesized that if capital punishment deters homicide, the homicide rate should increase in states where the risk of execution went down or was nonexistent. Instead, the states that ended the death penalty had smaller increases in the homicide rates than those that kept the death penalty.[46] Other studies have shown the same thing (see Chapter 9 for a further discussion of deterrence). Thus, if the death penalty is to be justified as a punishment for all murderers, it can only be justified on a moral basis: Society is extracting an "eye for an eye." But it should quickly be added that murderers are not all irrational and impassioned; some, indeed, might be deterred by quick and severe punishment, particularly the 25 percent or so who do not kill relatives or friends in altercations. Nonetheless, a blanket policy should not be used to cover all types of murderers and assaulters because they are a wide and varied lot.

SEXUAL OFFENDERS   One study of 300 sexual offenders who were referred to the New Jersey Diagnostic Center found that 50 percent were under 30, 50 percent were single, 44 percent had less than an eighth-grade education, and 70 percent were from a low-income background.[47]

That statistical profile shows what the "average" sex offender is like: a young man from a poor background with little education. But sex offenders are a highly varied lot. They include not only violent persons, who, in addition to rape may also kill, but also child molesters, exhibitionists, Peeping Toms, and lewd telephone callers. The circumstances surrounding such criminal behavior are extremely varied, but there are two common elements in most instances: Society's reaction to the crime is quite severe, but the sex offender seldom perceives of himself as a criminal.

In the case of statutory rape which involves sexual intercourse with a girl below the age of consent, the person who commits the offense does not at all think of himself as a criminal. In fact, the victim is usually a willing participant, though under age. The most common offender in this case is the soldier or sailor on leave or an adult who has a long-time relationship with a young person ("Lolita"). Most offenders regard themselves as law-abiding citizens and believe they are doing what everyone else is doing; only they get caught. They usually have no prior record, and have a normal family background and conventional peer group relationships.

The aggressive rapist, who uses force in varying degrees, is similar to the statutory rapist in self-conception, but he usually is young, as is his victim. A 1967 study reported that 50 percent of cases of aggressive rape are victim precipitated.[48] The traditional police view is that if a woman is known to the man, has had sex with him before, has a bad reputation, and is uninjured, she is not a victim and deserves what she got. This view has come under attack. Some women take the view that rape is simply another form of the male domination in American society. From this perspective the woman is not likely to precipitate the crime.[49]

Increased attention to the question in recent years shows that rape is one of the most unreported crimes. In the past, women were reluctant to report rape because of the hostile way they were treated in law as well as by law enforcement officials. This situation is rapidly changing. Public attitudes toward the crime of rape are altering, partly due to the influence of the women's rights movement. Increasingly, rape is recognized as a violent crime against the person, rather than a sexual act. This shift in attitude has brought about efforts to reform rape laws as well as to develop more enlightened and sensitive procedures for investigating and prosecuting rape cases.

This increase in public concern may account for the rate more than doubling from 12.1 per 100,000 reported rapes in 1965 to 26.1 in 1974. As a result law enforcement agencies have looked for ways to strengthen their ability to deal with rape offenses. A Law Enforcement Assistance Administration (L.E.A.A.) survey of rape conducted in 1977 turned up important findings. First, it found that there is a lack of uniformity in the way police agencies define rape offenses. Most agencies require penetration and the use of force before an assault is classified as rape. But 28 percent of these agencies also require the use of a weapon and/or evidence of the victim's resistance. In these jurisdictions the incidence of rapes is less, since the definitional requirements are more stringent.

The L.E.A.A. study reports some other interesting facts about rape. The researchers found that nearly one-half of all offenses occur between 8 P.M. and 2 A.M., and they occur more frequently on weekends. A large percentage (41 percent) occurs in the victim's residence, although a large percentage also occurs outdoors (34 percent). The third largest percentage is associated with hitchhiking (18 percent). Approximately one-third of rape victims come in contact with their assailants voluntarily. But, contrary to what was previously believed, the study found that in two-thirds of forcible rapes, the victim and offender were strangers. In only a quarter of reported incidents were they acquaintances. Alcohol or drug use is involved in over one-half of the cases. Resistance by the victims most often is verbal (one-third of reported cases), but in about 40 percent of the cases no resistance is offered. Finally, some physical injury is involved in about one-half of the reported cases; the injuries required medical treatment in about a quarter of the cases, and hospitalization in about 7 percent.[50]

The statistics about resistance and injury perhaps explain why rape is greatly underreported. If evidence of resistance exists in only a small percentage of cases, a woman is likely to be reluctant to report the crime, particularly since police are likely to be skeptical in those cases where there is no evidence of resistance. Police are likely to treat reported rapes as unfounded in these cases, and women are reluctant to go through the public humiliation an investigation entails. About 20 percent of all forcible rape cases reported to the police are considered by them to be unfounded, and about half of all individuals arrested and prosecuted are acquitted.[51] Little wonder that only 10 percent of all rape cases are reported according to some estimates.

Strong efforts by feminists have improved the process of investigating rape. Cities have created special units that are run by women, who are likely to be more sympathetic toward the victim. These efforts may improve reporting. This may reduce the incidence of rape in the future because better reporting should mean that more offenders will be prosecuted and this, in turn, may improve deterrence of the crime.

PROFESSIONAL CRIMINALS

The crimes that fall into this category are committed by individuals who are motivated by self-interest, much the same as everyone else in American society. In general, these individuals are as "normal" as everyone else in motivation and life habits. They have families, relatives, and homes. They recognize that the law places constraints upon criminal behavior, and they actually endorse this. "After all," they say to themselves, "when I get rich I don't want someone coming around and taking my property."[52] The difference, of course, is that these offenders cannot live by the norms of straight society, they cannot stand the routine of a nine-to-five job, and they prefer the excitement of crime. They recognize, however, that they are criminals. In contrast to amateurs, professionals maintain ties with others who facilitate their crime and enable the professionals to deal with the criminal justice system skillfully. Loyalty to their fellow criminals is an important value, even though they may frequently betray them. Scholars do not agree about what a professional criminal is, but one point on which there is agreement is that, to the professional, crime is a means of earning a living, while for the amateur it is not. There are other dimensions of importance for distinguishing the professional from the amateur, such as the amount of skill the criminal has, which we shall describe later. A close look at an ideal "professional job" should clarify the traits that make criminals professionals.

The famous Brinks' robbery that occurred in Boston in 1950 was one of the most sensational and successful robberies of all times.[53] The robbery was the product of the thought and experience of men who had known one another for many years. The gang spent more than a year in planning the robbery. They began by becoming thoroughly acquainted with the Brinks' premises. Each entered the building on a number of occasions after closing time and made a study of Brinks' schedules and shipments.

After thoroughly "casing" the Brinks' premises, the gang made a number of trial runs, during which the approach and getaway routes were practiced. One member was deployed on the roof of a nearby building to signal the others with a flashlight if the police appeared.

On January 17, 1950, the members of the gang met in the Roxbury section of Boston and entered the Ford stake-out truck they had stolen for the job during the previous November. Nine members of the gang were carried to the Brinks' building in this truck. They wore Navy-type peacoats, chauffeur's caps, Halloween masks, gloves, and crepe-sole shoes to muffle their footsteps. Each also carried a pistol.

As they approached the Brinks' building, they received the go-ahead signal from the lookout on the nearby roof. Using a side-door key previously obtained, they quickly entered the building. They proceeded to the second floor where they took five Brinks' employees by surprise. The employees were bound hand and foot, gagged, and left lying on the floor. The robbers then gathered the loot, loaded it on their truck, and made a clean getaway.

The loot was hidden in a home in Roxbury and divided among the gang several weeks later—several million dollars in all! The truck used in the robbery was cut up with an acetylene torch. Brinks' offered a $100,000 reward, and the F.B.I. conducted a six-year investigation, during which it interviewed thousands of possible suspects, witnesses, and other individuals in an attempt to solve the crime.

The Brinks' robbery is a good example of professional criminals at work. The heist was well planned; the planning took a great deal of patience and time. The robbery itself was exquisitely executed. The Brinks' robbers were not amateurs.

Professional criminals such as the Brinks' robbers pursue crime as a full-time endeavor for the purpose of making a livelihood and, in most cases, a good income. Amateurs, on the other hand, usually commit a crime once or twice and are much more likely to be caught. Professional criminals are seldom caught and sent to prison. Skilled criminals are less concerned with being caught (although they seldom are) than with avoiding conviction if caught. They therefore leave no evidence that would stand up in court.

Criminals themselves do not use the term *professional* and prefer the term *rounder* (or true criminal), referring to one who has devoted his or her life to crime. In the argot of the criminal, the word *square-John* refers to an amateur, someone who is arrested just once and goes to jail, someone who is not to be respected or admired. Rounders do not steal against their will, whereas a "bum" or square-John does not have the dedication and stability to be a good criminal. Rounders can be trusted. They are reliable and, contrary to popular myth, will not cheat on their partner. "Alkies" (alcoholics) or "dope fiends" (drug addicts), on the other hand, seldom achieve rounder status because they are unreliable.

Professional criminals are specialized. Each has his or her principal line, such as safecracking, hotel prowling, or pickpocketing. This does not mean that they never shift from one specialty to another. In fact, good professionals must be able to do more than one thing, otherwise they will not survive very long. Thus, the safecracker must be able to do some hotel prowling either when there are no good safecracking jobs available or when safecracking becomes less and less appealing as a specialty. In fact, professional criminals face the same dilemma that all professionals face: If they become too narrowly specialized they may become obsolete as society's needs change.

Professional criminals also must be good money managers, since they need capital to do the better jobs. The 11 men who did the Brinks' job needed a good deal of capital because the planning took a full year, and they needed money to live on during this period.

Three main types of skills are useful to professional criminals: (1) mechanical skills, which are needed for forced entries of all kinds; (2) organizational skills, which include group leadership and planning; and (3) social skills, which involve manipulating or handling people.[54] The skills are combined in various ways depending upon the type of crime.

Some crimes, such as safecracking, require mechanical skills. Crimes involving victims, on the other hand, revolve around social skills and require the ability to establish authority quickly. Bank robbers, for example, emphasize self-confidence as the key to a successful bank robbery—an undertaking where the ability to control people under stress is essential. The role of a strong voice in establishing authority and managing tension is crucial. Moreover, the successful robber must be familiar with the habits of the people and businesses he or she wants to rob. The robber must know its usual and unusual processes and cannot be ignorant of social convention.

Professional criminals presumably enjoy their craft. They prefer to avoid the responsibilities that burden more lawful citizens. They spend only one-fifth as much time in jail as amateur crooks. Arrest and jail are considered to be an occupational hazard—to be endured when they happen in somewhat the same way as football players endure injuries. Professional criminals enjoy a very high standard of living. Given the low risk and high probability of reward as well as the absence of guilt pangs, crime is a rational choice for them. Al Capone, for example, is said to have made $105 million tax-free dollars in one year alone, and he did not have many qualms about his activities.[55] One professional burglar put it as follows:

> There ain't no such thing as right or wrong in my world. Can you dig? Right or wrong is what a chump chooses to tell himself. And I choose to tell myself that stealing is right. I had a choice: to be a poor ass, ragged-ass math-a-fucker all my life or to go out into the streets and steal me some money. . . . I ain't ashamed of what I did or who I am.[56]

BURGLARS AND ROBBERS   The burglar may be an amateur or a professional. The principal distinction is that for the professional, burglary is not a haphazard operation. It is not based on a random selection of homes. Professional burglars are aware of the location of homes with valuable contents and when the occupants will be away. They are thus assured of a large haul and little trouble. Contemporary burglary is not restricted to residences; it now includes any type of structure, even ships and airplanes. However, about two-thirds of reported burglaries in 1978 involved residences and occurred during the day. Victimization surveys show that most burglaries of residences are not reported to the police because the victims believe the police are not effective in solving the crime. And they are right. Only 17 percent of all burglaries in 1978 were cleared by arrest. Thus, professional burglars who believe the pay is high and the chance of getting caught is low are right. In this case, crime does pay.

The professional burglar is not hostile toward police and usually not inclined to use violence. However, there are professional criminals who use a high degree of violence. This is true of the professional robber who takes property with the use of force. Most live in large cities. They are usually called upon as a "team." They define themselves as criminals, but they see crime as preferable to regular work. They usually are from lower-class backgrounds and begin their careers as predatory gang delinquents in the slums where they live. They are "admitted into the profession" and learn their "craft" through direct contact with other professionals, usually in prison.

CON ARTISTS   Con artists get their name from the fact that the principal tactic they use is to gain the confidence of their victims. John Ernest Warrell Kelley is a con artist who began a hoax in 1874 that made him a fortune and lasted more than a quarter century. His nonexistent perpetual motion machine, which he claimed would produce a force more powerful than steam or electricity, was used to extract money from many cities on two continents as well as from the United States Secretary of War. Before his career was over, he had written a 372-page book on his "discovery." Over $1 million in cash, a life of luxury for 25 years, and an international reputation were also his.[57]

Con artists such as Kelley are considered to be the cream of professional criminals. They are accorded considerable prestige by fellow criminals and often acquire great sums of money without being caught. Professional con artists usually begin their careers at a late age, moving into a criminal life after a period of selling or working in restaurants or hotels. They have great acting ability. And the schemes of con artists show fantastic ingenuity. One major area for the con artist is securities fraud. The Bank of Sark swindle is a good example. This swindle is estimated to have taken $40 million from banks, insurance companies, and small and large businesses around the world.

The Bank of Sark was chartered on Sark, a small island off the coast of England, where there are few banking regulations. However, the Bank of Sark was not really a bank at all. It was a small office with a Telex machine and a post-office box number. But it distributed handsomely printed brochures with a crest bearing the inscription *Nulli Secundus.* The mastermind of the swindle, Philip M. Wilson, hired an "accountant" to draw up a balance sheet for the "bank," showing assets of $72 million. The hired accountant was about as legitimate as the bank itself, having obtained his C.P.A. certificate through a correspondence school. Following this illegitimate accounting of the bank's assets, Wilson and his cohorts proceeded to issue phony securities, called the "First Liberty Fund." They not only sold millions of dollars of these stocks but they issued bank drafts as well to buy autos, pay for airline flights, acquire mortgage notes, and pay telephone bills.[58]

How is it possible for such a scheme to fool so many people in this way? The strongest tool in the swindler's kit is the ability to convince victims that they would be fools to pass up the opportunity being presented. Thus, the victims' own greed aids the swindler. The famous con artist Joseph "Yellow Kid" Weil said:

> The men I fleeced were basically no more honest than I was. One of the motivating factors in my action was, of course, the desire to acquire money. The other motive was a lust for adventure. The men I swindled were also motivated by a desire to acquire money, and they didn't care at whose expense they got it. I was particular. I took money only from those who could afford it and were willing to go in with me in schemes they fancied would fleece others.[59]

Con artists such as Weil are professionals who live by their wits, which are sharp indeed. Society does not generally condemn con artists and even romanticizes them, as was the case in the movies *The Sting* and *Paper Moon*. In each of these movies the con artists, including a young girl, were handsome, colorful, adventurous people who took money either from those who would not miss it or from greedy and dishonest people. But in real life the target of the confidence artist is the ordinary citizen who can ill afford to lose money. For example, in the mid-1970s, a rather clever confidence ruse was developed around the principle of a "pyramiding" sales scheme. In this scheme individuals are told they can make large profits if they become "distributors" of a particular product, such as a rug shampoo or perfume. Each "distributor" is asked to invest a few thousand dollars for which he or she will be supplied with a large quantity of the product. With the company's help, the victim is supposed to hire a small sales force to sell the product in his or her own neighborhood and receive a percentage of every product sold. But what actually happens is that the victim ends with a garageful of a fairly useless product. The money put up by many individuals usually represents their entire life savings.

CHECK FORGERS Although some professionals engage in check forging, most check forgers are amateurs; they usually pass a few bad checks, frequently their own or a relative's, after the breakup of a family or the loss of a job. Although the passing of bad checks is extremely commonplace and costly, a large portion of the bad checks are for small amounts. Merchants are reluctant to report these bad checks and prefer to add it to their cost of doing business. The amateur check forger generally is a white male, with a higher I.Q. and more responsible occupation than other offenders, and generally a bit older. It is likely that most of the bad checks will be written after a gambling or alcoholic spree.

The professional check forger, on the other hand, deals either with large bunches of fictitious checks that are made to look authentic or with stolen check forms. But professional check forging has declined as technology has improved and as the production of inks, papers, engraving, and check-writing machines have gotten better. It has thus become harder to make good counterfeit checks. Few professional check forgers exist today.[60] Most professional forgery is undertaken by solitary thieves with blank checks stolen from individuals or corporations.

SAFECRACKERS Safecracking also is a declining criminal activity. Safecrackers usually work in pairs; one does the actual safecracking and the other works as the "point man," who keeps watch. A safecracker resembles the craftsman whose reward is psychological rather than strictly monetary. One safecracker who was caught said in an interview:

> Maybe . . . it may be just that it's a crime, but I can tell you that I've had no greater thrill than the first time I opened a safe door. When I opened, you know . . . I went at it . . . I didn't peel it or nothing. I went at it in a sophisticated manner and it was a thrill.[61]

Among the reasons for the decline of safecracking as a criminal career are the increasing difficulty of making nitroglycerine as well as improvements in making burglar-proof safes. The development of a credit economy and night depositories also have made safecracking less lucrative.

SHOPLIFTERS   Professional shoplifting, or "boosting," on the other hand, has not declined in recent years. In fact, it has increased, probably as a result of the increase in self-service department and grocery ·stores. The professional shoplifter is likely to be a woman, partially because a dress affords greater opportunity to hide the loot. However, contrary to popular belief, most losses to stores are due to store employees rather than to professional shoplifters. It has been estimated that employee theft accounts for 75 percent of all store losses.[62]

The Department of Commerce estimated in 1977 that shoplifting costs stores up to $5 billion a year. Although shoplifting is done mostly by store employees or teen-agers on a spree, professional shoplifting, sometimes by rings, also accounts for a great amount of the loss. For example, if the target were a clothing store, a shoplifting ring might send out four-person teams who would enter a store and begin browsing. One member of the team would attract the salesperson's attention while the other three began to roll up suits and other items of expensive clothing. Hangers would be taken so that the salesperson would not suspect shoplifting. In addition, the person who first attracted the salesperson would usually buy a fairly inexpensive item to further allay suspicion. One member of such a ring indicated that they did not feel they were hurting anyone, because "the insurance company pays for the store's loss."[63]

THE DECLINE OF PROFESSIONAL CRIME   Professional crime began to decline in the early 1940s, when the number of specialized career criminals was reduced. The golden age of professional crime spanned the era from the Civil War to the Second World War. There may have been as many as 100,000 professional criminals in existence at one time. True, certain types of crime, such as bank robbery, have increased, going from 81 in 1950 to over 2,000 in 1970. But bank robbery was less than 1 percent of all robberies in 1978. And the increases that occured in the early 1970s were due to nonprofessional offenders rather than professionals. In the past a bank robbery was a smooth and slick operation. Today, however, it is different. In one recent case the robbers jumped from their car and dashed up to the door of the bank, only to find that the doors were locked; they departed quickly. In other cases, the robbers were thwarted by bank employees who either refused to comply, screamed, or merely ducked behind their cages. Professionals would not make such gross errors or misjudge the situation. A further indication that professional bank robbing has declined.is the fact that of those arrested in a recent year, half had no prior record.[64] And the total number of robberies declined between 1975 and 1979. In 1978, robberies comprised less than 5 percent of all property crimes; half of all robberies occurred in the streets, the rest taking place in gas stations, stores, and residences; and about two-thirds of all the robbers were armed.

What kind of policies are likely to be effective in reducing the number of professional crimes? Would there be fewer of these crimes if prison sentences were made longer for those caught and convicted? The answer is inescapably yes. Most professional criminals are rationally motivated and carefully weigh the costs and benefits of crime. If the risk of apprehension and conviction is too great, given the possible reward for a job, they are not likely to commit the crime. The problem is to develop police and security methods that can be effective against certain types of rather clever criminals.

The police and improved security measures have been effective in reducing and, in some cases, almost eliminating certain types of professional crime, particularly kidnapping, safecracking, and bank robbery. But sometimes the cost of reducing crime can be prohibitive. For example, the Rand Study of New York City subways mentioned earlier found that added police patrols on the subway system did reduce robberies—but at a cost of $35,000 per robbery.[65] Public officials were willing to bear this high cost because of the strong feelings that existed about crime in the subways. But public officials are not willing to spend more money to try to prevent shoplifting because the public is not as alarmed about this kind of crime. The professional crimes that have declined, particularly check forging and safecracking, have done so as a result of technological changes rather than more stringent police enforcement.

Does this mean that crime pays? Daniel Glaser argues that burglary and robbery do not pay. His argument is as follows: The probability of being caught and convicted for burglary is very low—approximately .10 (i.e., only 10 percent of those who commit burglary are convicted). This means the probability of success for a single job is .90—very high (i.e., 90 percent get away with the crime). However, most criminals do not stop at one job but commit, instead, a large number of jobs. They are almost certain to be caught sometime in their career, Glaser writes, because the probability of pulling 30 successful jobs *in a row* is only .04, even though the probability of being successful on any one job is .90. He arrives at this conclusion by applying the multiplicative rule of probability for independent events; thus, the probability of getting 30 successes in a row is $.90^{30}$, or .04.[66]

But there are two flaws to this argument. First, the multiplicative rule of probability does not apply in this situation because each burglary is not an independent event. The burglar learns more about the work each time a job is done. In other words the burglar gets better at it; however, the police may also learn more about the particular method being employed by this burglar. Thus, the chance of being successful on the second job is dependent upon how well the first job was done and how much was learned. But even if we concede that each burglary is an independent event, there is still a flaw in Glaser's argument—the paradox in probability theory called "gambler's ruin." Even though the chance of getting a run of 30 successful jobs in a row is .04, the chance of being successful on any particular job, if the events are truly independent, is always .90. In essence, this says that the chance of being successful on the thirtieth job is *not* .04, but .90, because the probability of independent events does not change from one trial to the next. In short, the probability of being successful in committing a burglary is very high, it remains high no matter how many jobs are done, and it is true that "crime pays" for burglary and robbery.

WHITE-COLLAR CRIMINALS

The persons designated by the F.B.I. as public enemies numbers one through ten in 1939 were burglars and robbers; they netted only $250,000. In that same year the sum stolen by a single stock manipulator was $25 million. Today, medical quackery takes at least $2 billion a year from the public, and it is estimated that some $350 billion in taxable income goes unreported by "law-abiding" citizens each year. The burglar and robber are usually given stiff penalties, while white-collar criminals are let off scot-free. The following cases are good examples of this.

Jack L. Clark, chairman of the Four Seasons Nursing Centers of America, Inc., was convicted of defrauding the public of $10 million in securities; he had "stashed" $4 million of this in a secret Delaware trust that could not be recovered. He received a one-year prison sentence and was eligible for parole after four months because he agreed to plead guilty to a few of the government's charges.

Austen B. Colgate, the managing partner of the brokerage house of Middendorf, Colgate & Co., was charged by the Securities and Exchange Commission with "gross abuse of trust" and "personal misconduct" in his handling of an in-house mutual fund. His penalty was a 90-day suspension from engaging in the securities business.

In 1973 Howard J. Arbel, senior vice-president and general counsel of International Telephone & Telegraph, sold some of his I.T.T. stock on the basis of inside information that, when it became public, caused the stock to decline. Arbel did not contest the finding. His punishment was an order not to repeat the performance.

These cases are only the tip of the iceberg for many white-collar criminals are not even prosecuted. Many are allowed to hide behind corporate façades since it is most often the corporation that is fined, while its officers escape prosecution.

But what is white-collar crime? There is not a universally accepted definition, perhaps because so little of it is actually prosecuted that we do not know enough about it. Also called "upperworld crime," white-collar crime has been defined by sociologists Edwin Sutherland and Donald Cressey as any illegal act committed by a person of respectability and high social status in the course of his or her occupation.[67] It also has been defined more broadly as any crime committed as a result of offenders being in a particular position that enables them to do it.[68] Business crime, embezzlement, and stock fraud are examples. However, some experts would distinguish between embezzlers, who take money from a business for personal gain, and those who engage in illegal actions in order to further the financial success of the firm (e.g., corporate officials who commit consumer fraud or rig prices).[69]

The last definition of white-collar crime, which emphasizes criminal acts committed by employees for the benefit of their employer, does not include dishonest and illegal acts committed solely for personal gain by labor union officials, government employees, politicians, doctors, and lawyers as well as business executives. Thus, the best definition of white-collar crime encompasses crimes committed for organizational as well as personal gain and includes such crimes as restraint of trade, false advertising, unfair labor practices, financial manipulation, embezzlement, misappropriation of public funds, bribery, making illegal narcotics prescriptions, and fraudulent reports.[70] White-collar crime has so many facets that it may ultimately be impossible to include them all in a single definition. For our purposes we shall accept the definition that includes criminal acts for either organizational or personal gain committed by persons in positions of trust in the course of their occupations.

White-collar criminals recognize that their acts are illegal, but they define these as acceptable or even essential to the success of their organization. Hypocrisy is the hallmark of white-collar crime. Offenders do not like to have their acts called "criminal." The standard explanation that attributes crime to poverty and broken homes does not apply to white-collar crime, for it is most often committed by wealthy and/or professional individuals such as business executives, lawyers, and medical doctors.

White-collar crime committed for the benefit of the company cannot be fully understood without reference to the structure and values of society. Many individuals feel that government should not regulate business, not just because they are against governmental interference with private enterprise but also because regulations become so complex and cumbersome that executives can almost not run their businesses without breaking the law.[71] However, much of this may simply be rationalizing, for there is a tremendous amount of deliberate crime committed by business executives in the ordinary course of their business. Some of this crime benefits the company but much of it also is for the personal gain of the executive who, in some cases, may be the owner of the company. Consumer fraud, for example, is quite prevalent, involving false advertising, deceptive pricing, misrepresentation, failure to deliver, undue delay, and performing unnecessary repairs. These crimes are committed for the benefit of the company and, therefore, for the personal gain of the owners and managers of the company because they lead to higher, and often illegal, profits. Crimes that are committed *against* business firms for the personal gain of those committing them include taking bribes, kickbacks, computer fraud, and embezzlement. The following discussion of embezzlers illustrates this latter form of white-collar crime.

EMBEZZLERS An Internal Revenue Service computer programer noticed a buildup of unclaimed tax credits in a computer printout. He then rigged the machine to transfer the money to a relative's account. Luck ran out on him when the real claimant showed up for the money.

Another I.R.S. programer used the computer to steal checks being held for someone whose mailing address had been changed and whose forwarding address had been lost. He was caught when he deposited ten checks at one time in his bank account—an act that aroused the suspicion of the bank's tellers.

An Air Force sergeant computerized a fuel-ordering system for Kelley Air Force Base in Texas and then used the system to purchase fuel from suppliers who did not exist. The computer issued checks to phony companies set up by the sergeant. He also manipulated the computer's memory so it did not notice the loss of the fuel. By the time he was caught he had stolen over $100,000.

Several college students who worked in the registrar's office at a large urban university changed the grades of fellow students and gave them credits for courses they never took, all for a fee. They were fired and expelled from college when discovered; the registrar also lost his job.

The computer revolution in American society has created an amazing number of new ways for people to embezzle money. But embezzlers do not always use the computer to steal. Embezzlement occurs when a person in a position of trust uses that position to make money or converts a large sum of his or her employer's money to personal use and keeps those acts secret. Traditionally, embezzlers altered books and accounts or failed to report money they received. More recently, embezzlers have been using computers because many firms have computerized accounting systems. A 1977 study by the General Accounting Office identified 69 computer crimes that in a period of two years defrauded federal agencies of $2 million. But this, of course, is only the amount that was *identified*. Less than 1 percent of such crimes is prosecuted. No doubt, embezzlers take many millions of dollars every year. There are many ways to cheat an employer—for example, taking property, misrepresenting the amount of work done, padding expense accounts, and manipulating books to siphon funds. Embezzlement is increasing more rapidly than other crimes, and it involves much more money than robberies and burglaries combined.

Embezzlers do not think of themselves as criminals, they usually have no prior record, and are from a middle-class background. However, they often become embroiled in difficulties with alcohol or gambling before they decide to embezzle. And they also engage in elaborate rationalizations before they steal; most embezzlers convince themselves that they are borrowing the money rather than stealing it.[72]

OCCASIONAL PROPERTY CRIMINALS

Crimes against property constitute 90 percent of all reported crimes. White-collar crime such as embezzlement and shoplifting are crimes against property, but the property crimes that police most often are occupied with are burglary and auto theft. White-collar crime has not yet found its way into the official crime statistics; it is not one of the index crimes reported in the F.B.I.'s *Uniform Crime Reports*.

Those who commit occasional property crimes are the opposite of the professional criminal. They commit offenses infrequently, and they use crude methods. They also are much more likely to be caught. And they commit the majority of most minor property crimes such as check forging, shoplifting, auto theft, and vandalism. The latter is a crime committed by amateurs, usually young people, who reject society's values and take their hostility out on buildings. Graffiti in subways is one form of vandalism. But the most frequent target of vandalism is the school or public housing project. School windows, doors, desks, fire hoses, and equipment are regularly destroyed or defaced. The cost of vandalism each year is enormous.

Most occasional property criminals, however, do not want to destroy or deface property. They want to use it for personal gain. They do not perceive of themselves as criminals and are usually "respectable" citizens. One good example is Ken Speck, a W.I.R.E. disk jockey in Indianapolis, who was indicted in 1977 for stealing 236 television sets from a truck that was traveling through Indiana. The F.B.I. recovered 64 television sets from Speck's barn at his home. Speck had never been in trouble before.[73]

Most property crimes reported in the *Uniform Crime Reports* involve the theft of fairly small items, such as bicycles, auto accessories, articles taken from cars or buildings, and shoplifting. Forty-three percent of those arrested for these crimes are 18 years old or younger.

In terms of the total value of items stolen, however, auto theft stands out. It is primarily a youth crime—64 percent of those arrested are juveniles. One of the main reasons for such theft is joy riding, so it is not surprising that those arrested do not see themselves as criminals.[74]

Arson is another major type of occasional property crime. Although it is usually committed by amateurs, it is rapidly emerging as the new big business in professional crime. "The sky is red," is the code message telephoned to clients by professional arsonists to let them know that their heavily insured property—a hotel, a warehouse, a pleasure boat, or a small business—has just been set ablaze. Arson accounts for five times as much property loss as robbery. It is estimated that arson losses amounted to $2 billion in 1976.

Although professionals are getting more involved in arson, the usual incident is a restaurant owner whose business is not doing well and who decides to have the restaurant burned to collect the insurance. The number of arsons has increased greatly from 1976 to 1978, mostly because it is an easy crime to commit and extremely difficult to detect.

Probably the majority of Americans have committed a relatively minor property crime at one time or another and are thus "occasional property criminals." As the comic strip character Pogo says, "We have seen the enemy and he is us." For example, Richie, who is 42 years old and the father of five children, works in a high-rise building that is under construction. In an average week he takes home a reasonably good income of about $300. But he feels it is not enough to support his family. So he supplements his income on weekends by wiring basements for homeowners who are trying to beat the high cost of regular contractors. He is doing well at this because he charges less than a regular electrician. His prices are cheap, he says, because "I don't have to pay for materials or tools. I just take what I need from the site I'm working on." His justification is that "you steal it instead of letting them steal it." [75]

TAKE THE MONEY AND RUN

After 55 years of being a "straight arrow," Charlie Walsh says he just didn't know how to be crooked. But when an unusual temptation beckoned, he yielded.

Walsh was down on his luck on Jan. 5, 1978. No family. No job. Few friends. More debt than he could handle. "Everything was going down the tubes for me."

He was a bachelor who had never earned more than $200 a week, and he owed $5,000 in back taxes on his house.

How bad was it? He had smoked cigarettes for 35 years, but quit cold turkey. "I was down to my last $12. It was either food or cigarettes."

But all that changed when a Commercial Trust Co. computer deposited $100,000 in his meager savings.

"I knew it was the bank's money, but you can't help but start to daydream," he says. "I was out of work for a couple of years, so I figured, 'What the hell. I'll take a chance.' What did I have to lose?"

So Walsh withdrew his $101,081.13 balance, bought a new car and took off. "I had a helluva ball," he says.

Walsh says he left New Jersey after he saw a newspaper article about the bank's mistake. He took a leisurely drive across the country, enjoying the scenery and doing "the whole tourist bit."

"I wanted the money to last. I didn't want to blow the whole wad. I ate out in fancy restaurants a few times. But I still had many meals at Mc-

Donald's," he says. "You don't change your ways and become a playboy overnight."

He stopped in Las Vegas, where he cashed several dozen travelers' checks for $250 each. But he didn't do much gambling.

"I'm no fool. I didn't want to risk going to jail for one wild weekend," he says. "I put seven nickels into a slot machine and won $7, but I got bored with pulling that stupid handle."

Walsh wanted to settle in the Pacific Northwest, open a small hobby shop and have security for the rest of his life. But his luck ran out.

He was caught in Portland, Ore., on June 23, when police with "a new-fangled computer system" ran a spot check on the license plates of his car and learned he was a fugitive.

When he was arrested by the FBI, agents seized a satchel containing $74,000 in cash.

Walsh now faces grand larceny charges and the bank is suing him for restitution. He's now on welfare, lives at the YMCA and is awaiting trial. But his "run for the money," he says, changed his life for the better.

"This whole thing brought me out of my shell. I was always pretty much of a loner. Now people on the street slap me on the back and say hello. And I'm friendlier."

Lawrence Journal-World, February 11, 1979, p. A18. Reprinted by permission of the Associated Press and the *Lawrence* (Kansas) *Journal-World*.

Richie, of course, is not unusual. A survey of auto mechanics and watch repair shops found that two-thirds of the former and one-half of the latter are dishonest. Thefts of small tools and supplies for do-it-yourself home projects are common among maintenance and construction workers. Firms do little to stop this, for they find it better to accept moderate theft by employees than to try to control it.[76] No effective means for controlling such crimes has yet been found.

Violence, said a critic of American society in the 1960s, is as American as cherry pie. Crime might have been included in that statement, for there is a great deal of crime committed by supposedly law-abiding average citizens. Besides the crimes mentioned above, another fairly prevalent crime committed by normally law-abiding citizens is income-tax cheating. Some income-tax cheating schemes are very clever indeed. For example, the Internal Revenue Service in 1977 caught a New York architect in a $13,000 tax-evasion scheme involving Xaviera Hollander, the "Happy Hooker." The architect and Hollander were neighbors in the apartment building where the latter operated her business. The prosecutor said the architect paid her $100 a month out of corporate funds, ostensibly for her services as an interior decorator. But, in fact, Hollander cashed the checks and turned the cash over to him, and he pocketed the money after claiming it as a legitimate business expense. This scheme, of course, is a bit more sophisticated than those practiced by most tax cheaters, but average citizens cheat on their tax bills in many ways. Many a waiter, dentist, and small business person regularly understates cash receipts. Many people hold part-time jobs while collecting unemployment compensation. This unreported income, called the "underground economy" by Professor Peter Guttmann of New York, may amount to 10 percent of the Gross National Product.[77] In a $2 trillion economy, this means that the government is losing billions of dollars in uncollected taxes from unreported economic transactions.

There are many other ways Americans cheat. Investigations of Medicaid have turned up overbilling and cheating by doctors, pharmacists, nursing homes, and laboratories of over $1.5 billion.[78] Hundreds of thousands of student

borrowers have defaulted—many deliberately—on their federally insured loans. Hotels and motels lose millions in stolen towels and bedding.

Most cheating goes unnoticed until it involves a rather big name—such as former President Nixon, who in the early 1970s did not pay any income taxes because of deductions he tried to take for donating his papers to the public. There was some question about whether he claimed too much for these papers and about whether some documents were backdated to take advantage of the law, which had expired. In short, occasional property crimes are so much a part of the fabric of American society that governmental strategies for reducing these crimes are likely to have only limited impact. Society's support for attacking such crimes is too weak to bring about any significant results.

ORGANIZED CRIMINALS

In August 1977 narcotics overlord Vincent Papa, the suspected mastermind of the notorious "French Connection" case, was found dead of multiple stab wounds in a courtyard of the Atlanta Federal Prison, where he was serving a 22-year sentence. He died of wounds inflicted while he was walking along a darkened rampway. A number of prisoners were in on the attack. "There's no question about it," one insider told newspaper reporters, "to kill him, it had to come from someone very high up." The killing, sources said, resulted from an old unpaid debt, possibly someone who felt he didn't get his money's worth in dealing with the slain mobster. The "contract" to kill Papa came from "very high" Mafia leaders.[79]

The killing of Vincent Papa fits the stereotype that most people have of the Mafia and of the activities engaged in by organized crime. In this view, the "Godfather" gives an order to have someone killed, and his lieutenants and soldiers carry it out with cold-blooded and ruthless efficiency. Further, the "syndicate" (or "Cosa Nostra," or "Mafia") is a national organization tightly controlled by one "family." Although other families dominate certain regions of the country, the national organization is hierarchically arranged, with the heads of each region subordinate to the "Godfather." The majority of organized criminals, according to this view, are of Italian (and specifically Sicilian) extraction. They engage in a host of illegal activities, including gambling, prostitution, loan sharking, extortion, and drug trafficking. The money made on these illegal activities (in the billions) is invested in legitimate businesses, such as night clubs and restaurants, that are then used as fronts for the Mafia chiefs.

How accurate is this stereotype? Is this actually the way organized crime is structured in the United States? The answer, not surprisingly, is no. An examination of each piece of the stereotype will show that most aspects are inaccurate—as is the overall picture.

Are there wars among families in organized crime in which members are killed? All known evidence indicates that this is indeed true. Members of organized crime often engage in bloody wars, in which one group will assassinate members of another group, and this may continue until one group wins and gains control of a particular kind of illegal activity, such as gambling, for a specific region. But violence in organized crime is diminishing today, and, most importantly, when it occurs, it is not random and sporadic. It is stark and businesslike, and done for business reasons alone.[80] There are rules governing the use of violence, and random, indiscriminate violence is frowned upon. It is the byproduct of other activities and not a raison d'être. For example, it might be used against an insider who is caught stealing from the organization, or someone who fails to repay a large loan. Thus, this part of the stereotype is somewhat true.

Is organized crime efficient and ruthless? Columnist Jimmy Breslin, in *The Gang that Couldn't Shoot Straight*, portrayed the Mafia as a bunch of bumbling idiots. But the truth is that they are neither exceptionally dumb or exceptionally efficient. They are as efficient or inefficient as any other organization. For example, in recruiting people the best person does not always get the position; nepotism and loyalty to organizational chiefs are more important than merit.

Is the "syndicate" a national organization that controls all organized crime activity? The answer here is a qualified no. Two separate issues are involved in this question. One is whether a single group such as the Mafia controls all organized crime, and the other is whether it is national in scope. It is helpful in addressing the first issue to use Frederic Homer's distinction between a *criminal society*, such as the Mafia, and a *matrix of crime*. According to Homer, a matrix of crime is a set of illegal activities—narcotics traffic, for example. Many different kinds of people are involved in this matrix, from the college kids who sell and distribute marijuana on campuses and who are not part of organized crime, to public officials who may accept bribes and therefore allow narcotics traffic to flourish, to members of a criminal society, such as the Mafia, who may be part of an international smuggling ring. But the Mafia does not control all the activities in this particular matrix, nor in any other matrix. In fact, the Mafia does not control all the activities in any specific matrix of organized crime (including gambling, prostitution, and loan sharking).

Researchers are somewhat divided on the issue of whether organized crime is a national organization. Homer believes that there may be a national commission of crime societies that meets from time to time, but it is at best a confederation rather than a tightly knit hierarchy. Members are linked to each other by mutual deference to a "commission" made up of the leaders of the most powerful families.[81]

Is organized crime a tightly knit hierarchy in which the members faithfully carry out the orders of their leaders—or get shot? Sociologists Marshall Clinard and Richard Quinney believe this is the case. At the top of the organization is the boss, who masterminds everything (see Figure 3-1). The middle echelon is made up of lieutenants who carry out the orders of the boss. At the bottom are soldiers and persons marginally associated with the organization—narcotics peddlers, prostitutes, bookies, and runners—who deal with the public.[82] However,

FIGURE 3-1

The Organization of Organized Crime

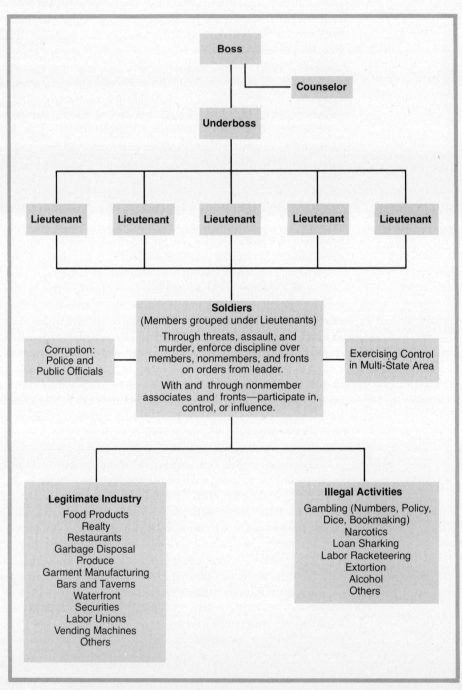

several other researchers doubt that there is such a tightly knit organization. They believe that the "Mafia" faces the same problems of control that all organizations face. Most organizations, including the army and police departments, are not able to attain complete control of their members. There are in any organization limits to how much discipline is possible.

Are most organized criminals of Italian (and specifically, Sicilian) extraction? Here the answer is pretty clearly no. In answering this question it is important to distinguish between the Mafia, which is mostly made up of Italians, and organized crime, which is not comprised solely of the Mafia. The Mafia is only one of the many different groups involved in organized crime. Moreover, different groups have dominated organized crime at different times in history. Frederic Homer has written that "it would be foolish to assume that when there is no more Cosa Nostra, there is no more organized crime, or that Italians invented or perfected what we know as organized crime."[83] Joseph Valachi, an organized crime figure himself, described the various people involved in organized crime as follows: "Besides us Italians, there were the Diamond Brothers, Legs and his brother Eddie, there were other Jew boys, and Irish guys from down around Yorkville. Sometimes you saw Lepke and Gurrah and also Little Augie from the East Side downtown."[84]

At the turn of the century organized crime was in the hands of the Irish, Jews, and native Americans rather than the Italians. One scholar says that organized crime played a major role in the upward movement of the Irish and Jews as well as the Italians.[85] And now the new entries into organized crime are the blacks, Puerto Ricans, Cubans, and Chicanos. As sociologist Gus Tyler has noted: "Like the Germans, Irish, Jews and Italians before them, the newly arrived and aspiring people reach upward through labor, crime, and politics."[86] The boss of organized crime in black Harlem, for example, is a man by the name of Nicky Barnes, known to the public and police as "Mr. Untouchable." He earned his nickname because he had been arrested innumerable times but escaped conviction for a long time. He would usually leave the police station after an arrest in an expensive Mercedes Benz.

The final question is, what are the activities engaged in by organized crime? Illegal traffic in booze and prostitutes was the major business of organized crime in the 1920s. It expanded to industrial racketeering (using strong-arm extortion tactics) in the 1930s. After the Second World War organized crime went into finance and banking. By the 1970s it had become a hydra-headed conglomerate. Among its many enterprises are traffic in illegal goods and services, such as drugs, gambling, and prostitution. In addition, organized criminals engage in racketeering and political graft, control some unions and businesses, and participate in corporate finance. But more traditional crimes are still a part of its activities. Organized crime is involved in stealing entire carloads of goods from airports, docks, shipping rooms, and trucks. Theft of clothing is another example, estimated to involve over $16 million a year in New York City's garment industry alone.[87] Organized crime is also involved in auto theft in a systematic way. One such operation was so refined that a customer who placed his order for a specific car at 9 A.M. could get delivery with all the necessary papers by 11 A.M. the same morning, right down to the color and style requested.

Organized crime has invested in business in a big way, from building materials and garbage collection, to casinos, night clubs, real estate, hotels, sports, wholesale food, and legitimate loan companies. Organized crime can provide capital for businesses. It can make a labor supply available to cooperating businesses—and generally does at bargain rates. It can maintain labor peace. It can ensure safe and speedy transport. "The trucking service itself," writes Gus Tyler, "is a most useful item in the portfolio of organized crime."[88] Control of trucking is crucial because more money can be made through manipulation of freight rates than through outright theft of goods.[89] For example, while about $16 million is lost to theft each year in the garment industry in New York City, much more is involved in the rates that truckers charge garment-industry owners to ship their goods. The total volume of business in the garment industry each year is about $5.5 billion. Trucking firms that ship these goods generally get about 5 percent of this amount; the profit thus comes to $285 million a year.[90]

But no one really knows how much organized crime makes each year. The gross income from prostitution, bookmaking, gambling, and numbers is estimated to be anywhere from $7 to $50 billion a year.[91] But Homer believes that figures on how much organized crime makes are just guesses. A United States Senate committee published a figure of $20 billion a year from gambling, which, says Homer, a staff member admitted was "picked out of a hat."[92]

What conclusion can be drawn, then, about the correctness of the public image of organized crime? It appears that the public image is only partially correct. On balance, the public is quite misinformed about the nature and structure of organized crime. And American society has an ambivalent attitude. On the one hand, it depicts organized crime as an evil fraternity. But it also gives support to organized crime every time it uses organized crime's services. "In fact," Clinnard and Quinney write, "it may be argued that organized crime is a result of the particular structure of our society." Playing the numbers and gambling, like other vices, survive because many people enjoy them, see no harm in them, and do not regard them as immoral, even when they are illegal.[93]

Behind every great fortune, the French writer Honoré de Balzac wrote, there is a crime. The ruthless robber barons in the nineteenth century, including Andrew Carnegie and John D. Rockefeller, made their fortunes by deals, blackmail, violence, and private crimes. The Watergate revelations made the public aware that there is also a great deal of corruption in American politics. While this does not constitute a defense of organized crime, it does say that moral posturing about organized crime is a form of scapegoating. Heat can be taken off of corrupt politicians and businesses by blaming organized crime for corrupting the system. Muckraker Lincoln Steffens long ago wrote about the shame of our cities. He argued that the culprits were not the individuals who took the bribes, but the corrupt businesses that offered the money. Attempts to reduce the activity of organized crime are likely to be only partly successful because organized criminals provide goods and services that are in high demand.

POLITICAL CRIMINALS

From one point of view all criminal behavior results from the political organization of a society because the decision about what to consider criminal is made by government. But political crime, more conventionally defined, attempts to change or harm the existing political system by force or violence. According to one categorization, political criminals are (1) those who are regarded as subversive by government, (2) religious or philosophical sectarians whose behavior is contrary to existing law, and (3) nonconformists who persist in outlawed behavior.[94] This typology makes one thing apparent: It is the state itself that determines what constitutes political crime. The specific political crimes that are mentioned in the United States Constitution are treason and sedition. Treason consists of waging war against the United States or giving aid and comfort to its enemies. State constitutions define treason in a similar manner, so that an act that is treasonable may violate both federal and state laws.

Sedition is criticism of the state calculated to cause people to overthrow the government violently. But the long history of interpretation of the First Amendment's protection of free speech makes it difficult to know exactly when statements are seditious libel or an exercise of free speech. Political criminals do not consider themselves criminals and rarely engage in illegal activity unless it achieves their political ends. Violence, even terrorism, is frequently used as a tactic by the political offender. The goal of terrorism is to increase general strife and bring down the government. Sharp increases in other forms of crime usually accompany increases in civil strife, as happened in the United States in the 1960s. Political scientist Ted Gurr found that "when social tension is widespread and intense, it is likely to provide different forms of disorder at the same time it spurs elites and officials to intensify efforts at control." But Gurr also found that attempts to maintain order are *not* merely the desire of the elite to maintain power, for the general public also pressures government to maintain order.[95]

Another form of political crime, not recognized until recent years, is governmental lawlessness. Here, instead of dissenters committing crimes against the state, the state itself—or rather, its leaders—are the criminals. Governmental lawlessness includes acts of individual corruption, such as when politicians and officials take bribes or use their powers to enrich themselves. Illegal activities by such agencies as the C.I.A. and F.B.I.—assassinations, surveillance and illegal wiretapping, burglaries committed for "national security" reasons, and harassment of dissenters—are also included in this category. In addition, political crimes aimed at promoting or bringing down government are sometimes committed by politicians who are promoting their own point of view. Political criminality has been almost ignored by scholars until recent years. As is the case with other crimes, devising policies to deal with political crimes requires an examination of how the criminal views his or her own behavior, how society reacts to the crime, and whether it is a crime against a person or against property.

Conclusion

There are, in fact, limits to how much we can do to eliminate criminal behavior. According to dean of the University of Chicago Law School Norval Morris and sociologist Gordon Hawkins, "The evidence is substantial that social, industrial, and commercial progress is accompanied by an increase in criminal activity."[96] Further, not only is it not desirable to rid society of all crime, it is not really possible to determine what the optimum level of a particular crime should be. For example, how much burglary is too much? Is the 1977 New York City rate of 9.4 per 1000 people too high, and, if so, by how much? The same question could be asked of the current rates of murder and rape. Crime rates cannot be reduced to zero, for that would cost far too much. To accomplish such an objective might require that this country become a police state—an obviously exorbitant price.

The amount that crime can be reduced, therefore, is a relative matter. Society's attitude about what constitutes a serious crime is important in determining what public policy should be with respect to various crimes. But "society" is not a homogeneous mass of individuals. It is composed of different classes, different ethnic and racial groups, different age and sexual groups, and different regional and professional communities. And they do not all agree upon what kinds of crime are most serious. The poor person, for example, sees the law in quite a different way than the rich person. As Robert Kennedy once said, to the poor person "legal has become a synonym for technicalities and obstruction, not for that which is to be respected. The poor man looks upon the law as an enemy, not as a friend. For him the law is always taking something away."[97]

Thus, public policies aimed at reducing the kinds of crimes described in this chapter have to be concerned with the question of who benefits and who pays when a crackdown on crime is ordered, for, as this chapter demonstrates, there are many different types of crime. Unfortunately, when the word *crime* is used, it is usually interpreted to mean "violent" crimes, which are the crimes most often committed by the poor. However, violent crimes comprise only about 10 percent of all reported crimes. And, if policies aimed at controlling crime apply only to violent crimes, the poor and minority groups will be more likely to end in prison.

Criminal behavior is varied, and different policies must be evolved to cope with different crimes. In some cases deterrence may work; in others rehabilitation may be the best; and in still others it may be best to have *no* public policy because nothing can be done to reduce or contain it. (A good example of the last is alcohol consumption as we shall see in Chapter 11.) The discussion in this chapter has emphasized that it is necessary to consider who the criminal is before making policy.

But the type of policy that should be adopted as a means of reducing crime must also be one that can be implemented by the system. It does no good to devise an ideal policy if it has no chance of being made into legislation or no chance of being carried out administratively once it becomes law.

SUMMARY

A number of theories have been developed to explain the causes of crime. These include biological, psychological, social-psychological, sociological, and crime-specific theories. Most of these theories attempt to explain the ultimate causes of criminal behavior, and are largely unconcerned with what the government can do about crime. For example, if crime actually is caused by low I.Q. or defective genes, as some biological theories state, there is little that public policy can do to reduce crime. Sociological and psychological theories also point to factors that cannot be changed through public policy. In this book we focus on the aspects of criminal behavior that are most relevent for public policy. The three important issues we deal with are: (1) how criminals perceive themselves; (2) how society views the crime; and (3) whether the crime is directed against property or a person.

Violent criminals who harm others, such as murderers, assaulters, and rapists, are looked upon with particular disfavor by the public and in public policy. But public policy may be least effective in controlling such criminals for they act from emotion rather than reason, giving little thought to possible consequences.

Professional criminals, on the other hand, are rational, calculating individuals who pursue their specialties as a way of making a living. They include the con artist, check forgers, safe-crackers and shoplifters. Public policy may be effective in controlling their activity, for these criminals calculate the risks of being caught against the benefits to be derived. Professional crime has declined in recent years, not so much as a result of public policy but because of technological advances that have made such crimes less profitable.

White-collar crime has grown at the same time that professional crime has decreased. But since white-collar crime has not been extensively studied or prosecuted, little is known about its exact magnitude and dimensions.

Amateur criminals tend to engage in occasional property crimes, such as shoplifting, petty thievery, burglary, tax cheating, and passing bad checks. They are more likely than the professional to be caught and prosecuted.

Organized crime and political crime have been around for a number of years and do not appear to be declining. Organized crime is not a nationwide hierarchy run by one ethnic group; it is a multifaceted affair that has spread from bootlegging, prostitution, and gambling to industrial racketeering, finance, and banking. It is extensive and flourishes because it is tied to political crime and because it supplies goods and services that people want. Political crime includes not only crimes against the state, such as treason and sedition, but also crimes committed by the government, including illegal surveillance of citizens, burglaries, and the use of public authority for private gain. Public policy could be effective in controlling organized and political crime, since these are crimes committed by rational and calculating individuals. But effective public policy is not likely to be developed in these areas because the public generally is not alarmed by them and because public officials themselves gain from the existence of this form of crime.

FOOTNOTES

[1] *Indianapolis Star*, June 26, 1977, p. 1.

[2] Quoted in A. Carl Kotchian, "The Payoff," *Saturday Review*, July, 9, 1977, p. 10.

[3] Larry Berg, Harlan Hahn, John Schmidhauser, *Corruption in the American Political System* (Morristown, N.J.: General Learning Press, 1976), p. 16.

[4] John Landesco, *Organized Crime in Chicago* (Chicago: The University of Chicago Press, 1929), pp. 10–11.

[5] Ibid., p. 23

[6] Martin Tolchin and Susan Tolchin, *To the Victor: Political Patronage from the Clubhouse to the Whitehouse* (New York: Vintage Books, 1972), p. 9.

[7] James Kobler, *Capone* (London: Michael Joseph, 1972), p. 210.

[8] James Q. Wilson, *Thinking about Crime* (New York: Basic Books, 1975).

[9] Ted R. Gurr, *Rogues, Rebels, and Reformers* (Beverly Hills, Calif.: Sage Publications, 1976), p. 109.

[10] Jerome Michael and Mortimer Adler, *Crime, Law, and Social Science* (New York: Harcourt 1933), p. 2.

[11] Quoted in the *New York Times*, March 23, 1975, p. 23.

[12] William Sheldon, *Varieties of Delinquent Youth* (New York: Harper & Row, 1949).

[13] Daniel Glaser, *Adult Crime and Social Policy* (Englewood Cliffs, N.J.: Prentice-Hall, 1972), p. 24.

[14] See David Lykken, "A Study of Anxiety in the Psychopathic Personality," *Journal of Abnormal and Social Psychology* 55 (July 1957), 6–10; and Stanley Schachter, *Emotion, Obesity and Crime* (New York: Academic Press, 1971).

[15] Larry Christensen, "Discriminating Criminal Types and Recidivism by Means of the MMPI," *Journal of Clinical Psychology* 30, no. 2 (April 1974), 192–93.

[16] Glenn Wilson and Alastair MacLean, "Personality, Attitudes and Humor Preferences of Prisoners and Controls," *Psychological Reports* 34, no. 3 (June 1974), 847–54.

[17] Vdai P. Singh, "Personality Profiles of Recidivists and Non-Recidivists," *Indian Journal of Social Work* 35, no. 3 (October 1974), 227–32.

[18] Jan M. Chaiken, Michael Lawless, and Keith Stevenson, *The Impact of Police Activity on Crime: Robberies on the New York City Subway System* (New York: Rand Institute, 1974), p. 23.

[19] Émile Durkheim, *The Rules of Sociological Method*, ed. George C. Catlin (Chicago: University of Chicago Press, 1938).

[20] Robert Merton, *Social Theory and Social Structure* (New York: The Free Press, 1957).

[21] See John Gillin, *Criminology and Penology* (New York: The Century Company, 1926); and Charles H. Cooley, *The Social Process* (New York: Scribner's, 1918).

[22] Don Gibbons, *Society, Crime and Criminal Careers* (Englewood Cliffs, N.J.: Prentice-Hall, 1973), p. 221.

[23] See, for example, Thorsten Sellin, *Culture Conflict and Crime*, Bulletin #41 (New York: Social Science Research Council, 1966), p. 29.

[24] Walter Miller, "Lower Class Culture as a Generating Milieu of Gang Delinquency," *Journal of Social Issues* 14, no 3 (1958), 5–19.

[25] M. E. Wolfgang and Frank Ferracuti, *The Subculture of Violence: Towards an Integrated Theory in Criminology* (London: Tavistock Publications, 1967).

[26] Howard Erlanger, "The Empirical Status of the Subculture of Violence Thesis," *Social Problems* 22 (December 1974), 280–92.

[27] Bruce Jackson, *A Thief's Primer* (New York: Macmillan, 1969).

[28] The term "differential association" was coined by E. H. Sutherland, *The Professional Thief* (Chicago: University of Chicago Press, 1937).

[29] Gibbons, op. cit., p. 254.

[30] Marshall B. Clinard and Richard Quinney, *Criminal Behavior Systems* (New York: Holt, Rinehart & Winston, 1967), pp. 12–20.

[31] Gibbons, op. cit., p. 253.

[32] Wilson, op. cit., p. 50.

[33] Daniel Glaser, *Crime in Our Changing Society* (New York: Holt, Rinehart & Winston, 1978), pp. 3–13.

[34] Peter Letkemann, *Crimes as Work* (Englewood Cliffs, N.J.: Prentice-Hall, 1973), p. 13.

[35] Donald Cressey, *Other People's Money* (Belmont, Calif.: Wadsworth, 1971).

[36] Commonwealth v. Pierce, 138 Mass. 165 (1884).

[37] Manfred S. Guttmacher, *The Mind of the Murderer* (New York: Farrar, Straus & Giroux, 1960).

[38] Marvin Voss and John Hepburn, "Patterns in Criminal Homicide in Chicago," *Journal of Criminal Law and Police Science* 59 (December 1968), 499–508.

[39] Marvin Wolfgang, *Patterns of Criminal Homicide* (Philadelphia: University of Pennsylvania Press, 1958).

[40] Reported by William K. Stevens, "Homicide No. 700: An Ordinary Man (with a Gun) Cracks," *New York Times*, December 26, 1973, p. 41.

[41] Theodore N. Ferdinand, "The Criminal Patterns of Boston since 1849," *American Journal of Sociology* 73 (July 1967), 84–99.

[42] Glaser, *Crime in Our Changing Society*, op. cit., pp. 210–11.

[43] Glaser, *Adult Crime and Social Policy*, op. cit., p. 34.

[44] David Pittman and William Handy, "Patterns in Criminal Aggravated Assault," *Journal of Criminal Law and Police Science* 53 (December 1964), 462–70.

[45] Don Gibbons, op. cit. p. 280.

[46] Margaret Garey, "Death Penalty Rarely Stops Potential Killers, Study Says," *Kansas City Times*, October 24, 1977, p. B2.

[47] Gibbons, op. cit., p. 380.

[48] Menachein Amir, "Forceable Rape," *Federal Probation* 31 (March 1967), 51–58.

[49] Susan Brownmiller, *Against Our Wills: Men, Women, & Rape* (New York: Simon & Schuster, 1975).

[50] National Institute of Law Enforcement and Criminal Justice, *Forcible Rape, a National Survey of the Response by Police* (Washington, D.C.: U.S. Government Printing Office, 1977).

[51] Charles Kirkpatrick and Edward Kanin, "Male Sexual Aggression on a University Campus," *American Sociological Review* 22 (January 1957), 9–15.

[52] Jonathan Casper, *American Criminal Justice, The Dependent's Perspective* (Englewood Cliffs, N.J.: Prentice-Hall, 1972), p. 48.

[53] This description draws heavily from Gibbons, op. cit., 253–54. See also Everett DeBaun, "The Heist: The Theory and Practice of Armed Robbery," *Harper's*, February 1950, pp. 69–77.

[54] Letkemann, op. cit., p. 49.

[55] Gwynn Nettler, *Explaining Crime* (New York: McGraw-Hill, 1974), p. 187.

[56] Quotation A. Hassan, "The Pit," *Maximum Security: Letters from Prison*, ed. Eve Pell (New York: E. P. Dutton, 1972), pp. 21–22.

[57] James A. Inciardi, *Careers in Crime* (Chicago: Rand McNally, 1975), p. 24.

[58] Jonathan Kwitney, *The Fountain Pen Conspiracy* (New York: Knopf, 1973).

[59] Joseph Weil and N. T. Brannon, *"Yellow Kid" Weil* (Chicago: Ziff-Dans Publishing, 1948), p. 293.

[60] Inciardi, op. cit., p. 26.

[61] Letkemann, op. cit., p. 83.

[62] Mary Cameron, *The Booster and the Snitch* (New York: The Free Press, 1964).

[63] Quoted in the *Kansas City Star*, November 27, 1977, p. A26.

[64] Gibbons, op. cit., p. 97.

[65] Chaiken, Lawless, and Stevenson, op. cit., p. vi.

[66] Glaser, *Crime in Our Changing Society*, op. cit., p. 215.

[67] Edwin H. Sutherland and Donald Cressey, *Principles of Criminology*, 8th ed. (Philadelphia: J. B. Lippincott, 1970), p. 51.

[68] Gilbert Geis, "Upperworld Crime," in *Current Perspectives on Criminal Behavior*, ed. Abraham Blumberg (New York: Knopf, 1974), p. 114.

[69] Gibbons, op. cit., p. 99.

[70] Clinard and Quinney, op. cit., pp. 30–32.

[71] See Robert E. Lane, *The Regulation of Businessmen* (New Haven, Conn.: Yale University Press, 1954).

[72] Cressey, op. cit.

[73] *Indianapolis Star*, July 21, 1977, p. 1.

[74] Gibbons, op. cit., pp. 317–70.

[75] Quoted in Nettler, op. cit., p. 184.

[76] Lawrence Zeitlin, "A Little Larceny Can Do a Lot for Employee Morale," *Psychology Today*, June 1971, pp. 22–26.

[77] Guttmann's findings were reported in Ernest Conine, "Is America Becoming a Land of Cheats?" *Laurence Journal World*, February 4, 1978, p. 4.

[78] Ibid.

[79] *New York Times*, July 3, 1977, p. 1.

[80] Frederic D. Homer, *Guns and Garlic, Myths and Realities of Organized Crime* (West Lafayette, Ind.: Purdue University Press, 1974), p. 111.

[81] Homer, op. cit., p. 13.

[82] Clinard and Quinney, op. cit., pp. 383–85.

[83] Homer, op. cit.

[84] Quotation Peter Maas, *The Valachi Papers* (New York: Bantam Books, 1968), pp. 66–67.

[85] James M. O'Kane, "Ethnic Mobility and the Lower Income Negro," *Social Problems*, Winter 1969, pp. 302–11.

[86] Gus Tyler, "The Crime Corporation," in *Current Perspectives on Criminal Behavior*, op. cit., p. 193.

[87] Dennis Palumbo, James Levine, and Michael Musheno, "Individual, Group and Social Rationality in Controlling Crime," in *Modeling the Criminal Justice System*, ed. Stuart Nagel (Beverly Hills, Calif.: Sage Publications, 1977).

[88] Tyler, op. cit., p. 203.

[89] Jack Newfield, "How the Mob Bleeds the Garment District," *Village Voice*, April 25, 1975, pp. 5–9.

[90] Palumbo, Levine, and Musheno, op. cit., p. 77.

[91] Tyler, op. cit., p. 201.

[92] Homer, op. cit., pp. 101–102.

[93] Clinard and Quinney, op. cit., p. 390. See also Thorston Sellin, "Organized Crime A Business Enterprise," *The Annals of the American Academy of Political and Social Science* 347 (May 1963), 12–19.

[94] George B. Vold, *Theoretical Criminology* (New York: Oxford University Press, 1958), pp. 299–300.

[95] Ted Gurr, op. cit., p. 94.

[96] Norval Morris and Gordon Hawkins, *The Honest Politician's Guide to Crime Control* (Chicago: University of Chicago Press, 1969), p. 78.

[97] Robert Kennedy, quoted in *Law and Order Reconsidered*, a staff report to the National Commission on the Causes and Prevention of Violence, eds. James Campbell, Joseph Sahid, and David Stang (Washington, D.C.: U.S. Government Printing Office, 1969), p. 27.

BIBLIOGRAPHY

Banfield, E. C. *The Unheavenly City.* Boston: Little, Brown, 1971.

Berg, Larry; Hahn, Harlan; and Schmidhauser, John. *Corruption in the American Political System.* Morristown, N.J.: General Learning Press, 1976.

Cameron, Mary. *The Booster and the Snitch.* New York: The Free Press, 1964.

Casper, Jonathan D. *American Criminal Justice: The Dependent's Perspective.* Englewood Cliffs, N.J.: Prentice-Hall, 1972.

Chaiken, Jan M.; Lawless, Michael; and Stevenson, Keith. *The Impact of Police Activity on Crime: Robberies on the New York City Subway System.* New York: Rand Institute, 1974.

Christensen, Larry. "Discriminating Criminal Types and Recidivism by Means of the MMPI." *Journal of Clinical Psychology* 30, no. 2 (April 1974), 192–93.

Clinard, Marshall B., and Quinney, Richard. *Criminal Behavior Systems.* New York: Holt, Rinehart & Winston, 1967.

Cressey, Donald. *Other People's Money.* Belmont, Calif.: Wadsworth, 1971.

Erlanger, Howard. "The Empirical Status of the Subculture of Violence Thesis." *Social Problems* 22 (December 1974), 280–92.

Ferdinand, Theodore N. "The Criminal Patterns of Boston since 1849." *American Journal of Sociology* 73 (July 1967), 84–99.

Geis, Gilbert. "Upperworld Crime." In *Current Perspectives on Criminal Behavior,* edited by Abraham Blumberg. New York: Knopf, 1974, pp. 114–138.

Gibbons, Don C. *Society, Crime and Criminal Careers.* Englewood Cliffs, N.J.: Prentice-Hall, 1973.

Glaser, Daniel. *Adult Crime and Social Policy.* Englewood Cliffs, N.J.: Prentice-Hall, 1972.

————. *Crime in Our Changing Society.* New York: Holt, Rinehart & Winston, 1978.

Gurr, Ted R. *Rogues, Rebels, and Reformers.* Beverly Hills, Calif.: Sage Publications, 1976.

Guttmacher, Manfred S. *The Mind of the Murderer.* New York: Farrar, Straus & Giroux, 1960.

Hassan, A. "The Pit." In *Maximum Security: Letters from Prison,* edited by Eve Pell. New York: E. P. Dutton, 1972, pp. 21–22.

Homer, Frederic D. *Guns and Garlic, Myths and Realities of Organized Crime.* West Lafayette, Ind.: Purdue University Press, 1974.

Inciardi, James A. *Careers in Crime.* Chicago: Rand McNally, 1975.

Jackson, Bruce. *A Thief's Primer.* New York: Macmillan, 1969.

Kwitney, Jonathan. *The Fountain Pen Conspiracy.* New York: Knopf, 1973.

Letkemann, Peter. *Crime as Work.* Englewood Cliffs, N.J.: Prentice-Hall, 1973.

Maas, Peter. *The Valachi Papers.* New York: Bantam Books, 1968.

Michael, Jerome, and Adler, Mortimer. *Crime, Law, and Social Science.* New York: Harcourt, Brace Jovanovich, 1933.

Miller, Walter. "Lower Class Culture as a Generating Milieu of Gang Delinquency." *Journal of Social Issues* 14, no. 3 (1958), 5–19.

Morris, Norval, and Hawkins, Gordon. *The Honest Politician's Guide to Crime Control.* Chicago: University of Chicago Press, 1969.

National Institute of Law Enforcement and Criminal Justice. *Forcible Rape, A National Survey of the Response by Police.* Washington, D.C.: U.S. Government Printing Office, 1977.

Nettler, Gwynn. *Explaining Crime.* New York: McGraw-Hill, 1974.

Palumbo, Dennis; Levine, James; and Musheno, Michael. "Individual, Group and Social Rationality in Controlling Crime." *Modeling the Criminal Justice System,* edited by Stuart Nagel. Beverly Hills, Calif.: Sage Publications, 1977.

Pittman, David, and Handy, William. "Patterns in Criminal Aggravated Assault." *Journal of Criminal Law and Police Science* 53 (December 1965), 462–70.

Rose-Ackerman, Susan. *Corruption: A Study in Political Economy.* New York: Academic Press, 1978.

Sellin, Thorston. "Organized Crime: A Business Enterprise." *The Annals of the American Academy of Political and Social Science* 347 (May 1963), 12–19.

Shaw, Clifford R., and Roth, Loren H. "Biological and Psychophysical Factors in Criminality." In *Handbook of Criminology,* edited by Daniel Glaser. Chicago: Rand McNally, 1974, pp. 236–59.

Sheldon, William V. *Varieties of Delinquent Youth.* New York: Harper & Row, 1949.

Sutherland, E. H. *The Professional Thief.* Chicago: University of Chicago Press, 1937.

Toeh, Hans. *Violent Men.* Chicago: Aldine, 1969.

Vold, George B. *Theoretical Criminology.* New York: Oxford University Press, 1958.

Weil, Joseph, and Brannon, N. T. *"Yellow Kid" Weil.* Chicago: Ziff-Dans Publishing, 1948.

Wilson, Glenn, and MacLean, Alastair. "Personality, Attitudes and Humor Preferences of Prisoners and Controls." *Psychological Reports* 34, no. 3, part 1 (June 1974), 847–54.

Wilson, J. Q. *Thinking about Crime.* New York: Basic Books, 1975.

Wolfgang, Marvin. *Patterns of Criminal Homicide.* Philadelphia: University of Pennsylvania Press, 1958.

Wolfgang, M. F., and Ferracuti, Frank. *The Subculture of Violence: Towards an Integrated Theory in Criminology.* London: Tavistock Publications, 1967.

Zeitlin, Lawrence. "A Little Larceny Can Do a Lot for Employee Morale." *Psychology Today,* June 1971, pp. 22–26.

Highland Park, Illinois, is a small, affluent town outside of Chicago that likes to keep its streets quiet and safe, especially at night. Because young people are the most likely to create disturbances, the Highland Park police rigorously enforce their laws concerning juvenile offenses. The town's policy is to lock up kids who gather into groups downtown looking for trouble. Until the state of Illinois adopted a new juvenile code in 1962, the police could arrest a youth on a juvenile delinquency charge for almost anything. But the new code made it considerably more difficult to make arrests. So Highland Park passed a municipal curfew law in 1963. The police chief remarked about the law, "It's in conformity with the state statute. . . . We still have to bring (the juvenile) into the station, but at least we've got a charge on him that we can use to get him off the streets."[1]

CHAPTER FOUR

THE MAKING
OF CRIMINAL JUSTICE POLICY

Thus it was possible for the town of Highland Park and its police to continue almost without change its practice of keeping youths off the street, even though the new law passed by the state of Illinois made it more difficult. This kind of local control in developing, interpreting, and enforcing the law is a major characteristic of the American criminal justice system. The direction that criminal justice policy takes is greatly influenced by the agencies that are supposed to implement it.

The Policy-Making Process

Policy making begins with the various legislative bodies—Congress, state legislatures, county commissions, and city councils—that formulate the laws specifying what constitutes illegal behavior. Administrative agencies—police departments, city and county prosecutors, sheriffs, the F.B.I.—implement these laws. In the conventional wisdom of public administration, legislative bodies make policy while administrative agencies implement it. But contemporary public administration rejects this dichotomy. Administrative agencies also make policy. They do this when they determine which of the vast number of laws will be given more attention and resources; by dragging their feet when they are asked to implement a law they do not like; by pressuring legislatures to change, rescind, or adopt laws; and by making administrative rules and regulations.

The policy-making process thus includes both the formulation of laws and their implementation. As Figure 4–1 shows, the policy-making process includes the formation, implementation, and impact of all of the actions taken by govern-

FIGURE 4-1

The Policy-Making Process

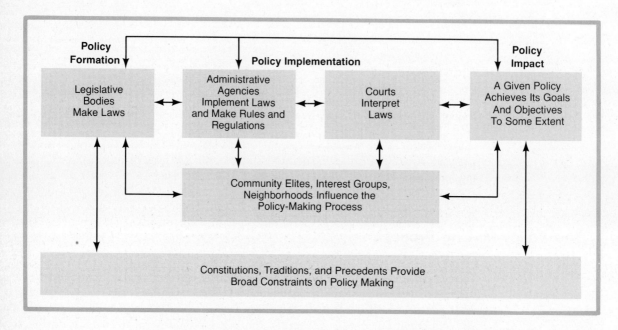

mental agencies. The word *policy* has been defined in various ways. It has been used to refer to the goals of individuals, groups, or agencies. A policy can be distinguished from a program. The former refers to goals, while the latter refers to a set of specific actions to attain the goals.[2] However, some writers believe that policies "normally contain both goals and the means for achieving them."[3] The reason for this is that goals are changed, redefined, and shaped while they are being implemented. It is not always possible to make a hard-and-fast distinction between a policy and a program anymore than we can always distinguish between means and ends. Means from one perspective can be considered to be ends from another. Thus, rehabilitation is not just a goal of corrections agencies but also a means of reducing crime. We shall use the term *policy* in this book to mean both the goals *and* strategies of action.

Public policy changes constantly, and the government pursues a number of different and often conflicting policies simultaneously. For example, such policies as deterrence, rehabilitation, decriminalization, and diversion (described in Part III of this book) are four different ways of trying to contain criminal behavior. Sometimes the government pursues two or more of these simultaneously to control crime even though two of them yield opposing results.

The *criminal justice system*, as this term most often is used, refers to the various agencies and institutions that are directly involved in the implementation of public policy, such as the police, courts, attorneys, and corrections (described in Part II of this book). But these agencies work within a broad policy-making environment, and it is essential to understand that environment in order to grasp criminal justice policy. That is the purpose of this chapter. We shall describe the policy-making process in criminal justice, including lawmaking institutions, the principal groups that influence policy, and how policy is implemented.

Formulating Criminal Justice Policy

LAWMAKING INSTITUTIONS: DECISION-MAKING CENTERS IN THE UNITED STATES

Criminal law is found in constitutions, legislation, judicial decisions, and administrative rules. Because there is no single source from which criminal law comes, many agencies and institutions help shape the nature of the criminal law.

All three levels of government—national, state, and local—are involved in making criminal law. Power at each of the three levels is usually divided among the three branches of government. First, there are legislative bodies such as the United States Congress, state legislatures, county commissions, and city councils. Then there are executive agencies—the president and all federal agencies dealing with law enforcement at the national level, the governor and various law enforcement agencies (e.g., the attorney general and the police) at the state level, and the mayor and/or city manager, as well as numerous police departments and sheriffs at the local level. Finally all three levels have a system of courts. The American judicial system, as shown in Figure 4–2, has a dual system of courts, both federal and state.

Although in theory state and municipal courts are supposed to be subordinate to the federal courts with the United States Supreme Court at the apex of the system, state and local courts retain most of their autonomy.[4] A variety of reasons can be cited for this. One is that constitutionally federal courts deal with violators of federal law, while state and local courts have responsibility for those accused of breaking state laws and local ordinances. But even more important is the fact that American jurisprudence has always recognized that state and local courts are somewhat independent. For example, the Bill of Rights was interpreted originally as applying only to federal agencies, and only through years of "incorporation" through the Fourteenth and Fifteenth amendments to the Constitution were the provisions of the Bill of Rights extended to the states. And besides the legal facts, state and local judges are elected or appointed locally, not by the federal government, and they therefore are accountable to local electorates or local officials. For these reasons state and local courts are likely to remain autonomous.

These legislative, executive, and judicial agencies are involved in criminal justice policy making in the following way: Legislatures pass the laws that define the kinds of behavior considered illegal (gambling, loitering, disturbing the peace, price rigging, murder, embezzlement, etc).

Infractions of laws passed by legislatures are handled, in the first instance,

FIGURE 4-2

The Dual System
of Courts

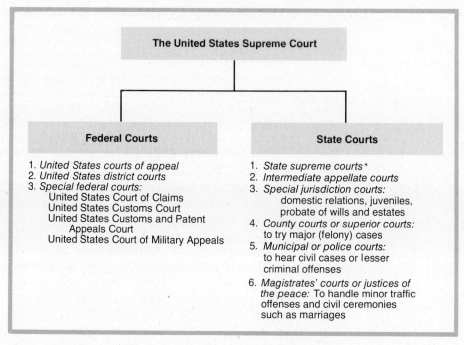

The United States Supreme Court

Federal Courts

1. *United States courts of appeal*
2. *United States district courts*
3. *Special federal courts:*
   United States Court of Claims
   United States Customs Court
   United States Customs and Patent
      Appeals Court
   United States Court of Military Appeals

State Courts

1. *State supreme courts* *
2. *Intermediate appellate courts*
3. *Special jurisdiction courts:*
      domestic relations, juveniles,
      probate of wills and estates
4. *County courts or superior courts:*
   to try major (felony) cases
5. *Municipal or police courts:*
   to hear civil cases or lesser
   criminal offenses
6. *Magistrates' courts or justices of
   the peace:* To handle minor traffic
   offenses and civil ceremonies
   such as marriages

[1] In some states (e.g., New York and Maryland) the highest court is called the "court of appeals."

by law enforcement agencies—the police, the F.B.I., and sheriffs. Courts and prosecutors determine if a charge will be brought and if an individual will be prosecuted. Finally, persons found guilty of violating a law are subject to many different kinds of correctional institutions, from city and town jails to county, state, and federal prisons. To a person caught up in this system, it may seem like a bewildering array of rules, agencies, and individuals—and it is. As we shall see below, the criminal justice system is a hodgepodge of institutions, agencies, and individuals.

SEPARATION OF POWERS AND FEDERALISM The "revolutionaries" who met in Philadelphia in 1787 to revise the Articles of Confederation ended by establishing two principles of government that have been with us ever since. These principles are so ingrained in the American system that they seem quite natural to us. Yet they often are pointed to as the major factors inhibiting rational and speedy action by public officials. These principles are the separation of powers and federalism.

Separation of powers means that each of the three major branches of government—legislative, executive, and judicial—has some power derived directly from the people; the other branches cannot formally exercise these powers. For example, the legislature is the only branch that can *make* laws: The mayor of

a city, the President of the United States, the police chief, or any other administrator cannot make laws. But this does not mean that administrators do not make
criminal justice policy. Laws and policy are not the same thing. A law is formally
passed by the legislature, and the writing of laws is the major function of legislatures. Laws are a part of policy, but they are not all of it. Administrators also
make policy every time they decide to enforce or not enforce a given law, or
when they decide just how the law will be enforced. For example, many state
legislatures have passed laws saying that sexual intercourse out of wedlock is
illegal, but few states enforce these laws. Administrators are able to make policy
because they have a great deal of discretion in determining when to enforce laws
such as these. We shall discuss the concept of "discretion" and its consequences
for the criminal justice system shortly.

Even though each of the three branches has independent powers, the
other branches are able to check and balance these powers. For example, a
police officer, who is part of the administrative branch of government, may
decide that a particular individual is guilty of "breach of the peace" and arrest
that person, perhaps even forcibly if the person resists. But the courts, a separate branch of government, may decide that the arresting officer violated the
person's rights at the time of the arrest—by searching the person's house without
a warrant, for example—and dismiss the charge.

The second major principle of government is federalism. Federalism is an
organizational system in which two of the levels of government—national and
state—have independent powers. The local levels of government—cities and
counties—do not have independent powers. Cities and counties are legal cre-
ations of states. Under federal principles the national government is considered
to be supreme in foreign relations and in the regulation of interstate commerce.
But the police powers generally are reserved to the states and local governments. Table 4–1 shows that state and local expenditures for criminal justice far
exceed those of the federal government, reflecting the fact that they are paramount in this area.

One of the risks citizens used to run because of the federal system was that
they could be brought to trial for violating laws of each jurisdiction and put in
jeopardy twice for the same crime; a person could be tried and acquitted of a
crime in a federal court and then be tried again for a similar or related crime in a
state court. The Fifth Amendment protection against double jeopardy applied
only to the national government, until recently. But the United States Supreme
Court has made this as well as all other provisions of the Bill of Rights applicable to state action as well. This was done by "incorporating" the Bill of Rights
through the due process and equal protection clauses of the Fourteenth Amendment.

Although the federal government is constitutionally supreme in certain
areas, it cannot order states or local governments to do things. It can offer inducements, such as grants-in-aid, or attempt to use negative incentives, such as
cutting off federal funds to state or local jurisdictions if they violate certain rules.
These positive and negative inducements have increased the federal govern-

TABLE 4-1

Expenditures for Criminal Justice Activities, 1975
(Dollar amounts in thousands)

| Type of Activity | | Level of Government | | | | | |
| | | Federal | | State | | Local | |
and Expenditure [1]	Total	Amount	Percent	Amount	Percent	Amount	Percent
Total criminal justice system	$17,248,860	$2,187,875	12.7	$4,612,373	26.7	$10,448,612	60.6
Police protection	9,786,162	1,460,625	14.9	1,512,130	15.5	6,813,407	69.6
Judical	2,067,664	165,332	8.0	497,660	24.1	1,404,672	67.9
Legal services and prosecution	933,126	177,275	19.0	215,997	23.1	539,854	57.9
Public defense	280,270	87,017	31.0	65,481	23.4	127,772	45.6
Corrections	3,843,313	216,778	5.6	2,193,000	57.1	1,433,535	37.3
Other criminal justice	338,325	80,848	23.9	128,105	37.9	129,372	38.2

[1] Figures are direct expenditures only. The table has been simplified; see the original for other types of expenditures.
SOURCE: U.S. Department of Justice, Law Enforcement Assistance Administration, and U.S. Bureau of the Census, *Expenditure and Employment Data for the Criminal Justice System—1975* (Washington, D.C.: U.S. Government Printing Office, 1977), p. 21, Table 2.

ment's role in law enforcement activities in the United States. In addition, the establishment of the Federal Law Enforcement Assistance Administration (L.E.A.A.) has done more to increase the federal government's role in law enforcement than any other single act in American history. The L.E.A.A. has given hundreds of millions of dollars to state and criminal justice agencies in an attempt to improve their effectiveness and efficiency. From the time it was created in 1967 until the end of 1979, Congress had appropriated more than $7 billion for the L.E.A.A. It is likely that it will become a permanent feature of the American criminal justice system.

Although the concept of federalism is fundamental to our governmental system, each level of government does not operate completely in its own jurisdiction, untouched by other levels. Rather than a layer cake, a better analogy for the system, developed by political scientists Morton Grodzins and Daniel Elazar, is that of a "marble cake."[5] There is a sharing and intermingling of powers in the federal system. For example, each level has some jurisdiction over certain crimes, such as selling illegal narcotics. But there are areas that fall mostly under one jurisdiction rather than another. For example, espionage falls under federal jurisdiction, while regulation of automobile traffic falls mainly under local jurisdiction. But even in these areas there is an intermingling of power at times. When President John F. Kennedy was assassinated, local law enforcement officials apprehended Lee Harvey Oswald and kept him in a Dallas jail, where he was murdered. Another example is the federal government's current attempts to have states enforce the speed limit of 55 miles per hour by threatening to cut off highway funds to those states that do not comply. There is thus intermingling, cooperation, overlapping, conflict, and exclusivity all operating at the same time in the American federal system.

Reformers would like to create metropolitan-wide governmental units with centralized authority so that the problem of crime (as well as problems like air pollution and transportation) can be tackled on a regional basis. The belief is that if government has sufficient legal authority, it will be able to take effective action to solve problems.

But others believe that the government cannot solve social and economic problems, no matter how much authority it has. And still others feel that the fragmented system is actually the best way to make decisions because it closely approximates the market mechanism—that is, a large number of semiautonomous government units (over 100,000 throughout the country), each competing with the others, allowing the widest possible range of values and views to be considered.[6] Particularly desirable, in this view, is the large degree of local control that exists in the fragmented system. One team of researchers, for example, has found that autonomous, small police departments are much more effective and efficient than large ones.[7] Thus, if these findings apply to metropolitan reorganization, we can conclude that creating large police jurisdictions encompassing entire metropolitan areas will not necessarily solve crime problems, and may even make matters worse.

The advantages and disadvantages of a federal system may never really be resolved, at least in terms of being able to find evidence that supports either position conclusively. The question is an ideological one to some extent, with conservatives generally supporting the fragmented system, and liberals hoping that it can be reformed and centralized.

INTEREST GROUPS AND POLICY MAKING   Criminal justice policy is formulated by many groups and agencies operating in the vast maze of government jurisdictions in the American political system. As noted above policy is formulated in the first instance by legislatures. But legislatures do not operate in a vacuum. A number of interest groups apply pressure to pass laws they favor. The gun control lobby, for example, which includes groups such as the National Rifle Association, deluges the Congress with letters and threats among other things, whenever the question of controlling guns is raised.

Generally we think of interest groups as being private organizations that have a special issue they want to promote. But government agencies themselves can and do become effective interest groups. For example, the police are probably one of the most politically autonomous and powerful groups of local government officials in the United States. They receive valuable assistance in building a favorable image from the outside, particularly from television "police" shows. But major sources of their power are their police organizations, generally called "Police Benevolent Associations." These groups have successfully prevented any encroachment upon police autonomy and have used their political clout on many issues. The question of civilian review of police behavior, which we now turn to, is a good example of their power.

Demands that civilians be given power to review police behavior are not new. For years civil rights groups have urged the adding of civilians to existing review boards. A proposal for creation of a civilian review board in New York City, made in 1965, created an intense controversy seldom equaled in the city's history. The police, through the Patrolmen's Benevolent Association (P.B.A.), vigorously opposed the proposal. The P.B.A. is the bargaining agent and union for all New York City police; about 90 percent of the city's police are members.

Mayor John Lindsay first made the proposal to add four civilians to the police department's civilian complaint review board during his 1965 mayoral campaign. After his inauguration he took steps to implement his campaign promise. On May 2, 1966, Lindsay announced the creation of a civilian-controlled review board consisting of four civilians and three police officers. He then appointed two blacks, one Puerto Rican, and one Irish Catholic as the four civilian members of the board; one of the three police officers he appointed was also black.

The creation of the board inflamed passions among the city's police. The P.B.A. through its president, John J. Cassesse, announced it would oppose the board and was prepared to spend its entire treasury to do so. It then collected 51,852 signatures on a petition for a referendum on the issue. The P.B.A. hoped that the people of the city would support them in their opposition to the board.

In the referendum campaign the police received the support of the Conservative party, the American Legion, the Brooklyn Bar Association, various parent and taxpayers' groups, and the Businessmen's Citizens' Committee—all conservative groups. The groups that favored the board were mainly liberal ones such as the Liberal party, the American Jewish Congress, the B'nai B'rith Anti-Defamation League, and the New York Civil Liberties Union.[8]

The P.B.A. spent $1 million on its campaign to defeat the board.[9] It argued that the board would impair the morale and efficiency of the police. Norman Frank, P.B.A. general counsel, argued that police officers would hesitate in the line of duty, fearing the possibility of unjust censure. The other side, in contrast, argued that the board actually would increase efficiency and would restore public confidence in the police department by guaranteeing fair hearings for complaints of brutality. But the real issue was race. A civilian review board was widely regarded as a means to satisfy the demands of blacks and Puerto Ricans for a channel to complain of police brutality. Once the race issue was introduced, those in favor of the board were identified with civil rights, and those opposed were identified with white backlash—a reaction to the movement for black rights.

The electorate overwhelmingly rejected the review board by a vote of 1,131,161 to 765,468.[10] Blacks and Puerto Rican voters were heavily in favor of the board. The white middle class—many of whom had relatives, friends, or neighbors on the police force—voted heavily against it. As researchers who studied the vote commented:

The magnitude of the outcome was stunning. For years, the white electorate of New York City had been dominated by a coalition of liberal forces—a coalition that had been especially willing to support the demands of blacks and other minority groups. . . . Yet, in the 1966 referendum, the presumed liberalism of white voters could not be translated into support for the Review Board.[11]

What happened? Some observers believe that the referendum was a critical election in which the city experienced the first shift of white voters toward a more conservative position. However, the election outcome also reflected how much power the P.B.A. and the police in general have in local politics and, consequently, the formulation of criminal justice policy. They usually succeed in stopping any encroachment on their independence. In the words of two researchers, "The police benevolent associations, the police unions, are among the most vociferous proponents of police independence from City Hall and oppose any real or imagined political interference."[12]

Not only did the P.B.A. in New York succeed in defeating the civilian review board, but it also fought with the mayor, and won, over the issue of changing the entrance requirements for the police department. The mayor's change would have allowed a person charged or convicted of petty larceny to be eligible for appointment to the department. This would have helped minority groups, since they are more likely than other citizens to have had a run-in with the law. The police also opposed the mayor in 1970 when he appointed an independent committee to investigate charges of police corruption. The police contended that the committee was a violation of a provision of the city charter, which reads: "Neither the Mayor, Police Commissioner nor any other administrative officer of the city may authorize any person, agency, board or group to receive, investigate, hear, recommend, or require action upon . . . civilian complaints [against policemen]."[13]

The example of the defeat of the civilian review board in New York City shows which interest groups are most likely to be involved in criminal justice issues in large cities. They include many of the same groups (e.g., the American Legion and the various business and taxpayers' groups) involved in most political questions. But the civilian review board incident also involved groups that were specifically interested in the particular issue, such as the Brooklyn Bar Association and the P.B.A. These latter groups—which also include other bar associations, chiefs of police associations, state trial lawyers' associations, and various government agencies—are considered permanent criminal justice interest groups because they are likely to take a position on almost every criminal justice question. On the other hand, some of the interest groups involved in the formulation of policy on the civilian review board were ad hoc groups. Their interest in criminal justice is limited to only one or two issues. This is true of the American Legion and American Jewish Congress. As another example of an ad hoc group, when states began changing their criminal codes on abortion provisions, the Catholic Church became very active in opposing liberalizations of the code. The

Catholic Church was an ad hoc group in this case. Or whenever gun control legislation comes up, the National Rifle Association acts as an ad hoc interest group opposing this criminal justice policy. It takes a stand only on the question of gun control legislation.

POLITICAL ELITES AND THE CRIMINAL JUSTICE ESTABLISHMENT Community elites can be considered a permanent interest group in criminal justice. In fact, former Supreme Court Justice Oliver Wendell Holmes Jr., believed that law is, in the main, the rationalization of the dominant group in a community. Who are the community elites? Lawyers are one of the most important of the elite groups. They are heavily represented in legislatures, giving testimony before legislative committees, in drafting commissions, and as lobbyists. Business people are another major elite group. Many communities in the United States are governed more or less directly by their big business interests, which usually include owners and executives of banks, department stores, newspapers, and real estate and insurance firms. Elected and appointed public officials such as governors, mayors, and city managers also are part of a community's elite. Political scientists have debated the extent to which various elites actually govern and the extent to which elites are responsive to the desires and needs of the public. But there is little doubt that elites have a major voice in determining both what kind of behavior will be considered criminal and the way in which the law will be enforced.

In small middle-class towns particularly the town elite and the police are likely to have a close working relationship.[14] In many of these communities the police force has about 40 to 50 members, and they have the support of the majority of citizens. For the most part the police in small towns do an honest and efficient job. But in some cases corruption exists, and both the police and the town's elite may be involved. The town of Wincanton, studied by political scientist John Gardiner, is a case in point.[15] Wincanton had a high degree of gambling, vice, and corruption. Mayors, police chiefs, and lesser officials were on the payroll of the gambling syndicate. The three county detectives who worked in the rural areas of the county and the state police as well took a "hands off" attitude toward city crime and worked only in rural areas unless invited into the city by the mayor.

Numbers, dice games, pinball machines, and prostitution in Wincanton all were controlled by one man and involved millions of dollars a year. This "boss" paid public officials of Wincanton for protection. Corruption in Wincanton was therefore partly the result of the bribes and payoffs given by those who profited from its existence. But the real reason why gambling and corruption existed in Wincanton (and continues to exist in other cities in the United States) was that most Wincantonites actually wanted it. One of the town's leading lawyers said in an interview: "When I was a little kid, my dad would lift me up so I could put a dime into the slot machine at his club. We never saw anything wrong in it."[16] Most people in Wincanton believed that the same kind of corruption existed in most cities in the country. Thus, it was impossible to get rid of gambling in Wincanton because a significant number of its citizens wanted to gamble. If the people had believed that illegal gambling produced corruption, it would have ceased.

The Wincanton example is an illustration of how elites can become involved in corruption in a community and thus how they can influence the administration of criminal justice and the enforcement (or nonenforcement) of laws in these kinds of towns. Of course, this does not mean that all small towns are corrupt. It simply shows how powerful the elite can be. Elites have a great deal to say about criminal justice policy in general as well. Of course, they do not get involved in day-to-day decisions such as how vigorously traffic laws will be enforced; but there are many important issues on which their influence is felt. They may influence decisions on how juvenile offenders will be handled, how much police protection will be afforded downtown business establishments, and what kinds of criminal justice ordinances will be enacted. In general, the elites of a community have a great deal to say about criminal justice in American cities.

THE ROLE OF THE COMMUNITY   The type of criminal justice system a community has is only partly determined by its elites. The community as a whole may be able to determine how hard to crack down on vice and may even be able to reduce vice, at least temporarily. But, as Harvard political scientist James Q. Wilson has concluded, "The prevailing police style is not explicitly determined by community decisions, though a few of its elements may be shaped by these decisions." [17] Nevertheless, the community influences the criminal justice system in a number of ways.

The political culture of a city can influence certain aspects of the criminal justice system. For example, cities with a professionalized, city manager form of government tend to have "legalistic" police forces. [18] This means that they are likely to view their principal role as enforcing the laws on the books; as a result, they may make more arrests than other kind of jurisdictions. This type of police force is most often found in suburbs. The influence of the average citizen in these towns is likely to be indirect. Larger cities, on the other hand, have partisan, mayoral-council governments, with candidates running for office on a party ticket. These cities are likely to have "watchman" style police departments, which generally focus on keeping public order and making arrests for disorderly conduct. [19] Police in such cities are less concerned with legal details and more preoccupied with street crime.

The community is related to criminal justice in yet another way. Communities vary widely in how favorably their citizens view the police. Large-city police have poorer police-community relations than small cities, partly because blacks and minorities, who live mainly in urban areas, have a less favorable attitude toward the police than middle-class whites (see Table 4-2).

In an attempt to overcome community mistrust of police, cities have hired more blacks and minority-group members for the police force. But blacks who become police officers face a dilemma. They are put into a position where they must make arrests for acts that are not regarded as particularly criminal in the

TABLE 4-2
Race and Attitudes Toward Police in Seattle, Washington

Attitude Toward Police	Race	
	White	*Black*
Favorable	73.5 percent	45.9 percent
Unfavorable	26.5 percent	54.1 percent

SOURCE: Information from Paul E. Smith and Richard O. Hawkins, "Victimization, Types of Citizen-Police Contacts, and Attitudes Toward the Police," *Law & Society Review*, Fall 1973, pp. 137–38. Although the data are for Seattle, Washington, the attitudes toward police are similar in other large American cities. Reprinted by permission of the Law and Society Association.

ghetto. Policy operations, street gambling, and drunkenness are not seen as very serious crimes in black ghettoes. If black police officers make an arrest for these offenses, they are seen as "Uncle Toms." If they fail to make an arrest, they violate the standards of a good cop. Their uniform is a symbol of their accomplishment in escaping the ghetto, but they come to despise it because it symbolizes those who have betrayed their race.[20]

Thus, there is considerable tension between the police and the community in central cities. But the tension is not because the poor do not want and need police protection. They do. In fact, they complain bitterly about the lack of law enforcement in housing codes, about the absence of due process when they are evicted from public housing, and about the way they are treated by the police and the criminal justice system.[21]

The tension between the police and the community, therefore, stems from the inner-city residents feeling that they do not have an adequate voice in determining criminal justice policy in general, and in controlling police behavior in particular. Moreover, the police are not as effective in controlling crime in the poor sections of a city as they are in other areas. As a result more and more cities have seen the development in poor neighborhoods of citizen action groups in an attempt to help control the spiraling crime rate. For example, a citizen action team was formed in Dayton, Ohio, in a racially mixed neighborhood. This group patrolled the streets at night and radioed information to the police when there was suspicion of crime.

The evidence on the effectiveness of these efforts is unclear. Are good community relations essential for the police to be able to do their job effectively? James Q. Wilson does not think so. In fact, he writes that it is impossible to have good community relations in large cities because such cities do not have a sense of community. According to Wilson, concern for community is manifested in the "observance of standards of right and seemly conduct in the public places in which one lives and moves." He writes, "Around one's home, the places where one shops, and the corridors through which one walks there is for each of us a public space wherein our sense of security, self-esteem, and propriety is either reassured or jeopardized by the people and events we encounter." Central cit-

Black police officers can sometimes overcome ghetto distrust of police

ies, Wilson says, do not have this sense of community, but middle-class suburbs do.[22]

Still, the cooperation of the community is essential for the police to do a good job. For example, in one large American city someone dropped a boulder from an expressway overpass and it smashed the windshield of a passing car, killing the driver. The police had very little information about who committed the crime, but they were able to solve the case by intensive questioning of people in the neighborhood. This, of course, is but one example of the kind of crime for which community cooperation is needed. The willingness of the community to cooperate may well be a function of the social class of the community. But, social class alone is not the only factor. Several studies have shown that the political system also has an impact upon how courts operate. For example, according to a study by political scientists James Eisenstein and Herbert Jacob, the political affiliation of judges was found to have an impact on conviction rates in a Detroit court.[23] In another study political scientist Martin A. Levin found that there was a significant difference in the sentencing behavior of judges in Minneapolis, a city that has nonpartisan politics (i.e., candidates cannot be given political party identification) as compared to Pittsburgh, a city that has a traditional, partisan political system. There was a greater percentage of offenders put on probation in Pittsburgh, incarceration was for a shorter length of time, and blacks received better treatment. The Minneapolis judges, Levin found, were more oriented toward professional doctrine and believed in the effectiveness of institutional rehabilitation and penal deterrence. For example, one judge stated, "I know I am considered a tough judge here, but that doesn't bother me, because punishment works. You won't sit on a hot stove if you have been burned."[24] The Pittsburgh judges, on the other hand, seek to help defendants and feel attachment to the "underdog." They believe they are realistic and feel blacks deserve special consideration because they have a "different code of morality." Their decision making is nonlegalistic.

Levin feels these differences in judges' views are the "indirect" product of the cities' political systems. Pittsburgh judges had political careers prior to becoming judges, and many have minority and lower-income backgrounds. Minneapolis judges, on the other hand, had legalistic careers prior to their service on the bench, and most are from middle-class and northern European, Protestant backgrounds. Thus, both class and prior career experience are at work. The influence of the political system is indirect and works through the selection process. As Levin concludes, "The judges' attitudes and decisions are the product of structural factors, such as the influence of the cities' political system on judicial selection and judicial socialization and recruitment, rather than simply the product of the individual personal characteristics of the eighteen judges in each city."[25]

The community, therefore, influences the criminal justice system in a number of ways. It helps determine the style of policing and types of decisions made by judges and other persons in the criminal justice system. Cooperation with and acceptance of police by a community influences how effective they will be in doing their jobs. The type of community determines how difficult the job of law enforcement will be since the extent and nature of crime varies from place to place. All such factors play a role in the formulation of criminal justice policy.

Implementing Criminal Justice Policy

On January 3, 1973, Governor Nelson Rockefeller, in his fifteenth State of the State message, proposed that all convicted peddlers of hard narcotics as well as violent drug addicts receive mandatory life sentences with no possibility of parole or plea bargaining. The harsh drug law was the New York governor's way of trying to reduce violent crimes, which were soaring at the time. He compared drug sellers to an invading army that threatens to destroy society.

The governor's proposal met immediate, harsh criticism from a number of sources. The New York Civil Liberties Union as well as a number of prominent judges called the plan unworkable unless accompanied by unimaginable court and prison expansion. Mayor Lindsay of New York City called it a piece of political demagoguery. Columbia University law professors said it would not accomplish its objectives because it would drive up the cost of drugs and thus increase street crimes as addicts tried to pay for their habits. A New York City

State of the State:

ROCKY ASKS LIFE FOR PUSHERS

Wants Watchdog Over Schools

1973, *above*

1979, *right*

Rocky's hard drug penalties softened

ALBANY (AP) — Hundreds of people in New York state prisons will soon be eligible for reductions in their sentences as a result of the repeal of the harshest features of the "Rockefeller Drug Laws."

Gov. Carey has signed into law a bill which leaves only a few provisions of the much-publicized 1973 anti-drug laws.

The new law, which takes effect Sept. 1, will reduce penalties for many types of hard drug sales and sharply restrict the "life sentence" provisions.

It will also reduce the sentences of hundreds already in prison under the laws pushed through the Legislature by then Gov. Nelson Rockefeller in 1973.

Even legislators who supported the 1973 laws now say they turned out to be as big a bust as Rocke-

feller's critics said they would.

Trafficking in hard drugs continued to flourish. Relatively few bigtime drug pushers have been convicted. Because of the stiff penalties, more and more people have gone on trial, rather than work out a plea bargain, adding to court backlogs.

And hundreds of people convicted of the sale or possession of small amounts of drugs are serving mandatory prison terms — often longer than sentences given to rapists and robbers.

The new law repeals outright the mandatory "life" sentences for anyone convicted of selling heroin, cocaine, morphine or other "hard" drugs, no matter the amount.

Only the most serious drug offenses will still be subject to "life."

police inspector called it an "Archie Bunker law" that would be completely unworkable. The New York State Bar Association warned that it could cost hundreds of millions of dollars. Even the New York State Conservative party asked the governor to modify his proposal.

But Governor Rockefeller pressed on. On March 5 he said he was giving very serious consideration to proposing the death penalty for members of organized crime convicted of trafficking in narcotics. However, on April 12 he said he was willing to accept some compromises and proposed a modified version to the legislature, including mandatory prison sentences, a limited form of plea bargaining, and a system of mandatory life sentences that would permit parole but require lifetime supervision of the parolee. On April 27 the New York State Senate, by a vote of 41 to 14, passed a modified bill very similar to the governor's proposal. And although the bill met more resistance in the assembly, a version, with further modifications, was passed there on May 3, similar to the senate bill, but deleting hashish from the list of dangerous drugs. On May 8, with much fanfare and some caustic criticism of his opponents, Governor Rockefeller signed the bill into law. The *New York Times* said in an editorial that the New York State legislature had succumbed to political hysteria over drug abuse.

Drug use and violent crime were not reduced as a result of the harsh new law. In fact, both continued to increase throughout the 1970s. This failure of the harsh drug law to stop drug abuse and street crime is by no means an isolated event. One of the chief discoveries in public policy in recent years is that the mere passing of a law and the development of machinery to institute and enforce that law do not guarantee that change will occur or that the law's intentions will actually be carried out. Putting a law on the books often assures very little in terms of realizing the goals of the law. The Safe Streets legislation that created the Law Enforcement Assistance Administration is another example of this. The money spent by L.E.A.A. from 1968 to 1980 did not make the streets of our cities any safer. In fact, street crime continued to increase from 1968 through 1977 and, although it declined somewhat in central cities from 1977 to 1979, it increased in the suburbs. Just establishing an agency does not guarantee a particular policy outcome for several reasons. First, there are limits to what can be accomplished by legislation. It may well be beyond the power of the police to reduce street crime short of instituting a police state, which is too high a price for a democratic society to pay. But even more important is the fact that the agency created to implement policy will develop a set of goals itself, and these goals may be quite different from those intended by the legislation. The formal goals of legislation often are sabotaged by the administrative agencies that have to implement them.

THE LIMITS OF POWER

"Off with her head," cried the Queen at the top of her voice. Nobody moved.

Lewis Carroll, *Alice's Adventures in Wonderland* (1865).

THE FORMAL AND INFORMAL ASPECTS OF POLICY MAKING

Up to this point in the chapter we have been focusing upon the formulation of criminal justice policy. From a strictly formal perspective, only legislatures—national, state, and local—are supposed to formulate criminal justice policy. But, in reality, administrative agencies, such as the police and courts, also are involved. As was shown above, police help establish policy when they bring pressure to bear on legislatures or on the community, as in the case of New York City's civilian review board. The courts help formulate policy when they apply the laws in particular cases.

Policy making is conceptually and institutionally distinct from policy implementation. Again, from a strictly formal perspective, once policy is determined, it is up to the administrative agencies to implement it. Administrations are supposed to be concerned only with finding the most efficient and effective way of carrying out policy. But, in fact, they actually formulate policy as they implement it. This is inevitable, and it is due to the great deal of discretion that exists at every point in the criminal justice system.

The distinction between the formally designated powers of institutions in the criminal justice system and the reality of their operations is an important one. A strictly formalistic picture of the criminal justice system is only partly correct because it does not contain the informal and more realistic aspects of the system, which may actually be more than 50 percent of the total picture.

The formal view of the criminal justice system is depicted in Figure 4-3. It shows that the criminal justice system becomes involved at the point where a crime is detected. The various events that can then occur are shown.

There are two possible outcomes at each step; the accused can be kept in the system or taken out of the system. The first step at which a criminal justice agency becomes involved (labeled 1 in the diagram) is when a crime is investigated by the police. The investigation can lead to an arrest (step 2) or to an unsolved case. If an arrest is made, the accused can be booked (step 3), which means that he or she is finally accused of having committed the crime, or released without prosecution. Sometimes juveniles are diverted from the formal criminal justice system at this point and turned over to a juvenile authority such as a state social service agency. Once a person is formally charged with a crime, he or she must make an initial appearance (step 4) before a judge, who, upon the advice of a prosecuting attorney, may decide that the evidence is insufficient and drop the charges. If the evidence is sufficient, the accused is given a preliminary hearing (step 5) to determine if he or she should be held for trial. The preliminary hearing can occur before a judge or a grand jury (step 6). If the accused is held over for a trial, he or she is arraigned (step 7). It is at this point that the accused may enter into plea negotiations with the prosecutor and either enter a guilty plea or ask for a jury trial (step 8). If a trial is held and the defendant found not guilty, he or she is acquitted. If the defendant is found guilty, he or she can appeal the decision, or be sentenced (step 9), either to probation or prison (step 10). If a person is given probation but later violates some of the conditions,

FIGURE 4-3

Step-by-Step Movement of Cases Through the Criminal Justice System

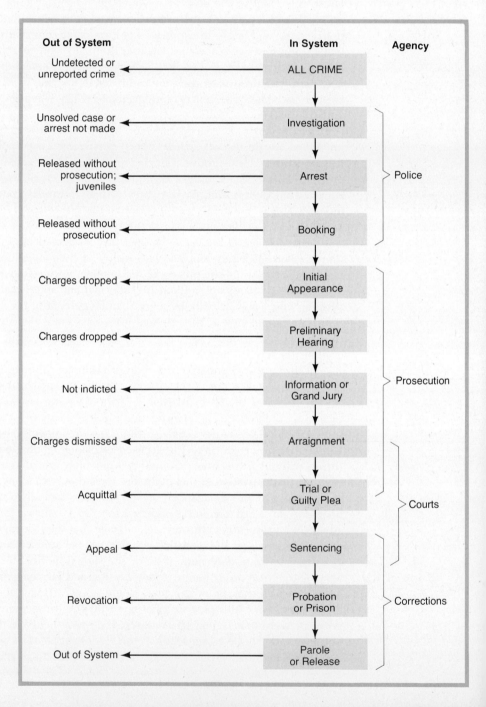

probation can be revoked and the person sent to prison. Finally, upon completion of the prison term, the offender may be released unconditionally or released on parole (step 11). The offender is then out of the formal criminal justice system unless he or she again commits a crime that is discovered by the police.

Notice that there are numerous points along the way at which offenders may be released. They may be released right after arrest (if the evidence is insufficient), booking, the preliminary hearing, the grand jury hearing, arraignment, or trial. At each one of these points, various criminal justice officials use the discretion they have to determine whether to release offenders. In fact, the police themselves, in making the decision to arrest, often use discretion. In all cases when discretion is employed, criminal justice policy is not only being implemental but it is being formulated as well.

Ideally, the police are supposed to arrest everyone who violates a law, and they are supposed to do so automatically. In fact, they do not. Similarly, prosecutors are supposed to bring charges against every person arrested, assuming that the arrest is a proper one in which the evidence of wrongdoing is adequate. Again, they often do not. That is because the police, prosecutors, and judges have considerable discretion. What is the nature of this discretion, what are its consequences, and how can it be controlled?

THE INEVITABILITY OF DISCRETION   The police have a great deal of freedom in determining whether or not to make an arrest, not only with regard to public inebriation but also in regard to a large number of other crimes. As one police officer noted:

> If the person is properly dressed, and if the officer knows him or knows where he lives, and if he's not disturbing anyone, the officer will take him home. Sometimes, though not often, we'll let him dry out in the station without booking him, and then we'll call his wife. But our obnoxious drunks—the tramps and the ones who get nasty—and anyone who gets rowdy in the business district or in a quiet residential area, we'll arrest.[26]

They have this freedom of action partly because it is impossible to observe every infraction of law, partly because the law on the books needs interpretation, partly because an officer can get information about major crimes by overlooking minor ones, and partly because society would not tolerate full enforcement of all laws. Of course, the police would not have much discretion in a situation where they directly observe someone in the act of a crime such as robbery. But relatively little of their job involves this direct kind of crime control. The principal activity of the police is maintenance of order—or keeping public places and the streets free from disorder. In fact, over 40 percent of all nontraffic arrests are for public drunkenness. The statutes that relate to this offense include the labels "loud and boisterous," "disorderly," and "vagrancy." What constitutes such behavior is a matter of subjective judgment.

Who gets arrested for disturbing the public order varies from place to place. In some locales a large number of arrests are made, but in others, relatively few. The basic reason for the variation is that it is not possible for a police chief to specify in advance whom to arrest or the conditions under which a person should be arrested for disturbing the public order. A patrol officer has a number of questions in mind when he or she confronts such a situation. The officer usually mentally asks: "Has anyone been hurt?" "Will an arrest improve the situation?" "What will the guy do if I let him go?" "Will I have to go to court on my day off?" Since the police administrator cannot predict what the proper behavior is for an officer, it is really not possible to determine if the officer is doing a good job.

Another reason for the wide range of discretion is the vagueness of laws. For example, the New York City disorderly conduct law is a complex statute that penalizes 11 different acts, ranging from abusive language to soliciting a man for a crime against nature, when these acts provoke a breach of the peace. But the decision as to when they do disturb the peace is a subjective one, and police frequently use the charge of disorderly conduct as a way of covering false arrests and brutality.[27]

Attorney Paul Chevigny, in a study of the New York City police, notes that vague laws giving police much discretion can be abused, particularly by those officers who identify so closely with their office that they consider any threat to it a very grave threat to public order. Chevigny calls this the "good guys versus bad guys" ethic.[28] The type of officer who displays this ethic tends to believe that deviants are undesirable and should be in jail. Thus, the legislature is to blame for giving police wide discretion when they pass vague statutes aimed at regulating morality and at forcing people into a certain way of life.

The police have less discretion when they are investigating crimes such as burglary and robbery. They also have little success in solving these crimes. Only about 24 percent of all robberies and 8 percent of all burglaries are cleared by arrest. But, since only a small part of total police activity is devoted to these crimes, the majority of police activity involves areas where their freedom of action really cannot be curbed.

The police, of course, are not the only law enforcement agency to exercise discretion. When the police are finished with their work, the prosecutor steps in and has much more latitude than the police. If there is sufficient evidence that a crime has been committed, a person may be held for trial. The decision to prosecute or not is one of the most important in the entire criminal justice process. The prosecutor, who makes this decision, has almost unlimited discretion; and this freedom to decide has been fully supported by the courts, unless it is used in a discriminatory manner.[29]

One case, illustrating several aspects of prosecutorial discretion, occurred in Vano County, California (a fictitious county). Two prosecutors at separate times handled two similar suspects arrested for drunk driving. Both suspects held jobs requiring a valid driver's license, and both would lose their licenses upon conviction for drunk driving. Both were in their mid-forties and supported families. However, one prosecutor permitted the suspect he interviewed to plead guilty to reckless driving, thereby saving the man's job; the other prosecutor insisted on a plea of drunk driving from the second driver, which cost that driver his job.[30]

To many people, this disparity in the handling of similar cases seems unjust. The same offense, by a sense of equal justice, requires the same punishment. But others feel that it is impossible to treat all cases similarly because prosecutors deal with uncertain environments and must have flexibility. Discretion and justice go hand in hand, according to this view, because justice requires individualized treatment rather than mindless and mechanical application of the law. Political scientist Lief Carter, who was a participant observer in a prosecutor's office for a year, recounts the story of how an individual arrested for possession of marijuana was treated.[31] The example shows that the outcome of a case can depend upon which prosecutor handles it, who the defense attorney is, and which judge hears the case. The case is important enough to summarize here.

On a fairly typical day in Vano County, California, Sergeant Hawk of the Condenado Police Department brought a number of felony arrest cases to the district attorney's office. Included among the felonies was a routine arrest of a male black in his mid-forties for possession of a matchbox of marijuana, which was found in his car when he was stopped for a routine traffic violation. The car was searched because the arresting officer thought he saw a packet of Zig-Zag cigarette papers in the accused's pocket. Most experienced prosecutors believe that the possession of one or two cigarettes of marijuana deserves to be treated as a misdemeanor rather than a felony. However, the case was given to a young deputy with only a half year's experience, who decided to charge the accused with a felony. Not only was the man unlucky enough to get a young, inexperienced prosecutor, he also was assigned a young public defense attorney, who decided to fight the case rather than bargain for a lesser plea because he doubted the legality of the search procedure used by the arresting officer. The young attorney felt that the principle was important, but his stand for principle caused a delay in the trial for more than a year. When the case finally came to trial the accused was acquitted by a jury based on the fact that no evidence of marijuana could be found in the accused's shirt, even though the matchbox that contained the marijuana leaked. The accused claimed that he did not know how the box of marijuana had gotten in his car, but he said he saw some young boys hanging around the car when he returned there after stopping for some beer. Because he was acquitted, the case turned out favorably. But if the case had been given to an experienced prosecutor, the accused might have been charged only with a misdemeanor and let off without the need to go to trial. He would have been saved the one-year wait for trial. And if a different defense attorney had been assigned to the case, he might have asked for a lesser plea from the prosecutor. Whether or not the defendant would have fared better in the latter situation is not important from our perspective here. What is important is the fact that the outcome would very likely have been different if a different prosecutor handled the case. This is a key part of prosecutorial discretion.

Prosecutorial discretion is inevitable. A prosecutor cannot be expected to mechanically charge every person the police bring in—and for obvious reasons. The police may have only weak evidence, or they may not have performed their duty properly, and it is up to the prosecutor to check the police in these cases. Someone must decide if the evidence is sufficient to invoke the awesome machinery of the criminal law, for it would be impossible to follow legal technicalities rigidly for every case. More than half of the felony arrests made in 1977 in five areas of the country (Los Angeles, Indianapolis, New Orleans, Detroit, and Milwaukee) were rejected by prosecutors or dismissed after charges were filed. The principal reasons were that not enough evidence had been collected by the police or the witnesses refused to cooperate. These findings, which were made by an L.E.A.A. computer system called Prosecutor's Management Information System, were contrary to the public's perception that the majority of cases are plea bargained (see below).[32] In these five areas, at least, prosecutors used their discretion in pursuit of due process. Prosecutorial discretion in some ways balances that of the police: Police discretion is frequently used in ways that violate due process, but prosecutors throw many of these cases out. We should hasten to add, however, that prosecutors usually do side with the police. Chevigny states that most prosecutors in the United States have chosen to side uncritically with the police. The courts, likewise, protect the police from criticism, not only because judges must rely upon police credibility in thousands of cases, but because they will open the door to damage suits for false arrest if they do not side with police.[33]

Prosecutorial discretion also tends to be used to support the police in cases that have sufficient evidence to warrant charging the accused. In the overwhelming majority of these cases, the disposition is handled through the process of plea bargaining. In these cases, prosecutors will charge the accused with the maximum offense allowable in order to be in a better bargaining position. Those accused, especially minority-group members, frequently accept the bargain because they would rather plead guilty to a lesser charge than run the risk of going to trial and being found guility of a greater offense.

Prosecutors play this bargaining game with accused persons or their attorneys in an attempt to elicit a guilty plea. Tremendous pressure exists to obtain a guilty plea because it serves the interests of the police, prosecutors, defense lawyers, judges, and corrections authorities. To the police it is an assurance that their suspicions were accurate. To prosecutors it is another case expeditiously handled. To defense lawyers it is the best deal they could get for their clients while remaining on good terms with the prosecutor and judge. To judges it places their conduct beyond the possibility of appeal. And to the corrections authorities, it suggests the accused can be rehabilitated because he or she admitted guilt.

Judges also have considerable discretion in sentencing so that there is very wide variation in sentences given for the same offense. One judge may free a check forger on probation while another will give a check forger ten years. Some of this disparity is justified because of differences in the records of each offender, but some simply results because judges do not know what other judges are doing. Proposals have been made to establish mandatory sentences as a way of limiting judicial discretion. But a recent L.E.A.A. study has proposed setting up guidelines that retain sufficient judicial latitude to ensure that justice can be individualized and humane as well as even-handed. The guideline system incorporates the collective wisdom of experienced judges and takes into account the seriousness of the offense and probability that the accused will again commit a crime. A suggested sentence length is given to the sentencing judge, and the judge decides how much he or she wants to stray from the guidelines.[34]

The final point in the system where considerable discretion exists is in corrections. Most individuals convicted of a crime and sentenced to prison are given indeterminate sentences with eligibility for early release on parole if they maintain the kind of behavior desired by corrections officials. But corrections officials themselves are free to determine if the offender, in fact, is behaving properly. Corrections officers thereby have considerable power to decide whether an offender has been "rehabilitated." This aspect of discretion in criminal justice will be discussed in more detail in Chapter 10.

THE CONSEQUENCES OF DISCRETION   Discretion frequently is abused by criminal justice officials. Police abuse it when they make arrests based on arbitrary whim—on how they feel that day or on the racial identity of the accused. Prosecutors abuse their discretion when they engage in plea bargaining for the sole purpose of obtaining as many guilty pleas as possible to make themselves look good. And judges abuse their discretion when they participate in plea bargaining that causes defendants to plead guilty to crimes they did not commit, or when they give widely disparate sentences to individuals accused of the same crime.

Discretion, however, cannot and should not be completely eliminated. It is inevitable and necessary at all stages in the criminal justice system. The real question is how to ensure that it is used to support the ends of justice. Take, for example, police discretion. When patrol officers exercise discretion, they are actually making criminal justice policy. When this occurs, criminal justice policy is being made, statistically speaking, by a white male whose median education is 12.4 years (in 1976) and who may well be racially prejudiced. Criminal justice policy in this case is idiosyncratic, uneven, and, very often, discriminatory.[35]

The crucial question is not whether or not this discretion should be eliminated or diminished, for it cannot be. The question is how to channel the discretion so that public interest goals are achieved rather than the narrow self-interests of administrators. This is a part of the broader question of how bureaucracies—the implementers of criminal justice policy—can be controlled.

BUREAUCRACIES:
IMPLEMENTERS OF CRIMINAL JUSTICE POLICY

The reason that the mere passing of a law does not guarantee the results intended by the law is that laws have to be implemented by people. Implementation can be compared to assembling a machine designed to turn out public policy. If the machine is put together perfectly and it runs flawlessly, public policy will be implemented precisely as planned in the law.

But implementation is not simply a mechanical act, as the machine analogy implies. Public administrators for years mistakenly believed that implementation was just a matter of carrying out the goals of legislation as efficiently and as economically as possible. In the "science of administration" implementation did not involve politics and, therefore, was not policy making. But we now know this is not true. The bargaining, maneuvering, and pulling and hauling that characterize the legislative process carry over into administration as well.

Implementation consists of a number of fragmented and isolated moves and countermoves by many different groups. Leakages of authority occur at numerous points because officials in charge of carrying out a given law do not all have the same goals. All officials (and all groups) affected by a law use their own discretion in translating goals and/or orders to fit their own particular self-interests.[36] As described by political scientist Eugene Bardach, the implementation process resembles "the maneuvering of a large number of semi-autonomous actors, each of which tries to gain access to program elements not under its own control while at the same time trying to extract better terms from other actors seeking access to elements it does control."[37]

The various administrative agencies that are involved in implementing policy are a part of what is more generally called "bureaucracies." Of course, not all agencies that carry out policies are bureaucracies in the strict sense. A small sheriff's office in a rural Kansas town is hardly a bureaucracy. Courts normally are not considered to be a part of the bureaucracy, if the term is used to designate the administrative branch of government, for courts are part of the judicial branch. But a large court system may have characteristics of a bureaucracy.

What then, are the principal characteristics of bureaucracies? In a strictly literal sense, the term *bureaucracy* means administration by government bureaus. In the everyday sense, it means red tape and incompetence. But the term cannot be discussed properly without reference to the classic work of Max Weber.

Max Weber is, according to some, one of the greatest social scientists of the twentieth century. Weber is responsible for developing the theory that a bureaucracy is the most efficient means of conducting large-scale operations that has ever been devised by humans. The problem is that Weber's model of a bureaucracy is an ideal type. It does not actually exist; instead, it is merely a tendency toward which large organizations in modern society are headed—rather like the Prussian army, which was the prototype upon which Weber based his analysis.

The modern criminal justice system in the United States does not even come close to Weber's idealized bureaucracy. First, it is not hierarchically arranged so that those at the top have more power and authority than those at the bottom. For example, in a police department the lower down in the ranks one moves, the more discretion (and, therefore, power) there is. Second, the criminal justice system is not formalized so that there are precisely written rules regarding how each job should be performed or each case handled. As we said above, a great deal of discretion is allowed in the system, and it is not always possible to have written rules about how the jobs should be performed. Third, the criminal justice system is not highly professionalized, although there are a number of professionals in it. A profession exists only if a written body of generalized knowledge can be transmitted in formal education, individuals are judged by their peers, and formal licensing is required before one can practice. James Q. Wilson claims that the police are not professionals as measured by these criteria. They can learn their job best by apprenticeship rather than by formal education. And there is not a generalized body of written knowledge about policing.[38] Nor are judges really professionals. They are likely to be appointed or elected without opposition and may well receive their position as a reward for good political service rather than on the basis of professional merit. And, although prosecutors are lawyers, and the practice of law generally is considered to be a profession, they do not conform to bureaucratic rules. Lief Carter's study of the Vano County district attorney's office led him to conclude that "a bureaucratic, rule-oriented administration model of management does not get [to] the nature of the job of criminal prosecution."[39] The reason is that a great variety of factors in addition to laws and policies affect the behavior of prosecutors. The effective supervisor cannot use rigid, programed rules in guiding the work of prosecutors. This, of course, is true of the entire criminal justice system as well. As political scientist Malcolm Feeley concluded, "Rather than the highly rationalized rule-bound and bureaucratically structured system that Weber depicted the process to be, one finds a highly decentralized and decidedly nonbureaucratic system of exchange, in which there are virtually no instruments to supervise practice and secure compliance to the formal goals of the organization."[40]

FORMAL AND INFORMAL COMMUNICATIONS NETWORKS   What an organization is *supposed* to be doing and what its members believe it *is* doing are often two quite different things. For example, according to the manual of the Garden City Police Department (which is a small, suburban department of 34 members serving a community of 25,000 people), the department is supposed to work to preserve the public peace and order, apprehend offenders, protect persons and property, and enforce the city's ordinances. But when the members of the department were asked what the goals are, they responded in a variety of ways. Each member emphasized a different goal, but there was some agreement among the 34 members. In order of importance, the goals they most frequently listed were: (1) crime prevention, (2) law enforcement, (3) traffic control, (4) public relations, (5) criminal investigation, (6) assistance to the public, (7) handling minority group problems, and (8) cooperation with other agencies.[41]

In the Garden City police department, therefore, there is a considerable difference between the formal definition of goals and the informal understanding of members about which goals are most important. Why does this difference exist? One reason is the existence of friendship groups in the department. What is considered to be most important depends upon the friendship group to which a person belongs. The formal lines of authority in the Garden City department run from the police chief to the lieutenant, thence to the sergeant, inspectors, and finally to the patrol officers. But the officials belong to a number of friendship groups as well. These groups cut across the formal lines of authority. Attachment to face-to-face groups is of prime importance for the members of the Garden City department. It provides a source of personal security for the individual in an otherwise impersonal environment.

The friendship groups within the police department are a part of the informal organization that cuts across the formal channels of authority. Such informal lines of communication and power exists at the upper level of an organization and among the chief, mayor, city manager, and leading citizens. These informal friendship ties, which may include golf or tennis games or membership in the same country club, are often as important as formal authority in determining what will be done. Of course, the informal groups need not be in conflict with or supplant the formal lines of authority. In fact, they often supplement and contribute to more efficient operation. The important point to recognize is that they exist, and the administrator who does not recognize their existence may not be able to function effectively.

BUREAUCRATIC GAMES   Administrators, we have said, frequently change the nature of a particular law in the process of carrying it out. They do not always do this intentionally. More often, the changes occur as a by-product of a number of games that administrators play. The term *games,* in this sense, does not designate sports and fun but relatively serious institutional processes that are part of the everyday reality of administration. Some of these games, identified by political scientist Eugene Bardach, are:

1. *The diversion of resources game:* In this game money meant for one goal is used for something else. For example, L.E.A.A. money was originally intended to fight street crime, but in the early years the states spent large amounts of such money on airplanes, helicopters, and traffic control. Also, states tended to divert the money to small towns rather than give it to the larger cities where street crime is a serious problem.
2. *The easy life game:* The goal in this game is to tailor the work environment to suit the interests of bureaucrats as much as possible rather than those of the clients; the self-interest in convenience, therefore, becomes paramount. Thus, judges in one eastern city sit on the bench an average

of three hours a day, even though court calendars are overcrowded. The extreme form of this game is when police pull over to the side of the road out of sight and take a nap.

3. *The deflection of goals game:* Goals stated in legislation often are re-negotiated, trimmed back, added to, distorted, or changed outright by the agencies charged with carrying them out. The reason is that most legislation is written in relatively ambiguous legal language, and often shot through with loopholes. For example, when public drunkenness was decriminalized, money was appropriated for detoxification facilities. But much of the money was used to help middle-class people overcome drinking problems rather than to help the skid-row drunk. As another example, mandatory capital punishment laws are usually subverted because juries and judges do not like to execute offenders. The result is that a person is seldom charged with a crime requiring mandatory capital punishment but is allowed to plead to a lesser offense.

4. *The reputation game:* In this game each administrator attempts to build his or her own reputation. A police captain will attempt to see to it that crime statistics show he or she is doing a good job; prosecutors will push to get a high percentage of convictions because this enhances their image and standing. Again self-interest predominates and public interest goals become secondary.

5. *The territorial imperative:* This is one of the favorite pastimes of administrators and is analogous to the more serious game played by animals. A program given to one agency may infringe upon the jurisdiction of another agency. It will, therefore, be fought tooth and nail by the latter agency. For example, in some cities welfare departments claim jurisdiction over juvenile offenders and fight any attempt to give police greater power in this area.[42]

TOKENISM

Tokenism involves an attempt to appear to be contributing a program element publicly while privately conceding only a small ("token") contribution. Other variations of Tokenism are procrastinating in making any such contribution or substituting a contribution of inferior quality. Since Tokenism often requires persistence and ingenuity, interests committed to a strategy of escaping from the implementation process as much as possible will not bother with it at all if they are in a secure enough position to do so by more direct assertions of refusal or defiance.

Although Tokenism has been most highly de-veloped in the area of compliance, and non-compliance, with court-ordered school desegregation and with civil rights laws more generally, it commonly turns up in many other policy and program areas as well. Federal officials have made only token efforts to enforce federal fair campaign practices legislation. The Berkeley Police Department makes only token efforts to enforce the laws against marijuana use.

Eugene Bardach, *The Implementation Game: What Happens after a Bill Becomes a Law.* (1977), p. 5.

These are only some of the games administrators play. In addition, classical bureaucratic "laws" help explain why legislation often fails. For example, the Peter Principle says that administrators are usually incompetent because of the way they are promoted. An individual will be given promotions in an agency until elevated to a job he or she cannot do; the promotions will then stop. The problem, of course, is that the unqualified person will remain in that position. For example, a patrol officer who does a good job may be promoted to sergeant. He or she may do this job beautifully and receive another promotion to captain. But the person may lack the personality or temperament to be a good captain, and there will be no further promotion—leaving the officer in the position he or she cannot do well.

And, of course, there is Parkinson's classic law that, loosely stated, says that work expands to fill the time available. Thus, if a job could be finished in four hours by one person, but there are eight hours and two people available, it will take sixteen hours to do it. In this manner bureaucracies tend to be born, expand, and grow; and once begun, they are almost immortal.

CAN BUREAUCRACIES BE MADE MORE EFFICIENT?   Do these various bureaucratic games mean that there is no way to try to see that goals are accomplished? Do they mean that the members of the criminal justice system do only what they want and nothing else? To both questions the answer is no, for a variety of incentives can be used to shape behavior, at least to a certain extent.

Suppose you were police chief in an average American city, and pressure is put on you to increase the enforcement of the traffic laws. How would you go about doing this? Of course, you would pass the word down to your lieutenants and officers that you want more enforcement of traffic laws. But this alone would not do it. What other steps could you take? A study of traffic control in four cities found the following factors important in getting more tickets written in one city. First, a number of police officers were assigned *specifically* to traffic enforcement on a long-term basis; the officers assigned this function could not say their production of traffic tickets was low because they were doing something else. Second, more of the available overtime work was given to those who wrote many tickets. Third, those assigned to traffic enforcement worked the daytime shift rather than the midnight-to-eight shift. Specialization increased the ability of the officers assigned to traffic control. As one officer put it, no officer could possibly know all the laws; by being responsible for only the traffic offenses, he could concentrate on the motor vehicle laws.[43]

The chief of police can use a variety of incentives to accomplish his or her objectives. Besides specialization, good schedules, and the reward of getting overtime work, there are promotions, pay increases, or the threat of demotion or cuts in salary. But to make these incentives effective, the police chief must be able to determine when someone is or is not complying with the rules. It is relatively easy to do this when traffic control is involved. But in general, what constitutes satisfactory performance in policing is difficult to determine for most activities. For example, what can be used as a measure for the effective handling of a noisy drunk, a family quarrel, a street disturbance, or a brawl? In such cases success is not simply a matter of increasing the number of cases handled but of improving the manner in which they are handled. For example, is the police officer who arrests a noisy drunk and responds to two family-quarrel calls on the same day doing better than the officer who spends an entire day on a single family quarrel? The latter is doing better if he or she succeeds in settling the feud without anyone being hurt, and the former is unable to do this. But on any given day the ability to settle a family quarrel will depend to a large extent upon luck rather than strictly upon the police officer's ability, even though some officers are better in this function than others. In general, the conclusion is unavoidable that it is difficult to develop performance standards for police work.

It is equally difficult to develop standards of good performance for other members of the criminal justice system. Prosecutors and judges resist any encroachment on their prerogatives. The criminal courts, for example, are a closed community, resentful of outsiders and strangers. District attorneys, judges, probation officers, lawyers, and even clerks arrange their official behavior to suit the expectations of those who will be watching.[44] Many of these individuals do not respond to formal orders or to the use of incentives such as pay raises or promotions. However, it is possible to get people to work toward achievement of goals by appealing to their self-interest. An individual will perform certain activities if it is in his or her self-interest to do so. The problem, of course, is to make achievement of the goals of the organization overlap with individual self-interest. This is one of the most important tasks of leadership.

LEADERSHIP: MAKING BUREAUCRACIES MORE EFFECTIVE

The view that individual self-interests are intrinsically in conflict with an organization's goals is found among administrative theorists who view organizations as totally rational and formal entities.[45] From the strict rationalist perspective informal lines of communications should not exist. Wherever they do, they are considered to be a deviation from the formal organization. Since they are, in effect, illegitimate, they cannot be up to any good.

But the informal structure can be supportive of the formal. In fact, the formal lines of authority and communication cannot function effectively without the support of the informal. The reason is that, for all the formal training one may undergo when joining an organization, one learns most about the organization through informal channels. It is there that one finds out who has real power, who can block various projects, which groups are in favor, and what gossip there is about the personalities, foibles, and indiscretions of key people in the organization.

How can the informal group be integrated into and made supportive of the formal organization? One school of thought argues that the more the members of the informal structure perceive that they can participate in decision making, the more they will tend to support the norms of the system.[46] Of course, not all organizations may be able to give members a feeling that they can participate in the making of decisions. In a prison, for example, inmates develop a subculture that helps them cope with the pains and pangs of imprisonment. This subculture is characterized by extreme authoritarianism and rigid stratification. The prisoner who has a high degree of self-control and composure and who is never subservient to the prison staff enjoys high status among fellow prisoners. In other words, the informal subculture of a prison, by the nature of the prison environment, is necessarily in conflict with the formal lines of authority. In fact, the inmate social system wields more authority over individual inmates than do members of the prison staff itself.[47]

Still, one sign of a good leader is the ability to give members of an organization the feeling that they are participating in policy making for that organization. A good leader helps reduce the feeling of conflict that develops between the informal and formal lines of authority.

WHO BECOMES A LEADER? The common view regarding leadership is that the person with charisma generally becomes a leader. The term is commonly defined as personal attractiveness and dynamism. It is easy to think of many leaders who most people would agree have "charisma"—John Kennedy, Franklin Roosevelt, and Martin Luther King, Jr., for example. However, this nation has had other leaders who had very little "charisma"—Gerald Ford or Ralph Nader—but who nevertheless were competent in guiding and rousing others. Thus it seems that "charisma" alone is not a sufficient condition for leadership. Some other factors must also be present.

Leadership theory stresses two different aspects of leadership. One is the group context, and the other is the situational factors. Theorists who emphasize the former think leadership is predominantly a group phenomenon; those who emphasize the latter think the situation determines who the leader will be.

Group theory holds that the individual who becomes a leader is the one who is most like the members of a group in many respects but at the same time is slightly above the group in intelligence, energy, and ability. He or she cannot be too far ahead of the group, for that would make the person too unusual. And

---

SPOTTING THE GOOD LEADER

Most of us believe that we possess the uncanny ability to identify outstanding leaders. This confidence in the ability to spot the "comers" is encouraged by the belief of many executives that they would not be where they are if (A) they were not excellent leaders and (B) they could not pick them. It may well be true that some executives and personnel men do have the intuition necessary to select good leaders for certain jobs. It is equally true—and considerably more relevant—that most executives do not, and that they share this lack of ability with psychologists, personnel men, and the rest of us mortals.

Fred E. Fiedler and Martin M. Chemers, *Leadership & Effective Management* (1974), p. 20.

since a leader gives the group its feeling of self-esteem, the person must be liked by the group. The difference between the leader and the group is not great. He or she is a "typical" group member—only more so. The statement, "All members of the group are equal, only some are more equal than others," seems to apply.

The situational theory, on the other hand, holds that particular events determine who the leader will be. For example, a series of events that are causing a problem for an organization may only be solved by someone with an informal and loose style. If one of the individuals at the top in the organization has the personality and background to fit this profile, he or she may emerge as the leader. Consider, for example, the so-called long, hot summer in New York City in 1969, when many feared that the ghettoes of Harlem and Bedford-Stuyvesant were going to explode in riots. At the height of the tension, Mayor John Lindsay made a point of walking the streets of Harlem, making sure he was plainly visible to the news media. Many believe that this dramatic move by the mayor helped prevent riots that year, and it gave Lindsay national publicity. A different mayor with a different personality, such as Abraham Beame who succeeded Lindsay, might not have done the same thing and the situation in New York might have turned out quite differently.

The question of which factor is more important, the group or the situation, has not been settled. But in either case, it is clear that a leader must perform two tasks to remain in power: One is affective in nature and the other requires an "instrumental" ability.

The affective task deals with interpersonal relations. The leader must remain on relatively friendly terms with the group. He or she must give group members the feeling that they belong to a team that gets along well and that they are all concerned with one another's welfare.

The instrumental role is the task-oriented part of the job. In this role the leader must see to it that goals are achieved with some degree of efficiency. Those outside the organization generally judge how well the leader is performing in this instrumental role. If he or she falters, the term as leader will be ended. On the other hand, if leaders drive the group too hard they may lose members' affection. For example, a police chief who constantly goads subordinates to maintain a high quota of arrests and citations for traffic violations may eventually earn the animosity of the department. A high arrest rate may help the chief look good to higher officials in the city, but after awhile it may cost the chief the respect of his or her officers. Maintaining a good balance between the two functions of leadership is not simple. How successfully it can be done depends, to some degree, on what style of management the leader follows.

MANAGEMENT STYLES To encourage people to work toward the achievement of certain goals requires more than the use of incentives and sanctions such as good assignments, promotions, or dismissals. The effective leader instills in subordinates a shared outlook, or ethos, that provides a common definition of the situations employees are likely to encounter. This ethos also gives the organization its distinctive character or feel. In many ways an organization is an extension of the personality of its director. It takes on many of that individual's personal characteristics. If the director is in the position long enough, the organization may become the mirror image of him or her. The F.B.I., for example, was almost the embodiment of one single person—J. Edgar Hoover. It is no accident that the agency lost much of its public esteem and image shortly after Hoover died and it was discovered that he abused his power and discretion, particularly in wiretapping, harassment, and illegal burglaries committed by members of the F.B.I.

Every chief administrator has his or her own personal style. But basically there are only two principal sorts. One is the traditionalist administrator. The traditionalist tends to use relatively authoritarian methods, which may involve centralizing a department or reshuffling assignments in order to break up personal relations and loyalties inimical to the style of the director. Technical efficiency is the goal of persons exercising this style. The desire is to produce as much output as possible with given inputs, even if the outputs do not serve the public interest. For example, in a prosecutor's office, the goal may be to get as many convictions as possible. Thus, the prosecutor will try to bargain for as many guilty pleas as possible. Such a prosecutor will tend to withhold information from defendants, and even from staff, if that facilitates more convictions. A police department run by this style is likely to keep many records, emphasize quick response time to calls, and be legalistic in its approach to law enforcement.

The second major type of administrator believes in participatory management. As the name implies, such management is relatively decentralized and informal, with lower-echelon people being encouraged to take a hand in policy making for the organization. For the most part this style is not believed to be appropriate for criminal justice agencies such as police departments. But there are some places where it may be appropriate and desirable. For example, it may be the best form of management in a prosecutor's office, especially as a way of supervising the assistant district attorneys in the office. It even is appropriate to some extent in the administration of prisons, given the movement toward unionization in prisons (See Chapter 8 for a further discussion of this point.)

PROFESSIONALISM IN CRIMINAL JUSTICE

Although most criminal justice officials cannot be classified as professionals, there has been a movement in recent years to increase the professionalism of criminal justice personnel such as police and probation officers.

Just what is "professionalism"? Earlier we mentioned that a profession has a generalized body of knowledge that can be transmitted through formal training, a code of ethics governing conduct of members, and entry requirements.

Professionalism may not always be a good thing in criminal justice agencies. Of course, because professionalism is highly respected in American culture, the label of professionalism has high symbolic value. But some studies have shown that small, nonprofessional departments frequently do a better job than professionalized departments. One study, for example, found that police departments in smaller communities are less professional, but they tend to have greater community approval.[48]

The issue of professionalism in police work raises the question of whether college training can help police do a better job. The assumption behind many college programs for police is that since a large part of their job entails public relations, they will do better if they understand something of the culture and feelings of the people they serve. A Rand Corporation study found that college-trained personnel did better than those without college background in the New York City Police Department.[49] They were less likely than their noncollege peers to be the subjects of civilian complaints and less likely to violate the rights of individuals they arrested.

Reformers have also tried for a number of years to increase the professionalism of judges. They advocate having judges appointed rather than elected or, if elected, chosen from a panel selected by members of the bar of a state. Again, as with police, some doubt that this suggestion would ensure better performance on the part of judges. For example, one study found that elected judges, in contrast to appointed ones, were more likely to be sympathetic toward and give better treatment to minority-group members.[50] To the extent that such treatment offsets the discrimination faced by minorities in the criminal justice system, it is desirable.

Whether or not professionalism of criminal justice personnel is desirable is highly debatable. But there are certain forces in contemporary society that seem destined to increase the amount of professionalism in criminal justice agencies willy-nilly. These trends will affect the way criminal justice policy is implemented in the future.

One trend is the increasing use of experts in evaluating criminal justice programs, both as assistants in crime analysis and as outside consultants. One example is the use of outside consultants by the New York City Housing Authority Police to evaluate a closed-circuit television monitoring system as a means of reducing crime in a Bronx public housing project. The consultants discovered that the system, which was very expensive, did nothing to reduce crime. The Housing Authority agreed not to expand the use of the system as a result of this evaluation.[51] Greater use of outside consultants frequently is accompanied by the hiring of experts on police department staffs so that they can better judge the worth of the research and also to conduct such studies themselves. This requires greater expertise and education and will therefore increase professionalism in law enforcement and other criminal justice agencies.

A second trend is the use of management information systems, computers, and communications technology both in police agencies and in the courts. Many of these techniques have been developed through L.E.A.A.-sponsored research. Large-city police departments, for example, use computer-based information systems for assigning officers to their duties, responding to calls, and investigating crime trends. This again will accelerate the trend toward professionalism in criminal justice agencies, for highly trained individuals are required to install and run such systems.

The third trend is a tendency toward greater professionalism in all public agencies. The amount of college education of criminal justice personnel has increased along with that of personnel in all public agencies. And there are continuous pressures to make public employees more professional. Criminal justice agencies, therefore, cannot remain aloof from the trends that are affecting all public agencies.

Increased professionalism will not decrease the amount of discretion that exists in criminal justice agencies. In fact, it is likely to enhance it, since one of the characteristics of a professional is the ability to be self-directed. Increased professionalism is likely, therefore, to have profound effects on how criminal justice policy is implemented, not the least of which will be an increase in the discretion of criminal justice personnel. If this is accompanied by the development of ethical standards for the use of such discretion, the trend toward increased professionalism can only be seen as a desirable development.

Conclusion

The making of criminal justice policy in the United States is to a great extent a political process involving both the formulation and implementation of laws. It is not entirely rational because agreement about what goals should be achieved is not always possible, nor is it possible to identify all alternative ways of achieving goals.

There are a number of independent agencies, institutions, and groups involved in the making of policy. Reform in such a system is difficult because changes in one agency, such as the police, may not correspond to changes made in another, such as the courts. Coordination of the great number of groups involved in formulating and implementing policy is also no easy task.

The many agencies in the system are, quite naturally, motivated by self-interest. Call it the law of bureaucratic survival or the law of human nature, but the fact is that agencies, like people, will take action if they believe it will promote their self-interest. Thus, accomplishing anything requires an appeal to the self-interests of the agencies involved.

This often means that only incremental rather than sweeping changes can be made. Radicals and reformers both dislike incrementalism. They believe that it leads to inaction or conservatism. But recognizing the reasons why incrementalism exists can lead to the adoption of effective change and realistic policy.

A realistic policy is a policy that administrators are willing to implement. A great deal of policy is developed during implementation. The principal agencies involved in implementation are the police, courts and judges, attorneys, and corrections institutions. In the next part of this book we shall describe these agencies.

SUMMARY

The policy-making process includes both the formulation as well as the implementation of laws.

Many different institutions are involved in formulating laws, including legislatures, executive agencies, and courts at the national, state, and local levels. Each performs a distinct role. The operation of these institutions is affected by two broad principles of American government—separation of powers and federalism—which greatly complicate the policy-making process. More generally, however, all policy is greatly influenced by interest groups. Most interest groups are private, but many public agencies, such as the police, often act as interest groups—and they are often extremely effective when they do so. Community elites as well as the structure of the community are also very important in formulating criminal justice policy.

Once laws are made, they must be implemented. Because a great deal of discretion exists in administrative agencies, policy is made when it is implemented. Implementation generally is in the hands of bureaucracies. A bureaucracy is hierarchically organized and operates on the principles of specialization and professionalism. The criminal justice system in

this country is not a bureaucracy, at least not in the ideal sense of that term.

An ideal bureaucracy is supposed to be a highly rational form of organization. But rationality is difficult to achieve. Emotions and feelings are important parts of any organization, especially in its informal relations. Bureaucracies respond to the imperatives of informal groups, which may undermine stated goals. However, bureaucracies can be made more effective and efficient.

One of the more important ways to improve bureaucratic performance is through leadership. An organization often will reflect the personal characteristics of its leader. Although it is commonly believed that a leader must have "charisma," many effective leaders do not have that gift. Situational factors may often determine who the leader will be.

An effective leader must fulfill both affective and instrumental roles. The leader must be liked by subordinates but at the same time ensure that tasks are accomplished. These two roles are often in conflict, but may be effectively integrated by good management styles. The tasks of leadership have been made more complicated by the growth of professionalism and use of experts in organizations.

FOOTNOTES

[1] Quoted in James Q. Wilson, *Varieties of Police Behavior* (Cambridge, Mass.: Harvard University Press, 1968), p. 178.

[2] Grover Starling, *The Politics and Economics of Public Policy: An Introductory Analysis with Cases* (Homewood, Ill.: Dorsey Press, 1979), p. 5.

[3] Jeffrey L. Pressman and Aaron Wildavsky, *Implementation* (Berkeley, Calif.: University of California Press, 1973), pp. xiii–xiv.

[4] Herbert Jacob, *Justice in America: Courts, Lawyers, and the Judicial Process*, 2nd ed. (Boston: Little, Brown, 1972).

[5] Morton Grodzins, "Centralization and Decentralization in the American Federal System," in *A Nation of States*, ed. Robert A. Goldwin (Chicago: Rand McNally, 1963), pp. 57–83; and Daniel Elazar, *The American Partnership* (Chicago: University of Chicago Press, 1962).

[6] Vincent Ostrom, "Policycentricity" (Paper presented at the annual American Political Science Association meeting, Washington, D.C., 1971).

[7] Elinor Ostrom and Gordon Whittaker, "Does Local Community Control of Police Make a Difference? Some Preliminary Findings," *American Journal of Political Science* 17, no. 1 (February 1973), 390–408. See also, Elinor Ostrom, Roger Parks, and Gordon Whittaker, *Patterns of Metropolitan Policing* (Cambridge, Mass.: Ballinger, 1978).

[8] David Abbott, Louis H. Gold, and Edward T. Rozowski, *Police, Politics and Race* (Cambridge, Mass.: The American Jewish Committee and the Joint Center for Urban Studies of the Massachusetts Institute of Technology and Harvard University, 1969).

[9] Sterling Spero and John M. Capozzola, *The Urban Community and Its Unionized Bureaucracies* (New York: Dunellen, 1973), p. 183.

[10] Abbott, Gold, and Rozowski, op. cit., pp. 69–70.

[11] Ibid., p. 70.

[12] Spero and Capozzola, op. cit., p. 182.

[13] Ibid., p. 186.

[14] Wilson, op. cit., p. 230.

[15] John Gardiner, "Wincanton: The Politics of Corruption," in *Criminal Justice: Law and Politics*, ed. George F. Cole (North Scituate, Mass.: Duxbury, 1972).

[16] Ibid. p. 126.

[17] Wilson, op. cit., p. 230.

[18] A city manager form of government is one that has an appointed city manager as the head of the administrative agencies. The city manager is usually appointed by and accountable to the city council. In some cities with a city manager, there may also be an elected mayor, but he or she is likely to be just a ceremonial figure, except in larger cities where the mayor may have substantial political power as well. But in most cities with a city manager there is no mayor.

[19] Wilson, op. cit., p. 274.

[20] Nicholas Alex, *Black in Blue* (New York: Appleton Century Crofts, 1969).

[21] Stuart Nagel, "The Poor, Too, Want Law and Order," *The Chicago Daily Law Bulletin*, Law Day Edition, April 26, 1968, p. 120.

[22] James Q. Wilson, *Thinking about Crime* (New York: Basic Books, 1975), p. 24.

[23] James Eisenstein and Herbert Jacob. *Felony Justice: An Organizational Analysis of the Criminal Courts* (Boston: Little, Brown, 1977), p. 254.

[24] Quoted by Martin A. Levin, "Urban Politics and Policy Outcomes: The Criminal Courts," in *Criminal Justice: Law and Politics*, op. cit., p. 342.

[25] Ibid., p. 353.

[26] Quoted in Wilson, *Varieties of Police Behavior*, op. cit., pp. 118–19.

[27] Paul Chevigny, *Police Power: Police Abuses in New York City* (New York: Random House, 1969), p. 280.

[28] Ibid.

[29] Brack v. Wells, 181 Md. 86, 40F.2d 319 (1944).

[30] Lief Carter, *The Limits of Order* (Lexington, Mass.: D. C. Heath, 1974), p. 1.

[31] Ibid., pp. 8–15.

[32] *Indianapolis Star*, April 25, 1977, pp. 1, 5.

[33] Chevigny, op. cit., pp. 250–51.

[34] Leslie T. Wilkins et al., *Sentencing Guidelines: Structuring Judicial Discretion* (Washington, D.C.: Criminal Justice Research Center, October 1976).

[35] See, especially, Kenneth Culp Davis, *Discretionary Justice, A Preliminary Inquiry* (Baton Rouge, La.: Louisiana University Press, 1969), p. 98.

[36] See Anthony Downs, *Inside Bureaucracy* (Boston: Little, Brown, 1969); and Graham Allison, *Essence of Decision* (Boston: Little, Brown, 1971).

[37] Eugene Bardach, *The Implementation Game* (Cambridge, Mass.: Massachusetts Institute of Technology Press, 1976), p. 51.

[38] Wilson, *Varieties of Police Behavior*, op. cit., p. 215.

[39] Carter, op. cit., p. 117.

[40] Malcolm Feeley, "Two Models of the Criminal Justice System: An Organizational Perspective," *Law and Society Review* 7, no. 3 (Spring 1973), 422.

[41] Robert Peabody, *Organizational Authority* (New York: Atherton Press, 1964).

[42] Bardach, op. cit., pp. 65–148.

[43] John A. Gardiner, *Traffic and the Police; Variations in Law-Enforcement Policy* (Cambridge, Mass.: Harvard University Press, 1969), pp. 70–76.

[44] Abraham Blumberg, *Criminal Justice* (Chicago: Quadrangle Books, 1967), p. 87.

[45] Sidney Verba, *Small Groups and Political Behavior, A Study of Leadership* (Princeton, N.J.: Princeton University Press, 1961).

[46] See Fred Fiedler and Martin Chemmers, *Leadership and Effective Management* (Glenview, Ill.: Scott, Foresman, 1974).

[47] David Duffee and Robert Fitch, *An Introduction to Corrections; A Policy and Systems Approach* (Pacific Palisades, Calif.: Goodyear Publishing, 1976).

[48] Ostrom and Whittaker, op. cit.

[49] Bernard Cohen and Jan Chaiken, *Police Background Characteristics and Performance* (New York: Rand Institute, 1972).

[50] Levin, op. cit.

[51] James Levine, Michael Musheno, and Dennis Palumbo, "Television Surveillance and Crime Prevention: Evaluating an Attempt to Create Defensible Space in Public Housing," *Social Science Quarterly* 58, no. 4 (March 1978), 647–56.

BIBLIOGRAPHY

Abbott, David; Gold, Louis H., and Rozowski, Edward T. *Police, Politics and Race*. Cambridge, Mass.: The American Jewish Committee and the Joint Center for Urban Studies of the Massachusetts Institute of Technology and Harvard University, 1969.

Alex, Nicholas. *Black in Blue*. New York: Appleton-Century-Crofts, 1969.

Bardach, Eugene. *The Implementation Game*. Cambridge, Mass.: Massachusetts Institute of Technology Press, 1976.

Barkun Michael, ed. *Law and the Social System*. New York: Leber-Atherton, 1973.

Blumberg, Abraham. *Criminal Justice*. Chicago: Quadrangle Books, 1967.

Carter, Lief. *The Limits of Order*. Lexington, Mass.: D.C. Heath, 1974.

Davis, Kenneth Culp. *Discretionary Justice, A Preliminary Inquiry*. Baton Rouge, La.: Louisiana State University Press, 1969.

Eisenstein, James, and Jacob, Herbert. *Felony Justice; An Organizational Analysis of the Criminal Courts*. Boston: Little, Brown, 1977.

Feeley, Malcolm. "Two Models of the Criminal Justice System; An Organizational Perspective." *Law and Society Review* 7, no. 3 (Spring 1973), 407–25.

Fiedler, Fred, and Chemmers, Martin. *Leadership and Effective Management*. Glenview, Ill.: Scott, Foresman, 1974.

Gardiner, John. *Traffic and the Police: Variation in Law-Enforcement Policy*. Cambridge, Mass.: Harvard University Press, 1969.

———. "Wincanton: The Politics of Corruption." In *Criminal Justice: Law and Politics*, edited by George F. Cole. North Scituate, Mass.: Duxbury, 1972, pp. 126–54.

Goldstein, Joseph; Derschowitz, Alan M.; and Schwartz, Richard. *Criminal Law: Theory and Process*. New York: The Free Press, 1974.

Jacob, Herbert. *Justice in America: Courts, Lawyers and the Judicial Process*, 2nd ed. Boston: Little, Brown, 1972.

Levine, James; Musheno, Michael; and Palumbo, Dennis. "The Limits of Rational Choice in Evaluating Criminal Justice Policy." In *Policy Studies and the Social Sciences*, edited by Stuart Nagel. Lexington, Mass.: D. C. Heath, 1975, pp. 89–105.

———. "Television Surveillance and Crime Prevention: Evaluating an Attempt to Create Defensible Space in Public Housing." *Social Science Quarterly* 58, no. 4 (March 1978), 647–56.

Morris, Norval, and Hawkins, Gordon. *The Honest Politician's Guide to Crime Control*. Chicago: University of Chicago Press, 1969.

Ostrom, Elinor, and Whittaker, Gordon. "Does Local Community Control of Police Make a Difference? Some Preliminary Findings." *American Journal of Political Science* 17, no. 1 (February 1973), 390–408.

Packer, Herbert. *The Limits of the Criminal Sanction*. Stanford, Calif.: Stanford University Press, 1968.

Spero, Sterling, and Capozzola, John M. *The Urban Community and Its Unionized Bureaucracies*. New York: Dunellen, 1973.

Wilson, James Q. *Thinking about Crime*. New York: Basic Books, 1975.

———. *Varieties of Police Behavior*. Cambridge, Mass.: Harvard University Press, 1968.

Ziegenhagen, Eduard. "The Reconceptualization of Legal Systems and Processes," In *The Politics of Local Justice*, edited by James R. Klonoski and Robert I. Mendelsohn. Boston: Little, Brown, 1971, pp. 26–35.

PART TWO

THE AGENCIES OF THE CRIMINAL JUSTICE ESTABLISHMENT

The American system of government often is described as a hodgepodge of overlapping agencies and units sewn together in a "crazy quilt" pattern. The same description applies to the criminal justice system. The main agencies of the system are the police, attorneys, judges, wardens, guards, and probation and parole officers. All are highly interdependent. What each does has an impact on all the others in both obvious as well as subtle ways. If the police institute a crackdown on criminals and increase the number of arrests, courts become overloaded and are forced to release or process those who are accused at a faster rate. If the courts sentence more offenders to prisons, this overloads all corrections agencies and forces them to spend more for prisons, change management practices, or adopt new rehabilitation programs.

The various agencies of the criminal justice establishment thus form a system of interrelated parts. Understanding criminal justice requires an appreciation of how the parts are connected. The outputs of one part of the system, such as the police, become inputs for another part, such as the courts, and what the courts do becomes feedback for the police, affecting the way they behave.

The fact that criminal justice agencies are interrelated does not mean that the various parts are well coordinated, that the actions of one part complement or support the behavior of another part, or that the operation of the whole establishment is rational and logical. In fact, the agencies of the criminal justice establishment often work at cross-purposes. Police are not happy when courts either fail to convict or release offenders on probation, and judges are not pleased if police make arrests that violate due process. Also, individuals in each agency of criminal justice come from different backgrounds and have varying values. Those who become police officers are often from different socioeconomic backgrounds than those who become lawyers or judges. The organizational culture of police departments is dissimilar to that of courts or prisons. The goals of police include making effective arrests and maintaining order, the goals of the courts include protecting the rights of citizens, and the goals of corrections agencies include trying to rehabilitate offenders. These goals often are in conflict.

An understanding of the criminal justice system requires an appreciation of the conflicts of interests and goals among the various parts of the system as well as a working knowledge of its collaborative and complementary parts. Can the overall operation of the criminal justice establishment be improved by reducing conflict in the system? Can criminal justice operations be made more efficient by making reforms within each agency rather than trying to improve interorganizational relations?

The aim of the chapters in Part II is to increase understanding of the criminal justice system by describing the workings of each of its major parts. In Chapter 5 the nature and degree of police power are described, with particular emphasis upon dispersal of that power among many different agencies and the extent of their discretion. The organizational and legal implications of police discretion are also considered, along with some suggestions for controlling and chaneling it in the right direction.

Although police are among the more powerful agents in the criminal justice establishment, lawyers have a tremendous amount of status and discretion as well. Two major categories of attorneys are involved in the criminal justice system—prosecutors, often called district attorneys, and defense lawyers. The discretion and power of prosecuting attorneys and the criteria they use in making decisions are discussed in Chapter 6. In addition, the role of the defense counsel, the practice of criminal law, and counsel for the poor are discussed there. Finally, the chapter deals with plea bargaining, the principal way in which decisions are made by attorneys in the system.

Because the great majority of cases are settled by plea bargaining between prosecuting and defense attorneys, judges and courts would seem to play a minor role in the overall decision process. But judges, like police and attorneys, have a great deal of discretion and power. Some stems from legal ambiguities and factual uncertainties that are described in Chapter 7. The points at which discretion is exercised are also described. In addition, the chapter considers the political nature of judgeships, the bail system, and the grand jury and jury-trial system, and it exposes the anarchy of sentencing in American courts.

Individuals who are unlucky enough to be processed through these parts of the system end up in corrections agencies, which are described in Chapter 8. Corrections agencies are in turmoil in this country today. There is confusion about what goals should be given priority. Prisons, which are overcrowded, antiquated, and inadequate, are fast becoming outmoded as a means of handling offenders. The complexity and cost of prison administration are important reasons why more and more states are seeking alternatives to prison. Probation, parole, and community-based corrections, as well as the future of corrections institutions, are all described in this chapter.

A police chief or superintendent of a large law enforcement agency commands a bureaucracy structured much like a branch of the military. The chief initiates directives in the form of general orders, which are intended to prompt the unquestioning attention of the department's chain of command.

For example, General Order 70-4, issued in 1970 by the Chicago superintendent of police, outlines the responsibilities of district (or precinct) commanders: "The district watch commander will direct the enforcement of all laws and ordinances and the rules, regulations, and orders of the Department during his tour of duty."[1] However, in studying the behavior of the Chicago police department in 1975, law professor Kenneth Culp Davis found that watch commanders often failed to carry out this order. He reports:

CHAPTER FIVE

POLICING IN AMERICA
Goals, Working Environment, and Tactics

More than nine out of ten patrolmen refuse to arrest for smoking marijuana in public even though the possession of even a tiny quantity of marijuana is a crime. Supervising officers have generally asserted in our interviews that the arrest should be made, but they generally acknowledge that they do not require their subordinates to comply with their views.[2]

The above example illustrates that police departments are, in fact, humanistic rather than mechanistic organizations and must cope with many of the motivating characteristics we outlined in Part I. They are expected to carry out a number of conflicting tasks or goals that in part mirror the public interest goals referred to in Chapter 1.

Also, police departments and the individuals who work in them are driven by self-interest that sometimes complements and sometimes detracts from their ability to meet public interest goals. Because of federalism and localism, there are many police departments operating in a single metropolitan area. As we will see below, these numerous departments become competitive, often working to outdo their neighboring departments.

In Chapter 2 we pointed out a number of myths that citizens have acquired about crime and the criminal justice system. In this chapter we show how one misperception—that most police officers spend their time pursuing career criminals—aggravates the stress of police work and confounds usually law-abiding citizens when they find the police interfering in their lives. If police officers enforce a traffic violation or intervene in a family quarrel, a citizen may respond by saying that the officers should be spending their time "pursuing criminals rather than interfering in the life of an average, taxpaying citizen."

In Chapter 3 we investigated a variety of serious criminal careers. This chapter shows that police tactics, especially patrol, provide very little opportunity to pursue the serious criminal. Instead, patrol exposes police officers to street people—pimps, prostitutes, drug addicts, and winos. Because of this ex-

159

posure, the police are as much a 24-hour social service agency as they are the vanguard against society's most serious crime.

In Chapter 4 we pointed out that one must trace the implementation of laws and public policies to comprehend the actual impact of crime-fighting policies, usually designed by distant legislators. Here, we explore the discretion, or administrative and street-level flexibility in interpreting legislative and judicial mandates, that police agencies and individual police officers possess. Often the discretion allowed street patrol officers is used to contradict what they see as unrealistic commands from supervisory personnel who rarely get out on the streets.

In short, we concentrate on police behavior rather than police structure to investigate the overall goals, environment, and tactics surrounding law enforcement in contemporary society. In doing so, we reveal that the police and the other agencies of the criminal justice system are complex social service organizations that have an enormous impact on translating the laws "on the books" into "policies in action."

Law Enforcement Functions:
Police as Society's Utility Infielder

> The policewoman pulls a disheveled wig from her shopping bag and crams it over her reddish curls. A dingy scarf follows, hiding her gold earrings. Then comes a decrepit coat and flopping shoes, and an aging woman derelict staggers from a station wagon, lurches past a seedy midtown hotel and collapses into a corner doorstep, her purse open at one side with a dollar bill protruding from its flap.[3]

The woman described above is a member of New York City's street crime unit with over 80 arrests to her credit. While this crime-prevention strategy has produced a reduction in crimes against such vulnerable victims as the elderly and taxi drivers, at least two groups have questioned it. Civil libertarians fear that innocent citizens may be lured into criminal conduct as a result of the agressive tactics employed by such units. Alternatively, some police officials are concerned over the increased dangers it poses for police officers who are a part of the unit as well as patrol officers who are usually unaware that decoys and their backup units are operating in their patrol areas.

While on the beat, patrol officers spend much of their time providing social services to the sick and the elderly. A "sick assist" call frequently requires an officer to aid someone who is bedridden or too frail to go to the bathroom alone. One call, reported by journalist Jonathan Rubinstein, occupied a patrolman and his partner for almost four hours on a New Year's Eve:

> They arrived at a dreary apartment building to find a terrified old woman in fear for her aged husband's life. Their electricity had gone out and the refrigerator contain-

A decoy police officer on duty

ing his medicine was getting warm. The patrolmen found the basement locked and they were unable to get to the fuse box. The landlord could not be reached; his babysitter said he was at a party. They scavenged some wire and extension cord from the apartment and returned to their station to pick up some more, in order to run a line from the refrigerator into a hallway where they had located a live socket. When the refrigerator was working again, they bid the couple good night [and returned to their car].[4]

As demonstrated by the two scenes described above, policing is complicated in part because law enforcement agencies have been assigned a wide range of functions. On the one hand, they are urged to enforce the law strictly against criminals who threaten the physical safety of law-abiding citizens. At the same time, they are supposed to deal compassionately with a range of society's down-and-outs, like the city's elderly, drug addicts, and skid-row inebriates, all of whom have few family ties and lack attention from most social service agencies.

These and other tasks are rooted in the history of policing in the United States and have accumulated over time, beginning in colonial days. As will be shown below, although the many functions have long been established, considerable controversy revolves around both the legitimacy of certain tasks and the overall ordering of priorities. In short, what the police should be doing with their time is a politically charged question, especially given the limited resources available for law enforcement.

HISTORICAL ROOTS OF POLICE FUNCTIONS

The earliest American towns relied heavily on self-policing to assure public tranquillity. Most of the colonists were similar in background and held to the same religious tenets, so that communal pressure rather than institutional oversight formed the backbone of law enforcement.

In addition to the impact of this common social heritage, town members recognized the realities of joining a wilderness settlement. There was little worth stealing and, due to limited mobility, virtually nowhere to hide from other citizens if one came upon something worth pilfering. Being part of a colony afforded fragile protection from the harshness of the vast wilderness, and this reinforced internal harmony. Still, as political scientist David C. Perry notes, certain conditions worked against complete order:

> These colonists were far from the cream of European society; in many cases they represented the legal and religious castoffs. Their migration served the dual purpose of removing socially undesirable persons from the Mother country and providing manpower for the outposts of imperial expansion. The governors of the new colonies were responsible for keeping such people in line.[5]

The British crown's representatives established the traditional English law officer, the constable, who was chosen by the townspeople from among themselves. He was expected to uphold the social order by suppressing visible violations of the community's religious edicts. As an official agent of social control, he enforced laws concerning public behavior and morality (now referred to as "victimless crimes"), and, as the upholder of the peace, he kept public order by dealing with problems that often revolved around excessive drinking. The dual functions of serving as a symbol of social control and maintaining order were clearly assigned tasks of constables in colonial New York City; they were charged with "keeping the peace, suppressing excessive drinking, gambling, and prostitution, and preventing disturbances while church services were in progress."[6]

Towns also adapted the European tradition of the "night watch"—a patrol by town volunteers, usually supervised by the constable, who upheld moral standards and maintained order during the evenings. According to Perry, "Members of the night watch were engaged to arrest drunkards and men who did not appear for military training, and to report single women or wives with husbands away who entertained (or) housed a man."[7]

Citizens could avoid night watch duty by paying for the services of another town member. In this way the night watch contributed to the evolution of a paid police force, which later became a springboard for upward mobility for new immigrants. Soon, wealthier citizens came to rely on these less-than-professional personnel to enforce standards of behavior. The night watch force frequently hesitated to invoke its authority against the well-to-do members of the community, who were often their employers. By 1757, members of New York City's night watch were described as:

[a] parcel of idle, drinking, vigilant snorers, who never quell'd any nocturnal tumult in their lives; . . . but would, perhaps, be as ready to join in a burglary as any thief in Christendom. A happy set indeed, to defend the rich and populous City against the Terrors of the Night.[8]

These colonial traditions of self-policing, constables, and the night watch fit nicely with the principles of low taxation, individual liberty, and direct democracy (town meetings), which were cornerstones of eighteenth-century government. Each political subunit within the town (a ward) maintained its own constable and night watch and relied heavily on self-policing to keep the peace and maximize individual liberty.

Under these old policing traditions, citizens, regardless of their economic status, were responsible for the identification and pursuit of offenders who victimized them. Historian Roger Lane once described the procedure thus:

The victim of robbery or assault called a watchman, if available, and afterward applied to a justice for a warrant and a constable to make or aid in the arrest. The business of detection was largely a private matter, with initiative encouraged through a system of rewards paid to informers.[9]

Thus, crime prevention was left largely to citizens while the maintenance of order and the enforcement of victimless-crime laws were the joint responsibility of the citizens and these early police personnel. As a result the late eighteenth century was marked by the toleration of a high level of lawlessness, especially in certain sections of a town. As Lane notes, "In districts inhabited by new arrivals and transients, . . . the agents of law were only occasional visitors, controlling little and simply exciting resentment."[10]

Conditions associated with urbanization prompted changes in policy on the East Coast. By the 1820s massive immigration, the transition of towns into heterogeneous and bustling cities, exploding health problems, and rampant public disorder led to the simultaneous abandonment of direct democracy and old policing practices. In fact, the word *police*, as it was applied in Boston, expressed both the need for elective government to replace direct democracy and the abandonment of the old law enforcement arrangement. In 1828 Noah Webster defined *police* to mean the entire government of a city, and he applied it to that part of a municipal government that was responsible for executing or enforcing the laws of a city.[11]

By 1823 Boston had appointed a city marshal, who became supervisor of the city's constables and chief health officer. During the transitional period that followed, the task of providing community service became central to Boston's emerging police department. Under the supervision of the city marshal, constables were assigned "the care of the streets, the care of the common sewers . . . and whatever else affects the health, security, and comfort of the city."[12]

Boston's movement toward a city police department paralleled a trend in England, which established a citywide police agency for London in 1828. While the London model placed the department under the authority of the national government, this country's law enforcement agencies were under the jurisdiction of municipal governments and therefore were controlled by local ward politicians and later by urban political machines. Initially, ward bosses appointed police captains, who wielded considerable influence in behalf of these political power brokers. While a citywide agency existed on paper in American cities, early law enforcement agencies were decentralized institutions; the central headquarters and chief of police played only minor roles. The policemen were also appointed at the ward level, and "direct payments to the police captain and the ward alderman for specific jobs [were] not unusual."[13] The function of police departments as supportive agents of cities' political and economic elites was cemented during this new era.

Few changes occurred until the early 1900s. Most of the twentieth-century changes in policing have involved loosening the hold of political influence (and corruption) over the departments and, consequently, giving the police a professional image that emphasized a task that seemed to be politically neutral—crime prevention. This task consists of catching lawbreakers in the act of a crime and of apprehending them after they commit crimes. The latter aspect of crime prevention is sometimes referred to as the law enforcement function. Technological innovations, such as the telegraph, telephones, radio patrol cars, and belt-size walkie-talkies, were used to improve police officers' accountability to a professional bureaucracy as well as to enhance their crime-prevention potential. For example, the 1930 Wickersham Commission, a presidential advisory panel formed to provide proposals to improve enforcement of criminal laws in the United States, issued a report on police that heralded the emergence of patrol cars as new "angels of death."

> With the advent of the radio-equipped car a new era has come. . . . Districts of many square miles, which formerly were officially patrolled by only a few men who . . . could not watch the area, are now covered by a roving patrol car, fast, efficient, stealthy . . . just as liable to be within 60 feet as 3 miles of the crook plying his trade.[14]

Like so many other technical advances in police work, the automobile in itself has not proved to be the deterrent to crime that was anticipated. But its arrival did signify the increased emphasis on crime prevention that took place during this period.

CONTEMPORARY POLICE FUNCTIONS

Today, the police are expected to carry out all of the functions that they have historically gathered. However, the relative importance of these functions has shifted as a result of both forces within law enforcement and pressures from the outside—including business, government, and community sentiments.

While their uniform symbolizes governmental authority, police officers are only periodically called upon to overtly support political and economic elites in operations that tend to reinforce the status quo in society and protect established elite groups. In one such operation during the late 1960s and early 1970s, the police were designated to lend their physical support to the Vietnam war policies of Presidents Johnson and Nixon by policing antiwar demonstrations, rallies, and marches. Their activities created hostility toward the police by those citizens who felt that their freedom of expression was being limited by the police. However, those same citizens wanted the police to prevent crime and maintain order in their own communities.

Most recently, the police have been used to enforce controversial busing policies that are intended to promote racial integration. Unlike tactics sometimes used in the late 1960s, police agencies have developed passive strategies that aim to calm citizens' displeasure over such policies rather than aggressively break up protests against government decisions.[15] Aggressive tactics designed to quell such protests sometimes incited riots, as, for example, during the 1968 Democratic National Convention when Chicago Mayor Richard Daley ordered his police department to "break up" antiwar demonstrations outside the convention hall.[16]

A second police function, enforcing social ethics, has been somewhat deemphasized in recent years. Decriminalization of public drunkenness and, in some states, decriminalization of possession of small amounts of marijuana represent legislative divestment of police responsibility for upholding social standards (see Chapter 11). However, thousands of arrests for such charges continue to be made each year, and during municipal political campaigns, the police are sometimes used to wage sporadic campaigns against "gambling clubs," "porno shops," and "massage parlors." Despite these occasional forays, this task, a primary responsibility of constables and night watches during colonial times, is somewhat receding, due in part to more permissive community sentiments, police professionalization, court decisions, and legislative reform. Of course, the extent to which police attention to these matters has been reduced depends on where one lives.

The remaining functions—community service, order maintenance, and crime prevention—have become the duties that the police are expected to perform regularly. Today, as in the past, most law enforcement officers spend the bulk of their time observing street life (in a patrol car rather than on foot), handling disputes among citizens, and providing 24-hour social service support for the most down-and-out citizens in society (e.g., the elderly poor, skid-row inebriates).[17]

These tasks of maintaining order and providing community services, which constitute the bulk of police work, frequently require restraint and verbal skills rather than the full exercise of police authority. For example, in the case of family disputes, patrol officers recognize once they begin working in the field that calming the situation and referring family members to social service agencies are often more productive means for dealing with such incidents than using force and relying on arrests.

Nevertheless, the media, politicians, citizens, and police administrators alike evaluate police officers' performance on the basis of crime prevention and the apprehension of criminals.[18] According to Herman Goldstein, a law professor who has written extensively on contemporary policing, the perpetuation of the

Contemporary police functions

community service

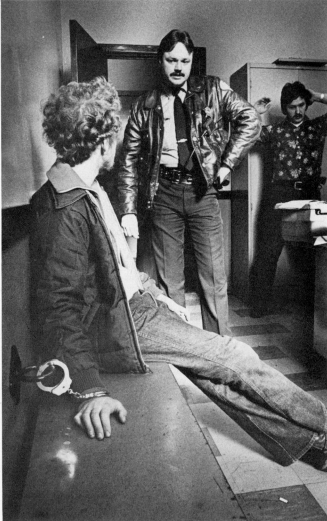

order maintenance

crime prevention

myth that the prevention of crime and the arrest of criminals are the major tasks of police has undermined the quality of police service in the United States:

> As a result, individuals are recruited into the field who may possess the characteristics required for dealing with criminals, but not necessarily the abilities that are essential for carrying out the multitude of other police tasks. The training they receive, which in the past has usually been based on the same stereotype of policing, does not provide instruction on how to deal with the incidents police most commonly handle.[19]

Further, the fact that this myth is promoted by police administrators as well as outsiders fosters alienation from work. Street officers often dislike their superiors and feel alienated from the department's hierarchy because they believe that the organization and those that run it are insensitive to the realities of patrol and are concerned only with their own administrative status.

The heavy emphasis on crime prevention is partly attributable to the actions of police administrators who, over the last century, have made this task a symbol of police professionalism and a basis for acquiring larger budgets. It is also the product of the focus by the media and politicians on street crime as a tool for selling newspapers and winning votes as well as of the legitimate concerns by citizens about victimization. Combined, these factors have greatly raised communities' expectations concerning police officers' ability to prevent street crime and apprehend criminals, especially in cities, where the fear of violent crimes runs highest.

The Atomization of American Police Power

In 1977, during his first year in office, Attorney General Griffin Bell came under attack for proposing a study of the feasibility of merging the F.B.I. and D.E.A. (the United States Drug Enforcement Administration).[20] Interest groups, such as the National Association of State Boards of Pharmacy (which had built up a working relationship with the D.E.A.), as well as law enforcement associations throughout the country opposed a consolidation.

Supporters of the F.B.I.'s position argued that even with consolidation the bureau would be unable to impose tighter discipline over the drug enforcement effort, and they feared that a merger might taint the bureau with the corruption that has surrounded the federal drug agencies. D.E.A. supporters also opposed the proposal; they insisted that the agency was making major strides to overcome its bad reputation and was in the midst of shifting its focus away from low-level street dealers to big-time drug wholesalers. D.E.A.'s advocates argued that the agency was finally coming into its own and, therefore, had a right to remain autonomous.

The attorney general's "trial balloon" illustrates how law enforcement agencies fight to maintain the status quo and protect their particular jurisdictional turf.[21] One reason why agencies do this is to retain the jobs and the power that they build over time. In part, this scrapping over territoriality is complicated by federalism and localism. In our federal system, there are three levels of law enforcement agencies, and each level has police forces that carry out tasks that infringe on the turf of the others. Localism refers to the fact that within a single metropolitan area there may be (and usually are) dozens of municipal police departments.

LOCAL, STATE, AND FEDERAL LAW ENFORCEMENT AGENCIES

The wrangling over territoriality among law enforcement agencies is a by-product of the historical precedent of local rule combined with the post–Second World War explosion of urbanization.[22] The result is the proliferation of autonomous municipal police departments as the predominant agencies for enforcing the law.

LOCAL AND STATE AGENCIES As shown in Figure 5-1(a), local government funds provide the bulk of support for the nation's criminal justice agencies. Within each local government, almost 65 percent of the criminal justice budget is spent on police departments (see Figure 5-1(b)). Law enforcement's dependency on municipal funds means that the available resources of police departments varies greatly from one local jurisdiction to another.

Despite the mushrooming of metropolitan areas beyond town, county, and in some cases state boundaries, municipalities within an identifiable metropolis usually maintain their own departments. In one metropolitan area, there may be as many as 50 autonomous departments, ranging from very small forces of under 20 officers to very large bureaucracies with thousands of sworn officers.

Small-town police departments that lie outside of a metropolitan area "usually have part-time, short-term [high turnover] nonprofessional police . . . often elected," according to David Perry.[23] Officers in these communities tend to be older and less educated than police personnel who operate within metropolitan areas.[24] These departments stress traffic control and the provision of public services to the community. Their crime-prevention efforts usually revolve around problems of juvenile delinquency.[25] Small towns that fall within metropolitan areas eventually move from this constable system to a full-time, salaried police agency that is a mini-version of the big central city agency.[26] However, even when a small-town police force begins to pattern itself after a large-city force, most activities still emanate from a central headquarters rather than being split between headquarters and substations, commonly called "precincts."

A central city's police agency is usually a mammoth bureaucratic complex. William Turner, a former F.B.I. agent, describes the central office of the New York City Police Department: "Headquarters is honeycombed with specialized units ranging from the Narcotics Bureau . . . and Bomb Squad, which are part

FIGURE 5-1

Distribution by Level of Government of Direct Expenditures by the Criminal
Justice System, 1975

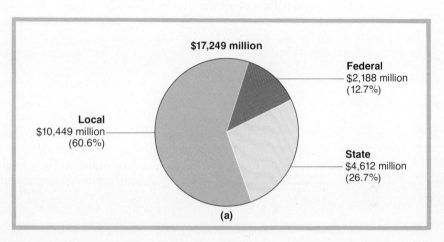

$17,249 million

Federal
$2,188 million
(12.7%)

Local
$10,449 million
(60.6%)

State
$4,612 million
(26.7%)

(a)

Local Criminal Justice Systems' Total Expenditures, 1975

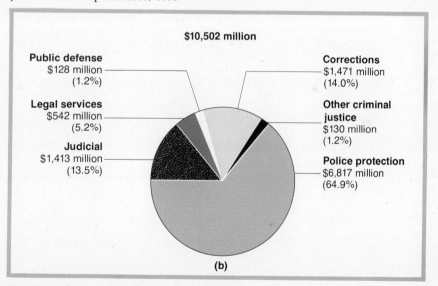

$10,502 million

Public defense
$128 million
(1.2%)

Corrections
$1,471 million
(14.0%)

Legal services
$542 million
(5.2%)

**Other criminal
justice**
$130 million
(1.2%)

Judicial
$1,413 million
(13.5%)

Police protection
$6,817 million
(64.9%)

(b)

SOURCE: *Expenditure and Employment Data for the Criminal Justice System—1975* (Washington,
D.C.: U.S. Government Printing Office, 1977), pp. 4–5.

of the Detective Division, to the Emergency Service Division of rescue specialists."[27] Most citizens living in big cities are exposed only to patrol officers who
operate totally out of local precincts. The New York City Police Department has
123 precincts, which serve many different people, from the 41st Precinct (sometimes called "Fort Apache" because of its dangerous nature), whose officers pa-

trol the ghetto of the South Bronx, to the 19th, which is responsible for the upper-income residencies and shops along Manhattan's fashionable "Upper East Side."

Additionally, many state legislatures have encouraged counties to retain a sheriff's office or a similar law enforcement agency. Such agencies usually are responsible for handling and detaining accused individuals as they are processed in the local court system or patrolling unincorporated areas of counties. Sheriffs, who are sometimes political patronage appointees, retain broad powers of arrest within their respective counties, which frequently contain many towns and municipalities.

The tenth Amendment to the United States Constitution reserves the police power for the states. The states, in turn, have delegated much of that authority to municipalities and counties. Still, most states have state police departments or highway patrols that regulate traffic on their road systems, provide law enforcement protection for some unincorporated areas, and offer smaller municipal departments support services, such as sophisticated crime laboratories. Many states also have created special purpose law enforcement agencies to muster statewide attacks on illicit drug traffic; other agencies have been created to regulate liquor laws.

THE F.B.I.　Based generally on Article One of the United States Constitution, which gives Congress the power "to regulate Commerce with foreign nations, and among the several states," a number of federal law enforcement agencies have emerged since the Civil War. The first such agency was the Treasury Department's Secret Service, created in 1865 to combat widespread counterfeiting.[28] Over the years the "commerce clause" of the Constitution has been interpreted broadly to stretch the authority of the federal government in dealing with domestic public policy issues, including crime. The Department of Justice, created in 1870, was charged with the responsibility of enforcing most federal criminal laws developed by the Congress. But, according to journalist Don Whitehead, it had to borrow agents from the Treasury; with a $50,000 appropriation from Congress, the Justice Department had to rely on an agents-on-loan system:

> Under this arrangement, no government official had any real check or control over the agents' activities. Most of them were hired on a part-time basis from a list of private detectives "approved" by the Secret Service; some were suspected of being ex-criminals, and they were called Secret Service men even though they were not regular Secret Service agents.[29]

In 1906 President Theodore Roosevelt's attorney general, Charles Bonaparte, who headed the Justice Department, requested that Congress replace the rent-an-agent system with a permanent law enforcement agency under his department's jurisdiction. Congress not only denied the request but removed financial support for the department's use of Treasury agents. Journalist Sanford

Unger maintains that congressional reaction was in part due to "the Secret Service agents' work in a land fraud investigation [which] had led to the indictment and conviction of several members of Congress."[30]

Bonaparte defied the action and issued a departmental order in July 1908 that created a small enforcement division in the Justice Department. The next year the new administration's attorney general, George Wickersham, upheld this action and named the new agency the Federal Bureau of Investigation.

After a shaky beginning, which was characterized by internal corruption and poor leadership through the mid-1920s, the F.B.I. began cultivating public opinion and gained wide-based congressional support for its law enforcement campaigns. This support grew under the leadership of J. Edgar Hoover, who not only "cleaned up" the agency's image but, through his relationship with many presidents, secured the bureau as one of the most powerful agencies in the federal bureaucracy even though it appears on an organizational chart as a subunit of the Justice Department.[31] Hoover accumulated so much influence that his leadership was ended only by his death in office after nearly three decades of running the agency almost single-handedly. The power of the F.B.I. within the Washington bureaucracy is symbolized by the J. Edgar Hoover Building on Pennsylvania Avenue, built at a cost of $126 million, which dwarfs the Department of Justice's building.

Part of the bureau's strong popular and official backing evolved from its enforcement of moral-behavior violations, such as those defined under the 1910 White Slave Traffic Act (the Mann Act), passed in response to the international and interstate trafficking of females as prostitutes throughout the United States.[32] The F.B.I. also acquired the reputation of being the country's elite law enforcement agency in the late 1920s and early 1930s when it captured a number of famous bootleggers and bank robbers.[33]

For example, when the infamous bank robber John Dillinger escaped from an Indiana jail in 1934 and stole the local sheriff's automobile to flee to Chicago, Illinois, he broke a federal law—the National Motor Vehicles Theft Act—that prohibits transportation of a stolen motor vehicle across a state line. The F.B.I. entered the case; several months later they had learned through a female informant that Dillinger would be going to a movie theater, the Biograph, on July 22, 1934, to see Clark Gable in *Manhattan Melodrama*. Don Whitehead records the ensuing event:

> The FBI men . . . recognized Dillinger when he entered the theatre that warm July evening with Polly Hamilton and Ana Cumpanas, who was to become known as "The Woman in Red" [the FBI's informant]. Despite plastic surgery, the outlaw was identified beyond doubt. Cowley (the FBI agent in charge) called Hoover, who was pacing the library at his home in Washington. The decision was made to take Dillinger as he came out of the theatre, rather than risk a gun battle inside the crowded show house.
>
> When the trio emerged, by prearrangement Purvis [an agent] lit a cigar. The trap began to close. Dillinger must have sensed that something was wrong. He glanced over his shoulder and saw an agent moving toward him. He darted toward an alley,

clawing a pistol from his pants pocket. But before he could get his gun in action, three FBI agents fired five shots. Slugs tore into Dillinger's body and he pitched on his face. The chase was over.[34]

But the bureau occasionally has been tainted by its continuous embroilment in national political upheavals. In the hysterical "Red Scare" episode of 1919–1920, it led raids on communist and socialist organizations—most of which had not really violated any laws. More recently, its agents bugged and infiltrated the offices and homes of civil rights leader Martin Luther King, Jr., and others who were perceived as political opponents.[35]

THE L.E.A.A. In addition to the direct impact of such agencies as the F.B.I. and D.E.A., the federal government has influenced policing throughout the country with the establishment of the Law Enforcement Assistance Administration (L.E.A.A.) in 1968. Responding in part to the "law and order" presidential campaign of Richard Nixon as well as to media and citizen concern over rising crime rates, Congress created the L.E.A.A. to improve the law enforcement and criminal justice systems of the states. According to a Department of Justice study group, "Its design was intended to maintain the delicate balance between Federal assistance in the pursuit of national objectives and local authority. . . . Thus, a new form of Federal financial assistance was developed: block grant funding for state activities embodied in comprehensive plans."[36]

The L.E.A.A. gave states large amounts of money and stipulated that the states develop comprehensive plans for the needs of their criminal justice systems. But in many states comprehensive planning meant no more than a "paperwork exercise" of drawing up a vague statement of intent to acquire these available federal monies.[37] Little, if any, research and consultation went into these so-called plans. Additionally, many states used the funds to purchase police hardware and gadgets (e.g., antiriot tanks) for their own state agencies, often allocating less than a fair share to the large metropolitan police departments.

Other expensive L.E.A.A.-developed programs earmarked to improve policing were based on untested assumptions. For example, under the assumption that better educated police officers improve the quality of law enforcement in the country, the Law Enforcement Education Program (L.E.E.P.) provided nearly $200 million in loans and grants for higher education to students who were pursuing or planning careers in law enforcement. This program originated in the 1960s, when a commission studying city riots and protest demonstrations discovered widespread misuse of authority by police, including many incidents of brutality.[38] But a recent evaluation of the program found no discernible improvement in police performance on the basis of educational attainment. The study stated that the curricula of most educational programs that emerged in response to these available funds poorly fit the stated goals of L.E.E.P., which were to combat misuse of authority by the police and improve police skills for effective crime control.[39] As in many new public service bureaucracies, L.E.A.A. officials moved quickly to spend L.E.E.P.'s full budget allocation, thus creating a hodgepodge of permanent programs rather than supporting experimental programs to determine the validity of their assumptions and the impact of various approaches in meeting stated goals.

On the other hand, even reports extremely critical of the L.E.A.A.'s overall performance still note several achievements for the agency. The study group mentioned previously found that "many jurisdictions have been better serviced by police agencies through the development, with L.E.A.A. funds, of more effective patrol techniques, police community relations programs, and minority recruitment efforts."[40] When it took office in 1977, the Carter Administration singled out the L.E.A.A. for major reorganization. But the agency had already developed a broad-based constituency, ranging from police departments to universities, and cemented the dependency of state and local criminal justice agencies on federal support. Therefore, presidents may redirect its goals somewhat and alter its organizational structure, but they are unlikely to kill the L.E.A.A.

THE PRIVATE SECURITY BOOM

On top of these local, state, and federal agencies, the nation's free-market economy has created a maze of nongovernmental policing institutions that are collectively labeled "the private security industry." Licensed by state legislatures, this industry is currently expanding because of the increased rate of property crimes; the enlargement of this country's armament industry, which requires tight security; the growth in political violence directed at the affluent and their institutions (e.g., corporate headquarters); the recent adjustments by insurance companies, which offer discounts in premiums for businesses with private security systems; and failure of public agencies to reduce the crime problem.[41] As shown in Figure 5-2, the combined number of public and private personnel directly engaged in law enforcement approached 1 million in 1975, and one-third of those are private security employees.

Most private security personnel are full- or part-time *direct* employees of this nation's business establishments. For the most part, in-house security personnel, like the rent-a-guards in smaller establishments, are assigned to protect the property of corporations from both employee and outside thefts. Most of these security people are guards, although businesses also employ nearly 24,000 private investigators and detectives. Combined, these in-house guards and detectives make approximately 500,000 yearly arrests.

The nation's growing reliance on the private security industry is alarming because of the negligence of some state governments in licensing personnel and firms. A national survey conducted by the Rand Corporation revealed abuses by the private security industry, including assaults, shootings, killings, security personnel theft rings, and gross violations of bugging and wiretapping laws.[42] Still, little progress has been made toward instituting stricter licensing requirements. According to one researcher, Milton Lipson, the industry is thus left to make high profits while its crime-prevention potential is being negated:

FIGURE 5.2

Trends in Law Enforcement Employment

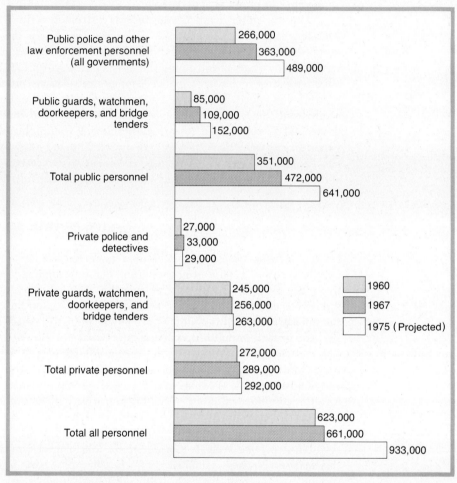

SOURCE: Adapted from Milton Lipson, *On Guard: The Business of Private Security* (New York: New York Times Book Company, 1975), p. 196.

It employs as guards the very types of persons that it advises management are high risks. . . . Need, temptation, and opportunity are among the inducing factors in our climbing crime rate. Yet, the makeup of security forces is often of low-paid, low-quality, under-educated, and untrained individuals . . . entrusted with all of the assets on the premises of the business they are hired to protect.[43]

Greatly compounding this problem is the fact that many states allow private security guards to be armed. At a recent hearing in Pennsylvania, in testimony discussing private security guards, Edward Lee, clerk of the Court of Quarter Sessions in Philadelphia, said:

These guards are armed with revolvers, mace, tear gas, knives, blackjacks, attack dogs, billy clubs, and occasionally 12-gauge shotguns. . . . It is a fact that security guards in this area shot 13 people. This is an alarming statistic because it seems to indicate any guard with a gun on his hip is inclined to use it.[44]

Some states deputize these personnel, granting them considerable statewide law enforcement status. Thus, in Texas selected security employees are designated as special Texas Rangers. In other states in-house security personnel of large retail establishments are granted arrest authority equivalent to officers of state highway patrols. Lipson notes that as a result of their special status, "Many of these officers . . . may obtain information from police files otherwise limited to sworn law enforcement agencies."[45] However, in comparison to police personnel, these security employees are held much less accountable to elected or appointed officials of government. Community accountability, a critical public goal for criminal justice (see Chapter 1), is eroded by this nation's increased reliance on the private security industry.

NEGATIVE AND POSITIVE EFFECTS OF ATOMIZATION

Is the atomization of this country's police power a universal good or does it mostly subvert the meeting of important public interest goals in criminal justice? We view localism and federalism in less than absolute terms. Indeed, many of the effects of atomization should be looked at in such a way, because atomization is a phenomenon that both contributes to and subverts the public interest.

THE QUALITY OF POLICE SERVICE   Some experts argue that localism leads to disparities in the quality of police services provided to citizens in the same state. In *Police in the Metropolis*, David Perry points out, "There is no way to compare the competencies of large central city police forces and single-man suburban police units. They often have similar duties, but not comparable resources."[46] For example, many of the larger departments have professional staffs to acquire state and federal funds from the L.E.A.A. for innovative programs, minority and female recruitment, and supportive technology. This grant-getting potential allows them to increase their resources without adding a burden on local taxpayers.

However, a group of university researchers led by Elinor Ostrom has challenged the argument that small police departments in a metropolitan area are less competent agencies than large, central-city ones.[47] Relying largely on citizen satisfaction as a measure of competence, this team of researchers found no evidence that officers working in the precincts of larger departments perform better than those from smaller departments, at least not in the eyes of the constituencies they serve.[48] From a public accountability perspective the police in smaller departments seem no less competent.

While admitting that most large departments deliver a wider range of police services, the team's most recent study, conducted in the St. Louis metropolitan area, found very few differences in the professional qualifications (e.g., training, education) of officers in small (less than 12 officers), medium-size (12 to 76), and large (over 76) departments.[49] They also determined that financing larger departments is no cheaper than maintaining smaller ones.[50] The greater purchasing power of large departments does result in savings, but these are offset by higher salaries and the costs of the additional services the larger agencies offer. The research team therefore questioned whether the public interest goal of efficiency is necessarily better met by large departments.

AGENCY OVERLAP It is not unusual for an officer patrolling a beat in a central city to have state police officers, F.B.I. agents, insurance investigators, and private detectives operating in the same area without the officer's knowledge or control. Some experts take a dim view of this uncoordinated concentration of personnel in a given area, pointing to duplication of effort, competition, and the emergence of "spillover" tactics, or the shifting of policing problems from one jurisdiction to another.[51] For example, a metropolitan police department may "dump" skid-row inebriates into subway terminals, where transit police are responsible for maintaining order. Or a police department bordering another in a single metropolitan area may temporarily solve its prostitution problem by using a paddy wagon to round up a large number of prostitutes and drop them off in a neighboring turf.

In addition, specialized elite units of major law enforcement agencies, in competition for prized arrests, are sometimes unwilling to share information or to coordinate strategies with rival agencies. These self-interest conflicts occasionally emerge between units of federal law enforcement agencies and those of major metropolitan police departments in investigations of key crime figures or crime syndicates. Often, creating working relationships between such units requires extraordinary personal efforts. According to one source, prior to the successful joint effort of the New York Police Department's Narcotics Bureau and the Federal Bureau of Narcotics (now the D.E.A.) to break up the "French Connection" drug syndicate, the New York Police Department's head, Ed Carey, worked hard to make use of the strengths of the two agencies:

> The Federals had resources, manpower and equipment that the locals could use to advantage. The New York Police had information, contacts and certain legal leeway—such as court authorized wiretapping—that the government agents found useful. At least weekly, Chief Carey met with the Federal Regional Director, George Gaffney, to trade reports and strategy.[52]

Still, such informal cooperative arrangements are sometimes inadequate, given the autonomous movement of law enforcement officers from a number of agencies throughout the same geographical area. In the "French Connection" case, during a joint New York City–federal stakeout of a cellar in the Bronx, the following incident occurred:

> It was shortly after 2:00 a.m. when the agent up front in the closet heard a faint shuffle of footsteps outside. He doused the light and opened the door of his hiding place a crack, hands gripping the shotgun. The cellar door opened, letting in a rush of cold night air. . . . The slight scraping of feet on the cement floor sounded like two men. Suddenly shafts from two flashlights pierced the darkness.
>
> One swept the entry hall, then in a quick step one of the visitors reached to pull the chain dangling from a ceiling bulb. Simultaneously the cellar entry was flooded with light and a voice barked: "All right! Police! Who's down here?"
>
> They were two patrolmen, massive in their heavy blue overcoats, revolvers, flashlights in their hands. One whirled as the agent pushed open the closet door and stepped out, shotgun laid aside. "Who the hell are you, Mister?" the cop demanded.
>
> There was no time for a reply, for the other officer cried: "What! Look out!" Two agents in the alcove were emerging from the shadows, revolvers in hand. The startled cops crouched, prepared for violence. But a sharp voice rang from the blackness of the boiler room: "Hold it, f'Chrissake! We're *all* police officers!"[53]

On the other hand, atomization can create opportunities for personnel to enhance their self-interests, and this may be beneficial to the public. For example, dozens of police chiefs can exist in a single metropolitan area. Like members of opposing football teams, they can compete for the glory and fame that result from a "prize bust." Competition, in this instance, prods them to do their best.

Overlap also diffuses police authority, preventing the emergence of a police state. Federalism and localism are structural assurances that no single law enforcement agency can acquire all of the nation's police power, thus limiting the impact of any one agency's violations of the law.

LOCAL VERSUS NATIONAL POLICY   Localism and federalism create the opportunity for municipal and even state agencies to block national policy when the latter runs counter to local community values. A primary example of such activity involved the unwillingness of local law enforcement agencies to halt the terrorism of the Ku Klux Klan during the early 1960s. When the F.B.I. entered the South to enforce federal laws against those who were victimizing civil rights workers, they received very little aid from local law enforcement agencies, especially those representing the rural areas of the Deep South.[54] A local law enforcement agency sometimes protects its community's practices at the expense of national policy. After all, a police department is ultimately dependent on the support of its community's political and economic elites for budget decisions and salaries.

COPING WITH ATOMIZATION

Several plans of action have emerged to reduce the negative impacts of atomization without significantly disturbing its role as a buffer to excessive police power. Many of these plans fall under the broad umbrella of "metropolitan reform," the overall attempt by urban municipalities to retard local government chaos and improve the efficiency of delivering public services.[55] The municipal reforms for improving local policing can be viewed either as permanent or as less formal, cooperative agreements, depending upon how easily they can be dissolved by participating governments.

Establishing a metropolitan government usually requires the vote of the electorate and new state legislation.[56] Permanent metropolitan-wide police departments have been created in Nashville, Tennessee, and Indianapolis, Indiana, to replace most municipal departments and provide all police services throughout these metropolitan areas. In the Miami, Florida, metropolitan area the municipalities provide basic police services, while Dade County supplies such supporting services as training and recordkeeping to balance the competencies of the many municipal departments.

Other municipalities have entered either less formal, cooperative arrangements or intermunicipal agreements that can be broken through the unilateral action of a participant's governing board (e.g., city council).[57] Thus, under the Lakewood Plan of Los Angeles County, California, municipalities sign contracts with the county and pay for the services of the county police department. Such purchasing plans are designed to offer citizens in smaller communities more economical and "professional" police services than smaller departments usually provide.

Those politicians and bureaucrats who advocate permanent metropolitan government as a solution to public service deficiencies in urban areas portray the problems as essentially technical ones.[58] They ignore the fact that many service problems, including policing, involve political issues—decisions of where and how to deploy available street officers, for example. And some of the advocates of metropolitan government also promote such "reforms" because they recognize that the beneficiaries of localism and police atomization in the 1970s have been blacks and other racial minorities.[59] Therefore, some who support this movement to reduce atomization want to offset the growing economic and political power of minorities in central cities by combining suburban and central-city jurisdictions into one political unit. In doing so, those who are currently in power feel they would be able to maintain their power, since large numbers of minority-group voters in the central cities would be outnumbered by the still largely white suburbs.

Atomization of police power creates many problems, but the establishment of metropolitan government is hardly an ideal solution because it is partly a political tool for retarding local self-government. Informal cooperative arrangements among autonomous jurisdictions within a metropolitan area generally overcome many of the negative effects of atomization without destroying localism and the protections it offers to citizens.

Police Tasks and Discretion

During the Newark, New Jersey, race riots of 1967, state troopers and city police officers on the scene were given broad authority to use their weapons. A commission that studied the riot reported the following incident:

> At 5:30 p.m. [July 14], on Beacon Street, W. F. told J. S., whose 1959 Pontiac he had taken to the station for inspection, that his front brake needed fixing. J. S., who had just returned from work, went to the car which was parked in the street, jacked up the front end, took the wheel off and got under the car. The street was quiet. More than a dozen persons were sitting on porches, walking about, or shopping. None heard any shots. Suddenly several state troopers appeared at the corner of Springfield and Beacon. J. S. was startled by a shot clanging into the side of the garbage can next to his car. As he looked up he saw a state trooper with his rifle pointed at him. The next shot struck him in the right side. At almost the same instant, K. G., standing on a porch, was struck in the right eye by a bullet. Both he and J. S. were critically injured.[60]

During the summer of 1977 New York City experienced a day-long power failure. Looting broke out in many sections of the city. The police were ordered to use restraint, and no police shootings of citizens occurred. However, the blackout cost businesses $135 million in theft and property damage.[61] Members of the business community accused the police department of excessive leniency, while the mayor praised their way of handling the massive breakdown in order. How should the police respond to outbreaks that threaten the political and social stability of communities?

Officer Mark Rockingham has great admiration for the way a fellow police officer handles family disturbance calls.

> He'd come into a family beef with a husband and wife throwing and yelling at each other. Then he'd set down on the couch and take his hat off, and he didn't say a word. Sooner or later the couple felt kind of silly. He'd take 45 minutes in each of these situations but he never had to come back.[62]

Another officer on the same police force usually entered a family beef to confirm his childhood sentiments over such quarrels.

> When the confirming clue appeared, he "knew" the whole story. Instead of arbitrating the dispute that was actually taking place, however, he constituted an inquiry to determine which parent was at fault for the assumed injury to the child.

Did the mother feed the child, or play around? Did the father get drunk, or was he trying to keep the house together? Once he found out, there were only two alternatives: the "no-good" parent left "willingly—or went to jail." Thus, sentimentality developed into an enforcement response.[63]

How should police officers go about handling family disputes?

As depicted in the first incident, police agencies have a significant degree of discretion and flexibility in deciding what tactics to employ in order to cope with a breakdown in a community's social order. They also have a good deal of flexibility in deciding what priorities to give to various police tasks and how to execute routine tasks like crime prevention. Of course, they do not make these decisions in a vacuum; they must be sensitive to certain norms of their communities as well as responsive to legal authorities and community elites.

Implementing police tasks is even more complicated because what law en-

---

A FAMILY BEEF

A depressed and jealous wife shot her husband while he slept, but he revived nearly 20 hours later and the couple then took turns shooting each other with her gun, police said. It began in bed and went on as they crawled bleeding from room to room.

The .32 caliber revolver changed hands several times. It ended after police arrived. They said the woman, who had turned the gun on herself by that point, fired a final shot at her husband, collapsed and died.

Her husband was hospitalized in critical condition.

Police said the bizarre episode began at 7 A.M. Tuesday in a second-floor condominium in a comfortable new building in the suburb of Homewood, southwest of Chicago. It ended at 3 A.M. Wednesday.

Police said Margaret Radovich, 50, shot her husband, Theodore, 56, twice in the chest while he slept Tuesday morning and later, for some unexplained reason, returned to the bed.

"When he regained consciousness early Wednesday, he found his wife next to him in bed and pulled the gun out of her hand, shooting her once in each leg," said Police Chief William Nolan.

Nolan said Radovich also fired a shot out the window to attract attention and tried to throw the gun through a closed window.

The window broke, but the gun fell back inside the room, and Mrs. Radovich found it and reloaded it.

Radovich managed to crawl to another room, followed by his wife, who then shot him in the mouth, Nolan said.

But he still was able to make his way to another bedroom. There he broke a window in another attempt to attract attention.

Meanwhile, Nolan said, Mrs. Radovich shot herself.

When police arrived, after being summoned by neighbors, they found Mrs. Radovich in a hallway. She was on the floor, and her husband was in the other room.

Police said that before they could reach Mrs. Radovich, she took one more shot at her husband through the doorway. The bullet missed, and she fell unconscious.

She was dead on arrival at a hospital.

"Spouse Shooting Ends Wife's Life: Husband Critical," *State Press*, September 8, 1977, 13. Reprinted by permission of the Associated Press and the Arizona State University *State Press*.

forcement agencies can accomplish depends to a large extent on the street wisdom of individual officers. An officer has a range of options available in almost any incident. Some options are taught in police academies as proper procedure; others are learned from fellow officers while on the beat. For example, in a family quarrel a police officer may decide to arrest one of the antagonists, informally calm the parties involved and leave, call in the help of other social service agencies, or, in many cases, decide to do nothing, leaving the matter to the family for settlement.

Acknowledging the discretionary nature of contemporary policing, social scientists have discovered a number of external, organizational, and individual characteristics that guide police decision-making and set limits on street-level enforcement practices. Police discretion is the vehicle by which departments and individual officers reduce the mass of tasks and criminal justice statues to a manageable set of priorities. If police arrested everyone they observed committing a violation, they would rarely get a block away from the station house. Also, a full-enforcement approach to policing would undoubtedly bring the court system to a standstill. Therefore, although there are serious problems with discretionary decision making, it is a vital component of policing and, as we will see in Chapter 6, an indispensable tool for court personnel as well.

ENFORCEMENT LEVELS

"Total enforcement"—carrying out all the criminal laws with unobstructed vigor and without concern for human rights—is neither a desired nor a legitimate goal for American criminal justice.[64] The requirements of due process are necessary for limiting the scope of police enforcement practices. If, as a result of enforcing certain laws, police might violate individual liberties, they are expected to exercise great restraint and care in implementing those laws. The due process guarantees are supposed to be given precedence over society's desire for crime control.[65]

American society expects "full enforcement"—the carrying out of all tasks and criminal statutes within the bounds of due process. However, full enforcement is an unattainable goal both because localism allows for the injection of community standards in shaping police practices and because police organizations and individual officers have limited resources as well as self-interest drives. Police departments operate within budgets; officers are dependent on court personnel (e.g., prosecutors) who have their own priorities in deciding what actions should be taken against arrested individuals; they must rely on citizens' reporting of crimes, which is quite sporadic; and police officers also have their own ideas about what laws should be given priority. All of these discretionary forces further restrict police enforcement practices, leaving communities with a low level of "actual enforcement." The three levels of enforcement—total, full, and actual—are schematically shown in Figure 5-3.

FIGURE 5-3

Discretionary Factors Influencing Law Enforcement

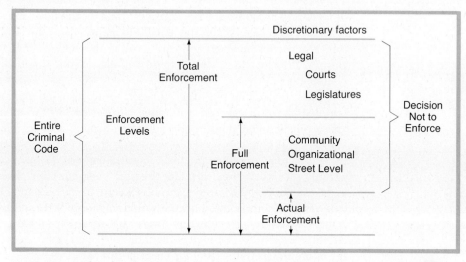

SOURCE: In part, based on Joseph Goldstein, "Police Discretion Not to Invoke the Criminal Process: Low-Visibility Decisions in the Administration of Justice," in *Criminal Justice: Law and Politics*, ed. George F. Cole (North Scituate, Mass.: Duxbury Press, 1972), pp. 59–80.

LEGAL FACTORS

COURTS   The appellate courts of states and the federal government take major responsibility for seeing that the police adhere to constitutional and procedural restraints against total enforcement of the law. Due process requirements tend to constrict the range of police activity, limiting discretion by setting rather strict standards for how police are to enforce the law. Consequently, these constitutional protections are often disliked by police and unpopular with many citizens. For example, some due-process requirements limit the use of sophisticated eavesdropping equipment that could be employed to retard white-collar and organized crime. A four-county Arizona police strike force investigating an organized-crime figure was disbanded when an officer from one of the participating departments discovered that an overzealous officer had neglected to ob-

---

REVISED MIRANDA WARNING

YOU HAVE THE RIGHT TO SWING FIRST IF YOU CHOOSE TO SWING FIRST, ANY MOVE YOU MAKE CAN AND WILL BE USED AS AN EXCUSE TO BEAT THE SHIT OUT OF YOU.
YOU HAVE THE RIGHT TO HAVE A DOCTOR OR A PRIEST PRESENT. IF YOU CAN NOT AFFORD A DOCTOR OR ARE NOT PRESENTLY ATTENDING A CHURCH OF YOUR CHOICE, ONE WILL BE APPOINTED FOR YOU.
DO YOU UNDERSTAND WHAT I JUST TOLD YOU, ASSHOLE?

From a police department bulletin board in a large western city.

tain court permission to wiretap the home of the suspected syndicate figure—an illegal practice.[66] Limitations on the use of available technology have influenced police to rely heavily on paid informants and offers of immunity for testimony.

However, the costs of maintaining a network of informants significantly affects the budgets of many law enforcement agencies, including the F.B.I. Sanford Unger notes: "As the importance of informants has grown in recent years, with other methods of investigation closed off, the confidential funds in the Bureau budget that are designated to pay sources have grown substantially larger, into the millions."[67] He describes one F.B.I. informant called "Jack," as an example of how police agencies often end up supporting small-time criminals.

> Jack is a well-dressed, middle-aged man, who, although short on education, is well spoken. He has a way of drawing people into his engaging narratives and would make a perfect companion on a long train ride; he is warm, and, in his own unpolished style, gentle. Jack is also a crook. Though he prefers the term "thief" he would not dispute the characterization. He has held a real job, in a factory, for only one of the last twenty years and instead has made his living mostly by gambling. When gambling goes poorly, he steals—not so much from people as from institutions. Some years back, Jack got into a jam and, as he put it, "made the decision to go with the Bureau." In FBI parlance, he is an "informant," but he prefers to think of himslf as a "source." Whatever the title for the relationship, it has been a mutually beneficial one: he has helped the Bureau solve some sticky criminal cases, has made some money, and has stayed out of jail.[68]

Other court action has relieved the police of some social-control, or victimless crime, responsibility. In *Robinson* v. *California* (1962), the Supreme Court held that heroin addiction could no longer be treated as a criminal act, while in *Easter* vs. *District of Columbia* (1966), a federal district court decriminalized public drunkenness, putting public inebriates in the hands of community service agencies in the capital city. The former police chief of Washington, D.C., Jerry Wilson, claims that such decisions enabled him to redirect police resources to more serious order-maintenance and crime-prevention problems.[69] Therefore, in addition to generally restricting police discretion by imposing due-process requirements on police action, the courts sometimes eliminate criminal laws, relieving the police of certain responsibilities in which they had exercised broad discretion.

LEGISLATURES State legislatures set the crime-prevention agenda for the activities of police departments by developing criminal statutes. However, police tasks such as order maintenance and community service have evolved historically without much oversight from policy-making bodies. Police agencies and street officers therefore carry out these latter functions on their own.

In regard to crime prevention legislators have been quick to enact statutes for nearly every crime imaginable, while remaining reluctant to remove laws that have long lost their bite or have proven impossible to enforce.

State legislatures have therefore created the problem of criminal law overreach—the extension of the criminal law into areas of behavior that might better be regulated by other public institutions or by informal means of social control, like the family, if regulated at all.[70] Some argue that criminal laws concerning narcotics use, gambling, and sexual behavior overload the criminal justice system with morality-enforcement activities (see Chapter 11). Until recently, for example, police officers throughout the country made 2 million arrests a year for violations of public intoxication statutes.[71] Also, laws regulating morality are believed to generate collateral crimes, like the burglaries that heroin addicts, who must purchase drugs on the black market, commit to pay for their habits.[72]

Legislative bodies also fail to address the realities of policing when they enact statutes concerning proper behavior of law enforcement officers. Many legislatures have developed laws that require all officers to enforce every law. For example, an Illinois statute outlining the duties of all police officers in the state reads:

> It shall be the duty of every sheriff, coroner, and every marshal, policeman, or other officer of any incorporated city, town or village, when any criminal offense or breach of the peace is committed or attempted in his presence, forthwith to apprehend the offender and bring him before some judge, to be dealt with according to the law.[73]

Such unrealistic requirements force police chiefs to issue general orders that include full-enforcement language. Police officers, however, see these orders as unresponsive to street realities, and they therefore develop their own policies for determining who to arrest and who to deal with in a less serious manner. In short, legislative mandates and orders by police agencies do little to guide street officers in finding proper levels and methods for enforcement.

COMMUNITY FACTORS

Since the advent of professionalism in many police departments, beginning in the late 1800s and early 1900s, local politicians have exercised less direct control over police priorities. Still, in many cities the local political elite use police resources for protective and ceremonial purposes to serve as bodyguards and chauffeurs. Direct political accountability of the police to local government is accomplished through an elected official's appointment of the police chief. In Minneapolis, for example, the short term and rapid turnover of mayors has meant the appointment of four police chiefs over the last six years.

Also, because of localism, community standards help shape police priorities. For example many small, homogeneous towns may prefer strict enforcement of Sunday blue laws that prohibit the sale of certain goods on the Sabbath, while large, heterogeneous cities in the same state may exhibit little sentiment for such use of police resources.

According to James Q. Wilson, today's police administrators and street officers are also responsible to an indirect barometer of community sentiment—the political culture.[74] He speculates that the chief promotes and officers are responsive to a style of policing that reflects the socioeconomic makeup of the community, the law enforcement standards of the political system, and the concerns of the community elite, such as the business establishments and the media.[75] Specifically, he identifies three styles of policing that tend to shape actual enforcement practices and to guide police officers in deciding what tasks to perform.

The "watchman style" emphasizes order maintenance, largely accomplished through informal policing techniques rather than arrest. The police encourage informal solutions of private disputes and, as in the days of the original watch officers, are less likely to invoke their authority when the disruptive actions are those of the respectable elements of the community. When the police do make arrests, they are less concerned about the proper category of arrest to invoke than they are in choosing a criminal sanction that will adequately restore order. Such a style often emerges in heterogeneous communities with many crime problems; these communities frequently are highly charged with the partisan politics surrounding the election of the mayor and city council.

The "legalistic style" reflects the orientation of police departments that project a professional image. Here, the police are prone to make frequent arrests to show that they are being productive. Order-maintenance issues (e.g., family disputes) are often reinterpreted as crime-prevention problems; the police are more likely to make an arrest than to urge private solutions or use informal tactics, such as calming the parties of a family quarrel. Such a style is most common in cities that rely on council-manager structures, which emphasize efficiency and productivity. In such cities the business community is often directly involved in local government and commands considerable police resources.

In homogeneous, middle-class, suburban communities as well as in smaller towns, the "service style" is likely to dominate policing. Police officers are encouraged to give high priority to all citizens' calls and requests for police assistance. According to Wilson, they "take seriously all requests for either law enforcement or order maintenance (unlike police with a watchman style) but are less likely to respond by making an arrest or otherwise imposing formal sanctions (unlike police with a legalistic style)."[76] Officers are judged on the basis of their interactions with citizens and are expected to project a courteous and responsive demeanor at all times.

ORGANIZATIONAL FACTORS

While police administrators can encourage a certain style of policing, they cannot command the officers in the streets like an army general overseeing troops in battle. As we said at the beginning of the chapter, this "paramilitary pretense" is unrealistic. Street patrol is the major tactic for meeting most police tasks, and officers at headquarters cannot fully control the "cop on the beat."

HEADQUARTERS   At police headquarters a set of yearly routines are performed that are unrelated to street patrol. As we mentioned above, chiefs develop police orders that reflect the orientation of state legislators and local politicians toward police conduct rather than the realities of street policing. Police administrators and headquarters staff spend much of their time preparing the budget, processing recruits, developing training programs, acquiring government grants for research and experimental programs (e.g., crisis intervention teams), and "putting out fires" (i.e., reacting to issues that reach the public agenda, like accusations of police brutality).

Many of the special field units (e.g., S.W.A.T. units, or Special Weapons Attack Teams) do operate under the close scrutiny of headquarters. Each of these special units is usually commanded by a field officer, who expects unit loyalty and disciplined responses to directives. For example, New York City's much heralded hostage negotiating team is under the direct supervision of a detective lieutenant, who participates in nearly all encounters for which the team is requested.[77] Because of the high visibility of this unit's activity, which automatically draws massive on-the-spot press coverage, the "brass" of the city's police department is usually well represented at the scene. When the team was called in to negotiate with an unsuccessful robber who was holding ten hostages inside a Manhattan bank, the commander of that police district, the chief of operations, and the police commissioner were all present and involved in directing overall tactics.[78]

PRECINCTS   The average patrol officer is far removed from routine headquarters scrutiny. Patrol officers work out of precincts or district headquarters and are attached to platoons divided according to the watches or working hours of officers. The principal link between the patrol officer and headquarters is the roll call, which in reality operates much like a locker room meeting of a football team. Loyalty to the platoon and the immediate field supervisor, usually a sergeant, is stressed in a highly informal atmosphere.

Sergeants use roll calls to foster a feeling of platoon harmony and cooperation (often against headquarters) and to present an overview of departmental news. The district or precinct commander's staff usually sifts through the mass of information that flows from headquarters, identifying what the sergeants should read to their platoons. Sometimes officers are given copies of police orders to read and put in their loose-leaf notebook, often called the "police manual." Some officers keep these massive notebooks in the front seat of their patrol cars, but

---

THE RIGHTS OF TAXPAYERS

I am standing at the precinct desk on a slow night and the desk sergeant is kidding with somebody on the phone. When he hangs up I ask whom he was talking to. "Oh, just some guy who likes cops. He calls periodically to tell us how he'd make love to us. Even cops get obscene phone calls." But why talk to him? "Why not? He's a taxpayer, too."

Dan Greenburg, "The Ninth Precinct Blues," *New York Times Magazine*, January 21, 1979, p. 73. 1979 by The New York Times Company. Reprinted by permission.

just as often they may be stored in the trunk while a clipboard with often-used report forms is kept close at hand.

Sergeants use much roll-call time to remind officers of issues relevant to the district and also to promote the self-interests of the assembled group. Officers usually are given only perfunctory warnings about their performance, although comments are sometimes more explicit when complaints have been lodged by local residents or merchants.[79] The warnings contain an appeal to self-interest, revolving around circumstances and conditions in the district that can affect the officers' well-being and the sergeant's reputation. As Jonathan Rubenstein notes, these issues are often presented in a we-against-them context, often pitting the platoon's reputation against snooping by headquarters:

> There is a funny wagon with fake door panels parked on the corner of the 1800 block of Vale Street. [The sergeant warns] "Don't hang around there, and if you get a job in the area do it right, do it quick, and get out." Everyone in the platoon understands that the funny wagon is a blind for a hidden camera used by the department's internal inspection unit, the finks, to conduct secret investigations of complaints against policemen.[80]

The sergeant is usually trusted by patrol officers as a street-level compatriot, but lieutenants and other police officials are closely scrutinized. Although headquarters and district-command positions offer tempting rewards including regular hours and better pay, many patrol officers disdain these positions and dislike those who aspire to such "soft, desk jobs."

This we-against-them attitude, which sociologist Jerome Skolnick has labeled the "working personality" of police,[81] was accentuated in the 1960s, when patrol officers faced increased hostility from blacks and students and perceived a lack of support from top police and city officials. During this era some patrol officers reacted by creating police unions; in the 1970s, these unions have gone on strike in several cities to better job conditions and material benefits.[82] The unions have also served as bastions against change, most recently opposing women on patrol despite recent studies that have shown women to be effective patrol officers.[83]

STREET-LEVEL FACTORS

Some of a patrol officer's decisions follow departmental mandates (e.g., taking down a burglary report). However, each officer is allowed a great deal of discretion in deciding what to do while on the beat, especially when encountering citizens in conflict with laws. Therefore, learning how to be a competent patrol officer usually requires on-the-job training rather than formal classroom learning. In an attempt to make academy and in-service training more realistic, some departments have turned to role playing—where recruits assume the identity of citizens as well as street officers—and to other exercises that simulate street experiences.[84]

When patrol officers are on the street, they are subject to pressures from a variety of sources, including street supervisors (usually sergeants) and radio dispatchers;[85] peer relationships, especially in two-person patrol cars;[86] local merchants and other community notables like the heads of civic organizations;[87] other bureaucrats on whom police depend, such as assistant district attorneys and public health people, who run shelters and detoxification centers for inebriates;[88] and citizens who come to the attention of the police officer. These street-level influences often shape a police officer's decision as to what action should be taken in a given situation. However, according to political scientist William Muir, these street-level influences are less important than organizational directives concerning how to handle a particular situation when the police are carrying out nonthreatening, routine tasks such as "taking reports of burglaries, lost dogs, and missing persons; teaching in school; testifying at trials; and driving the streets."[89]

But Muir also notes that when officers are facing a "critical incident," like a family quarrel or a street fight, they develop "defensive responses," which are based on the accumulation of their street-level learning.[90] Muir found that police officers' responses to these encounters with citizens can be described in one of four ways:

1. Professional—taking charge on the basis of one's ability to talk, on a readiness to explain and exhort, to establish hope, understanding, and fear.
2. Reciprocating—nurturing the citizen's sense of personal obligations to the police officer. In this response, the officer counts on the citizen falling into line out of a sense of gratitude to the officer.
3. Enforcement—an aggressive, impatient and unenlightened response. The officer is not concerned with any changes going on inside the citizen's head and heart. The officer uses words as weapons to incite, never to probe the soul.
4. Avoidance—almost invariably passive, ineloquent, and unintimidating. The officer's response is not luminous like the professional, lenient like the reciprocating, or lunatic like the enforcement response.[91]

How police officers displaying each of these responses are likely to react can be exemplified by a look at incidents on skid row. Three of the four types of responses described above (reciprocating, enforcement, and avoidance) fall outside of the law for handling street-oriented, public drunks. An officer following a reciprocating response may delegate policing skid row to a designated citizen, who represents the interests of the business-people and merchants who work in the area. Muir tells of "Captain Hook," a vigilante, who was paid by local merchants to keep skid-row inebriates in line by using bullying tactics.[92] The police officers in the area looked the other way, delegating the dirty job of handling drunks to this vigilante and allowing him to commit crimes against skid-row inebriates.

Using the enforcement technique, other officers maintain order on skid row by brutalizing certain inebriates (e.g., using force or the threat of physical force to scare them away) who harass merchants. Those brutalized serve as examples to the others, and officers are thereby able to strike fear into the community of street people who congregate in the skid-row area. Patrol officers who remain largely in their patrol cars, rarely interfering with the street scene on skid row, are demonstrating the avoidance response. When interviewed, such officers portray all of the symptoms of being overcome by the drive for personal security:

> A guy worries about the repercussions if you did get into a hot situation. . . . I'm lucky. I've just bought a new house. I got a family. If I got fired, I don't know what I'd do. I could get a job. I'm still young, but when I get older and get fired, what could I do. The salary, it's good, and you live right up to it. Two or three thousand less, and I'd be in a real bind. I earn fifteen thousand dollars but I've got no savings account. If I were to make less money, I'd have to make a lot of changes. I worry about security. I think of it more and more. My house, my daughter, more and more security. So when you see a job that looks like it might blow up, you sometimes want to say, "so what?" and move on.[93]

On the other hand, a professional response requires "developing the beat." The officer establishes relationships with all of the citizens, including the street people. For the skid-row inebriate the professional officer may represent someone to talk to when the street person is totally depressed. For merchants the officer becomes a "good public servant," who resolves problems that genuinely affect business (e.g., keeping inebriates from sleeping off a binge in the doorway of an establishment open for business). All of the citizens around skid row have something to lose if a professional officer moves to another beat.

NEGATIVE EFFECTS OF DISCRETION

While street discretion provides officers with an opportunity to take into account individuals' circumstances and the realities of street life on their beat, it also opens the door to stress, brutality, and corruption. In part, stress is associated with discretion because officers are overwhelmed by conflicting job pressures that come from a variety of organizational and street-level sources. As we depicted above, police orders drawn up at headquarters require police to make arrests for every violation they observe. On the other hand, a supervisory sergeant operating out of a precinct may tell his patrol officers that they are spending too much time in the station house processing petty offenders and too little time on the street maintaining order.

Officers also acquire symptoms of stress because police work is dangerous and unpredictable. While fewer police officers are killed on the job than construction workers, police must be constantly looking out for signs of potential violence. "As a result, the policeman is generally a suspicious person," according to Jerome Skolnick.[94]

Stress is also a by-product of the social isolation associated with police work. Police officers have the authority to arrest lawbreakers 24 hours a day, 7 days a week. As pointed out in the following case, recorded by Skolnick, police officers soon discover that their civilian friends and acquaintances are wary of the authority that they possess:

> Several months after I joined the force, my wife and I used to be socially active with a crowd of young people, mostly married, who gave a lot of parties where there was drinking and dancing, and we enjoyed it. I've never forgotten, though, an incident that happened on one Fourth of July party. Everybody had been drinking, there was a lot of talking, people were feeling boisterous, and some kid there . . . threw a firecracker that hit my wife in the leg and burned her. I didn't know exactly what to do—punch him in the nose, bawl him out, just forget it.
>
> Anyway, I couldn't let it pass, so I walked over to him and told him he ought to be careful. He began to rise up at me, and when he did, somebody yelled, "Better watch out, he's a cop." I saw everybody standing there, and I could feel they were all against me and for the kid, even though he had thrown the firecracker at my wife. I went over to the host and said it was probably better if my wife and I left because a fight would put a damper on the party. Actually, I'd hoped he would ask the kid to leave, since the kid had thrown the firecracker. But he didn't, so we left.
>
> After that incident, my wife and I stopped going around with that crowd, and decided that if we were going to go to parties where there was to be drinking and boisterousness, we weren't going to be the only police there.[95]

Undetected stress can contribute to police brutality or police breaches of due process by the physical abuse of citizens without cause. However, as documented by attorney Paul Chevigny in *Police Power* and a 1977 CBS news series on police brutality in Houston, Texas, a series of such wanton violations of due process usually occurs with the acquiescence of the police hierarchy, government officials, and the community.[96]

Police corruption, or the ignoring of illegal activity in exchange for payoffs, is often associated with drug trafficking, gambling, and prostitution. *The Knapp Commission Report on Police Corruption* uncovered many cases in New York City of uniformed patrol officers receiving regular payments of under $20 from illegal gambling operations run in their patrol areas. However, the commission found corruption to be much more widespread than these small payments to patrol officers:

> It took various forms depending upon the activity involved, appearing at its most sophisticated among plainclothesmen assigned to enforcing gambling laws. In the five plainclothes divisions where our investigations were concentrated we found a strikingly standardized pattern of corruption. Plainclothesmen, participating in what is known in police parlance as a "pad," collected regular bi-weekly or monthly payments amounting to as much as $3,500 from each of the gambling establishments in the area under their jurisdiction, and divided the take in equal shares.

The monthly share per man (called the "nut") ranged from $300 and $400 in midtown Manhattan to $1,500 in Harlem. When supervisors were involved they received a share and a half. A newly assigned plainclothesman was not entitled to his share for about two months, while he was checked out for reliability, but the earnings lost by the delay were made up to him in the form of two months' severance pay when he left the division.[97]

IMPROVING DISCRETIONARY STREET BEHAVIOR

Patrol officers have developed informal techniques for relieving the tensions that often result from unsympathetic and out-of-touch command structures combined with the barrage of critical incidents officers may face on a given day. They stick together, displaying police solidarity, even when a fellow officer commits a minor infraction.[98] They also socialize together, relieving tension by gathering in a safe place to drink and generally let off steam.

Citizens' groups have lobbied for more formal mechanisms to correct the negative effects of discretion. Minority communities have called for the creation of police-community review boards and other community controls to educate the police and make them more responsive to community standards.[99] These suggestions have met with stern opposition from patrol officers and administrators, who fear such actions would undermine police professionalism.[100] Where civilian review boards have been formed, the citizen representatives are given only advisory powers and the citizens are frequently coopted by police spokespersons that come before them, so that boards rarely recommend that officers be sanctioned.

Police departments have implemented a variety of approaches, including improved communication systems, to deal with the negative effects of the discretionary environment. However, relying on the "wonders" of communication technology to produce closer supervision has proven unsuccessful, because police officers always find ways to fall out of touch when they find it necessary. Also, administrative rule making, the attempt of police departments to explicitly spell out priorities and tighten guidelines for the use of the force, ignores many of the organizational realities outlined above.[101]

Still, a 1976 panel of police administrators, citizens, and academicians, formed in Minneapolis to suggest mechanisms for reducing excessive use of force and shootings, recommended rule making as the best solution. According to sociologist David Ward, a member of the panel, "Administrative rulemaking not only means narrowing the limits within which an officer can operate in potentially dangerous situations—the use of a gun, for example—but it also means grappling with . . . what laws are going to be enforced, under what circumstances, and against whom."[102] Other experts assert that street policing requires that patrol officers have considerable flexibility in meeting the unique demands of incidents they encounter. They see administrative rule making as a denial of "the human nature of lower-level public servants."[103]

The most recent attempts of academicians and police administrators to reduce stress, corruption, and brutality involve making the job more satisfying to officers by developing rewards that reflect the tasks that patrol officers usually perform and by injecting more interesting work into the patrol function. Police officers spend much of their time maintaining order and performing community service tasks, but the rewards in many departments are related to crime-prevention criteria. Some experts have proposed recently that police departments give officers credit equal to misdemeanor arrests in assessing their monthly performance record for such tasks as delivering skid-row inebriates to public health facilities or rushing heart attack victims to hospital emergency wards.[104] Police agencies are also starting to implement team policing—decentralizing decision making, assigning detectives to work with small patrol teams, and giving patrol officers investigative responsibility rather than requiring them to turn a crime over to a detective squad.[105] These innovations are designed to bring into harmony the self-interests of patrol officers with the tasks they can best perform. However, to some extent, increasing patrol officers' investigative authority conflicts with the self-interests of detectives, who want to maintain control over field investigations. The future of team policing depends on the ability of police administrators to accommodate the self-interests of both patrol officers and other field personnel, like detectives, in building decentralized systems of policing.

Crime Prevention and Police Tactics

Police are increasingly relying on special units for crime prevention. These new, special units are different than traditional crime-prevention units because they are oriented around proactive rather than reactive strategies. Reactive special units, like homicide detective squads, are formed to respond to a crime after it has occurred. In the last few years police have established proactive special units to defuse incidents before crimes occur (e.g., family crisis intervention units) or to catch perpetrators in the act of committing a crime.

One example of the new proactive units designed to catch law violators in the act is New York City's street crime unit. The street crime unit is made up of 250 policemen and women who focus on such street crimes as purse snatching and muggings by disguising themselves as decoy victims:

> A derelict slumped in the bank doorway, purse spilled open, may have a pistol in her pocket. Since 1970 the streets of New York have been infiltrated by police decoys. The program has paid off, with a drop in crime against the elderly and against taxi drivers, and an arrest rate that is rising.[106]

In the area of property crimes, the Metropolitan Police Department (M.P.D.) of Washington, D.C., along with several federal law enforcement agencies have developed elaborate hoaxes to infiltrate the world of fencing stolen goods.[107] Recently a team of M.P.D. officers, posing as a New York City "mafia don" and his "heavies," pulled a "sting" and recouped $2.5 million in stolen property. The arrests occurred after the police unit had run a successful whole-sale market for purchasing stolen goods for over five months. To celebrate a good year, the disguised don threw a lavish party for participating thieves in a local warehouse. A *New York Times* reporter described the gala:

> The guests, some in tuxedos rented for the occasion, were there for a party to cele-brate the buyers' and sellers' mutual profits from transactions in hot goods.
>
> "Pasquale," a "counterman" at the elaborate fencing operation, leaned over to kiss the leader's ring, admonishing the visitors to "show some respect for the don."
>
> Then the awed guests—burglars, armed robbers and a couple of suspected murderers—were led through a door and handcuffed.
>
> Arrests totaled 60-odd thieves who walked into the police trap—including two who came in on Monday, a day when the story of the Saturday party was headlined in local papers.[108]

Two major problems arise from heavy reliance of police on these proactive special units. First, the police stand the risk of trapping innocent citizens through the use of these aggressive tactics.[109] Second, the special units place police officers in much greater danger than many defensive, or reactive, units because of the possibility of mistaken identity. According to one researcher who has studied the problem, "During the past two years (1973–74), nine sworn members of the NYPD were shot and seriously injured because of encounters of the uniformed police with their civilian-clothed counterparts whose identities were unknown to them."[110]

Police use of proactive strategies to fight crime is likely to grow, especially in large cities. However, both small and large departments alike will undoubt-edly retain patrol as a major field tactic. Most police agencies expanded their budgets in the 1960s largely by increasing the size of support services for their patrol divisions. Most police officers and citizens view patrol as the mainstay of law enforcement agencies' fight against crime.

What needs to change is not the dismembering of patrol as a major police strategy. Instead, the law enforcement community should clearly acknowledge that patrol does and should serve as the bulwark for performing community ser-vices and maintaining order—both of which are traditional functions of law en-forcement agencies in the United States. Citizens should be informed about these critical tasks. Equally important, patrol officers should be trained and rewarded on the basis of their ability to meet these tasks.

Crime prevention should be emphasized as only one of several important functions that the law enforcement community is responsible for implementing. Of course, the performance of this latter task is also of critical importance to the lawyers and judges of the municipal courts, for they rely on the police to identify the clientele of accused individuals who must ultimately be judged innocent or guilty.

SUMMARY

Self-policing, the town constable, and the night watch served as the major instruments of law enforcement until the 1820s. After that era law enforcement agencies in the United States emerged first as politically dominated institutions and recently as professionally oriented agencies.

Today, law enforcement agencies are responsible for performing five essential functions: supporting political and economic elites' decisions, enforcing social ethics, performing community service, maintaining order, and preventing crime. Although order maintenance and community service generally consume the greatest amount of time for most police officers, law enforcement officials and community leaders emphasize crime prevention most.

This country's police power is dispersed among many municipal, state, and federal law enforcement agencies. The federal government has expanded its interest in law enforcement since the mid-1960s, but police power rests largely in local hands. These public law enforcement agencies are supplemented by the private security industry, which has also expanded in recent years.

This diffusion, or atomization, of police power undermines efficiency, creates disparities in the quality of police services, encourages spillover tactics, and leads to friction among competing law enforcement agencies. On the other hand, atomization prevents the emergence of a police state. Informal techniques for correcting the negative effects of atomization are more viable than the creation of metropolitan-wide government.

Policing requires discretion. Legal mandates, community sentiments, organizational realities, and street-level contingencies influence discretionary decision making. Street discretion enables police officers to develop responses that fit the situations they encounter. It also opens the door to police stress, brutality, and corruption. Informal techniques, administrative rule making, and incentive systems have been proposed to cope with the negative effects of discretion.

For crime prevention, police are increasingly relying on special units. Many of these newer units use proactive rather than reactive strategies in responding to crime problems.

FOOTNOTES

[1] Quoted in Kenneth Culp Davis, *Police Discretion* (St. Paul, Minn.: West Publishing, 1975), p. 59.

[2] Ibid., pp. 6–7.

[3] *Arizona Republic*, July 16, 1977, p. B8.

[4] Jonathan Rubinstein, *City Police* (New York: Ballantine Books, 1973), p. 93.

[5] David C. Perry, *Police in the Metropolis* (Columbus, Ohio: Charles E. Merrill, 1973), p. 24.

[6] James F. Richardson, *The New York Police* (New York: Oxford University Press, 1970) p. 7.

[7] Perry, op. cit., p. 27.

[8] Richardson, op. cit., p. 10.

[9] Roger Lane, *Policing the City* (Columbus, Ohio: Charles E. Merrill, 1975), p. 7.

[10] Ibid.

[11] Ibid., p. 3.

[12] Ibid., p. 17.

[13] Perry, op. cit., p. 33.

[14] Wickersham Commission, *Wickersham Commission Reports: No. 14, Report on the Police* (Montclair, N.J.: Patterson Smith, 1968), pp. 97–98.

[15] See *Arizona Republic*, September 6, 1977, p. A12.

[16] See Theodore L. Becker and Vernon G. Murray, eds., *Government Lawlessness in America* (New York: Oxford University Press, 1971), p. 8.

[17] George McManus, "What Does a Policeman Do?" in *Police Community Relations: Images, Roles, Realities*, eds. Alvin W. Cohn and Emilio C. Viano (New York: J. B. Lippincott, 1976), pp. 131–62.

[18] James F. Ahern, *Police in Trouble* (New York: Hawthorn Books, 1972), pp. 152–53.

[19] Herman Goldstein, *Policing a Free Society* (Cambridge, Mass.: Ballinger, 1977), pp. 8–9.

[20] *Arizona Republic*, July 2, 1977, p. A2.

[21] See Emmette S. Redford, *Democracy in the Administrative State* (New York: Oxford University Press, 1969), pp. 39–40.

[22] Perry, op. cit., pp. 8–21.

[23] Ibid., p. 107.

[24] John F. Galliher, L. Patrick Donovan, and David L. Adams, "Small-Town Police: Troubles, Tasks and Publics, *Journal of Police Science and Administration* 3, no. 1 (March 1975), 20.

[25] Ibid., 26.

[26] Perry, op. cit., p. 107.

[27] William W. Turner, *The Police Establishment* (New York: G. P. Putnam's Sons, 1968), p. 36.

[28] Don Whitehead, *The FBI Story* (New York: Random House, 1957), p. 26.

[29] Ibid.

[30] Sanford J. Unger, *FBI* (Boston: Little, Brown, 1976), p. 40.

[31] Ibid., pp. 37–66.

[32] Ibid., p. 41.

[33] Whitehead, op. cit., pp. 92–112.

[34] Ibid., pp. 105–106.

[35] Unger, op. cit., pp. 41–48, 284–88.

[36] Department of Justice Study Group, *Restructuring the Justice Department's Program of Assistance to State and Local Governments for Crime Control and Criminal Justice System Improvement, Report to the Attorney General* (Washington, D.C.: U.S. Government Printing Office, 1977), p. 6.

[37] Ibid., p. 7.

[38] *Report of the National Advisory Commission on Civil Disorders* (New York: E. P. Dutton, 1968).

[39] James B. Jacobs and Samuel B. Megdovitz, "At LEEP's End?: A Review of the Law Enforcement Education Program," *Journal of Police Science and Administration* 5, no. 1 (1977), 1–18.

[40] Department of Justice Study Group, op. cit., p. 29.

[41] Milton Lipson, *On Guard: The Business of Private Security* (New York: New York Times Book Company, 1975), pp. 45–52.

[42] Reported in ibid., p. 232.

[43] Ibid., p. 168.

[44] Quoted in ibid.

[45] Ibid., p. 181.

[46] Perry, op. cit., p. 103.

[47] Elinor Ostrom and Dennis Smith, "On the Fate of 'Lilliputs' in Metropolitan Policing," *Public Administration Review* 36, no. 2 (March/April 1976), 192–200.

[48] Elinor Ostrom et al., *Community Organization and the Provision of Police Services* (Beverly Hills, Calif.: Sage Publications, 1973).

[49] Ostrom and Smith, op. cit., pp. 195–96.

[50] Ibid.

[51] For a general discussion of this problem, consult Lowdon Wingo, "Introduction: Logic and Ideology in Metropolitan Reform," in *Reform of Metropolitan Areas* ed. Lowdon Wingo (Baltimore: Johns Hopkins University Press, 1972), p. 2.

[52] Robin Moore, *The French Connection* (Boston: Little, Brown, 1969), pp. 78–79.

[53] Ibid., pp. 260–61.

[54] Unger, op. cit., p. 411.

[55] Research and Policy Committee, *Reshaping Government in Metropolitan Areas* (New York: Committee for Economic Development, 1970).

[56] Wingo, op. cit., p. 9.

[57] Ibid., p. 33.

[58] See Francis Piven and Richard Cloward, "Black Control of Cities," *New Republic* 157, nos. 14 and 15 (1967), 15–19, 19–21.

[59] Ibid.

[60] *Report of the National Advisory Commission on Civil Disorders*, op. cit., p. 66.

[61] Peter Kihss, "Theft-Damage Cost in Blackout Put at $135 Million out of Total Business Loss in Hundreds of Millions," *New York Times*, (July 22, 1977), p. 19.

[62] Quoted in William K. Muir, Jr., *Police: Streetcorner Politicians* (Chicago: University of Chicago Press, 1977), p. 82.

[63] Ibid., p. 89.

[64] See Joseph Goldstein, "Police Discretion Not to Invoke the Criminal Process: Low-Visibility Decisions in the Administration of Justice," in *Criminal Justice: Law and Politics*, ed. George F. Cole (North Scituate, Mass.: Duxbury Press, 1972), pp. 59–80.

[65] See Herbert Packer, *The Limits of the Criminal Sanction* (Stanford, Calif.: Stanford University Press, 1968).

[66] Jack Swanson, "FBI Probes 4-County Unit for Illegal California Taps," *Arizona Republic*, August 19, 1977, p. A1.

[67] Unger, op. cit., p. 450.

[68] Ibid., pp. 453–54.

[69] Jerry V. Wilson, "Police Discretion and the Public Inebriate" (Unpublished paper from the American University College of Law, 1975).

[70] Norval Morris and Gordon Hawkins, *The Honest Politician's Guide to Crime Control* (Chicago: University of Chicago Press, 1969), pp. 1–29.

[71] Raymond Nimmer, *Two Million Unnecessary Arrests* (Chicago: American Bar Foundation, 1971).

[72] Morris and Hawkins, op. cit., p. 5.

[73] Cited in Davis, op. cit., p. 55.

[74] James Q. Wilson, *Varieties of Police Behavior* (New York: Atheneum, 1971).

[75] Ibid., p. 143.

[76] Ibid., p. 200.

[77] Barbara Gelb, "A Cool-Headed Cop Who Saves Hos-

tages," *New York Times Magazine*, April 17, 1977, pp. 30–33, 87–91.

[78] Ibid., p. 90.

[79] Rubinstein, op. cit., p. 60.

[80] Ibid., p. 61.

[81] Jerome Skolnick, *Justice Without Trial* (New York: John Wiley, 1967), pp. 42–71.

[82] See Harvey A. Juris and Peter Feuille, *The Impact of Police Unions: A Summary Report* (Washington, D.C.: U.S. Government Printing Office, 1973).

[83] Peter B. Block and Deborah Anderson, *Policewoman on Patrol: Final Report* (Washington, D.C.: The Police Foundation, 1974).

[84] Malcolm Bard, *Training Police as Specialists in Family Crisis Intervention* (Washington, D.C.: U.S. Government Printing Office, 1970).

[85] Rubinstein, op. cit., pp. 73–97.

[86] Egon Bittner, "The Police on Skid Row," *American Sociologist Review* 32 (October 1967), 699–715.

[87] David Aaronson, C. Thomas Dienes, and Michael Musheno, "Improving Police Discretion Rationality in Handling Public Inebriates," *Administrative Law Review* vol. 30, no. 1 (Winter 1978), 93–132.

[88] Ibid.

[89] Muir, op. cit., p. 59.

[90] Ibid.

[91] Ibid., pp. 144–46.

[92] Ibid., p. 75.

[93] Ibid., p. 65.

[94] Jerome Skolnick, "A Sketch of the Policeman's Working Personality," in *The Ambivalent Force*, eds. Arthur Niederhoff and Abraham Blumberg (San Francisco, Calif.: Rinehart Press, 1973), p. 136.

[95] Ibid., p. 138.

[96] Paul Chevigny, *Police Power: Police Abuses in New York City* (New York: Pantheon Books, 1969); and Ed Rabel, "CBS Evening News," August 24, 1977.

[97] Commission to Investigate Allegations of Police Corruption, *The Knapp Commission Report on Police Corruption* (New York: George Braziller, 1972).

[98] Skolnick, "A Sketch of the Policeman's Working Personality," op. cit., p. 140.

[99] Rita Mae Kelly, "Increasing Community Influence over Police," in *Police Community Relations: Images, Roles, Realities*, op. cit., pp. 434–61.

[100] Joseph Fink and Lloyd Sealy, *The Community and the Police: Conflict or Cooperation* (New York: Wiley, 1974).

[101] Davis, op. cit., pp. 98–121.

[102] Quoted in Sam Newland, "Review System for Policeman Has Advocates in City," *Minneapolis Tribune*, December 30, 1976, p. 4.

[103] David Perry and Paula Sornoff, *Politics at the Street Level: The Select Case of Police Administration and the Community* (Beverly Hills, Calif.: Sage Publications, 1973), p. 11.

[104] David Aaronson, C. Thomas Dienes, and Michael Musheno, "Improving Police Discretion Rationality in Handling Public Inebriates," *Administrative Law Review*, 29, no. 4 (Fall 1977), 449–52.

[105] Lee P. Brown, "Neighborhood Team Policing and Management by Objectives," *The Police Chief* 49 (November 1976), 72–76; and John Peterson and Mark Pogrebin, "Team Policing: A Modern Approach to the Decentralization of Police Decision-making," *Abstracts on Police Science* 5, no. 1 (January/February 1977), 1–11.

[106] *Arizona Republic*, July 16, 1977, p. B8. See also Andrew Halper and Richard Ku, *New York City Police Department Street Crime Unit* (Washington, D.C.: U.S. Government Printing Office, 1974).

[107] Ben A. Franklin, "Police Party is a Trap for 60 Thieves," New York Times, March 8, 1976, p. L18.

[108] Ibid.

[109] Halper and Ku, op. cit., pp. 57–70.

[110] James J. Green, "Plainclothed Police Personnel: An Identification Problem," *FBI Law Enforcement Bulletin* 44 (April 1975), 16–17.

BIBLIOGRAPHY

Davis, Kenneth Culp. *Police Discretion*. St. Paul, Minn.: West Publishing, 1975.

Jacobs, James B., and Megdovitz, Samuel B. "At LEEP's End?; A Review of the Law Enforcement Education Program." *Journal of Police, Science and Administration* 5, no. 1 (1977), 1–18.

Lane, Roger. *Policing the City*. Columbus, Ohio: Charles E. Merrill, 1975.

Lipson, Milton. *On Guard: The Business of Private Security*. New York: New York Times Book Co., 1975.

Muir, William K., Jr. *Police: Streetcorner Politicians*. Chicago: University of Chicago Press, 1977.

Ostrom Elinor, and Smith, Dennis, "On the Fate of 'Lilliputs' in Metropolitan Policing." *Public Administration Review* 36, no, 2 (March/April 1976), 192–200.

Perry, David C. *Police in the Metropolis.* Columbus, Ohio: Charles E. Merrill, 1973.

Rubinstein, Jonathan. *City Police.* New York: Ballantine Books, 1973.

Skolnick, Jerome. *Justice Without Trial.* New York: John Wiley, 1967.

Unger, Sanford J. *FBI.* Boston: Little, Brown, 1976.

Wilson, James Q. *Varieties of Police Behavior.* New York: Atheneum, 1971.

The New York law firm of Cahill, Gordon, and Reindel is composed of about 125 lawyers, most of them graduates of the nation's most prestigious law schools—Harvard, Yale, Columbia, and the like. The firm's offices are spacious and well decorated; secretaries abound. The firm has its own law library, replete with the latest volumes of statutes and court opinions. While doing work for one client, Trans World Airlines, in its antitrust suit against the financial empire of Howard Hughes, the firm's attorneys put in 58,600 hours on the 11-year-old case. For this work they received an average of $125 an hour, for a total fee of $7.5 million.[1]

In Philadelphia a lawyer nicknamed "Plead 'em Guilty Fenn" practices criminal law. His briefcase serves as his file cabinet, and the corridors of the courthouse are his office.

CHAPTER SIX

ATTORNEYS
Dealers in Justice

Like many criminal lawyers Fenn picks up his clients in courtrooms and jails. In exchange for arranging quick plea bargains, he has been known to take as little as a bottle of whisky. Once, when a client refused to go along in a rape case and insisted on trial, Fenn (who never tries cases) approached a younger lawyer and asked him to try the case for half of the total fee, saying, "There's seven-fifty in it for you." The implication was that the defendant was paying $1,500. However, after winning an acquittal, the astonished young lawyer was shocked to learn that Fenn meant $7.50, not $750—half of the measly $15.00 fee.[2]

The Legal Profession

These contrasting vignettes are not meant to portray the typical lawyer at work and indeed, no two descriptions can accurately represent a cross-section of all attorneys—but they do illustrate two very different worlds within the legal profession. The Wall Street lawyers, representing the rich and the powerful, can go all out for their clients. The criminal lawyer, often defending the poor and the helpless, does the bare minimum in many cases.

What both have in common, however, is their concern for money. Each departs enormously from the myth of the idealistic seeker of truth and justice. Lawyers, like everyone else, have their own interests to protect, and they must shape their practices to flourish or merely to survive within the environments in which they operate.

In this chapter we shall see that lawyers working within the criminal justice system must often manipulate the law and engage in tactics that depart enormously from the Perry Mason image. Shortcomings develop not because lawyers are by nature an evil breed. Rather, the hectic pace, the organizational pressures, the often seamy working conditions, and the frequent economic problems encountered in the practice of criminal law require attorneys to stray from norms of professional conduct in many cases. Prosecuting and representing defendants is a tough business, and lawyers involved in it must respond accordingly.

PERCEPTIONS OF LAWYERS

Americans have mixed feelings about lawyers. On the one hand, we admire and are in awe of the legal profession. Lawyers seem to possess skills of logic and expression that are highly valued, they have a near monopoly on the expertise that is necessary to deal with courts and other government agencies, they have access to people in power, and they can speak the strange language of the law.[3] Moreover, their occasional role in representing the underdog and pursuing justice has given them a heroic image and much popularity. Indeed, 23 presidents have been lawyers, and our legislative bodies are dominated by lawyers. Thus, lawyers have always had an exalted position in American society, and as early as 1830 the astute observer Alexis de Tocqueville claimed that they were the one aristocracy in the country.[4]

On the other hand, Americans have less flattering images of the lawyer. Typical stereotypes include the "Philadelphia lawyer" who uses legal technicalities to make simple matters complicated, the "shyster" who connives and deceives to accomplish dubious ends, the "ambulance chaser" who callously exploits other people's miseries by encouraging accident victims to sue and then skims off a good part of the dividends when other courses of action might be preferable. Many would agree with Dick the butcher, one of the rebels in Shakespeare's *Henry VI, Part II* who wants to take over England and turn it over to the common man. Says Dick, "The first thing we do, let's kill all the lawyers."[5] And surely many would share the opinion of the famous poet John Keats: "I think we may class the lawyer in the natural history of monsters."[6] Indeed, surveys have shown that the public has negative feelings about the legal profession, and those who have used lawyers tend to feel even more hostile toward them than those who have not.[7] While recently this antagonism has also been directed at other elites, like doctors and politicians, most people chuckle with approval when reading the following poem by Carl Sandburg, which captures common sentiments so well:*

> In the heels of the higgling lawyers, Bob,
> Too many slippery ifs and buts and howevers,

Too many hereinbefore provided whereas
Too many doors to go in and out of.

When the lawyers are through
What is there left, Bob?
Can a mouse nibble at it
And find enough to fasten a tooth on?

Why is there always a secret singing
When a lawyer cashes in?
Why does a hearse horse snicker
Hauling a lawyer away?[8]

LAWYERS AND SELF-INTEREST

Probably the major cause of the disdain of lawyers is that people intuitively recognize how devoted to self-interest many lawyers are. The truth about the legal profession contradicts the image of Daniel Webster selflessly trying to save the Union or Abraham Lincoln, the country lawyer who helps all comers at modest fees. In fact, most lawyers have been rather singularly interested in getting as high an income as possible, and the profession as a whole has sold its services to the highest bidder. In his recent scholarly treatise on the history of the legal profession in this country, Jerold Auerbach has documented how the best legal talent joined hands with the business community in the late 1800s to help both gain maximum profits in an expanding capitalist economy.[9] This pattern has continued, and the biggest and most successful law firms do most of their work for corporations, banks, investors, and other economic elites.[10]

The vast disparity in the type of work done by economically successful lawyers and less prosperous ones is a phenomenon sometimes referred to as the stratification of the legal profession. The most highly paid lawyers serve the business world, while other lawyers catering to the lower and middle class reap more modest rewards. Criminal lawyers, with a few well-publicized exceptions, are part of this latter group. Because of this economic fact of life as well as the lim-

A LAWYER'S UNKIND VIEW OF LAWYERS

The legal profession is a whorehouse serving those best able to afford the luxuries of justice offered to preferred customers. The lawyer, in these terms, is analogous to a prostitute. The difference between the two is simple. The prostitute is honest—the buck is her aim. The lawyer is dishonest—he claims that justice, service to mankind, is his primary purpose. The lawyer's deception of the people springs from his actual money-making role; he represents the client who puts the highest fee on the table.

Florynce Kennedy, "The Whorehouse Theory of Law," in *Law Against the People* (1971), pp. 81–82.

ited demand for defense attorneys, large cities have relatively few criminal lawyers. A survey in New York City showed that fewer than 1 percent of all attorneys in Manhattan and the Bronx practice criminal law.[11]

This paucity of criminal lawyers results from the fact that even lawyers of
lower stature have economic gain as their primary motivation. Favored fields of
law are those that are most lucrative—negligence law, where plaintiffs must give
one-third to one-half of their awards to their attorneys; probate law, where lawyers receive a certain percentage of an estate before any inheritors get a penny;
real estate law, where lawyers must receive their fees before the deal is legally
closed.

There are, to be sure, altruists in the law, lawyers who sacrifice good incomes to help the downtrodden and the dispossessed. The name of Clarence
Darrow comes quickest to mind, for he gave up a highly successful law practice
representing railroads to defend the impoverished employees of those same
railroads who were striking for better wages. More recently, Emanuel Bloch
devoted his entire savings, his health, and ultimately his life to defending Julius
and Ethel Rosenberg, who were executed in 1953 after being convicted of giving
the secret of the atom bomb to the Soviet Union.[12]

But in the main, lawyers have been self-serving rather than other-serving.
As we discuss the role of attorneys in the criminal justice system in the remainder of this chapter, we shall emphasize the self-interest that guides their behavior. Criminal lawyers, both public employees and private ones, are no worse
a breed than those who practice civil law. They are concerned about themselves,
as are police, judges, prison guards—and criminals. But the nature of criminal
practice, the limited resources of defendants, and the constricted opportunities
of those who work for the government require criminal lawyers to engage in activities that are more obviously self-centered and that depart greatly from the
model of the adversary system.

Prosecutorial Discretion: Verdicts Without Trials

The single most powerful figures in the criminal justice system are the prosecutors, or district attorneys, who represent the government in criminal cases.
They have enormous discretion and influence in important ways the fate of those
accused of crime. After arrests are made by police, and sometimes even before,
prosecutors make decisions that determine how justly and fairly those accused of
crime are to be treated. Their decisions on priorities in law enforcement effectively make some criminal behavior permissible and other criminal acts much
more serious. They are judges without robes.

We shall see that prosecutors are part lawyer, part bureaucrat, and part
politician. Their judgments are *not* routine administrative decisions but complex
assessments of many different factors. They are egocentric; yet their immediate

interest is not in money but in convenience and organizational approval. The justice they hand out is individualized, not standardized—for better or for worse.

THE DISTRICT ATTORNEY'S OFFICE: A STEPPING STONE

At the local level the prosecutors, who are normally called district attorneys, are elected officials serving entire counties. In most large cities candidates run for the office as members of political parties, but in some smaller areas there is no partisan affiliation listed on the ballot. Although many local elections are characterized by widespread popular indifference and massive ignorance of the candidates due to "voter fatigue" (the inability to keep track of many different offices), the race for district attorney often attracts a great deal of public interest as a result of the centrality of the crime issue. Police chiefs are appointed and judges are too numerous to keep track of, so, by default, the desire of voters to have a voice in criminal justice matters is focused on the district attorney's office.

District attorneys are responsible for pursuing all criminal matters on behalf of the government, and in most jurisdictions neither police nor victims of crimes can commence actions against suspects in serious cases without their participation. Thus, the office combines enormous legal authority with considerable political sensitivity.

Because of the visibility of the office (largely provided by the mass media), many aspiring politicians perceive it as an excellent position in which to make a name for themselves and to establish a supportive constituency. It has often been a launching pad for higher political office: Tom Dewey's climb to governor of New York and two-time presidential candidate started when he was district attorney of Manhattan; and Washington Senator Warren Magnuson's 40-year career in Congress was preceded by a stint as prosecuting attorney in Seattle. Over half of all state judges have held the position of state's attorney or district attorney, and the Ninety-fourth Congress had 17 senators and 58 representatives who were former prosecutors.[13]

Even those district attorneys who do not covet higher office rarely see the job as a career position. There are exceptions, such as Frank Hogan, who served so long as district attorney of Manhattan that he was dubbed "Mr. District Attorney." But for all elected prosecutors the average tenure in office is only one and a half terms.[14]

We shall see that many of the judgments of district attorneys are predicated on their need to maintain public approval, whether they are seeking to ascend the political ladder or are merely concerned about possible reelection. This was visibly demonstrated in New York City, when a suspect was captured in the case of "Son of Sam" (the .44-caliber killer who picked female victims at random). The killings had taken place in three of New York's boroughs (Brooklyn, Queens, and the Bronx), each of which has a separate district attorney. The night the suspect was apprehended, the three D.A.'s argued into the wee hours of the morning over where the defendant would be arraigned and tried first, each of them wanting the publicity that the court hearings would generate. Moreover, when a confidential psychiatric report concluding that the suspect was psychologically unfit to stand trial was delivered to the presiding judge in Brooklyn, district attorney of Queens John Santucci (who was in the midst of a tough reelection struggle) chose to violate confidentiality, leak excerpts of the report to the press, and take advantage of the opportunity to lambast any soft treatment of the defendant.[15]

In most urban areas, however, the elected district attorney has little to do with the day-to-day conduct of the office. He or she sets some general policies but leaves the routine processing of defendants to subordinates, who are variously known as assistant district attorneys (A.D.A.'s) or deputies. They occupy appointed positions: Some obtain their jobs as a result of competitive civil service examinations, but most are political appointees who have connections of some kind with the dominant political party. Salaries are not high; whereas some top Wall Street law firms hire new lawyers just out of law school for $25,000, most A.D.A.'s make between $12,000 and $15,000 as a starting salary. As a result, the best students from the top law schools rarely seek such positions, and those who do take the job normally stay for only one or two years.

Since few cases go to trial and what little trial work exists is sometimes reserved for the few senior people who remain on the job a long time, assistants are often relegated to the role of handling routine paperwork, showing up at court appearances, and arranging case dispositions without trial. Consequently, after the initial satisfaction of controlling people's lives has ebbed, the work can become quite stultifying. The job is used to gain practical experience which will be useful later in more lucrative private practice and occasionally as an entrée into politics.

In the federal system the structure of the prosecutor's office is somewhat different. Responsibility for prosecuting those accused of breaking federal laws (e.g., robbing post offices or transporting stolen cars across state lines) lies with the Department of Justice, which is headed by the attorney general who is appointed by the president with confirmation by the Senate. The Justice Department contains various divisions, such as the Antitrust Division, the Civil Rights Division, and the Criminal Division; each is headed by an assistant attorney general. However, these individuals are in charge of setting general policies, and the routine task of processing criminal cases falls to United States attorneys and their assistants, who work in 94 judicial districts spread throughout the country.

The position of United States attorney is clearly a patronage job: the president makes the appointments on the recommendation of the senators or representatives of his party who represent the state where there is an opening. While the assistants to the United States attorneys are sometimes hired on a merit basis, many are selected because of their affiliations with incumbent politicians. Thus, in September 1977 the highly rated United States attorney for northern New Jersey (Jonathan Goldstein), who had been appointed by President Nixon (a Republican), was forced to resign because Democratic Senator Harrison Williams prevailed upon President Carter (a Democrat) to put one of Williams's protégés in the office.[16]

Thus, politics plays a role in the selection of both local district attorneys and United States attorneys. How does this affect the running of the office? The answer depends on the type of case. Commonplace cases involving burglary or robbery, in which the media take little interest, are treated very differently from publicized cases involving powerful individuals in the community or particularly heinous crimes. The ordinary cases are treated routinely by assistants, whereas the highly visible cases with political ramifications receive the guidance of top officials.

Because assistants are highly autonomous in their handling of cases and the top prosecutors are rather remote from ongoing dispositions, the handling of ordinary cases is not affected very much by politics. Political scientist Herbert Jacob compared the performance of a "machine"-supported district attorney and his successor, who was a "reformer" and supported by very different elements in the city of New Orleans.[17] The way the office ran under both men was fairly similar in terms of numbers and kinds of dismissals, conviction records, and sentences meted out to those convicted. Likewise, a study of a district attorney's office in a large California city indicated that top officials had very little influence on routine cases.[18]

This does *not* mean that assistants were oblivious to the impact of prosecutorial decisions on the community; quite the contrary. First, some cases (such as those involving public figures) have immediate repercussions on those in power, and these tend to be treated specially. Second, depending on the ideology of the top prosecutor, certain law enforcement priorities do shift to some degree (such as the decline in prosecution of civil rights violators and the simultaneous crackdown on drug offenders when President Nixon's attorney general, John Mitchell, took office). Third, the assistants' interest in maintaining a good public image for the office and doing nothing to disgrace their politically oriented superiors transcends the outright favoritism of partisan politics.[19]

Thus, politics always lurks in the background in the prosecutor's office. But only occasionally does it become a conscious factor in decision-making.

THE RANGE OF CHOICES

Prosecutors, like police, invariably use their discretion to engage in selective law enforcement. What this means is that they choose whether to pursue, downplay, or altogether overlook possible criminality. Not only do they have the legal right to decline prosecution after the police make an arrest but they are able to make other kinds of decisions that determine how alleged criminals will be treated.

DISMISSING CHARGES Following an arrest, the prosecutor must determine whether to press charges or dismiss them. This decision is made through a variety of procedures, depending on the procedural law and customary practices of different localities. In many cities prosecutors simply take the police or citizen complaint that has been forwarded to them and announce at an early court hearing that they will not prosecute. This is technically called a *nolle prosequi*, and a dismissed case is said to be *nolled* or *nol. prossed*. In Detroit, this procedure is used little, but prosecutors scrutinize all police arrests and issue warrants legitimating the arrest only when they desire to prosecute. Elsewhere other technical procedures are used.[20] All have the same function—to screen out those cases that for one reason or another do not warrant prosecution in the prosecutors' estimation.

Dismissals account for a large percentage of the total case dispositions (i.e., the number of cases handled by the criminal justice system). For example, in Chicago narcotics courts prosecutors voluntarily dismiss 55 percent of all charges filed by the police.[21] In Los Angeles half of all felony cases are terminated by the prosecutor.[22] While the precise figures vary from place to place, it is clear that many defendants are absolved through the unilateral action of prosecutors rather than the verdicts of judges and juries.

While these decisions are usually ad hoc assessments of the merits of individual cases, sometimes they reflect general office policies. Thus, Manhattan District Attorney Robert Morgenthau authorized his assistants to dismiss all charges against persons caught with less than two ounces of marijuana as a means of unclogging court calendars. In effect, Morgenthau was legalizing the use of this drug by making his policy widely known.[23]

SELECTING THE CHARGES   Criminal incidents often entail the breaking of several laws. For example, a drunk person who mugs someone on a subway train with a gun may have committed the crimes of robbery, assault, larceny, possession of an illegal weapon, disorderly conduct, harassment, and public intoxication. After evaluating the situation, the police make a decision to allege certain specific criminal acts from among these possibilities, and the suspect is "booked" at the police station (i.e., a formal complaint is made against the suspect). While this judgment limits the discretion of a prosecutor, he or she still has enormous latitude.

In most jurisdictions the prosecutor may determine whether to institute a single charge (e.g., robbery) or multiple charges (e.g., robbery, assault, and larceny). The prosecutor chooses whether to select serious charges (e.g., armed robbery) or minor ones (e.g., disorderly conduct). Also, certain crimes, such as murder, are graded by degree of seriousness. The normal uncertainty about the facts prior to trial allows the prosecutor to make a choice.

These kinds of decisions are very consequential. The punishments attached to various crimes differ enormously. For example, in New York robbery is a felony punishable by up to 25 years imprisonment, while the misdemeanor of public intoxication calls for a maximum of 30 days in jail. Moreover, since a person faced with serious charges is exposed to greater risk than would be so with minor charges, he or she may feel more constrained to plea bargain to avoid a long prison term (see below).

A good example of the exercise of this kind of discretion was the decision of

Special Prosecutor Leon Jaworski to charge the many corporate executives who illegally contributed corporate funds to President Nixon's reelection campaign fund with misdemeanors instead of felonies. Jaworski himself points out that "the evidence in almost all instances would have supported the felony charge, but on balance it seemed fair to charge the volunteers [those who admitted guilt] with the misdemeanor violation."[24] As a result, not one of these executives served a day in jail, and the maximum fine imposed was $2,000.[25]

Another facet of selecting the charges is determining the number of "counts" of any particular crime to accuse the defendant of committing. A count is a specific criminal act, and an incident may entail a large number of distinct violations of the same law. Thus, a criminal who goes on a check-forging spree can be charged with a separate count for every wrongful check that is written. A person who commandeers a bus or a plane and demands ransom can be charged with separate acts of kidnapping against every passenger aboard. Again, deciding whether to charge a person with one, a few, or many counts may have a bearing on the ultimate penalty imposed if there is a conviction.

These decisions have a crucial bearing on subsequent plea bargaining. Prosecutors sometimes institute at the outset more charges than are warranted by the evidence so that they have flexibility in negotiating with the defendant. This practice, called "overcharging," often plays a key role in obtaining the defendant's cooperation, because it makes the defendant vulnerable to disastrous consequences should he or she opt for a trial and lose. Prosecutors risk nothing by overcharging because they can always reduce the charges later on their own initiative if they are faced with the task of proving guilt before a judge or jury.

INVESTIGATING POSSIBLE ILLEGALITY   Not only does the district attorney's office follow up on police arrests but it often is involved in prior investigations of criminal activity. To intercept certain kinds of crimes like fraud, price fixing, and vice (prostitution, gambling, etc.), authorities must actively and aggressively probe. District attorneys are often involved in this quest.

Decisions must be made concerning allocation of investigators. Should they be deployed in search of organized crime operations? Should political terrorists be scouted? What about corporate executives who engage in illegal business practices? Since public attorneys have limited resources, they must decide where to concentrate their attention.

A good example of the exercise of this kind of discretion was the choice by Cook County (Illinois) District Attorney Edward Hanrahan to pursue the alleged violent activities of the Black Panther party in Illinois. His decision to raid the headquarters of the party in search of illegal weapons resulted in the death of the leaders of the party and was the subject of much controversy. Critics lambasted not just his procedures (such as breaking down the doors of the leaders' apartment at 5:00 A.M. and commencing a fusillade of bullets) but the entire crusade against black political militants. Indeed, the political flak that resulted caused top leaders of the Democratic party, including Mayor Daley of Chicago, to "disown" him and led to his rejection by the voters in his bid for reelection.

In addition to deciding on targets of investigation, public attorneys must choose how intensively to go after various kinds of criminals. It was widely alleged that the United States attorneys for the District of Columbia were lax in their search for White House officials who might have been involved in the Watergate burglary and cover-up. Senator Sam Ervin, who chaired the Senate Watergate Committee, severely castigated them for being unable to discover high-level involvements and for ending their investigation with convictions of only those caught on the scene.

In contrast to these allegedly timorous forays by prosecutors were the vigorous efforts of the Pittsburgh district attorney's office probing the shooting of Joseph Yablonski, an activist in the United Mine Workers Union who tried to wrest control from the established leadership and who was killed during a campaign to become the union's president. Many assistants and thousands of dollars were allocated to this case, resulting in the amassing of evidence that tied Yablonski's opponent, Tony Boyle (the incumbent president), to the murder. Boyle was ultimately convicted of being an accessory to murder before the fact and of being in the conspiracy that plotted the crime.[26]

THE POWER TO DISCLOSE One of the most crucial elements in defending an accused person is knowing what kind of evidence the prosecution has obtained—who the witnesses are, what physical evidence has been found, what the results of any laboratory tests are, and so forth. Defense attorneys have a legal right to some access to these materials, but in actuality a great deal depends on the cooperativeness of the prosecutors. Their decision to provide maximum disclosure or to maintain secrecy (or to take some middle ground) can affect how well the defense is prepared at trial and, even more important, how rational the defendant's deliberations about plea bargaining can be.

IMMUNITY FROM PROSECUTION Prosecutors can give immunity from prosecution to persons knowledgeable about crime or even involved in it in exchange for their testimony against others. Because many of these people would incriminate themselves if they answered prosecutors' questions, they often invoke their Fifth Amendment right to remain silent unless they are given legally binding assurances that they themselves will not be accused (called "transactional immunity"). A less comprehensive variation of this privilege is called "use immunity": No testimony given will be used against a witness, but charges may be made on the basis of information that is independently obtained. Both kinds of immunity are a way of "buying" information from those involved in crime, and such immunity is frequently extended to small-time criminals (like street peddlers of narcotics) to obtain evidence against their superiors.

RETRYING CASES If a jury fails to reach agreement on a verdict, a mistrial is declared by the judge, which means that the entire trial is considered faulty and is terminated. Prosecutors then have the option of either dismissing charges or commencing a new trial. Similarly, if a conviction is overturned by an appellate court because of an illegal procedure used at the trial (e.g., admission of improper testimony), the prosecutor must decide whether to retry the case. For example, after the murder conviction of boxer Reuben "Hurricane" Carter was overturned by the New Jersey Supreme Court in 1977, the prosecutor decided to try him again even though the crime took place 11 years earlier and Carter had already served 10 years in prison. Some had urged the prosecutor to dismiss the charges in the interest of fairness and justice, which he had a perfect right to do; but he chose not to, and Carter was reconvicted (although he has appealed the verdict in the second trial).

Just how awesome prosecutorial control over retrying can be was manifested in the case of William Rose, Jr., a black Marine Corps sergeant and Vietnam veteran who was indicted for the murder of a white police officer in Brooklyn on March 18, 1972. Four trials were held, three of which failed to produce a unanimous verdict and one of which resulted in a conviction that was reversed on appeal. After each inconclusive outcome, the Brooklyn district attorney's office opted for another trial. Rose's ordeal did not end until the presiding judge dismissed the case at the beginning of the fifth trial, saying that "the defendant had been badgered enough." Before the case was terminated in 1977, however, the defendant had spent five years in jail while the prosecutor had vainly tried to convict him.[27]

OTHER PROSECUTORIAL OPTIONS   The prosecutor decides (often subconsciously) how hard to fight in those few cases that go to trial: The average trial preparation takes no more than a few days, and the average trial lasts less than two days. But in the case of mass murderer Charles Manson, Los Angeles Deputy Prosecutor Vincent Bugliosi worked exclusively on the case virtually seven days a week for a year and a half, producing a trial that cost $1 million, lasted seven months, and resulted in a trial transcript of 31,716 pages.[28] Prosecutors recommend sentences to the judge and must choose whether to be tough or lenient. They can also suggest alternatives to prosecution, such as drug treatment programs, commitment to mental institutions, or, in the case of youngsters nearing adult status (i.e., 15 or 16 years old), referral to juvenile court. They decide whether to appeal cases to appellate courts if trial judges rule against them on points of law. And finally, they negotiate with the defense concerning reduction of charges in exchange for pleas of guilty—a topic so important that we shall devote a whole section to it later in this chapter.

CRITERIA USED IN DECISION MAKING

A complex interaction of self-interest and the public interest dictates how the various choices described above are made. An underlying factor, of course, is that the system lacks the resources to cope with all offenders. Even plea bargaining requires the expenditure of funds (e.g., for keeping some defendants incarcerated) and the use of personnel. The several hundred assistant district attorneys in large cities would be overloaded and actually paralyzed if they pressed charges against all of the tens of thousands of people arrested for felonies annually by police. The crucial questions, then, are: Who gets acquitted (or mildly chastised) by prosecutors, and who is made to feel the full brunt of criminal sanctions?

NATURE OF THE EVIDENCE The most common reason for dropping charges is that the evidence is insufficient to make the charges stick if the case goes to trial. A study of one California city showed that prosecutors regularly dismissed cases where they were convinced that the police made a mistake and arrested the wrong person.[29] Even incriminating evidence obtained in an obviously illegal manner by police and likely to be excluded by a judge will not be accepted; prosecutors often dismiss charges under such circumstances in many narcotics cases.[30] Not only are prosecutors concerned about exonerating the innocent and (to a lesser extent) curtailing police irregularities, but they want to eliminate cases that they will probably lose. Dismissing the weak cases is a way of assuring that the rate of convictions will be kept high, and having a high "batting average" is in the self-interest of prosecutors.

COOPERATION FROM VICTIMS Often lack of evidence results from the unwillingness of victims to cooperate and testify against defendants. Such reticence is not uncommon, especially when the victim and the defendant had a prior relationship, which is frequently the case in crimes of violence. In fact, a study of felony dispositions in New York City shows that 69 percent of all dismissals result from such noncooperation, and the figure is as high as 86 percent for the crime of rape.[31] Often the parties become reconciled before trial, but in many cases the victim simply fails to show up in court for unknown reasons. Thus, prosecutors are critically dependent on assistance from victims to gain convictions, and if it is not forthcoming, they often have little recourse but to dismiss charges.

INTERPRETATIONS OF LAW Sometimes prosecutors base their decisions not to prosecute on interpretations of the law rather than assessment of the facts. Legislatures and appellate courts are continuously changing the precise definitions of various offenses, and prosecutors react accordingly.

For example, the definition of what qualifies as obscene literature has been fluctuating for many years, and prosecutors are constantly second-guessing police determinations. The criteria developed by the Supreme Court of what is obscene (and therefore *un*protected by the First Amendment's guarantee of free speech) include such vague factors as whether a book or movie appeals to "prurient interests," whether it violates "contemporary community standards" regarding sexual expression, and whether the work has "redeeming social value." These are very elusive legal standards made even more uncertain by the Court's vacillation and inconsistency in defining them. Thus while the Burger Court ruled in 1973 that localities were free to define their own standards concerning sexual expression,[32] a year later the same Court held that this discretion was not unbridled in over-

"JUDGING" BY THE PROSECUTOR: THE SCREENING PROCESS

Authorities have dropped charges against a 33-year old Vietnam veteran who began sniping at a police station [in the Boston suburb of Quincy] with a sawed-off shotgun, after a Veterans Administration doctor said he was a victim of "traumatic war neurosis" [commonly known as "shell shock."]

John R. Coughlin served in Vietnam during 1966 and 1967 and his severe leg wound required 18 months of extensive surgery before it healed. . . .

Coughlin, now 33, did his sniping from Mt. Wollaston Cemetery, across the street from the station, where two of his war buddies were buried.

Doctors later theorized that when Coughlin began hearing voices and seeing images, the cemetery became a battlefield in his mind, full of Viet Cong. . . .

At the insistence of Assistant Norfolk County District Attorney Gerald Kirby, the charges against Coughlin were dropped last week. District Attorney Willaim D. Delahunt conceded the veteran was not criminally responsible for his actions that May morning.

Sunday Freeman, February 4, 1979, p. 9.

turning the decision of a Georgia jury that had found the widely acclaimed movie, *Carnal Knowledge,* obscene.[33] This has created a difficult situation for the police who must make on-the-spot judgments in deciding whether to arrest booksellers or theater managers dealing with erotic materials. Prosecutors, who are more knowledgeable about constitutional law, often have different opinions and therefore drop charges against those arrested.

SERIOUSNESS OF THE CRIME   Another concern in the decision about whether to prosecute is an assessment of the seriousness of the offender's criminal behavior. Frequently cases are dismissed when the action of the suspect, though illegal, appears to be rather trivial. Thus, the Brooklyn district attorney recently dropped gambling charges against some old men who were playing small-stakes pinochle in a park and who were arrested by an overzealous police officer. Likewise, a New Jersey district attorney dismissed charges against a man who was caught carrying legally prescribed pills in a different container than the one in which they were originally dispensed. The law was intended to prevent the illegal transfer of narcotics from legitimate users to others rather than to keep people from using pillboxes for convenience; so, even though there was a technical violation of the law, the charges were dismissed. Prosecution of such cases would expose prosecutors to public ridicule, for it seems unjust to punish people for such minor harmless infractions.

SOCIAL CLASS OF OFFENDERS AND VICTIMS   When cases are either weak in terms of evidence or of only moderate seriousness, or both, sometimes the prosecutor's assessment of the relative equities of the victims and the defendant plays a role in the prosecuting decision. The prosecutor can be empathetic, hostile, or neutral toward either party, and that factor can be pivotal if there is doubt whether to press charges. Thus a courteous, well-dressed white businessman caught with liquor on his breath after a traffic accident might be treated quite differently from a belligerent black youth caught in similar circumstances.

PUBLIC OPINION   It is not always the personal preference of prosecutors that underlies the decision to prosecute but their assessment of the community's feelings about particular victims and offenders. If public opinion is especially strong, prosecutors may press charges to win popular support even if the legal or factual foundations of the case are weak. Many feel that the prosecution of Angela Davis, a Communist-affiliated, black philosophy professor at the University of California, for her alleged role in furnishing the gun to a defendant (Jonathan Jackson) who killed a California judge, was dictated by the prosecutor's desire to win political plaudits from conservatives.

Attorney General John Mitchell (appointed by President Nixon in 1969) may have been similarly motivated when he instituted federal antiriot charges against eight people involved in the battle between police and demonstrators during the Democratic National Convention in Chicago in 1968. His predecessor, Ramsey Clark (who served under President Johnson), did not think the evidence warranted prosecution in light of the provocative behavior of the police. But Nixon had been elected largely on the basis of his appeal for "law and order" and his condemnation of disruptive protests, and some say the decision to reverse Clark's decision and begin prosecution was intended to show that the Nixon Administration would fulfill its promises. Such, indeed, was Clark's own assessment. It was "politics, pure and simple," according to Clark. "The same lawyers in the Department who reported to me that proceedings against the demonstrators could not be justified must have reported the same thing to Mitchell. But with the same information he reached a different conclusion."[34]

BIASES OF THE PROSECUTOR   Sometimes the personal ideology of prosecutors is significant in pressing charges. For example, some argue that Manhattan District Attorney Frank Hogan's continued prosecution of nightclub comedian Lenny Bruce for obscenity and drug charges stemmed from his own puritanical nature rather than from a cool judgment about the evidence against Bruce or the seriousness of his crimes. For example, Vincent Cuccia, one of the assistant district attorneys who worked under Hogan, made the following observations after Bruce died in 1966 of a drug overdose:

> I feel terrible about Bruce. We drove him into poverty and bankruptcy and then murdered him. I watched him gradually fall apart. It's the only thing I did in Hogan's office I'm really ashamed of. We all knew what we were doing. We used the law to kill him.[35]

Occasionally outright favoritism or animosity toward particular individuals enters the decision on whether to prosecute. This is especially frequent with regard to politicians who engage in dubious conduct and who sometimes benefit from the fact that their allies hold the prosecutor's office; however, these same politicians can become vulnerable if the office shifts to the opposition. A good example is the fate of some of Mayor Daley's associates—including his right-hand man in the City Council, Alderman Tom Keane—who after years of engaging in corruption with impunity were prosecuted when Republicans gained control of the Cook County district attorney's office as well as the regional office of the United States attorney.

Another case of a personal vendetta was the successful attempt of Attorney General Robert Kennedy to convict Teamsters Union President James Hoffa. A special "get Hoffa" squad was created in the Justice Department with the job of finding some criminal charges that could be pinned on Hoffa. According to law professor Monroe Freedman:

> From the day that James Hoffa told Robert Kennedy that he was nothing but a rich man's kid who never had to earn a nickel in his life, Hoffa was a marked man. When Kennedy became Attorney General, satisfying this grudge became the public policy of the United States, and Hoffa was singled out for special attention by United States Attorneys.[36]

Clearly, cases involving prominent members of the community do receive special attention because of the political implications of deciding whether or not to prosecute. In Seattle all such cases are immediately referred to the district attorney for disposition rather than to an assistant.[37] Similarly, the decision to prosecute Bert Lance, President Carter's first director of the Office of Management and Budget, for violating federal banking laws was made at the highest level of the Justice Department because it so affected the political standing of the Carter Administration.

EXCHANGE RELATIONSHIPS   Finally, any decisions of prosecutors about prosecuting are made in light of their need to get along with others in the criminal justice system—what are sometimes called "exchange relationships." Prosecutors must be responsive to the needs of police, judges, defense lawyers, and corrections officers if some semblance of coordination is to be maintained. For example, because prosecutors are so dependent on police for effective testimony in many cases, special care is normally taken not to offend police. Thus, prosecutors are quite reluctant many times to press charges against police officers accused of brutality unless the evidence against the officers is overwhelming or the public furor is substantial.

The exchange relationships prosecutors have with defendants and their lawyers are of greatest consequence. Indeed, the process of plea bargaining is the single activity that occupies the greatest part of the average prosecutor's and defense lawyer's time. Working together, prosecutors and defense lawyers are responsible for the ultimate disposition of most criminal cases. Thus, to a very significant extent the fate of defendants depends on lawyer-to-lawyer interactions conducted out of court. It is this prevalent and decisive system of backroom justice to which we now direct our attention.

Plea Bargaining: A Cooperative Endeavor

Plea bargaining is a system by which the prosecution agrees to permit lesser punishment of offenders than might otherwise be possible in exchange for their agreement to plead guilty. State penal codes and legal procedures vary, so that the transaction is accomplished in a variety of ways. But the same basic process takes place and the same functions are served.

Plea bargaining is a common means of obtaining convictions. In fact, around 90 percent of all convictions are the result of guilty pleas, and most of these are secured through negotiation. Specifically, a study of all felony dispositions in New York City in 1971 shows the following: 98 percent of the convictions were disposed of by guilty pleas instead of trials; 74 percent of the guilty pleas were to misdemeanors or lesser offenses; 50 percent of the guilty pleas resulted in "walks" (no incarceration); and only 9 percent of the guilty pleas resulted in a sentence of more than one year in prison.[38] Another New York study showed that eight out of every ten persons accused of homicide in 1973 pled guilty to a lesser charge and received either probation or no more than ten years imprisonment.[39] Table 6-1 shows the percentage of guilty pleas in various jurisdictions, suggesting that the widespread use of plea bargaining in New York is typical. While guilty pleas in themselves do not indicate the presence of plea bargaining,

TABLE 6-1

Proportion of Convictions Represented by Guilty Pleas in Various Courts

State [1]	Total Convictions	Guilty Pleas as Percent of Total
California (1965)	30,840	74.0
Connecticut	1,596	93.9
District of Columbia	1,115	73.3
Hawaii	393	91.5
Illinois	5,591	85.2
Kansas	3,025	90.2
Massachusetts (1963)	7,790	85.2
Minnesota (1965)	1,567	91.7
New York	17,249	95.5
Pennsylvania (1960)	25,632	66.8
United States district courts	29,170	90.2
Average (exc. Pa.)		87.0

[1] Statistics are for 1964, unless otherwise stated
SOURCE: President's Commission on Law Enforcement and Administration of Justice, *Task Force Report; The Courts* (Washington, D.C.: U.S. Government Printing Office, 1967), p. 9.

it is implausible to assume that so many would plead guilty in the absence of any inducement to do so.

The most common method of plea bargaining involves a reduction in the number of charges against a defendant and, normally, the dismissal of the most serious ones in exchange for a plea of guilty to whatever is left. Sometimes the defendant may plead guilty to specific crimes that technically he or she did not commit. The crucial element is agreement (either explicitly or implicitly) among prosecutor, defense counsel, defendant, and judge about the sentence to be imposed—which may well be just (i.e., proportionate to the offense) even if the defendant really pleads guilty to the wrong crime.

Consolidation of several counts may also serve the purpose of reducing the maximum sentence that can be handed down. States like Ohio, which have indeterminate sentences that are set by the parole board rather than the judge, accomplish plea bargaining by negotiating on multiple-count indictments (i.e., reducing the number of crimes of the same type charged). Also the judge has latitude about imposing concurrent prison terms, which run simultaneously, or consecutive ones. Use of concurrent sentences restricts the length of time prison authorities can hold convicts, so it can be a major bargaining point.

Some cities, like Los Angeles and Pittsburgh, seem to carry on relatively little plea bargaining and hold a high percentage of trials, but in reality what takes place are many "slow pleas."[40] These are informal trials, sometimes simply relying on the transcript of the preliminary hearing, in which the defense presents mitigating material in order to obtain leniency. While the defendant formally pleads "not guilty," his or her willingness to accept an abbreviated trial is tantamount to an admission of guilt. There is the pretense of a trial, but actually the process is a disguised plea bargain.[41]

After an agreement has been reached, a court hearing must be held to secure formal approval. What follows is a typical courtroom dialogue that takes place during the judicial ceremony ratifying the plea bargain that has been made:*

> Bailiff: All rise.
>
> Court Clerk: People versus Randolph for trial.
>
> Assistant District Attorney: Your Honor, with leave of the Court the People move that the information [i.e., the formal accusation] in this case be deemed amended by adding Count Four thereto alleging that on or about the date alleged in the other counts the defendant, Peter Randolph, did unlawfully enter the premises in question, a misdemeanor.
>
> Assistant Public Defender: If Your Honor please, at this time the defendant Peter Randolph consents to the amendment proposed by the assistant district attorney and tenders a plea of guilty to the Count Four of the information charging the misdemeanor offense of unlawful entry.
>
> I should inform Your Honor that I have discussed this matter with Mr. Carbo, the assistant district attorney, and he has indicated that he will ask the

---

* Dialogue from pages 24–26 in *Justice by Consent* by Arthur Rosett and Donald R. Cressey. Copyright © 1976 by J. B. Lippincott Company. Reprinted by permission of Harper & Row, Publishers, Inc.

Court to dismiss the remaining counts in this information, charging first-degree burglary, simple burglary and grand larceny, at the time sentence is imposed on this charge.

Assistant District Attorney: That is correct, Your Honor.

The Court: Mr. Randolph, do you understand what your attorney has just said?

Peter Randolph: I do.

The Court: Have you been furnished with a copy of the information and discussed the charges contained in it with your lawyer?

Peter Randolph: Yes, sir. . . .

The Court: And do you understand that you are entitled to confront your accusers, to require that they testify in open court at a public trial and to cross-examine the witnesses against you, as well as to call by compulsory process witnesses on your own behalf.

Peter Randolph: Yes, sir.

The Court: And do you further understand that by your plea of guilty you are waiving all of these rights and subjecting yourself to sentence and punishment without a trial?

Peter Randolph: Yes, sir.

The Court: Were any threats, promises or inducements made to cause you to offer this plea?

Peter Randolph: No, sir.

The Court: All right, I will accept the plea, but I want a presentence investigation. Sentencing is set for two weeks hence in this courtroom. The defendant is remanded to jail pending sentence. Next case.[42]

This brief encounter shows that the judge, prosecutor, defense lawyer, and defendant all pretend that plea bargaining did not occur. But, in fact, promises, inducements, and sometimes threats are involved; and the participants all know it. What happened behind the scenes, however, is kept off the public record, so the entire proceeding acquires the appearance of legitimacy that might otherwise be lacking.

The Supreme Court has declared that the plea-bargaining process is constitutional. So long as a defendant has the benefit of counsel, his or her agreement to waive the right to trial is binding, even if it appears later that the chances of acquittal before a jury would have been good. Justice Byron White candidly referred to the "mutuality of advantages" inherent in the system, recognizing the many functions served by plea bargaining.[43]

FUNCTIONS OF PLEA BARGAINING

It might be thought that the primary reason for plea bargaining is court congestion. While it is no doubt true that many courts would be overwhelmed and perhaps paralyzed if most cases went to trial and that court personnel therefore have an incentive to encourage plea bargaining, more subtle factors sustain the practice. Available evidence suggests that case overload is a less instrumental factor than previously suspected.

First, plea bargaining has deep historical roots and was in frequent use long before the escalation in the number of arrests that occurred in the last couple of decades. Figure 6-1 shows that the percentage of defendants seeking trials remained fairly constant (and low) in Connecticut over a 75-year period beginning in 1880. Likewise, as far back as 1950 only 4 percent of all cases went to trial in New York.[44]

Second, a comparison of courtroom workload and the use of guilty pleas in three cities shows no clear relationship. In Baltimore there was an average of 671 defendants per courtroom in 1972, but only one-third of the cases were disposed of by guilty pleas. On the other hand, Chicago had less than half the number of defendants per courtroom (307) but used the guilty plea twice as often, even though we would expect it to be used less. Detroit had the heaviest courtroom workload (735 defendants per courtroom) but used guilty pleas no more than Chicago.[45] So the use of guilty pleas is not simply a response to overloaded courts.

FIGURE 6-1

Ratio of Trials to Total Dispositions for Connecticut Superior Courts, 1880–1954[1]

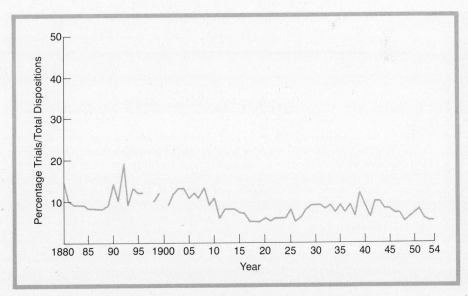

[1] Data unavailable for two years between 1895 and 1900.
SOURCE: Milton Heumann, "A Note on Plea Bargaining and Case Pressure," *Law & Society Review* 9 (Spring 1975), 519. Reprinted by permission of the Law and Society Association.

COPING WITH UNCERTAINTY   What then does account for plea bargaining? A hypothetical example may help answer the question. Assume that the police respond to a phone call that an intruder has broken into the caller's house at 11:30 at night in a high-crime ghetto area. When they arrive, they see a man running about a block away. They yell at him to stop, but he keeps running. A shot is fired in the air, and the police apprehend the man carrying a wallet belonging to the victim.

When the police take the suspect back to the house, the victim identifies him. The police question the victim about what happened, and he responds as follows:

> I heard the front window break downstairs and I ran to the landing while my wife remained upstairs in the bedroom and called police. I saw a man standing downstairs looking around. When he saw me he said something like "Get back upstairs or else!" He had something dark in his hand that looked like a gun. I went back to the bedroom and he ran out.

In a quick search the police find two other items belonging to the victim in the bushes—a tape recorder and a watch. They interrogate the suspect, who denies everything. He says that he was out buying a pack of cigarettes at a candy store, and on the way home he saw a wallet in the bushes, which he picked up. When he heard the police yell, he thought they were muggers after him, so he ran. The man is arrested and charged with robbery, burglary, larceny, possession of a deadly weapon, and resisting arrest.

It turns out the defendant is a Puerto Rican with a criminal record. He was arrested at age 14 for shoplifting, and the charge was dismissed in juvenile court.

WHY PROSECUTORS PLEA BARGAIN

One of the cases [in the study of criminal justice in Washington, D.C., done by the Vera Institute of Justice] helps explain why prosecutors avoid trials if they can: a seemingly guilty defendant was acquitted against all the odds. Charged with first-degree sexual abuse and assault, the defendant had a record of five convictions, including a prison term for rape. The case went to trial only because the defendant rejected his lawyer's advice and refused the bargain offered by the prosecutor; he also insisted on taking the stand, despite his prior record. "My client had a long record, his story was unconvincing, he was crazy," his attorney recalled. "He would jump up and down in the court yelling that everyone was lying," as a result of which he had to be handcuffed to the rail in the courtroom. "But he was my client and insisted on his innocence, so we went to trial—handcuffs and all." Despite the fact that the complainant—a fifteen-year-old girl—made an unusually credible witness, the man was acquitted. When asked about his prior record, he responded, "I pleaded guilty in the past—five times—because I committed those crimes. This time I didn't do anything and I didn't plead because I'm not guilty." The jury believed him, even though his own lawyer did not.

Charles Silberman, *Criminal Violence, Criminal Justice* (1978), pp. 272–73.

At 17 he was arrested for auto theft; he pled guilty and received probation. At 19 he was arrested for burglary; he again received probation. For the last two years he has been steadily employed at a car wash and earns the minimum wage. He has a wife and three children—ages one, three, and four.

From the standpoint of the defendant, the situation looks bleak indeed. He has been "caught with the goods" and positively identified. His record suggests that upon conviction he would receive a fairly stiff sentence, since he has yet to serve any time in jail. It will be hard to find witnesses who were out late at night and might confirm his alibi. The candy store owner might not remember him or might not want to get involved, even if he does recall the man's presence.

Aside from these legal factors racial prejudice on the part of some judges and jurors might be a strike against the defendant from the outset. Also, he might be quite wary about the skills of the public defender representing him.

On the other hand, the prosecutor does not have a perfect case. On the robbery charge, the words the defendant allegedly used ("or else") might or might not constitute a threat to use force. The weapons charge might be hard to prove because the gun was never found and the house was dark when the victim made his observation. Even the charge of resisting arrest raises questions because many people would think it perfectly reasonable to run when someone yells out in a dark, deserted crime-ridden area. Moreover, there is the slight possibility that a jury would acquit him altogether, believing his story (perhaps out of sympathy to his wife and three children sitting in the front row of the courtroom).

In short, the situation is fraught with uncertainty, and neither side can safely predict total victory (i.e., acquittal for the defendant or conviction for the prosecution). To avert the risk of complete loss (i.e., a long prison sentence or an acquittal for the defendant), both sides will probably be amenable to compromise—a negotiated plea of guilty. Both the prosecutor and the defendant might be quite happy to settle for a plea of guilty to simple burglary, a dismissal of the other charges, and a short prison sentence (perhaps equivalent to the time served in jail prior to trial). Both sides get something: The prosecutor gains a conviction, which makes his record look good, and the defendant wins his freedom in the immediate or not-too-distant future.

The logic of plea bargaining can be appreciated better by recognizing that negotiation is also the common mode for resolving civil cases. Indeed, 98 percent of all civil suits are settled prior to trial.[46] Why does this happen? The plaintiff is fearful that a jury might find the defendant totally blameless (e.g., non-negligent in a medical malpractice suit), while the defendant is afraid he or she will be held liable and the jury will assess the damages at a very high level. In short, in both civil and criminal cases, bargains are made to avert disaster.

Another complicating factor for criminal defendants is the uncertainty about what cohorts in crime may be doing in dealing with the prosecutor. This uncertainty is sometimes referred to as the "prisoner's dilemma." A defendant may be fearful that his or her partner is going to plea bargain and agree to testify for the state. Such an action will put the defendant who holds out for trial in a very vulnerable position, since the accomplice can provide damaging testimony.

If both partners plead innocent, the chance of acquittal for both improves. But the existence of distrust between them makes each leery of being caught "holding the bag" while the other gets preferential treatment.[47]

The fatal consequence of going for an all-or-nothing solution is revealed in a case handled by San Francisco attorney James McInner. His client was accused of murder, and the evidence against him was rather weak. The prosecutor offered to let the defendant plead guilty to voluntary manslaughter. The defendant refused, and he was ultimately convicted of first-degree murder and executed.[48] If the defendant had taken the deal, he would have been alive today, and perhaps even free.

This practice of "throwing the book" at defendants who turn down plea bargains was upheld by the Supreme Court in 1978. In *Bordenkircher* v. *Hayes*, the Court, in a five-to-four decision, sustained the prosecutor's right to threaten uncooperative defendants with more serious indictments.[49] In that case the defendant (who had two previous felony convictions) was convicted of violating Kentucky's habitual offender statute, for which he received a life sentence after he had refused to accept a five-year sentence if he pled guilty to forging an $88 check. The ruling may well increase the pressure on defendants to accept plea bargains by increasing the risk of rejecting the prosecutor's offer. The prospect of facing additional charges compounds the uncertainty inherent in the pretrial situation.

SEEKING A JUST PUNISHMENT Plea bargaining may also aid the search for a just punishment. In many cases the defendant may be guilty of something at the time of arrest. However, the punishment associated with the most serious charges often seems too heavy, while allowing the defendant to emerge scot-free is too light. In the previous hypothetical example, the individual probably does not deserve 25 years (a typical maximum penalty for armed robbery); nor, after his previous scrapes with law, does probation seem adequate. Some middle ground—perhaps a short stay in jail—may be the most fitting punishment. In short, most defendants are neither totally guilty nor totally innocent, so a halfway punishment is most appropriate for the crime if the goal being sought is justice.

SELF-INTEREST A third function served by plea bargaining is to make the job of court personnel and defense attorneys easier and safer. By avoiding trials, arduous preparation is rendered unnecessary and embarrassing courtroom defeats are avoided. The prosecutor's percentage of convictions is kept high, and these statistics can be publicized when the district attorney is seeking reelection.

In Chicago satisfying the interests of the attorneys is carried one step further. Judges there prescribe minimum and maximum sentences. To accommodate each others' interests, the defense attorney sometimes agrees to let the prosecutor set the maximum sentence, while the defense attorney selects the minimum. In this way the prosecutor appears to be acting severely; but since the minimum sentence *usually* is the time that is actually served, the defendant gets a good deal and is pleased with the defense attorney. Everyone comes out looking good.[50]

Because the self-interests of attorneys on both sides are so nicely met by plea bargaining (except for those few who are eager for trial work), the practice has incredible resiliency to attack. Top officials regularly try to eliminate or curtail this method of disposition to answer public criticism that it leads to overly lenient treatment of criminals, but they rarely succeed. For example, a Michigan district attorney once ordered the "abolition" of plea bargaining in drug sale cases when he took office. Because defendants had nothing to lose, they began demanding trials in record numbers; the rate rose from 2 percent prior to the new policy to 28 percent after it was implemented. Soon after, however, the number of defendants seeking trial plummeted, and 90 percent pled guilty to *original* charges. What happened? The judges simply agreed to make pretrial settlements on sentences and disregard the nature of charges, a way of reinstituting plea bargaining through the back door. The district attorney's policy was subverted, and the benefits of plea bargaining once again accrued to all participants.[51]

Boulder County (Colorado) instituted a similar attempt to eliminate plea bargaining on January 1, 1978. Once a person is charged with a felony, there can be no subsequent reduction of charges. Insufficient time has yet elapsed to assess the impact of this change, but Robert Miller, president of the Boulder Bar Association, claims that plea bargaining has remained but is done more surreptitiously than previously. According to Miller:

> What it really means is that the bargaining is now done before the charge is filed. They're investigating your client before charging him, so you go over and say, "Look, you can't get him on this, this, or this, and only maybe on that one, so why don't you just charge him with that?"[52]

Since both the assistant district attorneys and the public defender's office were besieged with work immediately after the new policy went into effect, there is every reason to believe that Miller's contention is correct and that plea bargaining has somehow been salvaged. Something so advantageous to all parties cannot be easily eliminated.

THE NEGOTIATING PROCESS: FACTORS AFFECTING AGREEMENTS

THE EVIDENCE   One of the most important factors in determining the kind of bargain that is made is the strength of the prosecutor's case against the defendant. Prosecutors distinguish between "dead bang" cases and "reasonable doubt" cases.[53] The former are cases with very strong evidence against the defendant and no plausible explanation by the defendant for innocence. The latter are cases entailing limited or conflicting evidence. Such categorization is important because it indicates the degree of risk a trial would create. Thus 85 percent of prosecutors surveyed by the *University of Pennsylvania Law Review* said that the strength of the state's evidence was decisive in determining the type of bargain to be made.[54]

This factor no doubt accounts for the decision of Bronx, New York, prosecutors to allow 12 men originally charged with the mass rape of 2 prostitutes to plead guilty to criminal trespass, a minor misdemeanor. The victims had agreed to sell sex to one man but were met by the whole group upon arriving at the appointed motel. Proving exactly what happened would have been very tricky.[55]

THE SERIOUSNESS OF THE CRIME   Another crucial factor in the bargaining process is the seriousness of the crime. Table 6-2 suggests that the more harm caused by the crime, the less likely "cheap" plea bargains will be arranged. The fewest number of pleas occur when defendants are accused of the crimes that carry the stiffest punishments in the penal code and that involve physical violence. In cases like homicide, kidnapping, and forcible rape, prosecutors are apparently resisting excessively lenient treatment through plea bargaining, even at the risk of freeing defendants as a result of acquittals.

THE DEFENDANT'S CULPABILITY   In figuring out the appropriate punishment, prosecutors and defense attorneys judge the defendant's culpability by "bargaining recipes" that go well beyond the statutory definitions and gradations of crime in the penal code. These guidelines are rough measures of the defendant's "badness," and they include all kinds of legally extraneous data, such as background, demeanor, motivation, and the degree of repentance shown. Especially important are the previous records of defendants as a means of determining whether they are wayward people continually in trouble with the law or relatively decent individuals who ventured into crime through unfortunate circumstances largely beyond their control. Blameworthiness depends not only on the degree of damage inflicted on victims but on the overall qualities of the defendant. Often the plea negotiations involve a more or less cooperative attempt by both lawyers to reach a consensus about the character of defendants—are they evil people, are they basically good, or are they somewhere in between?

Thus, in "sizing up" a burglary defendant, the lawyers will ask such questions as: Was the criminal an "amateur" or "professional"? Was the crime well planned or a thoughtless drunken escapade? Was the defendant a hard-working, responsible breadwinner who came upon hard times or a shiftless vagabond? Is the defendant mean or gentle? In short, was the defendant acting out of character, or was the criminal act exactly what we would expect from such a person?

None of these questions can be answered with certainty, and all of them are legally irrelevant in determining the proper charge—which is theoretically based only on the facts of the crime. But they are the stuff out of which moral

TABLE 6-2
The Use of Jury Trials in Criminal Cases in Los Angeles Superior Court, 1970

Offense	Total Defendants	Percent of Defendants Disposed of by Full Court or Jury Trial
Homicide	398	36.1
Kidnapping	189	28.0
Rape, forcible	391	27.1
Other sex offenses	769	22.9
Robbery	1,875	22.2
Assault	1,640	21.5
Opiates (primarily heroin)	1,250	16.8
Other	261	16.8
Hit and run	109	13.7
Theft, except auto	2,092	11.1
Deadly weapons	377	10.6
Burglary	4,670	10.4
Manslaughter, vehicular	69	10.1
Theft, auto	1,582	9.4
Drunk driving	371	8.6
Marijuana	5,529	8.2
Other dangerous drugs (e.g., cocaine)	6,851	8.2
Other drug violations	194	7.2
Forgery and checks	2,107	6.2
Bookmaking	701	5.0
Escape	146	2.7
Average		11.6

SOURCE: Lynn Mather, "Some Determinants of the Method of Case Disposition: Decision-Making by Public Defenders in Los Angeles," *Law & Society Review* 8 (Winter 1973), 213. Reprinted by permission of the Law and Society Association.

judgments are made, the major ingredients in determining what level of plea is acceptable. The very factors that enter into the judge's posttrial sentencing decisions impinge on the lawyers' pretrial negotiations. Assuming that there is general agreement that the defendant is in fact guilty of something, the crucial question often is: What punishment does he or she deserve?

THE ROLE OF THE LAWYERS Most attorneys are largely constrained by the facts of the case, but some differences in style can affect plea bargaining outcomes. Thus, some defense attorneys are widely known for the adamance with which they pressure their clients to plead guilty. One of the prisoners interviewed by political scientist Jonathan Casper characterizes such a lawyer:

> You know, his name in superior court is known as "cop-out Kujawski." This is what everybody in prison calls him cause that's the first thing as soon as he comes in your cell in superior court, that the first thing he says—cop out, cop out, cop out.[56]

However, Kujawski's distinctive characteristic may be his forthrightness rather than his conduct. Indeed, sociologist Abraham Blumberg's study of 724 defendants who pled guilty revealed that in 56 percent of all cases the defense counsel was the first person to suggest pleading guilty.[57]

The role played by defense lawyers is sometimes analogous to that of the real estate broker who deceives the prospective home buyer into thinking that the seller is intransigent about a high price and simultaneously deludes the seller into believing that the buyer will not budge from a lower price—in order to get both sides to accept a middle ground and consummate a deal. In handling clients defense attorneys may distort the prosecutors' position and make them look more unyielding about a tough sentence than is actually the case. By the same token, in dickering with prosecutors the defense lawyer may put up the pretense that defendants are adamant about a jury trial when in fact they are willing to bargain. By engaging in such deceptive tactics, the defense lawyer functions as a mediator who brings both sides together, persuades them to compromise their initial positions, and cements an agreement.

THE ROLE OF THE JUDGE   While judges ordinarily take a back-seat role in the plea bargaining process, in some cities they are more active participants. Thus, in Chicago and New York the judge and attorneys for both sides normally meet in pretrial conferences. If the judge is a party to the negotiations, he or she can approve of the terms of the plea bargain in advance of the formal court hearing. Judicial involvement serves the purpose of eliminating any residual uncertainty as to whether the reduction in charges will be accepted and whether sentencing recommendations will be followed. By dispelling any doubt that the arrangements worked out by the attorneys will be rejected, such conferences expedite the plea bargaining process.

At the same time judicial presence during plea bargaining puts extra pressure on the defendant to plead guilty. Many believe that judges hand out harsher sentences to defendants who insist on trials (although evidence on this point is unclear). Defendants may be particularly afraid of this risk if the judge is the one who has proposed the bargain. Moreover, if the judge suggests a plea of guilty, the defendant may well doubt whether the judge can remain objective in conducting a trial. So, while such pretrial conferences are useful in assuring that there are no misunderstandings or snags when the plea of guilty is entered, they may make it more risky for defendants to take advantage of their constitutional right to a trial.

If the judge remains aloof from negotiations, then both the prosecution and the defense must guess about the judge's probable decisions—whether the reduction in charges and the sentencing recommendations will be accepted. These guesses are sometimes wrong. In 1977 a California judge rejected an agreement allowing two leaders of the American Indian movement accused of killing a cab driver and robbing him of 50 cents to plead guilty to minor charges and go free on probation, thereby prompting a regular trial.[58] While this example of a judge upsetting prearranged accords is rare, it demonstrates how judicial passivity prior to trial complicates the plea bargaining process.

RELATIONSHIPS AMONG COURTROOM PERSONNEL If the same prosecutor and defenders regularly appear together in the same courtroom, they and the presiding judge are more likely to work out trusting relationships and establish norms about agreements than if they deal with each other only sporadically. This decreases uncertainty and facilitates plea bargaining.

Indeed, where officials have good working relationships, "bargaining" may be a misnomer for the process. "Plea discussing" is a better term, since the process of selecting a plea is a cooperative enterprise rather than a conflicting one. The guilt of the defendant is assumed, and everyone involved merely tries to work out an acceptable punishment.

On the other hand, in cities such as Baltimore, where judges frequently rotate from courtroom to courtroom and the turnover among assistant district attorneys and prosecutors is above average, greater suspiciousness prevails and more reliance is placed on formalities. Hence, there is less plea bargaining, and over one-third of all cases go to trial.[59]

THE INFLUENCE OF THE MEDIA In highly publicized cases political pressure may be put on prosecutors *not* to plea bargain lest they appear to look "soft" in the public eye. Thus, when Manhattan District Attorney Robert Morgenthau allowed Luis Velez to plead guilty to second-degree murder for killing two police officers in cold blood, Morgenthau received considerable criticism—even though the defendant received two consecutive 25-year prison terms.[60] Other prosecutors, aware of such negative publicity and less resistant to public pressure, might hesitate to accept pleas in cases involving heinous crimes or social outcasts.

WHETHER THE DEFENDANT IS INCARCERATED PRIOR TO TRIAL If a defendant is jailed prior to trial, he or she may be more predisposed to plea bargain than if allowed to remain free. To escape the ordeal of imprisonment, the defendant may be more willing to plead guilty (especially if the punishment is made equal to the time already served in jail and as a result he or she is set free). Moreover, the jailed defendant, less able to help with his or her own defense and often stigmatized in court because of being under guard, may feel more vulnerable to conviction if a trial is held. Consequently, a negotiated plea is more appealing.

ASSESSING PLEA BARGAINING

Politicians and editorial page writers commonly condemn plea bargaining as the curse of the criminal justice system, but a sober reflection leads to a more balanced evaluation. The motivations of the lawyers who engage in the process are primarily self-serving, but the results of that procedure are positive as well as negative.

Table 6-3 summarizes the apparent impact of plea bargaining on the various goals. The effects on crime-prevention strategies are the most uncertain. High conviction rates may contribute to deterrence by making punishment for crime more certain and the commission of crime more risky, but if the lenient sentences that are negotiated are insufficiently severe there may be an adverse effect. It is unknown whether the probation and short jail terms frequently agreed upon foster rehabilitation by quickly reintegrating criminals back into the normal life of the society or whether they promote crime repetition (i.e., recidivism) by permitting those convicted to return unchanged into their old, familiar criminal environment. One thing is clear: Such sentences undermine incapacitation, the exclusion of criminals from society, in that many criminals are able to bargain for their immediate freedom or for a very short prison term, so they can very quickly continue their life of crime if they desire.

TABLE 6-3
An Assessment of Plea Bargaining

	Impact of Plea Bargaining		
Goals	Positive	Negative	Uncertain
Crime prevention			X
Public tranquillity		X	
Justice	X		
Due process		X	
Efficiency	X		
Accountability		X	

Because much of the public equates plea bargaining with soft treatment of criminals, public tranquillity is diminished by its common usage. Many see it as a sordid practice that allows criminals back on the streets much too soon. The high conviction rates achieved through this practice do not seem to fool people into thinking they are any safer.

Are plea bargains just? To answer this question, we must make an overall judgment about the propriety of the hundreds of thousands of sentences imposed through this mode of disposition. The crucial criterion in assessing whether justice is done is whether the punishment inflicted fit the gravity of the crime.

By focusing on just the highly publicized cases of plea bargains, a negative evaluation seems proper. For example, many people were outraged that Patty Hearst, who had been kidnapped by a group of political militants and later joined hands with her abductors to commit a series of crimes, plea bargained for probation for her part in the armed robbery of a sporting goods store during which she repeatedly sprayed the store with submachine-gun fire. Likewise, the deal allowing former Vice President Spiro Agnew to go free after pleading "no contest," the equivalent of guilty, to tax evasion was widely condemned because federal prosecutors had amassed evidence that he was guilty of the far more serious crimes of taking large bribes while serving as governor of Maryland.[61] In both the Hearst and Agnew cases, it seemed that wealthy and powerful defendants charged with major crimes were getting far too good a deal.

However, if we judged each and every instance of plea bargaining on its own merits, we would probably find that the above-mentioned cases were anomalous and that as much justice is achieved through plea bargaining as results from sentences imposed after convictions. Since quite frequently the original charges made by the police and prosecutor are excessive, plea bargaining often serves to scale them down to the true nature of the offense. Moreover, the continuing option of both sides to refuse each other's offers and insist on trial normally acts as a check against gross injustices—negotiated sentences that are outrageously mild or unconscionably harsh.

Unquestionably due process suffers from plea bargaining. Defendants are deprived of their "day in court," and the informal, often clandestine dealings between lawyers seem anything but fair in many cases. Indeed, the pressures on defendants to yield to this process and forsake trials occasionally result in totally innocent prople pleading guilty in order to avoid the risk of being wrongfully convicted and severely punished. How this can happen is well illustrated by a plea bargaining scandal that was uncovered in 1976 in the small town of St. Albans, Vermont. Some years earlier, many young people seeking a rural way of life had migrated to the St. Albans area from various cities. Their divergent life style quickly brought them into conflict with the indigenous population, who resented the values and habits of the newcomers—the way they dressed and spoke, their occasional use of drugs, and the late hours that they spent in public.

An aggressive prosecutor was hired by the town council, and he soon obtained convictions for the possession and sale of drugs against several young people. Shortly thereafter, scores of others began plea bargaining with the prosecutor, even though they contended outside court that they were innocent. An investigation by the state's attorney later revealed that the prosecutor had no evidence whatsoever against many of those who pled guilty. The charges were completely trumped up to harass them and to break up the youth cult that had descended on the community. The governor of the state finally pardoned those victimized by this process, an act that had the effect of eliminating both their arrests and convictions from the record books.[62]

What is so unusual about the episode in St. Albans is the conclusion. Rarely are such unfair dealings uncovered, and no doubt some people acquire undeserved criminal records and unfair terms in prison because they are afraid to contest their innocence. The hapless person who has done nothing wrong but who is implicated in crime by unfortunate circumstances may well find that plea bargaining effectively eliminates the chance to be vindicated.

Plea bargaining seems to have opposite effects on the two remaining goals of the criminal justice system. Efficiency is enhanced because the astronomical expense of providing full-blown trials for all defendants is eliminated. On the other hand, accountability is diminished because the public is kept in the dark about the truth of criminal events as well as being almost totally excluded from the decision-making process.

To make a final judgement about the merit of plea bargaining, however, we must compare the settlements reached by lawyers with adjudication by courts (which is analyzed in the next chapter). In other words, while we may have misgivings about the efficacy and morality of plea bargaining, to assess it properly we must ask ourselves: How good are the alternatives? In a world of competing goals and varied self-interests, plea bargaining may be as good a method of deciding cases as can be expected from the criminal justice system.

The Practice of Criminal Law

Just as prosecutors choose how vigorously to pursue a case (if at all), so too defense lawyers must decide how aggressively to represent their clients. From the moment they take a case, they must exercise discretion about how much time, effort, and money to expend on behalf of their clients. Lawyers can offer a wide range of services in order to render the utmost of assistance to clients, and lawyers must make conscious or unconscious decisions about how far they are willing and able to go in mounting a criminal defense.

Prior to trial a lawyer has many responsibilities. At the outset clients must be interviewed; it sometimes requires time, patience and understanding to ferret out relevant information. Factual research such as questioning witnesses is usually necessary, and legal subtleties must be studied. If the defendant is incarcerated, attempts may be made to obtain release through a reduction of bail. Special motions may be made in court to secure dismissal of cases if procedural errors such as illegal searches were made. In order to obtain the best possible outcome in plea bargaining, ample discussion with the prosecutor must take place. The persuasiveness of a lawyer's presentation depends directly on the quality and quantity of earlier preparation.

If the case does go to trial the defense lawyer must perform additional tasks. Witnesses must be located and "prepared" for trial. Careful attention must be paid to jury selection. Defense strategy must be plotted (e.g. determining whether the defendant should take the witnesss stand). Facts must be carefully presented to the jury through thoughtful interrogation of witnesses. Legal errors such as the admission of improper testimony must be noted, and objections must be entered in a timely fashion. The law must be manipulated to assist the defendant—for example, by suggesting to the judge "instructions" to the jury that make it difficult to convict.

If the defendant is convicted, the lawyer has the option of at least one appeal to a higher court. Such appeals require written arguments ("briefs") that entail extensive legal research into past precedents and careful drafting. They also involve oral arguments in which the lawyer must respond effectively to the questioning of appellate judges. Knowledge, skill, devotion, and time—these are the ingredients of a sound appeal.

Clearly, a broad continuum of possibilities is available to criminal defense lawyers. They can do a bare minimum—simply standing next to their clients at formal hearings. They can do everything—fervently seizing any chance of exonerating their clients. Or, as is frequently the case, they can do just a little—helping defendants avoid the worst but forgoing the tasks which have better results. Why the last option is the most commonly chosen has to do with the inadequacies of legal education and the economics of defending clients who are often poor.

LEGAL EDUCATION AND CRIMINAL LAW

The entire law school curriculum is oriented toward civil law rather than criminal law. The totality of most students' contact with criminal law during the typical three-year law school program is one course in criminal law and one course in criminal procedure. Moreover, these courses concentrate almost exclusively on the theoretical and legal aspects of criminal justice, with scant attention paid to the practical realities of handling a criminal case. The subtle nuances of difference between fraud, embezzlement, larceny, and conversion are scrutinized, but little is said about how the criminal code is actually dealt with by practitioners.

This shortcoming reflects a narrowness in legal teaching that is pervasive in the law school curriculum—the neglect of the practical arts of using the law as one deals with people having legal problems. Law texts are primarily casebooks filled with statutes, appellate court opinions, and commentaries about the law together with questions about how the principles articulated in these documents should be applied to hypothetical situations.

What is missing from the books as well as from the classroom is tutelage in the real-life activities of lawyers—an area in which many law professors are themselves ignorant. The daily activities of lawyers include the tasks of interviewing, fact finding, advising, counseling, influencing, and brokering.[63] In years past, when people became lawyers by apprenticing with those already admitted to the bar, training in these skills was a dominant part of legal education. But in most states law school is now the only viable route to becoming a lawyer, and the bar examinations essentially test whether one has adequately absorbed substantive and procedural laws—not whether one is capable of being a lawyer.

Some law schools have taken steps to remedy these defects through "clinical programs" in which part of the student body spends time working side by side with legal aid personnel or public defenders. But these efforts have been modest, and the format of legal education has changed relatively little. Consequently, most people who enter the field of criminal law have learned nothing about advocacy skills. Furthermore, they quickly become immersed in a world of lawyers who have eschewed many facets of lawyering themselves and so are unable to pass the skills along. Hence, the failing of the law schools is never overcome and the average criminal lawyer never becomes truly comfortable preparing a full-scale criminal defense.

ECONOMIC INCENTIVES AND DEFENSE LAW

In running a business an entrepreneur normally chooses whether to seek profits by selling a low volume of goods at high prices or to go after low returns per unit but high turnover. One can cater to a small market of wealthy purchasers who can afford an expensive product of higher quality or appeal to the mass market, which must settle for lower-quality goods at cheaper prices. Because prospective clients in criminal law usually have limited resources, most defense lawyers (with some notable exceptions, such as Edward Bennett Williams, who has received upwards of $250,000 for representing a single defendant), usually opt for the latter strategy for making money.

These lawyers are sometimes called (derogatorily) "courthouse lawyers" because they roam around the courts and the police stations to solicit defendants. They often charge prices less than the recommended minimum fees established by the local bar associations. As a result of a Supreme Court decision,[64] they are now allowed to advertise their services; but even before the canon of ethics prohibiting advertising was struck down, they often let it be known that they could be hired cheaply. They offer "discount justice"; and as usual, the purchaser gets what he or she pays for.

In order to sell their services most of these lawyers agree to a relatively small fee (anywhere from $50 to $500), no matter how the case is resolved rather than charging according to the nature of their services or the hours devoted to the case (as is standard in business law). Moreover, sometimes fees are split with bail bondsmen, police officers, or courtroom "runners" (who refer defendants to lawyers), so the net return is less than what is paid by the client. Because of this flat-fee arrangement, the lawyers are tempted to press for a plea bargain that consumes a rather small amount of their time. Most criminal lawyers feel that $1,000 is the absolute bare minimum necessary to make even a one-day trial pay off, and few defendants can afford to pay such a price. Therefore, defense lawyers have a definite economic incentive to bargain with the prosecutor. One Boston attorney sums it up this way: "A guilty plea is a quick buck."[65]

Even though fees are low (by lawyers' standards), criminal lawyers have great difficulty collecting them; defendants are notorious "deadbeats" (especially those who end in jail).[66] Consequently, some lawyers engage in all kinds of sleazy practices to extract money from their clients. In fact, Abraham Blumberg has called the practice of criminal law a "confidence game" because the lawyer often pretends to be acting in the client's interest but in reality is engaging in tricks to maximize the chance of getting paid.[67]

PRESENTING A GOOD IMAGE   One such unethical activity is image making—allowing the client to think that he or she is getting many special services; in reality, it is a meaningless charade. Lawyers will file easy motions that are inconsequential, although they look important. They will make phone calls to court officials in the client's presence and adamantly demand a postponement, which they could get through a simple request. They will even fake payoffs to officials and tell the client that someone has been "bought," which squares with many defendants' cynical view of how the criminal justice system operates.

Other techniques are used to expedite fee collection. Lawyers often seek postponements and refuse to move a case along unless they receive regular payments. Often relatives are pressured to find funds to pay the lawyer. In Illinois defendants are allowed by state law to assign the bond that they have given to the court to secure release from jail to their attorneys, and many lawyers require them to do this before they will take the case.[68] This gives lawyers first claim on the money returned by the government if defendants faithfully show up in court as scheduled, and it guarantees at least partial payment of legal fees.

Sometimes court personnel cooperate to help the defense attorney "snow" the client. One prosecutor cynically describes how the accomplishments of the defense attorney can be glorified by "overfiling"—that is, charging the defendant with more serious crimes than are warranted by the facts:

> The defense attorney is selling a service, and if his client feels he hasn't done anything for him, then it's not being fair to him. You just file high and then deal it down a notch to what it should have been all along, and everybody's happy. We get what we want. The defendant thinks his attorney is great. The attorney gets his money.[69]

PREFERRED TREATMENT FOR SOME CLIENTS   Because of the profit-making orientation of most criminal defense lawyers, they will often seek special treatment for their clients only if a substantial fee is being paid. Nonpaying or low-paying clients are sacrificed so that influence with authorities can be saved for paying customers. Describing this "trade-out process," as it is occasionally called, a Texas attorney notes, "You naturally use what influence you have for the client who pays you well. If the D.A. owes you a favor, you don't waste it on a court appointed case. You've got to convert your connections into money. Maybe you shouldn't but you will."[70]

Occasionally lawyers will go all out and conduct an extensive trial for a client even when the fee is not high enough. This is done so that the lawyer maintains credibility as a fighter who will battle for a client under the right circumstances. Attorney Percy Foreman expresses this point well: "One never makes much money on the cases one tries, but they help to bring in the cases we can settle."[71]

LAWYER-CLIENT RELATIONSHIPS   The mercenary perspective that lawyers take toward legal practice sows distrust between lawyer and client. Attorneys are supposed to act as their clients' fiduciaries in that they are entrusted with their clients' intimate confidences. But because most defendants eventually do understand what their attorneys' prime motivations are, they are often bitter about the way they are represented. Even if a defendant fares as well as possible, he or she may feel "sold out" by the lawyer.

This antagonism can only compound any deeper resentments against the social and political system that defendants often feel. Such antagonism is contrary to the quest for rehabilitation. Eldridge Cleaver, the former leader of the Black Panther party, has expressed the prevalent attitude of inmates about lawyers:

> Convicts hate lawyers. To walk around a prison yard and speak well of a lawyer is to raise the downcast eyebrows of felons who've been bitten by members of the Bar and Grill. Convicts are convinced that lawyers must have a secret little black book which no one is ever allowed to see, a book that schools lawyers in an esoteric morality in which the Highest Good is treachery and crossing one's dumb and trusting client the noblest of deeds.[72]

One attempt to create a better attorney-client relationship is the establishment of prepaid legal services. These are plans in which groups of lawyers are hired by individuals or by employers for the benefit of employees to represent members in the plan should they need a lawyer. Theoretically, the client gets to know the lawyer or lawyers on a continuing basis, so that a feeling of mutuality develops that is lacking when people hire lawyers on a onetime basis. Also, the lawyers are paid salaries, eliminating the economic incentive to shortchange their clients. However, most middle-income people have rare occasions to see lawyers (in contrast to their continuing reliance on doctors), so it is unlikely that they will want to invest in services that they may never use.[73]

Counsel for the Poor

Earl Gideon was arrested for burglary in Florida in 1960 and forced to act as his own lawyer. Florida had no provision for providing counsel for indigents who could not afford to hire one of their own. After he was convicted, he took advantage of a special process called a writ *in forma pauperis*, which allows poor people in prisons to make appeals to the United States Supreme Court. In his own handwriting he scrawled a statement alleging that he had been denied his constitutional right to counsel stipulated in the Sixth Amendment. The Court agreed with him and reversed a precedent of long standing that said counsel must be provided in state courts only if there is a possible death penalty, if the defendant is particularly enfeebled mentally, or if the case is highly complex. The new rule, as announced in *Gideon* v. *Wainwright*, required counsel to be provided when a poor person was charged with *any* felony.[73] Ten years later the case of *Argersinger* v. *Hamlin* extended the right to counsel to indigents accused of any crime for which imprisonment is a possible sentence.[75]

Two subsidiary issues have gone unresolved by the Supreme Court. First, the Court did not specify any requirement to demonstrate indigency. While some states simply rely on the defendant's own insistence that he or she cannot afford a lawyer, others demand a full accounting of the defendant's resources. Even more restrictive are communities that assume that a person who is able to make bail is able to afford a lawyer; in reality, most people can finance one but not both. As a result, a person may go to jail prior to trial in order to have counsel provided, a sacrifice that in many ways vitiates the utility of a lawyer.

The second murky area of constitutional law deals with adequacy of counsel. The courts have not established any standard that assigned counsel must meet. Only egregious malfeasance on the part of state-provided lawyers suffices to overturn a conviction. When this reluctance of the appellate courts to exact a certain quality of performance from lawyers is coupled with the unwillingness of trial judges to dismiss lawyers when poor defendants complain and replace them with new ones, the helplessness of the dissatisfied defendant becomes apparent. As the Constitution stands today, by and large one has to take what one gets.

METHODS OF PROVIDING COUNSEL FOR THE POOR

Counsel to indigents is provided through various systems. Most large cities have public defenders who are salaried lawyers entrusted with the responsibility of respresenting all indigents. A public-defender office may have upward of 100 lawyers working for it. Since this permits specialization and routinization of tasks, it is the most economical way of meeting the constitutional obligation to provide counsel.[76]

Another system, used as an alternative or supplement to the public defender, is the assignment of private counsel. In most cities where this system is utilized, lawyers can request such assignments and receive prescribed fees, depending upon whether they get the case resolved with or without a trial. A few cities pay assigned counsel according to the specific work they do. In any case the fees are almost always substantially below the rate for private lawyers. Some small cities and one large one (Houston) assign cases of indigents to all members of the bar and expect them to represent their clients without pay as part of their public responsibilities.

Legal aid societies are a variant of the public defender systems. Such societies are in part privately funded and are controlled by a board of nongovernment officials. Therefore, they can be somewhat more independent than defenders, who are directly under government control.

Three other sources of legal advice are sometimes available on a case-by-case basis. First, private organizations with social purposes, like the National Association for the Advancement of Colored People, the Center for Constitutional Rights, and the American Civil Liberties Union, represent defendants if an extreme injustice is apparent or if an important social issue arises. Second, in certain notorious cases special fund-raising campaigns are used by supporters of defendants to hire private lawyers. For example, women's groups raised $325,000 to defend Joan Little, who was accused of killing a jail guard but who contended she did so in self-defense to ward off a sexual attack.[77] Third, many jail and prison inmates use their free time to become conversant in law and share their understandings with fellow prisoners; they are often called "jailhouse lawyers."

COMPARING PRIVATE LAWYERS AND PUBLIC DEFENDERS

How does the public defender (or the legal aid equivalent) compare with a hired, private defense lawyer? On the one hand, defenders deal with many cases on a regular basis, so they are more familiar with prosecutors, judges, and probation

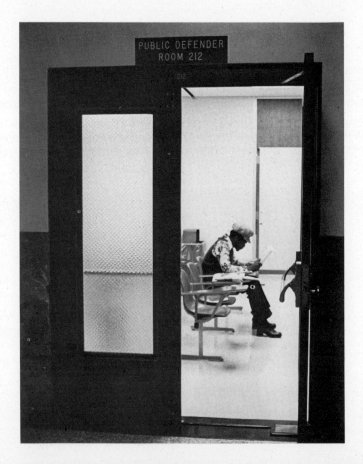

officers. As a result, they are able to predict probable outcomes better than the private lawyer, who usually has less experience. Also, prosecutors get to know and trust defenders whom they see repeatedly. They are consequently more willing to disclose evidence to them than to private lawyers whom they see only sporadically.[78]

These virtues are more than outweighed by the many drawbacks of the defender system. The most obvious is the caseload problem. In 1970 each defender in the Philadelphia office handled between 600 and 800 cases; in Oakland the average was 300 cases; in New York it was 922.[79] With so many clients, relatively little personal attention can be devoted to each case. Most cases must be plea bargained, and very, very few can be given the elaborate handling that we briefly described as a possibility earlier in the chapter.[80]

Public defenders usually have little or no experience when they are hired. A study of legal aid lawyers in Brooklyn, New York, showed that they had belonged to the bar an average of 5 years in contrast to the average private criminal lawyer who had belonged for 25 years.[81] Whether this differential in experience has a bearing on professional competence is problematic, but the relative youth and inexperience of the legal aid lawyers may upset defendants who would feel more reassured with seasoned lawyers.

In many large cities, the preponderance of defendants are black or Hispanic. However, due to the paucity of minority lawyers generally, most public defenders are white. For example, 83 percent of the felony defendants in Baltimore in 1972 were black, yet there was not one black defender at the criminal court level.[82] Many defendants may feel more comfortable relating to someone of their own race.

Because of low salaries and highly routinized work, personnel turnover is high in most defender offices. The average stay for lawyers in the Cook County (Chicago) public defenders office was 2.5 years from 1960 to 1968.[83] This kind of revolving-door staffing not only lowers morale among the entire work force but continuously deprives the office of its most adept lawyers.

A problem inherent in the defender's employment by the government is that clients perceive him or her as working for the prosecution as well as the defense. This is sometimes called the "double agent" problem in that defenders are not exclusively interested in protecting their clients' interests but also want to expedite the prosecutor's workload. Defenders may at first feign a tough bargaining posture to placate clients while in reality capitulating fairly readily to the prosecutor's demands.

Indeed, defendants often feel that their government-paid lawyer wants a conviction as much as the prosecutor so that the wheels of the system can keep on grinding. This was well put by one defendant in jail who apprised a fellow inmate of the merits of his newly appointed defender: "You got an asshole. That guy's just a messenger boy for the DA."[84] The divided loyalties of the defender are thus seen (whether correctly or not) as precluding the possibility of honest representation and "square dealing" with the prosecutor.

A structural problem in many defender offices is the so-called zone defense. Different lawyers are assigned to different stages of the criminal justice process (arraignment, preliminary hearing, etc.), which fragments the handling of any one case. Defendants are passed from one lawyer to another, stifling the development of a trusting relationship and resulting in a loss of information because attorneys often omit some things they learn about the case from the written file.

A final problem concerns the defense lawyer's loss of positive attitudes toward work. This sometimes leads to shirking responsibilities and devoting minimum energy to the job at the expense of clients.

Related to this phenomenon is what might be called "burn out"—a loss of exhilaration. As one lawyer in the Alameda County (Oakland) public defender's office commented, "in about two and a half years I felt a certain routine setting in. . . . There's just so many ways you can commit a burglary and just so many ways you can commit a robbery. . . . You're burned out, you know, you've done it . . . at some point you just poop out."[85]

This malaise can end in cynicism and hostility toward the very people one is supposed to be helping. Animosity is pointedly registered by another Oakland defender:

> The fact of the matter is that you're dealing with the scum of the earth and they'll stab you in the back at the first opportunity. They'll walk over you and anybody else to get what they want. They're one cut above the animal—in fact they're by and large worse. . . . They're just the lowest of the low.[86]

How can one possibly gain a client's confidence while harboring such seething antagonism?

CASE OUTCOMES   Somewhat surprisingly, the actual disposition of cases handled by public defenders is not all that different from the outcomes in cases with private attorneys. Comparisons are difficult because the kind of clientele is often different, but some studies have attempted to do so. A study of Baltimore, Chicago, and Detroit showed that clients of public defenders actually received lighter sentences.[87] On the other hand, several studies have indicated that the rate of plea bargaining is higher among those represented by state-provided counsel.[88] In Chicago clients with public defenders pled guilty 75 percent of the time versus 53 percent for those with private counsel.[89] Therefore, the findings are mixed, and no appreciable differences in case outcomes between the two types of lawyers have been demonstrated.

DEFENDANT DISTRUST OF PUBLIC DEFENDERS   One generalization that can be made with some confidence is that public defenders are distrusted much more than private lawyers. A study of defense counsel in Brooklyn showed that among defendants insisting on their innocence to their own attorneys, 43 percent of those with legal aid lawyers pled guilty while only 18 percent of those with private lawyers did so.[90] This may be interpreted two ways: Either legal aid clients who are innocent are doubtful of their lawyers' ability to gain acquittals, or a greater preponderance of them are in fact guilty and they simply lie more frequently to their attorneys about their culpability than privately represented clients. Either way, they are demonstrating a lack of trust; they either question their lawyers' effectiveness or have qualms about their loyalty and are therefore afraid to be honest with them.

These inferences are consistent with the findings of an interview study of convicts in Connecticut. That study found that 80 percent of the convicts thought that their court-appointed attorneys were actually working against them. This was in stark contrast to the 12 men in the study who were represented by private attorneys; they unanimously believed that their lawyers were on their side and fighting for them, even though nine of them received prison sentences.[91]

These findings do not imply that either fairness or justice was lacking for defendants represented by state-supported lawyers. Data from many cities indicate that differences detected in the ultimate disposition of cases handled by private lawyers and public defenders are not very profound. Perhaps the defects of one type of lawyer are simply matched by a set of deficiencies in the other class of lawyer. Or it may be that the impact of counsel on case outcomes is not nearly as significant as it is sometimes alleged to be so long as a minimal level of legal representation is forthcoming.

On balance, it appears that providing a public defender for the poor who are accused of crime does not solve all the problems that they face in dealing with the criminal justice system. Their alienation toward government officials is not lessened; in fact, the lack of rapport between defenders and their clients may aggravate these bitter feelings. Nor does the practice overcome some of the biases confronting the poor person accused of crime—the stereotypes used by police in making arrests, the insensitivity of some judges who almost invariably come from another social class, the unrepresentative nature of juries overloaded with nonpoor persons.

But assuring the poor the right to counsel undoubtedly has been a step in the direction of achieving the public interest goals of due process and equal justice. There are many flaws in public defender and legal aid systems, but giving the indigent defendant a harried and sometimes hard-bitten lawyer is better than leaving that person with no lawyer at all.

Conclusion

It is in the self-interest of both prosecutors and defense lawyers to resolve most cases cooperatively and search for compromises rather than to fight as adversaries for all-or-nothing outcomes at trials. Prosecutors and public defenders prefer this approach because it is administratively convenient and it lowers the risk of looking like a loser. Private defense lawyers have economic interests at stake in shunning costly trials for their clients, who often cannot afford to pay high legal fees. Ironically, however, the self-interest manifested by lawyers often is beneficial to the public and to defendants.

When cases do proceed to trial, winning becomes the key objective of law-yers, and other public interest goals become subsidiary. To advance their reputa-tions as skillful lawyers, lawyers are tempted to give short shrift to the ethical norms of the legal profession. Moreover, the verdicts that are reached may sometimes depend more on the competence of lawyers' pretrial preparation and trial advocacy than on the guilt or innocence of the accused. This raises the profound question of whether poor defendants could fare very well in such court-room battles if they chose to stand trial more frequently than they presently do.

Perhaps the real flaw in the role played by lawyers has more to do with the very nature of the adversary system than with the performance of the lawyers themselves. Jerome Frank, a long-time judge and highly respected legal thinker, years ago questioned the wisdom of using battles between conflicting lawyers who thrive on winning as a means of obtaining truth and justice.[92] The question is still a poignant one today. Quite possibly the public interest would be best served by granting legitimacy to a more cooperative form of decision making. In other words, instead of treating plea bargaining as a necessary evil, it may be wiser to conceive it as an unperfected good. Improving plea bargaining may hold more promise than trying to abolish it.

SUMMARY

After arrests are made, attorneys have a major impact on the way cases are decided in the criminal justice system. Prosecutors have enormous discretion to dismiss charges, down-play them, or pursue them aggressively. De-fense attorneys decide how much time, money, and effort to expend in representing their clients. Most importantly, lawyers on both sides arrange negotiated pleas of guilt, which is the most common way of obtaining convictions and fixing punishment.

Self-interest largely determines how deci-sions are made by lawyers. It is generally in the interest of both criminals and lawyers to plea bargain because of the uncertainty about possible verdicts and sentences posed by trials. In addition, prosecutors must worry about ex-pediting heavy caseloads, so that forgoing trials is in their interest unless a case is sensitive po-litically. Private defense lawyers (who are rela-tively less affluent members of the legal profes-sion) must bear in mind the limited resources of their clients. Poor defendants, who have a constitutional right to counsel paid for by the government, receive little personal attention from overburdened public defenders.

Thus, lawyers often function as politicians, bureaucrats, brokers, and business people rather than as professional advocates. Never-theless, the result of lawyer decision making is not all bad. Although due process often may be slighted and the public is distraught by the frequency of plea bargaining, the goal of ef-ficiency is significantly advanced—and more often than not, justice is done.

FOOTNOTES

[1] Paul Hoffman, *Lions in the Street* (New York: Saturday Review Press, 1973), p. 44.

[2] Albert Alschuler, "The Defense Attorney's Role in Plea Bargaining," *Yale Law Journal* 84 (May 1975), 1183.

[3] At the beginning of his *Law Dictionary for Non-Lawyers* (St. Paul, Minn.: West Publishing, 1975), Daniel Oran gives the following forewarning:

> This is a guidebook to a foreign language. The language of Law uses mostly English words, but they rarely mean what they seem. Many look like everyday English, but have technical definitions totally different from their ordinary uses. Some contain complex legal ideas compressed into small phrases. Others mean several different things, depending on the area of law, business or politics they come from. Also, the language of Law contains more "leftovers" than most languages. Hundreds of Latin, Old English, and Old French words are still used in their original forms. And the law keeps more outdated English words than any other profession.

[4] Alexis de Tocqueville, *Democracy in America*, vol. 1 (New York: Knopf, 1946), 278.

[5] William Shakespeare, *Henry VI, Part II*, act 4, sc. 2, line 83.

[6] Cited in *Time*, April 10, 1978, p. 56.

[7] See Martin Mayer, *The Lawyers* (New York: Harper & Row, 1966), p. 8.

[8] Carl Sandburg, "The Lawyers Know Too Much," *Complete Poems* (New York: Harcourt Brace Jovanovich, 1950), p. 189.

[9] Jerold Auerbach, *Unequal Justice: Lawyers and Social Change in Modern America* (New York: Oxford University Press, 1976), pp. 130–57.

[10] Erwin Smigel, *The Wall Street Lawyer* (New York: The Free Press, 1964).

[11] Jerome Carlin, *Lawyers' Ethics: A Survey of the New York City Bar* (New York: Russell Sage Foundation, 1966), p. 12.

[12] Louis Nizer, *The Implosion Conspiracy* (Greenwich, Conn.: Fawcett Publications, 1973).

[13] Robert Rhodes, *The Insoluble Problems of Crime* (New York: Wiley, 1977), pp. 102–103.

[14] James Eisenstein, *Politics and the Legal Process* (New York: Harper & Row, 1973), pp. 20–25.

[15] George Arzt, "Night of Arrest, 3 DAs Fought to Get Sam Case," *New York Post*, August 16, 1977, p. 3.

[16] Seymour Hirsch, "Bell, Deputy Split on Carter Pledge to Name U.S. Attorneys on Ability," *New York Times*, September 14, 1977, p. 1.

[17] Herbert Jacob, "Politics and Criminal Prosecution in New Orleans," in *Criminal Justice: Law and Politics*, 2nd ed., ed. George Cole (North Scituate, Mass.: Duxbury Press, 1976), pp. 193–211.

[18] Lief Carter, *The Limits of Order* (Lexington, Mass.: Lexington Books, 1974), pp. 21, 42–43.

[19] John Kaplan, *Criminal Justice: Introductory Cases and Materials* (Mineola, N.Y.: Foundation Press, 1973), pp. 230–38.

[20] In Chicago prosecutors request dismissals at the preliminary hearing through use of what is called the S.O.L. ("Stricken with Leave to Reinstate"), a device through which they can later prosecute if the defendant is arrested again within a certain time period. In New York the same procedure is called "Adjournment in Contemplation of Dismissal" (A.C.D.).

[21] J. A. Gilboy, "Guilty Plea Negotiations and the Exclusionary Rule of Evidence: A Case Study of Chicago Narcotics Courts," *Journal of Criminal Law and Criminology* 67 (1976), 92.

[22] Donald McIntyre and David Lippman, "Prosecutors and Early Disposition of Felony Cases," *American Bar Association Journal* 56 (December 1970), 1156.

[23] Carl Pelleck, "Cops May Issue Tickets to Manhattan Pot Puffers," *New York Post*, April 7, 1977, p. 17.

[24] Leon Jaworski, *The Right and the Power: The Prosecution of Watergate* (New York: Pocket Books, 1976), p. 316.

[25] Ibid., pp. 342–43.

[26] Trevor Arbrister, *Act of Vengeance: The Jablonski Murders and Their Aftermath* (New York: Saturday Review Press, 1975).

[27] *New York Times*, August 1, 1978, p. B5.

[28] Vincent Bugliosi with Curt Gentry, *Helter Skelter* (New York: Bantam Books, 1975), p. 619.

[29] Carter, op. cit., p. 154.

[30] Gilboy, op. cit.

[31] Vera Institute of Justice, *Felony Arrests: Their Prosecution and Disposition in New York City* (New York: Vera Institute of Justice, 1977), p. 20.

[32] Miller v. California, 413 U.S. 15 (1973).

[33] Jenkins v. Georgia, 418 U.S. 153 (1974).

[34] Quoted in Richard Harris, *Justice* (New York: Avon Books, 1970), p. 170.

[35] Quoted in Martin Garbus, *Ready for the Defense* (New York: Farrar, Straus, & Giroux, 1971), p. 81.

[36] Quoted in Victor Navasky, *Kennedy Justice* (New York: Atheneum, 1971), p. 395.

[37] George Cole, "The Decision to Prosecute," *Law and Society Review* 4 (February 1970), 342.

[38] Vera Institute of Justice, op. cit., p. 134.

[39] Selwyn Rabb, "Plea Bargains Resolve 8 of 10 Homicide Cases," *New York Times*, January 27, 1975, p. 1.

[40] Martin Levin, "Urban Politics and Judicial Behavior," *The Journal of Legal Studies* 1 (1971), 193.

[41] A special kind of plea is the posttrial, postconviction, postsentencing plea. Here, the defendant agrees to forsake an appeal on some questionable points of law in return for a reduction of sentence by the judge.

[42] Arthur Rosett and Donald Cressey, *Justice by Consent: Plea Bargains in the American Courtroom* (Philadelphia: J. B. Lippincott, 1976), pp. 24–26.

[43] In Brady v. United States, 397 U.S. 742 (1970).

44 Abraham Blumberg, *Criminal Justice* (Chicago: Quadrangle Books, 1967), p. 32.

45 James Eisenstein and Herbert Jacob, *Felony Justice: An Organizational Analysis of Criminal Courts* (Boston: Little, Brown, 1977), pp. 238–39.

46 H. Laurence Ross, *Settled out of Court: The Social Process of Insurance Claims Adjustment* (Chicago: Aldine Publishing, 1970), p. 4.

47 However, a recent study compared robbery cases involving multiple defendants with those involving single defendants. No significant difference in the percentage of guilty pleas was found, casting some doubt on the "prisoner's dilemma" hypothesis. See Brian Forst and Judith Lucianovic, "The Prisoner's Dilemma: Theory and Reality," *Journal of Criminal Justice* 5 (Spring 1977), 55–64.

48 Albert Alschuler, "The Prosecutor's Role in Plea Bargaining," *University of Chicago Law Review* 36 (Fall 1968), 62.

49 Case number 76-1334 (1978).

50 Alschuler, "The Prosecutor's Role in Plea Bargaining," op. cit., 108.

51 Thomas Church, Jr., "Plea Bargains, Concessions and the Courts: Analysis of a Quasi-Experiment," *Law and Society Review* 10 (Spring 1976), 377–401.

52 Quoted in Molly Ivans, "Plea Bargain Ban Adds to Court's Work in Boulder," *New York Times*, February 17, 1978, p. A14.

53 Lynn Mather, "Some Determinants of the Method of Case Disposition: Decision-Making by Public Defenders in Los Angeles," *Law and Society Review* 8 (Winter 1974), 187–216.

54 "Guilty Plea Bargaining—Compromises by Prosecutors to Secure Guilty Pleas," *University of Pennsylvania Law Review* 112 (1964), 865.

55 *New York Times*, June 12, 1977, p. 45.

56 Jonathan Casper, *American Criminal Justice: The Defendant's Perspective* (Englewood Cliffs, N.J.: Prentice-Hall, 1972), p. 107.

57 Blumberg, op. cit., p. 92.

58 *New York Times*, June 26, 1977, p. 19.

59 See Eisenstein and Jacob, op. cit., chap. 4.

60 *New York Times*, October 19, 1976, p. 33.

61 Richard Cohen and Jules Witcover, *A Heartbeat Away* (New York: Viking Press, 1974).

62 John Kifner, "Drug Raid Leader Jailed for Vermont Frame-ups," *New York Times*, August 2, 1976, p. 1.

63 Gary Goodpaster, "The Human Arts of Lawyering: Interviewing and Counseling," *Journal of Legal Education* 27 (1975), 5–50.

64 Bates v. State of Arizona, 433 U.S. 350 (1977).

65 Quoted in Alschuler, "The Defense Attorney's Role in Plea Bargaining," op. cit., 1182.

66 One of the most bizarre examples of the predicament of lawyers with nonpaying clients was the experience of New York attorney Richard Wynn, who represented a local pornography merchant. When the bill of $25,000 was submitted, the client said his funds were completely exhausted, and Wynn had to settle for payment in reels of obscene film that could be sold to peep shows. See

Murray Kempton, "Porn Merchants Aren't Reeling in Big Bucks," *New York Post*, July 28, 1977, p. 33.

67 Abraham Blumberg, "The Practice of Law as a Confidence Game: Organizational Cooptation of a Profession," *Law and Society Review* 1 (June 1967), 15–39.

68 Eisenstein and Jacob, op. cit., p. 120.

69 Quoted in Carter, op. cit., p. 73.

70 Quoted in Jackson Battle, "In Search of the Adversary System—The Cooperative Practices of Private Criminal Defense Attorneys," *Texas Law Review* 50 (December 1971), 60–90.

71 Quoted in Alschuler, "The Defense Attorney's Role in Plea Bargaining," op. cit., 1182.

72 Eldridge Cleaver, *Soul on Ice* (New York: McGraw-Hill, 1968), p. 19.

73 Lillian Deitch and David Weinstein, *Prepaid Legal Services* (Lexington, Mass.: Lexington Books, 1976).

74 Gideon v. Wainwright, 372 U.S. 335 (1962).

75 Argersinger v. Hamlin, 407 U.S. 25 (1972).

76 Stuart Nagel, *Improving the Legal Process* (Lexington, Mass.: Lexington Books, 1975).

77 Wayne King, "Joan Little's Lawyer Scorns Legal System and Says He 'Bought' Her Acquittal," *New York Times*, October 20, 1975, p. 23.

78 Alschuler, "The Defense Attorney's Role in Plea Bargaining," op. cit., 1225.

79 Ibid., 1248.

80 It is alleged by some that case overload can be turned around and put to good advantage by defenders who are able to threaten besieging the prosecutor with trials if the plea offers of the latter are unacceptable. However, this threat is only infrequently used.

81 James Levine, "The Impact of 'Gideon': The Performance of Public and Private Criminal Defense Lawyers," *Polity* 8 (Winter 1975), 222.

82 Eisenstein and Jacob, op. cit., pp. 89, 204.

83 Anthony Platt and Randi Pollock, "Channeling Lawyers: The Careers of Public Defenders," in *The Potential for Reform of Criminal Justice*, ed. Herbert Jacob (Beverly Hills, Calif.: Sage Publications, 1974), p. 251.

84 Quoted in Rosett and Cressey, op. cit., p. 17.

85 Quoted in Platt and Pollock, op. cit., p. 62.

86 Quoted in Ibid.

87 Eisenstein and Jacob, op. cit., p. 285.

88 See Lee Silverstein, *Defense of the Poor in Criminal Cases in American State Courts* (Chicago: American Bar Foundation, 1965); and Stuart Nagel, "Effects of Alternative Types of Counsel on Criminal Procedure Treatment," *Indiana Law Journal* 48 (1973), 404–26.

89 Dallin Oaks and Warren Lehman, "Lawyers for the Poor," in *The Scales of Justice*, 2nd. ed., ed. Abraham Blumberg (New Brunswick, N.J.: Transaction Books, 1973).

90 Levine op. cit., 228.

91 Casper, op. cit., pp. 17, 105, 115.

92 Jerome Frank, *Courts on Trial: Myth and Reality in American Justice* (New York: Atheneum, 1967), pp. 80–107.

BIBLIOGRAPHY

Alschuler, Albert. "The Defense Attorney's Role in Plea Bargaining." *Yale Law Journal* 84 (May 1975), 1179–1314.

———. "The Prosecutor's Role in Plea Bargaining." *University of Chicago Law Review* 36 (Fall 1968) 50–112.

Bailey, F. Lee. *The Defense Never Rests.* New York: New American Library, 1971.

Blumberg, Abraham. *Criminal Justice.* Chicago: Quadrangle Books, 1967.

Bugliosi, Vincent (with Curt Gentry). *Helter Skelter.* New York: Bantam Books, 1975.

Carter, Lief. *The Limits of Order.* Lexington, Mass.: Lexington Books, 1974.

Casper, Jonathan. *American Criminal Justice: The Defendant's Perspective.* Englewood Cliffs, N.J.: Prentice-Hall, 1972.

Eisenstein, James, and Jacob, Herbert. *Felony Justice: An Organizational Analysis of Criminal Courts.* Boston: Little, Brown, 1977.

Harris, Richard. *Justice.* New York: Avon Books, 1970.

Heumann, Milton, *Plea Bargaining: The Experiences of Prosecutors, Judges, and Attorneys.* Chicago: University of Chicago Press, 1977.

Jaworski, Leon. *The Right and the Power: The Prosecution of Watergate.* New York: Pocket Books, 1976.

Levine, James. "The Impact of 'Gideon': The Performance of Public and Private Criminal Defense Lawyers." *Polity* 8 (Winter 1975), 215–40.

Lewis, Arthur. *Criminal Lawyer.* New Haven, Conn.: College and University Press, 1967.

Mayer, Martin. *The Lawyers.* New York: Harper & Row, 1966.

Rosett, Arthur, and Cressey, Donald. *Justice by Consent: Plea Bargains in the American Courthouse.* Philadelphia, Pa.: Lippincott, 1976.

Silverstein, Lee. *Defense of the Poor in Criminal Cases in American State Courts.* Chicago: American Bar Foundation, 1965.

Vera Institute of Justice, *Felony Arrests: Their Prosecution and Disposition in New York City.* New York: Vera Institute of Justice, 1977.

In the fall of 1937 a shrewd check forger who had been victimizing banks throughout the country concocted a clever scheme to extract money from the lucrative McAlpin estate, which was managed by a New York accounting firm. He used a dummy key to enter the firm's office one night and stole two canceled checks bearing the names of two of the accountants authorized to pay money from the estate as well as five blank checks—but left no signs whatsoever of a burglary. A few days later he feigned the identity of George Workmaster, a reputable securities dealer with an impeccable credit rating, in whose name he opened up a checking account in the Trust Company of North America, an unsuspecting bank. He then deposited a check from the McAlpin estate that he had forged, made out to himself (i.e., Workmaster). After allowing sufficient time for the checks to clear, he next wrote two

CHAPTER SEVEN

DECISION MAKING BY COURTS
The Speculative Nature
of Adjudication

more forged checks totaling $4,160, payable to himself (Workmaster), which were routinely cashed by the Trust Company of North America. The forger walked off with a large pile of hundred-dollar bills, and the McAlpin estate was that much the poorer.

One of the few leads police found when they investigated was the phone number that the forger had listed as Workmaster's office phone when he had opened the bogus account. The number actually happened to be that of Wesley Mager, a stock broker. Mager was cleared of suspicion but provided the names of others who frequently visited his office, including Bertram Campbell, another broker who resembled the descriptions of the forger given by bank personnel. Further inquiries revealed that Campbell had recently been using hundred-dollar bills to pay merchants near his home in Freeport, Long Island. Campbell was called to police headquarters, where he was identified by one of the tellers who had cashed his check and the bank president who had authorized the opening of the phony Workmaster account. Soon thereafter Campbell was arrested and charged with the crimes.

The major evidence produced by the prosecution at Campbell's trial was the testimony of five witnesses who identified him as the forger—the bank officer who handled the establishment of the Workmaster account, the bank president, the teller who cashed the bad checks, and two tellers from a New Jersey bank who said they had cashed other forged checks for the defendant. The defense put eight character witnesses on the stand to testify about Campbell's integrity. Campbell himself swore that he knew nothing of the forgeries and that he had never set foot in either of the two banks where the forged checks were cashed. However, he lacked an alibi since he was unable to recall where he had been the day the checks were cashed at the New York bank. The jury found Campbell guilty, and the judge sentenced him to between five and ten years at Sing Sing Penitentiary, where he spent the next five years of his life until he was released on parole.

About four years after Campbell's release, a man named Alexander Thiel was arrested by the F.B.I. for a string of forgeries that used a strikingly similar technique to the crimes presumably committed by Campbell. He soon confessed to many of the crimes, including the ones for which Campbell had been convicted. All of the people who had previously identified Campbell as the criminal (nine years earlier) recanted and stated in sworn affidavits that Thiel was really the forger. Subsequently, a full investigation was made by the New York Board of Paroles, which issued a 40,000-word report totally absolving Campbell of any connection with the forgeries. The governor gave Campbell a full pardon, and the state court of claims awarded him $115,000 for wages lost and the humiliation suffered. As fate would have it, however, Campbell died of a cerebral hemorrhage only 82 days later.[1]

When the Democratic party held its presidential nominating convention at Chicago in August 1968, thousands of demonstraters gathered to protest the raging Vietnam war, which had been consistently widened by President Lyndon Johnson (a Democrat) and supported by Vice President Hubert Humphrey, who was about to become the party's candidate to run for the presidency. The demonstrations erupted into pitched battles with the police, causing a considerable number of injuries and resulting in many arrests. There is no doubt that many of the demonstrators were provocative toward the police and some were violent, such as the young people who were observed throwing human feces and balloons filled with urine. But the police reaction was also furious, and a government commission characterized their behavior as a "police riot," which included "unrestrained and indiscriminate police violence on many occasions."[2]

In the aftermath of these encounters federal prosecutors investigated the disorders and charged three police officers with willfully violating the civil rights of John Linstead, a *Chicago Daily News* reporter covering the events. When Linstead had observed police assaulting the occupants of a convertible car, he yelled out: "Cut that out, you mother fucker." Police responded by clubbing Linstead, causing him to receive six stitches.[3]

At the trial of the officers for violation of civil rights, the prosecution produced the testimony of nine eyewitnesses to the event. Also introduced into evidence was film of the entire incident, which was taken at close range and analyzed frame by frame by an F.B.I. expert. Indeed, there was so much evidence submitted that the judge admonished the prosecution that they were engaging in "overkill." Nevertheless, the jury exonerated the police officers, bringing in a verdict of not guilty.

What the two above cases have in common is the fallibility of the trial process. A truly innocent man is convicted, while three police officers are acquitted in the face of massive evidence against them. Due process is honored, both sides get their "day in court," and a jury of peers deliberates; yet the outcome is wrong in the first case and suspect in the second. While these extreme examples were intentionally selected to make a point and are not representative of routine cases, they do suggest the potential for error in all cases. Trial by jury is far from a perfect solution to the difficult problem of determining guilt or innocence.

In this chapter we shall show that the discretion allowed to courtroom personnel and participants and the speculation that occurs when cases are contested in court result in outcomes that are often unpredictable and frequently idiosyncratic. Even when judges and jurors act with the most noble of motives and put self-interest aside, the judgment process is inexact; it is a science of "muddling through." For the truly innocent person the route through the courthouse is a perilous maze in which bad luck can do one in; and for the guilty it is a set of golden opportunities for "beating the rap." Decision making by courts is in fact a strange amalgam: It is a semirational search for truth; it is an agonized groping for justice; it is a political process for resolving conflicts and choosing values; and, in surprisingly large measure, it is, like poker and roulette, a game of chance.

Discretionary Aspects of Adjudication

Societies use a variety of methods for settling disputes. Legislatures in democracies make choices on the basis of majority rule. In families, classrooms, and totalitarian countries controversies are often resolved by fiat: Parents, teachers, and dictators impose their own preferences and solutions. In the marketplace the give-and-take of bargaining is the customary means of determining prices and wages when buyers and sellers disagree. Small groups of all kinds engage in informal discussion, persuasion, and manipulation to overcome differences of opinion and to develop a consensus to which all parties can subscribe.

Adjudication is a special method of conflict resolution that is used by courts and some administrative agencies and that is intended to reduce the politics, the subjectivity, and the uncertainty of the other approaches by relying on reasoned argument and formal proof to decide who wins and who loses.[4] The distinguishing element of adjudication is the hearing, during which legal norms are debated and facts are garnered by systematic and rigorous procedures. The competing parties present their contentions, and the outcome is decided in a principled and neutral fashion by scrupulous adherence to the rule of law.

Not all decisions in the criminal justice system are made through adjudication. Cases of suspected juvenile offenders are normally handled informally through discussion by various interested parties. Most civil cases are settled out of court through negotiation, and, as Chapter 6 showed, most criminal cases are similarly resolved through plea bargaining. To deal with family quarrels and neighborhood strife, some jurisdictions are diverting cases away from the court system and turning to mediation to encourage conflicting persons and groups to work out their problems cooperatively; this procedure will be discussed in detail in Chapter 12. While these nonadjudicative alternatives have the virtue of flexibility and avoid some of the abrasive features of legal battles, they are inherently discretionary. The law is relegated to a minor role in arriving at settlements.

What is less obvious but equally true is that discretion is inherent in all stages of court decision making, although it is normally cloaked by legal rituals and arcane terminology. Adjudication is based on rules and does create regularities, but they are insufficiently fixed to give anyone enormous confidence that truth and justice will triumph in any particular case. The notion that decisions are reached mechanistically through the objective application of legal standards and rational fact-finding processes has long ago been debunked by a school of jurisprudential thinkers called "legal realists."[5] Only recently, however, has a vast amount of empirical research been produced that demonstrates the wide range of choice exercised by even the lowliest of courtroom personnel.

There are various reasons that the exercise of discretion is inevitable during the course of adjudication. Because these factors are so crucial to a proper understanding of the actual practice of adjudication, we shall examine each in some detail.

LEGAL AMBIGUITY

The terms used to define the meaning of the criminal law, like so many legal concepts, are fraught with ambiguity. Often distinguishing conduct that is prohibited from conduct that is allowed is very difficult. Disturbing the peace, for example, is against the law; but does this prevent people at a summer party from playing steroes loudly with the windows open? Does it matter if it is Saturday night at 11:00 P.M. instead of Tuesday morning at 1:00 A.M.? Does it make a difference if the party is taking place in an apartment building near a college comprised mainly of students rather than in the middle of a quiet residential area with many elderly people? And how loud is *too* loud—20 decibels, 50 decibels, 80 decibels? All of these questions (and others) arise in drawing the fine line between legal and illegal behavior.

Moreover, even when it is clear that a crime has been committed, it is not always clear *which* precise law has been broken. Deciding which law is applicable can be of enormous importance because it frequently portends the severity of punishment that will be imposed if a defendant is found guilty. Whereas rape in the first degree is punishable in New York State by up to 25 years in prison, the crime of sexual abuse is a minor misdemeanor that can bring no more than three months in jail.

The federal government and all states now have comprehensive statutes articulating the definition of various crimes, but filling in the precise meanings and applications still takes place on a case-by-case basis. Justice Oliver Wendell Holmes, Jr., once said, "What the courts do in fact is what I mean by law."[6] But what courts do is often a hodgepodge of inconsistent and unrelated decisions that leave legal definitions quite unsettled. A myth persists that the law of precedent (sometimes referred to by its Latin name, *stare decisis*) binds judges who decide cases today by the way other judges ruled earlier, but, in fact, ample leeway exists for discretion within the boundaries of previous rulings because no two cases are ever identical in all respects. For example, just because a previous court decides that the movie *Deep Throat* is judged to be obscene does not necessarily mean that exhibition of a similar film with the title *Behind the Green Door* in the same community is a violation of local obscenity law, even though both include graphic depictions of oral sex. Each new case requires a fresh appraisal of the meaning of the law, and how this determination is to be made escapes accurate prediction.

To be sure, previous court rulings can shed light on such questions as the definition of obscenity, but the answers of the past are not always decisive for present cases. Judges and juries must often make up the law as they go along. The law is "squishy"—as much as we have tried to pin it down in legal codes and appellate court interpretations, it remains subject to discretion that puts the outcome of many trials in doubt.

FACTUAL UNCERTAINTY

Facts are guesses. So said Judge Jerome Frank in 1949 in his influential book *Courts on Trial*, which pointed out how inaccurate courtroom reconstruction of events can be.[7] Because we have progressed quite a bit from the appeals to the gods that served as fact-finding methods in previous eras, we tend to be overconfident about the capabilities of the modern trial as a fact-finding process. But determining "whodunit" is a far more difficult enterprise than we are led to believe from watching Kaz systematically and unfailingly unravel mysteries on television. Indeed, the limitations of the trial process cast doubt on the correctness of some verdicts that are reached even when judges and jurors are scrupulously honest in their search for the truth. As we briefly examine the various kinds of evidence produced at a trial, it should become apparent how shaky the bases for determining guilt or innocence really are.

EYEWITNESS IDENTIFICATION   One of the most damaging kinds of evidence against a defendant is an identification made by eyewitnesses—either the victims themselves or bystanders to crimes. Some of the most dramatic moments at trials occur when a witness points across the room to the defendant and says, "That's the one!"

However, two vexing problems arise with regard to eyewitness identification. The first is the difficulty of locating disinterested witnesses who are willing and able to testify in court. Many crimes are committed in secluded places, and many criminals take great pains to make certain that no one besides the victim is present. Furthermore, many bystanders who do get a good view of what is going on are loath to get involved because of the personal cost—the risk of retaliation from the criminal, the possibility of lost wages during court appearances, and the sheer inconvenience of abruptly interrupting one's own activities and schedule.

Self-interest thus can ward off bystander participation in criminal justice matters, often leaving cases to be adjudicated without the benefit of the best possible evidence.

A second difficulty is the unreliability of eyewitness testimony. Many studies have shown that people often make mistakes when trying to recollect what they saw or heard in the past.[8] People are frequently unable to characterize accurately the fleeting events that take place when crimes occur, and their memories often fail when they try to recall what they did see. This is especially the case when the crimes that are seen entail furious activity and quick movements or when the emotions of the observer are aroused because he or she is horrified by the unfolding events. Trials are supposed to sort out good observations from bad ones, but judges and jurors are sometimes hard-pressed to assess the reliability of the observations told to them.

Many sophisticated studies have been done to show how erroneous people's observations of other people are. For example, researchers at Hayward State University in California faked a classroom attack on a professor in front of 141 students, who thus witnessed what they thought was a real crime.[9] Seven weeks later all of them were shown a set of six photographs, which included the "assailant" (i.e., the confederate of the experimenter) and a bystander situated nearby, who was also "planted." Only 40 percent of the students picked out the assailant, and 25 percent accused the bystander. When so many errors occur in conditions where lighting was good and vision was unobscured, it is easy to imagine how much more subject to error are the observations that take place in shadows or at night by people who are located some distance away. And surely the perceptions of many older people who have reduced vision or hearing are likely to be even more unreliable.

Mistakes do, in fact, happen in real life, where the consequences can be disastrous. Lawrence Berson, the individual on the left in the photos on page 249, was picked out of a line-up by several rape victims; George Morales, the man on the right, was identified by victims to a robbery. Both were arrested, but subsequent events showed that the two men had been mistakenly identified. Richard Carbone, in the center, was later arrested and convicted for both the rapes and the robbery, thus clearing the other two men. Fortunately for Berson and Morales, their cases never went to trial, and the real criminal was found. But had Carbone never been located, they might well have been found guilty by a jury and forced to serve stiff sentences for crimes they never committed.[10]

Frank J. Doto was another hapless victim of faulty eyewitness identification. Seventeen witnesses stated to police that he was the assailant in a supermarket robbery in Santa Barbara, California, during which a police officer was shot in the head. Doto was arrested and charged with this crime as well as with two others in which a similar method was used. As it turned out, Doto was later released when he was able to prove conclusively that he was in Los Angeles, about 100 miles away, when the Santa Barbara crime was committed.[11]

Berson and Morales were vindicated because the real culprit was captured. Likewise, Doto was fortunate in that he was able to come up with an ironclad

A case of mistaken identity

alibi that demolished the evidence against him. But the point is that eyewitnesses do err, and judges and jurors sometimes are unable to recognize their mistakes.

LYING Frequently the factual disputes in trials boil down to one person's word against another. The defendant claims, for example, that she was observing the speed limit, while the police officer claims she was speeding. The defendant says he beat up the assault victim in self-defense, and the victim says he neither touched nor threatened the defendant. The bank officer says she never used the computer terminal to appropriate customers' money to her personal account, but a fellow employee swears he saw such a manipulation of funds take place. Or, to use a real case, John Connally—who served as President Nixon's Treasury Secretary and who was accused of accepting a bribe—defended himself largely by emphatically denying that he ever did it, in the face of lobbyist Jake Jacobsen's equally emphatic assertion that he paid Connally the money.[12] Jurors must decide who is telling the truth, and this is not always an easy task.

Quite obviously, defendants have compelling motives to lie: Why worry about committing perjury if you are being charged with far more serious crimes (especially since it is very difficult to prove that a person is intentionally lying)? What is less clear but equally true is that accusers also may have personal incentives to lie. Police officers sometimes feel the need to justify arrests and the physical force used against suspects; complainants may lie to carry out personal vendettas against defendants whom they hate; people may fabricate accusations against others to cover up their own improprieties or embarrassments (e.g. pregnant women who claim they were raped when, in fact, they consented to sexual intercourse with defendants). Just because people who take the witness stand swear "to tell the truth, the whole truth, and nothing but the truth" does not mean that we can trust them. For many the oath to which they swear is an empty ritual that they forget the moment they take it. Self-interest may loom larger than moral or legal obligations to speak truthfully.

Theoretically, the trial process exposes the liars and separates fact from fiction. One of the main purposes of examining and cross-examining witnesses is to ferret out inconsistencies, hesitancies, gaps of information, and other indications of lying. However, anyone who has ever tried to interrogate a group of young children, all of whom deny some mischief that one of them *had* to have done (e.g., breaking the antique lamp, flooding the bathroom with water, etc.), will recognize the difficulty of getting at the truth. We cannot underestimate the ability of people to lie successfully by concocting plausible stories and appearing to look sincere.

What makes this problem most troublesome is that oral accusation, recriminations, and denials are frequently the only evidence presented in court. Most cases lack the "smoking gun"—physical evidence such as fingerprints or marked money that clearly links defendants with crimes. Minor cases in particular are likely to be resolved on the basis of relatively brief bits of verbal testimony because neither the prosecution nor the defense can commit the resources to secure concrete evidence or credible testimony from disinterested third parties that might create overwhelming proof in one direction or another. The "facts" are often simply various people's versions of events, and they may be in stark contradiction.

EVIDENTIARY RESTRICTIONS   In many European countries evidence is admissible in court proceedings no matter how it was obtained (legally or illegally), no matter how unreliable, and regardless of its relevancy. The fact finders (judge or jury) must evaluate how much credibility it should be given and what weight should be placed on it in the context of the totality of all the evidence. However, in this country courts operate according to rather strict rules of evidence, which sometimes cause crucial information to be barred from the case. Thus, illegally seized contraband often is declared inadmissible because proper search warrants were not obtained by police, forcing jurors to decide drug or gambling cases on the basis of circumstantial evidence (i.e., proof of facts established indirectly through inferences made from other facts). Likewise, hearsay evidence (secondhand evidence of what other people not present in court said), which may be quite germane to a case, often is ruled out of order. The rationale of these rules is to protect due process by preventing verdicts based on invalid evidence or on statements that cannot be scrutinized in open court, but the inflexibility of such procedures can undermine the ability of jurors to discover the truth.

CONFLICTING EXPERT TESTIMONY   A vital part of some criminal cases is the opinions of experts. In matters as diverse as ballistics, insanity, autopsies, and diagnoses of injuries, a vast assortment of professionals regularly proffer their opinion on matters within their expertise. Unfortunately, these "experts" often disagree: One says the bullet came from the left, while the other says that it came from the right; one maintains that the defendant was suffering from delusions, the other holds that the defendant was normal; one claims that bruises must have been caused by a blow, and the other asserts that they could have come from a fall. Since all those testifying have credentials and experience that seemingly qualify them to make judgments, the finder of fact is often bewildered in trying to figure out which one is right.

A study conducted under the auspices of the federal Law Enforcement Assistance Administration of 240 state and local police crime laboratories has shown pointedly how imperfect the scientific testing of physical evidence can be.[13] One-third of the laboratories could not differentiate among three paint samples; one-fifth could not correctly identify the nature of three metallic substances; and many were unable to distinguish human hairs from animal hairs. Perhaps even more disconcerting was the finding that 9 percent of the laboratories could not match test bullets with the weapons that fired them—an alarming failure in light of the deference often given to ballistics experts. Thus, even the so-called hard evidence produced by presumed experts at trials frequently has a shaky foundation in fact.

Moreover, experts sometimes have personal reasons either to distort their findings or to pretend that they are more reliable than they really are. Since they may be paid appreciable sums of money by one side or the other, the experts may well testify in a manner that gives the prosecutor or the defendant (whoever is paying them) the feeling they are getting their money's worth and serves to drum up business in the future. Aside from such mercenary objectives experts may well have an interest in enhancing their own reputation by appearing to be far more authoritative than their limited knowledge really permits. In some cases the fame of being called on repeatedly to testify at trials is sufficiently appealing to prompt experts to appear more "expert" than they really are. In any event the apparent objectivity of professionals sometimes is just as suspect as that of other participants in the trial—compounding the fact finder's quest for truth.

MAKING INFERENCES   Judges and jurors frequently must infer certain actions and states of mind from the evidence presented to them. Even if the evidence is absolutely clear that a man stabbed his wife, the jury must infer whether he intended to kill her and was therefore guilty of attempted murder rather than aggravated assault. Or if a defendant admits buying a new color television for $100 from a hawker on the streets but says he did not realize it was stolen, an inference must be made on the basis of the discrepancy between the purchase price and the normal selling price of $400 as to whether the defendant could have truly believed that the seller owned the goods that were being sold. The principles of logic are only partially helpful in making such determinations; judges and jurors often must use their own limited experiences to draw conclusions.

This reliance on common sense can lead to rather bizarre speculations. Thus, Judge Lois Jorer of the Philadelphia Court of Common Pleas has developed various rules of thumb to deal with the many cases in which the facts are uncertain or incomplete. Included among them is the following generalization that she applies in rape cases where the defendant claims the woman consented: "If he had time to take off his shoes, it wasn't rape."[14] The assumption is that most rapists are seeking quick satisfaction of their sexual drives or their hostilities and are not inclined to go through the amenities of getting undressed, but the validity of this generalization has never been proven. The example indicates the problematic nature of many deductions made by judges and juries.

There is really no solution to these dilemmas and obstacles confronting those seeking the truth. Re-creating the past is a difficult business even when all the parties involved have the purest of motives, as any historian will concede. When interests necessarily conflict, as in the case of most trials, the best that can be achieved is a certain probability of correctness, and the margin of error is likely to be greater than is customarily believed.

BIAS

Sometimes judges and jurors have preconceived notions about guilt and innocence based on their personal feelings about certain kinds of people or their stereotypes about how people behave. Consequently, they lack the open-mindedness that would enable them to deal with the matters before them rationally and objectively.

Cases are on record in which blacks and Hispanics have been convicted on the basis of the flimsiest of evidence due to race prejudice. One of the most egregious examples is the case of George Norris, one of the "Scottsboro boys" convicted of raping two white girls on a freight train in Alabama in 1931. Convictions were twice overturned by the United States Supreme Court, due to procedural irregularities, but the third time the conviction stuck, resulting in a death sentence that was later reduced to life imprisonment. Norris was paroled in 1946, and in 1976 Governor George Wallace pardoned him on the advice of the state parole board, which concluded that he had been innocent from the outset.[15] Although outright racism manifested in the Norris case may be diminished today, there are still numerous instances where the color of one's skin rather than the strength of the evidence seems to be the decisive factor on which verdicts and punishments hinge.

Sexual biases can also operate to determine outcomes. This is nicely demonstrated by comparing the handling of two rape cases decided within six days of each other by courts at either end of the country. A woman family-court judge in Ithaca, New York, sentenced a fourteen-year-old youth to the maximum sentence of three years imprisonment, saying that it would "serve as a symbol of public outrage."[16] But in California an appellate court manifested just the opposite attitude about the rights of women when it overturned a rape conviction involving a young woman who hitched a ride with the defendant in the San Fernando Valley, on the grounds that the victim's conduct was provocative. Said Justice Lynn D. Compton (writing for a unanimous court):

> The lone female hitchhiker, in the absence of an emergency situation, as a practical matter, advises all who pass by that she is willing to enter the vehicle with anyone

who stops, and in so doing advertises she has less concern for the consequences than the average female. . . . Under such circumstances, it would not be unreasonable for a man in the position of the defendant here to believe that the female would consent to sexual relations.[17]

So racism, sexism, and other prejudices can color perceptions of decision makers at every phase of adjudication—from the setting of bail to the resolution of appeals. Such prejudices are rarely the only factors operative, and in many cases they play no role whatsoever. But human likes and dislikes cannot be eliminated or overcome altogether.

SELF-INTEREST

The self-interests of judges and jurors can occasionally dictate certain kinds of decision making, but this phenomenon is much less apparent in the courtroom than in other stages of the criminal justice process. Not much is to be gained in personal profit by "tilting" one way or another once a criminal case has gone to trial. To be sure, there have been examples of sitting judges who are bribed, and some jurors have been threatened by associates of defendants if they do not return not-guilty verdicts. But because judges normally remove themselves from cases where they are directly or indirectly connected with defendants (a practice technically known as recusation) and because jurors are also excused if they are related to any of the principals in the case (including the lawyers), relatively little is to be won or lost by deciding a certain way. For most judges satisfaction is derived from the activity of judging itself and the status of the job—which are *not* normally dependent on the nature of their performance.[18]

On the other hand, the desire of both judges and juries to finish their judicial business quickly or to avoid work altogether can result in less thorough trials and a rush to judgment that precludes careful consideration of the law, the facts, and the defendant. Thus, a recent study of the New York City judiciary showed that Manhattan justices heard felony cases for an average of 3 hours and 23 minutes per day, which was partly the result of "boondoggling": Many arrived at court late and left early.[19] And the practice of jurors of fabricating excuses or feigning biases so they will be removed from cases can hinder attempts to secure a random cross-section of the population. But once judges and jurors are assigned to cases, self-interest plays a minimal role.

CROSS-PURPOSES

We shall see that the complexity of the public interest discussed in Chapter 1 is largely responsible for the subjectivity of decision making by courts. This is intuitively obvious with regard to sentencing: Some judges emphasize retribution; others focus on rehabilitation; still others concentrate on deterrence. However, varying conceptions of the public interest also account for other disparities in judicial dispositions. Bail administration often involves a clash between due process (the presumption of innocence) and crime prevention (incarcerating the dangerous offender); whether to dismiss cases for lack of sufficient evidence pits due process against democratic choice (i.e., letting the jury decide); jury selection can entail a conflict between economy and fairness insofar as the discovery of juror biases requires a tedious and time-consuming interrogation process. Because social priorities can change from judge to judge, from case to case, from locale to locale, and from era to era, the administration of the law by courts can never be constant. Stability is sometimes said to be the sine qua non of the law, but the many purposes to be served by law enforcement make this an ideal that can never be reached.

THE QUIRKS OF THE ADVERSARY SYSTEM

The adversary system of criminal justice leaves a great deal up to chance. People often assume that if two sides, the prosecution and the defense, engage in a vigorous series of courtroom battles to convince the judge and jury of the righteousness of their respective causes, then truth and justice will prevail. In fact, many idiosyncrasies having nothing to do with the law or the facts can determine outcomes of trials. The appearance or disappearance of witnesses, the demeanor of the defendant at the trial, the defendant's luck in obtaining a sympathetic jury, the mood of the judge on the day of sentencing—these and countless other contingencies can make a decisive difference in the disposition of cases.

Not the least of these fortuities is whether the lawyers in any given case have the ability and commitment to win. Relatively few cases are so open and shut that a concerted effort by the prosecution or the defense cannot alter the balance. Likewise, "easy" cases can be lost by inept legal representation.

Just how far the prosecution can go in converting a weak case into a conviction was well documented in a recent article contending that Bruno Hauptmann was *clearly* innocent of the kidnapping and murder of Charles Lindbergh's infant son in 1934, a crime for which Hauptmann was convicted and executed. Because the public was so outraged about a crime against such a hero (who was the first pilot to cross the Atlantic Ocean in a solo flight), the search for the culprit was intense. After discovering Hauptmann with some of the ransom money in his possession (which he insisted until his death that he had received accidentally), New Jersey prosecutors apparently manufactured and distorted enough of the evidence to convince the jury. According to author Anthony Scaduto, Hauptmann's lawyer "dozed drunkenly" throughout the trial and "allowed his client to be whipsawed." Whether this was in fact, "one of the most scandalous perversions of justice in our history," as Scaduto asserts, we shall never know for certain; but what is clear is that if the prosecution had been less vehement and the defense lawyers had been even moderately competent, Hauptmann might never have been convicted.[20]

Sometimes the defense is the party with the resources and dedication to gain a decisive advantage. This was true with regard to attorney Jerry Paul's handling of the celebrated case of Joan Little, a 20-year-old black woman who was acquitted of killing a 62-year-old white jail guard in North Carolina with an ice pick while she was serving a sentence for breaking and entering. Because Little claimed that she stabbed the guard to ward off a sexual attack, the case drew national attention and the support of both women's rights and black political groups, who raised $350,000 for her defense. With this inordinate amount of money, not only was Paul able to devote his time exclusively to her case for many months, but he was able, by his own admission, to manipulate the legal system to obtain victory against seemingly insuperable odds.[21]

His client had been sexually active from the age of 14 and had contracted syphilis at the age of 15; in addition, it was widely rumored that she was a prostitute. According to fellow prisoners of both sexes, she spent a large part of her 81 days in the Beaufort County Jail naked from the waist up, and she hinted at the trial that she had previously had sexual contact with the jailer.[22] In short, she was hardly a "model" defendant—prompting columnist Mike Royko to comment: "It was just as easy to believe that she had set up the old geezer for murder and escape as it was to believe that he forced her to defend herself."[23] And yet, the jury took only 1 hour and 18 minutes to acquit her.

How did attorney Paul do it? He used a team of five lawyers to go over all the evidence in painstaking fashion. He hired three social psychologists, a body-language expert (who assessed people's personalities on the basis of their facial expressions and body movements), and three statisticians to help him select the jury. A "change of venue" was obtained—moving the trial from a backwoods town likely to harbor racial prejudice to a relatively cosmopolitan state capital, where he was able to get six blacks on the jury. Paul secured the services of a role-playing expert to help train Little to deal with the prosecution's expected badgering when she took the witness stand. And Paul himself spent days with the defendant, going over every minute detail of her story to prepare her for her five days of testimony. While all this was taking place, a mail-order expert raised funds to pay for the whole operation.

All of this led Paul to conclude, after the trial was over, that "given enough money, I can buy justice. I can win any case in the country, given enough money."[24] While his remark is certainly an overstatement, the case demonstrates how the wheel of fortune can change with a vigorous defense. A prepared defense may well account for the results of a study showing that reputed organized crime figures fare much better in New York courts than ordinary persons: Of defendants allegedly involved in organized crime 45 percent received dismissals in contrast to the norm of 11 percent for all other felony defendants; and less than half (49 percent) were found guilty versus an average of 86 percent in other cases.[25] Organized crime figures often are indicted on gambling or drug charges, which are notoriously hard to prove, and they are able to hire good lawyers, who can take the time and money to exploit every legal and factual weakness of the prosecution's cases. The adversary system then takes its course—with justice often the loser.

As Chapter 6 explained, the average defendant has a quality of legal representation somewhere between the extremes of the Little and Hauptmann cases. In such cases the lawyers have less impact on case outcomes, but other equally idiosyncratic factors may be operative.

Social scientists, indeed all scientists, are usually seeking regularities in behavior—patterns, trends, correlations. But because so much is left to happenstance in the adversary process, the search for generalizations may be in vain. Some phases of the judicial process (like bail proceedings) are more routinized and predictable than others, as we shall see in the rest of this chapter. But the cumulative impact of the discretion, the uncertainty, the gamesmanship, and the sheer chance that affects the various judgment processes in the courts gives us little cause to be sanguine about the quality of the ultimate decisions. It is to these processes that we now turn our attention.

The Vast Authority of Trial Judges

The court system in this country is quite complex, as is shown in Figure 7-1. Each court has a different jurisdiction; that is, it can legally hear only certain kinds of cases—defined according to subject matter, seriousness, and geographical origin. Because our structure of government is based on the concept of federalism, which divides power between the federal and state governments, two relatively independent court systems operate side by side.

Within each system are trial courts (or courts of original jurisdiction), where cases are initially tried and appellate courts, which can review the lower court proceedings to determine if legal errors were committed. Although the United States Supreme Court is a federal court, it stands at the apex of the entire judicial system because it has authority to review the decisions not only of the lower federal courts but also some decisions emanating from the highest courts of the various states (which are normally called "state supreme courts"). State systems usually have separate courts for civil and criminal cases, which are located in each county, whereas the 94 federal district courts scattered across the country have general jurisdiction over all types of cases. Most criminal cases are handled in state court systems because they entail alleged violations of state law, and federal district courts hear only those cases involving federal crimes, like bank robbery, kidnapping, and postal fraud.

In addition, there are "layers" of courts in both the federal and state systems as well as specialized courts with very limited jurisdictions. The federal system has 11 courts of appeal to which federal cases must ordinarily be directed before they can be appealed to the United States Supreme Court. The larger states not only have such intermediate appellate courts, but also have other trial courts (called by various names, such as "magistrate's courts" or "municipal courts" in cities, and "justices of the peace" in small towns). These other courts have jurisdiction over misdemeanors, minor civil cases, and sometimes the early stages

FIGURE 7-1

The American System of Courts

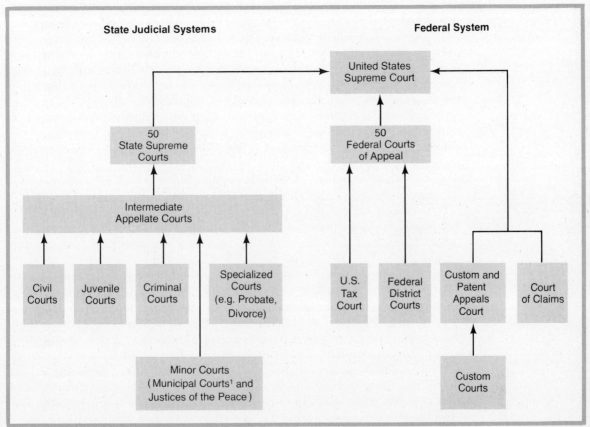

¹These exist only in some states.
SOURCE: Adapted from Harold Grilliot, *Introduction to Law and the Legal System*, 2nd ed., p. 40. Copyright © 1979 by Houghton Mifflin Company. Reprinted by permission of the publisher.

of felony cases. Moreover, both the federal and state systems have courts with very limited purposes, such as the United States Tax Court, which hears appeals from the Internal Revenue Service rulings, and state courts that deal with inheritance matters (called "probate" or "surrogate courts"). And finally the state systems have a distinct judicial apparatus for disposing of charges made against juveniles.

While this complicated structure would seem to limit the authority of trial judges in criminal cases and reduce them to cogs in an elaborate judicial machine, in reality few cases are appealed beyond the court in which they originate. Less than 5 percent of federal cases are appealed, and far fewer state cases are scrutinized by higher courts.²⁶ The United States Supreme Court has virtually total control over its docket of hearings and agrees to review only a fraction of the cases appealed to it. It accepted 9 percent of all appeals in 1977 and only 3 percent of the 2,075 criminal appeals filed by indigents (the so-called *in forma pauperis* docket).[27]

Moreover, appellate courts can only decide whether legal errors were committed in lower courts (e.g., improper testimony admitted into evidence or illicit jury selection procedures); they do not normally question findings of fact or sentencing. Thus, the two most crucial determinations in deciding a defendant's fate are almost exclusively within the province of the trial court.

In France and some other European countries, judges play a vigorous role in the fact-finding process. Utilizing the so-called "inquisitorial procedure," examining magistrates, who are part of the judiciary, make an independent full-scale investigation of the case prior to trial. Moreover, the trial judge usually dominates the questioning of witnesses at the trial and will not close the proceedings until satisfied that all the relevant information has come out.

Because judges in this country do not act in such a clearly aggressive fashion, a myth has developed that they play a modest role in the trial process. The judge's task is said to be limited to "the umpiring of competition" between the prosecution and the defense as well as the enforcement of appropriate substantive and procedural laws. One of the defendants interviewed by political scientist Jonathan Casper captured the essence of this myth in a pithy remark: "The judge's job is to sit on his ass and do what the prosecutor tells him to do."[28]

In reality, judges have a wide gamut of legal responsibilities that enables them to exercise enormous, if sometimes subtle, control over the disposition of cases. The ultimate fate of most defendants is determined by a succession of decisions made by judges, some seemingly minor and others obviously critical. Judges may often appear to be almost nonchalantly watching the proceedings as aloof outsiders when they sit quietly on the bench, but how they respond to motions, how they supervise various proceedings, and how they pronounce judgment decisively influence outcomes. To illustrate just how powerful judges can be, we shall now take an inventory of the many important options open to them.

PRETRIAL ADJUDICATION

THE ARRAIGNMENT The first appearance of a felony defendant before a judge is usually the arraignment. At this time the defendant pleads guilty or not guilty and is apprised of his or her legal rights. By the manner in which they explain these rights, (e.g., the right to counsel and the right to a jury trial), judges can subtly influence defendants either to cooperate with authorities by pleading guilty or to maintain their innocence. In some cities like Detroit these hearings function as "degradation ceremonies," which serve to stamp the badge of guilt on defendants in that judges treat them as if they were proven criminals.[29] Judges also determine at the arraignment whether the defendant is eligible to be represented by a state-provided attorney as a result of indigence. Guidelines are normally quite loose, so that judges have much discretion in deciding whether a poor defendant must scrounge for a lawyer or will receive one free of charge.

BAIL   The other important decision at the arraignment concerns bail. Judges have a variety of means at their disposal to try to guarantee that those arrested will return to court for trial. First, they can simply release the defendant on recognizance (R.O.R.), which means that he or she promises to appear in court at the scheduled times. A second related option is to release the defendant to the custody of some presumably reliable person, like a relative who is made responsible for the defendant's return to court. Third, judges can require a personal bond for a specified amount of money, which enables the defendant to go free without paying anything but makes him or her liable for the amount in the case of a failure to appear. Fourth, and most commonly used in serious cases, is the surety bond, which requires that a defendant post a certain amount of money or property or buy a bond from a bail bondsman, who will provide the money for a fee of about 10 percent. Fifth, in order to eliminate bondsmen, some states have introduced a "cash bail" program (sometimes called a "percentage deposit bail system"), which requires defendants to post a percentage of a bond in cash with the stipulation that most of this collateral is returnable if the defendant shows up in court. Finally, in most states and in the District of Columbia, persons accused of serious violent crimes can be denied bail altogether if the judge thinks they are dangerous; this is called "preventive detention."

Because most defendants have limited means, the dollar amount required for bail almost invariably determines whether or not the person is going to be incarcerated prior to trial. In other words, setting bail above a certain amount is, for all practical purposes, the same as preventive detention if even the 10 percent needed to buy a bond is unobtainable. A study of a sample of defendants in New York City in 1971 bears this out. Not one defendant out of 135 ordered to pay $2,000 or more was able to gain release, and only 2 percent of those required to pay at least $1,000 were released.[30]

By taking advantage of their enormous latitude in setting bond, judges are able to decide who they are going to detain—with the exception of the very rich, such as Nicky Barnes, the alleged "kingpin" of the Harlem heroin trade, who in 1977 came up with $300,000 to obtain his release.[31] Because the potential for great inequities is present in the very nature of the bail system and because the consequences of pretrial incarceration are quite large, we shall discuss the nature of the decision to set bail in some detail later in this chapter.

PRELIMINARY HEARINGS   Some time after the arraignment a hearing is held at which the judge determines whether there is "probable cause" to believe that the defendant is guilty of the offenses charged. If the judge decides that the evidence presented by the prosecutor is insufficient to warrant a trial, the case can be dismissed immediately. In some cities such as Detroit where prosecutors thoroughly screen cases, these hearings are rather perfunctory, since 95 percent of cases survive the evidentiary test; but in cities like Chicago well over half of all cases (74 percent) are terminated at this point.[32]

Other motions—challenging the use of certain evidence garnered by the prosecutor (e.g., seized drugs or the results of a police line-up)—are heard either at the preliminary hearing or in separate hearings. If the evidence is ruled inadmissible because of improprieties in acquiring it and it is central to the prosecution's case, the judge may dismiss the case or the prosecutor may drop the charges.

This is precisely what happened in the case of the key defendant in the "Dawson Five" case, in which five young black men were accused of murdering a white man in a grocery store in Dawson, Georgia. First, a judge threw out as evidence several ski masks allegedly worn by the holdup men that were found in the home of one defendant because the officer who made the search lacked the authority to do so. In a subsequent hearing, another judge (who had taken over the case) ruled that a confession taken from the defendant had been coerced and therefore had to be suppressed. (While he was wired to a polygraph, he was threatened with electrocution if he did not admit the crimes.) Soon thereafter, all charges were dropped. This indicates how judges can absolve defendants through procedural rulings if defects are apparent in the way the prosecution has developed its case.[33]

Judges have other powers at the pretrial stage. They must rule on a "change of venue" motion, in which the defendant asks that the trial be moved to a place away from the location of the crime because local pretrial publicity has made it impossible to select an unbiased jury. They must decide whether or not the defendant is sane enough to stand trial, the normal requirement being that the defendant must be able to understand the charges against him or her and assist with the defense. Alternatives to prosecution (often called "diversion"), such as drug therapy programs (to be discussed in Chapter 12), are recommended by the prosecutor and must be approved. Likewise, judges must put their stamp of approval on plea bargains arranged by the prosecution and the defense—an important act that provides both the legal cement that keeps these agreements intact as well as the legitimacy that makes them seem more proper. None of these decisions is a minor technical matter; all determine whether a trial will ensue and if so, which side will have the edge.

TRIAL SUPERVISION

The judge runs the trial. It takes only a few visits to any courtroom to realize how much the judge's presence dominates the scene. Both the robe and the elevated desk place the judge apart from all others, giving him or her an air of superiority. The deferential gestures that all other participants regularly make, such as rising when he or she enters the courtroom and using "Your Honor" as a form of address, are a recognition of this lofty status. Moreover, the real degree of control that the judge exercises matches this symbolic obeisance. For those judges eager for power, presiding over trials is an ideal means of satisfying this particular drive.

ADMISSION OF EVIDENCE   Judges continuously decide questions about the admissibility of evidence, and the typical trial features hundreds, even thousands, of decisions of this nature in response to objections of prosecution and defense attorneys. The relevance of testimony by witnesses is a persistent issue, as is the neutrality of lawyers' questions (e.g., whether the lawyer is improperly "leading" the witness). Many technical rules govern the introduction of physical evidence. Determinations about the propriety of "expert" testimony are another kind of judicial prerogative. Consequently, judges play an important part in screening the information available to the jury—and in so doing they may well influence final verdicts.

SETTING THE "TONE" OF TRIALS   Judges can reveal to the jury their sympathies toward the defense or the prosecution in a variety of subtle ways. Their attitude toward the lawyers on each side is sometimes quite transparent, and this sentiment can color the jury's perceptions of the opposing sides.

Sometimes judges are faced with unruly defendants. Such was the case when Bobby Seale, a leader of the Black Panther party, continuously cursed Judge Julius Hoffman while being tried for his part in the alleged conspiracy to cause a riot during the Democratic National Convention in Chicago in 1968. After Seale repeatedly jumped up and denounced Hoffman as a racist and fascist for not letting Seale represent himself, the judge ordered that Seale be chained to a chair and his mouth bound with adhesive tape. While Hoffman cautioned the jury that these measures had nothing to do with the defendant's guilt or innocence, such actions probably had a prejudicial effect on the jury's feelings about Seale and his seven codefendants (even though Seale was ultimately tried separately).[34] In their methods for handling such difficulties, judges can and do convey their own sentiments—and jurors are hardly oblivious to this state of affairs.

CONTROL OVER JURY SELECTION AND PERFORMANCE   The judge supervises the questioning of the jury pool (sometimes called the "venire") by the lawyers, deciding how much latitude they have in probing for hidden biases and occasionally asking questions himself. The decision to excuse jurors challenged "for cause" (i.e., for prejudice) by either of the opposing lawyers is in the judge's hands—and need not be justified formally. Administration of the jury pools is done by the judge who decides whether clerks are using proper procedures to secure cross-sections of the population.

Once the jury is chosen, the judge has the responsibility to acquaint jurors with trial procedures and to explain to them the many baffling technicalities to which they are exposed. It is the duty of the judge to admonish them about discussing the case with each other or with outsiders while the trial is taking place.

In a decision crucial to the well-being of jurors and sometimes affecting the ultimate outcome, the judge must decide if the jury is to be sequestered during the trial in order not to be influenced by the media. Thus, the judge determines whether jurors will be kept in seclusion away from their homes, their neighbors, their family, their friends, and their lovers.

One specific function of the judge in dealing with the jury—the providing of instructions to the jury about the meaning of the law that they must apply—can have awesome effects. Not only does the judge spell out the definition of the crime in question and the precise facts that the prosecution must prove, but he or she articulates many general notions about criminal law and procedure. The concept of guilt beyond a reasonable doubt is explained, presumptions about different kinds of evidence are discussed, and the notion of the burden of proof is elaborated. In some instances, the judge comments very specifically about the quality and quantity of the evidence on hand. Commonly, instructions consume several hours time, and in the process the judge can intentionally or inadvertently slant jurors' verdicts.

One facet of the judge's instructions can give him or her even more direct leverage over case outcomes. The judge ultimately decides, at the end of the trial, what verdicts are permissible—of exactly what crimes the defendant may be convicted. For example, the judge can decide whether a defendant who allegedly engaged in a street disturbance can be convicted of riot, unlawful assembly, or disorderly conduct—or all three.

In making these choices, the judge often has the alternative of giving the jurors an opportunity to find the defendant guilty of a less serious charge or of confronting them with the predicament of either convicting on serious charges or acquitting altogether. It is the latter course that the judge took in the Algiers Motel trial, in which a white police officer was charged with murdering three black teen-agers during the height of the destructive Detroit riots of 1967. During the riots the officer had discovered the boys (and seven others) having an orgy with two white prostitutes in the motel. Forty-two prosecution witnesses contended that the boys had been killed in cold blood after having been intimidated and beaten, but the defendant said he killed in self-defense while he was looking for snipers. In light of the volatile circumstances and pitched emotions that no doubt loomed large during the whole episode, some observers felt it logical to permit a finding of manslaughter—killing done in the heat of passion. But the judge gave the jury only two options—acquittal or conviction on a first-degree murder charge (requiring premeditation). Many commentators contend that in this way the judge preordained the verdict of not guilty that the jury reached.[35] Whether this speculation is true or not, the case does illustrate how the judge can encourage certain verdicts by structuring the jury's choices in a particular manner.

DIRECT CONTROL OVER VERDICTS   In about one-half of all cases that go to trial, the defendant waives the right to a jury trial. In those cases the judge decides both the legal and factual issues alone and thus has total control over the destiny of defendants. But even in jury trials judges can prevail over juries. Both before and after juries render verdicts, judges can legally take the decision out of their hands. They can dismiss cases after the prosecution has presented its case on the grounds that insufficient evidence was presented to allow the case to go to the jury, and they can upset a conviction to avert what they think is an injustice. Thus, a Colorado judge, Richard Green, overturned a verdict not long ago convicting a fellow judge of altering a trial transcript,[36] and Connecticut Superior Court Judge Simon Cohen acquitted a defendant in 1977 of drowning his wife just moments after a jury had convicted him.[37] A judge can also unilaterally decide case outcomes by barring a retrial of a defendant whose case resulted in a mistrial due to a "hung jury" that was unable to reach a unanimous verdict.

SENTENCING   Finally, judges have enormous leeway in sentencing those who are convicted after trial (in contrast to their more limited power if plea bargains have been arranged). The law generally allows a wide range of possible prison sentences for any given crime, and the judge is responsible for prescribing a maximum and minimum penalty. In some states indeterminate sentences are given, in which case the judge sets the lower limit but the correction authorities determine how long the defendant actually serves.

Even more important than control over the length of imprisonment is whether to impose a penal sanction at all. Judges normally have the right to impose fines in lieu of prison sentences or to grant probation even in the most serious of cases; thus a convicted defendant may go free but is subject to court supervision and restrictions on his or her behavior. Most states also allow judges to suspend sentences, which permits the convicted criminal to walk out of court with no formal punishment whatsoever.

Because all of these choices concerning sentencing are so forbidding in their proportions, we will devote an entire section later in this chapter to explaining how judges exercise this discretion.

SUMMARY JUSTICE IN MINOR CASES

When people are accused of serious felonies, a complicated time-consuming process commences, which may ultimately involve dozens of courtroom hearings and many decisions made by many different officials. However, most criminal cases are *not* of this nature; they involve defendants charged with minor crimes—misdemeanors—for which the maximum punishment is no more than one year in jail. Thus, in 1976 over twice as many people were charged with the crimes of disorderly conduct and vandalism than were charged with murder, rape, aggravated assault, and robbery—the serious crimes of violence.[38] One out of six arrests was for public drunkenness or liquor law violations. Approximately 7.5 million people were charged with misdemeanors in contrast to about 2.5 million persons arrested for felonies—a ratio of about three to one. Therefore, while we have emphasized the disposition of felonies in this book because they pose more serious consequences for defendants, victims, and the society generally, it should be borne in mind that the summary justice briefly described below predominates in the judicial system.

Misdemeanor cases are handled very quickly in a routine fashion, and the process has been likened to a conveyor belt or a "sausage factory."[39] What are usually quite distinct steps in the felony case (the arraignment, the preliminary hearing, the trial, the sentencing hearing, etc.) are all collapsed into one very brief hearing in which the judge reigns supreme, as the following transcript for the trial of a defendant charged with drunkenness makes clear:

> Magistrate: Where do you live?
> Defendant: Norfolk.
> Magistrate: What are you doing in Philadelphia?
> Defendant: Well, I didn't have any work down there, so I came here to see if I could find . . .
> Magistrate (who had been shaking his head): That story's not good enough for me. I'm going to have you investigated. You're a vagrant. Three months in the House of Correction[40]

The courts are simply overwhelmed with such cases and lack the resources to observe the niceties of legal procedures. For example, with three Atlanta judges disposing of 70,000 misdemeanors in one year and one Detroit judge handling over 20,000 such cases annually,[41] it is unrealistic to expect anything but the kind of exchange quoted above. A study of the handling of minor cases in Baltimore indicates that many defendants accused of similar crimes are actually processed in groups and that 72 percent of the courtroom encounters before the judge last no more than one minute.[42] Short sentences, such as "time served" or a small fine, are the norm, and certain misdemeanants, like prostitutes or numbers runners, are usually back on the street engaging in the same kind of crime within moments of their trial.

Perhaps even more routinized are traffic courts, the judicial institution with which the average citizen is most likely to have personal contact. In the mid-1960s approximately 21 million tickets for moving violations were issued annually, and countless more parking citations were meted out.[43] Most offenders simply mail in their fines and only a small fraction of these charges are contested, but in quantitative terms the traffic courts still handle far more cases than the regular criminal courts. And the ordinary traffic hearing bears little resemblance to the elaborate set of procedures sketched earlier in this chapter. The hearing is very standardized: The police officer gives one version of events; the motorist gives another; and the judge makes a split-second decision. Defendants barely know that their case is under way before they find themselves either at the cashier's window paying a fine or (in a small minority of cases) walking out of the courtroom with smiles on their faces after having been exonerated by the judge. This is justice by fiat—not adjudication.

Ironically, this assembly-line processing of defendants that characterizes both misdemeanor and traffic courts is somewhat freer of the chance and uncertainty described in the beginning of this chapter. Although little time is available to probe for facts, constitutional rights are minimally observed, and there is an underlying presumption of guilt, sentences are rather predictably based on the gravity of the charge. The person who is in fact guilty knows what to expect; but the innocent person caught up in incriminating circumstances has precious little opportunity to prove it. Only luck can normally save the latter—the good fortune to have the judge believe the story (as occasionally happens) or the break of having the complaining witness (usually the police officer) fail to appear in court (a common occurrence). But because luck may well operate without regard to truth or justice, guilty persons may benefit from it as often as the innocent. Conditions of mass justice make the task of discriminating between guilty and innocent almost impossible, so that treating almost everyone as guilty becomes the means of having a semblance of even-handedness.

This kind of mass justice clearly serves the public interest of economy in government: The costs would be astronomical if all defendants charged with misdemeanors were allowed the full panoply of rights and hearings furnished to felony defendants. Nevertheless, considerable resources are still expended adjudicating these rather minor cases of people accused of relatively harmless crimes, so a movement is afoot to reduce judicial cognizance of such matters drastically by decriminalizing some crimes and diverting others to other institutions that are less expensive to operate. These changes will be discussed in detail in Chapters 11 and 12.

JUVENILE JUSTICE

Whatever degree of discretion exists in the criminal courts must be multiplied several times over to describe adequately the operation of juvenile courts. The underlying philosophy of juvenile justice is *in loco parentis*—acting in the place of parents. This idea implies that courts should have the wide range of options and the high degree of informality that characterizes parental supervision of children. In coming to the assistance of children in trouble, the courts relax constraints such as legality, due process, and firm standards of responsibility so that they can concentrate on their main goal—helping wayward children.

To accomplish this, the jurisdiction of juvenile courts has been made very broad. Not only are such courts authorized to adjudicate all cases where young people under the age of 15 or 16 have allegedly committed crimes as defined in the penal code, but they can intervene in a broadly defined set of circumstances where the child has acted abnormally but not broken the law. All states also have what are called "Persons in Need of Supervision" (P.I.N.S.) statutes to deal with the so-called unruly child. The Ohio provision exemplifies such statutes:

As used in . . . the Revised Code, "Unruly Child" includes any child:

(A) Who does not subject himself to the reasonable control of his parents, teachers, guardian, or custodian, by reason of his being wayward and disobedient;

(B) Who is an habitual truant from home or school;

(C) Who so deports himself as to injure or endanger the health or morals of himself or others;

(D) Who attempts to enter the marriage relation in any state without the consent of his parents, custodian, legal guardian, or other legal authority;

(E) Who is found in a disreputable place, visits or patronizes a place prohibited by law, or associates with vagrant, vicious, notorious, or immoral persons;

(F) Who engages in an occupation prohibited by law, or is in a situation dangerous to life or limb or injurious to the health or morals of himself or others.[44]

One need not be a legal scholar to realize how far-reaching and ill-defined such a statute is and how, as a result, many children may find themselves at the mercy of judges in juvenile courts.

Procedures of the juvenile court are equally broad. All hearings are held in secret. Presumably this is done to prevent youths from being stigmatized; in actuality, these hearings function to shield very irregular processes from outside view. These are administrative proceedings: Little resemblance to the adversary process with procedural rights can be discerned, although some Supreme Court decisions in recent years have given children accused of serious crime some legal protections, such as the right to counsel.[45] Juvenile law allows dispositions to vary enormously with no regard for guilt or innocence. For example the courts may legally release killers to their parents' custody while incarcerating shoplifters. Moreover, all kinds of unusual "treatments" can be devised, limited only by the ingenuity or the inflexibility of the judges; thus, one judge in California sentenced a long-haired boy to wear girls' clothes to school.[46] In short, the judge is the boss of the juvenile court; his or her control is virtually unfettered.

The daily functioning of the juvenile courts is chaotic. The constitutional rights of juveniles are blithely ignored.[47] The police, social workers, probation officers, victims, parents, and the young people in jeopardy give their versions of what happened in brief and often disorganized hearings. Facts are thus obtained in a very casual and haphazard fashion, and only by happenstance, if there is a dispute about the young person's guilt, does the truth emerge.

Dispositions are made quite intuitively; they are characterized by laxity and seeming arbitrariness. In California over half of all cases disposed of by juvenile court were dismissed, and only 4 percent resulted in the youth's detention in a correctional agency.[48] The New York juvenile justice system is even more benign: Only 1 percent of youngsters arrested for violent street crimes was "institutionalized."[49]

Horror stories abound of dangerous individuals being put back on the street. After 18-year-old George Adorno killed a cab driver during a robbery, for example, it was discovered that he had twice before appeared in juvenile court for homicides and had admitted taking part in scores of armed robberies.[50] He committed most of the crimes while he was under the supervision of juvenile authorities.

On the other hand, nonviolent youngsters sometimes are detained because they make a bad appearance in court. The judgment process is basically a test of attitudes, and a certain demeanor is expected as a measure of moral character.[51] Deference, respect, politeness, and contrition—these are the qualities that pay off in leniency. Serious offenders who appear repentant often get off easy, while rebellious youths who have done little or nothing wrong may be designated "troublemakers" and treated accordingly.

Another form of inequity is the disparity in treatment accorded to criminals who commit similar crimes simply because they happen to fall on opposite sides of the age dividing line that separates juveniles and adults. Adults can receive life imprisonment or even death for crimes much less vicious than those committed by juveniles, who rarely serve more than one or two years in a detention center. This incongruity is most acute when cohorts to the same crime receive vastly different sentences due to age differences. For example, in New York City a 15-year old who pulled the trigger in a ghastly subway murder received 18 months, while his 17-year old accomplice who stood nearby and watched during the fatal holdup received 8½ to 25 years for his part in the crime.[52] Because such perversions of justice are not uncommon when two totally different judicial systems operate side by side, some states such as New York have changed their laws to permit some juveniles accused of certain violent crimes to be tried and sentenced as if they were adults.

To summarize, juvenile justice is often unjust and unfair. It has been largely unsuccessful in preventing future crimes. Its hearings are rituals, and youths who fail to play their assigned role are penalized. Nobody gains—except the people whose jobs depend on processing the overwhelming number of cases. These courts, in short, have virtually *no* redeeming social value.

The failures of juvenile justice are a cause for concern among advocates of diversion of adult offenders, a relatively new policy that subjects accused persons to "treatment" of one kind or another and spares them the ordeal of trial and punishment. As Chapter 12 describes, such informal treatment of adults has the potential for even greater arbitrariness than the regular institutions of the criminal justice system. The concept of treating people, whether adults or juveniles, in a humane and empathetic manner is quite appealing, and dispensing with the rigid formalities of the law seems on the surface to be a sensible way of achieving this objective. But the lesson of the juvenile justice system is that due process and justice may well be sacrificed through informal treatment of alleged offenders without any gain in crime prevention or public tranquillity.

The Political Nature of Judgeships

To understand how judges use all of this power, it must be recognized that the judiciary is a quintessentially political institution; judges are politicians in robes. The reason for this has more to do with the nature of the job than the way judges are selected (although we shall see that politics is often the key to being chosen). Judicial decision making invariably embroils judges in almost all the major conflicts and controversies in the society—those involving race, class, sex, life style, and moral values. Thus, appellate court justices regularly decide fundamental issues of public policy like abortion and integration when they use the power of judicial review to determine the constitutionality of laws and other government acts; and the range of views in such courts often parallels those in the larger body politic.

Decisions of lower courts are equally political, although the myth persists there that they are merely enforcing the legal norms created by others and implementing the policy choices made elsewhere. Sometimes lower courts play a direct role in allocating benefits to specific groups and individuals, as when probate judges assign favored lawyers to administer estates of people who die without a will or when federal judges divvy up the assets of bankrupt businesses among competing creditors who are making claims. Also, judicial discretion in imposing sanctions against certain political and economic elites who have been convicted of crimes can drastically curtail their power or wealth.

But far more important in terms of total social impact than these isolated decisions that can critically change people's fortunes or political standing is the aggregate effect of innumerable daily decisions made in criminal courts in cases far from public view involving totally unknown defendants. The patterns and trends established through countless decisions regarding bail, admission of evidence, jury selection, sentencing, and the like determine which kinds of criminal behavior are severely censured and which are treated lightly. Moreover, in making all of these decisions, judges are implicitly and incrementally determining which public interests (e.g., due process or efficiency) are to be given priority and which crime-prevention strategies (e.g., deterrence or rehabilitation) are to be preferred. Having a major voice in this area of public choice gives judges political power that matches their substantial legal authority described in the preceding section.

Various power structures generally decide on those who become judges. However, once judges reach the bench, they are able to pursue a remarkably independent course and are largely unbeholden to those who sponsored them. This independence may contribute to their integrity, but it also means that they are accountable to almost no one except themselves. Sometimes they are responsive to public dictates and particular interests, but only when they want to be. In its daily functioning, the American judiciary is a highly elitist political institution.

THE SELECTION OF JUDGES

A judge in a large Texas city keeps a cartoon on the blotter of his desk that shows a judge glaring down at a young witness and saying, "You better show me the proper respect, sonny, I kissed a lot of ass to get this job."[53] Nothing could depict more accurately the nature of judicial selection. Judgeships provide status, power, job security, and money—between $40,000 and $50,000 annually in most large states and $42,500 for federal district court judges. Thus, it should not be surprising that President Harry Truman received the following rather crass telegram one day: "Judge Smith died yesterday at his farm. . . . Jones would be an excellent man to fill the vacancy."[54] Judgeships are coveted positions and, therefore, one of the most lucrative forms of patronage used by those in political power and higher legal circles to reward friends and followers—or friends *of* followers.

Various formal methods are used to select judges. Federal judges are appointed by the president and must be confirmed by the Senate. State and local court judges are chosen in a variety of ways, with some states using a combination of methods: in 8 states appointment is primarily by the governor; in 4 states selection of most judges is by the state legislature; partisan election, in which the party affiliation of candidates is listed on the ballot, is used in 16 states; nonpartisan election is also used in 16 states; 12 states use some kind of "merit plan," according to which the governor appoints judges from a list of nominees submitted by a nominating commission (sometimes called the "Missouri plan" because it was first adopted in that state).[55]

PICKING FEDERAL JUDGES   Federal appointments are generally in the hands of the top leaders of the president's party in a state that has a vacancy (usually senators and occasionally representatives), and they make recommendations to the president. While the attorney general, the F.B.I., and the American Bar Association[56] do a check on these suggestions to eliminate any totally disreputable candidates, these groups and the president normally play a vetoing role rather than an initiating role in making appointments.

The Senate Judiciary Committee holds routine hearings to examine the credentials of nominees and to discern if any vehement opposition is raised from various quarters; but these sessions are ordinarily of a strictly formal nature, because rarely do senators oppose the choices of fellow senators. Even when it was revealed that Senator Edward Kennedy's protégé, Francis X. Morrisey, a long-time family friend and Boston politician, had received his law degree from an unaccredited "diploma mill" in Georgia where he had failed four courses and had failed to pass the state bar examination twice, the Judiciary Committee rec-

269

ommended his confirmation by a 6 to 3 vote. (Morrissey himself later withdrew from consideration as a result of the adverse publicity.)[57] The entire Senate is equally prone to back the nomination of one of their members, as is indicated by the 76 to 8 vote in favor of James Coleman, the segregationist ex-governor of Mississippi who was proposed by Mississippi's senators and nominated by President Johnson in 1965; this was the same year that the Congress passed some of the most far-reaching civil rights legislation in our history![58] The favorites of the party politicos almost always carry the day—regardless of ideology or competence.

The extent to which federal judgeships are used to reward the party faithful is indicated by the following figures: Since the presidency of Franklin Roosevelt, four Democratic and three Republican presidents have made at least 90 percent of their appointments from their own party. Moreover, the few federal judges who have spoken candidly about how they got their jobs have all acknowledged the primacy of political ties. Judge Joseph Perry, for example, tells how he jockeyed between the two parties several times until he "gambled" and supported Paul Douglas in his victorious campaign to become United States senator from Illinois in exchange for Douglas's promise to promote his candidacy to the federal bench.[59]

Another indication of the omnipresence of party politics in the selection of federal judges is the fact that when two prominent politicians in Illinois and Maryland were charged by federal prosecutors with corruption, a judge from out of state had to be brought in for both cases because every single judge within the two states had some kind of personal or political relationship with the defendants. Judge Robert Taylor of Tennessee presided over the trials of Maryland Governor Marvin Mandel and Governor Otto Kerner of Illinois, both of whom were convicted.[60]

The use of judgeships as patronage is by no means a new political phenomenon; the Founding Fathers themselves used these posts in an equally cynical fashion. Just before John Adams left office after losing the presidency in the election of 1800, he appointed several cronies from the Federalist party to judgeships in the District of Columbia that were not even needed, and he elevated Secretary of State John Marshall to the position of Chief Justice of the Supreme Court. The selection of these "midnight judges" was denounced by Adams's opponents as unsavory political contamination of the judiciary, but it has served as a precedent that politicians of all stripes have long since followed.

STAFFING THE STATE COURTS　When judges are chosen by the governors, both personal and political connections to these top officials are important considerations. In interviews with Texas judges who were appointed by two governors from 1949 to 1963, one-fourth of the judges said that their direct friendship with the governor contributed most to their appointment, and 60 percent alluded to other indirect ties.[61]

The appointment of 15 "midnight judges" by New York City Mayor Abraham Beame a few days before the expiration of his term of office in 1977 is an indication of how much more significant political considerations can be than other qualifications, such as court experience or legal knowledge. All 15 judges had been recommended by Democratic party leaders; 7 of them had been listed as unqualified by the New York City Bar Association, whose president accused Beame of "succumbing to narrow political considerations."[62] Yet all of the appointments had been approved by the mayor's screening committee (whose members he selected), and a journalist who studied the operation of this committee concluded that it was just a procedure for rubber-stamping the mayor's backroom deals.[63]

In the four states in which the legislature selects judges, politics also looms large. Almost all judges chosen have held previous political office, and many are former legislators. Again, a "buddy system" prevails.[64]

Where partisan election is the method of selecting state judges, patronage appointments are also the norm. Judicial nominations are generally controlled by party leaders, and since very few voters have any knowledge about the candidates for these offices, the dominant party almost always prevails in the general election. Indeed, a study of judicial elections in California showed a dropout rate of between 15 and 25 percent over a five-year period, meaning that up to one-fourth of the voters at general elections simply did not vote for *anyone* in the judges' races (in contrast to dropout rates of 4 percent for district attorney and 13 percent for the superintendent of public instruction).[65]

Since many local units of government (counties and cities) are regularly controlled by one party and manifest little seesawing between the parties, rarely do party nominees for judgeships lose at the polls. The blessing of the party leadership is tantamount to getting the job. So it should not be surprising that when judges greet Brooklyn Democratic leader Meade Esposito in a local restaurant they often say, "Hi, Boss"—an honest recognition that he is the one who staffs the judiciary.[66]

In addition, two special practices make the choices of the party even more invulnerable to electoral challenge. First, many elected judges resign or die in office before the expiration of their term. Governors (and sometimes mayors) then have the right to fill the vacancy by appointment (such as in Texas, where about two-thirds of all judges gain their initial appointment in such a manner).[67] Since incumbents have name visibility and can run for reelection with the prestigious title "Judge So-and-so," subsequent elections are normally one-sided events in which the challenger has little chance of winning. As a result, judges commonly run unopposed, which is the case in two-thirds of California elections.[68]

A device for assuring that each party gets a rather fixed share of judicial posts to be distributed to its favorite people is the practice of "cross-listing." Once agreement between leaders of opposing parties is reached on how many judgeships each party is to receive, one party agrees to list the other party's choices on the ballot; thus, for any given judgeship the voters' only choice is whether to select the same person as a Democrat or as a Republican. This is common practice in New York State; between 1970 to 1977, 126 out of 150 justices elected to the major trial courts ran with the prearranged endorsement of both major parties—giving voters no choice whatsoever except to throw their vote away on a write-in or minor-party candidate.[69]

A memo written by the former Democratic leader of Queens (New York), Matthew Troy, describing the pact he made with his Republican counterpart reveals how these deals on judgeships are part of an overall scheme to divide up the "spoils" of government positions. Excerpts from the memo read as follows:

> Five new Supreme Court judgeships (newly created by the legislature). Repubs to get three—Dems to get two (plus Dems to get replacement for Tony Liboti)—all on a bi-partisan basis. . . . If legislators go to Civil Court vacancies, then the special election for legis. vacancy will have no Repub. opponent. . . . Repubs agree to give bi-partisan endorsement to Boro Pres, District Attorney and Surrogate . . . [Troy himself] to receive bi-partisan Councilman endorsement in 1973.[70]

All this, and more, was carried out—with no influence whatsoever from the voters of Queens. Elections are intended to make officials accountable to the public, but such political machinations totally undermine that goal.

Elites are similarly in control of judicial selection under the Missouri plan, although it is the leadership of the bar associations rather than party bosses who dominate nominating commissions. The plan, however, does formally maintain one vestige of popular control—a referendum held near the expiration of a judge's term in which a majority of voters must agree that the sitting judge should be retained in office. This provision has been adopted in other states (e.g., Illinois) as the means for determining the judge's continuation in office, even though the initial choice was by contested elections. But in practice voter approval is almost automatic. In recent years only 1 out of 179 judges was turned out of office in Missouri, and in Illinois no judge has been voted out.[71] The "wrath of the voters" is an empty threat, and the public plays a negligible role in staffing the judiciary.

JUDICIAL AUTONOMY

Once judges are in office, they are able to pursue a quite independent course. Their terms of office are long: Most range from 5 to 8 years, although some are as high as 14 and 15 years; federal judges (plus judges in three states) have life tenure. Moreover, judges who must seek reelection are almost never unseated. Outraged voters in Madison, Wisconsin, in 1977 recalled a judge who attributed the rise in rape and the "normal" reactions of a juvenile rape defendant to the provocative way young women dressed; this action was noteworthy precisely because such results are so rare.[72]

The only way to remove federal judges is through the cumbersome and difficult process of impeachment, which requires a majority vote in the House of Representatives and conviction by two-thirds of the Senate; only four federal judges have ever been so removed in our entire history.[73] While most state constitutions also provide for impeachment of state judges by the legislature, the procedures are cumbersome and the option is almost never used. Many states also empower the top judges in the state to convene special judicial panels to investigate judges accused of impropriety and to discipline or oust those found to be malfeasant, but this too is a rarely utilized device.

Thus, judges really need not worry about losing their jobs if they offend the people and institutions instrumental in putting them on the bench in the first place. Some studies have shown modest correlations between party membership and whether judges lean more to the prosecution or to the defense;[74] but because American parties are relatively heterogeneous and nonideological, their behavior on the bench is not very predictable on the basis of party. Other aspects of judges' backgrounds, such as religion, do relate somewhat to their decision-making propensities,[75] but in no way do judges demonstrate the kind of allegiance to particular interests and groups that legislators do. Political leaders and economic institutions obtain years of fealty from those harboring judicial aspirations, but these obligations are largely relinquished when such service is rewarded with a judgeship. To the power brokers, judicial patronage is much more important in the way it constrains recipients *prior* to taking office; the behavior of judges *on the bench* is much less consequential.

Occasionally a trial involves a person connected to the power structure that brought the presiding judge into office, and it appears that judges are showing favoritism on the basis of party loyalty. This was the implication when a New York judge acquitted Democratic leader Matthew Troy of perjury charges while admonishing Troy that he "should be more careful with the English language."[76] When those on trial are judges, such judicial sympathy toward the defendant is sometimes even more obvious. Thus over a five-year period beginning in 1972, a special New York State prosecutor authorized to probe corruption in the judiciary secured indictments against 12 separate judges, but all of them ultimately had their cases dismissed or their convictions overturned by fellow judges.[77] While all of them may in fact have been innocent, they were treated far more favorably than the usual defendants appearing in court.

However, other judges have behaved in just the opposite way. Federal Judge John Sirica (a Republican) was meticulous in disdaining partiality toward the various Republican officials on trial before him in the Watergate affair and was adamant in insisting that President Nixon give up the famous White House tapes, which contained incriminating information. In short, judges cannot be counted on to save the party faithful or injure the opposition party once in office.

On the other hand, certain inherent biases in the selection process (such as the fact that all judges must be lawyers) have made the judiciary fairly unrepresentative; it is disproportionately made up of people who are white, male, affluent, middle-aged, and conservative. The intrusion of the American Bar Association into the federal judicial-selection process has reinforced this tendency by bringing to bear the distinctly conservative viewpoints of that organization (which opposed the nomination of social reformer Louis Brandeis to the United States Supreme Court in 1914 and has over the years taken positions against various liberal policies and programs).[78] Nothing forces judges to follow their previous ideology after they obtain office, but far more cases of continuity between pre- and post-judicial values are recorded than of radical departures. Judges who were "law and order" proponents while serving as district attorneys or state legislators are not likely to change political colors simply because they ascend to the bench.

Nevertheless, within the inescapable limitations of attitudes and philosophies acquired over a lifetime, judges are remarkably free to establish their own policies and therefore satisfy whatever self-interest in exercising power they may harbor. They are constrained by the law itself, but the latitude allowed by many statutes, the infrequency of appeals, and the virtual nonexistence of intrajudiciary administrative supervision permit enormous discretion. Like all political beings, they cannot and do not ignore the context in which they operate, so that the anticipated reactions of newspapers, other public figures, private groups, and the public can constrain their decision making. But since judges need not answer to a political constituency and are usually free of bureaucratic imperatives, they can let their own consciences and feelings be their guides more than other politicians.

Defendants embroiled in the criminal justice system are thus often at the mercy of the judges' individual proclivities. There are "tough" and "soft" judges—and which of them the defendants get will often determine their fate. *Who* the judge is—the identity of the courtroom—often helps us predict outcomes better than any other factors.[79] The assignment of cases to particular judges can be one of the most important decisions in the entire criminal justice process, and this is essentially a game of roulette. The unaccountability of the judiciary allows luck to play a central role in determining results.

The Administration of Bail: Justice by Formula

Bail decisions are fairly predictable. Most judges rely on similar criteria except in unusual circumstances, like riot conditions, where there is apt to be considerable variation among judges. Three factors loom largest—the severity of the charge, the defendant's prior record, and the strength of the prosecution's evidence.

The importance of the first two factors is shown in Table 7-1: The highest bail is demanded and the least number of persons are released on recognizance (without bail) when defendants with prior records are charged with the serious crimes of homicide, forcible rape, and robbery. The lowest bail is required and the most releases on recognizance are given when lesser felonies are involved and defendants have never been arrested before. Rarely are other factors given much weight, and motions for bail reductions are likely to be ritualistic denials unless charges against defendants are reduced or weaknesses develop in the prosecutor's case.

However, these factors have little to do with the ostensible purpose of bail,

TABLE 7-1
Bail Disposition According to Charge and Prior Record

Disposition	Major Charge	
	Prior Record	No Prior Record
Percent released on recognizance (*no* bail required)	1.8	5.3
Average bail required when release on recognizance denied	$3,863	$3,085
	Minor Charge	
Percent released on recognizance (no bail required)	8.7	46.4
Average bail required when release on recognizance denied	$1,587	$961

SOURCE: The data are based on 1,483 bail hearings observed from October to December 1964 in New York County Criminal Court. Adapted and reprinted, with permission of the National Council on Crime and Delinquency, from Frederic Suffet, "Bail Setting: A Study of Courtroom Interaction," *Crime and Delinquency*, October 1966, p. 321.

which is to guarantee that defendants appear as scheduled in court. For that purpose, careful screening of a defendant's background is necessary in order to discover the degrees of attachments he or she has to the community as well as his or her overall reliability. Various "point systems" have been developed as a quick means of aggregating information about a defendant's employment, residential stability, and family status in order to obtain a concrete measure of the person's social roots, but these are used in only a few jurisdictions. Even where a defendant is employed, point systems are avoided by judges when dealing with serious cases.

The standard practice of judges is well illustrated by the case of Bruce Ader, accused of a string of rapes and robberies in several New Jersey towns.[80] Ader was initially arrested after an informer identified him from a police sketch of the suspect printed in a local newspaper; he was jailed in lieu of $250,000 bail. When none of the seven witnesses to the various crimes could positively identify Ader or pick him out of a line-up, his bail was reduced to $12,000, which enabled him to win his freedom. The point of this example is that the change in Ader's status had little to do with his probability of disappearing (although the incentive to flee lessens slightly when guilt becomes more doubtful). Other factors probably loomed larger in the judge's mind.

The reason why judges may be reluctant to base their bail decisions on an estimate of defendants' risk of not reappearing is that such judgments cannot be made accurately without a great deal of information, which is often lacking. Even when such information is available, decisions based on it are far from perfect: A recent study in California showed that 15 percent of a sample of persons released on recognizance failed to appear.[81] While only a few released defendants become fugitives, studies have shown that it is not easy to discriminate between those who will and will not flee. Consequently, judges rarely concern themselves with the manifest purpose of bail and instead use their decision making to achieve different ends altogether—the prevention of recidivism, the imposition of pretrial punishment, and the spread of responsibility for mistakes in judgment.

THE REAL FUNCTIONS OF BAIL

Giving short shrift to the presumption of innocence (due process), most judges concern themselves with protecting society from additional crimes committed by those awaiting trial (crime prevention) and with making certain that the guilty receive punishment (justice). In the process the judges protect their own self-interest by warding off criticism and guarding their own reputations.

PREVENTING RECIDIVISM   The criteria used in deciding about bail, while having little relation to the probabilities of defendant nonappearance, are good predictors of whether defendants will commit crimes while out on bail or released on recognizance. Nothing can make judges look worse in the public eye than when people they release (with low bail or no bail) commit new crimes while awaiting trial. Thus, much anger was directed against the judge who had released a man being held on a weapons charge when the man later killed two police officers in New York City.[82] And a community uproar was caused in the Long Island community of Glen Oaks when a judge allowed an accused child molester living in the neighborhood to go free after posting only $650 in cash (10 percent of a $6,500 bond). Although the judge had reason to believe that the defendant would appear in court—he owned a $40,000 home, was married, had two children, and had a solid job—many people were afraid he would attack other children while free on bail. Said one parent from Glen Oaks: "We want to see what we can do about the judge. This is a community living in fear; we don't want this man on the streets."[83]

Because the media are able to fan such fears by publicizing the fact that

HIGH BAIL: PUNISHMENT BEFORE TRIAL

The Court Now, these boys, as I see it, have gone beyond children's acts. This is something that shows they don't know when to stop. Maybe a couple of days in jail may solve the problem. I don't know. I'm going to set $5,000 bail on each. Now, I'm leaving word that if a bond is presented, the matter is to be sent back to me, and I'll tell you right now, if they put up $5,000 bail, I'll make it $10,000, and if they put up ten, I'll make it $25,000. I want these boys to spend one or two nights in jail. Maybe that is the answer.

A report of the New York City Bar Association, cited in Ronald Goldfarb, *Ransom: A Critique of the American Bail System* (1965), p. 47.

suspected criminals are "at large," judges try to incarcerate the defendant whenever a substantial risk of crime repetition exists that may cause panic in a community. The prior record of the accused is important because it suggests the possibility of a "career criminal," and the seriousness of the charge is significant because the degree of harm that may occur is greater. In keeping potentially dangerous criminals in jail, the judges reassure the community—and they protect themselves.

PRETRIAL PUNISHMENT   Judges understand that detention prior to trial not only represents punishment in itself but makes it more probable that defendants will be convicted. Table 7-2 shows that incarcerated defendants are significantly more likely to plead guilty or be convicted than those who are free. Those in jail are under more pressure to plea bargain; they are unable to help very much with their own defense; and they are often stigmatized at their trial. Thus, in taking into account the guilt-implying prior record plus the strength of the prosecutor's evidence in setting bail, judges are in a sense prejudging the defendant and setting punishment in motion.

Pretrial incarceration also serves to punish those who may actually be guilty but manage to escape conviction. One study in Pennsylvania has shown that of 805 people who received pretrial detention because they could not pay bail, two-thirds were either acquitted or given no jail sentence.[84] This result is substantiated by a study of Baltimore, Detroit, and Chicago: As many as one-half (in Baltimore) of those who wound up winning in court spent at least one week in jail, and between one-fifth (in Chicago) and two-fifths (in Baltimore) of these

TABLE 7-2
The Effect of Pretrial Detention on Trial Outcomes

		Percent Acquitted	Percent Convicted
Baltimore	Released	41	59
	Unreleased	20	80
Chicago	Released	28	72
	Unreleased	22	78
Detroit	Released	29	71
	Unreleased	22	78
Los Angeles	Released	19	80[1]
	Unreleased	10	89[1]
New York City	Released	47	53
	Unreleased	27	73

[1] The figures do not add up to 100 percent due to rounding.
SOURCE: Compiled from data in James Eisenstein and Herbert Jacob, *Felony Justice* (Boston: Little, Brown, 1977), p. 261; Robert Rhodes, *The Insoluble Problems of Crime* (New York: John Wiley, 1977), p. 117; and James Eisenstein, *Politics and the Legal Process* (New York: Harper & Row, 1973), p. 239.

"winners" languished in jail for several months prior to their ultimate vindica-
tions.[85] What this implies is that the bail decision functions as a kind of insurance
to make certain that those who are in fact guilty pay a price for their crimes,
even if the complex criminal justice screening process results in their legal vindication. At the same time, it means that *some* of those who are absolutely innocent suffer wrongfully. This is one result of "justice by formula."

When people are arrested during riots or other kinds of mass disorders, it
is even more clear that bail decisions function both to keep participants from
going back onto the streets to do more damage as well as to make certain that
they receive some punishment. During ghetto riots in Chicago, Detroit, and Los
Angeles in the 1960s, a regular pattern occurred: Bail was set very high (e.g.,
$50,000 for those accused of looting and $200,000 for those accused of assault) so
that a disproportionately large number of those arrested were jailed; but the percentage of convictions was far below normal, and relatively few of those who
were convicted received jail sentences.[86]

Moreover, setting high bail in the riots was a form of pretrial sentencing
and had absolutely no relationship to the risk that the defendant would fail to appear in court. Table 7-3 shows that the treatment of those arrested during the

TABLE 7-3
Variation in Bail Decisions During the 1968 Washington, D.C., Riot

Judge	Number of Cases	Percent Requiring Money Bond [1]	Percent Permitting Immediate Release [2]
Korman	21	9.6	90.4
Alexander	53	13.1	79.3[3]
Edgerton	22	22.6	72.3[4]
Burka	10	30.0	70.0
McIntyre	15	33.4	60.0[3]
Hyde	56	48.1	50.0[3]
Murphy	28	50.0	46.5[3]
Kronheim	19	73.8	26.3[4]
Beard	56	73.1	25.0[3]
Halleck	60	81.9	18.4[3]
Pryor	44	84.7	14.2[3]
Daly	39	92.4	7.7[4]
Malloy	22	100.0	None

[1] Cash or a surety bond was required.
[2] Defendant was released on recognizance or to third-party custody.
[3] The figures do not add up to 100 percent because of some peculiar decisions falling outside the
two categories listed here.
[4] The figures do not add up to 100 percent due to rounding.
SOURCE: William Dobrovir, *Justice in Time of Crisis: A Staff Report to the District of Columbia
Committee on the Administration of Justice Under Emergency Conditions* (Washington, D.C.: U.S.
Government Printing Office, 1969), p. 129.

disturbances in Washington, D.C. that followed the assassination of Martin
Luther King, Jr., varied tremendously, depending on which federal judge was
setting bail. One judge required either cash or a surety bond from everyone
coming before him; another allowed virtually everyone (90 percent) to go free
without any bail; and the other judges took actions between these two extremes.
Although this may reflect differences in the times that the different judges were
handling cases (early in the riot versus late, when it may have seemed safer to let
more people go free), it no doubt also is a manifestation of differences in pretrial
sentencing policy. And just as the variation among judges in their sentencing behavior is a blow to the goal of equal justice, differences in bail decisions that are
based only on the judge's personal viewpoint are also unjust.

DIFFUSION OF RESPONSIBILITY   Another purpose served by the bail-set-
ting practices of judges is to make certain that blame for any crimes committed
by defendants who are out free awaiting trial and for any "bail jumping" is shared
among various parties rather than being borne entirely by the judge. In ordinary
cases judges tend to follow the recommendation of prosecutors rather closely and
are relatively unlikely to grant release on recognizance without the suggestion of
some investigative body. In this way judges can point the finger at someone else
if a defendant causes trouble after being released on low bail or no bail; at the
very least the judge need only share the blame with others.

Bail bondsmen are private entrepreneurs

Bail bondsmen are private entrepreneurs who provide the money necessary to enable defendants to make bail in exchange for some percentage of the amount paid. They provide important assistance to judges by assuming some of the responsibility for deciding who goes free. Because the bondsmen risk losing the money that they provided for a defendant's release if the defendant flees, they exercise some caution in screening out bad risks; they pay a price if defendants flee. Moreover, they possess special legal powers to capture defendants who have fled. Bondsmen can use professional detectives ("skip tracers") who, without a warrant, can force defendants to return to court at the point of a gun. The mere threat that such power might be used keeps some defendants in line and protects the judge from appearing to have set a foolishly low bail.

Ironically, it is in the economic self-interest of bondsmen to bail out as many defendants as possible and therefore support the presumption of innocence. They make more money if they sell more bonds, and they are insured to cover losses sustained from defendants who fail to appear. Because higher bonds are required for those accused of more serious crimes, they do not discriminate against such individuals; in fact, they prefer them as customers. Moreover, bondsmen are unconcerned about whether a bailed defendant will commit additional crimes because it has no bearing on their profits, as the following candid observation of one bondsman illustrates:

> We don't care and we can't care about protecting society. We have means and we have methods of making these people pay, so we take the risks and the gambles. That's what we're in business for. There is almost nobody I won't take out, including people I'm certain will repeat their crimes.[87]

Here is a case where private self-interest in money goes hand in hand with the public interest in due process but undermines the public interest in crime prevention. Bail bondsmen, who are business people, can afford to take the blame for recidivism in a way that judges, who are politicians, cannot.

THE ABSURDITY OF THE BAIL SYSTEM

The day before movie director Roman Polanski was to be sentenced in Los Angeles for having unlawful sexual intercourse with a 13-year-old girl, he fled to Europe, forfeiting the $2,500 bail he had posted to gain his freedom.[88] Polanski could have received up to 50 years in prison for the offense, and it was rumored that the judge was going to impose a stiff sentence. From the standpoint of sheer self-interest, fleeing abroad and losing the money made eminently good sense. Far better to lose the money (a mere pittance for someone of Polanski's wealth) and even give up one's home and livelihood than to face the onerous prospect of many years in jail.

Herein lies the absurdity of the bail system. A defendant's risk of disappearing has little logical relationship to his or her resources, but the latter determines most frequently whether that person will be allowed to go free. It is rather ludicrous to think that the mere fact of losing some money in itself will make one show up in court when there is the possibility of imprisonment, but the ostensible purpose of bail is based on just such a faulty premise. Most bailed defendants *do* show up at their trials, but it normally is for totally extraneous reasons—awareness that the chances of fleeing successfully are slim, a hope that they will be acquitted or receive a light sentence, and the horror of having to give up their identity and try to take up a new life. These factors also affect the poor defendant, who cannot make bail, but he or she is rarely given the opportunity to demonstrate this trustworthiness.

If the purpose of bail is to ensure appearance in court, "ransoming" defendants makes little sense because it usually is unnecessary and is no guarantee anyway when the stakes of the trial are greater than the loss of bail money. But other purposes like crime prevention, public reassurance, and pretrial punishment of the guilty as well as the innocent prevail. Justice and due process come out the losers.

The Grand Jury: Tool of the Prosecutor

The grand jury is a group of private citizens (usually 23 in number) selected from the community. It has two principal functions. First, it can investigate situations where apparent improprieties have been discovered to determine if criminality is involved, and, if so, who is responsible. Second, it decides whether to bring indictments against individuals, requiring them to stand trial for the crimes of which they are accused.

Historically, the grand jury arose in England centuries ago from the need to protect individuals from the trauma of unfair prosecution by requiring a group of ordinary people to see if there was sufficient evidence against an individual to warrant putting him or her through the ordeal of a trial.[89] It was transplanted by the American colonists to curtail abuses of British power against them. To protect people's reputations from unfounded charges, the proceedings were made secret, and the minutes of the hearing were sealed if no indictment was brought. Indictment by a grand jury as a prerequisite to trial was considered such an important protection against government repression of innocent people at the foundation of this country that this method of accusation was put into the Bill of Rights (although the Supreme Court has subsequently ruled that it is only required in federal cases).[90] However, in recent years the autonomy of the grand jury has diminished.

In those states that have retained grand jury indictment as a necessary step in the criminal justice process, it has become largely a rubber stamp of the prosecutor: If he or she asks for an indictment there is almost always one. Rare exceptions exist when the grand jury fails to indict, thus issuing a "no true" bill. These cases usually involve accused persons who, for one reason or another, evoke a great deal of sympathy (e.g., a Brooklyn grocer cleared by a grand jury of killing a man who only hours earlier had apparently murdered the grocer's wife during a robbery).[91] The opposite phenomenon is called a "runaway grand jury," which tries to indict more people than the prosecution requests (e.g., the Watergate grand jury wanted to charge President Nixon with conspiracy—against the wishes of the special prosecutor).[92] Normally, however, the grand jury overwhelmingly approves prosecutorial recommendations.

This acquiescence can be accounted for in several ways. First, the prosecutor dominates grand jury hearings. He or she presents all the evidence, asks most of the questions (although grand jurors have the legal right to interrogate witnesses) and is allowed to present illegally seized evidence (which cannot be done at a regular trial); persons under investigation can present no case of their own (not even being allowed to have a lawyer present in the room). Second, there is scant opportunity for critical judgment because the deliberation process is incredibly speedy. In 1971, 12 grand juries in Houston spent 1,344 hours on 15,930 cases—an average of five minutes per case, which includes the district attorney's summary of the evidence and recommendation, the presentation of testimony, deliberation, and voting.[93] Third, only a majority of the grand jury is required to indict, so the prosecutor need not worry much about a few skeptical jurors who might have doubts. Finally, in most large cities those under investigation are disproportionately poor and nonwhite, but due to the biased nature of the selection process very few such people make their way onto the grand jury, which means that the jury is frequently lacking members who might be able to empathize with the defendant.[94]

Not only are grand juries pawns of the prosecutors in the routine processing of cases but they are often used by prosecutors to harass and sometimes jail suspected criminals and political dissidents, against whom there is insufficient evidence to indict or convict.[95] What prosecutors sometimes do is to subpoena such individuals to appear before the grand jury and grant them immunity from prosecution—either "transactional immunity" or "use immunity." This means, in the first case, that they will not be prosecuted for any crimes they discuss, and in the latter case that nothing they say to the grand jury will be used as evidence against them, although they can be prosecuted for crimes they mention if other evidence is obtained. After receiving such legal protection, they are no longer allowed to invoke the privilege against self-incrimination of the Fifth Amendment. If they do not talk, they can be held in contempt of court and jailed for the length of time the grand jury sits (as much as a year).

This technique was used by federal prosecutors in 1965 to jail Sam Giancana, the purported organized crime leader in Chicago, who (perhaps fearing for his life) refused to discuss any of his alleged underworld associates.[96] The same device was used by several United States attorneys in the Nixon Administration to induce antiwar activists to talk about their political activities and those of their acquaintances. Forcing people to answer all kinds of intimate questions about their personal lives can be punishment in itself as well as a means for gathering political intelligence unavailable through standard surveillance. For example, members of a left-wing political group in Tucson, Arizona, were called before a federal grand jury that presumably was investigating the illegal purchasing of dynamite in the area; they were asked the following questions:

> I want you to tell the Grand Jury what period of time during the years 1969 and 1970 you resided at 2201 Ocean Front Walk [in Los Angeles] . . . who resided there at the time you lived there, identifying all persons you have seen in or about the premises at that address, and tell the Grand Jury all of the conversations that were held by you or others in your presence during the time you were at that address.[97]

While many feel such tactics are justified in dealing with the seemingly invincible organized crime figures, due process is unquestionably circumvented when people are given the coercive choice of talking or going to jail. Devices that can be used to cope with real social menaces can also be used against people with unorthodox views or deviant life styles. As a response to such abuses, some reform efforts are underway to give people under investigation some protection from grand juries, such as allowing witnesses to have counsel at their side when they testify and permitting the people being investigated to present evidence of their own.

It is ironic that the grand jury, conceived as a protector of individual liberties, has not only failed to protect defendants from flimsy prosecutions but on occasion has become an instrument of social repression. Aside from its dubious purpose of putting pressure on various people defined as public enemies, the grand jury is a vestigial organ of the criminal justice system. The interest of economy has outweighed that of accountability now that the professional judgments of the prosecutor have all but obliterated the independence of the grand jury.

Trial by Jury: The Enigma of Peer Judgment

In contrast to the grand jury, the petit jury that decides the guilt or innocence of the accused is quite autonomous, and the decision making of that body is unpredictable. While technically the jury is only supposed to analyze the facts and apply the law as explained by the judge, in practice many other considerations can affect its judgment. Factors such as the composition of the jury, the biases of individual jurors, and the social dynamics of deliberation make the decision-making process both chancy and mysterious. Although jurors may be the most disinterested of all people involved in criminal cases, innocent defendants can have only limited faith that juries will absolve them, and guilty persons can entertain realistic hopes that juries will get them off the hook. Popular justice is not always just.

Relatively few defendants avail themselves of the opportunity of jury trial, as was discussed in the last chapter. Only those with some exonerating evidence or those facing unacceptable plea bargains normally risk the uncertainty of jury dispositions. However, the fact that a small number of defendants do avail themselves of jury trials establishes certain realities about the propensities of juries to convict or acquit. Consequently, the threat of jury trial is an important ingredient in the plea-bargaining process, and it ensures that the bargainers take account of the possible reactions of outsiders selected from the general public. In other words, the predicted outcome of the jury trial is the "bottom line" of plea bargaining; what some juries do in the few cases that are contested gives both prosecutors and defense lawyers some basis for predicting what is likely to happen to them if they do likewise. Consequently, the outcomes of jury trials have repercussions far beyond those subject to the verdicts that are reached.

As we shall see, decision making by juries sometimes strays far afield from objectivity, which is the ideal of adjudication. Nevertheless, it does represent democracy in action—the right of the people to be wrong. But the people who do the judging are not *all* the people, as the following section shows.

THE VAGARIES OF JURY SELECTION

BIASES IN THE JURY POOL   As noted previously, jurors hearing individual cases are picked from jury pools called "venires." Theoretically these pools are cross-sections of the population, making it likely that over the long run the kinds of people on juries will reflect the general makeup of the population. However, in practice, most jury pools are quite skewed; they are made up disproportionately of people from certain walks of life and with particular social characteristics. Since prejudices do play a role in juror judgment (as will be discussed below), biases in the jury pool can alter an individual defendant's chances of success at the trial, for the defendant is likely to be judged by *some* of his peers—but not *all* of them.

A great deal of research has been done on the nature of these biases, and Table 7–4 shows how certain groups have been slighted in the selection of jury pools in four localities. In summary of this research, it can be said that there is a "middle America" coloration to most jury pools (although the specific biases vary from place to place): They overrepresent whites, males, the middle aged, the middle class, and those with moderate education; they underrepresent nonwhites, females, the very old, and the young.[98] Moreover, many of these biases against specific categories of people are cumulative in their impact. For example, the underrepresentation of blacks, women, and the young makes it highly unlikely that a young black woman will appear in the jury pool—and, in fact, not one such juror was to be found in the entire federal jury pool of 1095 serving the Boston area in 1970, although six should have appeared if there were proportionate representation.[99]

What accounts for these biases? The most important factor is the use of

TABLE 7-4

Jury Unrepresentativeness in Four Jurisdictions

Court and Category Underrepresented	Percent of Population	Percent of Final Jury Pool	Comparative Disparity of Final Jury Pool as a Percent
1. Superior Court of Beauford County, North Carolina			
Race			
Blacks	30.2	17.0	− 43.7
2. U.S. District Court for the Eastern District of Pennsylvania			
Age			
Under 30	25.5	18.6	− 27.1
Under 40	41.8	33.3	− 20.3
Race			
Nonwhites	15.7	12.8	− 18.5
3. U.S. District Court for the Northern District of Florida			
Race			
Blacks	22.8	16.0	− 29.8
4. Supreme Court of New York, Erie County			
Race			
Blacks	8.4	5.1	− 39.3
Age			
21 to 29	20.7	3.4	− 83.6
Sex			
Women	53.0	16.7	− 70.4

SOURCE: David Kairys, Joseph Kadane, and John Lehorzky, "Jury Representativeness: A Mandate for Multiple Source Lists," *California Law Review* 65 (July 1977), 804. Copyright © 1977, California Law Review, Inc. Reprinted by Permission.

names on voter registration lists as the source of the jury pool. From 30 to 50 percent of those eligible in various states do not register to vote, and voluminous research on voting behavior has documented that certain groups are much more likely to register than others. For example, the rate of registration of persons with family income of less than $3,000 is 61.2 percent; it is 70.9 percent for those with incomes between $7,500 and $9,999; and it is 85 percent for those making over $15,000.[100] Likewise racial minorities, young people, and the poorly educated more frequently ignore the electoral process, with the result that they do not appear on the list of potential jurors. To make jury pools more representative of the population, some areas have begun using multiple-source lists, such as the roster of licensed drivers as well as telephone directories to obtain additional names.[101]

THE UNRELIABILITY OF THE VOIR DIRE   After jurors are randomly selected from the jury pool, they are asked a series of questions by the judge (in federal courts) or by the judge and/or the lawyers (in most state and local courts) to determine whether they have prejudices that would prevent them from assessing the evidence objectively; this interrogation is known as the "voir dire" (pronounced *vwar deer*). The term is derived from two French words: *voir*, meaning true, and *dire*, meaning say. The phrase has thus evolved into the idea that prospective jurors should say the truth when asked questions about themselves. For example, they might be asked if they had ever been the victim of a crime similar to the one involved in the immediate case. Or, they might be questioned about their attitudes toward police officers if police testimony will be central to the case. After this questioning, the lawyers can challenge jurors "for cause," which is an allegation that they are incapable of being objective. The judge will remove them from the case if he or she believes that they have made statements that are indicative of bias.

However, to elicit revealing statements that demonstrate or even imply bias requires a searching and often subtle examination of prospective jurors, which can take days and even weeks. When seven antiwar radicals (including two Catholic priests) were tried in Harrisburg, Pennsylvania, for plotting sabotage, 465 panelists were interviewed over the course of a month-long voir dire.[102] Because lawyers' resources are limited, this detailed inquiry is normally absent, so that the jury pool is instead asked a number of rather superficial questions about their capacity to be neutral. Since most people intuitively understand what the socially acceptable response is when they are questioned about bias, they frequently conceal their true feelings (especially if they have a yearning to be on the jury). Moreover, if, for example, racist attitudes are held subconsciously, prospective jurors may honestly disavow these inner prejudices—of which they themselves may be unaware.

The voir dire conducted by attorney Charles Garry in selecting a jury to hear the 1968 murder trial of black militant Huey Newton for the murder of a white police officer revealed how thoroughly the background and attitudes of a prospective juror must be probed to ferret out prejudice. Garry asked a suburban woman many pointed questions about racism, radical politics, and police officers; he received nothing but reasonable responses that suggested that she was a fair-minded woman. But when Garry asked her to discuss her previous residences and her motives for moving, she finally admitted she moved out of a neighborhood in Oakland because too many blacks had moved in.[103] Only patient questioning led to this startling revelation, resulting in the dismissal of a juror who very well might have held the defendant's race against him.

So, the typical voir dire may eliminate people who are blatantly prejudiced; but without the time-consuming process used in the Newton case, it generally is quite unreliable as a screening device to eliminate those holding more deep-seated biases. Some observers claim that the voir dire contributes to jury impartiality more by educating jurors to the importance of fairness than by sifting out those who might have been unfair to begin with.[104] Its success in socializing jurors to their role is debatable, but there is little ground for confidence that it eliminates all but the most outspoken bigots from the jury.

PEREMPTORY CHALLENGES: A GUESSING GAME Another procedure intended to eliminate biased jurors is the peremptory challenge, the right of both the prosecution and the defense to strike a predetermined number of persons from the jury without giving any reason whatsoever. In most jurisdictions the number of such challenges increases with the seriousness of the crimes, and it is not uncommon for each side to be allowed 20 in murder cases. The assumption is that both sides can use their hunches as well as any information about people gleaned from the voir dire to exclude those people having the highest probability of bias among the group who survived challenges for cause and were pronounced fit to serve. The jurors who remain after the peremptories are supposed to be the most objective and open-minded jury that can be selected from the jury pool.

In reality, lawyers use these challenges to try to get partial jurors, not impartial ones—jurors who will be sympathetic to their side. While this is precisely what lawyers are supposed to do in our adversary system, the process obstructs the obtaining of juries that are true cross-sections of the population. Thus, prosecutors normally try to get conservative jurors, and defense attorneys usually seek liberals; the prosecution often strikes college professors; defense lawyers get rid of those related to police officers. These decisions can be decisive: The two trials of Black Panther Warren Wells for the murder of a police officer resulted in hung juries that voted 10 to 2 and 11 to 1 for acquittal; but the third time Wells was tried for this crime, he was convicted by an all-white jury created by the district attorney, who used all his peremptory challenges to eliminate blacks from the jury.[105]

Angela Davis . . . and the jury that acquitted her

Because the hunches of attorneys are often fallacious, attempts have been made in recent years to use more scientific procedures to discover what kinds of people are most likely to be sympathetic jurors. Thus when a black Communist professor (Angela Davis) was on trial in California for furnishing weapons to the murderer of a white judge, her black lawyers were faced with the inevitability of an all-white jury, since the district attorney had used his peremptory challenge to eliminate the only black member on the 150-person panel. In these circumstances they relied on the degree of eye contact between themselves and the prospective white jurors to determine how comfortable the whites were in relating to blacks. Jurors' facial reactions were deemed more important than their words as indicators of prejudice. Davis's acquittal is a measure of her lawyers' success.[106]

An even more elaborate technique is the use of public-opinion polls. This method was used in picking the jury for the 1972 trial of the so-called Harrisburg Seven, who were accused of conspiracy to kidnap National Security Advisor Henry Kissinger, to destroy the federal heating system in Washington, D.C. (a maze of underground steam tunnels), and to raid draft boards. A team of psychologists working for the defense surveyed the area and found out that four out of five residents held negative attitudes toward the defendants. Catholics and Lutherans were more favorably disposed to them, while Episcopalians, Presbyterians, Methodists, and fundamentalists were antagonistic. College graduates turned out unexpectedly to be quite hostile because those who were liberal-minded had left the area, leaving behind a contingent who were highly educated but very conservative. The ideal juror was a female Democrat with no religious preference and a white-collar job. Using the results of these surveys (along with more instinctive reactions), the lawyers obtained a jury that finally voted 10 to 2 to acquit after a two-month trial.[107] There was no retrial after the "hung" jury, so the defendants were exonerated.

The same team of social scientists helped select jurors who were to decide politically related cases in places as diverse as Camden, New Jersey; Gainesville, Florida; and St. Paul, Minnesota—and they were generally successful in obtaining acquittals for presumably unappealing defendants. Their findings often were surprising: Women were shown to be more friendly to the defense in Harrisburg, harsher in Gainesville, and the same as men in St. Paul.[108] But some of the predictions were wrong: in the Harrisburg case three presumed liberals voted to convict the antiwar activists—a black woman (who ultimately changed her mind), a juror who supported the grape boycott organized by Mexican farm workers in California, and a mother of four conscientious objectors. Thus, even using very scientific procedures, lawyers have no guarantee that their choices will be correct. As one commentator has written, "Social scientists can't rig juries."[109]

One intrinsic obstacle to shrewd selection is the fact that in most states peremptory challenges must be exercised at the time any individual juror is questioned rather than after all jurors have been interrogated. Such a sequential procedure makes it impossible for an attorney to know in advance if any sub-

THE JURY AND PUBLIC SENTIMENTS

Birmingham, Ala., November 17 [1977]. The case of Robert E. Chambliss, charged with the 1963 bombing here that killed four young black girls, went to the jury late this afternoon after the prosecution argued that conviction would prove to the world that Birmingham is a city of law and justice.

"You've got a chance to do something," Attorney General Bill Baxley told the jury of three blacks and nine whites at the end of four days of testimony about one of the most notorious racial incidents of the 1960's.

"Let the world know," he continued, holding up pictures of maimed bodies and shattered religious objects, "that this is not the way the people of Alabama felt then or feel now."

"It's not going to bring those little girls back, but it will show the world that this murder case has been solved by the people of Alabama. Give Denise McNair a birthday present."

Denise McNair was one of the four children killed by the blast, which occurred at the 16th Street Baptist Church shortly after 10 A.M. on September 15, 1963. She would have been 26 years old today.

* * * * * * *

Birmingham, Ala., November 18 [1977]. Fourteen years after a dynamite bomb exploded here at the 16th Street Baptist Church and killed four black girls in one of the worst racial incidents in Southern history, a jury of three blacks and nine whites delivered a murder conviction in the case today.

The jury, its integrated composition indicative of the vast changes that have taken place in Birmingham and the rest of the South since 1963, found Robert E. Chambliss, a 73-year-old former Ku Klux Klansman, guilty of first-degree murder in the bombing and sentenced him to life imprisonment.

B. Drummond Ayres, Jr., "Case Goes to Jury in Birmingham in '63 Church Bombing Fatal to 4," *New York Times*, November 18, 1977, p. A18; and "Alabamian Guilty in '63 Church Blast that Killed 4 Girls," *New York Times*, November 19, 1977, p. 1. © 1977 by The New York Times Company. Reprinted by permission.

sequent person on the panel may be more or less prejudiced than one he or she is thinking of removing. Even with the most reliable information about the jury pool's predispositions, unless all peremptory challenges are made simultaneously at the end of the voir dire (as occurs in the federal system), guesswork is involved in comparing the juror under observation with the untold possibilities in the rest of the jury pool. Without complete information the possibility of rationality is limited.[110]

JUROR JUDGMENTS: THE LIMITS OF OBJECTIVITY

The recollections of most people who have served on juries as well as experiments using "mock" jurors suggest that jurors conscientiously try to adhere to the role assigned to them—applying the law to the facts at hand. To be sure, they bring in their own ideas and experiences, but only insofar as they relate to the evidence before them and the inferences that they are required to make. Only rarely do they disregard the facts altogether and superimpose their own moral convictions.

However, very often the evidence is unclear. Under such circumstances jurors are much more at liberty to follow their own inclinations. The ambiguities produced by the trial free them to evaluate the law in question, the defendant's character, the victim's plight, and the appropriateness of the possible punishments.[111] Overall, this makes them more lenient than judges. In a famous study done at the University of Chicago Law School, judges who presided over 3,591 jury trials in every state in the country indicated that they would have convicted in 19 percent of the cases where the jury acquitted and would have acquitted in only 3 percent of the cases where the jury convicted.[112] Apparently, juries are more prone to give the benefit of the doubt to defendants—but only where legitimate doubt exists.

Not all defendants, however, are the recipients of jury kindheartedness. Jurors are more responsive toward defendants with whom they can identify or who evoke respect than toward those whose status or background is quite different from their own. Also, any sympathies or enmities that might be felt toward the victim may counterbalance any positive or negative reactions to the accused. Thus, in weighing evidence and deciding how the almost inevitable gaps in it will be filled in, jurors introduce their subjective feelings about the parties involved in the case.

In addition to evaluating the defendant's character, juries also sometimes take into account the seriousness of the harm the crime may have caused. Juries sometimes refuse to convict people who they think are guilty because they believe the law in question is wrong, the possible penalties are too severe, or the damage caused is negligible. This process—called "jury nullification"—is less common today than it was in the last century because judges often caution juries very emphatically about disregarding the law. However, jurors undoubtedly often go to great lengths to find exonerating evidence if they feel that, although a crime has been committed, punishment is undeserved.

JURY DELIBERATIONS: A PARTIALLY RATIONAL PROCESS

THE PERSUASION PROCESS   When jurors retire to the deliberation room at the end of a trial, a preliminary "straw poll" is normally conducted to see where people stand. If everyone is in agreement (in states requiring unanimity), the case is over and a verdict is reported to the judge. However, quite commonly the jury is divided, and a discussion ensues.

How rational is this discussion? On the one hand, jurors do spend many hours recounting testimony (since they are not allowed to take notes during the trial). They take great pains to try to decipher the judge's instructions, which are often confusing. Discourse centers on the case at hand, and jurors summon all of the reasoning skill that they possess to convince others of their point of view. Frequently, they return to the courtroom to get a reading of parts of the trial transcript or to have the judge clarify a point of law. Judging the fate of defendants is a serious business, and the jurors take it seriously.

On the other hand, where the issue or people in the case raise strong emotions (as is frequently the case if a brutal crime is involved or political figures are on trial), debate often degenerates into bitter conflict. The seven days of deliberations in the Harrisburg Seven case, which involved antiwar protestors, were characterized by some of the jurors as "blurred, quarreling, timeless periods of irrational arguments," during which two jurors nearly came to blows and another kept referring to himself as "serving God's will."[113]

Similarly, it was reported that jurors who found Juan Corona guilty of the mass murder of 25 people in California wept, shouted, and raged in the process of reaching a verdict. The intensity of this experience is illuminated by the comments of one of the jurors, a war veteran, during the course of the deliberations: "I need some more aspirins. God, I hate aspirins and yet here I am chewing them by the handful. I never got this strung-out in combat."[114]

The influence of all jurors is not always equal in these debates. Sometimes particularly aggressive or domineering jurors are able to sway those who are timid; this is due more to their personality than to the superiority of their reasoning ability. On the other hand, the calmly persistent juror who is very self-confident can win over those who are less sure of themselves.

The latter process occurred during the deliberations of the jury that decided the case of John Mitchell and Maurice Stans, two cabinet members in the Nixon Administration who were charged with conspiracy to impede a Securities and Exchange Commission investigation of a contributor to Nixon's reelection campaign fund.[115] The jury was made up of poorly educated and rather uninformed people, with the exception of Andrew Choa, a vice-president of the First National City Bank. After a ten-week trial the jurors intially voted 8 to 4 for conviction. However, Choa's status, self-assurance, and greater sophistication enabled him to sway the other jurors, who had been quite befuddled by the mass of complex evidence about the comings and goings of various government officials involved in the case. Choa, whose political ideology was described by bank colleagues as "to the right of Ivan the Terrible" was able to wield inordinate influence to vindicate two conservative politicians.[116] Thus, the goal of public accountability presumably served by jury trials can be undercut when elites are able to wield extraordinary influence.

COERCION OF SMALL MINORITIES   In the popular movie *Twelve Angry Men*, Henry Fonda plays a juror who, as the lone holdout for acquittal of a defendant charged with murder, is able to convert all other 11 jurors to his point of view. This made for a moving Hollywood drama, but in real life just the opposite usually happens: Small minorities eventually yield to the majority. In a study of 225 actual jury deliberations in Chicago and Brooklyn, only seven times did the minority prevail, and in no case did a minority of one succeed in changing the minds of all the others.[117] The building of a consensus is a process of wearing down recalcitrant dissidents, and the well-documented human need for conformity in small groups plays an important role. Most jurors who yield become intellectually convinced that the opposition is correct, but their change of mind may have been engendered by the uncomfortable feelings they had about appearing obstreperous.

These disconcerting feelings are accentuated when judges admonish juries about the importance of reaching a verdict and emphasize their obligation to listen to the opinions of others. Judges occasionally lecture juries that are having trouble reaching agreement, urging holdouts to consider the correctness of judgments rejected by the majority (although such remarks can be cause for reversal of convictions on appeal). Short of such coaxing (called a "dynamite charge" because it is intended to "blow open" the deadlock), judges can sequester juries that are deliberating for as long as they feel necessary; and the long days of draining conflict spent in isolation can wear down even the most stubborn of jurors.

COMPROMISE VERDICTS   Another means that juries use to resolve disputes is compromise. When the defendant is charged with several crimes (e.g., robbery, carrying concealed weapons, and larceny), jurors may agree to convict on the lesser charges and acquit on the serious ones. Another form of middle ground can be found if a trial has many defendants: Some are acquitted while others are convicted.

This is apparently the way the jury reached its verdict in the case of the so-called Chicago Seven, who were charged with the federal crimes of crossing state lines to incite a riot and conspiracy to do the same for their part in the Chicago disturbances during the 1968 Democratic National Convention.[118] After a six-month trial jury deliberations began on a Sunday. By Monday the jury seemed hopelessly deadlocked at 8 to 4 for conviction. On Tuesday one of the jurors came up with a compromise. She suggested that they acquit two of the most mild-mannered defendants (against whom the evidence was also the weakest) and convict the others—but only on the inciting charge (not conspiracy). By Wednesday everyone had convinced themselves that such a verdict squared with the evidence and a unanimous verdict was reached. The law and the facts were bent to accord with the results of what can only be called an old-fashioned political deal.

Thus, decisions made by juries can sometimes take on the qualities of plea bargaining. Because the facts are unclear and differences of opinion exist, both sides try to find a happy medium. In any given case, however, it is entirely problematic how close such verdicts come to capturing the truth of what really transpired.

THE IMPACT OF JURY SIZE AND DECISION RULES   Historically, trial juries were composed of twelve individuals who were required to come to a unanimous decision in order to reach a verdict. However, in recent years (and with the approval of the Supreme Court),[119] some states have reduced the size of the jury to six and require less than unanimity for conviction (e.g., ten out of twelve).

The avowed purposes of these measures are economy and the prevention of hung juries; and both goals are no doubt accomplished. The costs of paying jurors is at least cut in half, and far less courtroom time is spent in the selection of jurors when only six must be picked. Jurisdictions using majority verdicts have about 45 percent fewer hung juries per year.[120]

However, an unresolved question remains about whether such alterations sacrifice due process by allowing a greater number of innocent people to be improperly convicted. The Supreme Court has offered the opinion that "no discernible differences" are detectable in the results of juries of different sizes, but the results of empirical research are unclear on this point.[121] The smaller jury is likely to be less representative, which increases the probability that a member of some minority group will be excluded. If, for example, blacks make up 20 percent of the population and the jury is randomly selected from the population (which, as we have seen, it is not), there is about a one in four chance of no black appearing on a six-person jury, while there is less than a one in twelve chance of this happening with a twelve-person jury.[122] By the same token, however, the larger jury is more likely to include extremist jurors who may be antagonistic to minority defendants. Jury size is a two-edged sword, and it is as yet uncertain whether smaller juries convict more.

Experts also fail to agree about the effects of a nonunanimity rule.[123] Because of the group conformity effects previously discussed, these rules in themselves probably would not significantly alter the proportion of convictions. Those jurors who are outvoted where some kind of majority rule is required would, in most cases, have ultimately acquiesced had unanimity been required. In short, the net effect of substituting majority rule is normally an earlier suspension of deliberations and not a change in outcome.

However, some evidence has been collected to suggest that the reduced number of hung juries caused by majority rule results in additional convictions rather than more acquittals.[124] People are more willing to hold out for acquittal than conviction, and in some number of cases their resistance is simply overcome by majority vote.

Thus, at best, these changes in the form and functioning of juries leave the situation the same with regard to protecting the innocent. And possibly they increase the probability that the various opportunities for error and bias discussed earlier in the chapter will make their way into the final verdict.

The Anarchy of Sentencing

In 1923 a young boy collaborated with an older ex-convict to rob a grocery store in Mooresville, Indiana. The attempt was botched, and both were caught by police. The youth was sentenced to from ten to twenty years in jail, but his older accomplice went before a different judge and got from two to ten years.

While in jail the boy seethed with resentment about his inequitable sentence and vowed to get even. When he was paroled nine years later, he formed a gang that within a few months had netted $300,000 in a series of bank robberies and had killed 15 men in the process. On July 2, 1934, FBI agents shot him to death outside a Chicago theater. His name was John Dillinger.[125]

THE IDIOSYNCRASIES OF INDIVIDUAL JUDGES

The Dillinger story is just one of many notorious tales of sentencing injustice, although fortunately not all of them have such grim consequences. Although all phases of criminal justice decision making entail discretion, sentencing has the fewest legal guidelines to constrain judicial prerogatives. A highly respected federal judge claims that such sentencing arbitrariness verges on lawlessness. Says Marvin Frankel:

> In the great majority of federal criminal cases . . . a defendant who comes up for sentencing has no way of knowing or reliably predicting whether he will walk out of the courtroom on probation, or be locked up for a term of years that may consume the rest of his life, or something in between.[126]

As proof of such devastating criticism many outlandish examples can be given. Actress Claudine Longet received 30 days in jail from an Aspen, Colorado, judge for killing her boyfriend (to be served during the summer when her children were at camp), while a Long Island surgeon received 25 years in prison for murdering his wife in a triangle love affair.[127] Federal Judge Jack Weinstein sentenced two Grumman Aerospace Corporation officials to two-year sentences for illegally taking $20,000 from subcontractors in a kickback scheme, while federal Judge Morris Lasker suspended sentences for three Wall Street stock swindlers convicted of bilking millions of dollars from customers.[128] A group of Hanafi Muslims who seized several Washington, D.C., buildings and killed one man all received long prison sentences (up to 123 years in prison), while Patricia Hearst received probation for firing a submachine gun during an armed robbery.[129]

Statistical comparisons of the sentencing tendencies of various judges show that these disparities are not isolated. A study of Detroit courts showed that over a 20-month period one judge imposed prison terms upon 75 percent of those he sentenced, while a colleague imprisoned only 35 percent.[130] The proportion of convicted felons put on probation by various federal district courts ranges from 26 percent to 78 percent.[131] A study of the sentencing of those convicted of violating selective-service regulations in 1972 showed that most federal judges granted probation, but six judges always sentenced offenders to five years in prison—for the same crime.[132] Forgers sentenced by federal judges in the Southern District of New York (Manhattan) received sentences that are an average of 20 months longer than those meted out by judges in the Eastern District of New York (Brooklyn and Long Island).[133]

These comparisons may seem invalid because the judges may all have been dealing with crimes of varying degrees of seriousness and with criminals who were more or less deserving of punishment. But this comforting supposition is contradicted by the results of judges' workshops run by the Federal Institute on Disparity of Sentences as well as a study of federal judicial sentencing councils.

At the institute judges were given sets of hypothetical facts for several offenses and required to propose sentences. In one case a wealthy 51-year-old man with no criminal record who pled guilty to evading about $5,000 in taxes was "sentenced" to pay a fine by only three judges, was granted probation by 23 judges, and was given prison terms ranging from one to five years by 28 judges.[134]

Judicial sentencing councils operate in several federal district courts. They are meetings of all the judges in the district to discuss sentences and to exchange opinions prior to actual imposition of sentences. A study of the Chicago and New York councils showed 30 percent initial disagreement among judges *dealing with the same offenders* as to whether *any* prison sentence ought to be imposed. Furthermore, the disparities among judges in suggested sentence severity were 37 percent for Chicago and 46 percent for New York.[135]

The idiosyncratic nature of sentencing is a phenomenon well known to defense attorneys who often consider "judge shopping" one of the most important tasks in protecting their clients' interest. The lawyers realize intuitively what one researcher found out statistically: Information about the judge (which was obtained by in-depth interviews) is far more useful in predicting the sentence than knowing what the criminal or the crime is like. The judge's attitudes concerning the purpose of punishment, the gravity of various crimes, the importance of mitigating circumstances, and the nature of the criminal population are decisive factors in his or her sentencing policies.[136] Sentencing involves moral

---

THE IDIOSYNCRASIES OF SENTENCING

A 30-year-old paraplegic who pleaded guilty to a substantial narcotics charge has received a suspended sentence from a Federal judge who said that the law should not be "remorseless, implacable and without mercy."

The judge, Marvin E. Frankel, gave the suspended sentence in District Court in Manhattan last Thursday to Sylvester Mattox, a narcotics defendant who has been a paraplegic since 1971 when he was injured while fleeing from kidnappers.

Mr. Mattox pleaded guilty last April to having participated in a narcotics conspiracy involving what Judge Frankel described as "a large-scale wholesale and retail business in heroin and cocaine" in early 1971 before his injury and paralysis.

The judge observed that "the defendant was kidnapped, perhaps in connection with his criminal involvements, subject to various brutalities and finally injured when he jumped from a two-story window in an effort to escape.

"Since that episode," the judge added, "he has been a paraplegic confined to a wheelchair."

Mr. Mattox could have been sentenced to a maximum of 15 years in prison on the narcotics charge and an additional one year on a tax charge, but Judge Frankel released him on probation for three years.

[The judge said] "a society that sets an example of naked, pitiless vengeance will not promote respect for the law or compliance with the law's dictates."

"The line between sternness and cruelty cannot be seen with mathematical precision," the judge continued. "It must be espied by whatever right we can find. When the balance is uncertain, our law, like our professed morality, tells us to err on the side of mercy."

Arnold Lubasch, "Paraplegic Freed in Narcotics Case," *New York Times*, July 25, 1976, p. 44. © 1976 by The New York Times Company. Reprinted by permission.

judgment, which is an inherently subjective process. However, since defendants rarely know in advance of the trial whether they are going to be judged by a "hard liner" or a "bleeding heart" (or someone in the middle), their ability to predict what will happen to them is quite limited. For in the area of sentencing judges are in many ways a law unto themselves.

INFLUENCES ON SENTENCING

Within the confines of their own sentencing attitudes, judges do manifest some strains of consistency; they are usually not whimsical in their judgments. Moreover, legally significant criteria have greater impact than extraneous characteristics of the offender and the nature of the political environment. But the latter are not irrelevant.

THE LEGAL BASIS OF SENTENCING   The penal code specifies certain outer limits of judicial discretion—usually setting a minimum and maximum punishment for various crimes (but almost always leaving open the possibility of probation). These gradations in punishment are based largely on legislative determinations of the gravity of the injury caused by various crimes or their moral repugnance. Judges, too, apply these criteria; and some apparent discrepancies in sentencing of criminals charged with the same crime can be reconciled by examining precise details of the crime to assess its seriousness.[137]

Thus, all burglaries are not the same: Entering a vacant building to steal plumbing fixtures is not normally considered as reprehensible as breaking into someone's apartment and ransacking it. Likewise, there are degrees of guilt involved in assaults: Pushing someone during an argument over a place on line in front of a movie theater is hardly the moral equivalent of shoving a person off a bridge or pushing someone into a busy street. Judges do make such distinctions in handing out sentences.

They also pay heed to the "character" of the defendant. The "career criminal," who has a criminal record, is dealt with more harshly than the first-time offender. People with redeeming virtues (e.g., sustained employment) are punished more leniently than marginal types, like derelicts, who seem to be contributing nothing to society. Judges pay careful attention to the presentence investigations of the defendant's life style, and recommendations for probation by probation officers are followed closely.[138]

The culpability of the criminal is taken into account, and it is assessed by putting particular crimes into the context of a person's entire life. "Bad" people are punished more harshly than "decent" folks—even if they have committed the same crimes. The problem is, however, that making these kinds of judgments can very easily slide into choosing between preferred and disliked kinds of people. Making allowances for the moral strengths and weaknesses of a person can become an opportunity and an excuse for the naked exercise of prejudice.

THE OFFENDER'S STATUS   Many politicians, journalists, and scholars have alleged that sentencing disparities are primarily a reflection of social and economic cleavages: The "haves" get favored treatment at the expense of the "have nots." Tales of wealthy individuals receiving light punishment for serious crimes are common. For example, in 1978 a California judge sentenced Columbia Pictures executive David Begelman to three years probation and gave him a $5,000 fine for stealing $40,000 in Columbia checks and forging the signatures of the intended recipients. Begelman, who was earning $300,000 a year, therefore wound up netting $35,000![139]

However, a careful review of 20 separate studies correlating extralegal attributes with sentences shows that factors such as race and socioeconomic status contribute fairly little to explaining judicial dispositions.[140] Specific instances of racial and class prejudice working against convicted defendants can be cited, but differential sentencing as a result of these factors is not commonplace.

One major exception to such impartiality has been discovered. In the application of the death penalty in some cases in the South, the race of defendants and victims has loomed large. Between 1930 and 1972, 137 blacks were executed for rape in 11 southern states, but only 5 white rapists suffered that fate.[141] More recently a national study of criminals on death row suggests that race plays a more subtle role: Murderers of whites are far more likely to get capital punishment than those who kill blacks.[142] Conceivably, the emotions generated by the horrible crimes for which death is a possible punishment lead to more prejudicial reactions than is otherwise the case.

THE POLITICAL ENVIRONMENT   Political realities also can affect judges' sentencing predisposition. Some cities are noted for markedly harsher sentencing than others as a result of the prevailing conservative ideology. Thus, Baltimore and Minneapolis judges are much more likely to mete out stern punishments than their counterparts in Pittsburgh and Detroit, where a more liberal ethos prevails.[143]

Not only do general community sentiments about law enforcement play a role but reactions to specific crimes and criminals can be influential as well. The antiwar fervor in Oregon during the Vietnam war (which was fanned by its two senators) no doubt accounted for the fact that 18 out of 33 men convicted of resisting the draft received probation. This is in stark contrast to what happened in highly conservative southern Texas, where *no* draft violators received probation and 14 got the maximum five-year prison sentence.[144] Since most judges have spent years in political life, they cannot help but at least partially reflect public feelings.

The shifting climate of public opinion can also have a bearing on sentencing. Again, the draft evasion cases are illustrative: As the proportion of people who thought the war was a mistake rose from 3 percent in 1967 to 56 percent in 1970, the proportion of defendants receiving probation increased from 34 percent to 93 percent.[145] Political winds affect judges like everyone else, and the legal discretion in sentencing often enables them to be responsive to the turn-abouts.

ARBITRARINESS Sometimes sentencing decisions are inexplicable and have nothing to do with judicial ideology, the law, or politics. The point is well made by a cartoon appearing in a legal magazine. A judge peers down at the defendant and says: "Let's see. . . . the car you stole had a wheel base of 98 inches, and an overall length of 175 inches, 4 wheels . . . $175 + 98 = 273$; $\times 4 = 1092$. That'll be 1092 days in the county jail."[146]

The same point is made in Bob Dylan's song "Joey"* about the late Joey Gallo, a vaunted figure in the annals of organized crime. The words of the song describing how Gallo was sentenced early in his life for the crime of conspiracy to commit murder are apocryphal, but they do ring true:

> "What time is it?" said the judge
> To Joey when they met
> "Five to ten," said Joey
> The judge says, "That's exactly what you get."[147]

Such random sentencing wreaks havoc on the very concept of adjudication—decisions based on reason and legality.

Rarely do judges admit that their decisions are so utterly devoid of principle. However, Judge Anthony Critelli of Iowa has acknowledged that there is absolutely no justification for some of his sentencing decisions. Says Critelli:

> From my own experience, about ten per cent of the time involves a case in which I can't readily determine what I do. I've got to think about it for awhile, maybe confer with some of my colleagues. Figuratively speaking, it's a coin flip sometimes and that is rather drastic when you are talking about somebody's personal liberty.[148]

Judges' sentences can result from a wild assortment of arbitrary ruminations and chance events—none of which is likely to be repeated in that precise combination. As is true of earlier parts of the trial, plain and simple luck can affect outcomes. Thus, the murderer of a college student killed during a robbery on a New York subway was granted probation and spared a lengthy prison term after the victims' parents requested leniency.[149] Their fortuitous intervention made all the difference—and was more important than the nature of the crime, the criminal, the community, and the judge.

To the extent that sentencing decisions lack *any* patterns, both justice and due process suffer. If a defendant's future depends on some combination of the quality of the judge's breakfast, the humidity in the courtroom, and the surliness of the lawyer in the previous case, then adjudication is sheer caprice. Arbitrariness and legality cannot exist side by side.

SENTENCING REFORMS

A number of measures have been proposed or adopted to remedy the problem of sentencing disparities. Mandatory sentencing stipulating fixed penalties for specific crimes (e.g., the Bartley-Fox gun law in Massachusetts that requires a minimum one year prison term for illegally carrying a weapon) eliminates judicial discretion. Presumptive sentencing is a concept embodied in the new federal criminal code; it allows a narrow range of discretion but employs strict guidelines that normally must be followed and requires written justification when there is a departure from them. Equal justice is sought at the expense of individualized treatment of offenders.

Sentences are not usually subject to appeal, but some appellate courts have relied on the "cruel and unusual punishment" clause of the Eighth Amendment to overturn particularly outrageous penalties. For example, the California Supreme Court held that a life sentence for a second offense of indecent exposure (committed in the privacy of the defendant's car) violated the principle of proportionality inherent in the Eighth Amendment—the notion that punishment must fit the crime.[150] A similar appeal was filed by a Texan who had been convicted of three separate crimes over an eight-year period: He purchased $80 worth of tires on a stolen credit card in 1964, forged a rent check for $29.36 in 1969, and cashed a check for $120.75 in 1972 without doing the repair work for which the check was an advance payment.[151] After this third conviction he was given a life sentence as a "habitual offender" (one convicted of more than two felonies)—for crimes that netted him $230.11. But most higher courts are wary of reviewing any but the most extreme injustices lest they encourage mass appeals of sentences.

The least drastic reforms are sentencing councils and information retrieval systems that give judges the benefit of knowing how other judges would decide cases or have decided similar cases in the past. But these, like all proposed reforms, are likely to be opposed by the judges themselves, who jealously guard their sentencing prerogatives. Sentencing is the one area where they are totally in command and where they can act creatively; it is a source of both power and satisfaction. Thus, the indignant comment of Judge Joseph Mattina should not be surprising: "To do away with judicial sentencing is to improperly delegate a responsibility that is *rightfully* and *inherently* a part of the judiciary."[152]

The self-interest of judges may well prove the greatest obstacle to reforming the chaos of sentencing. The power to determine the destiny of criminals is awesome and is not likely to be relinquished very easily.

Conclusion

What this chapter has demonstrated is that disinterested decision making in the criminal justice system is not necessarily infallible decision making. Judges and juries do not usually gain much personally from siding with the prosecution or the defense, but this does not eliminate subjectivity and mistake. With the best of intentions, juries occasionally acquit the guilty and convict the innocent, while judges punish the meek and discharge those who are evil. Speculation is inherent in judging, and perfection is beyond the capabilities of the adjudication process.

However, the formalities of the legal process continue to support the myth of objectivity and fairness. Judges often sound as if they are above petty politics and base partiality. As they intone the seeming mandates of the law books, they appear to be pronouncing verities received from on high. But in reality they are exercising discretion and bringing to bear their own personal prejudices, values, and interests. The poet W. H. Auden expressed it well:*

> Law, says the judge as he looks down his nose,
> Speaking clearly and most severely,
> Law is as I've told you before,
> Law is as you know I suppose,
> Law is but let me explain it once more,
> Law is the Law.[153]

Judges disguise their political choices and speculation in the righteousness and certitude of the law, but an exploration of the real workings of the judicial process reveals how superficial such posturing really is. Occasionally judges will confess that their judgments really are often quite dubious, as when United States District Court Judge Joseph Hutcheson related how "hunches" affect his decisions:

> When the case is difficult or involved, and turns upon a hairsbreadth of law or of fact . . . I, after canvassing all the available material at my command, and duly cogitating upon it, give my imagination play, and brooding over the cause, wait for the feeling, the hunch—that intuitive flash of understanding which makes the jump-spark connection between question and decision, and at the point where the path is darkest for judicial feet, sheds its light along the way. . . . The purely contemplative philosopher may project himself into an abstract field of contemplation when he reasons, but practical men, and in that judges must be included, must have impulses.[154]

But these impulses may be wrong—in terms of justice, due process, crime prevention, or any other of the goals of the criminal justice system. Moreover, although the probability of error at any single stage of the adjudication process may be slim, the cumulative chance of error is far greater since initial mistakes compound the likelihood of wrongful decisions subsequently. If a judge jails a defendant prior to trial, it is less likely that the defendant can show at the preliminary hearing that he or she was wrongfully arrested. Likewise, at the trial

* From "Law Like Love," by W. H. Auden in *Collected Shorter Poems, 1927–1957* (New York: Random House, 1967). Reprinted by permission of Random House, Inc.

and sentencing, earlier decisions against a defendant may preclude an ultimate decision in his or her favor.

Hunches, guesses, feelings—these are the unreliable components of much court decision making. To be sure, they intertwine with reason, proof, evidence, and logic—the rational elements in the law. But the net result is always subject to doubt, and the chance of error and bias is omnipresent. To repeat Auden's telling words, "The Law is the Law"—but the people who apply it, interpret it, and manipulate it are people—for better or for worse.

SUMMARY

Adjudication is a form of conflict resolution that uses reasoned argument, formal proof, and systematic hearings to decide outcomes. It is intended to be an objective procedure, but it is inherently discretionary due to the ambiguity of law, the occasional biases of judges and jurors, the intrusion of self-interest, and the conflicting public interest. Fact finding is a particularly speculative enterprise because of the problems of eyewitness identification, evidentiary restrictions, the uncertainty of expert testimony, and the need to make inferences. While the resulting decisions have certain patterns and regularities, the adversary process can also produce idiosyncratic outcomes that appear to be arbitrary.

Judges can ordain outcomes most directly by their decisions about bail, dismissals, and sentencing; but they can slant the end result in a multitude of more subtle ways, such as in their control over jury selection and their rulings on evidence. Judges handling misdemeanor cases and juvenile court judges have even greater latitude because these proceedings are informal and quite abbreviated. While judges are picked largely because of their political connections (regardless of the formal method of selection), they have a great deal of autonomy once they are on the bench.

Bail decision making is quite routinized, and whether judges make it hard or easy for defendants to go free prior to trial depends largely on the severity of the charge, the defendant's previous record, and the strength of the prosecutor's evidence. While the ostensible purpose of bail is to prevent defendants from fleeing prior to trial, other latent purposes served by the nature of judges' decisions are the prevention of recidivism, the imposition of pretrial punishment, and the diffusion of responsibility.

There are two kinds of juries. Grand juries decide whether there is sufficient evidence to indict those accused of crime, but in recent years the grand jury has become subservient to the prosecutor and has had little independent authority. Petit juries, which decide guilt or innocence, are supposed to be made up of the defendants' peers, but, in fact, they are not usually representative of the population. Juries have a good deal of discretion since the evidence presented at the trial rarely is absolutely conclusive for one side or the other. Thus, jurors' feelings about the law and their empathies with either defendants or victims can play a role in how they apply the law and construe the facts. The jury deliberation process entails a good deal of rational discussion, but in the end the majority is normally able to convince the minority to change their minds to achieve a consensus.

Sentencing by judges is highly individualized. The tendencies of different judges vary, and each case is treated differently by the same judge. There are, however, some factors—the seriousness of the crime, the offender's status (including his or her prior record), and the political environment—that influence sentencing and provide some predictability. But there is also much sheer arbitrariness. Consequently, reforms have been proposed and some have been adopted to reduce the sentencing discretion of the judge.

While judges take pride in their independence and juries conscientiously try to put aside their own prejudices and sentiments, subjectivity and politics pervade the judicial process. Both criminal law and criminal procedures determine who bears the brunt of legal sanctions—but favoritism, guesswork, and luck also play a significant role.

FOOTNOTES

[1] Jerome Frank and Barbara Frank, *Not Guilty* (Garden City, N.Y.: Doubleday, 1957), pp. 136–51.

[2] Daniel Walker, *Rights in Conflict* (New York: Signet Books, 1968), p. xix.

[3] "Verdict in Chicago," *Newsweek*, June 23, 1969, p. 92.

[4] David Fellman, "Domestic Adjudication," in *Encyclopedia of the Social Sciences*, vol. 1 (New York: Macmillan, 1968), 43–49.

[5] Glendon Schubert, ed., *Judicial Behavior: A Reader in Theory and Research* (Chicago: Rand McNally, 1964), pp. 9–71.

[6] Oliver Wendell Holmes, Jr., "The Path of the Law," in *The Mind and Faith of Justice Holmes*, ed. Max Lerner (New York: Random House, 1943), p. 75.

[7] Jerome Frank, *Courts on Trial* (New York: Atheneum, 1967), pp. 14–36.

[8] Robert Buckhout, "Eyewitness Testimony," *Scientific American* 231 (December 1974), 23–31.

[9] Ibid., 29–30.

[10] Ibid., 23.

[11] *Los Angeles Times*, June 23, 1972, p. 27.

[12] "Trials: A Reputation Retrieved," *Newsweek*, April 28, 1975, p. 35.

[13] Daniel Greenberg. "Scientific Testing that Gets Low Marks," *Washington Post*, July 25, 1978, p. A15.

[14] Lois Forer, "View from the Bench: a Judge's Day," *Washington Monthly* 6 (February 1975), 35.

[15] *New York Times*, October 26, 1976, p. 20.

[16] Quoted in the *New York Post*, July 28, 1977, p. 16.

[17] Quoted in the *New York Daily News*, July 22, 1977, p. 5.

[18] Austin Sarat, "Judging in Trial Courts: An Exploratory Study," *Journal of Politics* 39 (May 1977), 368–97.

[19] Tom Goldstein, "New York Justices Said to Hold Trials only Half a Day," *New York Times*, April 13, 1977, p. 1.

[20] Anthony Scaduto, "Bruno Hauptmann Was Innocent," *New York Magazine*, November 22, 1976, pp. 59–76.

[21] Wayne King, "Joan Little's Lawyer Scorns Legal System and Says He 'Bought' Her Acquittal," *New York Times*, October 20, 1975, p. 23.

[22] James Reston, Jr., *The Innocence of Joan Little: A Southern Mystery* (New York: Times Books, 1977).

[23] Quoted in Wayne King, "Joan Little's Lawyer Scorns Legal System and Says He 'Bought' Acquittal," *New York Times*, October 20, 1975, p. 23.

[24] Quoted in ibid.

[25] Nicholas Gage, "Study Shows Courts Lenient with Mafiosi," *New York Times*, September 25, 1972, p. 1.

[26] Glendon Schubert, *Judicial Policy-Making* (Chicago: Scott Foresman, 1965), p. 89.

[27] "The Supreme Court, 1976 Term," *Harvard Law Review* 91 (November 1977), p. 21.

[28] Jonathan Casper, *American Criminal Justice: The Defendant's Perspective* (Englewood Cliffs, N.J.: Prentice-Hall, 1972), p. 136.

[29] James Eisenstein and Herbert Jacob, *Felony Justice* (Boston: Little Brown, 1977), p. 195.

[30] William Landes, "Legality and Reality: Some Evidence on Criminal Procedure," *Journal of Legal Studies* 3 (June 1974), 303.

[31] *New York Post*, April 30, 1977, p. 6.

[32] Eisenstein and Jacob, op. cit., p. 191.

[33] *New York Times*, December 15, 1977, p. A26.

[34] Jason Epstein, *The Great Conspiracy Trial* (New York: Vintage Books, 1971), p. 255.

[35] "'A License to Kill?'," *Newsweek*, June 23, 1969. p. 32.

[36] Donald Jackson, *Judges* (New York: Atheneum, 1974), p. 216.

[37] *New York Daily News*, July 21, 1977, p. 76.

[38] All of the figures mentioned in this paragraph are calculated from data in U.S Federal Bureau of Investigation, *Uniform Crime Reports—1976* (Washington D.C.: U.S. Government Printing Office, 1977), p. 173.

[39] Leonard Downie, *Justice Denied* (Baltimore: Penguin Books, 1971), pp. 18–51.

[40] President's Commission on Law Enforcement and the Administration of Justice, *Task Force Report: The Courts* (Washington D.C.: U.S. Government Printing Office, 1967), p. 31.

[41] Ibid.

[42] Maureen Mileski, "Courtroom Encounters: An Observation Study of a Lower Criminal Court," *Law and Society Review* 5 (May 1971), 470.

[43] This estimate is based on data on tickets obtained in a 1965 survey of 697 cities and towns with populations of more than 250,000. See John Gardiner, "Police Enforce-

ment of Traffic Laws: A Comparative Analysis," in *City Politics and Public Policy,* ed. James Q. Wilson (New York: Wiley, 1968), pp. 153–54.

[44] The law is *Ohio Rev. Code* §215-022 (Supp. 1975); it is quoted in Al Katz and Lee Teitelbaum, "PINS Jurisdiction, the Vagueness Doctrine and the Rule of the Law," in *Beyond Control: Status Offenders in the Juvenile Court,* eds. Lee Teitelbaum and Aidan R. Gough (Cambridge: Ballinger Publishing, 1977), p. 201.

[45] In re Gault, 387 U.S. 1 (1967).

[46] Robert Emerson, *Judging Delinquents* (Chicago: Aldine Publishing, 1969), p. 203.

[47] Norman Lefstein, Vaughan Stapleton, and Lee Teitelbaum, "In Search of Juvenile Justice: Gault and Its Implementation,'" *Law and Society Review* 3 (May 1969), 491–562.

[48] Emerson, op. cit., p. 276.

[49] Nicholas Pileggi, "How Fifteen Year Olds Get Away with Murder," *New York Magazine,* June 13, 1977, p. 42.

[50] Ibid., pp. 36–44.

[51] Emerson, op. cit.

[52] Mel Juffe, "Juvenile Justice-1½ Years for Killing—8 for Watching," *New York Post,* August 2, 1978, p. 5.

[53] Jackson, op. cit., p. 89.

[54] Ibid., p. 248.

[55] Kenneth Vines and Herbert Jacob, "State Courts and Public Policy," in *Politics in the American States,* 3rd ed., edited by Herbert Jacob and Kenneth Vines (Boston: Little, Brown, 1976), p. 251.

[56] For a discussion of the role of the American Bar Association in the selection of federal judges, see Joel Grossman, *Lawyers and Judges* (New York: Wiley, 1965).

[57] Harold Chase, *Federal Judges: The Appointing Process* (Minneapolis, Minn.: University of Minnesota Press, 1972), p. 176.

[58] Ibid., p. 172.

[59] Joseph Perry, "How I Got to Be a Federal Judge," in *Courts, Judges, and Politics,* eds. Walter Murphy and C. Herman Pritchett (New York: Random House, 1961), pp. 93–96.

[60] Ben Franklin, "Mandel Sentenced to Four Years, Suspended as Maryland Governor," *New York Times,* October 8, 1977, p. 1.

[61] Bancroft Henderson and T. C. Sinclair, *The Selection of Judges in Texas: An Exploratory Study* (Houston, Tex.: University of Houston Public Affairs Research Center, 1965), p. 21.

[62] Lee Dembart, "Beame Appoints 13 to Judgeships," *New York Times,* December 28, 1977, p. D13.

[63] Timothy Crouse, "Who Really Picks Our Judges?" *Village Voice,* April 25, 1977, pp. 24–27.

[64] James Eisenstein, *Politics and the Legal Process* (New York: Harper & Row, 1973), pp. 51–52.

[65] Paul Beecken, "Can Judicial Elections Express the People's Choice?" *Judicature* 57 (January 1974), 242–46.

[66] Hendrik Hertzberg, "Hi, Boss, Said the Judge to Meade Esposito," *New York Times Magazine,* December 10, 1972, p. 33.

[67] Henderson and Sinclair, op. cit.

[68] Beecken, op. cit., p. 243.

[69] Jack Newfield and Paul DuBrul, *The Abuse of Power* (New York: Viking Press, 1977), p. 219.

[70] Ibid., p. 220.

[71] Richard Watson and Rondal Downing, *The Politics of Bench and Bar* (New York: Wiley, 1969), p. 345; and Wesley Skogan, "The Politics of Judicial Reform: Cook County, Illinois," *The Justice System Journal* 1 (September 1975), 11–23.

[72] The exact comment of Judge Archie Simonson was:

I'm trying to say to women stop teasing. There should be a restoration of modesty in dress. . . . Whether women like it or not they are sex objects. Are we supposed to take an impressionable person 15 or 16 years of age and punish that person severely because they react to it so normally?

"Rape and Culture," *Time,* September 12, 1977, p. 41.

[73] Joseph Borkin, *The Corrupt Judge* (Cleveland: World Publishing, 1966).

[74] Stuart Nagel, "Multiple Correlation of Judicial Backgrounds and Decisions," *Florida State University Law Review* 2 (Spring 1974), 258–80.

[75] Ibid.

[76] Edith Asbury, "Troy Acquitted of Perjury Charge; Larceny Trial Is Still Facing Him," *New York Times,* July 2, 1977, p. 1.

[77] Charles Kaiser, "Special State Prosecutor Reports Fewer Convictions for Last Year," *New York Times,* July 23, 1978, p. A12.

[78] Herbert Jacob, *Justice in America,* 3rd ed. (Boston: Little, Brown, 1978), p. 62.

[79] Eisenstein and Jacob, op. cit., p. 277.

[80] *New York Daily News,* November 10, 1977, p. 94.

[81] Michael Gottfredson, "An Empirical Analysis of Pre-Trial Release Decisions," *Journal of Criminal Justice* 2 (Winter 1974), 287–304.

[82] Steve Dunleavy, "The Bail Scandal," *New York Post,* November 21, 1977, p. 1.

[83] Quoted in Jerry Schmetterer, "Glen Oaks in Uproar as Molester Suspect Is Freed in Low Bail," *New York Daily News,* September 12, 1977, p. 18.

[84] Ebbe Ebbeseb and Vladimir Konecni, "Decision-Making and Information Integration in the Courts: The Setting of Bail," *Journal of Personality and Social Psychology* 32 (November 1975), 805–21.

[85] Eisenstein and Jacob, op. cit., p. 272.

[86] Isaac Balbus, *The Dialectics of Legal Repression* (New York: Russell Sage Foundation, 1973), pp. 238–41.

[87] Quoted in Forest Dill, "Discretion, Exchange, and Social Control: Bail Bondsmen in Criminal Courts," *Law and Society Review* 9 (Summer 1975), p. 661.

[88] *New York Times,* February 2, 1978, p. B5.

[89] Lynn Cobden, "The Grand Jury—Its Use and Misuse," *Crime and Delinquency* 22 (April 1976), 149.

[90] Hurtado v. California, 110 U.S. 516 (1884).

[91] Dena Kleiman, "Grocer and Son Cleared in Slaying of Alleged Murderer of His Wife," *New York Times,* August 11, 1977, p. B10.

[92] "The Jury Points a Finger at Nixon," *Newsweek,* March 11, 1974, pp. 17–22.

[93] Robert A. Carp, "The Behavior of Grand Juries: Acquies-

cence or Justice?" *Social Science Quarterly* 55 (March 1975), 856.

[94] Ibid., 863.

[95] Leroy Clark, *The Grand Jury* (New York: Quadrangle Book, 1975), pp. 45–50.

[96] Paul Cowan, "The New Grand Jury," *New York Times Magazine*, April 1973, p. 18.

[97] Quoted in Cobden, op. cit., 154.

[98] Haywood Alker, Carl Hosticha, and Michael Mitchell, "Jury Selection as a Biased Social Process," *Law and Society Review* 11 (Fall 1976), 9–41.

[99] Ibid.

[100] Laura Rose Handman, "Underrepresentation of Economic Groups in Federal Juries," *Boston University Law Review* 57 (January 1977), 198–224.

[101] David Kairys, Joseph Kadane, and John Lehoczhy, "Jury Representativeness: A Mandate for Multiple Source Lists," *California Law Review* 65 (July 1977), 776–821.

[102] Paul Cowan, "What Went Right in Middle America?" *The Village Voice*, February 1, 1973, p. 9.

[103] Ann Fagan Ginger, ed., *Minimizing Racism in Jury Trials* (Berkeley, Calif.: National Lawyers Guild, 1969), pp. 157–60.

[104] Robert Balch, Curt Griffiths, Edwin Hall, and L. Thomas Winfree, "The Socialization of Jurors: The Voir Dire as a Rite of Passage," *Journal of Criminal Justice* 4 (Winter 1976), 271–83.

[105] Ginger, op. cit., p. xx.

[106] Howard Moore, "Redressing the Balance," *Trial Magazine* 10 (November–December 1974), 29–35.

[107] Jay Schulman, Phillip Shaver, Robert Colman, Barbara Emrich, and Richard Christie, "Recipe for a Jury," *Psychology Today* 37 (May 1973), 37–44.

[108] "Judging Jurors," *Time*, January 28, 1974, p. 60.

[109] Michael Saks, "Social Scientists Can't Rig Juries," *Psychology Today* (January 1976), p. 48.

[110] Steven Brams and Morton Davis, "A Game-Theory Approach to Jury Selection," *Trial* 12 (December 1976), 47–49.

[111] Harry Kalven and Hans Zeisel, *The American Jury* (Boston: Little, Brown, 1966).

[112] Ibid., p. 58.

[113] Paul Cowan, "The Long Ordeal of 12 Anguished Jurors," *The Village Voice*, February 8, 1973, p. 9.

[114] Quoted in Victor Villaseñor, *Jury: The People vs. Juan Corona* (Boston: Little, Brown, 1977), p. 164.

[115] Hans Zeisel and Shari Diamond, "The Jury Selection in the Mitchell-Stans Conspiracy Trial," *American Bar Foundation Research Journal*, 1976, pp. 151–74.

[116] Ibid., 172.

[117] Kalven and Zeisel, op. cit., pp. 487–89.

[118] Kay Richards, "Rereading of Indictment Leads to Compromise Plan for 'Chicago 7' Jury," *The Oregonian*, February 28, 1970, p. 3.

[119] Williams v. Florida, 399 U.S. 78 (1970); and Apodaco v. Oregon, 406 U.S. 404 (1976).

[120] Keith Mossman, "Justice and Numbers," *Trial Magazine* 10 (November 1974), 23.

[121] Richard Lempert, "Uncovering 'Nondiscernible' Differences: Empirical Research and the Jury Size Cases," *University of Michigan* 73 (March 1975), 644–708.

[122] Alan Gelfand and Herbert Solomon, "An Argument in Favor of 12-Member Juries," *Modeling the Criminal Justice System*, ed. Stuart Nagel (Beverly Hills, Calif.: Sage Publications, 1977), p. 208.

[123] See Bernard Grofman, "Jury Decision-Making Models," in ibid., p. 133.

[124] Angelo Valenti and Leslie Downing, "Differential Effects of Jury Size on Verdicts Following Deliberation as a Function of Apparent Guilt of the Defendant," *Journal of Personality and Social Psychology* 32 (1975), 655–63.

[125] Glynn Mapes, "Unequal Justice: A Growing Disparity in Criminal Sentences Troubles Legal Experts," in *Before the Law: An Introduction to the Legal Process*, eds. John Bonsignore et al. (Boston: Houghton Mifflin, 1974), p. 309.

[126] Marvin Frankel, *Criminal Sentences: Law Without Order* (New York: Hill & Wang, 1972), p. 6.

[127] *Sentinel Star*, January 27, 1977, p. 5A.

[128] Morris Kaplan, "Judge Bids U.S. Attorney Weigh Indicting Grumman," *New York Times*, June 28, 1974, p. 1.

[129] Ben Franklin, "12 Hanafis Get Long Prison Terms," *New York Times*, September 7, 1977, p. A18; and Robert Lindsey, "Patricia Hearst, Called No Threat, Given 5 Years Probation by Judge," *New York Times*, April 10, 1977, p. 18.

[130] President's Commission on Law Enforcement and the Administration of Justice, op. cit., p. 23.

[131] Robert Carter and Leslie Wilkins, "Some Factors in Sentencing Policy," *Journal of Criminal Law, Criminology, and Police Science* 58 (December 1967), 511.

[132] Beverly Blair Cook, "Sentencing Behavior of Federal Judges: Draft Cases—1972," *University of Cincinnati Law Review* 42 (1973), 597–633.

[133] William Zumwalt, "The Anarchy of Sentencing in the Federal Courts," *Judicature* 57 (October 1973), 96–104.

[134] President's Commission on Law Enforcement and the Administration of Justice, op. cit., p. 23.

[135] Shari Diamond and Hans Zeisel, "Sentencing Councils: A Study of Sentence Disparity and Its Reduction," *University of Chicago Law Review* 43 (Fall 1975), 109–49.

[136] John Hogarth, *Sentencing as a Human Process* (Toronto, Can.: University of Toronto Press, 1971).

[137] Edward Green, *Judicial Attitudes in Sentencing* (New York: St. Martin's Press, 1961).

[138] Carter and Wilkins, op. cit., 525.

[139] *New York Times*, June 9, 1978, p. C16.

[140] John Hagan, "Extra-Legal Attributes and Criminal Sentencing: An Assessment of a Sociological Viewpoint," *Law and Society Review* 8 (Spring 1974), 379; and Theodore Chiricos and Gordon Waldo, "Socio-economic Status and Criminal Sentencing: An Empirical Assessment of a Conflict Proposition," *American Sociological Review* 40 (December 1975), 753–72.

[141] Marvin Wolfgang and Marc Riedel, "Race, Judicial Dis-

cretion and the Death Penalty," *The Annals of the American Academy of Political and Social Science* 407 (May 1973), 119–33.

[142] *New York Times,* January 2, 1978, p. 18.

[143] Herbert Jacob and James Eisenstein, "Sentencing and Other Sanctions in Criminal Courts," *Political Science Quarterly* 90 (Winter 1975–1976), 617–35; and Martin Levin, "Urban Politics and Policy Outcomes: The Criminal Courts," in *Criminal Justice: Law and Politics,* 2nd ed., edited by George Cole (North Scituate, Mass.: Duxbury Press, 1976), pp. 372–406.

[144] Willard Gaylin, *Partial Justice* (New York: Knopf, 1974), p. 6.

[145] Diane Graebner, "Judicial Activity and Public Attitude: A Quantitative Study of Selective Service Sentencing in the Vietnam War Period," *Buffalo Law Review* 23 (Winter 1974), 465–98.

[146] William Zumwalt, "The Anarchy of Sentencing in the Federal Courts," *Judicature* 57 (October 1973), 101.

[147] From Bob Dylan's "Joey," 1975.

[148] Quoted in Leslie Wilkins, Jack Kress, Don Gottfredson, Joseph Calpin, and Arthur Gelman, *Sentencing Guidelines: Structuring of Judicial Discretion* (Washington, D.C.: U.S. Government Printing Office, 1978), p. xi.

[149] *New York Post,* July 17, 1976, p. 8.

[150] In Re *Lynch,* 503 p. 2d 921; 105 Cal. Rptr. 217 (1972).

[151] *New York Times,* November 13, 1977, p. 60.

[152] Joseph Mattina, "Sentencing: A Judge's Inherent Responsibility," *Judicature* 57 (October 1973), 105 (emphasis added).

[153] W. H. Auden, "Law Like Love," in his *Collected Shorter Poems: 1927–1957* (New York: Random House, 1966), pp. 154–156.

[154] Joseph Hutcheson, Jr., "The Judgement Intuitive: The Function of the Hunch in Judicial Decision," in *Courts, Judges, and Politics,* op. cit., pp. 519–20.

BIBLIOGRAPHY

Alker, Haywood; Hosticha, Carl; and Mitchell, Michael. "Jury Selection as a Biased Social Process." *Law and Society Review* 11 (Fall 1976), 9–41.

Balbus, Isaac. *The Dialectics of Legal Repression.* New York: Russell Sage Foundation, 1973.

Buckhout, Robert. "Eyewitness Testimony." *Scientific American* 231 (December 1974), 22–31.

Cardozo, Benjamin. *The Nature of the Judicial Process.* New Haven, Conn.: Yale University Press, 1960.

Clark, Leroy. *The Grand Jury.* New York: Quadrangle Books, 1975.

Downie, Leonard. *Justice Denied.* Baltimore: Penguin Books, 1971.

Eisenstein, James. *Politics and the Legal Process.* New York: Harper & Row, 1973.

Eisenstein, James, and Jacob, Herbert. *Felony Justice.* Boston: Little, Brown, 1977.

Emerson, Robert. *Judging Delinquents.* Chicago: Aldine Publishing, 1969.

Frank, Jerome. *Courts on Trial.* New York: Atheneum, 1967.

Frank, Jerome, and Frank, Barbara. *Not Guilty.* Garden City, N.Y.: Doubleday, 1957.

Frankel, Marvin. *Criminal Sentences: Law Without Order.* New York: Hill & Wang, 1972.

Hagan, John. "Extra-Legal Attributes and Criminal Sentencing: An Assessment of a Sociological Viewpoint." *Law and Society Review* 8 (Spring 1974), 357–83.

Hogarth, John. *Sentencing as a Human Process.* Toronto, Can.: University of Toronto Press, 1971.

Jackson, Donald. *Judges.* New York: Atheneum, 1974.

Kalven, Harry, and Zeisel, Hans. *The American Jury.* Boston: Little, Brown, 1966.

Murphy, Walter, and Pritchett, C. Herman, eds. *Courts, Judges, and Politics,* 3rd ed. New York: Random House, 1979.

President's Commission on Law Enforcement and the Administration of Justice. *Task Force Report: The Courts.* Washington, D.C.: U.S. Government Printing Office, 1967.

Schubert, Glendon, ed. *Judicial Behavior: A Reader in Theory and Research.* Chicago: Rand McNally, 1964.

Villasenor, Victor. *Jury: The People vs. Juan Corona.* Boston: Little, Brown, 1977).

Watson, Richard, and Downing, Rondal. *The Politics of Bench and Bar.* New York: Wiley, 1969.

"First we had the Mexican Mafia, and we still have them," Warden Harold Cardwell of the Arizona State Prison said in November 1977. "Now this Aryan Brotherhood [white supremecist gang] is getting real strong."[1] Warden Cardwell believed a struggle between these groups for control of the extortion and protection rackets in the prison was the cause of nine stabbing deaths in the prison in just ten weeks. Some believed, however, that the problem was due to poor prison administration. The governor of Arizona fired the director of the Corrections Department in November 1977, saying that the prison administration in the state was "in shambles."[2] Almost a year later the state still had not found a satisfactory replacement for the director.

The Arizona prison system is not unique. Administrative confusion and violence in prisons characterized many

CHAPTER EIGHT

CORRECTIONAL INSTITUTIONS IN TRANSITION

Alternatives for the Future of Imprisonment

prisons across the country during the 1970s. Many changes occurred during this period, including the recognition and development of prisoners' rights, the unionization of prison guards and inmates, the formation of gangs in prison that had their origins on ghetto streets, and the increasing numbers of minority-group offenders. Maurice Sigler, chairman of the United States Parole Board (which handles the parole of prisoners in federal facilities), stated: "We will have to agree that change has come to corrections later than for most other human endeavors. But it is now upon us in full force."[3]

The changing correctional picture has raised questions about what the purposes of corrections should be and even about whether or not we should continue to build traditional prisons at all. Indeed, the word *corrections* itself is becoming outmoded for some seriously doubt that correctional institutions actually correct anyone. And if correcting individuals should not or cannot be a goal, what should be the purpose of prisons and other correctional institutions? We shall try to answer this question before turning to a description of correctional institutions and policies in the United States.

Alternative Correctional Policies

Four different and often conflicting policies have been used to direct prisons and other correctional institutions—rehabilitation, deterrence, retribution, and incapacitation. The first two and the last are policies aimed at crime control. The third is related to achieving justice, which we shall discuss in more detail later in this chapter (p. 311).

For over 30 years correctional institutions have emphasized rehabilitation, defined as any measure taken to change an offender's character, habits, or behavior patterns so as to diminish his or her criminal propensities.[4] To rehabilitate means "to restore to a former status." The assumption underlying rehabilitation is that criminals are mentally sick and can be "cured" if the right treatment is applied. Although based on progressive and enlightened principles, rehabilitation has more recently been under attack for not only violating basic principles of justice but also meting out psychological torture that is worse than confinement itself. Chapter 10 will discuss this issue in detail. Here we want to describe how rehabilitation as well as the other three policies are related to correctional institutions.

Rehabilitation uses the same approach for treating criminals that physicians use for treating patients, and this has a number of important policy consequences. To make rehabilitation work requires that correctional institutions have professional staffs consisting of psychologists, psychiatrists, social workers, and counselors who are able to diagnose the ills of criminals and apply the proper treatment. It also requires individualized treatment, since each person who commits a particular crime may be suffering from a different form of illness. Thus, under the rehabilitation poilicy, individuals who commit the same crime should not be given the same sentence or treatment. For example, consider two individuals who have committed armed robbery: One is a first offender, is married, has a family, and is employed full time; the second is a repeat offender who is not working and has no family. Because the first offender is considered more stable, that person's treatment needs are different from those of the second. Thus, rehabilitation requires indeterminate sentencing—that is, confining individuals for open-ended periods of time, such as from one to five years, with eligibility for parole after serving a year. Offenders given such a sentence could be released at the end of a year if they have shown progress toward rehabilitation; and, if not, they could be kept confined until corrections officials (usually a parole board) decide they have made sufficient progress. Rehabilitation policy, therefore, gives corrections administrators a great deal of discretion in determining when an offender will be released.

Deterrence, on the other hand, has completely different consequences. Deterrence is meant to frighten. The idea is that individuals will not commit a crime if they are afraid of the consequences of being caught. Thus, it can only work with people who are afraid of being caught and punished. Those who commit a crime without thought of consequences, such as one who murders a spouse in a fit of rage, are therefore not likely to be deterred.

Deterrence can be both specific and general. Specific deterrence prevents the convicted offender from committing crimes outside of prison by putting him or her in prison. General deterrence uses the individual who is punished as an example to deter others. But, in reality, specific deterrence does not reduce crime rates very much. First, only a relatively small proportion of criminals are caught and incarcerated. Second, as long as the benefits of crime exceed the costs, it is rational to commit crimes; so we can expect, in theory, that for each person locked up in prison, at least one new person will start a criminal career. Finally, because the average prison term is only two years, specific deterrence works only for a short period. Specific deterrence as a policy goal, therefore, suffers from the fact that it deters only those who are convicted and only for a short period of time; moreover, it does not stop them from committing crimes *inside* prison while they are incarcerated.

General deterrence, as a result, has more deterrent effect. The individual sent to prison serves as an example to others who might contemplate committing the same crime. Therefore, punishing one person can possibly deter a large number of others from committing the same crime—as long as the others believe that they could be caught and subjected to the same punishment. Deterrence appears to work under some conditions. Recent studies show that both the probability of being caught and the severity of punishment deter homicide, robbery, burglary, rape, and assault.[5] Chapter 9 discusses deterrence in more detail.

Whereas rehabilitation is based on a medical model, deterrence is based on a utilitarian model. Utilitarianism, devised by nineteenth-century British philosopher Jeremy Bentham, says that individuals are rational, calculating beings who compute the costs and benefits of committing crime. If the benefits are greater than the costs (which include the probability of being caught and the severity of punishment), then the person will commit the crime. If deterrence is to be the major policy goal of corrections, then punishment must be sufficiently severe to increase the costs so that they are greater than the benefits. The probability of being caught also must be high for deterrence to work. For example, if the penalty for committing armed robbery were only a month in prison, and the chances of being caught were very low, many more people would commit armed robbery. The theory behind deterrence is that the sentence must be made just harsh enough, and the probability of being caught just high enough, to convince a rational individual that "crime does not pay."

Retribution is based on the idea of justice—the notion of an "eye for an eye"—in contrast to the medical model of rehabilitation and the utilitarian model of deterrence. In ancient times the family or tribe of a murdered person would take vengeance into their own hands by killing the murderer. Today, when retribution is the goal of policy, offenders are given punishment equivalent to the seriousness of the crime they commit. Of course, this does not mean that a spy's eyes should be gouged out, or a thief's hands cut off, as was the case in the past. But it does require that the more serious the crimes, the greater the punishment (i.e., the longer the prison sentence or the larger the fine). In addition, for justice to be attained, each offender who commits the same crime must be given exactly the same punishment.[6]

Incapacitation is the fourth possible policy goal of corrections. It is identical to specific deterrence in that individuals who are put in prison have effectively been deterred from committing crimes outside of prison, although they have not been stopped from committing crimes while in prison (e.g., killing a guard or assaulting a fellow prisoner). In order to deter offenders from committing crimes outside of prison, incapacitation requires that an individual be put in confinement for as long as is required to prevent future criminal behavior. Some criminologists believe that a small percentage of all offenders commit the largest proportion of all violent crimes. If these individuals could be identified and incarcerated, they believe, the rate of violent crime would diminish. In order for this sytem to work new violent offenders who are apt to repeat their crimes would have to be identified and incarcerated for as long as they are likely to continue a crime career. Thus, incapacitation requires a completely different kind of sentencing policy than rehabilitation, deterrence, or retribution. Some believe that most violent criminals continue their crime careers until about age 35. Persons identified as career violent criminals, those who are likely to repeat their crimes, would therefore have to be put away until they are about 35 years old, when they could be released. Prosecutor James Kelley of Indianapolis believes that career criminals are not educable; he says, "I used to think the way to reduce crime was to educate and reform the offenders. But . . . [now I believe] what you have to do is warehouse the repeat offenders and keep them off the street."[7] Those who advocate incapacitation do not speculate on what might happen to such individuals after they are released. Would they be able to find a job? If they could not find work, would they be likely to return to a life of crime, even if they are, statistically speaking, beyond the normal age when persons commit violent crimes?

Each of the four possible policies of corrections therefore leads to a different set of sentencing standards. Retribution requires that punishment fit the crime: The more serious crimes should carry more severe penalties than less serious crimes, and each person who commits a particular crime should receive the same sentence. Rehabilitation necessitates that punishment fit the therapeutic needs of the individual: Not every person should be given the same sentence. Incapacitation demands that violent individuals who repeat their crimes be identified and given long-term sentences. Deterrence requires that offenders be incarcerated for as long as is necessary to serve as an example to others.

Confusion over Which Policy Should Be Given Priority

The principal problem facing corrections today is confusion about which of the four policies should prevail. This has been called the "model muddle" by some experts. While all four policies cannot operate simultaneously, some may be compatible with others in some respects. Retribution, for example, may be compatible with rehabilitation since it may be possible to extract an "eye for an eye" while at the same time attempting to rehabilitate an offender.

Rational planning for the future of imprisonment is difficult because the political forces obstructing change are powerful, and reformers have no agreed-upon program. They may agree upon what is wrong, but they are not of one mind about what should be done.[8] Increasingly, reformers have asserted that rehabilitation does not work. For example, the report of the Committee for the Study of Incarceration, which was chaired by former Senator Charles Goodell of New York, concluded: "The simple fact is that the experiment has not worked out. Despite every effort and every attempt, correctional treatment programs have failed."[9] Journalist Susan Sheehan reported that in 1977 various corrections officials in New York, including the commissioner of corrections, made speeches in which they denounced rehabilitation, called for determinate, or fixed-term, sentencing, and demanded a "get tough" policy on prison discipline.[10]

As faith in rehabilitation has diminished, support for prison abolition has increased. Two national crime commissions of the past decade, the National Council on Crime and Delinquency, a number of federal judges, and a host of criminologists have all recommended the abandonment of prisons. They conclude that prisons should be abolished and other forms of correctional institutions be put in their place.

On the other hand, retribution has been gaining favor in recent years. In the eighteenth century the idea that punishment should fit the crime had a firmly established place in criminal jurisprudence; but it went into eclipse with the rise of rehabilitative ideology. Today, its star is rising again for a number of reasons: It reduces the amount of discretion that exists in corrections, which appeals to liberals who believe that discretion results in discriminatory sentences; and it offers certain and swift punishment, which appeals to "law and order" advocates.

Retribution looks to the seriousness of the offender's past crime or crimes. Deterrence looks toward the probable future behavior of criminals, as does the policy of rehabilitation. Rehabilitation requires that corrections officials be able to predict the likelihood that an offender will commit a crime if released. But prediction is a risky business, especially because of the number of "false positives"—erroneous predictions that some individuals will commit future crimes. It has been estimated that for every accurate prediction there are two faulty ones. This risk does not have to be taken if punishment is based upon retribution, when the only requirement is to determine if the person did in fact commit the crime and then make punishment commensurate with the seriousness of the crime.

Although there are many supporters of retribution, a substantial number of people believe that incapacitation should be the principal policy goal of corrections, especially for violent criminals. For example, in December 1977, a 26-year-old ex-convict from New York's Attica Prison, who had previously been imprisoned for rape, and who was at the time under indictment on additional sex charges, was accused of raping and then beating to death a college student who had been hitchhiking. The accused, a part-time tree surgeon, had been arrested as he was trying to move the body of the 18-year-old student from one area to another. Heinous crimes such as this alarm and anger the public, who ask why the individual who had a history of such crimes was allowed to be free to repeat his act. In this case incapacitation might have prevented the murder. But there are two problems. One is that this individual could have given every indication he was rehabilitated and was therefore released. The other is: How long should he have been held in prison—until he was too old to rape? As recently as 1940 in the United States castration was the punishment given to violent sex criminals. Today society does not condone this kind of punishment. So, will this individual be out on the streets again and free to commit the same crime when he is 30? It is possible since the average time served for rape in some states is 4.2 years; and the average prison term for all offenses, including second degree murder (with which this person was charged), is only 2.4 years.

The issues involved in corrections are complicated and not amenable to simple solutions. A look at the history of corrections in the United States will show us why.

History Of American Corrections

Early corrections techniques were as inhumane as the worst offenses committed by criminals. Mutilation was common, including whipping and branding. Spies had their eyes put out, perjurers lost their tongues, rapists were castrated, and thieves lost their hands. In the colonial period prisons did not exist and the pillory, stocks, ducking stools, whipping posts, gallows, ostracism, and banishment were the principal forms of punishment. In Philadelphia, the city of "brotherly love," bodies of those who had been executed were placed in an iron cage where all could see them decompose. This practice, known as gibbeting, was based on the assumption that this horrible sight would be an effective deterrent. A death sentence might include drawing and quartering or burning at the stake; and thieves had a large T branded on their foreheads.

Prisons developed after the American Revolution as a "diversion" from these barbaric forms of punishment. The prison, thus, was part of a reform movement toward more humanitarian forms of punishment. The birthplace of the American prison system was Philadelphia, the same city that practiced gibbeting. At a gathering in the home of Benjamin Franklin on March 9, 1787, the Philadelphia Prison Society was formed. It lobbied successfully for the construction of the Walnut Street Jail. A number of other states quickly followed suit, and jails were built in New York, Massachusetts, and other states. The first generation of fortresslike prisons was built in the 1820s. Eastern Penitentiary was built in Philadelphia in 1829. Auburn prison was built in New York in 1831; this prison was the model for many others throughout the nineteenth and even into the twentieth centuries.

These first prisons were called "penitentiaries," because it was expected that offenders would do "penance" while serving their time in isolated and silent confinement. The assumption was that prisoners would reform themselves through expiation and repentance. To do this, they had to be totally isolated so that they could think about their deeds. The typical early prison structure contained many individual cellblocks—each about seven feet long, three feet wide and seven feet high—and a small exercise yard just off each cell. But because this design was very costly, prison designers soon switched to multiple cellblocks with individual cells and a common exercise yard. Community influences were kept out of early prisons, and a huge thick wall was built around them. Not only was the prison isolated from the community but isolation from fellow prisoners in individual cells also was stressed. In the Pennsylvania system, inmates were to see no one while in prison. Work, exercise, and worship were the main ingredients of the daily routine.[11]

In the early prison inmates were taught to consider themselves dead to all outside the prison walls. Prison sentences tended to be longer than they are today in order to allow time for convicts to repent. Prisoners worked together in shops under the strict rule of silence. They were locked in their small cells at night. Warden Elam Lynd of Auburn Prison expressed the prevailing sentiment about the purposes and goals of prison when he said that reform cannot take place unless you first break the spirit of the prisoner.[12] But few prisoners were reformed, and many went insane. The state of New York, which fathered the silent system, also sounded its death knell when the state legislature declared that "silence does not reform anyone."

A new wave of optimism swept through corrections following the Civil War. In October 1870, the elite of the international corrections community gathered in Cincinnati for a convention on the new "reformatory" concept that was sweeping the country. The convention was in the hands of reformers who created a "new penology." Physical punishment, such as beating or deprivation of privileges, was opposed, indeterminate sentences approved, parole and early release for good behavior accepted, and the development of inmate self-respect through vocational and academic training was promoted.[13] Rehabilitation became the principal goal of American penology, but it was not fully tested at first. Conservatives, who preferred punishment and maximum security, dominated prison administration, and, by the turn of the century, the reformatory movement that was born in Cincinnati lost much of its impetus. Fortress-style prisons continued to be built, and they were located in sparsely populated areas, completely cut off from the community. Punishment and retribution continued to dominate corrections.

From 1900 to 1935 penal reform stood still. Prisons stressed custody, punishment of uncooperative prisoners by solitary confinement, deprivation of privileges, and hard labor. Reformers, most of whom were sociologists and psychologists, attempted to foster acceptance of the idea of rehabilitation. But most prison wardens ignored them. Prison life mirrored the authoritarian administrations, whose main goal was to prevent riots, escapes, and injuries. Prisoner organization was as authoritarian as prison administration, with the favored prisoners maintaining control through cooperation with the warden who, in turn, depended upon them. Some elements of rehabilitative philosophy that had been accepted posed a new and cruel uncertainty for prisoners because they provided guards and administrators with still other means of harassing and intimidating inmates. With indeterminate sentencing the jailers alone decided when a prisoner would be released, and this power was used as a means of controlling inmate behavior.

In 1935 another wave of reform began, and many of the reforms that had been proposed in Cincinnati 65 years earlier were finally implemented. Prisons attempted to classify inmates according to custody needs. Inmates thought to have a potential for rehabilitation were channeled into different treatment programs than those thought to be incurable. The California Institute for Men at Chino, built in 1941, became the model for the new penology. It had neither walls (but was surrounded by a cyclone fence) nor cellblocks and was less restrictive and less repressive. At places such as Chino, punishment came to be regarded as a "bad word."

By 1950 the reform movement became a major part of the prison establishment, and its consequences were far reaching. Under rehabilitation the responsibility for curing criminals was placed on prison administrators. Criminals were regarded as sick rather than wicked, disadvantaged by society rather than evil. As a result the prison staff was augmented with specialists who provided education, training, counseling, therapy, and a host of social services. Committees to classify inmates in accord with custody needs and diagnostic centers were established. Thus, some prisoners were given more freedom and trust than others. Prison organization became more bureaucratized. All of this gave prison administrators more discretion because they had great latitude in determining how each prisoner should be treated. Use of probation and parole radically increased, putting more offenders on the streets than ever before.

The effect of the policy of rehabilitation is shown in data about probation and the average time served in prison. In the 1960s and 1970s, more than 50 percent of all offenders were given probation. In addition, the time served of the average sentence length went down from about 61 percent in 1965 to just a little over 46 percent in 1975. At the same time, because more serious crimes were being committed, the average sentence length increased (see Figure 8-1).

From the beginning of the reform movement down to the present, not all prisons experienced the same degree of reform. Prisons have been run independently and enjoyed complete autonomy throughout most of American history. Each has been managed differently, reflecting the personal biases of its warden. Only recently has centralization of corrections administration in many states occurred. But contemporary prisons are facing a crisis; they are overcrowded, antiquated, and riddled with racial tension, violence, and crime. Consequently, even the very legitimacy and future of prisons is being challenged. We shall now explore the dimensions of this crisis as we describe the various kinds of correctional institutions in the United States.

Types of Correctional Institutions

Imagine yourself in a hot, tiny room without any means of escape. The noise is endless—people talking, swearing, and shouting; radios blaring. There is no privacy. The toilets are open to the gaze of fellow inmates. Foul odors waft through the air. Inmates are packed into cells so that they can hardly move around. The temperature reaches over 100 degrees, and there is neither cross-ventilation nor a fan. You are allowed to shower once a week, usually with cold water. You may be there for a few days or even for months. How would you react?

These are the conditions in most American jails, the institution that first offenders usually experience initially. Jails are used only to detain persons awaiting

FIGURE 8-1

Average Time Served and Average Sentence Length
of First Releases from Federal Institutions, 1965–1975[1]

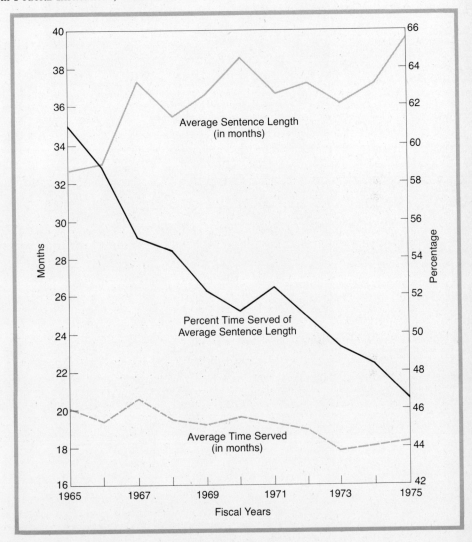

[1]Excludes Youth Corrections Act releases (i.e., those released because of their age).
SOURCE: U.S. Department of Justice, Law Enforcement Assistance Administration, and U.S. Bureau
of the Census, *Expenditure and Employment Data for the Criminal Justice System, 1975* (Washington, D.C.: U.S. Government Printing Office, 1977), p. 15.

A typical American jail

trial or to incarcerate those with short-term sentences. Drunks, juvenile offenders, and an assortment of different kinds of criminals are crowded into such jails. Many of the prisoners are young and poor blacks, Puerto Ricans, and Chicanos. Middle-class offenders seldom spend time in jails because they usually are set free on bail. Only those who cannot afford bail are forced to stay in jail. They are generally in a state of mental disarray. They are not likely to be career criminals because professionals are seldom caught and, if caught, are likely to make bail. Most jail inmates are rank amateurs who, if they are ever to become professionals, learn their first lessons in these jails.

Life in jail is hideously dull and maddening. Inmates' lives conform to the convenience of the staff. They eat when there is a change in guards, usually in cells or in a large day room. Between meals stretch long hours of boredom and monotony. Inmates may play games or write letters. A good day may bring a visit by a lawyer or social worker. But most of the time there is nothing to do. The overpowering helpless feeling brings on mental problems. Suicide by hanging is not uncommon in jails.

From time to time attempts are made to improve jails. Some states have a jail inspector who travels from county to county to determine whether jails meet certain statewide standards. Counties may be required by law to adequately fund and furnish detention facilities. However, even with state laws, the majority of jails are substandard. The Governor's Task Force on Corrections in Indiana recommended in 1977 that the state assume full legal control of local jails because of their substandard condition—for even though Indiana has a jail inspector, he does not have full authority over the jails. The report of the task force also recommended hiring rehabilitated ex-offenders; eliminating political patronage and establishing a merit system for jail administrators; limiting the holding period before trial; and providing hot showers, medical examinations, and counseling services as minimal requirements for the state's jails. Indiana is by no means unusual, nor are its jails regarded among the nation's worst.

County governments control most of the nation's jails. Offenders sentenced to less than one year are usually sent to a county jail or work farm. Most county jails suffer from the same inadequacies as city jails: they are old, unsanitary, and overcrowded. County jails are revolving doors for vagrants and drunks as well as warehouses for juveniles. They usually are managed by an elected sheriff and have low-paid, untrained staffs.

Beyond the county jails are the state and federal prisons. These institutions for long-term offenders housed nearly 280,000 men and women in 1978. Many of the federal prisons are mammoth institutions. The federal penitentiary in Leavenworth, Kansas, for example, is a small city, with 2,100 inmates and a staff of 500. Within the 22 acres enclosed by the prison are facilities for education, recreation, prison industries, and a prison hospital. The prison also has 2,250 acres of farmland on both sides of the Missouri River, which are cultivated by the inmates in the minimum-security prison camp. Leavenworth, built 50 years ago, is in fairly good condition, but it has 200 more inmates than it was designed to hold.

There were a total of 592 state prisons in 1975. Of these, 23 percent were more than 50 years old. However, a large number had been built since 1950—about 270, or 46 percent in the period from 1950 to 1974.

Rising crime rates and harsher punishments boosted the state and federal prison population by 22 percent from 1973 to 1977, compounding conditions that were already becoming major problems. In some facilities assault, theft, and homosexual rape are commonplace. Racial tension is the norm. Some prisons are run not by the guards or prison officials but by inmate gangs organized along racial lines. Conditions in the prisons have become so intolerable in some cases that federal courts have ordered large-scale reforms and, in some cases, have declared entire prison systems unconstitutional because they violate Eighth Amendment guarantees against cruel and unusual punishment. For example, the prison system of Arkansas has been declared unconstitutional. The Indiana Department of Corrections conceded in 1977 that a suit would be filed against it by the United States Department of Justice and that the state would lose. While the Indiana legislature refused to appropriate money needed to improve the prisons, the roof of the building used as a hospital for the state reformatory was literally falling in. The same reformatory's steam heating system needed replacing, but funds were not available. To guard against explosion, the system has been shut down from time to time, leaving prisoners crowded into areas where heat remains.[14]

The story is the same in many other states. Michigan's entire penal system has 3,000 more inmates than it was designed to hold. The Maryland State Penitentiary was built in 1841. Nearly 90 percent of its inmates are black, and 29 percent are serving life sentences. Inmates complain of filth, poor medical care, and inadequate food. Violence is commonplace in the Maryland prison as it is in many others. Assaults by inmates on other inmates or on corrections officers are common. In November 1977, 10,500 prisoners in the Illinois state system shared cell space that would be overcrowded with only 4,000. In San Quentin, California, violence and terror are a daily factor, much of it stemming from battles between racial and ethnic gangs.[15] The rapidly changing ethnic composition of the prison community is a major factor in the crisis facing American prisons. The majority of prisoners in most states are black or belong to other minority groups. Much prison violence is between gangs competing for control of illegal operations such as drug traffic. Learning how to adapt to, work with, and control such gangs is one of the major tasks facing prison administrators today.

The Prison Community

THE PRISONERS: A STATISTICAL PROFILE

In 1975 there were about 219,000 prisoners in state facilities and 24,000 in federal prisons. As Figure 8-2 shows, a large increase in the number of prisoners took place from 1971 to 1975, after the decline from 1960 to 1966. The other

FIGURE 8–2

Prisoners in State and Federal Institutions, 1925–1975

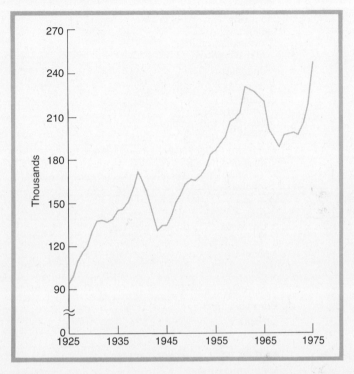

SOURCE: U.S. Department of Justice, Law Enforcement Assistance Administration, *Prisoners in State and Federal Institutions on December 31, 1975*, National Prisoner Statistics Bulletin No. SD-NPS-PSF-3 (Washington, D.C.: U.S. Government Printing Office, 1977), p. 13.

major decline in the number of prisoners occurred from 1939 to 1944, which corresponds with the Second World War. In general, there has been an increase in the number of prisoners since 1925 and declines during the two major war periods. Since most violent crimes are committed by young people between the ages of 16 and 24, there is usually a decline during war because many youths are in the armed services.

More prisoners in state institutions have been convicted of violent crimes and crimes against persons than prisoners in federal institutions, who are more likely to have committed a drug or property crime. For example, the largest number of federal prisoners in 1975 were confined for drug law violations (5,570 of the total 24,000), the second largest number were in for robbery (4,242), and the third largest for larceny-theft (3,303). Only 97 were in federal prisons for assault. Only 441, or 1.8 percent, of federal prisoners were in for homicide. In contrast, 34,000 inmates in state correctional facilities were in for homicide—18 percent of the total. As shown in Table 8-1, the largest percentage of inmates in state facilities are incarcerated for homicide, robbery, and burglary.

TABLE 8-1

Estimated Number of Sentenced Inmates in State Correctional Facilities, 1974

Offense	Number of Inmates	Percent of Inmates
Total[1]	187,500	100
Homicide[1]	34,000	18
Murder	21,400	11
Attempted murder	4,400	2
Manslaughter	8,200	4
Kidnaping	2,200	1
Sexual assault[1]	9,600	5
Rape	8,500	5
Statutory rape	600	([2])
Lewd act with a child	500	([2])
Other	([2,3])	([2,3])
Major drug offense (except possession)[1]	8,000	4
Involving heroin	2,800	1
Involving other specified drugs (except marijuana)	2,100	1
Involving unspecified drugs	3,200	2
Robbery[1]	42,400	23
Armed	28,800	15
Unarmed	5,900	3
Undetermined	7,700	4
Assault[1]	9,000	5
Aggravated	5,700	3
Simple	1,700	1
Undetermined	1,700	1
Burglary	33,800	18
Larceny	12,200	6
Motor vehicle theft	3,200	2
Forgery, fraud, or embezzlement	8,100	4
Minor drug offense[1]	10,700	6
Involving marijuana (except possession)	1,800	1
Possession of heroin	2,600	1
Possession of marijuana	1,100	1
Possession of other specified drugs	1,200	1
Possession of other unspecified drugs	2,100	1
Activity unspecified	1,800	1
Weapons offense	1,900	1
Arson	1,000	1
Stolen property offense	1,900	1
Other sex offense	2,100	1
Drunk or drugged driving	1,100	1
Escape or flight	1,000	1
Habitual criminal	100[2]	([2,3])
Jail offense	2,800	2
Other	2,000	1
Not reported	([2,3])	([2,3])

[1] Detail may not add to totals because of rounding. Percent distribution based on unrounded figures.
[2] Less than 100 inmates or .5 percent.
[3] Estimate, based on about 17 or fewer sample cases, is statistically unreliable.
SOURCE: U.S. Department of Justice, Law Enforcement Assistance Administration, *Survey of Inmates of State Correctional Facilities 1974—Advance Report,* National Prisoner Statistics Special Report No. SD-NPS-SR-2 (Washington, D.C.: U.S. Government Printing Office, 1976), p. 28.

TABLE 8-2

Age, Race, and Sex of Federal and State Prisoners

	Federal	State
Median age	30	27
Percent white	63	51
Percent black and other	37	49
Percent male	95	97
Percent female	5	3

SOURCE: U.S. Department of Justice, Law Enforcement Assistance Administration, *Prisoners in State and Federal Institutions on December 31, 1975*, National Prisoner Statistics Bulletin No. SD-NPS-PSF-3 (Washington, D.C.: U.S. Government Printing Office, 1977), p. 29.

In general, inmates in federal institutions tend to be older and a greater percentage white than state inmates. The median age of federal prisoners is 30.5 as compared to 27 for state prisoners. Almost one-half of state prisoners are black or belong to another minority group, while only about 38 percent of federal offenders fall into this category (see Table 8-2). The percentage of black inmates in state institutions increased from 1950 to 1978, the median age dropped so that there is now a greater proportion of younger prisoners, and the percentage convicted for violent crimes increased. These, plus other changes, such as the movement for prisoners' rights, have made administration of prisons far more difficult today than in the past.

THE ADMINISTRATION OF PRISONS

Until very recently, prison administrators enjoyed almost complete autonomy. Each prison was managed according to the personal biases of the warden. Stateville Prison in Illinois is a good example. Located 30 miles southwest of Chicago, Stateville was run by Warden Joe Ragen, a strict authoritarian, for almost 30 years. Ragen exercised personal control over every detail and cultivated an image that made him seem invincible.

Known as the tightest prison in the United States, Stateville witnessed not a single riot or escape during the entire period that Ragen was warden. Part of this was due to the fact that Ragen was a strict disciplinarian. Part, however, was due to his system of cultivating inmate allies and rewarding with better jobs those who went along with him.[16] The tough inmates were coopted into his system and cooperated with the guards.

The guards who believed prisoners were there to be punished reinforced stability and the status quo. They were rewarded for being able to uncover situations that would upset routine. Their upward mobility was a function of their ability to maintain order.[17] Prison organization copied military organization and terminology. The main job of guards was to maintain security and internal control. This required the help of inmates, which was obtained by rewarding those who cooperated.

Autonomy of the kind that made the Ragen system possible began to erode in the 1960s when the courts started rejecting the doctrine that prisoners were virtually "slaves of the state." They issued judgments affecting discipline, time off for good behavior, living conditions, health care, censorship, restrictions on religion and speech, and access to the courts. As the older convicts were paroled or released, the old system of working with guards and administrators died. The new black inmates asserted themselves and refused to be attracted by the rewards that guards and prison administrators used on the older inmates.

Along with the erosion of prison autonomy went an increase in professionalization of prison administrators. The first step was a growth of centralization and greater accountability of prison wardens to the director of a state department of corrections. Wardens were reduced in power to the status of middle managers. The rise of professional administration led to conflict among prison staff members, because the older staff did not accept it, a decline in the morale of the guard force as more minority group members were hired, and, as a result, a deterioration of the prison's ability to control the inmates.

PRISON SOCIAL STRUCTURE

Every organization, including prisons, has a formal authority structure and an informal group structure. Administrators cannot rely upon their formal authority alone to get things done. They must know how the informal system of power operates as well. Changes in this aspect of prison social structure have had very important consequences for prisons in the 1970s.

Prior to the changes that began in the 1960s, prison social structure was a

---

A FEW BRIEF DAYS OF GLORY

"Big Mac," as the Oklahoma State Penitentiary here is known, spent a few brief days in the glow of public attention in 1973, and has since been forgotten.

The glow came from fires in a riot that caused about $30 million in damage to the prison and killed three convicts. At one point, 4,000 lawmen and National Guardsmen ringed the prison walls, inside of which balky convicts had set up a shantytown in the ruins.

That atmosphere exists only in memory now. Bill Arends, deputy warden, said prison officials have complete control of the prison.

"The convicts used to run the place," he said recently. "Between 1973 and 1975 we regained control of the institution, and it was almost hand-to-hand combat on a daily basis."

J. J. Maloney, "Big Mac under Firm Control after 1973 Rioting," *Kansas City Star*, April 2, 1978, pp. 1, 2.

strict hierarchy manipulated by the prison administration. Murderers and robbers held the highest status in the prison; rapists and sex offenders had the lowest. Prison rackets, such as gambling, flourished. A thriving black market existed in coffee, cigarettes, and alcohol. A great disparity existed between the most comfortable and least comfortable inmates. Those prisoners who cooperated with the prison administration received the best jobs in prison. However, prisoners were not supposed to give the outward appearance of cooperating with prison officials. The inmate who appeared to oppose prison officials, who refused to give up his or her personal identity, was given much higher status and respect by fellow inmates than the ones who cooperated. But prison officials did have rewards they could give to the prisoners who quietly cooperated with them. In a prison such as Stateville, cooperative prisoners were rewarded with better jobs, and prison officials allowed them to control the black market, gambling, and liquor.

The first major change in prison social structure came when blacks, spurred on by the black power movement outside of prison, organized their own prison gangs. Many of these were offshoots of the gangs that had been organized on the streets of city ghettos and transplanted to prisons when gang members were arrested. In reaction, Chicanos and whites began to organize themselves into separate social systems. By 1972 more and more prisoners were associated with one or the other of these ethnic gangs.

The gang in prison serves various economic and social functions. It helps the inmates who have nothing by giving them food and cigarettes. It serves as a communications network, keeping its members informed. It distributes contraband liquor, marijuana, and heroin. But its most important function is a psychological one; it gives its members a sense of belonging. The chief of one gang in Stateville, the Vice Lords, said, "It's just like a religion. Once a Lord always a Lord. People would die for it. Perhaps this comes from lack of a father figure or lack of guidance or having seen your father beaten up or cowering from the police."[18]

Gangs have had a profound impact on the inmate social system. Inmates no longer identify primarily with their inmate status but with their organizational allegiance. The gangs have taken over the contraband traffic by force, and the older inmates, who previously controlled these rackets, have found their lives disrupted. The new inmates are much harder to control. They are not concerned with the rewards or punishments that prison officials can mete out. "The gangs have made our job a helluva lot tougher. . . . There is no regard for discipline; no request for officers; most of them hate us," one guard explained.[19]

Guard morale has seriously declined in the face of these changes. Older guards, who are generally white, from rural backgrounds, and extremely conservative, have no understanding of or sympathy for the strange urban groups they are obliged to watch. Racial animosity is often a factor in this. In the New York State prison system after the Attica riots, blacks and women were hired, and the older guards resented this. As a result turnover has increased among guards, and guards are unionizing to counteract inmate gangs.

The older guards believe it is a mistake to treat convicts as if they had rights like law-abiding citizens. Such privileges only make the inmate cocky and cause trouble.[20] Antagonism has increased between guards and inmates and assaults have gone up. George Jackson, a black prisoner who became something of a celebrity in the 1960s, saw guards as being less psychologically secure than the prisoners. The guard is more defensive and hostile, and can never relax because any inmate could kill him—even though he or she has superior armament. To be a prison guard in a modern prison is to be put in a situation of constant threat from within prison, with no social recognition from outside. Guards are prisoners of the system whose term is longer than the inmates they must watch.

The self-interests of guards and those of the top-level administrators of prisons also are in conflict. Guards, who live in perpetual fear of physical assault, must somehow come to terms with the prisoners. They may look the other way when prisoners violate rules or engage in illegal activities. They may even become involved in smuggling dope and other contraband. Their self-interest dictates that they remain on friendly terms with prisoners. The warden and other top-level administrators, on the other hand, are primarily concerned with maintaining peace and order in the prison. Consequently, they stress discipline and strict adherence to rules. For example, when Thomas Murton took over the Tucker State Prison Farm in Arkansas, he attempted to do away with the system of prisoner privileges. The guards revolted over this reform because it took from them a crucial instrument for controlling prisoners and protecting themselves.[21]

Prison life is unendingly dull, and all attempts to create meaningful work for prisoners have failed. Prisoners put most of their thoughts and energy into making their lives in prison as comfortable as possible. They steal prison food and sell, barter, and exchange dope and "punks" (homosexuals who sell themselves). One common problem facing prisoners is the short work day—usually only about two hours a day. Prison industry—the making of goods to be sold—has been ended in some states as a result of pressure from unions and the demand of reformers that prisoners be paid as much as comparable workers outside of prison.[22] For example, inmates in Indiana prisons make picnic tables, park benches, and maps and highway signs, which state agencies are required to buy. But in 1977 it was reported that an untold number of city, county, and state officials refused to purchase the prison goods, which were being sold at about 20 percent below the price charged by private firms. The officials complained that the goods were inferior, but one state official candidly noted that they simply do not want to buy from prisoners.[23] Such opposition has effectively ended the possibility of prison industry in Indiana and elsewhere, thus making useful job training for prisoners or productive prison work all but impossible. This is a major factor in the idleness, boredom, and futility of prison life.

Prison industry is still important in some prisons, however. For example, the federal penitentiary at Leavenworth, Kansas, employs inmates to manufacture brushes, furniture, and shoes, paying them $45 to $150 a month. The products are sold to federal agencies such as the Department of Defense. In 1977 sales totaled $13.5 million, and profits, which go to support prison training programs, were $2.6 million. But not many prisons are as successful as Leavenworth in this regard. More are like the prisons of Indiana.

In most prisons inmates spend from 14 to 16 hours in their cells every day. Work would be a welcome break from the deadening confines of cell life if it were productive—but it is not.[24] For prisoners serving long-term sentences, the boredom of prison life can become extremely oppressive. Life there can become so bad that it causes some offenders to take extreme chances to escape. Henry Barker is a case in point. He was convicted at the age of 26 for the fatal knifing of his 76-year-old employer, a painting contractor. In 1975 he was in the maximum-security House of Detention for men on Rikers Island, New York, awaiting transfer to an upstate prison. He was given an opportunity to escape by three "tougher cons" who had befriended him. The men sawed through the bars of their cell, wriggled through 40 feet of the ventilating system to the roof, climbed down a makeshift rope made of bedsheets, then plunged into the icy East River. Barker was unable to swim, but he brought along an empty two-gallon milk jug that he used to keep him afloat. "I could hardly walk and didn't know how to swim," he said, but "I was so desperate to get out I didn't think of the danger."[25]

Rikers Island is a notoriously bad prison, but others are just as bad. Thomas Murton, the former superintendent of the Tucker State Prison Farm in Arkansas, has written that when he first entered the system in 1967, death was common and the natural result of the system's brutality. "Discipline was routinely enforced by flogging, beating with clubs, inserting of needles under fingernails, crushing of testicles with pliers, and the last word in torture devices: the 'Tucker telephone,' an instrument used to send an electric current through the genitals."[26]

Another example of the futility of life in prison is the Lifer's Club in Lansing Prison in Kansas. Members include 350 inmates serving life sentences. The organization was formed in 1975 to help lifers survive. Consider Richard Lee Thomas, who was convicted on two counts of first-degree murder and two counts of arson and sentenced to three life terms and five years. A short man with sideburns, Thomas earns $5 a month as a prison toolroom clerk, and most of that income goes to buying tobacco that he uses to roll his own cigarettes. He suffers from bronchitis and severe hypertension. The warden calls him an "agitator." "My life could be taken at any time," Thomas said in a newspaper interview. "Anytime you step out of your cell, you're taking your life in your hands. There's not enough programs, not enough positive activities to make life safe here. You have a tinderbox that could blow up at any time." Another member of the club, George R. Kennelly, drew three life sentences for first-degree murder, rape, and grand larceny. "It ain't been a good life," says Kennelly, who readily admits he is not rehabilitated. "If I had a chance to do my life over, I wouldn't do it any different. I'm not proud of what I've done. But I'm not ashamed either." Kennelly is 51 and says he has done time in Montana, Florida, Washington, Colorado, and Kansas on charges of robbery and murder. The warden believes that the kind of lifer Kennelly represents is trouble. The prison is his life, he knows the ropes and will kill another inmate or guard if crossed because he knows he will never get out. The lifer who is in for a crime of passion, such as murdering his wife, on the other hand, is the best prisoner. "He's not really a criminal," says the warden. "He thinks of behaving, of being good and getting back home."[27] But the majority of the prisoners are like Thomas or Kennelly; they are really not interested in rehabilitation.

Susan Sheehan describes prisoner interest in vocational training in another prison as follows:

> Only four of the eleven men who were supposed to be in the sewing-machine repair shop were there. Two were playing basketball in the gym, one was refereeing the game, one was at the prison's Protestant Center, one was at the prison's Sankore Mosque, one was keeplocked [locked in a cell] and one was at a Reality House meeting [rehabilitation program].[28]

The prison Sheehan investigated has over $100,000 worth of machines in the machine shop purchased with federal funds that are not being used because the men lack the training to use them.

The federal courts have intervened in a number of cases in an attempt to improve conditions. For example, the Federal District Court in Alabama, in *Pugh* v. *Locke*, ruled that the entire prison system violated the Eighth Amendment. In that decision, Chief United States District Court Judge Frank M. Johnson, Jr., found that the following violated the United States Constitution: warehousing of aged and infirm prisoners; the lack of protection for prisoners; the total absence of any meaningful vocational, educational, or other programs, all of which result in overwhelming idleness; the serious health hazards caused by unsanitary conditions; the total absence of adequate health care; and the lack of adequate staff resources. In the court's opinion, "Prison conditions are so debilitating that they necessarily deprive inmates of any opportunity to rehabilitate themselves or even maintain skills they already possessed."[29]

Recreation in most prisons consists mostly of card games, dominoes, checkers, and some organized sports. A single television set may be available in a recreation room. Drugs and alcohol are available, and clandestine gambling is a big business.

Overcrowding of prisons produces tension, hostility, and homosexual rape. It is not surprising that men segregated from women, living lives of desperate boredom in crowded conditions, seek solace with other men. Journalist Tom Wicker quotes one inmate of the Attica State Prison as saying:

> I remember the first time I forgot what it was like to fuck a woman. That day, man, was a helluva day. I lay there all night trying to remember. I couldn't remember how it was like. And that was a year and a half ago. That's a helluva experience, man—to forget.[30]

Violence is also common, not just between guards and prisoners but among prisoners. Inmates fight for various reasons—sometimes over "punks," for collec-

The idleness, boredom, and futility of prison life

tion of debts, for blackmail, because of racial tensions, or because rival gangs are feuding. The beating of inmates by guards is not uncommon. Guards fear and despise prisoners and feel that force is a necessary means of coping with them. But even if they are not physically punished, inmates suffer psychological pain from the loss of identity as well as the degradation and humiliation of prison life.[31]

To cope with the loss of identity, inmates develop their own status system, as is reflected in their language. The "right guy" does not allow custodians to strip him of his identity and undertakes risks for the benefit of the prison community. The "square john" cooperates with the prison staff and is not held in high esteem. The "ball buster" antagonizes the prison staff. The "punk" sells homosexual favors. The "hipster" acts tough. The "fag" betrays other inmates. And the "fish" is a new inmate.

In many cases, prisons are ready to "jump," as Attica was in the early 1970s, just before it exploded. Prisoners during the Attica riot used revolutionary language, charging that the prison administration was part of the general repressive conspiracy of American society. Such rhetoric led New York State Commissioner of Corrections Russell Oswald, a reform penologist, to decide that the leaders of the uprising were revolutionaries. Whether or not this was true, the Attica situation is similar to what existed in many other prisons in the 1970s. Prison administrators have become defensive in the face of rising racial tensions, and the principal incentive for change has therefore had to come from the courts.

THE RISE OF PRISONERS' RIGHTS

Until the early 1970s the courts took a "hands off" attitude toward prisons. Inmates were totally controlled by the state. As late as the early 1970s the sign that hung over the entrance to San Quentin stated, "When you enter these doors you lose all your rights." But beginning in the 1970s the courts began to hold that constitutional protections do indeed follow a prisoner into prison.

After the Attica prison riot, the issues could no longer be ignored. Attica started as a battle between guards and convicts in the exercise yard. But this was only the symptom of deeper problems. The majority of the prisoners in Attica at the time of the riot were youthful, violent man, 54 percent of whom were black and 9 percent Puerto Rican. Moreover, most (64 percent) were sent there for violent crimes. The conditions that led to the riot were expressed by one prisoner as follows:

> The entire incident that has erupted here at Attica is not a result of the dastardly bushwacking of two prisoners September 8 of 1971, but of the unmitigated oppression wrought by the racist administrative network of their prison throughout the year. We are *men!* We are not beasts and we do not intend to be beaten or driven as such.[32]

One of the first cases to follow Attica was *Wolff* v. *McDonnel,* in which the Supreme Court of the United States said that although prisoners' constitutional rights are diminished, there is no iron curtain drawn between the Constitution and the prisons of this country. The Court ruled that before a prisoner could be punished for a disciplinary violation, certain minimum due-process rights must be provided. These include 24-hour written notice, the right to call witnesses, an impartial hearing, and a right to a written statement by the hearing body as to the evidence and the reasons for the ultimate decision. But, the Court said, prisoners do not have a right to counsel in such hearings or to cross-examination of witnesses, nor can they remain silent without the hearing body drawing adverse conclusions about their silence. Furthermore, prisoners are entitled to due process only if they are faced with serious penalties such as the loss of time off for good behavior or solitary confinement.[33] In other cases the courts have found a number of Eighth Amendment violations, including overcrowding, inadequate

Attica, 1971: New York State Commissioner of Corrections Russell Oswald (*left*) negotiating with inmates

medical treatment, physical abuse by guards, solitary confinement for excessive periods of time, lack of outdoor exercise and recreation, inadequate diet, and all forms of corporal punishment.

The courts have not gone as far in regard to censorship. Prisoners have the right to free, uncensored communications with courts, counsel, and government officials. But, other than this, they may not write to whomever and whatever they please. Administrators can even stop all correspondence with given individuals, such as between prisoners in different institutions. However, in *Procunier* v. *Martinez* the Supreme Court ruled that administrators can censor personal communications only if the letter jeopardizes the prison's security and order or the rehabilitation of the prisoners.[34] Books, magazines, and other reading material can be censored, including controversial political, religious, and social literature. And interviews with the press may be barred.[35]

The courts have also held that religious freedom does not end at the prison gate. Officials may limit religious practices only if the security, safety, and discipline of the prison is disrupted by religious exercise.[36]

With regard to prisoners' political rights the courts have allowed some restrictions. The right to assemble as well as the right to free speech can be curtailed whenever prison officials believe it endangers prison security. In *Jones* v. *North Carolina Prisoners' Union* a federal appeals court overruled a decision by a lower court and held that a state regulation prohibiting prisoners from soliciting others to join a union did not violate the First Amendment.[37]

Medical care must be provided for a prisoner's serious medical needs, and officials cannot overrule a doctor's medical judgment. Moreover, in *Kamowitz* v. *Department of Mental Hygiene* a federal court ruled that prisoners cannot be subjected to medical experimentation without stringent safeguards.[38]

Finally, prisoners have a right to be protected against violence or sexual assault. Claims by prisoners that prison authorities have not provided adequate protection have been upheld.

However, the implementation and enforcement of prisoners' rights are still in the hands of prison administrators. Litigation is slow and costly and not a very good method of ensuring prisoners' rights. A study by M. Kay Harris and Dudley P. Spiller, two researchers who worked under a grant from the L.E.A.A. focused upon several major court decisions about correctional institutions.[39] They found that while the court decisions did significantly improve conditions, they also created a number of problems and did not result in ideal conditions. For example, in *Holt* v. *Sarver* the Eastern District Court in Arkansas issued 40 separate orders relating to the Arkansas prison system.[40] Harris and Spiller found that the impact of these orders was broad and profound. The decision educated the public about defects in the prison system, it provided the momentum for reform, and it changed the administrative structure of corrections in the state. Before the *Holt* case each prison was an independent entity, which was deemed to be a major reason for the chaos existing in the state's prisons. A unified department of corrections was created after the decision. In addition, the prison system was put on a sound financial footing. Management problems were lessened by the elimination of inmate trustee guards and the hiring of additional outside guards. But there were negative results as well. Administrators spent a substantial amount of time implementing court orders, compiling records to document compliance, and preparing for and participating in court hearings. In addition, inmates became even harder to handle than they already were because of the developments described above. They lost respect for authority, were testy and belligerent, and harrassed the administration. A number of correctional officers resigned because of the pressure created by allegations brought by inmate complaints. However, incidents of brutality and reprisals against inmates decreased dramatically. One attorney involved in the litigation best summarized the impact of *Holt* by saying it brought the Arkansas prison system into the twentieth century—though not very far into that century.[41]

Thus, while court litigation helps, other forms of action also are necessary. Better legislation and more adequate prisons are needed. But modern prisons cost more than legislators and the public are willing to pay. It is estimated that, in 1978, the cost of constructing a modern prison was over $30,000 per bed. Thus, corrections experts are looking increasingly to other ways of handling offenders.

Alternatives to Prison

PROBATION

It costs anywhere from 10 to 13 times more to maintain a person in prison than to put him or her on probation. Cost is one reason why the courts are turning more and more to probation and other methods of punishment. More than one-half of all offenders are now either placed on probation or otherwise diverted from prison.

Probation originated in the nineteenth century. A bootmaker by the name of John Augustus took a special interest in poor offenders he believed in and persuaded the judge of the Boston police court in 1841 to allow offenders to stay in his home. He convinced the court that he could produce results, and this set in motion other programs. Practices he began using in 1841—investigation and screening, interviewing, supervision of those released, and services such as employment, relief, and education—have stood the test of time. His efforts were so successful that legislation formally establishing probation and providing for paid staff was enacted in Massachusetts in 1878. By 1900 six states had enacted probation legislation. In 1907 there were 795 probation officers listed in the first directory of probation officers, mostly serving juvenile courts. By 1937 more than 3,800 persons were identified as probation officers, of whom 80 percent worked full-time. By 1970 the number of probation officers had increased to 25,000.

Originally, probation was a humanitarian strategy. Supervision of offenders was provided by volunteer workers. But by the middle of the twentieth century a new concept had emerged. Probation became a treatment strategy employing officers trained in counseling techniques similar to those employed by social workers. It also came to be considered to be a sentence in itself. For example the American Bar Association Project on Criminal Justice Standards now describes probation as:

> a sentence not involving confinement which imposes conditions and retains authority in the sentencing court to modify the conditions of sentence or to re-sentence the offender if he violates the conditions. Such a sentence should not involve or require suspension of the imposition or execution of any other sentence. . . .
>
> A sentence of probation should be treated as a final judgment for purposes of appeal and similar procedural purposes.[42]

Probation usually is controlled by a centralized state agency, although in some states it is operated by local agencies under the direction of a judge. It may be under the jurisdiction of the state's department of corrections or under the courts. Those who favor control by the judicial branch argue that probation is more responsive to court direction. The judiciary obtains automatic feedback on the effectiveness of dispositions, judges may place more trust in presentence reports written by probation officers, and there may be an increase in the use of pretrial diversion because courts will not lose discretion over the cases. Others, however, do not believe such arguments are persuasive. They believe the executive branch can be more effective than the courts. The executive branch controls other subsystems for carrying out court dispositions of offenders; it contains the allied human service agencies—including social and rehabilitation services, medical services, education, and housing. Probation officers will be in a position to negotiate and present their cases before these executive agencies more strongly if they are in the executive system rather than the judicial system.

Even though probation is now considered to be a means of rehabilitating offenders, many probation officers have no special training in the behavioral sciences. Many have changed fields after first serving as priests, ministers, insurance salesmen, or army officers. But since the 1920s the emphasis on education in social work as a prerequisite for entering probation has increased. The preferred standard is a master's degree in social welfare. Many probation officers are social workers, but a large percentage of such officers leave their jobs in frustration because they lack opportunity for using their knowledge and skills. Rather than counsel and help those on probation (probationers), they wind up doing little more than making sure their charges do not violate rules.

One result of the influence of social work on probation is the emphasis on casework. The terms *diagnosis* and *treatment* began to appear in the corrections literature in the 1920s and 1930s. The good probation officer was supposed to be able to understand the cause of the offender's problem and to treat it, just as the medical practitioner treats physical diseases. Casework became equated with a therapeutic relationship with the probationer. A study manual published by the National Probation and Parole Association in 1942 entitled two of its chapters "Case Study and Diagnosis" and "Casework as a Means of Treatment.'[43] But recently a broader view of the practice of social work has been developed—the view that the social worker should be involved with individuals, groups, and communities, with less emphasis on individual therapy.

Whether located in the executive branch or with the court system, the principal task of probation officers is to make presentence reports to the court, in which they diagnose offenders and predict their chances of being rehabilitated. They also supervise cases, provide surveillance, keep records, and keep the court informed about the progress of their charges. They are supposed to guide and help those on probation and attempt to change or modify their behavior. But if the probationer is arrested, it is a black mark against the officer because the first question likely to be asked is when the probation officer last saw the client. The natural reaction is for the probation officers to learn quickly that they must protect themselves. The system demands accountability, so that probation officers consider self-protection as the major factor in their decisions.

Some decisions about a case, such as recommendations for probation revocation, may be made only by the head of the probation agency, while other decisions about the same case may be made by officers. The necessity for self-protection pushes decision making in the direction of being sure to recommend revocation of probation at the first sign of danger rather than releasing the offender. The probationer may have to obtain permission to buy a car, move, marry, or change jobs. Violations of these conditions can result in revocation. The probationer may also be *required* to utilize some services offered by probation, such as psychiatric examination or testing, even if they prefer not to.

Most research indicates that probation is not much better than prison in reducing recidivism.[44] But even if probation is no more successful than prison—which is to say that it is not very successful—it would still be preferable to prison since it is so much cheaper. If society is protected as much when offenders are placed on probation as when they are put in prison, then probation is a better way of handling offenders. Of course, it may not work for all offenders. There may be some particularly violent offenders who must be imprisoned. But that may be true of only a small percentage of all offenders. We will return to this question after we discuss some other alternatives to prison.

PAROLE

Parole is similar to probation in that it is a conditional release, but it is offered only after an individual has served a portion of his or her sentence. The supervisory techniques used are similar to those used for probation. The idea began as an application of "good time" (time off for good behavior) laws. Parole also is used as a transitional stage, to see if the individual is able to adjust to life outside of prison. Parole, therefore, is a part of rehabilitation because it is a conditional release of an offender who has been "rehabilitated."

A parole board usually is appointed by the governor of a state on political grounds. Thus, board members seldom are experts, and parole boards seldom make their decisions on the basis of expert and pertinent information. Moreover, they make their decisions in secret and are not required to give reasons for their decisions; until recently, prisoners had no right to appeal. The United States Supreme Court has not established minimum due-process requirements for parole revocation hearings, and so it is possible for an offender's parole to be revoked for arbitrary reasons.[45]

Parole officers perform the same functions as probation officers. But in most cases, actual supervision is cursory. Surveillance is stressed, and the officers' foremost concern is protection of their own self-interests.

The reason why self-interest predominates is related to bureaucratic priorities. The department of corrections evaluates a parole officer's performance strictly on the basis of how much trouble develops from the parole officer's caseload. If parole officers can control their parolees, the caseload generates no trouble for the department of corrections, and the parole officer's performance is evaluated favorably. The officer is able to control parolees by "typing" them.[46] Parole officers classify their clients as being either "dangerous men," noncriminals, or sincere clients. The decision is based on whether the parole officer believes the parolees will make trouble and whether they can be controlled. Those who indicate they cannot be controlled or who are not docile are called "dangerous men." They do not respond rationally to threats or promises; and an officer will send them back to prison before they make trouble. The parole officer may test a parolee by challenging him. For example, one parole officer told a new parolee: "I've got your number, Ike. If you want to start a new life with me, I'll let you. But if you want trouble from me, mister, that's cool too. I know all about you and will be watching.[47]

If the parolee appears frightened and docile as a result of an attack like this, the parole officer considers him to be a good parolee. Some parolees are so docile after years of run-ins with authorities that if the parole officer tells them to jump, they'll ask "How high?" on the way up.

Parolees are usually classified as noncriminals if they are on drugs or are alcoholics. If they turn out to be troublemakers, the parole officer can blame it on their pathological condition. The sincere clients, however, are interested in being rehabilitated, and parole officers enjoy working with them. They may spend extra time on those they type as sincere and ignore all the others. However, the officers' supervisors downplay the importance of sincerity and even see it as something the parole officer invented because they are unable to determine if they will make trouble. But supervisors have a different interest than parole officers in the typing system. Parole officers are interested in trying to rehabilitate their charges, but supervisors are interested only in whether parolees are likely to make trouble. Thus, there is pressure on the parole officer simply to emphasize surveillance and ignore counseling.

WORK RELEASE AND COMMUNITY CORRECTIONS

Until recently, the only alternatives available to a judge were probation or prison. Now there are a large number of institutional and noninstitutional alternatives. Work release, a program in which individuals are permitted to leave jail or prison to pursue regular employment or to obtain academic or vocational education, is increasingly used. Although not all programs have been successful, others have; these have been found to be a good way to keep families intact, to introduce individuals to new skills, and to have a positive psychological impact on prisoners. Under some programs offenders must return to prison without stopping, but under others they can eat their meals at home and return to prison to sleep. Some programs enable individuals to contribute toward their room and board, pay child support, and make restitution for their crimes.

The federal work-release program began with the passage of the Prisoner Rehabilitation Act in 1965; and in 1967 a Division of Community Services, which was responsible for administering work release and related programs, was created in the United States Bureau of Prisons. It has been widely used for federal prisoners and has been successful. Work release is not given to those serving time for violent crimes, and it is not automatic for any prisoner.

Community treatment centers are largely the innovation of the federal government. The first one opened in 1961. Most house between 25 and 30 people and have very few restrictions. During the week, an 11:00 P.M. curfew is observed but weekend passes are allowed. A community treatment center usually has a director, administrative assistant, caseworker, and employment placement officer.

Halfway houses originally were started by religious and private agencies in the late nineteenth century. At that time they were not highly structured in their programs (i.e., they did not have family and job counselors or psychological testing), but most are structured now—and some claim to be highly successful. They provide shelter for those released, and they offer more structure and guidance than probation. More and more are being operated by private agencies under the direction of nonprofessionals and self-help groups. We shall describe their programs in more detail in Chapter 10.

The principal belief of community-based corrections alternatives is that re-habilitation cannot occur unless the wall between the prison and the community is broken down. The fortresslike prison of the past was designed to keep the community away from the offender and thus was placed in remote countrysides. Contemporary corrections theory requires that offenders be kept in contact with the community. Thus there is a movement to abolish prisons as we have known them. However, community-based corrections is no cheaper than incarceration, and the recidivism rate for persons placed in the community is not better than for those incarcerated. So, the principal argument in support of community cor-rections is a humanitarian one.

The Future of Corrections

A number of different changes and reforms are hitting corrections at the same time, including movements to abolish prisons, to establish sentencing guidelines and mandatory sentencing, and to maintain the status quo (although the last can-not really be called a "movement"). These changes do not move in the same di-rection, but because they are all important, we shall briefly discuss each before looking at what the future may hold.

PRISON ABOLITION

Half a century ago, Otto Hagenbeck, a zoo specialist in Hamburg, Germany, realized that caging was detrimental to the health and well-being of animals ac-customed to roaming free in nature. Zoo specialists have since tried to design zoos that replicate natural settings as closely as possible. Columnist Tom Wicker has written about the "revealed truth" he experienced when he realized that the men in Attica prison "were caged." He "saw in the same instant of blinding truth that to cage a human being was to place the person caged in the condition of a beast in the zoo."[48] Wicker should have added that the condition of prisoners in Attica is not the same as animals in a modern zoo; the animals are better off.

Gerhard Mueller, director of the Criminal Law Education and Research Center, New York University, asks, "Who would doubt that the sentence of cag-ing a claustrophobic human being in a seven-by-seven-by-seven-foot grilled cage is cruel and unusual punishment?" He answers, by nature "all human beings are claustrophobic, since ranging and roaming are natural instincts of the human being, requiring satisfaction as much as the hunger drive and the sex urge."[49] Mueller thinks that caging should be declared a violation of the Eighth Amend-ment to the Constitution, and indeed, in a few states the United States Supreme

Court has declared that the prisons, as they stand, do violate the Eighth Amendment.

The noted psychologist, Karl Menninger, has urged the state of Kansas to parole *all* of its prison inmates who have not committed a violent crime. Persons who commit crimes against property—a group that constitutes more than one-half the inmates in Kansas state institutions—should be released on parole, Menninger argues. Menninger does not go as far as Mueller, for he recommends that violent criminals not be released and that those who are caught a second time for homicide or rape should be permanently confined, though not in prisons. Menninger's basic message is that prisons are not good for either the individual or the state.[50]

Criminologist Calvert Dodge writes that "the time is here for planning a nation without prisons. Our major prison facilities . . . are not adaptable to current correctional concepts and programs. Sixty-one of the American adult prisons now in use were opened before 1900, and twenty-eight of these are now more than one-hundred years old."[51]

Voices from a number of different sources have been heard to support the prison abolition movement. Liberals, who formerly supported prisons for the rehabilitation offered there, now believe that they should be eliminated because rehabilitation is a cruel hoax. Some believe that rehabilitation gives a great deal of discretion to prison officials and this has been used to create a nightmare. Rehabilitation is punishment when it is made a condition of release. Political scientist David Greenberg writes that "the desire to help when coupled with a desire to control is totalitarian."[52] Part of the prison abolition movement is thus based on the conclusion that if prisons fail to rehabilitate, then they should be abolished, because none of the other objectives of incarceration—retribution, deterrence, or incapacitation—are proper objectives for a civilized society.

SENTENCING GUIDELINES AND MANDATORY SENTENCING

The therapeutic goal underlying rehabilitation policies violates principles of justice because two different individuals who have committed the same crime will be given different punishments. Furthermore, because any "treatment" that is given in prison is by definition compulsory, it will not work. Criminologist Ernest Van Den Haag believes that instead of trying to rehabilitate them, offenders should be punished according to the principle of just deserts. Punishment should fit the crime, and everyone who commits the same crime should be given the same punishment. Justice should be the principal goal of sentencing. If justice is the guiding principle, an offender is released at the conclusion of his or her sentence; release does not depend upon the approval of one's jailers.[53] This idea has gained momentum in recent years and has been the basis of sentencing reform.

The therapeutic goal requires indeterminate sentencing: An offender is given an open-ended sentence (instead of a fixed-term sentence), such as from one to five years, and then is told that early release on parole depends on his or her "rehabilitation." Of course, it is prison officials who decide just when a prisoner is rehabilitated; in effect, the parole board, not the court, actually decides the length of imprisonment.

Indeterminate sentencing has come under heavy criticism because it leads to great inequities. As we said in Chapter 7, a judge's sentence sometimes resembles the rolling of dice. One judge may give bad-check writers probation, and another may give them ten years. Two approaches have been taken as a solution—sentencing guidelines and mandatory sentencing. The first sets a range of terms for various crimes and judges are to select a prison term from within the range. The second—mandatory sentences—specifies exact sentences for each crime, and judges are not allowed to deviate from them. The state legislatures in Maine, California, Indiana, and Minnesota have adopted mandatory, or fixed-term, sentencing. Senator Edward Kennedy sponsored a bill in 1978 that would establish sentencing guidelines in federal cases.

The Indiana Parole Board was phased out with the adoption of mandatory sentencing. Many prisoners welcomed this because they felt that parole board decisions were arbitrary, unjust, and based on inaccurate bad conduct reports. But prisoners complained most about the lack of certainty as to when they would be released. With indeterminate sentencing, prisoners can serve the entire 10 years in a 1 to 10 sentence, or be released after a year. They are never sure.

Mandatory sentencing and sentencing guidelines are not panaceas, for they have problems. The difficult question in mandatory sentencing is determining how long sentences should be. The tendency has been to make the sentences long. Under Maine law, for example, a person convicted of armed robbery or rape must go to jail for 10 years and will actually serve 6 years with time off for good behavior. Under the old law, the average times served for armed robbery and rape before parole were 3.3 years and 4.6 years, respectively. Thus, Maine's prison population will increase under fixed-term sentencing. This means a large expense to the state to build adequate prison facilities

One possible solution to determining length in fixed-term sentencing is to adopt guidelines. A guideline system takes advantage of and incorporates the collective wisdom of experienced judges by developing sentences based on actual court policies. Under a project funded by the L.E.A.A. sentencing guidelines were developed that relate the seriousness of the offense and the probability of recidivism to an expected time to be served before release on parole. A small range is provided within which parole hearing examiners must usually set the exact length of incarceration. Departures are permitted outside these limits, but written reason must be given for each departure. These are then reviewed by a panel.

Both sentencing guidelines and mandatory sentences will reduce the discretion of judges, reduce the wide disparity that exists in sentences, and, therefore, yield a more just result in that all offenders who commit the same crime will receive the same punishment. But mandatory sentences take determination of punishment out of the hands of the courts and put it in the hands of the legislature. This can be bad because legislators are more likely to yield to public pressures to increase the length of sentences while, at the same time, not approving the large increases in expenditures that would be necessary to build additional prisons to handle the extra load mandatory sentencing generates. Sentencing guidelines are better because they are based on the average sentences of all judges for a particular crime. Thus, guidelines make the sentences for a given crime approximately the same and still allow some discretion for judges within the limits set by the guidelines. If equal (or nearly equal) punishment for the same crime is an important corrections goal—and many believe it is—then it is good policy to adopt sentencing guidelines.

MAINTAINING THE STATUS QUO

There are those who believe that prisons still serve a useful purpose and that rehabilitation still is a legitimate and important goal of corrections. Norval Morris, dean of the University of Chicago Law School, is optimistic about the need for prisons and for rehabilitation. First, he points out that prisons are not likely to disappear in the near future. Four new federal penitentiaries, for example, are opening in 1980. When the state of California attempted to close an unnecessary medium-security facility at Susanville, local citizens protested to their state senators, who applied enough pressure to keep it open. The Susanville citizens claimed that closing the prison would hurt the town's economy.

Nationwide, corrections is a multibillion-dollar industry with most of the money going for institutional maintenance and salaries for prison employees. There are more than 200,000 employees working under federal, state, and local jurisdictions, which process about 2.5 million offenders annually. These operating costs would be extremely hard to eliminate or drastically change.[54]

Morris believes that rehabilitation programs can work. The main reason why they do not is that they are not truly voluntary. Prisoners will "volunteer" for any kind of treatment if they think it will get them out of prison and they will try to satisfy the authorities. The connection between release on parole and involvement in prison treatment programs must therefore be broken. The way to do this, Morris thinks, is to make parole decisions in the first two weeks of imprisonment. Offenders can be told then when they will be released and their subsequent participation or nonparticipation in a rehabilitation program will not affect this release date. Predictions of possible future criminal behavior is just as accurate two weeks after an offender is imprisoned as after a few years in jail.

As a consequence, we should not get rid of parole, Morris argues, for two reasons. The first is that reforms that call for a complete abandonment of personnel and institutions are not likely to be implemented. Getting rid of parole is therefore not a very practical idea. A second reason is that the system is a useful way of gradually testing the ability of individuals to adapt to life outside of prison. As long as prisons are retained—and they are likely to remain for some time—parole is a good method of monitoring the progress of released prisoners.

Parole boards also serve an important interest of judges. Judges share sentencing power with parole boards. This sharing of power allows the judge to appear to be strict in sentencing while the parole board mitigates and lightens the sentence, which, of course, is in the self-interest of judges. Thus, the judge may impose a 10 to 20 year sentence on an offender to placate community sentiment, but the parole board can mitigate this by allowing the offender to be eligible for parole in less than 10 years. This helps a judge when he or she is up for election, for it is never good for a public official to appear to be too soft on criminals.

While not everyone who commits a crime can be rehabilitated, there may be some who can be. The evidence concerning the possibility of rehabilitation is not overwhelmingly negative. Some offenders are successfully rehabilitated. It seems to be a wiser course to maintain rehabilitation programs at least on a voluntary basis, but rehabilitation should not be the only policy goal of corrections. Retribution may be achieved as well. Retribution serves justice, but still allows room for rehabilitation programs to operate, providing, of course, that the temptation to establish long prison terms for crimes is avoided. The United States has the harshest and longest prison sentences in the world, but still it has one of the world's highest crime rates. Harsh sentences alone are not the answer to the crime problem.

PREDICTING THE FUTURE

A number of relatively small reforms are developing that seem certain to become accepted new programs in corrections. One of these is the idea that criminals should help compensate the victim. Embezzlers often are given light prison sentences if they pay back the money they have embezzled. Why not have robbers, burglars, and even those who commit assault compensate their victims? Part of their punishment might be a fine that, if paid, would be considered sufficient punishment, and the fine could be used to help compensate the victim. Fines as punishment are now used for minor crimes such as traffic offenses, parking violations, noise, and littering. To be workable for more serious crimes, they would have to be severe enough to deter yet equitable enough to be accepted as just. They will not work if they are used simply as a way of allowing the well-to-do to escape imprisonment.

A second reform, small in terms of its potential impact on corrections but large in cost, is the question of physical design of prisons. Most corrections experts agree that the day of the huge, fortresslike prison, with its imposing walls that cut off the community, is a thing of the past. Criminal justice expert David Fogel believes that perfectly secure institutions housing about 300 individuals can be built. Such facilities can be subdivided into living units of thirty individuals. This sytem will avoid the oppressive aspects of large cellblock prisons; it can aid in the classification of individuals by work, education, or treatment; it is more easily managed by staff; and it may be possible for guards to find new roles in these small units.[55]

The costs of making such a transformation will be expensive. The public, as yet, does not seem to be ready to support large-scale expenditures for corrections. The attitude still exists that criminals should not be coddled—that the key to the crime problem is the one that is turned in the prison door and then thrown away. But as we saw in Chapter 3, what can be done to curb crime depends upon how serious the public feels a criminal act is.

A third change that is waiting in the wings, which can have a large impact on corrections but that has a low probability of being implemented, is statewide criminal justice planning. Such planning is being supported by the L.E.A.A., and, if successful, it can help promote coordination among the different criminal justice agencies. The behavior of police, who receive the largest percent of the total criminal justice budget, has a large impact upon what can be done in corrections. The police see themselves as crime fighters and generally look with disfavor on corrections policies that allow individuals to be released quickly. They tend to see an arrest as a "success" and expect persons arrested to be quickly removed from the community. Contemporary corrections theory, however, holds that an offender's adaptation to social norms can be facilitated if he or she is put back into the community as soon as possible. In fact, the assumption underlying community corrections is that rehabilitation can be facilitated if the offender is not cut off from the community. Thus, community corrections institutions, it is said, should be built in urban areas rather than in isolated rural settings. David Fogel, for example, recommends that new prisons be built in or very near urban centers because that is where the majority of prison inmates come from.[56]

The incentive system and self-interests of prosecutors likewise run counter to the assumptions underlying contemporary corrections policy. Prosecutors emphasize obtaining guilty pleas, which tends to overload the prisons. Pressure caused by this emphasis has resulted in an increasing number of offenders being given probation.

The interdependence of each of the elements of the criminal justice system is obvious. If prosecutors decide not to prosecute because of the prison overload, then police may decide not to arrest, and the already low probability of being caught for various offenses will drop even lower, greatly lessening the deterrent effect of the total system.

Conclusion

Thomas Murton has written:

> Prison reform across the country is dead. . . . The law-and-order folks have spawned a new breed of writers who have rushed into print acknowledging the futility of reform and, instead, have advocated a return to longer sentences, more punishment—consequently, less humanization of the confined. And they shall prevail for a time. Prevail until the cost of new prisons becomes prohibitive, the harshness of the law once again becomes self-defeating, and the cycle of change is complete.[57]

By prison reform Murton means correcting the multiple deficiencies in prisons that have caused the courts to declare that some prisons are in violation of the United States Constitution. A number of developments tend to support the conclusion that there is more sentiment for getting harsher with offenders than for making things better for them, but several states are moving in both directions at the same time. For example, Kansas in 1978 adopted community corrections and rejected the recommendation by the then-governor (a Republican) that a new prison be built (a liberal move); but a year later in the 1979 session it passed a new death penalty law (a conservative measure), which the new Democratic governor vetoed. Also, several states have adopted mandatory sentencing laws that are aimed both at promoting justice (because they eliminate inequality in sentencing) and at serving the goal of retribution (because prison sentences are longer under these laws). The "get tough" sentiment that hit corrections in the late 1970s was expressed by the new warden of Leavenworth Federal Penitentiary in early 1978 when he said that prisons are for punishment and protection of the public: "In recent years prisons have moved in that direction. We've moved away from a medical model. We've spent time being a doctor; crime was a disease and if it wasn't cured, it was the doctor's fault."[58]

As the 1980s began the pendulum swung in the direction of harsher laws and treatment of offenders, but it never swings all the way in any one direction because not all states follow national trends. Several states are trying to make community corrections work. And, often, trends started in a few states become future policy in a large part of the country a few years later.

SUMMARY

Four different policies guide corrections. These correspond to the different purposes that correctional institutions can serve: rehabilitation, deterrence, retribution, and incapacitation.

Each of these policies has different consequences. Rehabilitation requires indeterminate sentencing and a host of professional workers. Retribution requires fixed sentencing, with the sentence fitting the crime. Deterrence requires a long enough sentence to frighten or convince others that crime does not pay. And incapacitation requires lengthy sentences for those who are deemed dangerous and likely to commit a crime again if released.

Correctional institutions throughout American history have followed one or the other of these four policies. Originally, prisons were built as a way of diverting offenders from the more barbaric forms of punishment then common. The original prisons were places for offenders to do "penance" for their sins. Although there were attempts to make rehabilitation a guiding force in prisons in the nineteenth century, not until the twentieth century did the attempt to reform offenders become the guiding purpose of prisons.

Correctional institutions include municipal and county jails as well as state and federal penitentiaries. Conditions in the jails are abysmal in most states. Overcrowding and lack of adequate medical, vocational, recreational, and other facilities are common.

The largest percentage of prisoners are incarcerated in state and local correctional facilities. Most inmates of these institutions are black or members of other minority groups, and they have been incarcerated for violent crimes.

Prison administrators have enjoyed almost complete autonomy until recently. Wardens ran their prisons and sheriffs ran their jails with little interference from central administrators. Prison social structure tended to reflect this hierarchical arrangement. However, with the infusion of large numbers of minority-group members, the rise of prisoners' rights, and the growing influence of gangs, prison administration has become much more difficult, and assaults and riots have increased. In addition, prison life is dull and boring, compounding the administrative difficulties. Thus, rehabilitation programs are likely to be failures.

Probation, parole, and various forms of community diversion programs are the principal alternatives to prison. Probation is being used increasingly as a sentencing alternative, not because it is more successful than prison in reducing recidivism or rehabilitating offenders but because it is cheaper. Probation officers are likely to be concerned with controlling rather than counseling their charges because they are evaluated on the basis of how much trouble their probationers cause. Work-release programs and community-based corrections, while much more humanitarian than prison, are not much more successful in reducing recidivism and are not less expensive than prison.

The prison abolition movement has a great deal of support from liberals, who are appalled at the abominable conditions of prisons and believe that rehabilitation gives too much discretion to corrections officials—discretion that often is abused. Conservatives believe that rehabilitation should be abolished and that retribution should be the principal purpose of corrections. This requires mandatory sentences and, in the states that have gone in this direction, sentences tend to be longer.

A great deal of confusion exists about which purpose should be given priority in corrections. This "model muddle" pervaded corrections policy in the late 1970s as the pendulum swung away from rehabilitation to punishment. Whether the latter will become stronger or whether there will be a return to rehabilitation is difficult to determine. One thing is certain: Correctional facilities are in a state of physical deterioration and will be very costly to rebuild and maintain. In an economy where the demands on the tax dollar are intense, corrections is not likely to be given increased support.

FOOTNOTES

[1] *Kansas City Star*, November 13, 1977, p. 6A.

[2] Quoted in Greg O'Brien, "State Constantly Fumbles Corrections Football," *The Arizona Republic*, February 19, 1978, sec. 13, p. 1.

[3] Quoted in David Fogel, *We Are the Living Proof: The Justice Model for Corrections* (Cincinnati, Ohio: Anderson, 1975), p. 283.

[4] Andrew Von Hirsch, *Doing Justice: The Choice of Punishments* (New York: Hill & Wang, 1976), p. 11.

[5] See Charles R. Tittle and Charles H. Logan, "Sanctions and Deviance: Evidence and Remaining Questions," *Law and Society Review* 7, no. 3 (Spring 1973), 371–92; Gordon Tullock, "Does Punishment Deter Crime?" *The Public Interest* 36 (Summer 1974), 103–11; Frank Bean and R. Cushing, "Criminal Homicide, Punishment and Deterrence: Methodological and Substantive Recon-

siderations," *Social Science Quarterly* 52 (1971), 277–89; George Antunes and A. Leittunt, *The Impact of Certainty and Severity of Punishment on Levels of Crime in American States: An Extended Analysis* (Evanston, Ill.: Center for Urban Affairs, Northwestern University, 1972); and Isaac Ehrlick, "Participation in Illegitimate Activities: A Theoretical Investigation," *Journal of Political Economy* 81 (May–June 1973), 521–65.

[6] This is sometimes referred to as a "flat," or "fixed-term," sentence. A "flat" sentence is one that strictly specifies the length that a person must spend in prison. This is discussed in more detail below.

[7] Quoted in the *Indianapolis Star*, January 30, 1977, sec. 4, p. 1.

[8] Norval Morris, *The Future of Imprisonment* (Chicago: University of Chicago Press, 1974), p. 1.

9 Quoted in Von Hirsch, op. cit., p. xxxviii.

10 Susan Sheehan, "Annals of Crime," *New Yorker*, October 31, 1977, p. 98.

11 Harry Elmer Barnes and Negley K. Teeters, *New Horizons in Criminology*, 2nd ed. (Englewood Cliffs, N.J.: Prentice-Hall, 1955), p. 406.

12 Quoted in David Duffee and Robert Fitch, *An Introduction to Corrections; A Policy and Systems Approach* (Pacific Palisades, Calif.: Goodyear, 1976), p. 406.

13 Barnes and Teeters, op. cit., pp. 524–25.

14 *Indianapolis Star*, June 19, 1977, p. 20.

15 "Crisis in the Prisons: Not Enough Room for All the Criminals," *U.S. News and World Report*, November 28, 1977, pp. 76–79.

16 James B. Jacobs, *Stateville* (Chicago: University of Chicago Press, 1977).

17 Fogel, op. cit., p. 201.

18 Quoted in Jacobs, op. cit., pp. 152–53.

19 Quoted in ibid., p. 162.

20 Sheehan, op. cit., p. 80.

21 Thomas Murton and Joe Hyams, *Accomplices to the Crime* (New York: Grove Press, 1969).

22 Tom Wicker, *A Time to Die* (New York: Quandrangle Books, 1975).

23 Byron C. Wells, "Public Officials Ignore Law Requiring Buying of Inmate-made Goods," *Indianapolis Star*, June 23, 1977, p. 6.

24 Sheehan, op. cit., p. 70.

25 Quoted in the *New York Times*, February 23, 1978, p. B1.

26 Thomas Murton, "The Arkansas Effect," *New York Times*, February 17, 1978, p. A27.

27 The warden and prisoners are quoted in Richard A. Serrano, "Lifers: Time on Their Minds," *The Kansas City Times*, January 21, 1978, pp. 1B, 3B.

28 Sheehan, op. cit., p. 70.

29 Pugh v. Locke, 406 F. Supp. 318 (E.D. Ala. 1976).

30 Quoted in Wicker, op. cit., p. 85.

31 Erving Goffman, *Asylums: Essays on the Social Situation of Mental Patients and Other Inmates* (Garden City, N.Y.: Anchor Books, 1961); and Donald Clemmer, *The Prison Community* (New York: Holt, Rinehart & Winston, 1966).

32 Quoted in Wicker, op. cit., p. 28.

33 Wolff v. McDonnel, 418 U.S. 539 (1974). See Alvin J. Bronstein, "Reform Without Change: The Future of Prisoners' Rights," *Civil Liberties Review* 6 (September–October 1977), 27–45.

34 Procunier v. Martinez, 416 U.S. 396 (1974).

35 Saxbe v. Washington Post Company, 417 U.S. 843 (1974).

36 Cruz v. Beto, 405 U.S. 319 (1972).

37 Jones v. North Carolina Prisoners' Union, 21 Cr. L. RPTR. 3190 (1977).

38 Kamowitz v. Department of Mental Hygiene, 2 Prison L. RPTR 433 (1973).

39 M. Kay Harris and Dudley P. Spiller, *After Decision: Implementation of Judicial Decrees in Correctional Settings* (Washington, D.C.: U.S. Government Printing Office, 1977).

40 Holt v. Sarver, 309 F. Supp. 362 (E.D. Ark. 1970).

41 Quoted in Harris and Spiller, op. cit., p. 114.

42 American Bar Association Project on Standards for Criminal Justice, *Standards Relating to Probation* (New York: Institute of Judicial Administration, 1970), p. 9.

43 Helen D. Pigeon, *Probation and Parole in Theory and Practice* (New York: National Probation and Parole Association, 1942).

44 Dean V. Babst and John W. Mannering, "Probation Versus Imprisonment for Similar Types of Offenders: A Comparison by Subsequent Violations" *Journal of Research in Crime and Delinquency* 2, no. 2 (July 1965), 60–71; California Youth Authority, *California Probation Subsidy Program: A Progress Report to the Legislature* (Sacramento, Calif.: California Youth Authority, 1975); H. J. Vetter and Reed Adams, "Effectiveness of Probation Caseload Sizes: A Review of the Empirical Literature," Criminology 8, no. 4 (1971); Law Enforcement Assistance Administration, *State and County Probation Systems in Crisis.* (Washington, D.C.: U.S. Government Printing Office, 1976).

45 Morrissey v. Brewer, 408 U.S. 471 (1971); and Gagnon v. Scarpelli, 411 U.S. 778 (1973).

46 Richard McCleary, "Dangerous Men" (Unpublished manuscript, 1978).

47 Quoted in ibid., p. 6.

48 Wicker, op. cit., p. 59.

49 Quoted in Calvert R. Dodge, ed., *A Nation Without Prisons: Alternatives to Incarceration* (Lexington, Mass.: D.C. Heath, 1975), p. 235.

50 Laura Scott, "Parole Nonviolent Convicts, Menninger Urges," *Kansas City Times*, September 8, 1977, p. 3A.

51 Dodge, op. cit., p. 240.

52 David Greenberg, "Rehabilitation Is Still Punishment," *The Humanist* 3 (May–June 1972), 24–43.

53 Ernest Van Den Haag, *Punishing Criminals* (New York: Basic Books, 1975), p. 9.

54 Robert Sommer, *The End of Imprisonment* (New York: Oxford University Press, 1976), p. 180.

55 Fogel, op. cit., pp. 263–64.

56 Ibid. p. 274.

57 Murton, op. cit.

58 Richard Alm, "Warden Emphasizes Dual Role: Punishment, Protecting Society," *Kansas City Times*, January 19, 1978, p. 8D.

BIBLIOGRAPHY

Babst Dean V., and Mannering, John W. "Probation Versus Imprisonment for Similar Types of Offenders: A Comparison by Subsequent Violations." *Journal of Research in Crime and Delinquency* 2, no. 2 (July 1965), 60–71.

Barnes, Harry Elmer, and Teeters, Negley K. *New Horizons in Criminology*, 2nd ed. Englewood Cliffs, N.J.: Prentice-Hall, 1955.

Bronstein, Alvin J. "Reform Without Change: The Future of Prisoners' Rights." *Civil Liberties Review* 6 (September–October 1977), 27–45.

California Youth Authority. *California Probation Subsidy Program: A Progress Report to the Legislature.* Sacramento, Calif.: California Youth Authority, 1975.

Clemmer, Donald. *The Prison Community.* New York: Holt, Rinehart & Winston, 1966.

Dodge, Calvert R., ed. *A Nation Without Prisons: Alternatives to Incarceration.* Lexington, Mass.: D.C. Heath, 1975.

Duffee, David and Fitch, Robert. *An Introduction to Corrections: A Policy and Systems Approach.* Pacific Palisades, Calif.: Goodyear, 1976.

Fogel, David. *We Are the Living Proof: The Justice Model for Corrections.* Cincinnati, Ohio: Anderson, 1975.

Goffman, Erving. *Asylums: Essays on the Social Situation of Mental Patients and Other Inmates.* Garden City, N.Y.: Anchor Books, 1961.

Greenberg, David. "Rehabilitation Is Still Punishment." *The Humanist* 3 (May–June 1972), 24–43.

Harris, M. Kay, and Spiller, Dudley P. *After Decision: Implementation of Judicial Decrees in Correctional Settings.* Washington, D.C.: U.S. Government Printing Office, 1977.

Jacobs, James B. *Stateville.* Chicago: University of Chicago Press, 1977.

Morris, Norval. *The Future of Imprisonment.* Chicago: University of Chicago Press, 1974.

Murton, Thomas, and Hyams, Joe. *Accomplices to the Crime.* New York: Grove Press, 1969.

Pigeon, Helen D. *Probation and Parole in Theory and Practice.* New York: National Probation and Parole Association, 1942.

Sommer, Robert. *The End of Imprisonment.* New York: Oxford University Press, 1976.

Van Den Haag, Ernest. *Punishing Criminals.* New York: Basic Books, 1975.

Von Hirsch, Andrew. *Doing Justice: The Choice of Punishments.* New York: Hill & Wang, 1976.

Wicker, Tom. *A Time to Die.* New York: Quadrangle Books, 1975.

Zimring, Franklin E. "Measuring the Impact of Pretrial Diversion from the Criminal Justice System." *University of Chicago Law Review* 41 (1974), 224–41.

PART THREE

POLICIES FOR COPING WITH CRIME

Although most citizens and many businesses often make an effort to fight crime, Americans tend to believe that efforts to cope with crime should be led by the government. Thus, the government makes and implements policies for dealing with crime—policies that often are rejected and readopted over time. A major purpose of this section is to analyze realistically the effect of four such policies currently being followed in the United States—deterrence, rehabilitation, decriminalization, and diversion. The first two are old and established and are widely in use throughout the country; the latter two are generally regarded as experimental, with only limited application to date.

A second, equally important purpose of this section is to describe the dynamics of the American criminal justice system. In order to understand why a particular policy emerged and how it actually is administered, one needs to keep in mind certain themes established earlier in the text. Before a policy is put into force, there are major political debates over the priority of public interest goals, and each policy requires the cooperation of criminal justice personnel and their agencies to be successfully implemented. Further, all policies contain certain assumptions about the nature of crime as well as the nature of criminals. As we will show in this section, each policy is best suited to attack particular crimes and certain categories of criminals.

In this part of the book we go beyond a discussion of the intellectual foundations of various policies to an analysis of the political realities involved in formulating and implementing these strategies. The form a particular policy ultimately takes is as much a product of legislative and bureaucratic politics as it is a reflection of whether it is logically and intellectually sound.

Chapter 9 begins with an analysis of whether deterrence is a reasonable approach for attacking crime. We show that deterrence is based on the theory that sanctions can inhibit criminal behavior. Next, the chapter identifies the basic requirements for setting up deterrence strategies. For example, deterrence requires that sanctions against criminal behavior must be fairly certain and sufficiently severe.

Further, we explore the practical obstacles to achieving deterrence strategies, including problems of implementation. The tangible and intangible costs of deterrence are exposed, including threats they present to due process. Last, the impacts that deterrence strategies like saturation policing, mandatory punishment, and capital punishment have on public interest goals are investigated.

Chapter 10 begins with a discussion of the theory of rehabilitation. This is followed by an analysis of the modes of rehabilitation, such as therapeutic treatment and alternative community-based programs.

The problems of implementing these various rehabilitation strategies are also explored, and an assessment is made of the difficulties in gaining community and social service agencies' support. Finally, we discuss whether or not rehabilitation meets its stated goals.

Chapter 11 treats two interrelated strategies for shrinking the scope of the criminal sanction—decriminalization and legalization. The chapter begins with a detailed examination of the political factors that have led to the proliferation of victimless crimes in our criminal codes. Next, decriminalization and legalization are viewed as policies that enable legislatures to cope with the problem of "overcriminalization." Special attention is given to the conditions required for the reform of criminal codes as well as to the role the federal government has played in encouraging state governments to adopt these strategies. Finally, the impact of two decriminalization policies are assessed—those dealing with marijuana and public drunkenness.

Chapter 12 looks at diversion as a form of mediation as well as an alternative to adjudication for settling disputes. The many facets of diversion are discussed, including the distinction between traditional or informal diversion, which relies on the discretion of individual court personnel, and "new diversion," which aims to establish diversion programs as agencies of government.

The political forces that support diversion policies are studied, including the role of the federal government. Three types of diversion programs are discussed in the context of what kinds of support are needed to implement them in various communities. Last, we assess the extent to which diversion meets stated goals.

In order to determine whether the threat of punishment deters people from violating rules, two professors in Florida performed an experiment on their students in which they examined whether fear of sanctions would curtail cheating on tests.[1] They gave objective quizzes once a week over the course of a term, graded the quizzes, recorded the grades, and returned them at the next class period with no marks on the paper. Students were told that in order to save time they were to grade their own quizzes according to an answer key that they were given. The difference between the grades that students assigned themselves and the real grades that the instructors had previously assigned them without their knowledge was taken as a measure of cheating.

Three groups of students were subjected to this procedure. In one (a control group), no mention was made of

CHAPTER NINE

DETERRENCE
Crime Prevention
Through Intimidation

cheating throughout the entire term. In the other two groups students were told after the fourth week about their moral obligation to grade themselves honestly. After the seventh quiz, students were informed that there was an apparent problem of cheating, which was going to be handled through spot checking of some of the tests. Before students graded the eighth quiz, they were again warned about cheating and falsely told that someone had been caught giving himself a higher grade than he deserved and that this person was being penalized. By comparing the amount of dishonest grading that materialized throughout the term, the professors were able to discern the relative effectiveness of appeals to the students' conscience as opposed to the threat of punishment.

The results of this experiment are reported in Table 9-1. From the outset cheating was abundant; large numbers of students submitted scores much higher than they actually obtained. The degree of cheating in all three classes remained relatively constant the first six weeks and was totally unaffected by the speech about morality given after the fourth week. However, the amount of false reporting in the two classes who were warned about sanctions near the end of the term plummeted dramatically. Quite clearly, the fear of getting caught and receiving the same fate as the unfortunate offender who was presumably being punished for cheating was sufficient to intimidate many students. In short, deterrence worked.

In another deterrence experiment the offenders were errant college professors at a large midwestern university who repeatedly violated parking regulations and refused to pay the tickets written by campus police.[2] To crack down on these violators, fines were increased from the previous figure of $1 per offense to $1 for the initial offense, $3 for the second, and $5 for every additional offense. The campus police force was enlarged to permit more patrolling, and police were authorized to tow away illegally parked cars at the owners' expense, which was done in a number of cases. The results were impressive: Of the 13 frequent violators, 11 stopped parking illegally, and the violations of the other two dimin-

351

TABLE 9-1

The Effect of Threats on Student Cheating

Sociology Classes or Groups	Average Percentage of Cheating Opportunities Utilized				
	Examinations 1–3, with No Moral Appeal or Threat	Examinations 4–6, with Moral Appeal	Examinations 1–6 Combined	Examination 7, with Threat of Spot Check	Examination 8, with Sanction Threat
Treatment Group *A*, a total of 30 students	31	41	34	13	11
Treatment Group *B*, a total of 51 students	41	43	42	32	22
Control Group, a total of 26 students	27	33[1]	30	24[1]	28[1]

[1] No moral appeal or threat.

SOURCE: Charles Tittle and Allan Rowe, "Moral Appeal, Sanction Threat, and Deviance: An Experimental Test," *Social Problems* 20 (Spring 1973), 491. Reprinted by permission of the Society for the Study of Social Problems, which publishes *Social Problems*, and of the authors.

ished markedly. The imposition of stiffer fines and more intensive surveillance engendered a great deal of compliance with the rules, which was previously lacking. Again, deterrence succeeded.

New York City used the threat of punishment to cope with a similar problem—the ubiquitous use of slugs to avoid paying the parking meters located on most commercial streets. In several selected areas where slug usage was high, police attached labels to the meters informing motorists that slug use was a violation of the law. One-third of the meters stated that the use of slugs violated a New York City ordinance and could result in a $50 fine; another third invoked a state law carrying a $500 fine and three-month sentence in prison; the remaining meters warned that slug usage was a federal crime (violating counterfeiting laws) punishable by one year's imprisonment and a $1,000 fine. All of the signs were made quite visible; they were placed right on the meter windows and printed in contrasting colors.

The results of this campaign were negligible: While slug use declined where notices about violation of state law were affixed (in comparison with a control group of meters using no special stickers), the impact did not last long. Within a few months slug usage in all labeled meters had climbed back to previous levels and significantly surpassed the citywide average.[3] This attempt at deterrence was a flop.

In Miami a special "STOP Robbery" investigative strike force was created in 1971 to reduce the escalating robbery rate in that city, which had gone up about 25 percent annually for the preceding several years. This special police unit used stakeouts, informants, surveillance, and new equipment. The force concentrated exclusively on robberies in progress or already consummated. Although the robbery rate declined substantially during the first 27 months of the project (from 9.6 percent in 1972 to 6.4 percent in 1973), by 1974 the robbery rate was again climbing—increasing 35 percent over the previous year, even though the number of robbery arrests had gone up substantially.[4] Apparently many robbers were insufficiently frightened by the increase in police capabilities to be deterred; in the long run, the "STOP Robbery" project simply did not stop robbery.

What these four examples suggest is that threats of punishment can prevent wrongdoing in some circumstances and be ineffectual in others. Students gave up cheating and faculty members obeyed parking rules, but neither slug users nor robbers were frightened into stopping their illegal pursuits. To explain these disparate results, we must examine both the theory and the practice of deterrence.

We shall see that the fear of legal sanctions can be a powerful constraint on human behavior and that people often decide whether or not to follow the law by judging the likely consequences of disobedience. But we shall also show that the limited capabilities and multiple purposes of the criminal justice system often thwart the development of effective policies aimed at crime deterrence. Moreover, the same attention to self-interest that makes potential criminals hesitate to commit crimes if the risks are great also can inhibit law enforcement officials from implementing various deterrence schemes that are formulated if adverse repercussions from so doing might result. Consequently, as the last section of this chapter will demonstrate, the impact of deterrence policies often falls far short of expectations. "Get tough" policies can deter crime—but only if the criminal justice system actually practices what it preaches.

The Theory of Deterrence

The first step in understanding deterrence is to clarify its meaning.[5] Various definitions of this concept have been offered, but deterrence essentially is the threat of punishment to inhibit wrongful behavior. This strategy of crime prevention is built on the premise that there is a significantly large population of amoral individuals who harbor criminal motivations for a variety of reasons—economic need, frustration, hedonism, and so on. However, people with these inclinations experience cross-pressures; while they may badly want to steal, cheat, or even kill, they also want to escape the onerous burden of criminal sanctions. The main idea of deterrence is to encourage people to suppress their criminal instincts in order to protect themselves from the grievous consequences of getting caught. They may continue to think evil thoughts, but they refrain from carrying them out. Deterrence tries to control *objective* behavior rather than change *subjective* feelings about crime.

TYPES OF DETERRENCE

Various types of deterrence are identifiable. In this chapter, unless otherwise indicated, we will refer to what is called "general deterrence"—the restraining effect of punishing offenders who are caught on the total population of potential offenders. Examples of such deterrence abound: Drivers who see tickets on the cars parked by expired meters are more likely to pay for the privilege of parking; robbers generally avoid selecting post offices as targets because the thoroughness of federal investigations makes the odds of success relatively low; department store shoppers who get a sudden craving for a particular item on display may well forgo the temptation to steal when they see the rotating cameras pointed at them and read the sign that says "All shoplifters will be prosecuted to the full extent of the law"; and politicians ready to accept a bribe to secure a government contract may desist if they read about colleagues going to jail for engaging in such corruption.

The essence of general deterrence is the use of punishment against apprehended criminals to serve as examples that will show the rest of us what may lie in store if we do likewise. The miserable fate of those who fail at crime threatens the rest of us—and keeps us in line.

Within the category of general deterrence we must distinguish absolute, partial, and marginal deterrence. Absolute deterrence occurs when a particular crime is forgone altogether out of fear of the legal consequences. The key idea is total abstinence—refusal to commit the crime to any degree and under any circumstances. The person who unequivocally resists trying marijuana for fear of arrest has been absolutely deterred, as has the juvenile delinquent who refuses to carry a gun in order to avoid "real trouble."

Partial (or restrictive) deterrence is a reduction in the intensity or brazenness of criminal activity to ward off the chance of punishment. Crime is not prevented, but the damage inflicted by it is scaled down. This occurs when drivers who see state troopers reduce their speed to 10 miles per hour over the limit instead of 20 or 30—still violating the law but making themselves less of a road menace and reducing the risk of accident. Likewise the millions of taxpayers who keep income tax fraud within "moderate" bounds to avoid being audited no doubt save the government billions of dollars, although the law has failed to keep them completely honest. While such curtailed criminality in some ways represents a failure of deterrence, the many obstacles to absolute deterrence that we shall analyze later suggest that such impacts are a more reasonable expectation of criminal justice policies.

Marginal deterrence is the difference between the deterrent efficacy of two alternative policies. It is the additional crime prevented by some stiffening of criminal justice operations—adding extra police, eliminating parole, restoring capital punishment, and the like. In other words, it is the total number of people who refrain from committing crimes because of a particular deterrence measure who would otherwise break the law. Because every policy aimed at deterring crime has costs associated with it, this concept is especially important insofar as it draws attention to the commensurate incremental gains of getting tougher.

In assessing the soundness of deterrence strategy and the effectiveness of our present system, absolute deterrence is informative: We want to know how many crimes would occur if there were *no* police, *no* prisons, and *no* penal laws so that we can assess the social dividends resulting from the current investment of so many resources in law enforcement measures that are intended to deter crime. However, no one seriously suggests dismantling the entire criminal justice system and relying solely on public virtue to maintain social norms. The relevant question is *not* what would happen if we emptied all the jails, but what would happen if we reduced jail sentences (or lengthened them) by 10, 20, or 30 percent. Business people are generally concerned with marginal revenue in deciding whether to add new products, install new equipment, or hire extra employees—the additional revenues to be generated by expenditures for such goods and services. In assessing whether reforms are sound investments from the standpoint of deterrence, a similar emphasis on marginal gains is appropriate.

The other major type of deterrence is specific deterrence, the extent to which punishment prevents those experiencing it from repeating their crimes in the future in order to avoid a repetition of the suffering they have undergone. Although this kind of deterrence is conceptually a subcategory of general deterrence (since the threat of sanctions is expected to inhibit future crime), there are additional complexities that require that it be analyzed separately. On the one hand, the actual misery wrought by the imposition of punishment makes the reality of potential sanctions much more salient to offenders. On the other hand (as Chapters 8 and 10 show), the debilitating negative consequences of prison (or even arrest) may be so acute that they reinforce criminal tendencies and therefore offset deterrent effectiveness. Attempts at specific deterrence can breed crime as well as inhibit it.

THE DYNAMICS OF DETERRENCE

The rationale of deterrence was set forth long ago by the eighteenth-century philosopher Jeremy Bentham.[6] According to his theory of utilitarianism, people generally guide their everyday behavior by rationally weighing the probable benefits to be derived from a course of action (i.e., the "utilities") against the probable costs (i.e., "disutilities"). While he recognized that human wants and aspirations were varied, it was assumed that people were by and large hedonistic—trying to maximize pleasures and minimize pain.

According to classical deterrence theory, people consciously or unconsciously refer to this "felicity calculus" and rationally determine whether it is worthwhile to commit particular crimes. If the punishment associated with criminal behavior detracted from their "net" happiness more than the gains from committing the crimes added to it, people would ordinarily restrain themselves. On the other hand, such criminality might be sensible if the harm caused by the punishments was less than the corresponding good derived from the crime. The key to deterrence, then, is to instill so great a fear of repercussions from breaking the law that potential criminals will gauge such illegal activities to be irrational risks. Crime is checked by frightening the population into obedience.

The appeal of this theory is that it so nicely comports with so much ordinary human behavior. Almost everyone can point to many instances in which they have resisted impulses to do something wrong because of fear of what would happen if they got caught. Children often abandon some mischief because they fear parental discipline. A parent routinely capitulates to outrageous demands of children ("I want more candy!") to avoid their crying and having tantrums—one of the worst forms of punishment for a parent. Employees will dutifully perform unpleasant chores if they fear a reprimand or dismissal. A student often refrains from cheating to avoid being censured, failed, or suspended from school. And soldiers on the battlefield fight savagely against the enemy because they are afraid of the prospect of harsh military sanctions for disobeying orders.

Likewise, most of us can point to times when we were sorely tempted to violate the criminal law but desisted from so doing out of fear. We often resist the urge to speed on the roads, to use some illicit drug, to pilfer some item from a store in which we are browsing, or even to strike an adversary during a quarrel because we are worried about getting caught and punished. Even during angry fits of passion, when we really feel like killing someone who has enraged us, the terror of arrest, conviction, and punishment makes us hold back our violent impulses. "I could have *killed* him" or "I've *got* to have that" are sentiments many have experienced; and it is legal threats as much as moral scruples that cause people to refrain from acting out such feelings.

Rational attention to self-interest dictates that people use their best efforts to protect themselves from deleterious consequences, and to a remarkable extent such rationality shapes and constrains the choices they make. The prime virtue of deterrence as a crime-prevention strategy is that it takes advantage of the inherent egocentrism in human nature and makes it serve the public interest.

In addition, other side effects to the punishing of offenders may reinforce the primary inhibiting effect of fear. First, penalizing offenders can impress upon people the moral turpitude of committing certain crimes; this has been called the "sermonizing function" of punishment. In everyday life many laws are routinely broken and many criminal acts are countenanced by the criminal justice system. When the system severely punishes particular kinds of offenders, a symbolic message about the gravity of the crime is communicated to the society. The horror of the punishment demonstrates the gravity of the evil.

Thus, the common knowledge that few people are prosecuted, convicted, or imprisoned for income-tax evasion suggests that such an offense is not really so bad—an acceptable way of padding one's income. On the other hand, the stiff treatment afforded check forgers and counterfeiters implies that these are much more loathsome acts. People's consciences are fluid, and in making moral judgments about the proper limits of satisfying their desires, individuals may well take cues from the decisions of the criminal justice system.

Just this kind of moralizing effect may have accounted for the deterrent effect of abortion laws prior to their repeal by legislation or their nullification by the courts. A study of abortion in Hawaii by Professor Franklin Zimring of the University of Chicago Law School suggests that the ease of obtaining an illegal abortion and the minimal level of law enforcement before legalization occurred in 1970 made it unlikely that pregnant women really feared arrest or prosecution if they obtained an abortion. However, many women have mixed feelings about the morality of terminating pregnancies, and the laws prohibiting abortion apparently reinforced such women's moral compunctions and feelings of guilt. The criminal law, in short, may have had more impact by gnawing at women's consciences than by creating a realistic risk of punishment.[7]

Another way in which legal threats contribute to crime prevention has been called "habituation": Threats get people in the habit of complying with the law. Individuals may initially shrink from violating rules because they are fearful of the consequences, but after a prolonged period of self-restraint they may simply become accustomed to acting lawfully. Children's learning again provides the most vivid example: The small child who resists the urge to run in the street for fear of being spanked gradually incorporates the notion of staying on the sidewalk into his or her normal mode of behaving. Likewise, obeying traffic laws may originally stem from fear of being caught, but after a while this responsiveness to threat is converted into good driving habits. Deterrence receives a big boost as a crime-prevention strategy to the extent that compliance with the law becomes "second nature"—an accustomed way of behaving.

Finally, it has been suggested that the regular use of punishment engenders a greater respect for law and the legal system. When laws are ignored or only occasionally enforced, the legitimacy of the legal system can be undermined and a justification for anarchy is provided. The erstwhile political radical Abbie Hoffman appealed to such cynicism when he wrote *Steal This Book*—a handbook of schemes and gimmicks for "ripping off" various capitalist establishments (stores, restaurants, etc.). Rubin was able to cite the widespread lawlessness by the rich and the powerful that was blithely tolerated by the criminal justice system as a license for the less privileged to show similar contempt for the law in their quest for material gain.

Presumably, more consistency in the use of punishment limits the effectiveness of such appeals and provides support for obedience to law as a compelling ethical norm, regardless of the merits of the particular law in question and the limitations it places on the pursuit of self-interest. The integrity of the legal system, it is said, acts as a model for the citizenry to emulate. Not only does faithful enforcement of the law make legal threats more credible, but it may also make them less necessary by strengthening people's moral obligation to follow the law. Paradoxically, the more deterrence works, the less it may need to work.

It should be emphasized that although *external* controls on behavior posed by government threats can be a powerful means of preventing crime, voluntary compliance prompted by the *internal* self-restraints of most people is responsible for much obedience to the law. This was well illustrated by the apparent effectiveness of a New York City "canine litter" ordinance, which requires dog owners who walked their pets on streets or sidewalks to clean up after them or face a $100 fine. Although very few summonses have been issued by police, who can hardly afford to spend much of their time enforcing this rather minor law, considerable compliance has been noted.[8] Many people probably recognized how filthy the city had become as a result of dog droppings, and their instincts to be good citizens inspired them to respond positively to the new law.

On a more profound level, personal security is probably far more dependent on the respect that many people have for one another's rights and property than on deterrence. We focus on threat and coercion because our emphasis in this part of the book is on how government policy can prevent crime. But in light of the ease of committing so many kinds of crime and the clear-cut need of so many people for things they are unable to obtain lawfully, the extent of compliance with the law is rather remarkable and must be attributed in good measure to the integrity of large segments of the population. Political scientist Andrew Hacker has made this point well: "My own considered—and by no means capricious—view is that we ought to count ourselves fortunate that so small a part of our population has taken to thievery. That so many Americans remain honest, while being treated so shabbily, has never ceased to amaze me."[9]

The Requisites of Deterrence

If the theory of deterrence is so persuasive, it might be asked, why has the crime problem been so hard to solve? If people can be so readily manipulated by incentives and threats, why are some laws routinely violated? If politicians across the nation of virtually all ideological orientations have embraced deterrence as a primary crime prevention strategy, why has the criminal justice system failed to produce the intended results?

The answer is that deterrence is easier said than done; translating theory into practice is no simple feat. Four (and possibly five) conditions must be satisfied for legal coercion to work: (1) there must be adequate communication of threats to the targeted group—the criminals; (2) there must be a relatively high degree of certainty that crime will in fact result in punishment; (3) punishment must be of sufficient severity to make it frightening; (4) the criminal population must have a rational aversion to legal threats that makes them responsive to deterrence attempts; and (most debatably) (5) there must be swift administration of punishments (sometimes called "celerity"). Due to the infinite complexities of crime and the criminal justice system, bringing all these elements together can be an almost insuperable task.

COMMUNICATION OF THREATS

Deterrence is, fundamentally, a state of mind. People refrain from crimes because they *think* there is a good chance of getting caught and they *think* that severe punishments will follow. While the objective reality about such dangers no doubt affects perceptions, neither efficient nor harsh law enforcement will deter those contemplating crimes if they are unaware of penal sanctions or ignorant about actual risks. Threats must be communicated, formally or informally, to be effective.

Public knowledge about the details of the penal code is quite limited. The California legislature some years ago commissioned a public-opinion survey in which people were asked to state the maximum sentence for various crimes. Between 21 and 47 percent of the respondents were unable to offer any guesses (depending on the crime in question), and among those who did answer, incorrect responses ranged from 61 to 92 percent.[10]

Not only do people have gross misconceptions about the penalties for various crimes but often they are confused about what is legal and what is illegal. This was nicely demonstrated in a study of illegal check writing in Nebraska, a state in which legal penalties are more severe than anywhere else in the country but where the rate of bad-check passing is as high as most other states.[11] A major reason for the high rate is that most people did not think it a crime to write a check with insufficient funds in one's account to cover the check. It was generally thought that "bounced" checks were merely embarrassing incidents to be settled one way or another through discussions between the check writer and the payee—somewhat akin to disputes between car dealers and purchasers about warranty coverage. Because only a few citizens had the vaguest inkling that they could be sent to jail for writing "rubber" checks, the harsh penalties on the law books were irrelevant to their behavior.

To confound matters more, people may not have accurate knowledge about the credibility of legal threats—the chances of being apprehended and convicted.[12] Because of certain statistical problems even crime analysts have trouble determining the odds of getting caught; it would therefore be folly to assume that the average person has such knowledge. What is worse (for deterrence enthusiasts), there are some indications that those *most* inclined to break the law underestimate their personal chances of arrest.[13] Such overoptimism may cause them to miscalculate what the cost to them will be in relation to the benefits received; they may attempt crimes even when it is more risky than they think to do so. And since the *actual* chances of success are fairly good for many crimes (as the next section will show), this irrationality caused by imperfect information may nonetheless lead to more successes than failures.

This misinformation about the possibility of arrest would seem to wreak havoc on all attempts at deterrence, but in fact a high degree of *public* knowledge about potential sanctions may not be essential. First of all, those who have committed crimes or are planning to do so generally have far better knowledge of criminal law than the public at large. The California study mentioned above

TABLE 9-2
Public Knowledge and Prisoner Knowledge of Penal Sanctions

	Percentage Correctly Stating Minimum and Maximum Penalties for Various Crimes	
	Public	Prisoners
First-degree robbery	8	85
Assault	35	59
Rape with injury	16	43
Forgery	17	50

SOURCE: Reprinted from *Deterrence: The Legal Threat in Crime Control* by Franklin Zimring and Gordon Hawkins (Chicago: University of Chicago Press, 1973), p. 145, by permission of The University of Chicago Press.

(demonstrating the abysmally low levels of public knowledge of the penal code) showed that prison inmates who were also interviewed were very familiar with the punishments for the various crimes in which they were involved.[14] Table 9-2, which contrasts public knowledge and prisoner knowledge, shows how much more sophisticated convicted lawbreakers are than others in the population. What this implies is that the criminally inclined have a greater self-interest in obtaining precise facts in order to assess rationally the risk of crime. Moreover, to the extent that criminals do associate more with like-minded individuals, they may have better access to information about the law than the average person for whom the law is a remote abstraction.

Second, special communications can be directed at the class of potential offenders above to publicize, emphasize, and dramatize the consequences of violations. One of the more vivid examples of such publicity was the practice of the Chinese government in the early 1900s of exhibiting the skulls of drivers executed for speeding next to the speed limit signs.[15]

A less gruesome but equally stark type of notice is the "Wanted" poster that appears in many banks. Ostensibly it is a solicitation for information about criminals at large, but its prime impact is to show the number of recent robbers apprehended. In fact, "no longer wanted" labels are continuously stuck on the faces of those shown at the top half to remind those who might approach tellers with guns in their pockets that successful bank heists are rare.

A rather ingenious experiment designed to prove whether better information about penalties for income-tax evasion reduces such crime was conducted by two sociologists.[16] In cooperation with the Internal Revenue Service, they randomly selected as subjects a group of high-income taxpayers, who have the greatest opportunity to cheat because they normally itemize many deductions and often have sources of income other than salaries. These taxpayers were visited by interviewers (purportedly doing a routine survey). One group was reminded of the possible prison sentences for tax evasion; another was subjected to appeals to conscience centering on the citizen's duty to pay what is owed; a third group (the control group) received no message that might prompt them to pay more. Tax returns of the various groups were later analyzed (along with another control group not visited at all), showing that those exposed to sanction threats and those sermonized about civic obligations paid considerably more taxes than they had in the previous years, while the "control" groups paid less. Although all taxpayers receive a fine-print notice about legal penalties for perjury on their tax return just above the line on which they sign their names, personal face-to-face communication of this fact is far more persuasive in securing compliance with the law. What this suggests is that persons who might be contemplating crime may well be receptive and responsive to campaigns attempting to educate them about legal sanctions.

In the income-tax experiment, the "threat" made by the interviewers was highly veiled—discretely worded questions about the law hidden in the context of a lengthy inquiry dealing with many issues. It is possible to use modern media techniques to communicate threats much more boldly. The Florida Sheriffs' As-

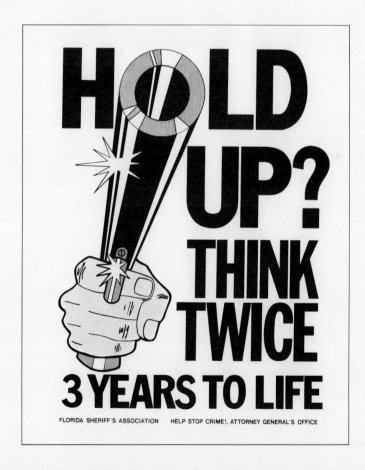

sociation has distributed a slick, eye-catching poster to merchants about the repercussions of conviction for robbery. This conversion of a provision of the penal code into an unmistakably clear threat may overcome part of the gap in public knowledge of criminal sanctions.

Finally, some experts have suggested that detailed personal information about punishments is not required for the sake of deterrence.[17] Just as buyers and sellers make many rational marketplace decisions without exact knowledge about relevant price structures, a general awareness about penalties may be sufficient as a basis for making sensible calculations about the risk of crime. People *do* know that murderers can receive long prison terms, that burglary is a serious offense with the possibility of prison, that prostitutes spend a few days in jail at the most, and that traffic violators are usually fined. These rough approximations may well be adequate for sanctions to make their mark.

Deterrence often fails when there is a low probability of punishment

CERTAINTY OF SANCTIONS

If there were 100 percent certainty that all criminals would be caught, convicted, and imprisoned, crime would no doubt plummet dramatically; few welcome punishment masochistically. But, in fact, certainty is a probabilistic notion, and foolproof apprehension and punishment systems are unobtainable. For people contemplating crimes, the chances of getting caught are often uppermost in their minds. This is especially the case regarding those who are seeking material gain, such as muggers, embezzlers, and price fixers, who spend endless time plotting how to get away with their crimes. Deterrence depends on closing the law enforcement net tightly enough around the criminal population so that the risk does not justify the probable payoff.

The importance of certainty in making deterrence effective is suggested by several studies that show that people's perception of risk relates to their self-reported criminality.[18] For example, 321 undergraduates were asked if they had ever smoked marijuana or engaged in petty theft. As Table 9-3 suggests, those who felt the chances of apprehension great were much less likely to commit crimes than those who thought they could get away with it. This is especially

TABLE 9-3

The Effect of Fear of Arrest on Admitted Criminality of Undergraduates

Perceived Likelihood of Arrest	Admitted Marijuana Use by Perceived Likelihood of Arrest For Marijuana Possession[1]			
	Percent Having Used Marijuana	Percent Never Using Marijuana	Total	(N)
Likely	0.0	100.0	100.0	(28)
50/50	10.7	89.3	100.0	(28)
Unlikely	38.9	61.1	100.0	(265)

Perceived Likelihood of Arrest	Admitted Theft by Perceived Likelihood of Arrest For Petty Larceny[1]			
	Percent Having Stolen	Percent Never Stealing	Total	(N)
Likely	40.6	59.4	100.0	(32)
50/50	48.5	51.5	100.0	(68)
Unlikely	62.4	37.6	100.0	(221)

[1] Data for these items were obtained from responses to the questions, "If someone like yourself used marijuana occasionally in Tallahassee, how likely are the police to catch him (her)?" "If someone like yourself stole something worth less than $100 in Tallahassee, how likely are the police to catch him (her)?"

SOURCE: Gordon Waldo and Theodore Chiricos, "Perceived Penal Sanctions and Self-Reported Criminality: A Neglected Approach to Deterrence Research," *Social Problems* 19 (Spring 1972), 535. Reprinted by permission of the Society for the Study of Social Problems, which publishes *Social Problems*, and of the authors.

true with regard to the drug offense, where moral scruples play a lesser role in securing compliance with the law and fear of sanctions is more decisive.

The success of crackdowns on skyjackers attests to the significance of certainty of apprehension.[19] Two significant steps were taken to make apprehension more certain, and both were effective in curbing the rash of skyjacking attempts. The first important step was Cuban President Fidel Castro's return of six skyjackers to the United States in 1969 to face air piracy charges, indicating that Cuba would no longer grant asylum to these criminals. Whereas 19 attempts had been made in the six months prior to this action, only 10 occurred in the six months following.

Even more effective was President Nixon's order in January 1973 requiring that domestic airports screen all passengers for weapons and inspect all baggage taken aboard. Attempts went down sharply—from 18 in the preceding six months to 4 in the six months after the search program was implemented. A decrease in international political tension may have reduced the incentive of terrorists to take over planes, but the heightened chances of apprehension and punishment for skyjacking attempts no doubt deterred many who were contemplating such crimes.

Draft evasion is another crime that was apparently curtailed by consistent use of imprisonment against offenders. Researchers have shown that during 1970 and 1971, when the Vietnam war was still very much in progress, states in which a higher proportion of evaders were found guilty of Selective Service Act violations experienced much less resistance to the draft.[20] This was a particularly good test of the certainty hypothesis because almost all evaders who failed to report when called were detected, but how they were treated in the 94 federal district courts across the country varied greatly. Where judges were unsympathetic to defenses such as conscientious objection or psychological unfitness for service, the frequency of evasion was much lower than in areas where judges often acquitted defendants for one reason or another. Thus, in the face of moral reservations about the legitimacy of the war and fear of injury or death, many men succumbed to the military in places where severe punishment for doing otherwise seemed inevitable. The certainty of punishment suppressed the intense desire of many to violate the law.

Voluminous research, using many statistical methods, has indeed shown that in parts of the country with higher probabilities of arrest, conviction, and imprisonment, lower crime rates generally prevail.[21] However, there are some indications that certainty must reach a particular level before differences in deterrent effects show up; one study showed a 50 percent arrest rate to be the "tipping point."[22] In other words, if the chance of apprehension is slim, minor differences in risk are insignificant. If the chances are 2 in 100 of getting caught instead of 1 in 100, the risk is doubled but the gamble is good in either case.

Indeed, it is abundantly clear that a major reason why deterrence often fails is the ease of committing many crimes. The old adage, "crime does not pay," is nonsense, at least in regard to certain kinds of offenses. Moreover, certain inherent limitations on the capabilities of the criminal justice system coupled with the vulnerability of an urbanized society to crime make it very difficult to appreciably raise the probability of punishment. Police, prosecutors, courts, and prisons are overwhelmed—giving criminals a tremendous advantage.

INVULNERABILITY TO ARREST The limited ability of police to capture criminals is indicated by Table 9-4, which estimates the proportion of unsolved crimes. Apprehension ratios are determined by comparing arrests by police with a rough approximation of total crime based on police reports and victimization surveys (which uncover much unreported crime).[23] Clearly, for most crimes success is far more likely than failure, and for crimes such as burglary the chances of being caught are quite remote.

Moreover, for certain undetected crimes like shoplifting, the probability of being arrested is truly minuscule. This was demonstrated by an experiment conducted in the largest supermarket in Freiburg, Germany, where, during a three-hour period, researchers working in cooperation with top store executives successfully accomplished 40 separate thefts. Either a pound of coffee or a pound of meat was placed in a private bag rather than in the shopping cart, and *not once* was the "thief" caught.[24] If these amateur thieves were able to do so well, one can well imagine the manifold opportunities for professionals skilled in the art of stealing.

Crimes that do not have direct victims and that are routinely committed by a large part of the society are also easy to execute successfully. For example, the chances of apprehension for relatively minor traffic violations are infinitesimally small. One study showed that the probability of receiving a speeding citation for going ten miles per hour over the limit for a two-mile stretch in Michigan was 1 in 7,600![25] Likewise, the odds of being arrested for using illicit drugs, gambling, or engaging in illegal sexual acts are truly minute. Under such circumstances people need not fear punishment and may commit crimes with impunity.

The main reason why arrests are so infrequent is that the police generally

TABLE 9-4
Nationwide Apprehension Ratios

Crime	Arrests	Crimes Reported to Police	Crimes Estimated from Surveys	Estimated Percentage of Crimes Solved
Forcible rape	25,720	51,000	153,000	17
Aggravated assault	208,100	416,270	1,313,180	16
Robbery	127,530	382,680	1,214,884	10
Vehicle theft	155,800	923,600	1,330,470	12
Burglary	434,000	2,540,000	7,818,026	06

SOURCE: Adapted from Wesley Skogan and George Antunes, "Information, Apprehension, and Deterrence: The Missing Theoretical Link" (Paper presented at the Midwest Political Science Association meeting, 1978). Reprinted by permission of the authors.

receive very little information about crimes until some time after they have occurred. Police officers are very unlikely to happen upon crimes in progress: Only
1 percent of all arrests result from the police witnessing criminal acts.[26] When
the police are dispatched to the scene of a crime as a result of a victim's call, the
criminal has normally departed and little can be done but report the crime.

Research based on victimization surveys of the public (to be discussed in
Chapter 13) shows that victims can normally contribute very little to the solving
of crimes. In crimes involving interpersonal violence like rape and assault, where
there is often a prior acquaintanceship between criminal and victim, only 17 percent of the latter can make a positive identification of the assailant. Robbery victims have a chance to observe directly those accosting them, but since the
average robbery takes between 60 and 90 seconds, they get only a fleeting,
unreliable glimpse of attackers and can make identification in only 7 percent of
all cases. If victims are not present when crimes occur, even less is known about
the predators: They can be identified in only 1 percent of all thefts, .2 percent of
all burglaries, and .5 percent of all vehicle thefts.[27] When information is so
scant, the police are virtually helpless in solving the crime.

Consequently, the law enforcement system is simply unable to make legal
threats very credible. This is obvious with regard to laws prohibiting littering,
jaywalking, or spitting in subway stations, but it is equally true with regard to
many of the more serious crimes. Not only are the odds of success good, but professional criminals are often able to improve the odds due to their expertise,
cunning, or sheer audacity. Even if police act with the utmost of efficiency,
dedication, and aggressiveness, they are incapable of arresting a very high proportion of criminals.

IRREGULAR IMPOSITION OF PENAL SANCTIONS Because of courtroom
congestion, due-process guarantees, plea bargaining, the failure of witnesses to
appear in court, and the extensive granting of probation, only a small percentage
of felons spend time in prison for their crimes. According to one estimate the nationwide ratio of arrests to conviction is 8 to 1, and at a maximum only 1.5 percent of felons receive prison sentences.[28] Thus, even when police do solve a
large number of crimes, their strict enforcement is undermined by the lenient
actions of others in the criminal justice system. While certain legitimate goals
may well be served by freeing many of those apprehended (e.g., attention to
due process, attempts at rehabilitation), such policies may well decrease the
criminal's concern for being severely punished if caught.

The combination of low apprehension rates and postarrest opportunities for
avoiding punishment is a criminal's paradise. This is the case concerning the
serious crime of arson, which is estimated to kill 1,000 people annually and cause
over $1 billion in property loss—more loss than any other crime.[29] Those setting
fires are usually far away from the scene when the smoke or flames are first reported, so they are infrequently implicated in the crime. Moreover, because the
materials used to start the blaze are often destroyed by the crime itself (e.g., the
gasoline that is spread around), police find it very difficult to make arson charges

stand up in court. Therefore, for every 400 cases of arson, there are 12 arrests, 3 convictions, and 1 person who goes to prison.[30] Since the returns from arson are quite lucrative (e.g., business people collecting large insurance payments, welfare tenants securing better quarters), this minimal risk is often well worth taking. The *possible* punishment under these conditions is virtually meaningless since the probability of *any* punishment is almost nil.

A study of prosecutions in sex assault cases shows that an inability to convict may also handicap efforts to deter rape. Only 22 percent of rape arrests made in the District of Columbia in 1973 resulted in conviction. Since the estimate is that no more than one in five rapes is solved, it follows that only about 4 or 5 percent (20 percent of 22 percent) of rapists are punished for their crimes. Under these conditions legal threats lack credibility.[31]

PERCEPTIONS OF LEGAL IMMUNITY Calculating criminals are realists about the law. They gauge risks according to how the criminal justice system really operates, not how it is supposed to work. Consequently, the many points in the law enforcement process where prosecution can be terminated may be perceived as loopholes providing immunity against severe punishment. Also, the persistent possibility of leniency due to the common practice of individualizing punishments may be seen as an escape hatch that can save a criminal from a harsh fate.[32]

The experience of a highly successful professional safecracker reported by Sociologist William Chambliss illustrates this point. The safecracker had been arrested for this crime over 300 times during a crime career that spanned 45 years, but he had received only three rather brief prison sentences as a result. Not only

---

BEATING THE SYSTEM: HOW TO AVOID PUNISHMENT

Steal from large numbers of people as indirectly as possible.

. . . You risk more jail time if you scare a little old lady into giving you $10 than if you steal $10 from 10,000 little old ladies through consumer fraud. . . .

Commit a crime the judge can relate to.

Judges are people, too. Commit a crime the judge can understand, either because he has reflected that there were certain temptations to which he (but for the grace of God) might have succumbed, or because he, when a practicing lawyer, had likable clients who committed similar crimes. . . .

Look prosperous and have many influential friends who can vouch for your character.

This may even get you acquitted, but if you're convicted it will likely get you a lower sentence. The more like the judge and the prosecutor you and your friends appear, the more they will personally identify with you and the harder it will be for them to send you away. . . .

Have someone to turn in.

It is statistically provable that if you give the prosecutor a "bigger" fish you will get a lesser sentence or possibly not be prosecuted at all. Unfortunately, not everyone knows bigger fish. If you don't, try to hang around with a better class of criminals. . . .

Stephen Gillers, "How to Make Crime Pay," *New York Times*, February 16, 1978, p. A3. © 1978 by The New York Times Company. Reprinted by permission.

had he been able to win case after case on legal technicalities but he was able to "fix" some of the charges against him by bribing officials. In a sense, the criminal justice system was proscribing illegal behavior in one breath but countenancing it in the next.[33]

General information about the risks of serious punishment most probably circulates in the criminal world.[34] In high-crime areas especially, considerable first-hand knowledge about the criminal justice system is likely to exist, and consequently many understand that there are manifold opportunities for getting "off the hook." The realities about detection, arrest, conviction, and sentencing may lead some criminals to think they are nearly invincible.

While the degree of risk is sometimes overestimated, in the long run deterrence requires a relatively high probability that sanctions will be imposed. Potential criminals are not ordinarily fooled by empty threats; "bluffing" by the criminal justice system will not work.

SEVERITY OF SANCTIONS

For deterrence to work, punishment must be sufficiently painful to scare those thinking about crime. Even with efficient law enforcement, small fines will not deter traffic violators and short jail terms will not not deter hired killers; the gains from these crimes offset the possible losses. What is troublesome, however, is determining *how* severe punishments must be to instill adequate fear in those who might consider various crimes. Inflicting punishment is a costly business that takes its toll on both government resources and those subjected to it, so ascertaining the threshold necessary to deter particular kinds of offenders is very important.

The sanctions available to the criminal justice system are differentially onerous. It is generally acknowledged that the order of severity, from most harsh to most lenient, is capital punishment, imprisonment, probation, suspended sentences, and fines. While some contend that capital punishment is actually less severe than life imprisonment because there is no pain after death, the human quest for survival under the worst possible conditions suggests that death is the worst punishment our society is willing to inflict. Certainly, the desire of most convicts on "death row" to get their sentences commuted to life in prison implies that they prefer life, with its hope of a better future, to the certain bleakness of death.

Prison is for most individuals a debilitating, oppressive, and often brutal experience that is highly feared. There may be some social outcasts whose daily existence is so miserable that prison life represents an improvement in living conditions, but for most people the deprivations of freedom, privacy, and autonomy are so grim that they react with horror to the thought of spending even a short time in prison. Even minimum security prisons that offer some amenities of life and greater freedom of choice are no substitute for life outside.

Probation, although allowing the criminal freedom, imposes constraints on behavior, supervision of daily activities, and the continuing potential for revocation and consequent imprisonment. Fines can create financial hardships, but they are generally reserved for the affluent, who can often afford them. Indeed, they are perceived by some "upper-world" criminals as simply a business expense that is far less costly than complying with business regulations. Thus, the average fine received by landlords for housing code violations in Chicago from 1950 to 1962 was $32; in New York the average fine per case was $16.86 and $.50 per violation.[35] This is a pittance compared to the cost of repairing the buildings.

Suspended sentences allow convicts to go free; but, unlike probation, they set no limits on behavior. This may therefore seem like a negligible punishment, but in fact it does result in certain costs. Convictions for felonies in most states result in the loss of some privileges, such as the right to vote, the right to hold public office, and the right to engage in certain occupations. In some states convicts are deprived of the right to engage in activities that require licenses, such as driving.

In addition to these formal sanctions, there are informal punishments that may deter. Arrest itself, no matter what the final disposition, is a humiliating experience except for the most hard-bitten recidivists. Moreover, its stigmatizing effect not only makes it more difficult to obtain employment[36] but can expose one to all kinds of social ostracism. And if a person is arraigned and prosecuted, he or she suffers "procedural punishment"—the financial and emotional strain of mounting a defense. The threat of this trying ordeal is no doubt sufficient to inhibit some crime without the necessity of anything else.

While a great deal of consensus exists in ranking the severity of various punishments, it is not at all clear what the proportional severity of alternative penalties is (i.e., just how much more intimidating a harsh penalty is than a more lenient one). When legislatures double the length of sentence for a crime from five to ten years, the punishment is presumed to be twice as onerous. But beyond a certain level of severity additional increments of punishment may easily be fathomed by those contemplating crime. However, smaller differences in punishment at the *low* end of the scale (say, between a fine and a month in jail) may have a greater impact than larger differences at the high end (e.g., a 20-year sentence versus a 30-year sentence). As penalties are increased to awesome levels, diminishing returns may set in.

Consequently, although research has clearly linked higher certainty of punishment with lower crime rates, no such direct relationship has been uncovered between severity of punishment and crime, with the possible exception of homicide.[37] It may be that those plotting felonies are much more concerned with the chances of being caught than the subsequent ramifications if they are caught. If the odds of getting away with the crime are great, the penalties may seem like far-fetched possibilities.

One reason why murder may be a special case is that the high rates of apprehension make penalties worth contemplating, and the longer prison sentences applied in some areas give some murderers a more intense foreboding of what could happen to them. This idea squares with other research that shows that the *combined* effects of certainty and severity of punishment do yield less crime, suggesting that severity deters *only* when certainty levels are high enough to make severity a salient concern.[38] Experience with various marijuana laws substantiates this. Although marked differences are discernible in permissible punishments from state to state, no evidence indicates less use of the drug in the "tough" states as opposed to the lenient ones. Where chances of apprehension are negligible, raising penalties seems to make little impression.

In fact, making sentences more severe might sometimes foment additional crime instead of stopping it, for several reasons. First, if prescribed penalties are excessively high, juries may be loath to convict at all and may lean over backward to find exculpating evidence. In eighteenth- and nineteenth-century England, for example, over 200 crimes carried the death penalty (including pickpocketing), but juries failed to convict—in which case the criminal received no punishment whatsoever. One study comparing severity of sanctions with certainty of sanctions in different states actually found a modest *inverse* correlation: As severity went up, certainty went down.[39]

Second, if a whole range of crimes carries very severe penalties, then criminals who might otherwise have committed a lesser crime may see nothing additional to lose by attempting a more serious one. For example, if punishment for burglary is upgraded and made equivalent to robbery, a criminal has every incentive to use physical force against a resident in trying to obtain the latter's property. Not only can such coercion turn up money or goods that a burglar roaming around a house might not find but the use of a weapon can fend off captors. Likewise, if rape is made a capital crime along with murder, self-interest might dictate that the rapist kill his victim afterward so that she is unable to testify against him. For this reason many deterrence theorists have advocated a "stepladder" approach to punishment schedules that makes the level of severity dependent on the seriousness of the crime; this would be used instead of a "fortress" strategy, which seeks to stop all major crimes with very severe penalties.[40]

Third, some evidence has been found that stiffer penalties cause more recidivism (i.e., they undermine specific deterrence).[41] For example, a study in Israel showed that 53 percent of drivers who were simply warned after their first traffic offense committed no further offenses, while 79 percent of those who lost their licenses for a period of time returned to the roads and had subsequent infractions.[42] Perhaps more telling is a mammoth F.B.I. study that traced the criminal career of 17,000 persons released from prison in 1963 and found that those who served long terms were rearrested more frequently than those who served shorter terms.[43] Although these studies are inconclusive because those who received the stiffer sentences may have been so treated because they appeared to be worse offenders, it is certainly conceivable that long prison terms breed antisocial attitudes and behavior. Whether the postrelease criminality caused by such embitterment and hostility is offset by the prevention of crime during prison (i.e., incapacitation) is an empirical question that has not been resolved.

Thus, it is relatively easy to increase severity by simply amending penal laws and building more prisons, but this tactic may simply not deter more crime. The United States uses longer prison sentences than most other countries. Going further in that direction is pointless according to most theory and research on deterrence.

CRIMINAL RESPONSIVENESS TO DETERRENCE

Deterrence is predicated on the assumption that offenders choose to commit crimes by rationally assessing the opportunities for competing legal and illegal activities. If the payoffs for crime are small but the risks great, crime will be avoided. The keystone of this strategy, then, is rational individuals carefully nurturing their own self-interest.

However, under several conditions such assumptions are unwarranted. First, many crimes are committed during fits of passion or on the basis of impulse; they are not premeditated. This is particularly true of violent crimes like willful homicides and aggravated assaults, which often result from personal quarrels. Indeed, one-fourth of all murders committed during 1972 were slayings of family members, and only 27 percent were felony murders, in which the killing was incidental to the execution of other crimes.[44] Many criminals who are motivated by intense emotion are oblivious to the legal consequences of their acts.

A few concrete examples can show how irrelevant deterrence is in these situations. During an argument over who was responsible for a minor traffic accident in New York, one motorist was fatally stabbed six times by the other driver.[45] In Fremont, California, a 16-year-old boy used his semiautomatic rifle to kill his sister and her two girlfriends in a sibling dispute over ownership of a Yo-Yo.[46] In the aftermath of a marital feud, Meadowlark Lemon, the "clown" of the Harlem Globetrotters basketball team, was stabbed by his wife on a busy New York City intersection *at the very moment* he was complaining to two police officers about her conduct.[47] That she would obviously be arrested on the spot was apparently the last thing on her mind. In all these cases the anger that welled up in the criminal precluded any contemplation of legal ramifications.

Lesser crimes, too, can be irrationally motivated. Thus while a study of traffic offenders showed that drivers generally were more likely to obey the law when they perceived the risk of getting caught to be greater, young drivers who were the most common violators broke the law without regard for the threat of sanctions. The urge to speed—whether to show off to peers, to rebel against authority, or just to get "cheap thrills"—was apparently so powerful that concern about punishment never even arose.[48] Surely many of the "follies" of youth, from stealing cars to tormenting old people, are also spur-of-the-moment decisions, totally lacking in foresight about consequences.

Another bar to deterrence can arise when the felt need of the criminal is so great that careful weighing of risks is impeded. Clearly, unemployed school dropouts and drug addicts desperate for money will often engage in "street" crimes, which sometimes defy success, because they are so eager to alleviate their destitution. The desire for a couple of hundred dollars may be so keen that bizarre crimes are attempted and almost insane chances taken. Deterrence is stymied when the attraction to the fruits of crime is so great that it leads people into foolhardy courses of action, which nevertheless sometimes succeed.

Persons who are more affluent are more likely to commit crimes because of greed than because of need. Because such individuals have much more to lose (status, property, good jobs, etc.) and their material concerns are less urgent, they are much more likely to be attentive to risks than those who are living more marginally. Therefore, white-collar criminals are much more feasible targets of crime-prevention strategies that stress deterrence because they will often insist on a far more favorable set of odds before gambling on some criminal endeavor.

Sometimes the pressures from peer groups are so strong that rational calculation of risks is precluded. Members of youth gangs can be subjected to intense pressure to commit crimes in order to demonstrate their courage and machismo. Under these circumstances, the fear of being labelled a "chicken" is far greater than the fear of legal repercussions because approval from friends is more important than worrying about punishment. Being punished can actually become a status symbol that wins accolades—resulting in just the opposite of the intended effect.[49]

Antinuclear demonstrators being arrested in Seabrook, New Hampshire: the failure of deterrence

Besides those acting out of emotion or desperation, a third kind of criminal who may be unaffected by sanctions is the fanatic. Those who are committing crimes for political or moral causes may feel so passionate and righteous about their activities that they would gladly suffer jail rather than yield to authorities. The words sung by many in the civil rights movement of the 1960s in defiance of southern law enforcement officials characterizes this state of mind: "I don't care about your jail because I want my freedom. . . . I want my freedom NOW!"

More recently, the thousands who fought nuclear power installations that were thought to be dangerous in Seabrook, New Hampshire, willfully trespassed on private property where the plant was to be located in full knowledge of the fact that the conservative governor of the state planned to arrest them all. The sanctimonious feeling that engulfs such protestors may well make them immune to any hardships that they are forced to endure. Some criminals who are severely punished by the government become martyrs, and the subsequent adulation that they receive from their followers enables them to bear the pain of punishment.

SWIFT PUNISHMENT

An old cliché says that justice must be swift to be effective. This sounds plausible, and it certainly agrees with psychological research on conditioning that shows that unwanted responses are best extinguished when the punishment immediately follows the behavior to be eliminated. However, since delay in criminal justice represents sustained punishment and the anxiety caused by prolonged uncertainty may be as disturbing as receiving a clear-cut sanction right away, the long ordeal that defendants go through on the way to conviction and sentencing may be functional for deterrence (whatever the negative implications for due process). In the large number of instances when defendants are incarcerated prior to trial, delay may be most effective because the miserable conditions of most local jails must be endured.

In only one important regard do delays undercut deterrence. Possibilities of proving guilt decrease as facts about a case recede into the distant past. Prosecution witnesses sometimes disappear or suffer memory lapses, and jurors may be less inclined to accept their version of what transpired. This may lead to more acquittals than usual or very lenient plea bargains, which make sanctions less certain or insufficiently severe.

Practical Obstacles to Deterrence Policies

The preceding section has indicated that achieving deterrence is ordinarily an uphill battle. The normal operation of the criminal justice system does not make legal threats very credible. Beyond that, however, policies aimed at intimidating criminals by making punishment more certain or more severe are often undermined by political indecisiveness, bureaucratic resistance, and the adaptability of the criminal population. These factors, to which we now turn our attention, can sabotage the adoption, implementation, or effectiveness of deterrence tactics.

POLITICAL UNFEASIBILITY

The political process often squelches or dilutes promising deterrence plans. The self-interest of politicians, interest groups, and individual citizens can frustrate the adoption of sensible policies that might thwart crime.

Thus, politicians sensitive to the power of the gun lobby may oppose legislation cracking down on the possession or use of guns. Ironically, Governor George Wallace of Alabama, who was permanently paralyzed from the waist down by the bullets of an attempted assassin, continued to oppose tough gun laws because so much of his political support came from groups that favored the use of firearms. Stiff gun laws have been shown to decrease murder and serious assaults by discouraging people from taking them outside their homes and businesses, but in many states provoking organizations in favor of guns is political suicide. Many voting analysts contended that Senator Joseph Tydings of Maryland, a popular politician from a prominent Maryland family, was defeated in 1970 for reelection largely because of the mail campaign conducted by gun groups offended by his support of a federal gun registration law. Such ominous results may deter legislators from advocating similar measures—even though they seem to work.

Liberals, too, can block deterrence. In England, Parliament had debated whether to allow spot checks on drivers to test for drunkenness, but legislators concerned about due process and the right to privacy stopped such a measure.[50] Many so-called bleeding-heart liberals in this country have opposed prison sentences for juveniles on the grounds that they deserve almost unlimited opportunities for redemption—notwithstanding the fact that juveniles account for an increasingly large number of violent crimes and that some of them commit crimes in anticipation of juvenile court leniency. Also, groups such as the American Civil Liberties Union and the National Association for the Advancement of Colored People have put considerable pressure on policy makers to steer clear of crime-prevention plans that run contrary to due process or justice.

The expense of deterrence programs may also lead to political opposition. Many financially strapped school districts, for example, have been forced to abandon the use of security police in schools troubled by student violence because taxpayers refuse to approve budgets to pay for them. Deterrence does not come cheaply; many intriguing plans are scuttled because politicians fear the retaliation of voters if additional taxes must be levied to finance them or if more visible services, like garbage pickup, have to be curtailed in order to obtain the additional funds.

Political resistance to deterrence schemes sometimes emanates from bureaucrats disturbed about new institutions usurping their responsibilities. Thus, some police departments have been quite cool to the idea of civilian patrol operations and have rebuffed attempts to establish direct radio linkage between these units and police precincts. Such civilian efforts have the potential for increasing surveillance capabilities at no cost to the taxpayer, but many police officers feel that this task should be exclusively theirs. The organizational self-interest in safeguarding their role in the criminal justice system looms larger than their commitments to crime prevention.

IMPLEMENTATION DIFFICULTIES

Before President Dwight Eisenhower took office in 1953, his predecessor, Harry Truman contemplated the problems Eisenhower, a former general in the army, would have in office. Truman remarked: "He'll sit here [in the Oval Office] and say 'Do this! Do that!' *And nothing will happen.* Poor Ike—it won't be a bit like the army." [51]

As difficult as a president's job is in controlling the gigantic, sprawling federal bureaucracy, it is simple in comparison with trying to coordinate the chaotic, uncoordinated criminal justice system. Even if political stumbling blocks are overcome and sound deterrence policies are adopted, those policies are frequently undermined by the autonomy of individuals charged with carrying them out. Increasing either the certainty of conviction or the severity of punishment requires a consistency in bureaucratic decision making that is not always forthcoming. Sometimes this is the result of self-interest, and on other occasions it represents commitment to other goals or strategies. But, whatever the motive, the result is the same: A deterrence policy on the books is never really implemented.

Examples abound. Consider the various "crackdowns" on traffic offenders that have been periodically attempted throughout the country. Two days before Christmas in 1955, Governor Abraham Ribicoff of Connecticut announced a new policy to stem the record number of accident fatalities that had occurred that year on his state's highways. He ordered all judges to suspend the drivers' licenses of first-time offenders for 30 days and two-time offenders for 60 days; those convicted a third time were to receive indefinite suspensions. Judges who failed to comply were threatened with nonreappointment.

A dramatic decline in traffic deaths occurred in the six-month period that followed, but not long thereafter fatalities began to climb. A careful analysis of the fluctuations over a number of years demonstrated that the program was actually ineffectual and that the brief drop in deaths was a "regression effect"—a decline that would normally occur after a period of record highs. [52] The failure was accounted for by two factors: Some speeders who previously would have been given tickets by police were let off because of the harshness of sanctions, and the courts acquitted more of those accused of speeding. The harshness of the governor's edict was mitigated by the more compassionate treatment afforded by law enforcement officials.

The British had a similar experience in response to the Road Safety Act of 1967, which made it an offense to drive with more than a .08 percent blood-alcohol level (the equivalent of three drinks of hard liquor taken in quick succession), regardless of whether "drunkenness" could be proved. Police were permitted to give drivers on-the-spot breath tests with special equipment called "breathalysers" if a traffic offense was committed, an accident took place, or they suspected alcohol consumption. Those failing the test could be brought to police stations for more definitive blood or urine tests. A minimum punishment of either a £100 fine or a four-month imprisonment was mandated in addition to suspension of driving privileges for a year. Enormous publicity about the act was generated prior to the date it took effect.

For several years this combination of increased opportunities for detecting alcohol-impaired drivers and relatively harsh sanctions clearly reduced drunk driving and the casualties caused by it.[53] After a thorough analysis, researchers concluded that drinkers were curtailing their driving, especially during holidays and on weekends when most accidents occurred. The act saved lives and prevented injuries.

However, as in Connecticut, the success was short-lived, and by 1972 alcohol-caused casualties had returned to their levels prior to the act.[54] Apparently, the police began to underenforce the law because they resented having to administer complex and unpleasant tests rather than use their own personal discretion in judging whether drivers were drunk. In 1970, 70,000 breath tests were given in England (with a population of 58 million), in contrast to 48,000 such tests in Sweden (with one-sixth the population) and 93,000 in Los Angeles County (which has one-eighth the number of people). This lackadaisical enforcement—and lessened risk—became known to drivers, who resumed their illegal practices.

Many other examples could be cited of policy directives aimed at deterrence fizzling due to uncooperative or careless behavior among lower-echelon personnel. The making of sound arrests is a cornerstone of many deterrence policies, but the evidence is growing that many police are remiss in this aspect of their work. A study of the District of Columbia showed that fewer than 10 percent of all police made over half of the arrests that result in conviction and that 78 percent of the force yielded only 16 percent of such conviction-producing arrests.[55] Many police in Washington, D.C., and elsewhere are sloppy in the procedures they use and the evidence they secure, creating opportunities for criminals to escape punishment. To understand such slipshod work, we need only return to self-interest: Police are rewarded in most departments for the quantity of their arrests and not the quality. Contributing to deterrence by making arrests "stick" does not necessarily lead to promotions.

Criminal investigations, another crucial link in the deterrence process, are also sometimes stymied by the boondoggling mentality. Patrol officers sometimes make the most perfunctory of inquiries when responding to crimes that have already occurred because they have little chance of personally making an arrest for which credit can be received. Moreover, the jealousy and enmity of detectives felt by many patrol officers may discourage the latter from doing anything that will help their rivals do the follow-up investigations.[56]

One reason that so few arson arrests are made is that investigators often shirk their duty, failing to dig through the ashes, soot, and rubble left by a fire to discover clues. This neglect is understandable since such searches are arduous, sometimes dangerous, and always unpleasant. This point was pithily made in a study of the arson problem: "An investigator's wife may be able to adjust to his late night calls, but may find the inevitable filthy and foul-smelling clothes intolerable."[57] The pursuit of self-interest leads to many fires receiving only the most superficial investigations.

Implementing deterrence strategies requires coordination and esprit de corps within the criminal justice bureaucracy. Because just the opposite condition often prevails, the commands made at the top are often disregarded at the bottom. Consequently, what seem to be policies that failed are often policies that have never really been tried.

CRIMINAL ADAPTABILITY

Rational criminals are often able to outwit deterrence policies directed at them. The "Fuzzbuster"—a device to alert speeders on the highways to radar patrols—is a particularly clear example of an opportunity to circumvent law enforcement efforts. It also shows how the fancy equipment of police can be countered by the ingenuity and enterprise of a manufacturer.[58] Modern technology is a two-edged sword; it can work for criminals as well as against them.

While the use of sophisticated techniques to hamper deterrence efforts is rare, criminals can and do use common sense to figure out ways of protecting themselves. First of all, many learn to distinguish credible threats, which really increase risks, from spurious ones, which are illusory. Thus, professional shoplifters are not bothered by rotating television cameras because they know that images are blurred, the area viewed at any one time is quite limited (leaving many blind spots), and store personnel rarely look at monitors. Likewise, competent burglars become adept at differentiating signs on house doors warning them of burglar systems that are actually in place and operating from phony signs threatening them with a nonexistent system. Criminals often have an uncanny ability to recognize and disregard ineffectual law enforcement efforts—those that are more "bark" than "bite."

Another means of foiling deterrence plans is for the criminal to change tactics by shifting operations away from high-risk situations to safer domains. This effect of intensified law enforcement is known as crime displacement, a change in the nature and location of crime but not in the amount of it. For example, the result of one street-illumination program in Kansas City was that street crime was reduced on blocks that received good lighting, but crime rates in adjacent blocks, which remained darker, went up.[59]

This is but one of many instances where criminals have changed their locations, times, or targets rather than succumb to deterrence attempts. The ease of physical mobility and the anonymity of large cities make this means of averting apprehension especially attractive. Thus, many prostitutes who were subject to massive police "sweeps" of the Times Square area in New York apparently left this setting for a while and resumed business in the less patrolled East Side.[60] Robberies of bus drivers fell drastically when exact fare systems were introduced on buses in many cities, but, simultaneously, holdups of subway booths soared— implying a displacement effect.[61] In response to the increased security measures of stores and offices on commercial streets (e.g., central burglar alarms, guard dogs, and steel gates), many burglars began preying on homes and apartments where thefts are less lucrative but also less risky.[62] Fortifying one environment sometimes simply makes another more vulnerable, without contributing to any appreciable curtailment of total crime.

The remarkable adaptability of criminals was well illustrated by the experience of "Operation Drugs"—an attempt by the federal Drug Enforcement Agency to curb the extensive heroin trafficking in Harlem, which has been called the "drug capital" of the nation. Working with New York City police, the agency produced 11,000 drug arrests in 11 months, seizing 21,242 envelopes of heroin and 7,972 packets of cocaine—but failed to put a dent in the drug trade. The city's special drug prosecutor, acknowledging defeat in the war against drug peddlers, explained the reason:

> There is still as much drugs up there [in Harlem] as before. They're not out in the street hawking like when they had 600 or 700 people on a corner and they were selling dope like it was on the floor of the stock exchange.
>
> Now they're in the bars, in hallways. They've gone underground.[63]

These examples may seem to spell disaster for all deterrence efforts aimed at increasing apprehension of criminals, but there are certain limits to crime displacement. Criminals must be quite familiar with the area in which they work (e.g., to learn unguarded spots, to know good escape routes, etc.), and they therefore have a tendency to stay close to their own communities, even if the risks of crime are lower elsewhere. The importance of "knowing the turf" is suggested by the fact that the average distance between a place that a robbery occurs and an offender's home is three-fifths of a mile.[64]

Furthermore, to avoid detection criminals try to refrain from looking conspicuous. In our race-conscious society nothing draws attention to a person as much as being a different color than everyone else in the vicinity; blacks stand out in white neighborhoods and vice versa. This may well explain why 84 percent of all ghetto burglaries are committed by blacks, while 93 percent of all suburban burglaries are committed by whites.[65] Geographic displacement of street crime may be constrained by the criminal's worry about appearing out of place in alien environments.

Forcing offenders to switch locales may increase their fear of being caught, and some of them may decide that it is safer to give up crime than to explore an uncharted terrain. However, the shrewdness and versatility of criminals often enable them to outsmart the many attempts to foil them.

The Costs of Deterrence: Competing Public Interests

As is true of all crime-prevention strategies, achieving deterrence may result in the sacrifice of other public goals. Thus, even if all the theoretical and practical obstacles to success are overcome, the question must always be asked if the results in crime reduction are worth the price.

ECONOMIC COSTS

The most obvious costs are economic ones. Deterrence is not cheap; it can require extra personnel, special equipment, and additional facilities within the already expensive criminal justice system. As of 1978, it cost about $13,000 per year on the average to maintain a convict in prison (including capital expenditures on new buildings and facilities).[66] Inflation raises this figure with every passing year, so that policies that increase the use of incarceration can be quite costly.

Increasing the probability of arrest is also costly. For example, investigations of the complicated and technical world of white-collar crime can entail almost interminable scrutiny of minute details—financial records, bank statements, payment vouchers, and the like. Simply obtaining one fraud or corruption conviction is an enormously costly process, and to get sufficient convictions to make the threat of sanctions credible would take prodigious resources.[67]

In evaluating the returns from deterrence attempts, researchers must compare benefits with costs. When this was done in an examination of the relatively harsh law enforcement process against bad-check writers in Nebraska, one researcher showed what a poor economic investment this exercise in toughness was.[68] About one-third of the state's entire prison population in 1957 was made up of bad-check writers—a high allocation of resources to deal with criminals whose gains in over half of all cases were less than $20. Indeed, the total loss annually from uncollected bad checks was about $500,000 (about 30 cents per capita)—considerably less than the overall cost to the criminal justice system of convicting and punishing the offenders. Whether the moral wrongs committed by such felons justified these policies is debatable, but, in light of the minimal deterrence accomplished, this was not a very prudent allocation of government funds.

In contrast to Nebraska's dubious expenditure is the payoff from hiring so-called meter maids to give citations to parking-meter violators. Not only does rigorous enforcement of traffic offenses actually prompt many drivers to pay their fines, but the substantial revenue from fines is far more than the personnel costs. It is therefore a cost-benefit analyst's dream—a workable deterrence program that pays for itself!

Careful attention to costs can lead to decisions to abandon a deterrence policy that is relatively unsuccessful. A government report issued by the state of California showed that liberalized drug laws reduced the number of marijuana arrests by half, generating a savings of $10 million. Moreover, a state survey indicated that no more than 3 percent of the population first tried marijuana after the law was passed, and only one out of eight of this small number of new users claimed that they took the drug because legal penalties had been reduced.[69] Thus the state obtained a fiscal bonanza without inducing more crime.

These examples suggest the importance of measuring the costs of crime. Crimes that do more damage may well deserve a more expensive government attack. Such measurement, however, is easier said than done for attaching monetary figures to losses from violent crimes is hazardous. For victims of assaults, rapes, and robberies, what is lost in terms of property, money paid for medical costs, and wages is often nothing in comparison with the psychological damage inflicted—shock, fear, trauma, and the like. Nevertheless, assessing the social and economic impact of such crimes is essential if a balanced view of the value of deterrence strategies is to be obtained.[70]

THREATS TO DUE PROCESS

Deterrence methods frequently threaten due process. Indeed, in many ways the two concepts are inherently incompatible. The former entails government suppression of the individual, while the latter is meant to protect the individual from the government. For deterrence to work, it is better that a few innocent people be wrongfully convicted if it tightens the law enforcement network around criminals. Priorities are totally reversed when due process is the goal: It is far better to let some guilty persons free in order to spare the innocent from wrongful treatment.

This dilemma emerges most clearly with regard to police surveillance tactics. The use of undercover police disguised as civilians is enormously successful in generating arrests and therefore making conviction of criminals more certain (a crucial element in deterrence). When criminals are unaware they are being observed, they are unable to guard against police detection and are more likely to be caught in the act. Randomly circulating undercover police can thus unnerve criminals and may create sufficient doubts in their minds about whether they are, in fact, under surveillance that they may abstain from committing a crime.

The effectiveness of this technique is even greater if plain-clothes police are decoys made to resemble typical victims. Thus, in Los Angeles two police decoys posing as streetwalkers were able to arrest 91 men illegally making propositions for prostitution.[71] And in Washington, D.C., in a more elaborate use of such a tactic, a fictitious fencing operation run in a huge warehouse by the F.B.I. trapped over 100 unsuspecting muggers, robbers, burglars, and purse snatchers who came to sell their wares and were arrested.[72]

The other side of these seeming success stories is the danger posed to the right to privacy. The presence of large numbers of unannounced police in places where they are not normally expected can inhibit unorthodox but perfectly lawful activity and make people suspicious of one another. This is even a greater problem if undercover police officers take a further step—infiltrating organizations suspected of criminal activities. While this can be quite successful in ferreting out information about crimes such as political terrorism and gang violence, it can at the same time have a chilling effect on freedom of association. If carried to an extreme, images of a Gestapo-like police state emerge. The fear that grips the criminal can also engulf the entire society.

Another form of aggressive police activity that points up the due-process–deterrence conflict is the use of field interrogations. This is the practice of stopping, questioning, and occasionally searching persons who appear suspicious but who are not in the midst of committing a crime or directly linked to the commission of a past crime. A study of this practice in several sections of San Diego, California, indicated that it was successful in reducing certain kinds of street crime.[73] Although relatively few arrests stemmed from these interrogations, the visibility of the process to others apparently discouraged some political criminals from chancing such an encounter with the police.

However, these practices were condemned by many minority-group citizens. They perceived it as a form of harassment—a means of discriminating against blacks and Chicanos. Many innocent people who simply looked odd in the eyes of police were forced to submit to inconvenient and embarrassing questioning about their personal lives. So, while increasing police discretion beyond normal bounds may have enabled them to intimidate some criminals, it also opened the door for the unjustified harassment of many people and the application of racist criteria in law enforcement. Being stopped is punishment in itself—meted out without the benefit of procedural rights, equal treatment, or legal standards.

To those who have been victimized by criminals or are afraid of such a fate, these sacrifices of due process may seem warranted. But to people victimized at the hands of the police, the price of crime deterrence may be too high.

INJUSTICE

The use of punishment is the essence of deterrence, but inflicting serious harm on those who are convicted can create unjust outcomes. First, the use of "exemplary" punishment is said by some to be unfair. Is it right, it is asked, that a few unlucky individuals who are caught during a crackdown period are singled out for harsh treatment while many others who did the same criminal acts went unscathed or were lightly chastised in a previous period? Is it proper to ruin the lives of a few people, even if they are guilty, to keep others in line?

This issue was raised acutely by the sentencing of an F.B.I. informant to ten years in prison for a burglary he committed to obtain information about political radicals. The avowed purpose of the relatively harsh sentence was to warn others that such illegal conduct, even when done under F.B.I. auspices, would not be tolerated.[74] However, not only was this stiffer punishment than the average home burglar gets, but it was a gross departure from the acceptance of such semiofficial lawbreaking that had previously been the norm.

Another problem is the use of punishments that are so horrid that they violate fundamental standards of civilized conduct. In some New Guinea tribes, an adultress found guilty used to be subjected to gang rape in public.[75] In the present era almost everyone would consider such punishment barbaric and deem it unacceptable, no matter how well it might serve as a deterrent. The impropriety of such a punishment is self-evident, but where to draw the line on the legitimate scope of punishment is a highly controversial question.

The emotional debates about capital punishment often pivot on this point. Regardless of whether capital punishment actually deters (discussed at the end of this chapter), some consider it to be a heinous act of bestiality on the part of the government. The horrible nature of killing by the government is an argument often used to justify abolition of this punishment.

In resolving whether capital punishment is morally repugnant, the physical realities about its imposition need to be clearly understood. Brief descriptions of the two forms of inflicting death most commonly used in this country reveal the truly gruesome nature of this punishment.

Lewis Lawes, a former warden of Sing Sing penitentiary, has described electrocutions that he has seen. The victim is strapped to an electrified chair and electrodes are attached to the head and legs. Says Lewis:

> As the switch is thrown into its sockets there is a sputtering drone, and the body leaps as if to break the strong leather straps that hold it. Sometimes a thin gray wisp of smoke pushes itself out from under the helmet that holds the head electrode, followed by the faint odor of burning flesh. The hands turn red, then white, and the cords of the neck stand out. . . . The initial voltage of 2,000 to 2,200 and the amperage of 7 to 12 are lowered and reapplied at various intervals.[76]

Two or three shocks, which take several minutes, are often required for death to occur.

Another method of execution is the use of lethal cyanide gas, considered by some to be the most humane method. However, this too is a grim process, involving gasping and groaning. An eyewitness account of the last execution in the United States prior to its suspension for ten years from 1967 to 1977 describes the gassing of Luis José Monge of Colorado:

> According to the official execution log unconsciousness came more than five minutes after the cyanide splashed down into the sulphuric acid. Even after unconsciousness is declared officially, the prisoner's body continues to fight for life. He coughs and groans. The lips make little pouting motions resembling the motions made by a goldfish in a bowl. The head strains back and then slowly sinks down to

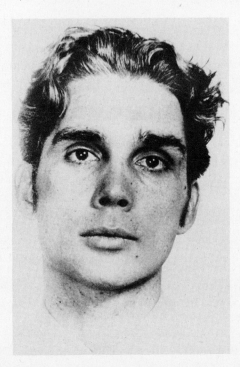

John Spenkelink: executed in Florida's electric chair, May 1979

the chest. And in Monge's case, the arms, though tightly bound to the chair, strained through the straps and the hands clawed torturously as if the prisoner were struggling for air.[77]

Clearly, imposing the death sentence is a ghastly business, no matter how many attempts are made to make such actions more humane. Its legitimacy cannot be resolved objectively. Two economists tried to do so by arguing that the probability of being a murder victim would change so little even if capital punishment does deter that it cannot possibly be worth the infinite losses to those undergoing it and the repulsion of those opposed to the taking of human life.[78] Ultimately, however, the question can only be answered with reference to value judgments that are subjective in nature.

Whether the pain rendered to criminals is warranted by the protection deterrence affords society is a very personal matter. No objective formulas are available to determine whether *any* of the costs of deterrence are worthwhile—money, deprivations of due process, injustice, or inhumanity. Individual preferences for these values versus the concern about particular crime problems must be weighed. Whether deterrence *works* is *not* the only appropriate question in deciding whether it is wise social policy. Evaluation must encompass the entire set of public interest goals in criminal justice.

The Impact of Deterrence Policy

While there are innumerable schemes aimed at deterring, over the years three policies have been continuously advocated and attempted to suppress crime—adding police patrols, requiring mandatory imprisonment for certain kinds of felons, and capital punishment. The theory of deterrence developed in this chapter might not give us grounds for optimism about their efficacy, but many politicians and large sectors of the public believe in them. They pass the tests of political and administrative feasibility, but the acid test is whether they stop crime. It is to this topic, an analysis of the impact of three popular deterrence policies, that we now turn our attention.

ADDING POLICE PATROLS

PREVENTIVE PATROL   The presence of police patrols meandering through the streets and alleys of cities is supposed to deter crime by enabling police officers to see some crimes in progress and to be in a position to respond quickly when dispatched to the scene of a crime. Logically, then, enlarged police departments should have increased deterrence capability because the risk of apprehension for criminals should go up. Adding more "cops on the street" is a plausible crime-prevention strategy.

However, the vulnerability of urban areas is so great and the territory to be covered is so vast that even significant additions to citywide personnel are so diffused that they have had imperceptible impacts on crime rates. The meager number of convictions stemming from long hours of police toil attest to this: In Kansas City the police achieve one felony conviction per 14,720 patrol hours—or one conviction for the equivalent of seven years of patrol for one person—notwithstanding the fact that the department is considered one of the most professionalized in the country.[79] With many inclined to commit crime at one time or another, police are grossly outnumbered. The presence of an extra officer here or there makes relatively little difference.

A number of studies have demonstrated this. Among cities with a population of over 500,000, the 13 cities that bolstered police strength the most during the 1960s incurred about the same rate of increase in violent crime as the 13 cities that added the least number of officers.[80] Another study of 155 cities of over 100,000 people showed that year-to-year personnel changes over a 12-year period bore no relationship to changes in the rate of serious crime.[81] Although some economists using alternative methods of statistical analysis reached opposite conclusions about the efficacy of adding police, even their findings suggest only modest gains in crime reduction.[82]

The plight of the nation's capital dramatizes the futility of police efforts aimed at containing rampant crime. In 1971 the District of Columbia had about twice as many police per capita as any other force in the nation, but it also had the dubious honor of being the most robbery-ridden city in the country—with 11,222 reported robberies. It is useful to contrast that city with Indianapolis, which is about the same size and which had only 2,109 reported robberies in 1971, even though the police force is about one-fifth the size of Washington's.[83]

Just how insignificant a role the police play in law enforcement is indicated by their helplessness during the mass disorders in New York City during the blackout of July 1977. About 100,000 people took part in the looting and burning of about 1,600 stores, and in the entire city only about 3,428 officers and detectives were on patrol when the lights went out at 9:30 P.M.[84] Moreover, in the city's ghettoes, where most of the looting took place, the "thin blue line" was stretched even thinner. The Brooklyn North command, covering the communities of Williamsburgh, Bushwick, Bedford-Stuyvesant, Brownsville, Crown Heights, and East New York—1 million people—had 189 officers on duty to deal with a total breakdown in law. Police were hopelessly outnumbered, and police frustration was well articulated by a high-ranking police official: "In the beginning we attempted to chase people with cars. But seeing this they became like flies in the kitchen; you hit over here, and they move over there."[85]

The irrelevance of police to crime has been shown in another set of circumstances, where police patrol is entirely removed. Without a police presence, we might expect a serious crime spree if the police contribution to crime deterrence were extensive. But when police in Albuquerque, New Mexico, went on strike for 10 days in 1975, leaving only a small number of nonstriking supervisors to cover the whole city, no such rampage materialized. Ironically crime actually seemed to go down slightly, and neither a single murder or traffic fatality took place.[86] The most serious crime was an armed robbery of a savings and loan asso-

ciation by gumen who were captured three days later. The reasons for this quie-
tude are obscure, but it suggests that the importance of police patrol in law enforcement is overestimated.

Underenforcement of traffic laws by police during a so-called police holiday
in Detroit in 1967 produced similar results. As part of a job action to protest
wages and working conditions, for seven months police issued about half the normal number of citations to errant drivers. Violators might have seen this as an incentive to ignore traffic laws, since they knew so many offenses were being
overlooked, but the evidence indicates no change in compliance with traffic laws;
the accident rate remained constant.[87]

Criminals are perhaps less afraid of police than is commonly realized, and
people inclined to obey the law are checked less by their fear of police than we
might expect. The relative presence or absence of police ordinarily therefore
seems to have a relatively minor impact on crime rates.

SATURATION POLICING   It may be unreasonable to expect more police to
do much good in deterring crime if they are spread out all over a city. The District of Columbia police force was doubled in size in a decade, but perhaps the
impact of the additional police was dissipated by their deployment in many locations and on various shifts. The visibility of police officers and their proximity to
crimes may improve only marginally when they are so scattered.

Whatever the shortcomings of normal police patrol even in large departments, it might be hypothesized that saturating a limited area with police does
deter by appreciably raising the risk of apprehension. This notion accords with
common sense: A person does not usually commit robberies in police stations
unless he or she is self-destructive. Presumably a point is reached in the inten-
sification of police surveillance beyond which the odds favoring a criminal's success are reversed and crime is therefore deterred.

An important experiment in Kansas City found that this point is *not*
reached by quadrupling patrol manpower.[88] Over the course of a year, five sections of the city were allocated four times the usual number of cruising squad
cars. In five other sections whose populations were comparable, all circulating
cars were removed from the streets, and police only responded to calls for assistance. Five additional sections served as a "control:" the normal number of cars
was maintained.

The results were startling. The annual crime rates in the areas with intensified policing were identical to the rates in the normal and "depoliced" sections.
This failure to deter may have been expected for crimes like assault, which normally occur indoors, but it was also true for crimes like auto theft, which almost
always takes place outside, as well as commercial burglary, which is usually visible from the street. Apparently, either the objective threat of apprehension or
the criminal's subjective perception of danger was insufficiently increased to warrant giving up crime or moving to a different locale. The areas were saturated,
but they were not saturated enough.

However, other research shows that Kansas City may simply have stopped short of what is required to make additional police effective. In Nashville, Tennessee, for about two weeks experimental zones also received four times the regular number of squad cars, but the areas were much smaller than those in Kansas City (less than one-half of a square mile each), which meant that in Nashville the police presence was more concentrated. Two other significant differences from the Kansas City saturation were introduced: Circulating police answered *no* calls except emergencies and crimes in progress, so they spent more actual time on patrol; and cars were required to drive no more than 20 miles per hour, which increased so-called slow patrol 3,000 percent (as measured by tachographs attached to cars that produce a continuous written record of speed and distance). The net result of this grossly expanded and much more attentive police presence was a significant reduction in crime.[89]

Another successful use of massive policing was the creation in the 1960s of 5,000 transit police officers in New York City whose jurisdiction was almost exclusively limited to subway trains and stations. The officers were used primarily in evening hours to deal with the soaring rise in violent crime during that time period. A long-term study of subway crime reveals that nighttime crime dropped enormously and remained low. Assigning a police officer to virtually every train and to many individual stations checked the rise in crime, for criminals knew that police were almost always very close at hand.[90] Eventually crime rates returned to and exceeded previous rates, for reasons that are unclear, prompting another bolstering of manpower in March 1979 that police claimed produced some initial success.[91]

But even "supersaturation" can be ineffective in the face of a crime epidemic. Prior to the sixth and deciding game of the 1977 World Series in Yankee Stadium, about 700 police and uniformed guards were stationed in and around the stadium. As the game neared completion with a Yankee win probable, police completely ringed the periphery of the playing field to protect the ballplayers from being mobbed and the field from being ruined by the postgame revelers. Simultaneously, several announcements were made warning spectators that anyone caught entering the field would be committing criminal trespass and would be arrested. What happened? Thousands of fans surged onto the field, oblivious to the police, knowing full well that they had the upper hand and that nothing would happen to them. A large police brigade suffered an ignominious defeat—powerless in dealing with a crowd bent on disorder.[92]

Such examples of mass lawlessness are rare, and large contingents of police are not usually so easily overcome. But a bigger obstacle to saturation policing is cost. To cover high-crime areas with police in sufficient numbers to deter requires astronomical outlays. Tactical forces can be sent to trouble spots to provide protection over and above normal levels, but they cannot be everywhere at once on an around-the-clock basis. For limited purposes, such as crowd control, strike peacekeeping, and guarding dignitaries, an imposing police presence may deter. But as a general deterrent to crime, it is not a promising solution.

MANDATORY IMPRISONMENT

Other approaches to deterrence focus on the postarrest treatment of offenders. Various proponents and proposals have dealt with three different purposes to be achieved by requiring incarceration—general deterrence, specific deterrence, and incapacitation.

Concerning general deterrence, it was thought that mandatory imprisonment prevents the relatively lenient treatment of serious criminals resulting from plea bargaining. By making the probability of a harsh sentence certain upon conviction, a giant loophole in the criminal justice process was supposed to be closed. Because criminals could no longer hope for a sympathetic judge who might grant probation or a token jail sentence and because indulgent plea bargains concluded by overly cooperative prosecutors were prohibited, the prescribed punishment on the books might be more credible. Theoretically, such provisions made the threat of sufficiently severe sanctions more realistic and thus would deter crime.

Two full-scale attempts to implement such a policy were tried and evaluated. A New York State law adopted in 1973 required all drug peddlers to go to jail, and a Massachusetts law that became effective in 1975 made imprisonment mandatory for all those convicted of illegally carrying firearms. The impacts have been mixed. The drug law clearly failed, while the gun law has been a partial success.

The New York law, dubbed the "Rockefeller Drug Law" because it was a major crime-fighting proposal of the then-governor, established the toughest punishments in the country for those selling narcotics. Even those selling small amounts of "soft" drugs like marijuana were to get an automatic one-year sentence unless they were first offenders, and heroin peddlers were to receive between 15 years and life imprisonment. Six days after the law took effect, Rockefeller announced that "heroin seems to be diasappearing, drying up in the city."[93] Subsequent evaluation by the Committee on Drug Law Evaluation showed this victory statement to be premature—and dead wrong.[94]

Though 31 judges were added to deal with drug cases and the anticipated decline in plea bargaining and $76 million was spent to enforce the law between 1973 and 1976, most cases totally bogged down in the cumbersome criminal justice system. Fewer cases were adjudicated during this period than during a comparable period under the old drug laws. To cope with the additional demands placed on them and the attempts to limit their discretion, prosecutors, defense lawyers, and judges found various means of circumventing the law and watering down its stern punishments. Because of delays in dispositions, greater use of jury trials, and the adaptive behavior of criminal justice personnel, risk of imprisonment under the new law actually went down.

This was a deterrence policy that, in practice, never saw the light of day. It was sabotaged by the deficiencies of the criminal justice bureaucracy and perhaps by the sensitivity of some prosecutors and judges who thought that the law was too harsh. The conclusion of the evaluators bears quoting, because they so aptly draw attention to the obstacles that imperil policies of mandatory imprisonment:

> The key lesson to be drawn from the experience with the 1973 drug law is that passing a law is not enough. What criminal statutes say matters a great deal, but the efficiency, morale, and capacity of the criminal justice system is even more of a factor in determining whether the law is effectively implemented. . . .
>
> Without implementation, there is no policy; there are only words.[95]

In contrast, the apparently positive impact of the Bartley-Fox gun law in Massachusetts substantiates the importance of bureaucratic follow-through. The law required a minimum one-year sentence—without possibility of suspension, furlough, or parole—for those convicted of carrying a gun without authorization. It was an attempt to deter the use of guns in the commission of crime by eliminating the opportunity to plea bargain for a light sentence.

This law seems to have worked at least in part. Police made arrests in almost all cases where they were warranted, prosecutors pressed charges, and judges did impose the mandatory sentence even though some said they resented doing so.[96] Consequently, there was a five-fold increase in the number of offenders who went to jail over the pre-law period.

The Massachusetts data suggest a marked deterrent impact—reflecting, among other things, the crucial importance of implementation.[97] But, paradoxically, the crimes that were affected were aggravated assault and homicide, which are supposedly committed irrationally in most cases, rather than the calculated crime of robbery, which was the main target of the law. The proportion of assaults with firearms dropped in 1976 (the year after the law took effect) to a new low of 17 percent.

Since most murders are simply the outgrowth of assaults, the assailant wants to injure the victim but the results go beyond what was sought. The decline in the use of guns in such attacks resulted in a dramatic decline in homicides—from 135 in 1973 to 82 in 1976. Whereas 1 in 10 assaults with firearms results in death, only 1 in 40 assaults with other weapons has such dire consequences. The law apparently gave people second thoughts about casually carrying a gun, and thus many assaults that previously would have resulted in death had less destructive impacts. Fear of prison dissuaded many from putting themselves in the position of becoming murderers.

The contrast between the New York drug law and the Massachusetts gun law points to a clear moral. Potential criminals must really believe that they will be in serious trouble if they are caught. The title of the research article evaluating the gun law—" 'And Nobody Can Get You Out' "—is well put. That message was not conveyed with regard to the drug law, based on an appraisal of what the criminal justice system was capable of accomplishing. Mandatory minimum prison sentences can deter, but only if the minimum is *really* mandatory.

A second purpose of mandatory imprisonment is specific deterrence. It is argued that insisting on substantial imprisonment for some offenders will jolt them into "going straight"—giving up their criminal ways and complying with the law. A tradeoff undoubtedly is made between the increased fear of future punishment, which a dose of prison may create, and the reinforcement of criminality, which immersion in the prison subculture may produce, but some research data suggest that the crime-inhibiting effects outweigh the crime-sustaining ones. Various studies tracing criminal careers and examining the impacts of imposing sanctions imply that those punished, while still committing more crimes than the general populace, commit fewer than those who manage to avert apprehension, arrest, and conviction.[99]

Finally, there can be no doubt that totally apart from deterrent effects, the purpose of incapacitation is served by mandatory imprisonment. Because some degree of crime repetition is unquestionably thwarted by taking offenders out of circulation, it is a policy gaining widespread support from legislators and citizens alike. But like other approaches to crime prevention, estimates vary widely on the potential effectiveness of incapacitation, as will be discussed in Chapter 15, where we examine new policies "on the horizon" in the field of criminal justice.

CAPITAL PUNISHMENT

The theory behind capital punishment as a deterrent is straightforward. Death represents the ultimate punishment; it is a fate that conflicts with the human instinct for survival, and it is thus feared even by the most downtrodden. Also, it is irreversible since it allows not as much as a glimmer of hope of a reprieve, unlike life imprisonment, which can eventually result in parole or clemency. Rational individuals will therefore stop short of some crimes if they foresee the prospect of death as a penalty. According to the Los Angeles police, robbers have told them many times that they often use toy guns or empty guns "rather than take a chance on killing someone and getting the gas chamber."[100]

However, even ardent advocates of capital punishment generally acknowledge that certain killers cannot be deterred—by the death penalty or anything else. Psychopaths such as Charles Whitman, who killed 27 students from his perch in a tower on the University of Texas campus, are unmindful of any consequences of their actions. So too are many emotional assailants who are totally out of control when they unleash their fury on their victims. But it is commonly argued that premeditated homicides of various kinds could be stopped. Thus, the hired killer, the felony murderer who kills to preclude apprehension, and the "lifer"—the person under life sentence who without capital punishment has nothing to lose by killing a guard to escape—may be deterred. Several Supreme Court justices based their decision supporting the constitutionality of the death penalty on the possibility that it might deter,[101] and a belief in deterrent effectiveness is the prime reason that public-opinion polls show a rise in sentiment favoring capital punishment, from 42 percent in 1966 to 65 percent in 1976.[102]

Although both advocates and opponents of the death penalty hold firm views on the issue, voluminous empirical research has left the question of the crime-inhibiting effects of capital punishment unresolved. Methodological problems in studying this question are enormous, because ethical reservations stand in the way of experimenting with the death penalty in a scientific manner.

Most people, for example, would be horrified by a proposal facetiously made by University of Chicago Law Professor Hans Zeisel that all convicted murderers born on even-numbered days would be given life imprisonment while those born on odd-numbered days would be killed.[103] Assuming that date of birth is a random event and over the long run people born on different days are comparable, studying the impact of such a policy could show whether those facing certain death were more restrained in their crimes than those who knew they would be spared. Because such an experiment is morally objectionable and politically unthinkable, only after-the-fact research linking crime and the death penalty has been undertaken, and therefore only the loosest inferences about cause and effect can be made.

One genre of research has compared trends in crime rates before and after the abolition or introduction of capital punishment in a particular jurisdiction.[104] Although such studies have generally showed no significant changes in crime incidence after such events, they carry little weight because real effects of the death penalty may be camouflaged by other factors, such as economic depressions or natural disasters, that simultaneously affect the murder rate. Another approach has been to compare states with and without the death penalty. The soundest examples of this type of research have tried to control for extraneous factors, such as cultural support for violence, by "matching" states to be compared. One way to do this is to examine adjacent states that are presumably similar in many respects but happen to differ regarding their policy on the death penalty. Table 9-5 reproduces a classic study of this nature, showing that over

TABLE 9-5

Homicide Rates in Contiguous States With and Without Capital Punishment

Matched Group 1			Midwest Matched Group 2			Matched Group 3		
Michigan	D[1] Indiana	D Ohio	Minnesota	Wisconsin	D Iowa	North Dakota	D South Dakota	D Nebraska
3.5	3.5	3.5	1.4	1.2	1.4	1.0	1.5	1.8

	Matched Group 1		New England	Matched Group 2	
Maine	D New Hampshire	D Vermont	Rhode Island	D Massachusetts	D Connecticut
1.5	.9	1.0	1.3	1.2	1.7

[1] Indicates a state with the death penalty.
SOURCE: Reprinted from *Deterrence: The Legal Threat in Crime Control* by Franklin Zimring and Gordon Hawkins (Chicago: University of Chicago Press, 1973), p. 265, by permission of the University of Chicago Press. Adapted from "Homicide Death Rates in Contiguous Abolitionist and Retentionist States, 1920–1963" in "Homicides in Retentionist and Abolitionist States," by Thorsten Sellin from *Capital Punishment*, edited by Thorsten Sellin. Copyright © 1967 by Thorsten Sellin. Reprinted by permission of Harper & Row, Publishers, Inc.

the years the homicide rate has been no higher in states lacking the death penalty than in neighboring states that permit it.[105]

There have been refinements of this kind of analysis. Researchers have demonstrated statistically that the contiguous states are demographically similar, making the results of Table 9-5 more persuasive. Other studies have looked only at first-degree murder rates, which involve premeditation when concern about consequences is more plausible, and the killing of police officers, which engenders the greatest risk of the death penalty. Again, no deterrent effects have been revealed.[106]

Both the before-and-after and the state-versus-state comparisons, however, may suffer from a major flaw. Conceivably, calculating murderers respond to the number of actual executions in a state and the real possibility of suffering the death penalty upon conviction rather than to the mere existence of capital punishment in the law. If the death penalty is legal but unused, that may be tantamount to abolishing it altogether.

One way of tackling this problem has been to examine murder rates before and after *actual* executions. Results are still negative. Murders did not go down in Philadelphia in the eight weeks following well-publicized executions,[107] nor were they lower in California in the days immediately following "execution day."[108]

The controversial but influential work of economist Isaac Ehrlich has pursued another line of inquiry. Using the statistical technique known as regression analysis, which permits one to predict one variable (e.g., the murder rate) on the basis of another variable (e.g., execution rates), he found that the trend in the nationwide incidence of murder *was* related to changes in the use of capital punishment.[109] As the number of executions dropped to zero in the year 1968 because of appeals wending their way up to the Supreme Court, the murder rate soared. Ehrlich concluded that had there been one additional execution per year between 1935 and 1969, 7 or 8 fewer murders would have occurred each year. To support his statistical evidence, Ehrlich argued that even murderers who are emotional make self-serving choices, and they consider the degree to which acting out their feelings might lead to the loss of their own life as a punishment.[110] Accordingly, if the death penalty is used only sporadically, it loses its potential to inspire intense fear.

Ehrlich's highly technical work has led to equally complex critiques. In particular the work has been faulted for including in the analysis the years after 1964, when so few executions actually occurred, on the grounds that the negligible import of capital punishment during most of the 35-year time span was eclipsed by including a few years where the disparity between executions and murders was so great. By reanalyzing the data excluding those years, the relationship disappears; in addition, it has been claimed that other factors, like urban tension, led to the zooming murder rate in the late 1960s.

Other objections have dealt with the quality of the data, the legitimacy of the mathematical techniques, and the use of national data, which are insensitive to fluctuations in state policy.[112] While all of this work has produced endless formulas, equations, and computer output, it has not settled the basic issue. Claims and counterclaims continue to be made, findings, rebuttals, and rejoinders to the rebuttals continue to pour out; analyses are followed by reanalyses. At the present time agnosticism seems to be the only safe conclusion: We really do not know, for certain, what impact the previous use and nonuse of the death penalty may have had on crime.

Nor will the basic policy dilemma be resolved even if the debates in the scholarly community are resolved. Demonstrating a clear-cut linkage between capital punishment and crime will still leave open the fundamental moral issues of whether the government should engage in killing and whether some criminals deserve death as just retribution totally apart from deterrence. These are questions that cannot be answered empirically.

Furthermore, a conclusive demonstration that capital punishment was an ineffectual deterrent in the past would not quell the controversy about its utility today. The argument could be made that it was ineffective only because it was never really tried with the degree of fervor and consistency necessary to make it work. A high certainty of execution may be needed for it to be a credible threat, and the soft-heartedness of previous prosecutors, judges, and juries, even in the heyday of its imposition, may have limited its effectiveness. Another hypothesis is that publicity surrounding executions has been inadequate: What is necessary is profuse mass media coverage (perhaps including live television with close-up shots) to demonstrate poignantly the real agony of death. These contentions are incontrovertible because we cannot reject out-of-hand that which has never been attempted.

THE INFREQUENCY OF EXECUTION

At the time of [Gary] Gilmore's death [before a firing squad in Utah on July 17, 1977], opponents of capital punishment believed that a rash of executions would result once the psychological barrier built up over the previous decade had been breached.

That has not proved to be the case, largely because of the implacable legal opposition put up by opponents of executions. . . .

Thus, since July 2, 1976, when the Supreme Court of the United States upheld discretionary death penalty statutes in Georgia, Florida, and Texas while striking down mandatory penalties in North Carolina and Louisiana, only one execution—Mr. Gilmore's—has taken place [as of April 6, 1979].

Since the decision, state and Federal courts have struck down other state statutes on varying grounds, with the result that 504 death row inmates have been freed.

An additional 141 persons facing the death penalty had their convictions or sentences reversed on appeal. Four others committed suicide.

As of February 20 of this year [1979], 32 states and the Federal Government had capital punishment laws, and 483 persons awaited execution.

Wayne King, "Slayer Again Asks Death; Court Bars Execution Delay," *New York Times,* April 5, 1979, p. A20. © 1979 by The New York Times Company. Reprinted by permission.

However, the political feasiblity of attempting mass executions is dubious. Use of the death penalty was resumed in January 1977 after a ten-year hiatus with the shooting of Gary Gilmore by a firing squad in Utah, but it is unlikely to be followed by a flurry of executions. Indeed, as of June 1979, only one additional criminal had been executed in the 2½ years since Gilmore's death. In the 1972 decision of *Furman* v. *Georgia*,[113] several justices toyed with the notion of requiring that executions for specified crimes be mandatory in order to make the action constitutional, but this idea was withdrawn five years later in *Gregg* v. *Georgia*,[114] which held that aggravating and mitigating circumstances of crimes *must* be considered if the "cruel and unusual punishment" prohibition of the Eighth Amendment is not to be violated. Also, the substantive and procedural laws of each state regarding capital punishment and the application of these laws to indiviudal cases will probably continue to be scrutinized thoroughly by the courts.

Consequently, the prospect of extensive executions is small, and the very real possibility of murderers escaping the death penalty will persist. The public interest in individualized justice will triumph over the requisites of successful deterrence. By the same token, the goals of civility and public decency are likely to preclude vivid communication of the grisly details of executions, regardless of whether such portrayals contribute to deterrent effectiveness.

Whatever the future of capital punishment, it has virtually no bearing on the crime problems confronting most Americans. Murder is a rare crime, and stranger-to-stranger murder is still rarer. While resurrection of the death penalty may reassure the community that *something* is being done about vicious criminals, the whole issue addresses a low-risk crime. The moral issues are profound, but the tangible impacts are destined to be minuscule. Whether capital punishment succeeds or fails as a deterrent is in many ways beside the point, and concentration on this question by both policy makers and policy evaluators is a diversion from the critical task of fighting crime.

Conclusion

Deterrence is much better in theory than in practice. People do respond to sanctions, and imprisonment is almost universally dreaded. But the criminal justice system is not very efficient in imposing punishments. While it is almost impossible to determine how many law-abiding people would commit crimes if they were not afraid of legal consequences, it is clear that the millions who violate one law or another are *un*deterred.

People are sensible enough to be able to assess the costs and benefits of crime, and in making those judgments they include estimates of being apprehended and (within limits) the harm that such a fate poses. The self-interests of those within the criminal justice system are rivaled by the self-interests of the criminals: If the latter have a good chance of outfoxing the former, they will often take the risk. The driver who slides through a red light, the merchant who deducts a family vacation as a business expense on a tax return, and the mugger who accosts someone in a dark alley all share a common sentiment: Crime pays—it is a good investment.

However, under some circumstances deterrence works better than under others. Calculating criminals who are acting rationally are more likely to be deterred than impulsive ones who are acting emotionally. People who are less desperate for the fruits of crime and have more to lose if they are punished will normally take fewer risks than those who feel compelled to commit crime because of dire need.

In formulating policy, decision makers must be selective in choosing targets for deterrence strategies. While considerable resources may be needed to convict and imprison real estate swindlers, contractors who overbill the government, and physicians who take more than is justified from Medicare, it may be necessary to punish only a small proportion of such white-collar criminals in order to intimidate the rest. This is the opinion of a former director of the Antitrust Division of the Department of Justice: "No one in direct contact with the living reality of business conduct in the United States is unaware of the effect of imprisonment of seven high officials in the Electrical Machinery Industry on the conspiratorial price-fixing in many areas of the economy."[115]

As to the street criminals who directly prey on people's safety and whose crimes result in more immediate losses, deterrence is inevitably an uphill battle. The politically expedient solution is to stiffen sentences, but if the odds of avoiding arrest remain sufficiently good, the tougher penalty is generally ignored. The legislative abolition of plea bargaining and the judge's stern pronouncement in sending a defendant to prison for many years are in some ways a sedative for the public; public tranquillity goes up a notch, but crime is relatively unaffected. Determining ways to apprehend more burglars, robbers, rapists, and auto thieves is far more crucial, but that task requires complex policies and almost infinite patience.

Criminals are in many respects a clever and persistent lot; they are not easily intimidated. They will sometimes desist from crime in the face of legal threats, but only when the threats are genuine and capable of being executed. Merely exposing them to bigger government—more police, more courts, more prisons—is insufficient to deter them. What is needed is *more punishment;* and obtaining *that* is no mean feat. Raising levels of arrest, conviction, and incarceration of criminals requires a set of finely tuned and coordinated policies implemented by a variety of agencies and entailing the active cooperation of the public. There are no shortcut solutions.

Unfortunately, the only sure means of drastically increasing the incidence of punishment accorded to criminals is the creation of a police state in which due process and justice are disregarded. For most Americans this is an unacceptable alternative. A free society must content itself with modest successes in its attempts to deter crime.

SUMMARY

Deterrence is a plausible crime-prevention strategy that uses the threat of sanctions to inhibit crime. General deterrence is the restraining effect on the entire population of punishing those offenders who are caught. Specific deterrence is the curtailment of future crime on the part of those who have actually been subjected to punishment. While the basic rationale of deterrence is that people try to avert pain, the imposition of sanctions can also stop crime by impressing people with the immorality of crime, by habituating them to compliance, and by creating greater respect for law.

For deterrence to work, five conditions must be satisfied. First, threats must be sufficiently communicated to potential criminals so that they appreciate the risk and consequences of getting caught. Second, the threats must be genuine: The certainty of apprehension, conviction, and punishment must in fact be relatively high. Third, the threatened punishments must be severe enough to instill fear among those contemplating crime. Fourth, deterrence must be directed at people who are rationally concerned about their own self-interest rather than at those who are emotional and therefore indifferent to the repercussions of their actions. Fifth, swift punishment may be important, although the impact of delay is not clear.

There are some practical obstacles to suc-

cessful deterrence. First, some seemingly sound deterrence policies are politically unfeasible. Second, those that are adopted may suffer implementation difficulties; the bureaucracy charged with enforcement may sabotage them. Third, criminals may be able to outwit the attempts to foil them by adapting their behavior; crime may be displaced rather than deterred. Finally deterrence policy may be too costly—either financially or in terms of other values like due process that are at stake.

Consequently, three approaches commonly proposed or tried produce only limited results. Adding police is generally ineffectual unless saturation levels are reached. Mandatory imprisonment has been partially successful, but it has sometimes failed because police and prosecutors can use their discretion to temper laws they think are too harsh. The deterrent effectiveness of capital punishment is unclear due to the many complexities in studying its impact.

The threat of punishment often fails because the benefits of crime outweigh the risks. The most promising way of strengthening the deterrence capabilities of the criminal justice system is to increase the risk of apprehension. But because this is very difficult to achieve, the policy of deterrence is not a panacea to the crime problem.

FOOTNOTES

[1] Charles Tittle and Allan Rowe, "Moral Appeal, Sanction Threat, and Deviance; An Empirical Test," *Social Problems* 20 (Spring 1973), 488–98.

[2] William Chambliss, "The Deterrent Influence of Punishment," *Crime and Delinquency* 12 (January 1966), 70–75.

[3] John Decker, "Curbside Deterrence? An Analysis of the Effect of a Slug-Rejection Device, Coin-View Windows, and Warning Labels on Slug Usage in New York City Parking Meters," *Criminology* 10 (August 1972), 127–42.

[4] Peter Greenwood and Joan Petersilia, *The Criminal Investigation Process: Summary and Policy Implications*

(Washington, D.C.: U.S. Government Printing Office, 1975), pp. 23–24.

[5] For discussions of deterrence terminology, see Franklin Zimring and Gordon Hawkins, *Deterrence: The Legal Threat in Crime Control* (Chicago: University of Chicago Press, 1973), pp. 70–74; and Jack Gibbs, *Crime, Punishment, and Deterrence* (New York: Elsevier, 1975), pp. 29–40.

[6] See Zimring and Hawkins, ibid., for a brief explanation of his views at pp. 75–77.

[7] Franklin Zimring, "Of Doctors, Deterrence, and the Dark Figure of Crime—A Note on Abortion in Hawaii,"

University of Chicago Law Review 39 (Summer 1972), 717.

[8] *New York Times*, August 3, 1978, p. B3.

[9] Andrew Hacker, "Getting Used to Mugging," in *Whose Law? Whose Order?* eds. William Chambliss and Milton Mankoff (New York: Wiley, 1976), p. 224.

[10] Richard Henshel, "Deterrence and Knowledge of Sanctions," in *Crime Prevention and Social Control*, eds. Ronald Akers and Edward Sagarin (New York: Praeger, 1974), pp. 51–64.

[11] Frederick Beutel, *Some Potentialities of Experimental Jurisprudence as a New Social Science* (Lincoln, Neb.: University of Nebraska Press, 1957), pp. 256–379.

[12] Zimring and Hawkins, op. cit., pp. 160–67.

[13] Nigel Walker, *Sentencing in a Rational Society* (New York: Basic Books, 1969), p. 30.

[14] Zimring and Hawkins, op. cit., p. 145.

[15] Ibid., p. 11.

[16] Richard Schwartz and Sonya Orleans, "On Legal Sanctions," *University of Chicago Law Review* 34 (Winter 1967), 274–300.

[17] See, for example, Jan Palmer, "Economic Analysis of the Deterrent Effect of Punishment: A Review," *Journal of Research in Crime and Delinquency* 14 (January 1977), 4–21.

[18] Gordon Waldo and Theodore Chiricos, "Perceived Penal Sanction and Self-Reported Criminality: A Neglected Approach to Deterrence Research," *Social Problems* 19 (Spring 1972), 522–40; and James Teevan, "Subjective Perception of Deterrence (Continued)," *Journal of Research in Crime and Delinquency* 13 (July 1976), 155–64.

[19] Robert Chauncey, "Deterrence: Certainty, Severity, and Skyjacking," *Criminology* 12 (February 1975), 447–73.

[20] Alfred Blumstein and Daniel Nagin, "The Deterrent Effects of Legal Sanctions on Draft Evasion," *Stanford Law Review* 29 (January 1977), 241–76.

[21] For a list of citations, see William Bailey and Ruth Lott, "Crime, Punishment, and Personality: An Examination of the Deterrence Question," *Journal of Research on Crime and Delinquency* 67 (March 1976), 99–109.

[22] William Bailey, "Certainty of Arrest and Crime Rates for Major Felonies: A Research Note," *Journal of Research on Crime and Delinquency* 13 (July 1976), 145–54.

[23] Wesley Skogan and George Antunes, "Information, Apprehension, and Deterrence: The Missing Theoretical Link" (Paper presented at the Midwest Political Science Association meeting in Chicago, 1978). See also Michael Musheno, Dennis Palumbo, and James Levine, "Evaluating Alternatives in Criminal Justice: A Policy Impact Approach," *Crime and Delinquency* 22 (July 1976), 281.

[24] Erhard Blankenburg, "The Selectivity of Legal Sanctions: An Empirical Investigation of Shoplifting," *Law and Society Review* 11 (Fall 1976), 109–30.

[25] Roger Cramton, "Driver Behavior and Legal Sanctions: A Study of Deterrence," *Michigan Law Review* 67 (January 1969), 421–54.

[26] Albert Reiss, *The Police and the Public* (New Haven, Conn.: Yale University Press, 1971), p. 100.

[27] Skogan and Antunes, op. cit., p. 14.

[28] President's Commission on Law Enforcement and the Administration of Justice, *The Challenge of Crime in a Free Society* (Washington, D.C.: U.S. Government Printing Office, 1967), pp. 262–63.

[29] John Boudreau, Quon Kwan, William Faragher, and Genevieve Denault, *Arson and Arson Investigation: Survey and Assessment* (Washington, D.C. U.S. Government Printing Office, 1977), pp. 14–18.

[30] Ibid., pp. 29–31.

[31] The findings are from a study done under the auspices of the Law Enforcement Assistance Administration and reported in *The Daily Freeman* [Kingston, New York], September 4, 1978, p. 16.

[32] Gibbs, op. cit., p. 144.

[33] William Chambliss, "Types of Deviance and the Effectiveness of Legal Sanctions," *Wisconsin Law Review*, Summer 1967, p. 716.

[34] Zimring and Hawkins, op. cit., p. 165.

[35] C. W. Hartman, *Housing and Social Policy* (Englewood Cliffs, N.J.: Prentice-Hall, 1975), p. 66; Judah Gribetz and F. P. Grad, "Housing Code Enforcement: Sanctions and Remedies," *Columbia Law Review* 66 (November 1966), 1276; and G. J. Castrataro, "Housing Code Enforcement: A Century of Failure in New York City," *New York Law Forum* (Spring 1968), 60–75.

[36] Richard Schwartz and Jerome Skolnick, "Two Studies of Legal Stigma," *Social Problems* 10 (Fall 1962), 133–42.

[37] William Bailey, J. David Martin, and Louis Gray, "Crime and Deterrence: A Correlation Analysis," *Journal of Research in Crime and Delinquency* 11 (July 1974), pp. 124–43.

[38] George Antunes and A. Lee Hunt, "The Deterrent Impact of Criminal Sanctions: Some Implications for Criminal Justice Policy," *Journal of Urban Law* 51 (November 1973), 145–61; and George Antunes and A. Lee Hunt, "The Impact of Certainty and Severity of Punishment on Levels of Crime in American States," *Journal of Criminal Law and Criminology* 64 (December 1973), 486–93.

[39] William Bailey and Ronald Smith, "Punishment: Its Severity and Certainty," *Journal of Criminal Law, Criminology, and Police Science* 63 (December 1972), 530–39.

[40] Zimring and Hawkins, op. cit., pp. 203–08.

[41] Antunes and Hunt, "The Deterrent Impact of Criminal Sanctions: Some Implications for Criminal Justice Policy," op. cit., 156.

[42] Giora Shoham, "Punishment and Traffic Offenses," *Traffic Quarterly* 28 (January 1974), 61–73.

[43] U.S. Federal Bureau of Investigations, *Uniform Crime Reports—1968* (Washington, D.C.: U.S. Government Printing Office, 1969), pp. 34–40.

[44] U.S. Federal Bureau of Investigations, *Uniform Crime Reports—1972* (Washington, D.C.: U.S. Government Printing Office, 1973), pp. 8–9; fn. 15.

[45] *New York Post*, July 28, 1977, p. 9.

[46] *New York Times*, August 3, 1977, p. A10.

[47] *New York Times*, April 26, 1978, p. A26.

[48] Harold Grasmick and Herman Milligan, "Deterrence Theory Approach to Socio-Economic Demographic Correlates of Crime," *Social Science Quarterly* 57 (December 1976), pp. 608–17.

[49] Zimring and Hawkins, op. cit., pp. 209–17.

[50] H. Laurence Ross, "Law, Science, and Accidents: The

British Road Safety Test of 1967," *Journal of Legal Studies* 2 (January 1973), 1–78.

[51] Quoted in Richard Neustadt, *Presidential Power: The Politics of Leadership* (New York: Wiley, 1962), p. 9.

[52] Donald Campbell and H. Laurence Ross, "The Connecticut Crackdown on Speeding: Time-Series Data in Quasi-Experimental Analysis," *Law and Society Review* 3 (August 1968), 33–54.

[53] H. Laurence Ross, Donald Campbell, and Gene Glass, "Determining the Social Effects of a Legal Reform: The British 'Breathalyser' Crackdown of 1967," *American Behavioral Scientist* 13 (March–April 1970), 493–510.

[54] Ross, op. cit.

[55] Cited by Tom Goldstein, "Police Study Views Low Conviction Rate," *New York Times*, September 19, 1977, p. 25.

[56] Skogan and Antunes, op. cit., p. 26.

[57] Boudreau et al., op. cit., p. 32.

[58] The courts in several states (e.g., Virginia, Michigan, and New York) have struck down laws against the possession of radar detectors. See Ben Franklin, "Radar-Detector Convictions Upset," *New York Times*, June 10, 1978, p. 7.

[59] Roger Wright et al., *The Impact of Street Lighting on Street Crime* (Ann Arbor: University of Michigan, 1974), pp. 112–20.

[60] *New York Times*, August 11, 1973, p. 52; and *New York Daily News*, May 19, 1974, p. 32.

[61] Jan Chaiken, Michael Lawless, and Keith Stevenson, *The Impact of Police Activity on Crime: Robberies on the New York City Subway System* (New York: Rand Institute, 1974), pp. 25–30.

[62] U.S. Federal Bureau of Investigation, *Uniform Crime Reports—1972*, op. cit., pp. 18–20.

[63] Quoted in the *New York Post*, October 26, 1977, p. 3.

[64] Thomas Reppetto, "Crime Prevention and the Displacement Phenomenon," *Crime and Delinquency* 22 (April 1976), 174.

[65] Ibid.

[66] John Kaplan, *Criminal Justice: Introductory Cases and Materials*, 2nd ed. (Mineola, N.Y.: Foundation Press, 1978), p. 541.

[67] Robert Ogren, "The Ineffectiveness of the Criminal Sanction in Fraud and Corruption Cases: Losing the Battle Against White-Collar Crime," *American Criminal Law Review* 11 (Summer 1973), 959–88.

[68] Beutel, op. cit., pp. 405–407.

[69] Cited in the *New York Times*, March 14, 1977, p. 18.

[70] For examples of attempts to do this quantitatively, see Eugene Swimmer, "Measurement of the Effectiveness of Urban Law Enforcement—A Simultaneous Approach," *Southern Economic Journal* 40 (April 1974), 618–30; and Isaac Ehrlich, "Participation in Illegitimate Activities: A Theoretical and Empirical Investigation," *Journal of Political Economy* 81 (May 1973), 521–65.

[71] Gary Marx, "Undercover Cops: Creative Policing or Constitutional Threat?" *The Civil Liberties Review* (July–August 1977), 40.

[72] Ibid., 34.

[73] Frances Gallagher, "An Annotated Bibliography of Deterrence Evaluations, 1970–1975," in *Deterrence and Incapacitation: Estimating the Effects of Criminal Sanctions on Crime Rates*, eds. Alfred Blumstein, Jacqueline Cohen, and Daniel Nagin (Washington, D.C.: National Academy of Sciences, 1978), pp. 174–77.

[74] *New York Post*, January 6, 1977, p. 16.

[75] Gibbs, op. cit., p. 8.

[76] Quoted in Austin Sarat and Neil Vidmar, "Public Opinion, The Death Penalty, and the Eighth Amendment: Testing the Marshall Hypothesis" *Wisconsin Law Review*, 1976, p. 206.

[77] Quoted in ibid.

[78] David McKee and Michael Sesnowitz, "Welfare Economic Aspects of Capital Punishment," *The American Journal of Economics and Sociology* 35 (January 1976), 41–47.

[79] Skogan and Antunes, op. cit., p. 33.

[80] James Levine, "The Ineffectiveness of Adding Police to Prevent Crime," *Public Policy* 23 (Fall 1975), 523–45.

[81] E. Terrance Jones, "Evaluating Everyday Policies: Police Activity and Crime Reduction," *Urban Affairs Quarterly* 8 (March 1973), 267–79.

[82] Eugene Swimmer, "The Relationship of Police and Crime," *Criminology* 12 (November 1974), 293–314.

[83] Levine, op. cit., 530.

[84] Robert Curvin and Bruce Porter, *Blackout Looting! New York City, July 13, 1977* (New York: Gardner Press, 1979), p. 60.

[85] Quoted in ibid., p. 63.

[86] *New York Times*, July 24, 1975, p. 32. The evidence is less clear with regard to the New Orleans police strike of 1979. Concern about the impact of the strike on crime was sufficient to cause curtailment of the traditional Mardi Gras festivities.

[87] Zimring and Hawkins, op. cit., pp. 168–69.

[88] George Kelling, Tony Pate, Duane Dieckman, and Charles Brown, *The Kansas City Preventive Patrol Experiment: A Summary Report* (Washington, D.C.: Police Foundation, 1974).

[89] John Schnelle et al., "Patrol Evaluation Research: A Multiple-Baseline Analysis of Saturation Police Patrolling During Day and Night Hours, "*Journal of Applied Behavior Analysis* 10 (Spring 1977), 33–40.

[90] Chaiken, Lawless, and Stevenson, op. cit.

[91] Robert McFadden, "War Begins on Crime on Subways as 900 Police Officers Join Patrol," *New York Times*, March 20, 1979, p. 1.

[92] Leonard Buder, "Panel Finds Police Overreacted to Unruly Crowd at Series Final," *New York Times*, March 15, 1978, p. B7.

[93] Quoted in David Bird, "Rockefeller Sees Heroin 'Drying Up,' " *New York Times*, September 8, 1973, p. 17.

[94] Franklin Zimring, "Policy Experiments in General Deterrence, 1970–1975," in *Deterrence and Incapacitation*, op. cit., pp. 157–60.

[95] The evaluation was done by the Committee on Drug Law Evaluation and was reported in Tom Goldstein, "Stiff New York Law on Drugs Is Termed Ineffective by Study," *New York Times*, June 22, 1977, p. B18.

[96] James Beha, " 'And Nobody Can Get You Out': The Im-

pact of a Mandatory Prison Sentence for the Illegal Carrying of a Firearm or the Use of Firearms and on the Administration of Justice in Boston—Part I," *Boston University Law Review* 57 (January 1977), 96–146.

[97] James Beha, " 'And Nobody Can Get You Out': The Impact of a Mandatory Prison Sentence for the Illegal Carrying of a Firearm or the Use of Firearms and on the Administration of Justice—Part II," *Boston University Law Review* 57 (March 1977), 289–333.

[98] Franklin Zimring, "The Medium Is the Message," *Journal of Legal Studies* 1 (1972), 97–123.

[99] See Charles Tittle and Charles Logan, "Sanctions and Deviance: Evidence and Remaining Questions," *Law and Society Review* 7 (Spring 1973), 375.

[100] Quoted in Hans Zeisel, "The Deterrent Effect of the Death Penalty: Facts v. Faiths," in *The Supreme Court Review, 1976*, ed. Philip Kurland (Chicago: University of Chicago Press, 1977), p. 320.

[101] Furman v. Georgia, 408 U.S. 238 (1972).

[102] Brian Forst, "The Deterrent Effect of Capital Punishment: A Cross-State Analysis of the 1960's," *Minnesota Law Review* 61 (May 1977), 743–67.

[103] Zeisel, op. cit.

[104] Thorsten Sellin, "Homicides in Retentionist and Abolitionist States," in *Capital Punishment*, ed. Thorsten Sellin (New York: Harper & Row, 1967), pp. 135–38.

[105] See Zeisel, op. cit., at p. 322 for citations.

[106] See David Baldus and James Cole, "A Comparison of the Work of Thorsten Sellin and Isaac Ehrlich on the Deterrent Effect of Capital Punishment," *Yale Law*

Journal 85 (December 1975), 171; and William Bailey, "Murder and Capital Punishment: Some Further Evidence," *American Journal of Orthopsychiatry* 45 (July 1975), 669–88.

[107] Leonard Savitz, "The Deterrent Effect of Capital Punishment in Philadelphia," in *The Death Penalty in America: An Anthology*, ed. Hugo Bedau (Garden City, N.Y.: Anchor Books, 1967), pp. 315–22.

[108] William Graves, "The Deterrent Effect of Capital Punishment in California," in ibid., pp. 322–32.

[109] Isaac Ehrlich, "The Deterrent Effect of Capital Punishment: A Matter of Life and Death," *American Economic Review* 65 (June 1975), 397–417. Regression analysis is discussed in detail in Chapter 14, which explains various statistical methods used in evaluation research.

[110] Isaac Ehrlich, "Capital Punishment and Deterrence: Some Further Thoughts and Additional Evidence," *Journal of Political Economy* 85 (August 1977), 741–88.

[111] Forst, op. cit.; and William Bowers and Glenn Pierce, "The Illusion of Deterrence in Isaac Ehrlich's Research on Capital Punishment," *Yale Law Journal* 85 (November 1975), 187–208.

[112] Bowers and Pierce, op. cit.

[113] 408 U.S. 238 (1972).

[114] Gregg v. Georgia, 428 U.S. 153 (1976).

[115] Quoted in Johannes Andenaes, "General Prevention Revisited: Research and Policy Implications," *Journal of Criminal Law and Criminology* 66 (September 1975), 358.

BIBLIOGRAPHY

Blumstein, Alfred; Cohen, Jacqueline; and Nagin, Daniel, eds. *Deterrence and Incapacitation: Estimating the Effects of Criminal Sanctions on Crime Rates*. Washington, D.C.: National Academy of Sciences, 1978.

Chambliss, William. "Types of Deviance and the Effectiveness of Legal Sanctions." *Wisconsin Law Review*, Summer 1967, pp. 703–19.

Ehrlich, Isaac. "The Deterrent Effect of Capital Punishment: A Matter of Life and Death." *American Economic Review* 65 (June 1975), 397–417.

Gibbs, Jack. *Crime, Punishment, and Deterrence*. New York: Elsevier, 1975.

Kelling, George; Pate, Tony; Dieckman, Duane; and Brown Charles. *The Kansas City Preventive Patrol Experiment: A Summary Report* (Washington, D.C.: Police Foundation, 1974).

Palmer, Jan. "Economic Analysis of the Deterrent Effect of Punishment: A Review." *Journal of Research in Crime and Delinquency* 14 (January 1977), 4–21.

Tullock, Gordon. "Does Punishment Deter Crime?" *Public Interest* 36 (Summer 1974), 103–11.

Wilson, James Q. *Thinking about Crime*. New York: Vintage Books, 1977.

Zeisel, Hans. "The Deterrent Effect of the Death Penalty: Facts v. Faiths." In *The Supreme Court Review, 1976*, edited by Philip Kurland. Chicago: University of Chicago Press, 1977, 317–43.

Zimring, Franklin, and Hawkins, Gordon. *Deterrence: The Legal Threat in Crime Control*. Chicago: University of Chicago, 1973.

Alex is a violent sex offender who is finally caught after he and his gang invade the house of Mr. Alexander, a well-known political reformer, and brutally rape his wife while he is forced to watch in horror. Under the government's program of dealing with the tremendous increase in crime, Alex is subjected to behavioral modification therapy in the Ludovico Medical Facility.

He is injected with a drug, bound up in a strait jacket, and has his eyes clamped open so that he cannot avoid viewing movies portraying violence and rape—all to the accompaniment of Beethoven's music. As the treatment progresses, Dr. Brodsky, the psychiatrist in charge, notes that Alex will very soon experience a deathlike paralysis together with deep feelings of terror and helplessness as he views the violent rape scenes. Dr. Brodsky explains: "Onc of our early test

CHAPTER TEN

REHABILITATION
The Orthodox Cure
for Criminal Behavior

subjects described it as being like death, a sense of stifling or drowning, and it is during this period that we have found that the subject will make the most rewarding associations between his catastrophic experience-environment and the violence he sees."

After a number of sessions of this kind, Alex finally shouts: "'You needn't take it any farther, sir. You've pointed out to me that this ultra violence and killing is wrong, wrong, and terribly wrong. I've learned my lesson, sir. I see now what I've never seen before. I'm cured, praise God!"

The therapy worked well on Alex, and so he is used as an example by the government in a public demonstration. Pointing to Alex after the demonstration, the prime minister announces that as a result of treatment like this "the problem of criminal violence is soon to be a thing of the past." [1]

Stanley Kubrick dramatized this behavioral modification program in *A Clockwork Orange*. Because it appeared in a film context, many people are inclined to believe it is not true to real life. But this is incorrect, for behavioral modification programs such as the one Alex went through, which included drug therapy, are actually being tried. For example, journalist Phil Stanford, describing the program at the Patuxent Institution for Defective Delinquents at Jessup, Maryland, provides the following account of a hearing for a teen-age inmate: *

An 18-year-old black takes his seat and folds his hands quietly before him on the table. The record says he was convicted of rape.

"At this time I would like to ask the board for leave," he says.

"All right," says Dr. Boslow.

"Tell us why you think you are ready for leave."

"When I first came to this institution I was a very confused and mixed-up 15-year-old boy. I had a low opinion of myself," he says.

He says he hated his father and mother. He tells how, when he was a small boy, his father would come home and beat him, then lock him in his room. He had come to have a low opinion of his mother because she hadn't done anything to stop it.

Boslow: Do you like yourself now?
Patient: Yes. I've come to accept myself. I accept my mother for what she is.
Boslow: How about your father?
Patient: He's dead.
Boslow: But that doesn't help. You know that you still carry your father with you in your mind. Until you come to accept your father too, you won't be able to solve anything.
Patient: Oh yes, I accept my father too.

The board votes unanimously to grant the leave.[2]

At Patuxent, as in the fictitious *Clockwork Orange*, the patient is released only after he demonstrates he is actually cured. When Alex is released from the Ludovico Medical Facility, he returns home and gives all indications of being permanently cured of his love for sex and violence. But he finds he cannot escape being the *object* of violence, first from the man who rented his room in his parent's house, then from a group of tramps, one of whom he had beat up before being sent to Ludovico, then from two policemen who were former gang members and rivals of his, and finally from Mr. Alexander, whose wife committed suicide after Alex and his gang had raped her. In the end we are not sure if Alex's cure held up in the face of all the violence directed at him after his release. In the final scene of the movie Alex is shown making love to a woman while saying, "I was cured, all right."

The Theory of Rehabilitation

The Patuxent and *Clockwork Orange* examples dramatize two important points. One is that behavioral modification, although it seems to produce a cure of violent criminals, may in fact be fiendish and sinister and, in the end, not really produce a cure at all. The second is that it may not matter if the individual is cured as long as society itself is shot through with violence, vengeful police, and ambitious, short-sighted politicians. In short, rehabilitation will not work if it aims only at curing violent individuals; society itself must be rehabilitated as well.

Behavior modification as practiced on Alex is only one aspect of the general policy of rehabilitation. More broadly, rehabilitation is the restoration of a criminal to a state of physical, mental, and moral health through treatment and training. The practice of rehabilitation is based on the belief that an offender's character, habits, or behavior patterns can be changed so as to diminish that person's criminal proclivities. Some psychiatrists believe that anyone can be cured by treatment. However, it generally is the impulsive criminal who ends in a treatment program. Professional criminals do not exhibit the same personality characteristics as the impulsive criminal. According to the director of the Patuxent Institution, the professional gunman cannot be distinguished from any other person: "He may very well have a wife and kids he's devoted to. . . . He'll probably live in a decent neighborhood, in a decent home. You know, it's just that he picks this peculiar way of earning a living."[3] So, if all of those who view themselves as professionals (as described in Chapter 3) are "normal" in all respects except in regard to how they make their living, they cannot be "restored" to a state of mental health. Rehabilitation, therefore, can be successful only with those who are "mentally" and/or "socially defective" in some way.

A number of rehabilitation methods have been tried in addition to behavior modification (a method, incidentally, that has been heavily criticized by professionals as well as through films such as Kubrick's). These methods include psychiatric therapy, education, religious conversion, group counseling, and community corrections. Each mode of rehabilitation is based upon a different underlying theory. Some are based upon psychological theories that relate criminal behavior to personality disorders, others are founded upon moral theories that postulate that criminal behavior is due to a failure of purpose, and still others derive from sociological theories of criminal behavior as a direct result of the failure of social institutions. Each of these theories leads to a different form of therapy, but all share the optimistic view of the positivist school of criminology that individuals *can* be convinced that they should turn away from criminal behavior. The positivist school of criminology dates back to the English philosopher Jeremy Bentham (1738–1842), who theorized that all individuals seek to avoid pain and seek pleasure, and will engage in an activity only if it is pleasurable.

The theory of self-interest underlying this book is similar to the positivist school's hedonistic theory, except that hedonism does not explain enough. Crime cannot simply be reduced by inducing individual offenders to amend their errant ways. For a successful crime-fighting strategy to work, it is necessary, in addition, to consider the self-interest of the victim, the police, judges, prosecutors, psychiatrists, and others. Crime will be reduced or controlled only if it is in the self-interest of enough groups affected by the particular crime to do something about it. An efficient crime-reduction strategy requires building a coalition of those whose self-interests are harmed by the continuation of a particular crime. If a coalition cannot be built because the groups affected by a crime have conflicting interests, or if such a coalition cannot include enough people to become a majority, then it is unrealistic to believe that crime can be reduced by rehabilitating those few offenders who are caught.

Not only is it unrealistic but it can be socially wasteful and harmful as well. Consider the "crime" of gambling. There are not enough groups whose self-interests are sufficiently harmed to reduce gambling very much. In fact, attempts to stop it may make its continuation more profitable for some groups. For example, corrupt police and government officials who receive payoffs profit more by the continuation of gambling than by its discontinuation. To attempt to "rehabilitate" individual gamblers in the hope that this will reduce the amount of gambling in society seems almost futile. Even if some gamblers can be cured, the individual offender is only one of a number of individuals and groups involved in this particular crime "subsystem," and not necessarily the most important one. If it is in the self-interest of others to see that gambling continues; they will ensure that gambling goes on, even if some individual gamblers are "rehabilitated."

What is true for gambling is equally true of other crimes, even violent crimes. Rehabilitating individual criminals will not necessarily reduce the general crime rate as long as economic, social, political, and psychological factors contributing to crimes are left uncorrected. The dean of the University of Chicago Law School, Norval Morris, notes ironically: "Virtually all criminals can have their subsequent violent crime dramatically reduced by detaining them in prison until their fiftieth birthday."[4] But, unfortunately, this will not reduce the general crime rate as long as others are out there ready to take the place of those who are incarcerated or rehabilitated.

Of course, rehabilitation can be justified on grounds other than its effect on the general crime rate. Some argue that society has a moral obligation to try to "straighten out" every criminal who is unfortunate enough to be caught, regardless of whether this policy reduces the general crime rate. This idea is similar to the religious notion that it is the moral duty of believers to try to convert others, whether it is sucessful or not—or even if the effort does not improve the general religious condition of society. In fact, this principle motivated the founders of rehabilitation programs in the United States. The first prisons were constructed as a "humanistic diversion" from the more cruel forms of retribution that were then practiced, such as drawing and quartering, and maiming. These early prisons ("penitentiaries") were places of silence and solitude aimed at providing time for the individual to reflect upon his or her ill deeds, repent, and be saved (rehabilitated). But over the years rehabilitation came to be justified more and more on the basis of its crime-reducing potential. The belief seems to have been that those who committed crimes constituted a small percentage of society, and if they could be identified and "cured," then the problem of criminal violence could be eradicated.

The same argument underlies the principle of incapacitation. It is believed that a relatively small percentage of all criminals commit the majority of violent crimes. If these few individuals can be identified and locked up permanently, the belief goes, society will be freed of violent crime. Unfortunately, the unstated assumption here is that these violent criminals will not be replaced by other violent criminals and that no one else will find such crime in his or her self-interest, or be socially, emotionally, and politically driven—or even accidentally fall—into violent criminal behavior. The assumption, of course, is wrong for it is likely that for every violent criminal who is caught and incapacited or rehabilitated, at least one other will begin a new career of violent crime.

Why will new individuals begin a life of violent crime or other forms of crime? A number of hypotheses have been forwarded in answer to this question. Bad social conditions produce in some individuals, alienation and hostility, which find expression in violence and crime. Political conditions necessitate violence as a method of reform and change. Individuals inherit certain genetic characteristics that predispose them toward violence. Particular and sometimes accidental circumstances of family life teach some individuals that violent behavior is a desirable mode of expression. It is in the self-interest of some, such as poor people, to engage in certain kinds of crime, such as gambling, because the potential benefits far exceed the costs.

Other hypotheses could be generated to explain why people turn to crime, but it is not our purpose here to discuss the causes of criminal behavior (see Chapter 3). The point we want to make is that rehabilitation will not work if the only goal (and justification) is to reduce the general crime rate.

But, it might be asked, can rehabilitation work in the sense that it can cure particular individuals and thus turn them away from a life of crime? If so, sufficient justification may then exist to follow a policy of rehabilitation. Moreover, rehabilitation for this purpose may be more effective because we will not have unrealistic expectations of what it can accomplish. Suppose we know that we can successfully rehabilitate 60 percent of all criminals who are caught and given a chance to participate voluntarily in various rehabilitation programs, even if this does not have much impact on the general crime rate; should we then pursue it as a major criminal justice policy? The answer seems obvious. Of course we should. While rehabilitation may not have a large impact on the crime rate because only a small number of criminals are caught while at the same time, new people are beginning criminal careers, we should still not neglect to rehabilitate that 60 percent; to do otherwise would be morally remiss. The situation is analogous to not providing a cure for skin cancer simply because others might contract the disease.

Of course, other factors besides society's moral obligation have to be considered. Cost is one such factor. If it costs society $100,000 to rehabilitate one offender, is the policy then justifiable? The answer to this question is more difficult because it involves the important issues of how much society is obliged to help its wayward members and what the cost to society may be if it does not rehabilitate an offender. Is it just for society to spend $100,000 on one who has broken the law, as is often done, when we spend only about $16,000 for the education of a child in a typical city?

Another factor that must be considered is the state of the art in rehabilitation. If present techniques of rehabilitation do not work but we know we are on the verge of discovering effective techniques that will work if society gives them adequate support, is a policy of rehabilitation then justifiable? The answer to this depends upon how close the techniques are to working, how much support is needed, what alternative policies can be pursued with this same level of support, and whether or not key individuals and officials are willing to continue to risk supporting a policy that has not fully demonstrated its worthiness.

This, approximately, is the situation facing the policy of rehabilitation today. Corrections officials and the general public still have a great deal of faith in rehabilitation as a policy. But some believe it is now a relatively conservative policy because it is supported by the criminal justice establishment and the general public and because it has been in existence for more than 30 years.[5] Rehabilitation is, in fact, a large industry consisting of professional psychologists, psychiatrists, sociologists, social workers, probation and parole officers, prison officials, reformers, and a number of others. And more and more criminologists have come to question the effectiveness of this rehabilitation industry. The principal objections to rehabilitation are that it has not been shown to actually work, it has not helped reduce the crime rate, and it has been used as a means of controlling offenders without due process, thereby violating the principles of justice, because individuals subjected to rehabilitation programs are completely at the mercy of those running the program.[6] We shall evaluate these arguments in the remainder of this chapter.

Modes of Rehabilitation

A number of different rehabilitation methods have been developed. Some are more likely to be successful with one class of offenders, while other methods may work better with different classes. One of the more difficult problems in rehabilitation is matching the right treatment method with the appropriate patient. Some of the failure of rehabilitation may be due to this problem. Also, it may not be possible to rehabilitate some kinds of criminals. Earlier, we mentioned professional criminals and described them in Chapter 3. Quite possibly professional criminals cannot be rehabilitated because they are not suffering from mental problems, as is assumed by all methods of rehabilitation. Professional criminals engage in crime because they believe the benefits exceed the costs, not because they hate society or because they have an uncontrollable impulse to do something violent. Thus, the only approach for professional criminals may be deterrence. For the most part in the discussion that follows, we shall concentrate on criminals who do not believe they are professionals.

THERAPEUTIC TREATMENT

The psychiatric approach to rehabilitation is based on the assumption that some criminals suffer from personality disorders. If these disorders can be properly diagnosed and treated, then it is possible to rehabilitate or "cure" such criminals.

406

What are those personality disorders? They include antisocial traits that display personal hostility. Researchers at the University of California, Davis, Medical School, compared 25 nonviolent male offenders, 25 nonhabitually violent male offenders, and 25 habitually violent male offenders on a number of psychosocial descriptors. They found that all violent offenders tended to report less provocation when involved in a fight, to be more alone, and to act more impulsively than the nonviolent offenders. The habitually violent offenders had more childhood problems such as tantrums, enuresis, nail biting, hyperactivity, and fighting.[7] A number of other studies have correlated certain personality characteristics with criminal propensity, including a less favorable attitude toward law, greater negativism toward others, more suspicion of others, and fewer feelings of guilt when they did something wrong.[8]

The most frequent diagnosis of a criminal's personality is "sociopathy"— behavior that violates social norms. Thus psychiatrists frequently classify as mental illness behavior that is socially defined as deviant—behavior such as aggression, negativism, and hostility.[9]

The term *sociopathy* has recently been dropped by some psychiatrists, who now prefer the term *defective delinquent* for youthful offenders. One of the psychiatrists at the Patuxent Institution for Defective Delinquents describes those he treats in the following way:*

> My own feeling is that probably the most basic thing is their inability to make any strong identifications with other people, and by that I mean they don't become a real member of the group. They are not team players; they don't have strong loyalties to their country, toward their family, toward anyone. Their affectionate relationships are very shallow. They become involved in numerous affairs with women, frequently with multiple marriages. . . .
>
> Then there is this underlying hostility which manifests itself in many ways. As I said before, there is, in a sense, a war with society, and they get great satisfaction in seeing what they can get away with in their acting out against society. . . . They frequently have conflict with teachers because part of their pattern is to be in conflict with authority figures. . . . They can't take criticism with any degree of equanimity, so that their work records are almost universally very fugitive. They rarely stick to anything for any length of time. They are basically hedonistic, and they must satisfy their needs as rapidly as they possibly can and at the expense of others.[10]

In short, the picture developed here of the juvenile offender is one of a "rebel without a cause." When James Dean portrayed this role in the film of that name, the personality type that is called a "defective delinquent" by psychiatrists became the antihero and idol of a generation of youth. Apparently, young people do not agree with psychiatrists that hostile youths are defective.

Some researchers no longer classify antisocial behavior as mental illness. A 1978 study of the criminal personality by psychiatrists Samuel Yochelson and Stanley E. Samenow concluded that habitual criminals possess thinking patterns that distinguish them from noncriminals and that the development of these criminal thinking patterns has little or nothing to do with either social circumstances or mental illness. The habitual criminal, they say, is a liar and a deceiver; he has little capacity for friendship and love; he can commit brutal acts without a twinge of conscience and yet continue to believe he is a "good" person. He finds the "restraints of responsible living unacceptable and even contemptible," the authors write. Further, they say, "the criminal disregards other people's right to live safely, but demands that others show him the utmost respect and consideration. . . . Untrustworthy himself, he demands that others trust him."[11] This study, which was based on clinical interviews of 240 men over a period of years, has been severely criticized both because it is methodologically defective (the sample is not random) and because it leads to the conclusion that nothing can be done to correct criminals. The authors say that violent criminals are cruel people who, while they are young, tear the heads off cats and are brutal and vicious. The blame is thus placed on the individual criminal rather than on society or the institutions that are unable to correct him.

Another group of researchers, who studied murders, found that some murders are committed by individuals who are constantly frustrated by people, agencies, and institutions, and who suddenly lose their composure. Among the individuals studied were an 11-year-old boy in Phoenix, Arizona, who stabbed his brother 34 times with a steak knife, and a "gentle, easy going, good-natured" young man who five days after graduation killed three unarmed people during a bank robbery.[12] The researchers found that individuals such as these, who are normally extremely shy, lack social and verbal skills. They tend to be more passive and see themselves as more feminine than the other violent criminals included in the study. Unable to adjust to a situation in which they feel frustrated and belittled, they build resentment. Then one day a minor provocation pushes them over the threshold, and impulse turns into action.

Can such individuals be cured? The researchers who conducted the study concluded that several kinds of treatment can be effective in curing individuals who suddenly become violent. Training in social skills is effective, they believe. This includes basic conversational skills—how to make demands in assertive rather than aggressive ways, for example. The overcontrolled shy murderer must also learn basic social skills, but different ones, the researchers write: "He must express feelings directly, to identify and respond to frustrations as they occur, instead of letting them build up."[13]

But others disagree. The therapy referred to above is based on talking, a middle-class skill that lower-income individuals often lack. Moreover, the patient is under the control of the therapist only for a short while. How can the therapist correct deficiencies that have been implanted in individuals at some unknown time during their youth? These "root causes" of crime may well be something that cannot be changed by government.[14]

The research team that investigated shy murderers maintain: "The social skills we've outlined should be learned by every child as a normal part of socialization. Children should be encouraged to express their feelings and to like themselves."[15] Perhaps they should, but there is no way to ensure this.

While psychiatrists may have succeeded in identifying certain personality traits of criminal behavior, they have not shown how these might be changed so as to reduce criminal proclivities. In fact, the "personality disorders" may be of such a nature that they cannot be corrected through conventional psychotherapy. The rehabilitation rate of institutions that are supposed to correct offenders, such as the Patuxent Institution for Defective Delinquents, indicates that personality disorders cannot be cured through psychotherapy. Once patients are committed to an institution such as Patuxent, they must stay there until the staff believes they are cured. The majority of inmates serve beyond their original sentences. In nearly 18 years of operation, out of a total of 985 patients committed to Patuxent, only 115 were released as cured—not a very high rate of success.[16]

Psychiatrists cannot agree in their diagnosis of what is wrong with criminals. Their diagnostic skills are not refined enough to enable accurate predictions about who is likely to engage in violent criminal behavior in the future. The case of the notorious "Son of Sam" murderer in New York demonstrates how much disagreement can exist. The two court-appointed psychiatrists who were asked to examine David Berkowitz, the person who was later convicted for the murders, concluded that he was "emotionally dead" and therefore unable to take part in his own defense. But another psychiatrist appointed by the Brooklyn prosecutor's office argued that Berkowitz was competent. Justice John R. Starkey agreed and ordered Berkowitz to stand trial, commenting that psychiatry is a "very inexact science." Another justice, when asked if he was surprised about the contradictory findings replied, "I learned a long time ago not to be surprised by anything a psychiatrist says."[17]

The conflicting testimony of psychiatric experts in court trials have raised serious questions about the role of psychiatry in diagnosing and treating criminals. One study has found that psychiatrists are unable to spot and predict which offenders are likely to be dangerous. The study, conducted by Joseph Cocozza and Henry Steadman, researchers with the New York State Department of Mental Hygiene, looked at 257 men indicted for felonies but found mentally incompetent to stand trial. In each case the judge relied on the advice of court-appointed psychiatrists to decide in which state facility to place the defendants. The psychiatrists' duty was to evaluate the defendants and determine which were dangerous. Those considered dangerous were sent to maximum-security mental hospitals. A total of 118 psychiatrists evaluated the 257 men and labeled 154 of them dangerous. Researchers followed the 257 men for three years. They found that the "dangerous" group was slightly more violent during the months of hospitalization. But, once released, only 14 percent of those labeled dangerous were later arrested for violent crimes, compared to 16 percent of those considered not dangerous. In other words, the ones labeled dangerous by the 118 "expert" psychiatrists were no more dangerous than those labeled not dangerous.[18]

Other studies support this conclusion. A study by M. J. R. Harper of the Smith College School for Social Work concluded that "the use of psychiatric professionals lies more in their consultative, diagnostic, and treatment skills and less in the area of prediction and social control where psychiatrists with their medical authority have been functioning as arms of the court."[19] Another study examined what happened to nearly 1,000 patients transferred from two New York State hospitals for the criminally insane to private mental hospitals in 1966 as a result of a United States Supreme Court decision. Four years later, about 50 percent were still in private mental hospitals, 27 percent were back in the community, and 14 percent had died. Only 3 percent had been returned to a correctional facility or a hospital for the criminally insane.[20] And a study of 60 men who had been released from a maximum-security hospital concluded: "Men who had been found unfit to stand trial or not guilty by reason of insanity before their admission were less likely to get into difficulty upon release than men who had been admitted for other reasons."[21]

Psychiatrists have not been very good at predicting or diagnosing criminal behavior and their record in curing criminals is not much better. Psychiatry thus does not seem to hold much promise as a way of rehabilitating criminals.

GROUP THERAPY

In recent years group methods of therapy and counseling, including role playing and reality therapy, have become increasingly popular. Role playing involves acting out criminal situations in a group setting, and reality therapy forces offenders to recognize the gravity of their offenses. One study reports a project for misdemeanants in a county workhouse involving 18- to 31-year-old males who

Prisoner acting out a criminal situation in a group session

were given intensive prerelease and postrelease group counseling. Compared to a matched group of misdemeanants who were not given such therapy, they committed fewer total offenses and had a much lower rate of serious felonies in the follow-up period.[22]

Another large-scale experiment in Dannemora, New York, was based on the idea that the entire staff, including the guards, had to be involved in what was called the "therapeutic community," defined as a community where all relationships are deliberately used as a social learning experience. In such a community the treated patients work along with the professionally trained staff. The goal is to rehabilitate as many offenders as possible. The Dannemora project was for persistent offenders only. Different from incidental offenders, persistent offenders are unable to conform to life around them either in or out of prison. Their regression from the responsibilities of life is deeper, and prison confirms their attitude of being unwanted and unwelcome.[23] According to a Rand Corporation study, persistent offenders are more likely to see themselves as professional criminals who engage in progressively more rational criminality, are more likely to be "losers," and steal as a reaction to frustration and humiliation; they are also more likely to be caught.[24]

Logically, we might expect it to be difficult to rehabilitate persistent offenders, since they have rationally calculated that crime pays. The best approach should be to deter them by increasing the likelihood of their being caught and punished. The Rand Corporation study cited above concluded that the most effective way to prevent crime for persistent offenders is to imprison them while they are young, since their crimes taper off after reaching a peak from about 25 to 31 years of age. The Dannemora experiment, however, attempted to reeducate and resocialize persistent offenders who volunteered for treatment. They were given the greatest possible freedom and flexibility in the program. Although the inmates were allowed to turn up for work and any other activity when they wanted, the project nevertheless emphasized good work habits, self-discipline, and toleration of inevitable daily frustrations. A community meeting of inmates and staff was held five days a week. On Saturday morning two other therapy techniques—role playing and sociodrama—were used. The daily sessions included corrections officers, who, it was discovered, rapidly learned psychiatric techniques. The program was based upon the idea that "the greater the aversion to work, the more evident is other pathology in the personality." A man's work record can be seen, the study director believed, as an extension of his school record and, earlier still, of his family relationships. "Persistent delinquency is only one aspect of a complex pathology, only one aspect of a person who is unable to relate, unable to remain free in society."[25]

The researchers were unable to demonstrate that the project succeeded in reducing the recidivism of those who participated. In fact, the director of the program believes that recidivism is a poor criterion for evaluating the program. Changes in the person's habits, thinking, and ability to learn are considered better criteria, and, the researchers were able to show improvements in behavior based in these factors.

It is difficult to see how an individual who has improved in work habits, thinking, and in the ability to work, but who still commits a crime when released, can be considered a success. Recidivism may not be the best criterion for measuring the success of a rehabilitation program, for reasons we shall discuss below, but rehabilitation can only be said to occur when an offender turns away from a life of crime. Apparently, this did not happen at Dannemora.

Like the Dannemora program, treatment at the Patuxent Institution relies heavily upon group therapy. Patients attend weekly group sessions where "they are made aware of their feelings and attitudes and how these are related to their antisocial behavior."[26] The Patuxent system uses both positive and negative reinforcers such as rewards and greater freedom, on the one hand, and greater restrictions, on the other hand. The positive reinforcers are based on a four-level program. Patients move from a lower to the next level as they demonstrate socially acceptable behavior. Each level provides more privileges and responsibilities. For example, fourth-level patients can stay up as long as they want, whereas third-level patients must go to bed by 11:30 P.M. Fourth-level patients are allowed to have Sunday afternoon picnics with guests, while others are not. When they convince the Board of Review they are cured, they are released. The indeterminate sentence, therefore, is essential to the operation of the program. The director at Patuxent believes that indeterminate sentencing is a mechanism for making patients realize that they need help. Because the inmates cannot defer gratification, their primary drive is to return to society, and the indeterminate sentence is thus used as the ultimate positive reinforcer. Negative reinforcement includes solitary confinement and sensory deprivation, such as no lights in the small cell where offenders are placed if they are not cooperative. Those who do not change are not released or are reassigned to the state penitentiary.

As we said above, the therapy at Patuxent has not shown a very high degree of success. This may be due to the fact that the Patuxent program focused on "defective delinquents," the impulsive and incidental offender. The problem facing group therapy is the same as all therapeutic approaches: it can only work on those offenders who are suffering from personality disorders. These are most likely to be the hardest to rehabilitate. The negative self-image that the impulsive criminal has is not likely to be corrected through individual or group therapy alone. A sense of self-worth and esteem, some believe, can be instilled only in a community setting. Offenders must come to see that society believes they are worthy people, and this can only be accomplished through community acceptance—the assumption underlying community-corrections approaches, such as halfway houses.

HALFWAY HOUSES

A halfway house is a small residence that people released from prison may use as a temporary residence while they adapt to society. The Delancey Street Foundation in San Francisco, started by an ex-offender named John Maher, is one of the

Group therapy at the Delancey Street Foundation.

better known of these programs. The program's success has been judged by political scientist Charles Hampden-Turner to be due to the games played in group-therapy sessions, during which rage and hostility are discharged "in a kind of psychic toilet."[27] Criminals who are admitted have decided to heal themselves. Based upon Maher's philosophy that criminals are not nice guys gone wrong but nasty, twisted characters, the program emphasizes discipline and authority coupled with a belief in the therapeutic value of the community.

Convicts, Maher believes, must accept responsibility for their own condition and become stronger than the forces that victimize them. Delancey Street is seen by Maher "as a cure for the disease of the self-destructive personality who uses drugs, and other people, and himself, badly."[28] From infancy onward, Delancey Street convicts lacked the opportunity and failed to develop the capacity for intimate personal relations with parents or partners. Yet they want to be successful in life just like law-abiding citizens. Group therapy makes them confront these conflicts. John Maher (speaking as an ex-convict) says:

> We don't admit this to ourselves, but *most convicts are scum*. Of course, social conditions *made* them that way. They've been fucked over, and they fuck each other. Point is, that's never going to change, *until we take responsibility for our condition*. To see that we're scum is to realize we don't have to be.[29]

Halfway houses such as Delancey Street are based on the notion that individuals are best treated in a setting located within society, not in isolation from it, and, like Delancey Street, many have had some success. They are usually located in neighborhoods that provide a range of resources for integrating the individual into the community. They serve juvenile offenders as well as adults, drug and alcohol offenders as well as the mentally retarded. Usually manned by ex-offenders and small in size, they are based upon the notion that everyone should be involved in the treatment process. In addition, the community's attitudes and perceptions of itself and of offenders must change for rehabilitation to work. The community must develop a tolerance for deviant behavior and be willing to work with offenders.

However, many communities are unwilling to accept halfway houses or convicts in their midst, fearing a potential threat to their safety. Just like integrated housing projects, they are usually supported as long as they are located in someone else's neighborhood.

Some states have moved toward relying upon community corrections as an alternative to prison. Kansas, for example, enacted a Community Corrections Act in 1978. The act provides that counties be given incentives, in the form of grants by the state, to retain individuals convicted of nonviolent crimes in community corrections programs within their own boundaries rather than send them to state prisons. However, evaluation of the success of community corrections programs is spotty. One controlled study of a halfway house took all offenders sentenced to the county jail and randomly assigned them to a halfway house or to the jail. The recidivism rate for the two groups was about the same, but the halfway house group had a higher level of employment.[30]

Another program that grew out of a unique collaborative effort involving a university, a large steel corporation, and federal, state, and local agencies included 77 participants assigned to a halfway house rather than to jail. When they entered the house, they were assured that they could expect a well-paying job with the steel corporation and that each would be given shelter and an allowance for at least six weeks if they were temporarily unemployed. The focus of the program was vocational but included other supportive measures such as recreation, psychological testing and counseling, medical care, and education. Contrary to expectations, the recidividm rate for the inhabitants was not lower than the rate for all state reformatory releases.[31]

An evaluation of the community corrections program in Des Moines, Iowa, concluded that it was successful in reducing recidivism, but a study of community treatment centers in Oklahoma found that recidivism was higher than for individuals sent to medium- and maximum-security prisons.[32] Thus, there is evidence both pro and con that community corrections may be a better alternative than incarceration. It is really too early to reach any final conclusions about halfway houses and community corrections because they are relatively new types of approaches to rehabilitation and there is not enough experience to allow definite conclusions.

EDUCATION AND WORK RELEASE

Programs involving education and vocational training in prison have not had any more success in rehabilitating criminals than therapy and halfway houses. A number of studies have shown that vocational training in prison is not used outside of prison.[33] An intensive review of evaluative studies found that education and vocational training for inmates have not been shown to have consistent or positive effect on recidivism.[34] An earlier study by criminologist Daniel Glaser found that prison educational and vocational programs failed to rehabilitate.[35] Work-release programs have fared a little better. Work release permits a prisoner to leave prison each day to go to a job and return to the prison at night. Work-release programs, used in 41 states, usually accept prisoners near the end of their term. Sometimes they will be housed in a county jail or halfway house while working. Prisoners work in a variety of jobs, including welding, small appliance repair, and health services. The participants usually sign an agreement in which they agree to travel by the quickest route to and from work without stops, not to visit family or friends, and to refrain from taking drugs or drinking liquor.

Evaluations of work-release programs have concluded that they are generally successful. There are some failures, however, including New York City's work-release program, in which 4,000 prisoners participated. From 1970 to 1977, 50 percent of these prisoners either escaped or were returned to prison for breaking the rules of the program. An investigation of the program found serious deficiencies in security, administration, and operations. Studies were made of the program in 1970 and 1971 and from 1974 through 1976 by agencies such as the New York City Rand Institute, the Urban Coalition, and the Corrections Department itself, all of which recommended changes. But they were all ignored.[36] For reasons we shall discuss in Chapter 14, it is not unusual for studies of programs to be ignored. As we shall show later, only under special circumstances is information about the success or failure of programs followed.

Although the New York City program was a failure, many others have been successful. A job is the most important need for a released prisoner since unemployment has been found to be a major factor contributing to further violations.[37] Most released prisoners have to find a job themselves, and the successful ones rely upon friends or former employers. However, ex-convicts face severe obstacles in the way of finding jobs. Among the obstacles they must overcome are licensing restrictions, civil service rules, and bonding requirements. Bonding usually is required of persons who handle valuables on their job, and it guarantees that a bonding company will pay for any valuables that are missing. Until recently, ex-convicts had a hard time acquiring bonds, but a federally funded bonding-assistance program enables an employer or applicant to apply for a bond through their state employment service. Over 6,655 bonds were issued by the program through July 1974 with a default rate of less·than 2 percent. This has helped overcome the bonding barrier, but the other two areas—licensing restrictions and civil service rules—have been less successfully dealt with. Consequently, released prisoners, whether or not they participate in a work-release program, are likely to end in a dead-end job such as waiter or clerk; and they usually last only two to three months in such jobs. Obviously, changes in society's rules and attitudes about ex-convicts are required for work-release programs to work.

PAROLE

Shortly after Alex in *A Clockwork Orange* blurted out that he was cured and the officials who were treating him agreed, he was released from prison and allowed to return home. If he had not been cured, he would not have been released. This, of course, is the idea upon which parole decisions are supposed to be based. An offender is given an indeterminate sentence by the judge, such as 5 to 20 years, and the parole board decides how long the offender will actually serve. In making that decision parole board members consider a number of factors, among which the most important is supposed to be whether or not the offender has been "cured." In fact, of course, this is seldom the major factor in the decision.

All states have parole boards, usually consisting of from three to five members. The National Advisory Commission on Criminal Justice Standards and Goals recommends that parole members have training in fields such as criminology, education, psychology, psychiatry, law, social work, or sociology as well as "a high degree of skill in comprehending legal issues and statistical information and an ability to develop and promulgate policy."[38] But 24 states have no statutory requirements at all, and 21 states refer only very broadly to experience and training. The remaining states have some requirements, but these do not meet the national commission's standards. Most appointments are based on political patronage. The term of a parole board member is usually from four to six years, and the median salary of an associate member of the parole board was $21,280 in 1975.[39] Most parole boards have a professional staff, consisting of case analysts, who keep records and prepare reports.

In making its decision, the parole board holds hearings in the prison. A hearing focuses on the individual's prison record as well as some acknowledgment of responsibility for his or her crime. Thus, time is spent going over the details of the crime, including the offender's motivation, personal background, criminal record, whether a weapon was used, the parole plan, and the recommendation of the prison staff. But not much time is given to each prisoner. A parole board hears about 30 cases a day in a 6-hour period, so each case receives about 12 minutes. The hearing thus serves more as a symbolic than an information-gathering function.

Most parole boards are more concerned with whether the offender will commit a crime or be a danger to the community than with whether the offender has been cured. Commission of a violent offense by a parolee may damage a board's reputation, and the wish to avoid embarrassment is a strong motivating factor for parole board members.[40] But parole boards are not very successful at predicting criminal behavior. One study divided 592 male offenders into two groups—those who were not predicted to be dangerous and those who were. The study found that 8.6 percent of the former and 6.1 percent of the latter subsequently committed a violent crime.[41] This small difference between the two groups shows that predictions were not reliable.

Individual behavior is never very predictable. We can predict that a group of heavy cigarette smokers is likely to have a higher rate of lung cancer, but we cannot say that any specific individual in the group will get lung cancer. An individual can have the characteristic statistically associated with higher recidivism, such as minority-group status, unemployment, drug use, and a prior record, but we cannot say that he or she will definitely be a recidivist. One who is predicted to be a recidivist but who does not relapse into crime is known as a "false positive"—and it is nearly impossible to identify such a person. The most that can be done is to arrive at a *probability* that an individual will be a recidivist. Thus, it is statistically legitimate to say that the probability is very high that a person will commit a violent crime in the future, but the prediction may turn out to be wrong. Since all predictions are necessarily probability statements, errors in prediction cannot be avoided.

Parole boards will continue to base their decisions on the criterion of protecting the community more than on whether an offender is rehabilitated because parole boards are very susceptible to community sentiment. For example, the parole board in Washington, D.C., greatly diminished the number of prisoners assigned to community centers after the chief of police announced that many of the city's crimes were being committed by individuals on parole.[42] Only a few bad decisions that receive a lot of publicity are needed to cause a parole board to become more strict in granting parole.

Once the parole board decides to release a prisoner, the individual is assigned to a parole officer, who is responsible for keeping the person under surveillance, attempting to help, and providing services such as job counseling or making contacts with social service agencies, as well as deciding whether or not to revoke parole. Little attempt is made to match the parolee and the parole officer in making these assignments. The example of a stern, middle-aged parole officer who told a young parolee to go to church regularly and not cause trouble is not unusual. The parolee remarked, "I need white trash advice like that like I need a private jet."[43] There is evidence that matching would help. One study of the matching of probation officers (whose job is similar to that of parole officers) and clients concluded, "Evidence suggests possible improvement through planned matching of clients to officers based on client and officer personality profiles."[44] But just how much improvement would occur is hard to determine. Certainly a great deal of improvement could not be expected because factors other than matching are much more important contributors to success or failure.

Given existing caseloads, a parolee can expect to receive less than six and one-half hours of supervision from the parole officer a year, which consists mostly of checking to see that the parolee is not violating any of the conditions of release. One of the important recommendations made by experts is that the caseload of parole officers be reduced to 30 per officer. Caseloads tend to be as high as 80 to 90 per officer.[45] But the evidence about whether the parole officer can do better with a smaller caseload is negative. In fact, smaller caseloads and greater contact increase the chances of detecting a violation. Of course, this would not be bad if it usually involved violations of serious rules, but most often parole is revoked for violation of relatively minor rules, such as traveling out of town without permission or for speeding.

Decisions to revoke or take away parole from those who are released on parole are based on bureaucratic factors rather than on how well the released prisoner is behaving. A study by criminologists James Robinson and Paul Takagi found that decisions to revoke parole frequently are based on who happened to be in charge and the attitude the boss held about the offenders. Robinson and Tagaki write:

> There are tendencies toward agreement among agents within a given office, but large differences in recommendation patterns between officers. While there is some indication that the agent's personal background (his educational specialty and prior types of jobs) has a bearing on these judgments, and that his current value orientation is involved, the most definite correlate shown in the present study was the agent's assessment of his supervisor's orientation.[46]

Changes in the revocation rate, especially a drop in the rate, are attributable to increased pressure upon agents to recommend continued parole supervision for many types of violators—a pressure originating from headquarters and transmitted through unit supervisors.

Evaluating parole officers' work is difficult because they aim to achieve contradictory goals. On the one hand, they supervise released prisoners and thus act as society's control agents to ensure the safety of society. On the other hand, they are supposed to be friends, counselors, and helpers to the offender. These are incompatible roles. It is difficult to act as a friend while at the same time spying on an individual to see if he or she has violated a rule. Frustration over their inability to perform both roles, plus bureaucratic pressures such as those discussed above, force parole officers into shallow, meaningless exchanges with their charges that usually involve checking on them to see if they are following the rules.

Seventy-five percent of those released on parole succeed, 5 percent abscond, 15 percent have their parole revoked as technical violators, and 5 percent are returned for a new crime.[47] Parolees are successes if they complete their time without having parole revoked or being returned for a new crime. The question is whether the 75 percent who succeed would do so regardless of whether they were placed on parole. Would their recidivism rate be any higher if they were simply released from prison and not placed on parole? The evidence is unclear.

So, too, is the evidence unclear concerning the success or failure of probation. We can look to probation to provide clues about the success of parole programs, for parole and probation are similar in all respects except in regard to when the offender is released. Those on probation are released without incarceration (and thus are more likely to have committed less serious crimes or be first offenders), whereas those on parole are released only after having served some time in prison. We discussed probation in detail in Chapter 8 because it technically is considered a sentencing option. Persons placed on parole, on the other hand, presumably have demonstrated that they have been rehabilitated. In both parole and probation, however, the method of supervision used is similar enough to enable us to evaluate their effectiveness together. First, the best risks are placed on probation or parole, and we should *expect* their success rate to be higher than those who are not given probation or parole.[48] Second, the outcome in both cases depends somewhat on the type of offenders. An Australian study of 223 juvenile offenders given probation and 223 committed to detention, matched on a number of characteristics, found recidivism was higher after detention than after probation; however, for behavior problems (i.e., vandalism, truancy, running away) results were the same for both groups, auto theft offenders responded better to detention, and offenders previously in institutions responded better to probation.[49] In a study by criminologists Robert Martinson and Judith Wilks, recidivism was compared for persons released under parole supervision and those released directly from prison after serving their maximum sentence. The authors controlled for seriousness of crimes, age, sex, race, and a number of other factors that might explain differences in recidivism. The results showed that the mean recidivism rate was lower for those given parole than for those released without supervision. They concluded, "The evidence indicates that abolition of supervision may result in substantially increased rates of arrest, conviction, and return to prison."[50]

However, the problem in evaluating the success of parole and probation is finding measures that show the extent to which parolees refrain from criminal behavior as a result of what happens in the parole system. The principal question relates to whether recidivism should be used as a measure of failure or success. We shall return to this question later in the chapter.

Problems with Rehabilitation

The evidence about what mode of treatment will succeed in rehabilitating criminals is uneven. But regardless of the evidence, there are a number of social and intellectual forces working against rehabilitation that threaten to overwhelm it. Intellectually, a number of "objective" studies have been produced documenting the failure of rehabilitation. The social opposition comes from a number of different quarters. Civil libertarians find that indeterminate sentences make a prisoner's freedom dependent upon highly arbitrary judgments of corrections officials and open to abuses by behavioral modifiers. Conservatives believe that the increase in crime is due to coddling of prisoners in such rehabilitation programs.

Some believe that justice should be the principal goal of corrections, and it is not well served by rehabilitation; others believe that crime prevention should be given more attention than "curing" criminals after the fact. Some critics base their opposition upon sheer economic and cost considerations, whereas other opponents are simply disenchanted with prisons as institutions. Are all of these forces likely to bring about the end of rehabilitation in the United States?

Seeing the possible imminent demise of rehabilitation, a number of experts have begun to rally to its defense. But the social forces and evidence against rehabilitation are formidable. Former Attorney General William Saxbe declared in 1974: "Rehabilitation is a myth. I think that punishment has a place, and if you catch people and you prosecute them, and you punish them, it is a deterrent to crime." Saxbe's successor, Edward Levi, told a national governor's conference that the "rehabilitative idea" is dead. Former President Gerald Ford said in his last State of the Union Address: "To keep a convicted criminal from committing more crimes, we must put him in prison so he cannot harm law-abiding citizens. To be effective this punishment must be swift, and it must be certain." And the United States Justice Department put a veritable freeze on prisoner rehabilitation programs in 1975–1976. The mass media has joined the chorus. On television, Mike Wallace of "Sixty Minutes" dolefully announced, "Rehabilitation doesn't work. Nothing works."[51] Senator Edward Kennedy supported a Senate bill in 1978 that would put an end to indeterminate sentencing in federal courts and eliminate the possibility of rehabilitation. The negative conclusions that his actions expressed about rehabilitation have been reached outside the United States as well. A report from Sweden, the country that boasts one of the world's most progressive and humane prison systems, states that the rate of recidivism there is 70 percent. "Our philosophy of rehabilitation has been shipwrecked," says Sweden's chief prosecutor. "Criminality will not be cured through prison rehabilitation."[52]

A number of reasons have been cited for rehabilitation's apparent failure. Some believe that it has not been given adequate support. Some think that it cannot work as long as it is forced upon prisoners. Some argue that it can work only in a community setting, not in prisons. Some point to the fact that, to be successful, rehabilitation requires collaborative efforts on the part of a number of groups and agencies that realistically are impossible to attain. And some attack the fundamental assumption underlying rehabilitation philosophy. Harvard political scientist James Q. Wilson, for example, writes:

> It requires not merely optimistic but heroic assumptions about the nature of man to lead one to suppose that a person, finally sentenced after (in most cases) many brushes with the law, and having devoted a good part of his youth and young adulthood to misbehavior of every sort, should, by either the solemnity of prison or the skillfulness of a counselor, come to see the error of his ways, and to experience a transformation of his character.[53]

Liberal criminologists such as Sol Chaneles point to the modest sums of money being spent on rehabilitation programs as the principal reason for their failure. "It's odd that the government is making such a fuss about it," Chaneles writes.

> The cost of all forms of federal, state, and local rehabilitation amounts to less than five percent of the $5 billion annually spent on prison operations and construction. In general, the U.S. spends less than $100 per inmate per year for recreation, religion, social work, medical care, psychotherapy, counseling, education, job training, and placement for the more than two million men, women, and youths who pass through the country's prisons each year.[54]

Chaneles believes that bad prisons make bad prisoners worse. George Bernard Shaw said that you cannot expect to turn a tiger into a Quaker by putting him in a cage. If the purpose of prison is to resocialize inmates, that cannot occur in an isolated place apart from society.[55]

So, part of the problem may be inadequate support of rehabilitation programs, and part may be that rehabilitation cannot work in a prison setting, where the prisoner is forced to participate in rehabilitation programs as a condition for release. It is this last aspect of rehabilitation that particularly disturbs advocates of civil liberties. The rehabilitation system leaves experts with unrestrained discretion. Used arbitrarily, discretion in the hands of parole boards, psychologists, counselors, and other corrections officials is antithetical to notions of fairness. People should not be sentenced to receive help; it should be made available, but not mandatory.[56]

Rehabilitation in a community setting is not necessarily better because it does not make participation any more voluntary than in prison settings, and it requires the cooperation and coordination of a number of groups and agencies whose self-interests may often be in conflict. Police, for example, would have to relinquish somewhat their self-perception as "crime fighters" and attempt to help rehabilitate offenders. But they tend to be uncomfortable in the role. A number of conflicts arise among police, courts, and corrections institutions that might militate against achievement of rehabilitation goals. To make community rehabilitation work requires a change in the entire criminal justice system. A study by Daniel Glaser notes that the chaotic cross-purposes begin with legislators who make victimless behavior, such as drinking and gambling, criminal even though they know police cannot enforce laws aimed at this behavior. This places discretion in the hands of police, overloads courts, promotes disrespect for law, and helps organized crime. Judicial efforts to regulate police behavior on a case-by-case basis make police seek convictions in fewer cases. There is therefore a large number of situations where police can be lawless because they do not seek convictions. Parole is impeded because parole officers are rewarded more for report writing then supervising parolees. Prisons turn treatment programs into ways of fostering inmate adjustment rather than preparing them for self-sufficiency after release.[57] And all of these agencies are operating in their own self-interest rather than trying to achieve the public interest goal of rehabilitation. The failure of rehabilitation, therefore, may be due more to the negative effects of self-interest than to other factors.

In summary, then, there are three general reasons for the failure of rehabilitation. First, many criminals—those who rationally weigh the costs and benefits of crime—cannot be rehabilitated. Second, most programs have inadequate support or are poorly designed (although there have been some very good programs that have been fully supported and still failed). And third, various groups and agencies whose support is essential for the success of rehabilitation pursue their narrow self-interests and fail to cooperate. This last reason seems to be the most important underlying cause of the failure of rehabilitation. Rehabilitation seems to be an area in which each agency pursues its own self-interest and does not contribute to the achievement of the public interest. The interrelationships are so complex that it is unlikely that any single policy change could increase achievement of rehabilitation.

Measuring the Success and Failure of Rehabilitation

When a person who has been injured in an automobile accident undergoes rehabilitation, we are quite clear about what it means and when it has been successfully accomplished. For example, if the injury is a broken leg or hip, rehabilitation involves mending the broken bones and providing physical therapy to enable the individual to walk again. And no doubt exists about when the process is completed or whether it has worked. The meaning of rehabilitation as applied to one who has been convicted of a crime is not quite so clear. Nor is it as easy to tell whether it has worked.

A conceptual definition of criminal rehabilitation seems easy enough. We defined it earlier in this chapter as any measures taken to restore a criminal to a state of physical, mental, and moral health through treatment and training. But how can we tell when this has occurred? Can we rely upon the word of the criminal, as when Alex claimed to have been cured in *A Clockwork Orange?* Obviously not, for the criminal has a self-interest in claiming to be cured—and, indeed, many have learned how to make just such claims in prisons so as to better their chances of being released. Can success be measured by whether or not the released person is again caught in a criminal act? No, because a person may engage in a number of criminal acts and not be caught. We know that reported crime is much lower than actual crime and that many crimes go undetected.

Evaluating the success or failure of rehabilitation programs depends upon finding a proper measure. The usual measure that is used in evaluating rehabilitation programs is recidivism, but there is no universal agreement about what that means. How much recidivism is said to exist depends upon (1) what is counted as the operational index that one has recidivated (arrest, conviction, parole, or probation violation); (2) how long a period must elapse before the event occurs; and (3) how serious the offense must be.

The first question in measuring recidivism is whether we should use arrest, conviction, and/or probation and parole violations as the operational index. Arrest alone cannot be used as a measure of recidivism because of the unevenness of police performance from place to place. A person is more likely to be arrested in some places than in others, and thus whether a person is a recidivist or not depends somewhat upon where a person lives rather than upon whether a crime has been committed. Studies of victimization, to be discussed in Chapter 13, show that in some cities five times as many crimes occur as are reported, while only two times as many occur as are reported in other cities. Thus, the chances of being caught for the same crime vary widely.

Conviction is a better measure since more evidence has to be presented that an individual actually has committed the crime than is the case for an arrest. But convictions also are not the same from place to place. The probability of being convicted for a particular crime (which most often results from pleading guilty) is higher in some places than in others. The variation occurs for a number of reasons. Some crimes are defined differently in different locales. For example, forcible rape is defined differently from one jurisdiction to another. In some jurisdictions penetration and evidence of resistance are required, but not in other jurisdictions. Hence, one can be convicted of rape in one place if there is evidence of penetration, but this would not be sufficient for a conviction in another jurisdiction, which may require evidence of resistance in addition.[58] Another reason for variation in conviction rates is that the police may be more efficient in obtaining evidence in certain locales, or the prosecutors may be more diligent and effective in obtaining a conviction. Thus, while conviction is a more valid and reliable measure than arrest, it still suffers from biases that are difficult to control.

Probation and parole violation suffer from the same defects as arrest and conviction; whether or not one is deemed a probation or parole violator depends more on the diligence of the probation or parole officer and upon chance factors than upon the objective facts. James Robinson and Paul Takagi report that parolees think, "Whether or not you make it on parole all depends on which agent you happen to get."[59]

The second question in measuring recidivism involves how long one must be free from being arrested or convicted for rehabilitation to be deemed successful. It obviously is too much to ask for freedom from involvement in crime for the rest of an ex-offender's life, for that would pose insurmountable and unreasonable measurement problems. But if a released offender is free from criminal involvement for one year, is that too little time for a meaningful measure? Statistics do show that if recidivism is going to occur, it most likely will happen the first six months after release. Nevertheless, can we say that one who commits a crime two years after release is not a recidivist? Most researchers solve the problem by picking an arbitrary number that does not offend common sense and is of sufficient duration to make the measurement problem relatively uncomplicated. The most frequently used time period is three years.

The final question that must be dealt with is how serious the offense must be in order to be called a case of recidivism. For example, should a person who has violated traffic laws and therefore has had his or her parole revoked be considered a failure? To call a criminal act "serious" can mean a number of things. The legal system makes distinctions between relatively minor crimes—misdemeanors—and more serious offenses—felonies. Various degrees or classes of offenses are defined within each of these categories. But these legal distinctions do not precisely measure seriousness. Generally, the more serious the crime, the longer the sentence it carries. But we cannot use length of time served as a measure of seriousness of crimes. The crime of first-degree manslaughter, for example, is much more serious than breaking and entering, and it carries a heavier penalty. But not every jurisdiction attaches the same sentence to the same crime. The degree of seriousness of a crime depends upon the social and cultural context in which it occurs. The sentences for committing forcible rape vary widely from place to place, depending upon such things as the race and age of the offender and that of the victim. Moreover, the sentence imposed by the court is not always the actual time a person serves. As we said earlier, the parole board determines the length of a sentence in most cases when it grants or denies parole. But the time served before being given parole for the same crime and sentence varies from jurisdiction to jurisdiction. Parole boards make the decision as to when an individual will be given parole, but since the criteria used by parole boards vary from state to state, the differences in length reflect administrative and personal characteristics of parole boards as well as the seriousness of the crime. Thus, the time served before receiving parole is also a somewhat arbitrary measure of the seriousness of the crime committed.

There are therefore no precise answers to the three questions that must be answered in finding a good measure of recidivism. A Brookings Institution study recommends that the following be used to define recidivism:

> On the basis of the present analysis, the most defensible indicators of a return to criminal behavior would be conviction of a new felony, of a misdemeanor punishable by 90 days or more imprisonment, or of more than one misdemeanor whose penalties add up to 90 days or more; all this to apply within three years after release.[60]

This, of course, is a long definition, and it points up the difficulties involved in measuring the success or failure of rehabilitation.

Recidivism is a measure of the ultimate impact of rehabilitation programs. While impact measures are an essential component of an evaluation, they should not be the only ones. It is important to measure how well rehabilitation programs are being run as well. An important part of the success or failure of rehabilitation is the amount of error parole boards make.

Parole boards can make two different kinds of errors when they release offenders under the assumption they have been rehabilitated. The first, which we will call a "Type 1" error, occurs when the parole board releases an offender who subsequently lapses into crime. This kind of error can be avoided by tightening up the requirements for release of an offender. But when this is done, the chances of making a different type of error increase. That error, called a "Type 2" error, occurs when an offender who would not actually lapse into crime is not released. Both errors should be considered in evaluating rehabilitation programs—though it is difficult to avoid both since they are inversely related. Thus, a rehabilitation program that attempts to avoid Type 1 errors is more likely to make Type 2 errors. This is the direction in which most parole boards go because they are more concerned with protecting the public safety and their reputation than with trying to meet the demand for justice by releasing those who have been successfully rehabilitated. A parole board that wants to avoid a Type 1 error (releasing prisoners who subsequently commit a crime) releases fewer offenders, and thus the aggregate recidivism rate for such boards is lower than that for boards that are more concerned with a Type 2 error (failing to release prisoners who will not subsequently commit crime). The decline in the recidivism rate occurs completely independent of the nature of the rehabilitation program. Actually, the recidivism rate of offenders could be drastically cut by simply keeping them incarcerated until they reach the age of 50, and this could be done without making any improvements in rehabilitation services whatsoever. Thus, measuring the success or failure of a rehabilitation program by its impact as reflected by whether or not an offender becomes reinvolved in crime takes attention away from the content and substance of the rehabilitation program itself.

Using recidivism alone as a measure of rehabilitation's success also ignores the nature of the persons involved in the rehabilitation program. The situation is somewhat akin to measuring the success or failure of high-school education programs by the number of individuals who go on to college. Very often, the type of student in the school is more important in determining who will go to college than what the school itself does. Similarly, a rehabilitation program that includes only first offenders who have been convicted of a minor crime, who are white, who are employed, and who have a family is more likely to be successful than one that has repeat offenders who are guilty of committing violent crimes and who are poor and black.

It seems clear, then, that an evaluation of rehabilitation programs should consider not just recidivism but the nature and substance of the program itself and the type of person in the program as well. Many factors affect outcomes, including the social and demographic characteristics of the offender, the efficiency and effectiveness of the entire criminal justice system, and the attitude and structure of society itself. A rehabilitation program is only one variable related to recidivism, and it may be the smallest component. Many factors in addition to rehabilitation programs determine whether or not an offender will return to a life of crime, and they should be included in an evaluation of rehabilitation. Most evaluation studies use recidivism rates and do not control for the quality of therapy, supervision, and vocational and educational programs, nor for the availability of community support programs, nor for how well rehabilitation programs are administered.

Conclusion

It seems premature to say that rehabilitation has failed. Until evaluation studies include a discussion of the nature of the rehabilitation programs themselves, judgment about whether it can work should be suspended. Those studies might well conclude that present rehabilitation programs are misdirected. From one perspective it may not be possible to rehabilitate an offender without changing the social system itself, if we regard criminal behavior as the result of inadequacies in the social system rather than as a result of individual pathology. If this perspective is valid, rehabilitation might be directed more effectively at social institutions than at individuals. There is a parallel with public health in this view. Treating the victim of a communicable disease such as smallpox is not as effective in controlling such diseases as eliminating the source of the infection itself. When people are exposed to the infectious conditions, it is only natural that they will contract the disease. The victim, then, should not be blamed.

Today, diversion from the entire criminal justice system (discussed in Chapter 12) is being turned to more and more because of dissatisfaction with the criminal justice system itself. Diversion involves taking individuals out of the criminal justice stream because it is believed that they cannot be rehabilitated within it. In essence, those who advocate diversion believe that the concept of rehabilitation itself is sound, but the way it is implemented in the existing system is faulty. Criminologist C. Ray Jeffery writes: "There are no criminals, only environmental circumstances which result in criminal behavior. Given the proper environmental structure, anyone will be a criminal or non-criminal."[61] Jeffery believes that changing criminal behavior requires changing the environment by decreasing the reinforcement available for criminal acts and increasing the risk involved in them.

The environmental position of Jeffery reminds one of the old debate among social scientists about which factor is more important in determining intelligence—heredity or environment. It is likely that it will be just as impossible to unravel the two in regard to criminal behavior as it is to determine which is more important for behavior in general. But the environmental argument alerts us to the fact that some attention must be paid to environmental factors if we want an adequate evaluation of rehabilitation. Thus far, this has not been done.

SUMMARY

Rehabilitation is based on the belief that an offender's character, habits, or behavior patterns can be changed so as to diminish criminal proclivities. Some criminals, such as the professional, cannot be "cured" since they are not mentally or socially defective. But it may be possible to rehabilitate some types of criminals. However, rehabilitation cannot be used as a way of reducing crime. Crime cannot be reduced by curing the relatively small number of criminals who are ultimately caught. The goal of rehabilitation instead should be to help individuals whether or not this reduces the general crime rate.

There are a number of different modes of rehabilitation. Therapeutic treatment is based on the assumption that criminals suffer from personality disorders. Violent offenders, for example, tend to act more impulsively and to have suffered from more childhood problems such as enuresis, hyperactivity, and fighting. The term *defective delinquent* is used by psychiatrists to describe the juvenile offender who has these characteristics. A defective delinquent is one who is at war with society, has negative feelings toward authority, and is unable to defer gratification. However, a successful therapy for such individuals has not yet been discovered. The rehabilitation rate of institutions that are supposed to "cure" offenders is not very good. Psychiatrists have been able to diagnose personality disorders, but they are unable to accurately predict if an individual will become a criminal.

Group therapy appears to have had more success in rehabilitating some offenders, but not persistent or professional ones. The impulsive offender is, theoretically, more amenable to group therapy, but he or she is also harder to cure.

Halfway houses such as the Delancey Street Foundation have had some success in rehabilitating offenders. But other community corrections programs, even those that operate under ideal conditions, have not been very successful.

Vocational-training programs have not had much success. Work release programs, on the other hand, seem to have had moderate success, but this may be due to the selectivity exercised in choosing candidates. One of the more difficult problems facing a released prisoner is finding a job, which is why both types of programs work.

Parole generally is granted to those offenders who give evidence that they have been successfully rehabilitated. However, parole officers are not able to provide counseling or other services for parolees, partly because of organizational pressures and heavy caseloads. The evidence about the success of parole is inconclusive.

Regardless of the evidence, there are a number of groups and forces working for the end of rehabilitation. The groups do not agree on the basis of their opposition, but they all conclude that rehabilitation should be ended regardless of the evidence for or against it.

One of the difficulties in evaluating rehabilitation is that recidivism is most frequently used as the sole criterion for evaluating programs. Various events, such as arrest, conviction, or reincarceration, are used to define recidivism. But recidivism is not a good criterion, not only because it is difficult to measure but also because it ignores other factors that contribute to the success or failure of rehabilitation programs.

FOOTNOTES

[1] Stanley Kubrick, *A Clockwork Orange* (screen play) (New York: Abelard-Schuman, 1972).

[2] Phil Stanford, "A Modern Clockwork Orange," *New York Times Magazine*, September 17, 1972, p. 74.

[3] Quoted in ibid.

[4] Norval Morris, *The Future of Imprisonment* (Chicago: University of Chicago Press, 1977), p. 80.

[5] Philip Bean, *Rehabilitation and Deviance* (Boston: Routledge & Kegan Paul, 1976), p. 6.

[6] Ibid., p. 15.

[7] Joe Tupin, Dennis Maher and David Smith, "Two Types of Violent Offenders with Psychosocial Descriptors," *Diseases of the Nervous System* 34, no. 7 (October 1973), 356–63.

[8] Barry Brown, "The Impact of Imprisonment on Selected Attitudes of Recidivists and First Offenders," *Journal of Clinical Psychology* 26, no. 4 (October 1970), 435–36; Samuel Guze, Donald Goodwin, and Bruce Crane, "Criminal Recidivism and Psychiatric Illness," *American Journal of Psychiatry* 127, no. 6 (December 1970),

832–35; W. A. Black, and R. A. Gregson, "Time Perspective, Purpose in Life, Extroversion and Neuroticism in New Zealand Prisoners," *British Journal of Social and Clinical Psychology* 12, no. 1 (February 1973), 56–60; Udai P. Singh, "Personality Profiles of Recidivists and Non-Recidivists," *Indian Journal of Social Work* 35, no. 3 (October 1973), 227–32; and Glenn D. Wilson and Alastair MacLean, "Personality, Attitudes and Humor Preferences of Prisoners and Controls," *Psychological Reports* 34, no. 3, pt. 1 (June 1974), pp. 847–54.

[9] C. Ray Jeffery, *Crime Prevention Through Environment Design* (Beverly Hills, Calif.: Sage Publications, 1971), pp. 115–17.

[10] Quoted in Stanford, op cit., p. 74.

[11] Samuel Yochelson and Stanley E. Samenow, *The Criminal Personality* (New York: Jason Aronson, 1976), as discussed in Michael S. Serrill, "A Cold New Look at the Criminal Mind," *Psychology Today*, November 1977, pp. 69ff.

[12] Melvin Lee, Philip G. Zimbardo, and Minerva Bertholf, "Shy Murderers," *Psychology Today*, November 1977, p. 69.

[13] Ibid., p. 148.

[14] James Q. Wilson, *Thinking about Crime* (New York: Basic Books, 1977).

[15] Lee, Zimbardo, and Bertholf, op. cit., p. 69.

[16] Stanford, op. cit., p. 76.

[17] Quoted in Jonas Robitscher and Roger Williams, "Should Psychiatrists Get Out of the Courtroom?" *Psychology Today*, December 1971, p. 85.

[18] Ibid., pp. 85, 91.

[19] M. J. R. Harper, "Courts, Doctors, and Delinquents: An Inquiry into the Uses of Psychiatry in Youth Correction," *Smith College Studies in Social Work* 44, no. 3 (June 1974), 158–78.

[20] Henry Steadman and Gary Keneles, "The Community Adjustment and Criminal Activity of the Baxstrom Patients," *American Journal of Psychiatry* 129, no. 3 (September 1972), 304–10.

[21] Vernon Quinsey, Manfred Pruesse, and Robert Fernly, "Oak Ridge Patients: Pre-Release Characteristics and Post-Release Adjustment," *Journal of Psychiatry and Law* 3, no. 1 (1975), p. 65.

[22] Marian Pew, David Speer, and James Williams, "Group Counseling for Offenders," *Social Work* 18, no. 1 (January 1973), 74–79.

[23] Bruno Cormier, *The Watcher and the Watched* (Montreal, Can.: Tundra Books, 1975).

[24] Joan Petersilia, Peter Greenwood, and Marvin Lavin, *Criminal Careers of Habitual Felons* (Santa Monica, Calif.: Rand Corporation, 1977).

[25] Cormier, op. cit., pp. 172–73.

[26] Stanford, op. cit., p. 74.

[27] Charles Hampden-Turner, *Sane Asylum* (San Francisco, Calif.: San Francisco Book, 1976), p. 71.

[28] Quoted in ibid., p. 71.

[29] Quoted in ibid., p. 134.

[30] Richard H. Lamb and Victor Goertzel, "Ellsworth House: A Community Alternative to Jail," *American Journal of Psychiatry* 131, no. 1 (January 1974), 64–68.

[31] Robert Vasoli and Frank Fahey, "Halfway House for Reformatory Releases," *Crime and Delinquency* 16, no. 3 (July 1970), 292–304.

[32] See David Boorkman, Ernest J. Fazio, Jr., Noel Day, and David Weinstein, *An Exemplary Project: Community Based Corrections in Des Moines* (Washington, D.C.: U.S. Government Printing Office, 1976). See also H. P. White, *Community Treatment Centers: Corrections Evaluation Report* (Oklahoma City, Okla.: Oklahoma Crime Commission, 1978).

[33] David T. Stanley, *Prisoners Among Us: The Problem of Parole* (Washington, D.C.: The Brookings Institution, 1976), p. 17.

[34] Robert Martinson, Douglas Lipson, and Judith Wilks, *The Effectiveness of Correctional Treatment, A Survey of Treatment Evaluation Studies* (New York: Praeger, 1975).

[35] Daniel Glaser, *The Effectiveness of a Prison and Parole System* (Indianapolis, Ind.: Bobbs-Merrill, 1964).

[36] Paul Meskil, "City Probe: Work Release Is at Least Half Bad," *New York Daily News*, December 26, 1977, p. 17.

[37] Stanley, op. cit., p. 150.

[38] National Advisory Commission on Criminal Justice Standards and Goals, *Corrections* (Washington, D.C.: U.S. Government Printing Office, 1973), p. 420.

[39] Stanley, op. cit., p. 32.

[40] Joseph Scott, "The Use of Discretion in Determining the Severity of Punishment for Incarcerated Offenders," *Journal of Criminal Law and Criminology* 65 (1974), 214–24.

[41] Harry L. Kozal, Richard Boucher, and Ralph Garofalo, "Diagnosis and Treatment of Dangerousness, *Crime and Delinquency* 18 (October 1972), 371–92.

[42] Stanley, op. cit., p. 69.

[43] Quoted in ibid., p. 85.

[44] Romine Deming, "Valence as a Measurement of the Effectiveness of Probation Officer–Client Relationship," *Journal of Criminal Justice* 2, no. 2 (Summer 1974), 158.

[45] Stanley, op. cit., p. 128.

[46] James Robinson and Paul Takagi, "The Parole Violator as an Organizational Reject" (Unpublished manuscript, School of Criminology, University of California, Berkeley, 1968), p. 366.

[47] Stanley, op. cit., p. 106.

[48] F. R. Scarpitti and R. M. Stephenson, "A Study of Probation Effectiveness," *Journal of Criminal Law, Criminology, and Police Science* 59, no. 3 (1968), 361–69.

[49] John Kraus, "A Comparison of Corrective Effects of Probation and Detention on Male Juvenile Offenders," *British Journal Criminology* 14, no. 1 (January 1974), 49–62.

[50] Robert Martinson and Judith Wilks, "Save Parole Supervision," *Federal Probation* 41 (September 1977), 24.

[51] All quotes cited in Sol Chaneles, "Prisoners Can Be Rehabilitated—Now," *Psychology Today*, October 1976, p. 131.

[52] Quoted in the Law Enforcement Assistance Administrator *Newsletter*, 6, no. 15 (November 1977), 7.

[53] Wilson, op. cit., p. 43.

[54] Chaneles, op. cit., p. 134.

[55] See Benedict S. Alper, *Prisons Inside-Out: Alternatives*

to Correctional Reform (Cambridge, Mass. Ballinger, 1974).

[56] Bean, op. cit., p. 144; and Morris, op. cit., pp. 26–28.

[57] Daniel Glaser, "From Revenge to Resocialization: Changing Perspectives in Combatting Crime," *American Scholar* 40, no. 4 (1971) 654–61.

[58] National Institute of Law Enforcement and Criminal Jus-

tice, Law Enforcement Assistance Administration, *Forcible Rape: a National Survey of the Response by Police*, vol. 1 (Washington, D.C.: U.S. Government Printing Office, 1977).

[59] Robinson & Takagi, op. cit., p. 352.

[60] Stanley, op. cit., p. 176.

[61] Jeffery, op. cit., p. 177.

BIBLIOGRAPHY

Alper, Benedict S. *Prisons Inside-Out: Alternatives to Correctional Reform.* Cambridge, Mass.: Ballinger, 1974.

Bean, Philip. *Rehabilitation and Deviance.* Boston: Routledge & Kegan Paul, 1976.

Black, W. A. and Gregson, R. A. "Time Perspective, Purpose in Life, Extroversion and Neuroticism in New Zealand Prisoners." *British Journal of Social and Clinical Psychology* 12, no. 1 (February 1973).

Brown, Barry. "The Impact of Imprisonment on Selected Attitudes of Recidivists and First Offenders." *Journal of Clinical Psychology* 26, no. 4 (October 1970), 435–36.

Cormier, Bruno. *The Watcher and the Watched.* Montreal, Can.: Tundra Books, 1975.

Glaser, Daniel. *The Effectiveness of a Prison and Parole System.* Indianapolis, Ind.: Bobbs-Merrill, 1964.

Guze, Samuel; Goodwin, Donald; and Crane, Bruce. "Criminal Recidivism and Psychiatric Illness." *American Journal of Psychiatry* 127, no. 6 (December 1970), 832–35.

Hampden-Turner, Charles. *Sane Asylum.* San Francisco, Calif.: San Francisco Book, 1976.

Jeffery, C. Ray. *Crime Prevention Through Environment Design.* Beverly Hills, Calif.: Sage Publications, 1971.

Kozal, Harry L.; Boucher, Richard; and Garofalo, Ralph. "The Diagnosis and Treatment of Dangerousness." *Crime and Delinquency* 18 (October 1972), 371–92.

Lamb, Richard H., and Goertzel, Victor. "Ellsworth House: A Community Alternative to Jail." *American Journal of Psychiatry* 131, no. 1. (January 1974), 64–68.

Lee, Melvin; Zimbardo, Philip G.; and Bertholf, Minerva. "Shy Murderers," *Psychology Today*, November 1977, pp. 68–71, 148.

Martinson, Robert; Lipson, Douglas; and Wilks, Judith. *The Effectiveness of Correctional Treatment: A Survey of Treatment Evaluation Studies.* New York: Praeger, 1975.

Miller, E. Eugene, and Montilla, M. Robert. *Cor-*

rections in the Community: Success Models in Correctional Reform (Reston, Va.: Reston, 1977).

National Advisory Commission on Criminal Justice Standards and Goals. *Corrections.* Washington, D.C.: U.S. Government Printing Office, 1973.

National Institute of Law Enforcement and Criminal Justice, Law Enforcement Assistance Administration. *Forcible Rape: A National Survey of the Response by Police*, vol. 1. Washington, D.C.: U.S. Government Printing Office, 1977.

Petersilia, Joan; Greenwood, Peter; and Lavin, Marvin. *Criminal Careers of Habitual Felons.* Santa Monica, Calif.: Rand Corporation, 1977.

Scarpitti, F. R. and Stephenson, R. M. "A Study of Probation Effectiveness." *Journal of Criminal Law, Criminology, and Police Science* 59, no. 3 (1968), 361–69.

Serrill, Michael S. "A Cold New Look at the Criminal Mind." *Psychology Today*, November 1977, pp. 83–87.

Stanford, Phil. "A Modern Clockwork Orange." *New York Times Magazine*, September 1977, pp. 9–10, 74–84.

Stanley, David T. *Prisoners among Us: The Problem of Parole.* Washington, D.C.: The Brookings Institution, 1976.

Steadman, Henry, and Keneles, Gary. "The Community Adjustment and Criminal Activity of the Baxstrom Patients." *American Journal of Psychiatry* 129, no. 3 (September 1972), 304–10.

Tupin, Joe; Maher, Dennis; and Smith, David. "Two Types of Violent Offenders with Psychosocial Descriptors." *Diseases of the Nervous System* 34, no. 7 (October 1973), 356–63.

Vasoli, Robert, Fahey, Frank. "Halfway House for Reformatory Releases." *Crime and Delinquency* 16, no. 3 (July 1970), 292–304.

Wilson Glenn D., and MacLean, Alastair. "Personality, Attitudes and Humor Preferences of Prisoners and Controls." *Psychological Reports* 34, no. 3, pt. 1 (June 1974), 847–54.

Wilson, James Q. *Thinking about Crime.* New York: Basic Books, 1977.

Criminal justice personnel devote a good deal of their resources to handling "street people"—addicts, pimps, winos, vagrants, and prostitutes. Some treat street people with considerable disrespect. Eve Merriam's poem about a wino captures this attitude:*

Wino Will who's drunk his fill
Gets chased by law and order.
Knock him down and kick him around,
That's the way of law and order.
Don't complain or they'll do it again,
Just a law-and-order caper;
Bloody his head and leave him for dead
And keep it out of the paper.[1]

But others approach this often messy task by displaying professional and humanitarian ethics. In *Police: Streetcorner*

*Reprinted by permission of Eve Merriam, % International Creative Management. Copyright © 1969 by Eve Merriam.

CHAPTER ELEVEN

DECRIMINALIZATION AND LEGALIZATION
Shrinking the Scope of Criminal Codes

Politicians, political scientist William Muir records the professionalism of walking patrolman Mike Marshall whose work with skid-row types has helped transform them into good citizens. The patrolman describes his work in these terms:

> I think I know everybody on my beat. Maybe 5,000 persons. And I try to learn all their first names and their faces. . . . I prefer to have them call me "Mike," and they prefer to have me call them that way. A wino comes up and by calling you by your first name he gets a feeling of equality. By giving them a feeling of equality, you are making a friend of them. Even though I put a lot of them in jail, they are friends, so-called friends. A lot will get drunk for a week; then they'll want you to put them in jail a week or so. They know when they've had enough. Otherwise, they'll die. An awful lot ask to go to jail.[2]

In part, the tremendous disparities in the way that criminal justice personnel treat such people raise a basic question about criminal justice priorities: Should the police and the courts be in the business of regulating street people whose crimes are more a reflection of their social or individual condition than a threat to the lives and property of the more stable citizenry? Some say they should not, that the law should be purged of such crimes as prostitution, public drunkenness, and vagrancy. The two methods by which this might be done are decriminalization and legalization.

It would be a mistake to assume that only street people commit crimes commonly associated with decriminalization and legalization policies. The range of crimes usually discussed as potential candidates for such policies include, in addition to those mentioned above, drug use, gambling, and sexual behavior between consenting adults.[3] Collectively these crimes are often referred to as "victimless crimes" in which "any harm done is committed by the actor . . . against himself, to him with his own consent, or against a consenting partner."[4]

Of course, by defining harm broadly to include "societal harm" and "indirect harm," one could argue that there are *no* victimless crimes. For example, cohabitation, the practice of an unmarried couple living together, can lead to the birth of an illegitimate child. Such a child may be psychologically harmed and discriminated against throughout his or her life by individuals who reject families that are not bound together by traditional marriage vows. One could argue that the parents of illegitimate children are partially responsible for the harm rendered to these "victims."

The meaning of "harm" cannot be settled here.[5] We use "victimless crimes," "folk crimes," and "morality crimes" as interchangeable terms to refer to that class of crimes that deal with morality. Victimless crimes involve acts in which an offender-victim relationship is more difficult to identify than in murder, robbery, auto theft, or most other actions commonly thought of as being criminal in nature.[6] These crimes usually are characterized by the exchange of sought-after goods (e.g., drugs) or services (e.g., gambling) by consenting adults rather than by one individual's direct seizure of another's property or injury to another's life.

Potential Crimes for Decriminalization and Legalization

Nearly all citizens have been involved in a victimless crime on one or more occasions. For example, have you ever gone to a park and consumed liquor out of an open container (a violation of open-bottle laws)? Have you lived with a member of the opposite sex without having taken marriage vows (defined in some states as illicit cohabitation), or practiced sexual acts other than missionary-position intercourse with a mate (referred to as "crimes against nature" in some criminal codes)? Have you experimented with an illicit drug like marijuana (against many state narcotic laws), or read a "dirty" book (a violation of obscenity laws)? If so, you must plead guilty to participating in a victimless criminal act.

This chapter investigates first the prevalence of lawbreaking associated with several folk crimes in contemporary American society. Later, the chapter focuses in on public drunkenness and marijuana use to study the impact of decriminalization policies. These two victimless crimes were chosen because: (1) several impact studies have already been completed that evaluate the effectiveness of public drunkenness and marijuana decriminalization policies, (2) they are significant concerns of the general public and the news media, and (3) police agencies and municipal courts have traditionally devoted significant resources to enforcing these laws.

WHAT ARE THE OFFENSES?

PUBLIC DRINKING   The consumption of alcoholic beverages is an American pastime engaged in by millions, mostly at home, in restaurants, or in bars. Public drunkenness and open-bottle laws are designed, in part, to curtail "excessive" drinking in public and to prohibit drinking in certain areas (e.g., parks). How many Americans routinely break these laws? Because only a small fraction of those who violate open-bottle statutes and ordinances are actually detected and booked by the police, we must look beyond arrest statistics to estimate the size of such populations.

The size of the "problem drinking population" gives some clue. A person is considered to have a drinking problem if he or she either drinks frequently or uses alcohol to escape interpersonal relationships. A national survey conducted in 1967 estimated the size of the problem-drinking population in the United States. Taking only that group of problem drinkers who scored high on both frequent intoxication and interpersonal problems, the survey estimated that 7 percent of the adult male population and 2 percent of the adult female population are in the group of severe problem drinkers.[7] Taking the 1977 population estimates for males and females whose age is 20 and over, we find 4.7 million males and 1.5 million females who drink frequently and as a result end in conflicts with fellow workers, casual acquaintances, friends, family, and the police.

Some of the problem drinkers no doubt confine their drinking to private places such as their own homes, so that they do not really violate the law. On the other hand, there are many occasional (nonproblem) drinkers who sometimes imbibe in public. So, while the above estimates of the number of problem drinkers must be adjusted somewhat they do suggest, when taken with estimates of occasional drinkers, that illegal drinking is a widespread phenomenon.

SEXUAL PRACTICES   Many states retain criminal statutes that prohibit sexual activity among consenting adults other than traditional marital coitus. Yet the sexual practices of Americans deviate significantly from this norm. Alex Comfort, a medical doctor, sold over 4 million copies of a book entitled *The Joy of Sex*, which encourages couples to enlarge their sexual horizons and includes a how-to section on the use of boots, bondage, and leather for expanding sexual pleasure.

Sparked by the studies of sexual behavior by Alfred Kinsey and his associates in the late 1940s,[8] many sex researchers have reported on sexual deviancy in the population. According to one such study, "Among the college educated . . . about 45 percent of the men and 58 percent of women have engaged in oral sex."[9]

The study also noted that about 5 percent of men and 2 percent of women are exclusively homosexual.[10] For the 1977 adult population, that means that 2.7 million males and nearly 1.5 million females are homosexual. Since some states still consider homosexual acts a crime, millions of these people are potential criminals.

MARIJUANA CONSUMPTION   Possession, cultivation, and sale of marijuana remains a criminal offense in most states today. Despite its criminal status, use of the substance has grown rapidly. A recent National Governors' Conference report stated that approximately 22 percent of the United States population over the age of 12 (which represents some 37 million individuals) had used marijuana at least once.[11] The same conference noted that current users—those that have used marijuana at least once in the last month—constitute 8 percent of all adults and 12 percent of all youth, age 12 to 17. In fact, among high-school seniors nearly 19 percent have used marijuana over 20 times in the last year. For those 18 to 25, the conference concluded, "What was once clearly statistically deviant behavior had become the norm."[12]

Times Square, New York City

SMUT PEDDLING "Smut," or pornographic material, is produced in at least four forms—movies, books, magazines, and mail-order erotica. How many Americans have viewed or own obscene material and what are the socioeconomic characteristics of these citizens? A national survey indicates that "approximately 85 percent of men and 70 percent of women report specific instances of having been exposed to explicit sexual materials depicting a minimum nudity with genitals exposed."[13] Fourteen percent of the men (approximately 9.5 million) and 5 percent of the women (3.7 million) report extensive experience with pornographic material.

Millions of minors have sampled obscene material. In national surveys adults have been asked when they first viewed explicit sexual materials. Among the adult males, almost three quarters reported having been exposed before age 21, one-half before age 18, and one-third before age 15. In general, females report being exposed about two years later than males.[14]

Users of adult bookstores and patrons of adult movie theaters are representative of American mainstream culture. Researchers have conducted observations of individuals entering adult bookstores and found that most patrons are white, middle-aged, and dressed either casually or in suits and ties.[15] The same seems to be true of adult movie theaters. Observation and follow-up studies of 2,791 customers at three adult theaters in San Francisco showed that the largest percentage of patrons were age 36 to 45 (32 percent), white (70 percent), wore a suit and tie or neat casual clothes (88 percent), and were married (60 percent).[16] Clearly, many perfectly normal people break obscenity laws on a routine basis, and it is sheer misperception to assume that this is a crime committed only by sexual perverts.

434

SOCIAL AND ECONOMIC EFFECTS OF MORALITY CRIMES

In *The Honest Politician's Guide to Crime Control*, Norval Morris and Gordon Hawkins argue that the proliferation of victimless crime statutes has caused millions of people to live in fear of being caught and labeled criminals. In addition, such widespread use of the criminal sanction eats away at citizens' respect for the law and contributes to an unnecessary expansion of the criminal subculture.[17]

There are other consequences of the "criminal overreach" problem, as it is sometimes called. Crime tariffs, or exorbitant purchasing costs, are levied for the supply of criminalized goods and services, making criminal activity a highly profitable and risk-worthy undertaking. For example, increases in demand for marijuana and an emerging "connoisseur class" of users, combined with improvements in federal law enforcement agencies' abilities to disrupt international trafficking of the substance, have caused the cost of marijuana to skyrocket in recent years. One writer describes the relationship between these factors in the following way:

> Marijuana is scarce and expensive today, though according to U.S. Customs, between 15 and 20 million pounds of the stuff were smuggled into the country last year. . . . In 1950, a pound of the best Mexican weed was worth $100. Today, the same pound costs eight times as much, if you can get it. What today's more sophisticated smokers want, however, is even more expensive: Columbian "gold" at $75 an ounce, or better still, the really costly "exotics" from Thailand, Afghanistan, and Brazil. The price of these connoisseur strains has escalated as smokers have become more discerning. Thai sticks—six-inch plant-tops gathered about a sliver of bamboo and bound with dental floss by deft Oriental hands—were as cheap as $20 an ounce during the height of the war in Southeast Asia. Today, they command from $200 to $350 an ounce—more than the price of *real* gold![18]

Besides increasing the profit associated with such activity, enforcement of statutes dealing with morality crimes may also damage the priorities and practices of criminal justice agencies. Scarce criminal justice resources are diverted away from more serious criminal matters. Also, since these crimes lack clearly identifiable victims, police use broad, discretionary street tactics to apprehend violators, which leads to selective enforcement, infringement of due-process guarantees, and increased opportunities for police corruption.

Enforcement of folk crime statutes also forces citizens identified with such crimes to pay significant costs outside of the criminal justice system. Job applications, qualifying codes for entrance into the professions, and standards for job promotion often include references to victimless crime association. Many homosexuals, for example, are denied career advancement unless they hide their sexual orientation.[19] The perceived need to keep their identity secret exposes such citizens to blackmail and other threats that jeopardize their employment and social relations.

FORCES BEHIND VICTIMLESS CRIMES

Given this list of costs, why has American society adopted and held on to so many of these crime statutes? Some argue that the growth of laws concerning victimless crimes is simply a product of legislative laziness. Legislatures give low priority to reviewing old criminal statutes. This argument ignores the powerful societal forces that have led to the creation and retention of so many such laws in this country. Three forces in particular have been significant—moral crusaders, the ruling class, and bureaucracy itself.

MORAL CRUSADERS   Beginning with the days of the original Puritan settlements on the continent, groups of "moral entrepreneurs," as criminologist William Chambliss has referred to them, have used the criminal law as a way to imprint certain precepts of right and wrong and to establish guidelines of moral responsibility for the entire citizenry.[20] Howard Becker, a sociologist who studied the formulation of the Marijuana Tax Act, a federal law that made simple possession a crime, identified three values that lie behind the efforts of these moral crusader groups. The first is the "Protestant ethic," one precept of which is that individuals "should never do anything that might cause loss of self-control."[21] Thus, alcohol and drugs are considered moral evils because they foster such a loss. A second value, "utilitarianism," stresses pragmatism and condemns peo-

Carrie Nation, temperance crusader (*left*); wrecking a bar during Prohibition

ple's pursuit of "ecstasy for its own sake."[22] Hence, sex is looked upon as a means for reproduction of the species, not for pleasure seeking. Finally, "humanitarianism" is often invoked by those who want to create or retain victimless crime statutes, because they see victimization in the personal and social harm caused, for example, by the use of drugs and alcohol.[23] The law is invoked to save people and their families from the misery sometimes produced by the use of these goods.

THE RULING CLASS   Historian Michael Hindus reports that in the late eighteenth and nineteenth centuries a shift is noticeable away from the criminal justice system's enforcement of prohibitions against private moral crimes (e.g., premarital sex) to prohibitions against public moral crimes such as drunkenness and vagrancy.[24] This shift to maintaining order in the street marks the rise of a second societal force that lies behind overcriminalization—ruling elites protecting their favored class status. An historical tracing of the origin of many victimless crime statutes lends considerable support to the arguments of conflict criminologists, who contend that class bias lies behind the labeling of a good deal of criminal behavior.

As early as the 1300s, England's ruling class of landowners had created offenses like vagrancy to keep free men (formerly serfs) from moving about the country in search of better working conditions and wages.[25] Later, with the emergence of the Industrial Revolution and the abundance of cheap labor, these same laws were revitalized as catchall crime-prevention tools to detain people on the road who might prey on merchants moving their goods. These laws were so broadly worded that any suspicious individuals could be arrested. For example, a 1547 vagrancy law read:

> Whoever man or woman, being not lame, impotent, or so aged or diseased that he or she cannot work not having whereon to live, shall be lurking in any house, or loitering or idle wandering by the highway side, or in the streets, cities, towns, or villages, not applying themselves to some honest labor, and so continuing for three days; or running away from their work; every such person shall be taken for a vagabond. And . . . upon conviction of two witnesses . . . the same loiterer (shall) be marked with a hot iron in the breast with a letter V, and adjudged him to the prison bringing him to be his slave for two years.[26]

These public nuisance laws were codified as criminal laws by American legislatures and, as in England, the laws were often created and enforced in response to periods of social and economic turmoil. Sociologist Sidney Harring recently documented the enactment and enforcement of "tramp laws" during the depression years of 1893 and 1894. During this period, several hundred thousand Americans "took to the rails" in search of work. To stop the movement of the unemployed and to provide the police with a means of controlling such individuals when they arrived in towns, legislatures enacted tramp laws, often worded like the following statute:

All persons who rove about from place to place begging, and all vagrants living without labor or visible means of support, who stroll over the country without lawful occupation, shall be held to be tramps. . . . Every tramp, upon conviction as such, shall be punished by imprisonment at hard labor in the nearest penitentiary for not more than six months.[27]

The enforcement of tramp laws became a more pressing concern as the traveling unemployed increased in numbers, began to organize, and gained support from workers in local communities. For example, in Buffalo, New York, the "police force was created at the initiative of wealthy businessmen" and controlled by economic elites into the early 1900s "through a series of businessmen commissioners . . . and superintendents."[28] The *Buffalo Evening News* reported violent police crackdowns on tramps by the mid-1890s, including the following account:

The policemen swung their long nightsticks right and left, left and right, and every time they hit a man he fell bleeding like a stuck pig, and whining and moaning like a kicked dog. . . . The horses were pulled upon their hind legs; they pawed the air with their front legs and mowed down the hobos like grass, tearing their scalps open and bruising and wounding them.[29]

Open-ended statutes prohibiting disorderly conduct and loitering continue to remain critical tools available to police for maintaining public order during times of societal tension and for keeping undesirables like skid-row inebriates out of commercially important sections of cities. Indeed, legal expert Caleb Foote states that the chief significance of these laws is their administrative utility to law enforcement agencies for solving small and large problems that arise in maintaining order.[30]

BUREAUCRACY A third force behind the continued prosecution of victimless crimes is law enforcement agencies seeking new tasks to expand their bureaucratic territories. One of the best-documented examples of this bureaucratic game is the role the Federal Bureau of Narcotics played in the 1930s to push for national legislation prohibiting marijuana use. During this period the agency was relatively young and lacked a wide range of tasks.

The agency played a dual role in pushing through the legislation by first initiating a publicity campaign to arouse public concern over marijuana use and then utilizing the effects of this campaign to justify before Congress the need for the Marijuana Tax Act of 1937.[31] In fact, the act is an example of how a bureaucratic agency can play three important roles in the policy-making process—creating public interest in legislation, drafting the initial wording of legislation, and lobbying before Congress for its passage based on expert testimony as well as documentation of public concern.

More recently, the passage of the Comprehensive Drug Abuse Prevention and Control Act of 1970 by Congress represents the combined impact of a governmental agency, the Federal Bureau of Narcotics and Dangerous Drugs, seeking more territory and the drug industry, seeking to protect its legal production of "uppers and downers" (amphetamines and barbiturates). William Chambliss recorded the impact of these two very powerful policy-making forces on this particular act:

> The bill, as drafted by the Nixon administration with consultation from representatives of the drug industry, was tantamount to providing heretofore unheard of powers to law-enforcement bureaucracies of the state and federal governments in the enforcement of laws controlling the distribution and possession of "drugs." Significantly, however, the drugs that received the greatest emphasis were those that were either imported or produced easily by individuals: heroin, marijuana, and LSD being the principal examples. Drugs which were produced by pharmaceutical manufacturers, even though they were generally sold illegally, were left virtually uncontrolled in the bill.[32]

SHAPING PERCEPTIONS OF VICTIMLESS CRIMES

In order to gain citizen support for criminally prohibiting certain goods and services, those who benefit from the creation of folk crime statutes—bureaucracies that expand their territoriality, newspapers that increase their sales, and politicians who gain votes—sometimes present unsubstantiated and misleading information about a newly proposed victimless crime. Such propaganda, once digested by the public, becomes a justification for including the problem in the criminal code. The following are some examples of these political forces creating misperceptions about victimless crimes.

BUREAUCRATIC PROPAGANDA In the 1920s, the commissioner for the Federal Bureau of Narcotics, Harry Anslinger, enlisted an army of civic groups and media supporters by dramatizing the evils of marijuana. One of the bureau's major tactics for increasing citizen awareness was to present a series of criminal atrocity stories, connecting them to marijuana use. The bureau's approach played upon citizen's natural fears of violent crimes. For example, the bureau circulated the following gruesome tale:

> Within a month after the passage of the Uniform Narcotic Drug Act in the State of Florida, twenty-two arrests were made in the city of Tampa for the sale of cannabis in the form of marijuana cigarettes and in bulk. A short time later, a young boy, who had become addicted to smoking marijuana cigarettes, murdered his family in a fit of frenzy, because, as he stated while under the marijuana influence, a number of people were trying to cut off his arms and legs. He seized an axe and killed his father, mother, two brothers and a sister, wiping out the entire family except himself.[33]

Warnings about the use of impressionistic data from the bureau's own legal advisor as well as testimony from medical scientists refuting the linkage of marijuana consumption to violent criminal behavior failed to halt the agency's "educational" campaign. Congress, too, seemed struck by the case examples and the growing focus on atrocity stories by the media. It finally enacted the Marijuana Tax Act over strong objections from the scientific community.[34]

When the New York State legislature was developing a new code on prostitution that would significantly reduce criminal penalties, the New York City Police Department and local business people teamed up to invoke public indignation over the liberalized law. As the legal revisions were about to take effect, the police began massive roundups of prostitutes in the Times Square area, and rumors were circulated that there was a large influx of prostitutes into the city.[35] While civil-libertarian interest groups and legislators sympathetic to the liberalized law won out over this combined police-business community campaign, it demonstrates another tactic available to law enforcement agencies for arousing community sentiments over victimless crimes—inflating arrest statistics and arranging crackdowns at times of critical legislative debate.

On January 27, 1978, a task force of 200 law enforcement officers from Maricopa County, Arizona, raided and closed 60 massage parlors in the valley, issuing civil summonses based on a public nuisance law. The raid coincided with the convening of the state legislature for a new session. An article in the *Arizona Republic* quoted law enforcement officials who claimed the need for a "clean-cut criminal law" to deal with these "fronts for organized prostitution."[36]

MEDIA FABLES Newspapers and magazines often unknowingly serve as conduits for bureaucratic and politicians' propaganda campaigns over victimless crimes. Also, some publishers and editors are themselves moral entrepreneurs who see taking a particular stand as both proper and potentially profitable.

The rising number of criminal statutes against marijuana, beginning in the 1930s, was supported by many newspapers. Editorial cartoonists also adopted the tactic of linking marijuana use to violent felonies. Even though the Federal Bureau of Narcotics encouraged newspaper support, agency officials became alarmed over the hysterical approach taken by some newspaper chains. By 1938 the commissioner reversed his position on promoting agency cooperation with the media, fearing the publicity "would lead children and impressionable youngsters to try the drug."[37] Of course, by this time, the bureau's campaign had led to stiff criminal codes in many states as well as federal legislation banning marijuana use.

Media crusaders used a second approach to arouse public concern—the "enemy from without" tactic. The tactic was used during the McCarthy era of the 1950s to link the need for a federal crackdown on drug use to communism. According to one source, "Political cartoons and commentaries quite often attributed increased drug traffic to the efforts of Chinese Communism to dominate and demoralize American young."[38] This accusation was never substantiated and usually was based on interviews with law enforcement officials, who speculated on the role of communists in directing the flow of drugs to the United States.

The Idol of Both

New Orleans *Times-Picayune*, 5 June 1930

ASSAULT WITH INTENT TO KILL

Arlington County, Virginia, *Daily Sun*, 19 March 1955

Antimarijuana propaganda

SYMBOLIC POLITICS Politicians often acquire or retain their offices by promoting stiff governmental responses to morality crimes. In addition to using the tactics of connecting morality crimes to more violent crimes and outside enemies, they also link people associated with folk crimes to a minority group lying outside of the American mainstream culture. In *Symbolic Crusade*, sociologist Joseph Gusfield labels such linkages "symbolic gestures of differentiation."[39] Gusfield stresses the importance of symbolic gestures in officeholders' decisions to create particular laws. Legislation against morality crimes is meant to convey the impression that politicians are doing something for the public's good.

In 1914 when the "drys" in Congress opened their legislative debate to win support for the prohibition of alcoholic beverages, they began by describing that part of the citizenry who use and gain from the open sale of liquor as:

the allied powers that prey, the vultures of vice, the corrupt combinations of politics, the grafters and gangsters, the parasites that clothe themselves in the proceeds of woman's shame, the inhuman ones that bathe themselves in the tears of little children, the wastrels who wreck and ruin material things while they contaminate childhood, debauch youth, and crush manhood; . . . the Hessians in the black-bannered troop whose line of march is over wrecked homes and broken hearts and ruined lives.[40]

441

Certainly, no casual consumer of alcoholic beverages would personally associate with such individuals. Throughout the debate over Prohibition, the "drys" were careful not to use rhetoric that would offend the great majority of drinkers who would ultimately be influenced by Prohibition.

In times when politicians, the media, and bureaucracies work together to criminalize certain goods or services, objective scientific data concerning the subject under debate are often ignored. Expert testimony and scientific evidence about the actual effects of controversial substances or activities are buried under an avalanche of political rhetoric and self-interest drives by members of these groups. Later in this chapter, we will see how changing the attitudes of these political forces is critical to the successful passage of decriminalization or legalization policies.

POLICING VICTIMLESS CRIMES

American law enforcement agencies have long been hooked on policing victimless crimes. In fact, the enforcement of morality crime statutes has resulted in the largest number of arrests by law enforcement agencies throughout our history. Today, enforcement of victimless crimes continues to be the bread-and-butter task of modern law enforcement bureaucracies. In 1975 law enforcement agencies throughout the country made over 4.1 million arrests for victimless crimes, constituting 52 percent of all arrests made for that year.[41] This figure includes nearly 1.2 million arrests for public drunkenness[42] and over 400,000 marijuana arrests.[43] Of course, such law enforcement concentration on victimless crimes has a tremendous impact on the courts and the prison system, especially on their capacity to adjudicate and house offenders who commit other kinds of crime (e.g., white-collar criminals).

In studying crime trends in Suffolk County, Massachusetts, from 1839 to 1870, Michael Hindus compiled prison commitment rates for two categories of crime—all serious crimes (e.g., theft, crimes against persons, white-collar crimes) and all crimes against morals and order (e.g., creating a nuisance, public drunkenness). Between 1839 and 1841 commitments for victimless crimes ran 695.4 per 100,000 population while commitments for all serious crimes totaled 536.6 per 100,000. Between 1869 and 1870 both categories of crimes showed increases in rates of enforcement, but detentions for victimless crimes continued to outstrip commitments for all serious crimes (1,096 to 813 per 100,000).[44]

Sidney Harring's study of tramping laws in Buffalo, New York, between 1892 and 1894 showed that police arrests for public-order victimless crimes, such as drunkenness and vagrancy, represented between one-half and two-thirds of all yearly police arrests during that period.[45] By the mid-1960s federal commissions and experts reported that national arrests for public drunkenness had reached nearly 2 million a year, placing an awesome burden on the entire criminal justice system.[46] For example, in Washington, D.C., the Metropolitan Police Department made nearly 40,000 yearly arrests for public drunkenness throughout the early 1960s.[47] This rate was typical of that for many large city police departments.

As we will see when discussing policy making below, the enforcement record of police departments in the 1950s and 1960s served as the basis for one argument put forth by reformers wanting decriminalization of public drunkenness. This country needed to free up its criminal justice agencies to fight more serious crimes. However, those making this plea failed to take into account historical realities. Policing and enforcement of victimless crime statutes have grown together. As examplified above, American law enforcement agencies have used victimless crimes to maximize their own self-interest.

Today, even with over 30 states passing decriminalization legislation concerning public drunkenness, law enforcement agencies have continued to stress arrests for morality crimes. As in the past, reducing enforcement of one victimless crime law is often offset by increased enforcement of a newly politicized offense. Despite a slight decline in 1975, marijuana arrests have increased sharply over the last decade. Costs to the public for the massive enforcement of marijuana laws alone has approached nearly $1 billion a year.[48] But for police agencies, coping with victimless crimes is a relatively easy (and safe) way of boosting arrest statistics that make them look aggressive and dedicated, thus justifying the tremendous amount of resources allocated to them.

Of course, police do exercise discretion in enforcing victimless crime statutes. A violator may or may not be arrested, depending upon whether the community is tolerant or intolerant, what area (business district or depressed area) is affected, whether someone complains, and what the socioeconomic status of the individual is.[49] For example, in *Police Discretion*, legal scholar Kenneth Culp Davis records the following example of how patrol officers in Chicago use disorderly conduct to harass certain individuals:

> One officer proudly told us in an interview that he "knows" that X is a big narcotics dealer so that whenever X comes out on the street the officer searches him and often finds some excuse to arrest him. . . . The officer says he goes through a ritual to keep such an arrest "honest." He says "move on" and then in the same breath says: "You didn't move fast enough and I'm arresting you for disorderly conduct." The officer chuckles that X has to put up bail money and then appear in Court to get it back. He knows that X has no practical remedy against such a false arrest.[50]

Most individuals studying the contemporary enforcement of victimless crime statutes agree that the latitude of police and court personnel is widest in this area.[51] The laws are usually quite vague, and police departments rarely develop more precise administrative guidelines to aid their street-level officers in determining who should be arrested for such offenses. The vagueness of these statutes has become a second major justification for decriminalization and legalization of several such criminal areas. As discussed below, civil-libertarian groups claim that many current laws fail to meet common law and constitutional guidelines for shaping criminal statutes.

Policy Making and Victimless Crimes: Decriminalization and Legalization

Broadly speaking, the debate over legalization and decriminalization of victimless crimes revolves around competing values as to what is the proper scope of the criminal law. Libertarians, like the philosopher, John Stuart Mill, argue that the criminal law should only address a very narrow range of antisocial behavior.[52] Criminal laws should be developed only to protect persons and property against harm from other individuals in society. Thus, government has no authority to interfere with personal moral decisions pertaining to the use of goods and services through the formulation of the criminal code.

At the other extreme, scholars like Patrick Devlin believe that the criminal outlawing of private immorality is perfectly legitimate: "The suppression of vice is as much the law's business as the suppression of subversive activities; it is no more possible to define a sphere of private morality than it is to define one of private subversive activity."[53] Thus, those arguing for a broad scope for the criminal law refuse to distinguish between private morality and societal vice. They view immorality, defined in terms of majority sentiments, as a socially harmful phenomenon.

As one can see, the definition of "harm" is at the crux of this debate. Are individuals and property harmed if an intoxicated individual is urinating near a park bench, if street people are hanging out on a corner of a residential community, or if a prostitute is soliciting customers in a hotel bar? Also, should harm to oneself, to one's family, or to the community be the criterion for determining the involvement of the criminal justice system? These questions cannot be factually investigated and answered because they ultimately rest on an individual's value judgment of social harm.

Still, some of the crimes under discussion produce victims; individuals and communities do suffer indirect harm, especially from those victimless crimes associated with alcohol use and/or that are transacted in public places. For example, a public inebriate may be a problem drinker who subjects his or her family to psychological trauma or possibly physical violence. Also, some central-city parks are overrun with street people disrupting the tranquillity of a beautiful day for poor, law-abiding families. However, proponents of decriminalization and legalization argue that much of the indirect harm associated with certain victimless crimes is attributable to the use of the traditional criminal sanction and criminal justice agencies to solve what are essentially social problems.

MIDDLE-OF-THE-ROAD STRATEGIES

Often when sharp political debates are rooted in diverging positions, middle-ground policy strategies emerge that attempt to walk a tightrope between extremist views. In the case of victimless crimes, one extreme position is to retain these acts as criminal violations with sanctions that may result in imprisonment while the other is to completely eliminate the role of government in dealing with these problems. Decriminalization and legalization occupy pragmatic, middle-of-the-road positions over what to do about a particular class of crimes. They are policies without deep theoretical underpinnings about the nature of criminal behavior. Therefore, they minimize the fact that many morality crime statutes were created to protect the "prevailing social order" and protect certain social classes.[54]

Instead, decriminalization and legalization are rooted in questions about what is the proper scope of the criminal sanction. Even more important, their proponents assume that any reduction in the scope of the criminal law can be brought about only by engaging in the political arena. As stated by political scientist Charles Lindbloom this arena is one of "mutual adjustment" or compromise, where all-or-nothing victories are nonexistent.[55]

Both policy options are part of an overall strategy to discourage the trafficking and use of the goods and services associated with victimless crimes. However, these strategies are aimed at either ending or significantly reducing the role of the criminal justice system in suppressing simple use of currently illicit goods and services.

LEGALIZATION This policy relies on a regulative approach to discourage and channel the public's use of goods or services. The legalization strategy has been applied to tobacco, alcohol, and gambling. Tobacco and alcohol are now almost universally available, and gambling is now permissible in several states. However, consumption of these goods and services is state regulated through licensing (e.g., of liquor establishments), state ownership of distribution facilities (e.g., liquor and gambling outlets), or taxing and pricing requirements (e.g., on alcohol and tobacco). Also, their use is discouraged through educational programs, restrictions on advertising, and, in the case of tobacco, increased prohibitions against consumption in public places like university classrooms.

DECRIMINALIZATION This policy is an adjustment to, but not an end of, government prohibitions against goods and services associated with victimless crimes. In the case of a product like marijuana, for example, the product continues to be legitimately available only for medical purposes. Trafficking of the product remains criminally sanctioned usually through unchanged stiff felony charges. Recreational use of the good (i.e., possession) is discouraged but through considerably reduced sanctions. Possession usually subjects a person to a misdemeanor charge (a criminal offense) or a civil fine. Thus, at the heart of decriminalization is protecting the recreational user from both criminal confinement and the criminal label. President Carter acknowledged this goal in his 1977 call for decriminalization of small amounts of marijuana nationwide:

> I am deeply concerned that over the past two years between 400,000 and 450,000 Americans have been arrested on marijuana charges, comprising an average of 69 percent of all drug arrests which occurred in this country. These were individuals who in other respects were normal law abiding citizens.[56]

As of July 1978 eleven states had decriminalized the possession of small amounts of marijuana by adopting fine-only punishment provisions.[57] Still, only six of these states—Mississippi, Minnesota, Maine, Nebraska, Oregon, and Alaska—had removed the criminal label.

As for victimless crimes involving the public order, public drunkenness has been decriminalized in over 30 states.[58] These states have removed the criminal label, but most such decriminalization laws contain provisions that allow for the mandatory commitment of public inebriates to detoxification facilities for up to 72 hours.

This latter brand of decriminalization is quite severe since confinement is a legal option. Some scholars have argued that such reforms are potentially dangerous because due-process guarantees do not extend to detention in civil facilities. One scholar has called for the writing of a therapeutic bill of rights to protect citizens committed to public health facilities like detoxification centers.[59]

IMPACTS ON OTHER GOALS

In addition to reducing the breadth of the criminal label and criminal confinement, legalization and decriminalization have been promoted as meeting additional public interest goals. For folk crimes such as gambling, recent efforts at legalization are designed, in part, as crime-prevention measures directed against organized criminal elements in society.

CRIME PREVENTION   Gambling and prostitution have been sources of massive revenues for organized crime syndicates. Legalization, it is felt, is one way to take the profit out of such activities and thereby thwart such syndicates. Of course, government has an organizational self-interest in promoting legalization of these services as well. Significant state revenues have been raised through the regulation of gambling, providing financially strapped states with opportunities to pay for increased demands in public services and to meet the rising costs of maintaining public service bureaucracies.[60]

EFFICIENCY   Advocates of legalization and decriminalization expect increased efficiency as a by-product as well. Theoretically, police and court personnel will be able to concentrate on more serious crimes, enhancing their professionalism. However, as pointed out in Chapter 5, police departments' abilities to decrease violent street crimes is also dependent on their willingness to shift tactics.

States that have adopted decriminalized and legalized stances on morality crimes have not reduced their emphasis on patrol. But patrol as a police tactic is an unreliable approach for reducing street crimes. Therefore, movements toward decriminalization and legalization are unlikely alone to produce more efficiency and professionalism.

Decriminalization and legalization policies are also promoted as ways to reduce official corruption. As described in Chapter 5, gambling and prostitution kickbacks to plain-clothes and street officers are a major source of contemporary police corruption. However, decriminalization aims to reduce sanctions only against those who possess drugs, not those who traffic in them. For this reason decriminalization of substances such as marijuana is unlikely to reduce the potential for official corruption. Also, historically, scandals have arisen over government-run lotteries, indicating that corruption may simply take a new form;[61] moreover, legalized gambling hardly means that crime syndicates will lose their opportunities to gain significant revenues.[62] Therefore, legalization of victimless crimes is no sure route to ending official corruption or organized crime.

CONFORMITY TO LEGAL PRINCIPLES   Civil-libertarian groups have been heavily involved in the promotion of many decriminalization and legalization policies. In order to win decriminalization of public drunkenness in over 30 states, these groups secured appellate court approval that the application of public-drunkenness statutes to chronic alcoholics did not conform with sound legal principles.

For example, Bernard Fearon of Minneapolis, Minnesota, was a chronic alcoholic who had been arrested on numerous occasions for public drunkenness. The Supreme Court of Minnesota agreed to review his arrest by a Minneapolis police officer on April 7, 1967. Nearly two years after his arrest the court ruled, in *State* v. *Fearon* (1969), that the public-drunkenness statute did not apply to chronic alcoholics, in part because "the necessary *mens rea* is lacking."[63] As we will see below, such court rulings served as the springboard for legislative decriminalization of public drunkenness.

PUBLIC TRANQUILLITY   Advocates of decriminalization and legalization policies have given very little consideration to how such reforms would affect the desires of residents and business people in cities for public tranquillity. Citizens want to be able to walk the cities free of street people's panhandling and general intrusions into daily activities. Store owners object to public inebriates sleeping in their doorways or prostitutes soliciting customers in front of their shops. These problems have become especially acute for downtown merchants since suburban shopping malls offer antiseptic environments as well as convenient parking for customers.

Disturbances of tranquillity are often associated with public-order victimless crimes such as public drunkenness. Although decriminalization statutes permit authorities to commit public inebriates up to 72 hours, recent studies have shown that chronic skid-row inebriates are often back on the streets within a few hours.[64] The increased street presence of these individuals has negatively influenced public peace, especially in downtown business districts of major cities. This observation confirms our statement in Chapter 1 that one of the serious problems facing American criminal justice is the conflict over public interest goals. Policy revisions, like decriminalization of public drunkenness, tend to accentuate the incompatibilities among the several public goals assigned to our criminal justice system.

CONDITIONS FOR REFORM

In order to win legislative support for decriminalization and legalization, new forces must enter the political arena and take root. These new political forces are needed to offset the weight of those that support victimless crime statutes—moral entrepreneurs, bureaucrats, and the ruling class. While all of the forces described below may not be operating when a given appellate court or legislature decides to promote legal reforms, some of these countervailing political forces should be detectable.

PERSUASIVE EXPERT TESTIMONY Experts, often medical scientists and lawyers, frequently issue individual statements and reports refuting popularly held assumptions about a particular folk crime. When organizations representing

---

THE THIRD LARGEST BUSINESS IN AMERICA?

America's taste for marijuana is no longer just a law enforcement issue. It has become a staggering economic headache, a balance-of-payments problem.

Frederick Rody, DEA chief for the South, estimated up to 3 million young people supplement their incomes by dealing small quantities of marijuana.

Rody said DEA officials can only speculate about the actual volume in the marijuana industry. "We think there is a good chance that marijuana dealing does a volume of maybe $48 billion per year," he said.

"If that is true, then marijuana is the third biggest business in the U.S. today. General Motors is No. 1, Exxon is No. 2, and marijuana is No. 3."

Today, said Rody, marijuana accounts for more than 20 percent of Colombia's gross national product—far more than coffee.

One CIA agent described factories in Colombia, where raw marijuana weed enters on a conveyor belt and later emerges wrapped in burlap with trademarks stamped outside. Each bale is worth about $40,000.

James Coates, "Marijuana, the Pot of Gold: No. 3 Business in America?" *San Francisco Examiner*, September 17, 1978, p. 1.

prestigious permanent interest groups, such as the American Medical Association (A.M.A.) and the American Bar Association (A.B.A.), testify, policy-making bodies and the media pay even more attention.

In the case of public-drunkenness laws, medical and public health organizations (including the A.M.A.) have empahsized that those citizens most influenced by the statutes—chronic skid-row inebriates—suffer from a disease—alcoholism—and that therefore such criminal laws should be voided. The Minnesota Supreme Court's ruling against the state's public-drunkenness statute documents that such declarations affect policy makers. The court justified its decision, in part, on the basis of the experts' position. According to the court, " 'Voluntary drinking,' as defined under [the public drunkenness statute] means drinking by choice. Therefore, the statute does not apply to the chronic alcoholic whose drinking is caused by his disease and, as such, cannot be controlled."[65]

MEDIA ATTENTION   In the early 1970s experts also testified in favor of decriminalizing marijuana, but law enforcement officials and politicians dissented. The flood of expert testimony and the growing gap between politicians and experts within the federal government caught the media's attention. National magazines started emphasizing a new kind of human-interest story surrounding marijuana use.

The emphasis was on the severity of punishment for marijuana use. For example, *Life* magazine devoted a feature article to the case of Frank LaVarre, an individual found guilty of possessing four containers of marijuana in Danville, Virginia. He was sentenced to 25 years in the state penitentiary, and *Life* used the LaVarre case to illustrate the nation's antiquated and inhumane drug laws.[66]

In regard to the decriminalization of public drunkenness, newspapers in Minnesota and Washington, D.C., devoted many human-interest stories to the plight of public inebriates caught in the "revolving door" of the criminal justice system in the 1960s. The media in these states also registered direct support for decriminalization through editorials when policy makers began deliberating over the issue.[67] Thus, the media plays critical roles both in promoting a shift in public sentiments by tracing the plight of those charged with victimless crimes and in directly registering a position on a victimless crime when policy makers are weighing a change in the law.

COMPETING GOVERNMENTAL INTERESTS   Chapter 4 noted that public service bureaucracies are in competition with one another over the scope of their respective jurisdictions. This "territorial imperative" becomes a critical ingredient in shrinking the scope of the criminal sanction. For example, jails lose their jurisdiction over housing public inebriates when public drunkenness is decriminalized, but the new statutes usually require the creation of detoxification centers to provide emergency treatment and promote rehabilitation for those picked up for civil commitment.

A shrinkage in the territorial responsibilities of criminal justice agencies offers the opportunity for expansion by other bureaucracies. A research team found that one of the groups promoting decriminalization legislation in both Minnesota and the District of Columbia was the public health bureaucracy that later assumed responsibilities for establishing and running such detoxification centers.[68] Even more recently, some of these agencies have received funds for training public health personnel and purchasing pickup vans to relieve or replace police street responsibilities for handling public intoxicants.[69] In some states, then, the public health bureaucracy has both expanded its facilities and created new field operations as a result of such legislation. Of course, from the perspective of an organization's self-interest, decriminalization means more jobs and more territorial turf for health agencies.

At the federal level the Department of Health, Education, and Welfare introduced reports criticizing the criminal justice system's handling of public inebriates and funded experimental detoxification facilities throughout the country. Police departments have not reacted and, in fact, were little involved in the deliberations over decriminalization. The former police chief of Washington, D.C., Jerry Wilson, stated that the impetus for decriminalization came at a time when the police were particularly pressed on other matters:

> the city was in a state of crisis, with street disorders occurring or threatening to occur almost weekly, with the Poor People's Campaign absorbing much of the time of senior officials of the department as well as diverting patrol officers to special details, and with sharp upward trends developing in serious crime and narcotics traffic.[70]

Police ambivalence coupled with the aggressiveness of alternative bureaucracies that stand to gain from decriminalization policy can influence greatly the opportunity for successful passage of such measures.

As for legalization measures, states seem to be significantly motivated to support such policies when they have a budget problem. The recession of the early 1970s prompted several states, including New Jersey, to seek financial relief through the legalization of gambling. This competing government interest in meeting expenses seems to overpower the arguments of traditional forces that led to the creation and retention of criminal sanctions against gambling.

CITIZEN INDIGNATION   Chapter 3 pointed out that one important dimension for assessing the potential of government to lower the incidence of a crime is the general public's perception of the particular criminal act. When large segments of middle-class society routinely indulge in a particular folk crime, societal support for the retention of the criminal sanction is significantly eroded.[71] Additionally, if police agencies continue to enforce strongly the relevant law by arresting many violators, public indignation or resentment about the crime escalates even more. Widespread violation and stiff enforcement are conditions associated with the marijuana laws since the early 1970s. Well-organized and solidly financed opposition seems to flow out of these social conditions.

RIVAL INTEREST-GROUP STANDS   Financed initially by the Playboy Foundation, the National Organization for the Reform of Marijuana Laws (N.O.R.M.L.) was created in 1970 as a one-issue interest group promoting decriminalization of marijuana. Since 1970 the organization has gained political respectability by developing a professional staff and lobbying for the gradual reform of state marijuana policies. In the ten states that have adopted some form of decriminalization, N.O.R.M.L. has played an active role by providing information to state legislators and the media to build support for such policies. In short, the organization has utilized the traditional tactics associated with interest-group politics.

Howard Becker, in his historical study of the 1937 Marijuana Tax Act, argues that organized groups that had an interest in continued use of marijuana faired well by the legislation. For example, birdseed manufacturers successfully lobbied for changes in the language of the legislation so as to allow for continued use of oil from marijuana plants in their products. However, marijuana smokers, who at that time were powerless, unorganized, and lacking publicly legitimate grounds for attack, sent no representatives to the hearings and did not secure attention for their point of view.[72] Today, individuals who consume the goods and services associated with morality crimes have discovered that engaging in interest-group politics is a potential route to legal reform of these criminal statutes.

FEDERALISM AND VICTIMLESS CRIMES

When the federal government favors decriminalization or legalization, it uses two basic strategies to launch an attack on victimless crimes. First, through the dissemination and promotion of information accumulated by experts, the federal government lends symbolic support to such efforts. President Carter's Fall 1977 speech favoring decriminalization of marijuana and congressional deliberations over the president's proposal are largely designed to prod state action. While the purging of folk crimes from the federal criminal code would slightly lessen the criminal justice system's involvement in such crimes, most criminal justice activity surrounding these violations occurs at the state and municipal levels. Morality crimes have rarely been a major concern of federal criminal justice agencies.

Second, the federal government sometimes supports decriminalization or legalization by appropriating experimental or seed funds for the creation of alternative facilities when needed. Both the Department of Health, Education, and Welfare and the Law Enforcement Assistance Administration have made money available to states and municipalities for staffing detoxification facilities. They have given grants for a three-year period, but they expect states to assume fiscal responsibility for facilities and staffs when the experimental funding period ends. Thus, both the enactment and permanent funding of decriminalization and legalization policies largely rest on the shoulders of state governments.

TABLE 11-1

State Variations in Marijuana Decriminalization Laws

State	Maximum Fine Imposed	Maximum Amount Possessed	Classification of Offense	Effective Date
Oregon	$100	1 ounce	Civil	October 5, 1973
Alaska[1]	$100	Any amount in private for personal use or 1 ounce in public	Civil	September 2, 1975
Maine	$200	Any amount[2] for personal use	Civil	March 1, 1976
Colorado	$100	1 ounce	Class 2 petty offense—no criminal record	July 1, 1975
California	$100	1 ounce	Misdemeanor—no permanent criminal record	January 1, 1976
Ohio	$100	100 grams (approx. 3½ ounces)	Minor misdemeanor—no criminal record	November 22, 1975
Minnesota	$100	1½ ounces	Civil	April 10, 1976
Mississippi	$250	1 ounce	Civil	July 1, 1977
North Carolina	$100	1 ounce	Minor misdemeanor	July 1, 1977
New York	$100	25 grams (approx. ⅞ ounce)	Violation—no criminal record	July 29, 1977
Nebraska	$100	1 ounce	Civil	July 1, 1978

[1]The Supreme Court of Alaska ruled in 1975 that the constitutional right of privacy protects the possession of marijuana for personal use in the home by adults. This decision invalidates the $100 fine for simple possession in the home.

[2]There is a rebuttable presumption that possession of less than one and a half ounces is for personal use and possession of more than that is with an intent to distribute.

Note: Distribution of marijuana by gift, or for no remuneration, is treated the same as simple possession in four states: California, Colorado, Minnesota, and Ohio (for up to 20 grams).

Only one state, Mississippi, has a mandatory minimum fine—$100 for the first offense and $250 for the second offense within a two-year period—but state judges can suspend payment of these fines.

In five states—Minnesota, Mississippi, New York, North Carolina, and Nebraska—subsequent offenses are subject to increased penalties.

SOURCE: National Organization for the Reform of Marijuana Laws, "Marijuana Decriminalization Laws: Summary Chart." Reprinted by permission.

Because each of the 50 state legislatures ultimately possesses the legal authority to decriminalize or legalize certain activities, this country lacks a national policy for any particular victimless crime let alone for victimless crimes in general. A citizen can be arrested in one state for possessing less than an ounce of marijuana and go to prison, while in another state, a citizen may receive only a fine similar to the sanction for a minor traffic violation. In this respect, federalism contributes to negating the concept of equal treatment.

Table 11-1 shows that even in the states that have decriminalized possession of marijuana, policies vary in two basic respects. First, the act may be classified as either a civil or a criminal offense, and a criminal offense may or may not carry with it a criminal record. Second, the maximum fines range from $100 to $250 in these states, another violation of equal treatment.

SEPARATION OF POWERS AND FOLK CRIMES

Appellate courts at both the federal and state levels of government have sometimes rendered decisions in support of decriminalization and legalization policies. As with public drunkenness, these appellate court decisions are only partial victories, serving to prompt comprehensive state action.

Both *State* v. *Fearon* and *Easter* v. *District of Columbia*[73] (a similar federal district court decision affecting Washington, D.C.) applied only to public inebriates who were chronic alcoholics. Therefore, these decisions served as legal beacons to legislative bodies, which are responsible ultimately for the enactment of decriminalization and legalization statutes. In the case of public drunkenness, the Minnesota state legislature enacted a comprehensive decriminalization policy, ending the criminal sanction and setting up an alternative treatment process.[74]

Impact of Decriminalization Policies

Passage of decriminalization or legalization policies by state legislatures is only the first step in the policy-making process. The new statutes must be administered by public service bureaucracies with wide discretionary powers. As described in Chapter 4, these agencies strive to meet public interest goals associated with new legislative decisions; but they also play a number of administrative games to enhance organizational goals and the self-interest of individual administrators.

In the remainder of the chapter, we will treat the administration of decriminalization policies regarding marijuana and public drunkenness. Marijuana decriminalization is an example of reform that requires little new administrative machinery for implementation and that is not traditionally associated with the police functions of maintaining public order and tranquillity. Public-drunkenness reform, on the other hand, is strongly associated with the enforcement of community tranquillity and requires significant new administrative machinery that does not involve the police or jails to be properly implemented. It is in this latter case study that we particularly can observe the dynamics of self-interest.

IMPACT OF MARIJUANA DECRIMINALIZATION POLICIES

Marijuana decriminalization measures attempt to meet a modest set of public interest goals. Simply through the enactment of these policies, the scope of criminal behavior is significantly reduced. This is especially true in those states that have adopted civil penalties rather than criminal sanctions. As pointed out in a 1977 study by the National Governors' Conference on marijuana policies, "loss of respect for the law [is] alleviated simply by virtue of adopting the change in the law."[75] Other public interest goals are met as well.

FISCAL SAVINGS   Implementation of decriminalization policies in several states has apparently reduced costs to criminal justice agencies without creating new costs for other public service bureaucracies. Preliminary studies in California and Minnesota have shown that police costs for dealing with marijuana use have been favorably reduced. For example, in California the cost of enforcing marijuana statutes has gone from $7.6 million in the first half of 1975 to $2.3 million in the first half of 1976, a savings of 70 percent.[76] Estimates of savings to the courts are also quite high, with reductions for handling marijuana use cases producing a yearly savings of $7 million in California.[77] Because correctional systems were rarely used for first offenders in those states that have decriminalized, savings for these criminal justice agencies appear to be minimal.

SPILLOVER   Savings for one public service bureaucracy may represent increased costs for another, thus resulting in no real reduction in costs to taxpayers. But this spillover effect has not occurred in the case of marijuana decriminalization. On at least a short-term basis, no new costs for the public health care system seem likely to result from decriminalization. In fact, Minnesota has realized savings of nearly $3 million to its health care system, because decriminalization legislation shifted emphasis from medical treatment to an educational program on drug abuse for offenders.[78] The five-hour mandatory educational program is far less expensive than putting marijuana users through the state's public health care system.

Long-term costs to states' health care systems cannot yet be tracked for two reasons. First, medical researchers still are unsure as to whether marijuana use produces any long-range health hazards. However, to date, no medical tests have revealed any long-term health hazards equivalent to those produced by alcohol or tobacco use.[79] Second, decriminalization policies have been in effect for less than five years in most states—too little time for medical and social science researchers to trace the full impact of the substance on either the health care or criminal justice system.

USE AND PUBLIC TRANQUILLITY   Critics of the legislation in several states argued that decriminalization would increase use of the substance. They further asserted that marijuana would be more openly displayed, exposing youths to this substance. What do we know about the use and public display of the substance following decriminalization?

Very little reliable research has been completed yet to answer this question conclusively. The study by the National Governors' Conference reviewed surveys conducted in Oregon and California on usage patterns. A moderate increase in use was recorded in the third annual Oregon survey, but no substantial increases in overall use have been revealed by these surveys.[80] Reporting on interviews with officials from the criminal justice system and other relevant agencies, the study concluded:

> It appears that reduced criminal penalties for possession do not generally lead to an immediate increase in total marijuana use, although the long-term effects of penalty reductions are less clear. The apparent short-term stability of use in the face of penalty reductions implies that harsh penalty structures do not in themselves deter personal possession.[81]

The cautious wording is just one indication of how little we know about usage patterns. Unfortunately, research undertaken following decriminalization is inadequate for testing the impact of decriminalization because almost no reliable research had been completed on usage patterns prior to decriminalization. In short, research efforts that look at usage patterns before and after decriminalization are necessary to conclusively answer the question of the effect of new marijuana statutes on public tranquility. States anticipating revisions of their laws should begin to make assessments of use under the criminal sanction.

IMPACT OF PUBLIC-DRUNKENNESS DECRIMINALIZATION POLICIES

Decriminalization of public drunkenness is a much more complex policy change. Reform legislation in many of the states is worded so as to assume that a wide range of conflicting public interest goals can be met by decriminalization. Also, as mentioned above, decriminalization legislation usually calls for the creation of new facilities—detoxification centers—while greatly reducing the responsibility of criminal justice agencies. Further, some state legislation calls for the training of new pick-up agents, who transfer public inebriates from the streets to public health facilities. Thus, officers from two very different public service bureaucracies are put side by side to handle the public-drunkenness problem in the streets. For all of these reasons, implementing the decriminalization of public drunkeness is much more difficult than administering the new laws governing marijuana use.

CONFLICTING AGENCIES A research team has recently studied the conflicts among public service bureaucracies set off by decriminalization legislation.[82] For example, the policies formulated in several state legislatures assume that decriminalization can achieve improved handling of skid-row inebriates who cause public tranquillity problems for the police and at the same time allow public health personnel to rehabilitate individuals who use excessive alcohol in public.

Detoxification centers are usually controlled by the public health bureaucracy, and public health workers prefer to concentrate on the more motivated client. In short, detoxification centers focus on "rehabilitative success." On the other hand, police officers are more oriented toward preserving public order by removing the emergency-case skid-row inebriate from the streets. Ultimately, this difference in focus between the police and public health personnel leads to a partial breakdown in service, negatively influencing those individuals for which the legislation was initially championed. As the research team studying the problem noted:

> Since the police, as pick up agents, usually emphasize the delivery of skid row type emergency cases, it becomes necessary for the detoxification center to stress voluntary intake mechanisms rather than the police delivery system. . . . The system becomes, over time, more specialized and more discriminating regarding who will be treated. Success becomes defined not in terms of servicing the emergency case, but rather in terms of recidivism rates or other measures of rehabilitation.[83]

PUBLIC TRANQUILLITY Because the new system of treating public drunkenness emphasizes a different clientele (those motivated enough to commit themselves), the police must resort to more informal mechanisms of keeping the streets clear of nuisance drunks. All of these informal techniques have as their control purpose keeping the drunk out of sight in important commercial and tourist areas of cities. For example, the police designate "safe zones," informally letting inebriates know that they are allowed to gather in run-down sections of the city or in isolated parks without police interference.[84]

Police officers must resort to these techniques because business people and residents complain and hold the police responsible for this unanticipated impact of decriminalization policy. A simple solution to the problem would be for citizens to grow more tolerant of skid-row inebriates, but few retailers or shoppers seem satisfied with this historical solution to public tranquillity problems.[85]

COSTS While significant savings for courts and correctional facilities result from the decriminalization of public drunkenness, police costs tend to remain quite high. Even where public health pick-up units are created, some studies have shown that police costs remain high because law enforcement agencies deal with a different clientele, usually the skid-row inebriate or the problem drinker who causes fights and other public order problems.[86]

Most studies that calculate overall savings ignore the spillover problem mentioned above. Decriminalization of public drunkenness places heavy financial burdens on state health care systems. The few studies that have attempted to estimate the costs of involving many agencies indicate that therapeutic programs are often more expensive than their criminal justice counterparts. Thus, the financial impact of freeing criminal justice resources has been smaller than anticipated.[87]

OVERALL EVALUATION

Those decriminalization polices that establish a modest set of goals, require few new public service bureaucracies, and continue to be largely handled within the criminal justice system are most likely to be implemented successfully. Such measures have the least severe impact on the policy hurdles (e.g., conflicting goals, territoriality) that are critical to the successful implementation of the law as outlined in Part I of this book.

Still, for nearly all decriminalization and legalization measures our knowledge becomes most limited when we move to a discussion of policy impact. More evaluation research from medical scientists and social scientists is needed to trace the intended and unintended consequences of the efforts to shrink the scope of the criminal law.

Conclusion

Because of changing societal values in the 1960s and 1970s many victimless crimes have been decriminalized at least in fact if not by law. But scholars concerned about due process and contemporary application of justice are convinced that practical nonenforcement of victimless crimes is not enough. Harassment remains a possibility whenever rarely enforced laws remain on the books, and criminal justice agencies enjoy wide discretionary latitude.

Also, while many states are formally or informally practicing decriminalization and legalization of a number of folk crimes, the discussion over whether the law should be used to regulate morality continues. A reminder that retrenchments are possible in the future while such discussion continues was made clear in a 1978 article of the Phoenix newspaper, the *Arizona Republic*. The article revealed that on February 9, 1978, the lower house of the Arizona state legislature had passed an amendment that would include cohabitation and adultery in the definition of criminal prostitution. The newspaper account went on to reveal that a state legislator representing the retirement community of Sun City was chastised by other representatives for maligning his constituents when he said, "a great many adults of geriatric age . . . live together in Sun City and other retirement communities. There are elderly people who live together in order to obtain additional Social Security [benefits] which they would not obtain if they were married."[88]

Crackdowns on such morality crimes continue. For example in 1978 the Boston police department conducted an undercover operation involving a homosexual hangout in the city's public library. Responding to citizens' calls and a plea from the library's trustees, an undercover team of 10 police officers made over 90 arrests in the spring: According to one report, "Police arrested a college professor, business executives, school teachers, students and doctoral candidates. . . . Some of those arrested went to the library only to solicit in the men's room, but others were scholars who also used the upstairs card catalogue.[89]

Proponents of doing away with all laws regulating sex argue that such incidents only occur because the law forces homosexuals to search out people of similar persuasion clandestinely. Staunch opponents counter that the criminal law must be used to reduce the potential for such public displays of immoral sexual interactions. As demonstrated in this chapter, decriminalization and legalization represent policy strategies that attempt to walk a tightrope between these very different positions.

SUMMARY

Both "deviants" and the more stable citizenry routinely commit victimless crimes. Depending upon how broadly one defines harm, one could argue that there are no victimless crimes. However, crimes such as marijuana use, public drunkenness, and cohabitation differ from other criminal acts. Victimless crimes (also called folk crimes or morality crimes) are acts in which identifying an assailant-victim relationship is more difficult than in murder, robbery, auto theft, or most other actions commonly thought of as being criminal. The chapter concentrates on those folk crimes that are usually associated with decriminalization and legalization.

Criminalizing such acts has (1) eroded citizens' respect for the law, (2) created exorbitant purchasing costs for such goods as marijuana, which makes criminal activity a highly profitable undertaking; and (3) misdirected the priorities of the criminal justice system. Forces that have supported the criminalization of these acts include moral crusaders, the ruling classes, and bureaucracies. Newspapers, politicians, and law enforcement agencies have benefited from criminalization legislature. Enforcement of morality laws continues to be the

bread-and-butter task of modern law enforcement agencies despite the contemporary movements toward decriminalization and legalization policies.

Decriminalization and legalization policies are pragmatic strategies aimed at either ending or significantly reducing the role of the criminal justice system in suppressing simple use of goods and services associated with morality crimes. Legalization relies on a regulative approach to discourage and channel the public's use of these goods and services. Decriminalization involves an adjustment to, but not an end to, the criminal prohibition of goods and services associated with folk crimes.

Both policies attempt to meet the public interest goals of crime prevention, efficiency, and conformity to legal principles. Advocates of these policies give little consideration to how these reforms affect public tranquillity.

To win legislative support for these policies, a state must rally expert support, media coverage, some government agencies, indignant citizens, and supportive interest groups, or some combination. Federal governmental support and favorable court rulings are also significant contributors to the formulation of decriminalization and legalization policies in state legislatures.

Decriminalization policies that require little new administrative machinery for implementation and that are not traditionally tied to public order and tranquillity problems can be success-

fully implemented. An example of such policies is decriminalization of marijuana use. Decriminalization of public drunkenness, a policy that is associated with public tranquillity and requires the creation of new agencies, has been less successfully implemented to date.

FOOTNOTES

[1] Eve Merriam, *The Inner City Mother Goose* (New York: Simon & Schuster, 1969), p. 38.

[2] William K. Muir, *Police: Streetcorner Politicians* (Chicago: University of Chicago Press, 1977), pp. 78–79.

[3] See, for example, Ronald Bayer, "Heroin Decriminalization and the Ideology of Tolerance: A Critical View," *Law and Society Review* 12 (Winter 1978), 312.

[4] Ibid.

[5] For a discussion of the issue, see Edwin M. Schur and Hugo Bedau, *Victimless Crimes: Two Sides of A Controversy* (Englewood Cliffs, N.J.: Prentice-Hall, 1974).

[6] Gilbert Geis, *Not the Law's Business?* (Rockville, Md.: National Institute of Mental Health, 1972), p. 2.

[7] Don Cahalan, *Problem Drinkers* (San Francisco: Jossey-Bass, 1970), pp. 52–53.

[8] Alfred Kinsey, Wardell Pomeroy, and Clyde Martin, *Sexual Behavior in the Human Male* (Philadelphia: W. B. Saunders, 1948).

[9] Daniel Coleman and Sherida Bush, "The Liberation of Sexual Fantasy," *Psychology Today*, October, 1977, p. 48.

[10] Ibid.

[11] National Governors' Conference, *Marijuana: A Study of State Policies and Penalties*, vol. 2 (Washington, D.C.: National Governors' Conference, 1977), p. 4.

[12] Ibid., p. 5.

[13] *Report to the Commission on Obscenity and Pornography* (Washington, D.C.: U.S. Government Printing Office, 1970), p. 119.

[14] Ibid., p. 123.

[15] Ibid., pp. 128–29.

[16] Ibid, p. 131.

[17] Norval Morris and Gordon Hawkins, *The Honest Politician's Guide to Crime Control* (Chicago: University of Chicago Press, 1970), pp. 5–6.

[18] Albert Goldman, "Marijuana: The Highs and Lows of Turning On," *Cosmopolitan*, March 1978, p. 236.

[19] Grace Hechinger and Fred M. Hechinger, "Homosexuality on Campus," *New York Times Magazine*, March 12, 1978, pp. 15–17.

[20] William Chambliss, "The State, the Law, and the Definition of Behavior as Criminal or Delinquent," in *Handbook of Criminology*, ed. Daniel Glaser (Chicago: Rand McNally, 1976), p. 8.

[21] Howard Becker, *Outsiders* (Glencoe, Ill.: The Free Press, 1973), p. 136.

[22] Ibid.

[23] Ibid.

[24] Michael Stephen Hindus, "The Contours of Crime and Justice in Massachusetts and South Carolina, 1767–1878," *The American Journal of Legal History* 21 (1977), 221.

[25] William J. Chambliss, "A Sociological Analysis of the Law of Vagrancy," *Social Problems* 12 (1964), 68.

[26] Ibid.

[27] Sidney L. Harring, "Class Conflict and the Suppression of Tramps in Buffalo, 1892–1894," *Law and Society Review* 11 (Summer 1977), 909.

[28] Ibid.

[29] Cited in Ibid., 873.

[30] Caleb Foote, "Vagrancy Type Law and Its Administration," *University of Pennsylvania Law Review* 104 (1956), 603–50.

[31] John Galliher and Allynn Walker, "The Puzzle of the Social Origins of the Marijuana Tax Act of 1937," *Social Problems* 24 (February, 1977), 371–73.

[32] Chambliss, "The State, the Law, and the Definition of Behavior as Criminal or Delinquent," in op. cit., p. 18.

[33] Richard J. Bonnie and Charles Whitebread, *The Marijuana Conviction* (Charlottesville, Va.: University Press of Virginia, 1974), p. 148.

[34] Galliher and Walker, op. cit., 372–73.

[35] Chambliss, "The State, the Law, and the Definition of Behavior as Criminal or Delinquent," in op. cit., p. 33.

[36] Jack West and Frank Turco, "Officers Close 60 Businesses in Parlor Raids," *Arizona Republic*, January 27, 1978, p. 1.

[37] Quoted in Bonnie and Whitebread, p. 179.

[38] Ibid., p. 209.

[39] Joseph R. Gusfield, *Symbolic Crusade* (Urbana, Ill.: University of Illinois Press, 1963), pp. 171–72. See also Murray Edelman, *Politics as Symbolic Action* (Chicago: Markham Publishing, 1971).

[40] Quoted in Andrew Sinclair, *The Era of Excess: A Social History of the Prohibition Movement* (New York: Harper & Row, 1964), p. 71.

[41] U.S. Federal Bureau of Investigation, *Uniform Crime Reports for the United States—1975* (Washington, D.C.: U.S. Government Printing Office, 1975), p. 191.

[42] Ibid.

[43] National Organization for the Reform of Marijuana Laws, "Marijuana Arrests Climb in 1976," *The Leaflet* 6, no. 4 (October–December 1977), p. 1.

[44] Hindus, op. cit., p. 226.

[45] Harring, op. cit., p. 886.

[46] See the President's Commission on Law Enforcement and Administration of Justice, *Task Force Report: Drunkenness* (Washington, D.C.: U.S. Government Printing Office, 1967); and Raymond Nimmer, *Two Million Unnecessary Arrests* (Chicago: American Bar Foundation, 1971).

[47] David Aaronson, C. Thomas Dienes, and Michael Musheno, "Improving Police Discretion Rationality in Handling Public Inebriates," *Administrative Law Review* 29 no. 4 (Fall 1977), 456–63.

[48] National Organization for Reform of Marijuana Laws, op. cit.

[49] See James Q. Wilson, *Varieties of Police Behavior* (New York: Atheneum, 1971).

[50] Kenneth Culp Davis, *Police Discretion* (St. Paul, Minn.: West Publishing, 1975), pp. 16–17.

[51] See, for example, Wilson, op. cit., p. 85.

[52] John Stuart Mill, *On Liberty* (London: Oxford University Press, 1966).

[53] Patrick Devlin, *The Enforcement of Morals* (New York: Oxford University Press, 1965).

[54] Bayer, op. cit., 315.

[55] Charles E. Lindbloom, *The Intelligence of Democracy* (Glencoe, Ill.: The Free Press, 1965), p. 64.

[56] National Governors' Conference, op. cit., pp. xi–xii.

[57] Ibid., vol. 3, pp. 110–11.

[58] Aaronson, Dienes, and Musheno, op. cit., p. 449.

[59] Nicholas Kittrie, *The Right to Be Different* (Baltimore: Johns Hopkins Press, 1971). See also Herbert Titus, "The Perils of Decriminalization" (Paper presented at the Conference on Criminal Justice, Santa Barbara, Calif., November 7–9, 1973).

[60] Council of State Governments, *Gambling: Source of State Revenue* (Lexington, Ky.: Council of State Governments, 1973).

[61] Ibid.

[62] Howard Blum and Jeff Gerth, "The Mob Gambles on Atlantic City," *The New York Times Magazine*, February 5, 1978, p. 10.

[63] State v. Fearon, 238 Minn. 90; 166 N.W.2d 722 (1969).

[64] Aaronson, Dienes, and Musheno, op. cit., 474–85.

[65] State v. Fearon, 166 N.W.2d 722–23 (1969).

[66] Bonnie and Whitebread, op. cit., p. 240.

[67] David Aaronson, C. Thomas Dienes, and Michael Musheno, "Changing the Public Drunkenness Laws: The Impact of Decriminalization," *Law and Society Review* 12, 3 (1978), 407–15.

[68] Ibid.

[69] Ibid., 426.

[70] Quoted in ibid., 410–11.

[71] See Chambliss, "The State, the Law, and the Definition of Behavior as Criminal or Delinquent," op. cit., pp. 30–34.

[72] Becker, op. cit., p. 139.

[73] Easter v. District of Columbia, 361 F.2d 50 (D.C. Cir. 1966).

[74] Aaronson, Dienes, and Musheno, "Changing the Public Drunkenness Laws," op. cit.

[75] National Governors' Conference, op. cit., vol. 2, 27.

[76] Ibid., p. 42.

[77] Ibid., p. 44.

[78] Ibid., p. 39.

[79] See, for example, Robert Carr, "Update/What Marijuana Does (and Doesn't Do)," *Human Behavior* 7, no. 1 (January 1978), 20–29.

[80] National Governors' Conference, op. cit., pp. 23–28.

[81] Ibid., p. 36.

[82] Aaronson, Dienes, and Musheno, "Improving Police Discretion Rationality in Handling Public Inebriates," op. cit., 454.

[83] Ibid., 480–81.

[84] Aaronson, Dienes, and Musheno, "Changing the Public Drunkenness Laws," op. cit., p. 431.

[85] See Edward Banfield, *The Unheavenly City Revisited* (Boston: Little, Brown, 1974), pp. 23–24.

[86] See, for example, Cathy Winslow, "Public Inebriate Diversion System: Mobile Assistance Patrol," Evaluation Report 45 (Paper submitted by Mayor's Criminal Justice Council, San Francisco, Calif., 1976).

[87] Aaronson, Dienes, and Musheno, "Improving Police Discretion Rationality in Handling Public Inebriates," op. cit., 460.

[88] Quoted in Joel Nilsson, "House Bill Labels Adultery and Cohabitation Criminal," *Arizona Republic*, February 10, 1978, p. B1.

[89] *Arizona Republic*, March 28, 1978, p. A20.

BIBLIOGRAPHY

Aaronson, David; Dienes, C. Thomas; and Musheno, Michael. "Changing the Public Drunkenness Laws: The Impact of Decriminalization." *Law & Society Review* 12, no. 3 (1978), 405–36.

———. "Improving Police Discretion Rationality in Handling Public Inebriates." *Administrative Law Review* 29 (Fall 1977), 447–85.

Bayer, Ronald. "Heroin Decriminalization and the Ideology of Tolerance: A Critical View." *Law & Society Review* 12 (Winter 1978), 301–18.

Becker, Howard. *Outsiders*. Glencoe, Ill.: The Free Press, 1973.

Benjamin, Harry. *Prostitution and Morality*. New York: Julian Press, 1964.

Bonnie, Richard J., and Whitebread, Charles. *The Marijuana Conviction*. Charlottesville, Va.: University Press of Virginia, 1974.

Chambliss, William. "A Sociological Analysis of the Law of Vagrancy." *Social Problems* 12 (1964), 67–77.

Gusfield, Joseph. *Symbolic Crusade.* Urbana, Ill.: University of Illinois Press, 1963.

Harring, Sidney L. "Class Conflict and the Suppression of Tramps in Buffalo, 1892–1894." *Law and Society Review* 11 (Summer 1977), 873–911.

Hindus, Michael. "The Contours of Crime and Justice in Massachusetts and South Carolina, 1767–1878." *The American Journal of Legal History* 21 (1977), 212–37.

Kittrie, Nicholas. *The Right to Be Different.* Baltimore: Johns Hopkins Press, 1971.

Morris, Norval, and Hawkins, Gordon. *The Honest Politician's Guide to Crime Control.* Chicago: University of Chicago Press, 1970.

National Governors' Conference, *Marijuana: A Study of State Policies and Penalties.* 3 vols. Washington, D.C.: National Governors' Conference, 1977.

Schur, Edwin M., and Bedau, Hugo. *Victimless Crimes: Two Sides of a Controversy.* Englewood Cliffs, N.J.: Prentice-Hall, 1974.

Sinclair, Andrew. *The Era of Excess: A Social History of the Prohibition Movement.* New York: Harper & Row, 1964.

The way Americans commonly solve crime problems today is not universally accepted. Certain Indian cultures, such as the Cheyenne, have used other methods with good results. The following are examples of how the Cheyennes handled crimes during the mid-1800's:*

> Cries Yia Eya had been gone from the camp for three years because he had killed Chief Eagle in a whiskey brawl. The chiefs had ordered him away for his murder, so we did not see anything of him for that time. Then one day he came back leading a horse packed with bundles of old-time tobacco. He stopped outside the camp and sent a messenger in with the horse and tobacco who was to say to the chiefs for him, "I am begging to come home."

* From *The Cheyenne Way: Conflict and Case Law in Primitive Jurisprudence*, K. N. Llewellyn and E. Adamson Hockel. Copyright 1941 by the University of Oklahoma Press.

CHAPTER TWELVE

DIVERSION OF THE ACCUSED
Community-Based Conflict Resolution, Counseling, and Treatment

The chiefs all got together for a meeting, and the soldier societies were told to convene, for there was an important matter to be considered. The tobacco was divided up and the chiefs' messengers were sent out to invite the soldier chiefs to come to the lodge of the tribal council, for the big chiefs wanted to talk to them. "Here is the tobacco that that man sent in," they told the soldier chiefs. "Now we want you soldiers to decide if you think we should accept his request. If you decide that we should let him return, then it is up to you to convince his family that it is all right." The soldier chiefs took the tobacco and went to gather their troops. Each society met in its own separate lodge to talk among themselves, but the society servants kept passing back and forth between their different lodges to report on the trend of the discussion in the different companies.

At last one man said, "I think it is all right. I believe the stink has blown from him. Let him return!" This view was passed around, and this is the view that won out among the soldiers. Then the father of Chief Eagle was sent for and asked whether he would accept the decision. "Soldiers," he replied, "I shall listen to you. Let him return! But if that man comes back, I want never to hear his voice raised against another person. If he does, we come together. As far as that stuff of his is concerned, I want nothing that belonged to him. Take this share you have set aside for me and give it to someone else."

Cries Yia Eya had always been a mean man, disliked by everyone, but he had been a fierce fighter against the enemies. After he came back to the camp, however, he was always good to the people.[1]

Shoots Left-Handed, though not a tribal chief, met the situation in a dignified way. . . . When this man returned from a long absence on the warpath, he found his wife was fat with child. He asked the name of her lover "in a good way." She revealed it as his friend, Sharp Eyes. Shoots Left-Handed convened the Elk troop to lay the matter before his soldiery, asking for their advice. In the meantime, Sharp Eyes' father had engaged a chief to take horses to Shoots Left-Handed, saying, "I am going to send my son to join his troop." When the emissary found Shoots Left-Handed in the society lodge, the husband refused to smoke the pipe until the soldiers had acted. "I won't have a word to say, because I have turned it over to my soldiers. Whatever their answer may be, that shall be mine," are his reputed words.

Sharp Eyes was sent for. He was given a pipe, and then was addressed by another chief. Was he guilty? Sharp Eyes confessed, offering to make amends by aiding Shoots Left-Handed in the care of the child after its birth. The society then informed their aggrieved chief that he should accept the offer and keep his wife. True to his word, he followed their judgment.[2]

Foundations of Diversion

Diversion in criminal justice refers to a policy in which adults accused of certain criminal offenses have their prosecution halted for a period of time. The two cases of Cheyenne crime-settlement mechanisms with which we began the chapter reveal two prominent characteristics of diversion policy that set it apart from such traditional policies as deterrence and rehabilitation. First, many diversion programs aim to resolve crime problems using methods other than adjudication. The alternative to adjudication used by the Cheyenne was mediation, or treating crime as a dynamic event that must be resolved among the accused, the victim, and the community. As we will see below, some diversion programs use mediation as an alternative to adjudication for settling family disputes and other controversies.

Other diversion programs offer counseling and treatment to clients. However, unlike traditional rehabilitation programs (see Chapter 10), these diversion programs usually rely on the resources of the community rather than established criminal justice institutions—and this is a second distinguishing characteristic. Because they are community based, many diversion programs are quite similar to the community corrections programs discussed in Chapter 8. In fact, the Minnesota Community Corrections Act places both diversion programs and community corrections centers under the direction of the commissioner of corrections.[3] Still, most community corrections programs treat clients that have already been convicted, while most diversion programs work with clients whose hearing in court has been halted short of conviction. Thus, diversion attempts to sidestep prosecution by inducing interested parties to negotiate an agreement to participate in community-based conflict resolution, counseling, or treatment programs.[4] Note that diversion policy encompasses three kinds of programs—one to resolve conflicts, another to offer counseling, and a third for treatment. Some diversion programs actually provide a mix of these services. Also, as noted above, in a few states diversion programs are quite similar to community corrections alternatives. Figure 12-1 illustrates the overlap among diversion programs as well as the intersection of diversion with community corrections programs. Before exploring the many goals and program alternatives that come under the umbrella of adult criminal diversion, we must determine whether the intellectual foundations of diversion identified above are viable ideas for contemporary American society.

ADJUDICATION VERSUS MEDIATION

As outlined in Chapter 6, adjudication uses the objective application of legal standards and rational fact findings in a hearing setting (i.e., a trial) to establish the guilt or innocence of an accused individual. It is a competitive game that

FIGURE 12-1

The Overlap of Diversion Programs and Community Corrections

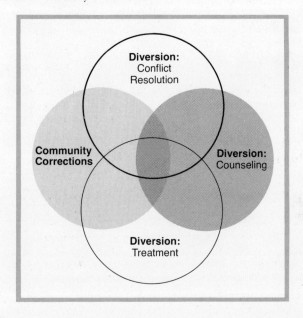

focuses the machinery of justice almost totally on the accused. The accused either wins and is set free or loses and is incarcerated. The victim and the citizens residing in the community where the crime occurred play only secondary roles, often as witnesses to supply evidence of the guilt or innocence of the accused. In short, adjudication is designed to determine guilt as as an end in itself.

HISTORICAL ROOTS OF MEDIATION   As an alternative to adjudication, mediation focuses on the situation, treating crime as a dynamic event involving the accused, the victim, and the community. The sought-after end for mediation is a settlement acceptable to all of the parties involved in the criminal event. Cries Yia Eya, who killed Chief Eagle, could return to his original home only after receiving support from the society of soldiers to which he once belonged and the explicit approval of the dead victim's father. To win the acquiescence of these parties to the event, he was required to refrain from ever again raising his voice against any member of the community.

Mediation relies on a third party to informally negotiate an agreement suitable to the accused, the victim, and the community. In the case of Sharp Eyes' adultery, a chief invited Sharp Eyes to tell his version of the event and also requested that the accused offer a means of compensating the man whose wife was impregnated.

CONTEMPORARY USE   Mediation has deep roots in comtemporary American society outside of the criminal justice system. Restoring peace in families often relies on parent mediation. Out in the garage two teen-age members of the

Nomads in Iran meet in council to determine the fate of a thief

family are screaming at one another over the use of the second car. In another home two young children playing together get into an angry wrestling match over the use of a dump truck. Parents arrive on the scene to negotiate a settlement by dividing use of the car or the toy so that each family member has an opportunity to enjoy the item without hoarding it.

Labor disputes are often settled by mediation or a companion technique, arbitration, which involves the assignment of a specialist trained in resolving disputes and usually requires participants to accept the decision of the specialist. States and the federal government have offices of mediators whose personnel are available to aid disputing companies and labor unions when direct bargaining between the parties breaks down. Specialists who have studied the procedure in labor disputes describe the rationale behind it in this way:

> Many, if not most, strikes and lockouts occur before the matters in dispute have been thoroughly thrashed out and before either side has indicated the utmost that it is willing to concede to secure a settlement. The strike or lockout usually throws the parties apart in irritation, if not anger, and neither is in a mood for calm discussion or frank bargaining. . . . The service which the successful mediators have rendered in situations of this kind is that of getting before each party the fact that there are terms which both sides are willing to accept as a settlement. The method which has been followed in most cases by the state mediators is that of bringing the parties together in a conference with the mediator and persuading them to discuss their differences calmly and frankly.[5]

MEDIATION IN CRIMINAL JUSTICE   Mediation and bargaining techniques have worked their way into the courtroom, displacing adjudication in its own home. In Chapter 7 we point out the many problems and pitfalls associated with adjudication in the courtroom. As legal expert and former judge Jerome Frank notes, in adjudication, one's right to life, liberty, or property are subject to such uncontrollable factors as "crooked lawyers, crooked witnesses, mistaken witnesses, absence or death of witnesses, loss of documents, competence of lawyers, mistaken judges, biased judges, inattentive judges, stupid judges, crooked judges, inattentive juries, and biased juries."[6] Even though plea bargaining has many pitfalls, several experts argue that this process, with its emphasis on mediation, is as just as the trial process (see Chapters 6 and 7).

COMMUNITY PARTICIPATION

As in the cases mentioned at the beginning of this chapter, the services of the community are often critical to the resolution of crime problems. Also, central to the successful implementation of contemporary diversion programs is the cooperation of the community and the utilization of its resources (e.g., job opportunities) to reform an accused person's crime habits. But does the community of people in present day American society have the resources and the commitment to facilitate this approach to criminality? Before we can answer this question, we must briefly examine the historical meaning of the term "community."

In its purest sense, "community" refers to a group of people who spend most of their lives in close contact with one another and who share many common experiences.[7] In his classic analysis of deviance in the Puritan's Massachusetts Bay Colony, sociologist Kai Erikson points out how the sense of community slipped away from the settlers once they established their dominance in the area and tamed the surrounding wilderness. In fact, he shows that once the natural threats to the survival of the Puritan communities were overcome, the settlers could only re-create their sense of community by finding deviants from within.[8] To regain their identity, they literally created a crime wave, searching out the earthly allies of demons and other evil spirits in the person of witches. Thus, creating deviant behavior as much as correcting it may be critical to the maintenance of community identity.

In contemporary American society many scholars fear the total dissolution of community or neighborhood identification as a result of poverty, discrimination, and urbanization.[9] The late 1960s and early 1970s represented a period of abundant rhetoric about, and limited government support for, rebuilding neighborhoods as basic units of social and political life.[10] Despite this effort most central cities continue to deteriorate, leaving little spirit or resources to lend to the fight against crime except in the relatively few areas where young professionals have returned to renovate old houses (e.g., on Capitol Hill in Washington, D.C.). Certainly, for areas like the South Bronx in New York City, the establishment of diversion programs makes little sense given the "battlefield environment" for personal survival.[11] However, we would be mistaken to write off most ghettoes as lifeless environments lacking any sense of community.

In all major cities as well as in smaller towns and suburbs, better conditions exist than those associated with the South Bronx. But it is questionable whether sufficient community spirit and social resources exist in many parts of the country to provide a strong enough foundation for diversion programs to build on. But before analyzing the implementation of diversion programs in communities, we must first take a closer look at the characteristics of contemporary diversion programs.

The Many Faces of Diversion

Diversion is an old practice, recently recycled as contemporary reform. As it has traditionally been practiced, diversion derives from the discretion possessed by patrol officers on the beat and assistant district attorneys. It is akin to screening, the process by which police officers ignore many crimes and prosecutors dismiss charges after initially reviewing police arrests. As Figure 12-2 demonstrates, screening creates a funneling effect for the disposition of criminal cases. It is the initial mechanism for fitting priorities to scarce criminal justice resources.

FIGURE 12-2

The Funneling Effect of Screening

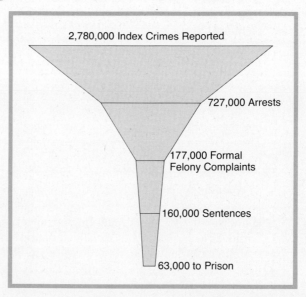

2,780,000 Index Crimes Reported

727,000 Arrests

177,000 Formal Felony Complaints

160,000 Sentences

63,000 to Prison

SOURCE: President's Commission on Law Enforcement and Administration of Justice, *Task Force Report: Science and Technology* (Washington, D.C.: U.S. Government Printing Office, 1967), p. 61.

Police see many more criminal acts than they care to pursue; rigid enforcement would tie up most of their patrol time in routine paperwork for minor traffic violations, victimless crimes, and misdemeanors. Also, prosecutors screen police arrests, eliminating cases on the basis of evidence and other discretionary factors that reflect the priorities of their office.

TRADITIONAL DIVERSION

Police officers and prosecutors also use discretion to provide themselves with more than the basic options of ignoring potential criminal activity or using the full machinery of the law to convict accused citizens. Specifically, in many localities they use "informal" or "traditional diversion" to handle crimes involving personal disputes (e.g., disorderly conduct), health-related problems (e.g., public drunkenness), and minor property crimes (e.g., shoplifting). In *Diversion: The Search for Alternative Forms of Prosecution*, legal scholar Raymond Nimmer argues that traditional diversion emerged because of a "dispositional dilemma": Police and prosecutors viewed some crimes as nonserious or marginally criminal but too important as social problems to be condoned or ignored.[12] Diversion serves the self-interests of criminal justice personnel on two counts. First, it allows them to reduce their workload, and second, it gives them increased street-level flexibility in handling the cases they decide to do something about.

Much like the crime-fighting strategies of decriminalization and legalization, diversion is a reponse to criminal overreach, or the extension of low enforcement into areas perhaps better handled by other social service agencies. Also, like the strategies of decriminalization and legalization, diversion is often used for those crimes in which offenders do not see themselves as criminals and society reacts leniently to their crimes. Traditional diversion, then, is quite limited in scope, focusing on many marginal, nonserious crimes that citizens least fear. But, it is these very crimes that comprise the bulk of the business handled by the criminal justice system. So, strictly in terms of numbers, diversion policies can have a significant impact on the criminal justice system.

Because traditional diversion evolves from the discretionary practices of police officers and prosecutors, the crimes that receive diversionary dispositions may vary from one municipality to another. For example, shoplifting cases may be fully prosecuted in one jurisdiction as serious property crimes while being diverted in another. In Albuquerque, New Mexico, judges provide unsupervised diversion, suspending prosecution indefinitely, for over 80 percent of the shoplifting cases reaching their courts. Judges who were interviewed argued that "defendants in such cases are not truly criminals and that conviction is unwarranted."[13] However, in Charlotte, North Carolina, less than 5 percent of those accused of shoplifting are diverted. Officials frequently use nearly maximum sentences in an attempt to deter shoplifting.

Traditional diversion has been attacked because its ad hoc nature violates the principle of equal treatment across jurisdictions, and even within the same jurisdiction individuals may receive very different treatment depending on the police officer, prosecutor, or judge they encounter. One police officer may seek to affix blame in a family dispute, hauling the male participant in the dispute off to jail. Another officer may react to a similar call by deferring arrest and instead personally contacting social service agencies to set up counseling for a quarreling family. These inequalities coupled with the desire of agency officials to gain some control over street discretion have led to recent refinements in diversionary practices.

NEW DIVERSION: FORMALIZING DISCRETION

The "new diversion process," a phrase coined by Raymond Nimmer, has four characteristics: (1) it represents a planned reaction to both the problem of formal prosecution and the insufficiencies of traditional diversion; (2) it reduces the discretion available to individual prosecutors and judges in the final disposition of offenders; (3) it relies heavily on formal relationships with agencies outside the criminal justice system; and (4) it regularly involves the staff of noncriminal agencies in the disposition of cases.[14] Rather than depending on the ad hoc decision making of individual actors, new diversion relies on programs with established eligibility criteria, a variety of ways to help clients (e.g., treatment, counseling), and full-time staff positions filled by trained community residents and professionals. In short, it attempts to use organizations and rules as means to assure that when the criminal label is withheld, it is done within a legal framework.

Funds from the federal government in the last decade have been used to establish experimental adult diversion programs in over 50 metropolitan areas.[15] These programs differ from those mandated by decriminalization legislation in that they are essentially voluntary in nature. For example, with decriminalization of public drunkenness, many states require the involuntary confinement of public inebriates in detoxification centers for up to 72 hours. With diversion, police and court personnel offer the resources of these programs as an alternative to arrest or prosecution. Although participation is not required, new diversion does use a carrot-and-stick approach to solicit "voluntary" participation by offering a choice between program involvement and full-fledged criminal prosecution.

Paradoxically, the explosion of adult diversion programs has ocurred at a time of disenchantment with and retrenchment in the area of juvenile diversion. Few critics of juvenile diversion advocate the wholesale elimination of such programs because they fear that a drastic cut would lead to the total collapse of the juvenile justice system.[16] The informal, mediatory atmosphere surrounding deliberations over diverting juveniles does allow for the rapid disposition of many cases.

However, several scholars and practitioners argue that juveniles are coerced into such programs rather than volunteering for them through deliberative bargaining.[17] Coercion is the natural outcome of an organizational syndrome that attorney Paul Nejelski calls "the omnipresence of guilt." He notes, "To many people in the juvenile justice system, it is inconceivable that a client could be innocent and not need help."[18] Originally intended to avoid stigmatizing youths with the label of "delinquent," diversion programs have expanded the institutionalization of youthful "clients," a fate as socially damaging as any delinquent label.

To correct this slippage away from deliberation to determine the need for institutionalization critics call for a fresh injection of due process into the juvenile justice system. They want closer supervision of discussions surrounding whether or not a youngster requires any of the treatment offered by diversionary programs. As we will see below, this same criticism has been lodged against adult diversion programs.

Policy Making and New Diversion

As discussed in Chapter 11 decriminalization and legalization strategies require state legislative action in order to be instituted. Once passed, these crime-fighting strategies are carried out by criminal justice personnel on a statewide basis. But most adult diversion programs have emerged in municipalities and metropolitan areas because of federal aid rather than state appropriations.

Many diversion programs are set up in cities because major metropolitan areas have experienced the effects of overcriminalization most acutely. Rather than continuing to wait for state legislatures to clean up their criminal codes and institute decriminalization and legalization policies, these hard-hit areas turned to the federal government to set up substitute ways of dealing with a variety of less serious crimes.[19] Specifically, then, how has the federal government contributed to the emergence of diversion programs throughout the country?

FEDERALISM AND DIVERSION

COMMISSIONS: THE MERGING OF LIBERAL AND CONSERVATIVE SENTIMENTS The national crime commissions of two presidents—Lyndon Johnson and Richard Nixon—endorsed the creation of adult diversion programs on the local level. President Johnson's Commission on Law Enforcement and the Administration of Justice advocated diversion for narcotics addicts, alcoholics, mentally disordered persons, and offenders "when full criminal disposition does not appear required."[20] Government agencies interpreted this latter phrase to refer to first-time or infrequent offenders who have been charged with nonserious offenses. They instituted a wide range of social services as treatment for these offenders, including manpower development.[21]

In 1973 President Nixon's National Advisory Commission on Criminal Justice Standards and Goals called for local jurisdictions to develop and implement diversion programs in cooperation with state agencies. The commission saw diversion as a means to redistribute the resources of the criminal justice system. The feeling was that if less serious first-time offenders were diverted, more criminal justice resources would be available for apprehending and prosecuting serious offenders.[22]

While Johnson's commission emphasized the social benefits of diversion in providing treatment for the most downtrodden of those caught up in the criminal justice system, Nixon's commission stressed the economics of a significant shift to diversion. Combining these two perspectives provides a powerful political argument for convincing localities to support diversion. But the federal government offered more than just supportive ideas to the diversion movement; it made available to communities funds for setting up experimental programs.

FEDERAL EXPERIMENTAL DOLLARS   Federal agencies began supporting experimental diversion programs in the mid-1960s.[23] In 1967 the Department of Labor funded the Manhattan Court Employment Project in New York City and Project Crossroads in Washington, D.C., both pretrial intervention programs emphasizing education and training for underemployed defendants. Relying on project staff evaluations of these programs' performance, the Department of Labor labeled the initial projects "models for diversion" and funded second-round programs in seven cities. Although researchers questioned the accuracy of these evaluations, the Labor Department ignored critics and invested over $5 million in pretrial diversion between 1967 and 1972.[24]

The Law Enforcement Assistance Administration (L.E.A.A.) began funding a hodgepodge of diversion programs in the late 1960s. Rather than directly funding all of these programs, the L.E.A.A. issued lump sums of federal dollars, or block grants, to state criminal justice planning agencies. The agencies were given wide latitude to disperse the money in support of innovative programs. Because funding was indirect and discretion was used in dispersing funds, no estimate is available on the level of L.E.A.A. financial support for diversion over the years.[25] Also, the Washington headquarters of the L.E.A.A. continues to directly fund several diversionary programs. For example, in 1977 the agency announced financial support for three experimental neighborhood justice centers—community, store-front centers for settling disputes.[26]

Other federal agencies, including the National Institute of Mental Health, have funded a variety of diversion programs. The proliferation of federal agen-

---

DIVERSION: PRO AND CON

Diversion of the first offender is unimportant since they would go on probation anyway. (Judge)

Diversion spends too much time with participants who won't get into trouble again. (Prosecuting Attorney)

In this country the penalty for conviction is so severe it stays with you forever. (Prosecuting Attorney)

The guilty plea has too many ramifications—in jobs, federal law—even when dismissed. (Defense Attorney)

Roberta Rovner-Pieczenik, *Pretrial Intervention Strategies* (1976), p. 112.

cies involved in supporting diversion programs leads to duplication and overlap in funding efforts. In fact, researchers have found that some programs have received experimental funds from more than one agency. For example, program directors who understood the inner workings of federal funding for experimental programs were able to pick up financial support from the L.E.A.A. once their experimental budgets from the Department of Labor had been spent.[27]

Although some project directors may know the politics of grant getting well enough to keep their program running on federal experimental dollars for several years, they eventually need to gain permanent municipal or state funds to establish their programs in communities. Therefore, state and local governments may need to appropriate little money at the start, but they will eventually be required to pick up a large share of the price to retain diversion options in communities. Some state legislatures have already moved to fund statewide diversion programs for drug offenders and other accused lawbreakers.[28] They view such undertakings as more cost-effective than expanding traditional courts and correctional agencies to handle such individuals.

THE THREAT TO SELF-INTEREST

Because the diversion programs usually apply to a narrow range of criminal activities and because prosecutors and judges still retain the discretionary authority to determine what individuals will be diverted away from court proceedings, diversion is not a threat to the self-interests of these personnel or the court system. Courtroom personnel gain both better control over caseloads and retain discretionary powers related to who may or may not be diverted from full prosecution. Of course, if diversion programs were used to handle most crimes, then they could become a threat to the self-interests of lawyers and judges. They might interfere with the process of plea bargaining, which is the desired mechanism for processing cases (see Chapter 6). They might also conflict with the self-interests of trial lawyers, who depend on a certain number of cases being decided by trial (see Chapter 6).

PUBLIC INTEREST GOALS

Because of the concerns of court personnel, diversion policy is often formulated to meet certain personal and organizational self-interest goals associated with the courtroom. But the pursuit of these narrow self-interests may nonetheless lead to the achievement of several broader public interest goals.

EFFICIENCY   Citizens expect efficiency from all government agencies that deliver services. Diversion is supposed to reduce costs associated with courtroom procedures by substituting conflict resolution, counseling, or treatment programs that draw heavily on existing community resources. In order to meet the goal of efficiency these community-based programs must be able to process "clients" less expensively than the courts are able to plea bargain or adjudicate outcomes for accused individuals.

Because the courts economically deal with individuals charged with minor crimes (e.g., shoplifting, public drunkenness), diversion probably does not increase the efficiency with which these offenders are handled. But when diversion is used to process individuals accused of more serious crimes (e.g., felonies), this policy may contribute to improving the efficiency of both courts and correction institutions.

A word of caution is in order, though. Diversion can only increase efficiency if the individuals who are diverted are indeed those that normally would go through all police and courtroom procedures. If individuals are being diverted who would be screened out of the criminal justice system routinely through nonarrest or dropped charges, then no significant increase in efficiency can be realized from new diversion strategies. In *The Future of Imprisonment* legal scholar Norval Morris speculates that individuals are being diverted who would normally be screened out, but not enough research has been concluded to support his suspicion.[29]

JUSTICE   As we pointed out in Chapter 1, Americans do not agree on the definition of justice. For those who interpret justice to mean equal treatment, new diversion is a considerable improvement over traditional diversion because it uses formal criteria for program entrance (e.g., first offenders only), and individuals are specifically hired to assure that these criteria are equitably applied when recommendations for diversion are made to the court. However, despite this oversight judges and prosecutors make the final decisions as to which individuals may enter a diversion program. Also, once individuals are enrolled in a diversion program, the staff attempts to work out individualized solutions to cases rather than using the same techniques to resolve all cases. Equal treatment is therefore not the operating norm for handling clients once they are in a program.

If one defines justice as retribution, many diversion programs are in conflict with this public interest goal. Specifically, those programs that emphasize treatment and counseling view accused citizens as clients who require services rather than as criminals who deserve punishment. Still, some of the conflict resolution programs do require clients accused of taking property (e.g., shoplifters) to compensate victims as a means to settle their cases. This kind of diversion program is compatible with still another definition of justice, that of restitution. Thus, whether justice is met by diversion programs depends on both one's definition of the public interest goal and the type of diversion program considered.

ACCOUNTABILITY   New diversion is partly an attempt to involve the community in efforts to prevent crime. As shown in Chapter 6 plea bargaining is fully under the control of professional courtroom personnel. Citizens both resent and distrust these dealers in justice and lawyers in general. Diversion attempts to promote a different image of criminal justice deliberations. Residents from high-crime areas may be hired to work on diversion projects, and ex-offenders may also be employed to counsel clients of these programs.

In addition, many of the diversion projects that focus on settling disputes attempt to involve the victim of a crime in working out a solution in much the same way the Cheyenne Indians encouraged participation. The purpose is to bring the complainant and defendant together in order to reach a settlement. Raymond Nimmer cites a case from Philadelphia's Community Rights Division:

> The charge was assault and battery. The complainant (C) lived across the street from defendant (D). C and witnesses described D and his friends as nuisances. D repairs his auto on the street and leaves it parked in front of others' homes for as long as two weeks. They also complained that D's friends disrupt the neighborhood by racing the engines of their noisy cars. C alleges the he was twice almost hit by rockets fired by D. He confronted D on the street and a fight ensued. D claims that the rocket incident was accidental. No physical injuries are alleged by C.[30]

The mediator's settlement required an avoidance of future contact between the parties and the designation of when and where the defendant could work on his car.

The infusion of "new blood" into the criminal justice system through the hiring of community residents and the central concern over the victims of crimes are positive attributes of diversion policy that can significantly enhance respect for the machinery of justice. However, control over major diversionary decisions remains in the hands of police and courtroom personnel.[31] Specifically, decisions of who to divert and determinations of successful participation in diversion programs ultimately rest with criminal justice officials. For this reason program staff members are extremely sensitive to maintaining cooperation with these officials.

As mentioned above diversion programs are often located in central-city neighborhoods with high crime problems rather than in rural areas. The advantage of housing these programs in such neighborhoods is that many participants in the programs can be close to their urban families and friends. However, sociologist Andrew Scull, who studied diversion and other community-based programs, argues that the "decarceration movement," as he calls it, is no more than a guise for fiscal (or financial) conservatism. He claims that it "forms yet one more burden heaped on the backs of those who are most obviously the victims of our society's inequities. And it places the deviant in these communities least able to care for or cope with him."[32] From Scull's perspective the goal of such programs is not to increase accountability but to reduce governmental support for serious social problems.[33]

CRIME PREVENTION   As with all strategies discussed in this text, diversion is supposed to relieve this country's crime problem. And like all crime-fighting strategies, diversion is based on certain assumptions about the nature of crime. As outlined in Chapters 2 and 3, crime can be seen as a product of social conditions that heighten personal stress. Both violent crimes and property crimes have been associated with personal stress and its accompaniments in many cases, heroin and alcohol.

Diversion programs attempt to lessen crime problems by relieving personal stress through job counseling, drug treatment, and on-the-spot dispute settlement. Much like traditional rehabilitation, diversion attacks crime problems on an individualized basis. However, it is different from traditional rehabilitation in that diversion attacks social stress in the community rather than from inside the walls of large bureaucratic institutions. Diversion is also different from rehabilitation and other community corrections programs because it protects participants from being labeled "criminals" by deferring prosecution while clients go through the program. Still, like the other crime-fighting strategies discussed in this text, diversion's success must be judged in part on whether it ultimately reduces the relapse rate of offenders. As we will see below, the existing data on recidivism rates of those in diversion programs are contradictory and inconclusive.

DUE PROCESS   Chapter 1 showed that a critical problem in American criminal justice is that we expect our machinery of justice to accomplish many conflicting public interest goals. Due process may be one goal that diversion cannot accomplish. Civil libertarians have attacked diversion because it does not promote "true voluntariness."[34]

As described above, clients are coerced into participation through a carrot-and-stick process. For that reason a 1977 study of alternatives to criminal adjudication completed by the American University's Institute for Advanced Studies in Justice makes the following recommendations:

> (1) Every pretrial intervention and pretrial release program should subject its policies and procedures to independent review, to insure their fairness and to guarantee that they provide adequate protection for participants' rights. . . . (2) Every pretrial intervention program should assure participants and potential participants access to meaningful legal advice at every stage of the intervention process. . . . (3) Every pretrial intervention program should institute a hearing procedure to be employed in all decisions to extend program participation or to terminate unfavorably.[35]

Although implementing such proposals would plug many due process holes in diversion programs, these legal requirements would at the same time lower the potential for efficiency, a goal very much desired by legal practitioners.

Implementing New Diversion

What kind of diversion programs have taken root in American society to meet public interest goals? One way of classifying diversion programs is on the basis of the point at which diversion occurs. Sociologist Nora Klapmuts uses this approach when she categorizes diversion programs, community absorption programs, police alternatives to arrest, and pretrial intervention by court personnel:

> The first is a decision by community residents to handle the problem without reporting it to police; the second is the decision by the police not to arrest or not to refer to court; the third is a decision by the court or prosecutor's office not to proceed to trial."[36]

Alternatively, new diversion programs can be analyzed on the basis of the kind of service they deliver to clients. For example, Raymond Nimmer identifies counseling, dispute settlement, and treatment programs.[37] Below we give program examples of each of these types of service before discussing the complexity of implementing new diversion in the field.[38]

COUNSELING SERVICES

Counseling programs have emphasized personal, employment, educational, and health counseling. Several communities have developed counseling projects for unemployed offenders including Washington, D.C. (Project Crossroads), Hennepin County, Minnesota (Operation De Nova), and New York City (Court Employment Program). Although it has expanded its programs in the 1970s to become a court-related, social service agency, offering counseling to individuals already convicted of crimes, the Court Employment Program (C.E.P.) continues to maintain a deferred-prosecution counseling program in the borough of Queens.[39]

Like most new diversion programs, the C.E.P. was originally funded as a demonstration project through the Manpower Administration of the United States Department of Labor. When its experimental funds ran out, New York City contracted its services and expanded its operations to the boroughs of Brooklyn, Bronx, Manhattan, and Queens.

Like other counseling programs, C.E.P. has gone through two essential stages. At the beginning in the first stage of the program's life, clients had to meet very restrictive criteria. They had to be young offenders (16–19), male, unemployed, charged with a misdemeanor, have little or no previous record, and be free of drug involvement or alcoholism. Later, in the second stage the program expanded age limits for clients (16 and over), removed employment status and sex as criteria for admission, and allowed admission of a restricted class of individuals charged with felony crimes.

As for its procedures, the Queens program has liaisons present in the courts who intervene immediately after the arraignment of accused adults. These liaisons have access to all of the court papers, initiate contact with eligible defendants and their respective lawyers, and ultimately seek permission of a special assistant district attorney to grant a 120-day adjournment and release without bail for potential clients. The naming of a special assistant district attorney to work directly with the program liaisons has meant high approval rates by the district attorneys' offices as well as frequent grants of requests for admission to the program from judges.

The counseling services are provided by two sets of C.E.P. employees. One set of "career developers" establish job and job-training accounts with 400 companies. Self-interest and the public's interest often mesh in the program. Businesses have a pool of cheap labor made available to them, and clients learn job skills that are in demand throughout the community. While prisons often offer jobs to inmates, their work assignments rarely provide inmates with skills they can capitalize on when they return to their communities.

Clients make the initial contact with a potential employer, or, alternatively, they can opt for vocational and academic training programs available in New York City. Career developers work closely with counselors, the second set of C.E.P. employees. Counselors, who actually provide available services to clients, come from many backgrounds, ranging from those who are college-educated to ex-convicts. After administering a series of tests to clients, counselors develop individual programs for each client. They also are important staff members to clients because they write a summary of performance that is reviewed by a supervisor and serves as one source of C.E.P.'s recommendation for dismissal, further adjournment, or termination of participation. Ultimately, the decision to dismiss charges rests with the prosecutor's office and the municipal court judges.

DISPUTE SETTLEMENT

Dispute settlement programs can be community-, police- or court-based. The earliest forms of these new diversion programs emerged as special police responses to family violence. Spurred usually by a combination of factors including poor police relations with minority neighborhoods, patrol officers' dislike for intervening in family incidents, and a recognition of the inadequacy of police resources to deal effectively with family violence,[40] police departments nationwide have developed special units that regularly handle calls concerning potential or actual violence between family members.

Although recently abandoned for fiscal reasons, the New York Family Crisis Intervention Unit (F.C.I.U.) was formed in the late 1960s and served as a model for such programs that have sprung up throughout the country.[41] Like most units, it was originally experimental, relying on the funding of federal agencies such as the L.E.A.A. Its principal goal was to use intervention and rehabilitative techniques to resolve domestic problems with a potential for violence. As one researcher notes, diversion involves a search for causes: "Domestic problems can be deemed to be significantly diverted from the criminal process only when the result of a police service call is not only restoration of order, but activation of a process which at least has the potential to resolve the source of the conflict."[42]

Because successful intervention requires the ability to identify and treat the source of family disputes, family crisis units need the cooperation of social service agencies to counsel family members. New York's F.C.I.U. experienced a great deal of disillusionment over available referral services as the program matured. Members of the intervention team soon recognized that many of the potentially relevant referral agencies were geared to middle-class clients and were not equipped to handle the host of unfamiliar, bureaucratic, red-tape requirements.[43] The differences in organizational goals between the social service agencies and the intervention unit forced F.C.I.U. members to develop informal mediatory skills to replace the use of some referral services as well as to develop ties with individuals in the social service agencies that they could informally tap for particular cases. While some heads of public service bureaucracies turn down new tasks because their resources are already drawn thin, many do so because cooperative ventures threaten the security of doing things according to routine.

Family crisis intervention programs are supplemented by a standardized set of staff training programs that have been used throughout the country and are administered by a group of psychologists from the City University of New York.[44] The training includes skits put on by professional actors to reveal family crisis situations and to prompt hypothetical police responses. Also, several of the programs include weekly in-service sessions to assure continued thinking about the task by the staff and to update the police officers' knowledge of potential referral services.

TREATMENT ALTERNATIVES

Several diversion programs emphasizing treatment have been initiated by state legislative action rather than experimental federal funds. For example, the Massachusetts legislature enacted a drug diversion program in 1972 that provides deferred prosecution for individuals who are charged with a drug offense and are "drug dependent persons who would benefit from treatment."[45]

The legislation allows any defendant charged with a drug offense to request an examination by a court-appointed psychiatrist or physician to determine whether the individual meets the criteria for diversion. For diversion to occur, the court must find that the individual depends on drugs and can benefit from treatment, and the defendant must decide to accept diversion rather than traditional criminal processing. The final decision to divert rests with the judge, who through the power of judicial discretion may elect to disregard the doctor's report and the client's request.[46]

The legislation designated the Division of Drug Rehabilitation in the Department of Mental Health to set up in-patient and out-patient facilities for this

Patients participating in a drug rehabilitation program in Phoenix, Arizona

diversion program. With very limited funds available, the division dispersed funds to a variety of private drug treatment programs in Massachusetts, ranging from hotlines and self-help groups to special units in state hospitals.[47]

The director's office of the Division of Drug Rehabilitation is responsible for reporting to the court on the outcome of an individual's performance in the program. If a defendant has either successfully completed the treatment program or completes the term of treatment ordered by the court, whether a cure is effected or not, the judge is required to dismiss the charges pending against the defendant. Thus, the Massachusetts drug diversion program provides limited judicial discretion over final disposition and weights the outcome in favor of diverted defendants.

IMPLEMENTATION QUAGMIRES

In Part I of the text, we pointed out that many well-formulated policies for fighting crime require proper implmentation before they can be deemed successful undertakings. In the implementation stage of policy-making, programs must be steered through the quagmires of personal and organizational self-interests within the criminal justice system.

Like all crime-fighting strategies discussed in this book, diversion programs depend greatly on decisions made by criminal justice agencies and personnel. But these programs are themselves bureaucracies, driven by organizational and personal self-interests much like those of the traditional criminal justice agencies. In short, all diversion programs face problems that must be overcome in order to have a fighting chance to meet their intended public interest goals.

ADEQUACY OF INFORMATION   Like the traditional criminal justice agencies, diversion programs make decisions about who is eligible for certain treatments. Critical to meeting efficiency goals, these projects must be able to distinguish between individuals who would routinely be screened out of the criminal process and those who might benefit from program offerings and who would normally be processed through the criminal justice system. Likewise, to meet crime-prevention goals and to assure public tranquillity in communities where diversion programs exist, they must be able to sort out clients that are too high a risk.

Sometimes programs fail to develop proper eligibility and selection processes, and as legal scholar Wallace Loh argues, such failures endanger "realization of one of diversion's stated goals—efficient use of resources in the criminal justice process." [48] One reason for the failure to develop eligibility schemes and scales is the program administrators' self-interest in maximizing client intake as a justification for larger budgets. Permanent social service agencies, including diversion counseling programs, are assessed, in part, on the basis of how many clients they actually serve.

RESOURCES   Many diversion programs never obtain the necessary resources to meet their intended goals. Legal scholar John Robertson studied the Massachusetts drug diversion program and showed that while legislators developed broad-based eligibility criteria, they failed to provide funds to compensate psychiatrists and physicians for conducting their evaluations of client eligibility:

> The courts were thus faced with providing examinations for an unpredictable number of persons, yet given no doctors to perform or resources to pay for them. To many judges who were hostile to the law because of its liberal or idealistic approach, this deficiency was further proof of impracticality. In one court where there were over 400 drug offenders in 1971 no defendants were examined for several months because of a lack of doctors. [49]

In the same study, Robertson points out that little money was allocated to set up community treatment programs for diverted clients. However, because the director of the Division of Drug Rehabilitation invested the funds he had in a mix of private drug treatment programs and because the courts were able to develop their own sources for referral, the program has been able to maximize its limited resources for treatment. [50] As we will see in Chapter 15, strong leadership must be exercised to overcome such implementatation quagmires.

COORDINATION   As pointed out in Part II of the text, the criminal justice system suffers from a lack of coordination of its agency components. This deficiency leads many scholars to label criminal justice a "nonsystem." Diversion programs face coordination problems even more complex than police departments or prosecutors' offices.

On one front diversion programs must gain the cooperation of personnel in traditional criminal justice agencies in order to meet basic goals. These personnel retain broad discretionary authority over both admission and ultimate disposition of clients, which gives them life or death power over a program. Although many of the programs serve the self-interests of traditional criminal justice personnel by expanding the discretionary options available to them for disposing a case, their cooperation cannot be assumed.

The Court Employment Program suffered early coordination problems with the prosecutor's office because each assistant district attorney had a personal view of the program's worth. As noted above this serious problem was overcome only when the district attorney agreed to appoint a special assistant prosecutor to work directly with program screeners in recommending cases for diversion. This example shows that the cooperation of rank-and-file personnel like assistant district attorneys or patrol officers is every bit as critical as gaining the endorsement of supervisory personnel in criminal justice agencies.

Diversion programs also must gain the cooperation of other government agencies and private community organizations like local businesses. New York City's Family Crisis Intervention Unit initially tried to rely on the city's social service agencies to provide clients with counseling and treatment. As we pointed out, the officers soon learned that the preferences of these agencies for middle-class clients and the enormous red-tape problems prohibited the immediate flow of services to clients. Soon after initiation of the program, police officers had to develop informal ties to these agencies in order to tap any of their available resources.

Evaluating New Diversion

Many programs end up viewing survival as an indication of success, given these organizational roadblocks. Still, taxpayers, funding agencies, and state legislators ultimately assess the worth of diversion programs on the basis of their ability to meet public interest goals. Too few reliable evaluations of diversion programs exist to date. Many evaluations are conducted by program staff members who lack the expertise to conduct objective assessments and who are strongly motivated to show successful outcomes for their own programs. Also, comprehensive evaluation research of diversion is difficult to carry out because of the special nature of each program. All programs were funded as experiments, and each program therefore has unique operating procedures, making it impossible to generalize about a category of diversion programs from the results of one study.

Still, some of the early pretrial diversion programs funded by the Department of Labor have been monitored closely. These program evaluations can serve as a basis both for looking at the viability of counseling programs and identifying the problems of conducting evaluative research in the area of diversion.

CRIME PREVENTION

As pointed out above, one of the major public interest goals of diversion is reduction of offender recidivism. Thus, a critical question is whether individuals who complete diversion programs in counseling show a lower recidivism rate than a comparable group of individuals who do not participate in the programs. The key to such recidivism research is the nature of the comparison group (see Chapter 14).

To date, the rearrest figures for diversion programs are usually compared with the much higher rearrest rates of individuals who are convicted of like crimes and sentenced to probation or jail. Many researchers, such as Wallace Loh, argue that these comparisons are biased in favor of the diversion programs because many individuals entering the programs would have been screened out of the criminal process rather than convicted and sentenced.[51]

Until like groups are compared that differ only on the basis of whether they received the benefits of diversion counseling, we can only speculate about the contributions that diversion makes to crime prevention. The ideal way to achieve such a comparison is through "random assignment." The technique is discussed in greater depth in Chapter 14, but when it is applied to diversion research, it has the following characteristics:

> People eligible for diversion are divided by lot into a test group that receives services in the program and a control group that returns to the criminal justice system for normal processing. If the project has more impact than the regular criminal justice system on factors such as employment or tendency to be rearrested, this impact should appear as a difference in employment or subsequent arrests between the test and control groups.[52]

The staffs of deferred prosecution programs have refused to conduct such reliable comparisons. They claim that denial of participation to some eligible clients for research purposes violates humanitarian tenets and their own sensitivities.[53]

Franklin Zimring, who conducted an independent evaluation of the Court Employment Program, rejects their reasoning. Pretrial diversion projects often fail to admit eligible individuals for bureaucratic reasons. For example, the Court Employment Program only conducts screening of individuals who are arraigned on weekdays. Defendants arraigned on weekends are automatically denied consideration because program screeners do not work on Saturdays or Sundays.[54] Since under normal operating procedures many otherwise deserving defendants are precluded from diversion, it is no worse a violation of equal treatment to randomize defendants in order to assess the impact of this relatively untested policy. Still, it is a violation of equal treatment to carry out such an experiment.

EFFICIENCY

Even if diversion programs produce the same crime-prevention results as traditional methods of processing the accused, they could be deemed successful by simply showing a savings in costs to the criminal justice system. Again, establishing a standard of comparison is difficult. Loh points out that comparing the costs of pretrial diversion programs with incarceration costs is misleading because "most pretrial diversion participants, if they had not been diverted, probably would not have been sentenced to prison."[55] Also, despite the claims of several government-sponsored studies,[56] independent researchers argue that too little reliable comparative analysis has been completed to assume that diversion programs increase the efficiency of the criminal justice system.[57]

Conclusion

In a comprehensive study of existing evaluations on diversion, sociologist Roberta Rovner-Pieczenik reveals more than just inconclusive research on the benefits of diversion. She claims that criminal justice personnel and public officials are actually unwilling to rely on evaluative research to determine whether or not diversion programs should be retained. Court personnel, who often have the power to retain or kill a program, are skeptical of such research. Rather than depending on scientific research to determine program retention, key decision makers are deciding on the basis of: "(1) whether a system is innovative; (2) whether a court is overloaded enough to 'risk' pretrial intervention ; (3) whether a political situation exists in which influential groups support the program; or (4) whether the system desires the economic 'carrots' being held out to it by state and federal governments to initiate changes."[58] In other words, political considerations, rather than objective evaluations, are helping to shape criminal justice policies in this area. But, given the lack of hard evidence on the effectiveness of such programs in preventing crime and saving tax dollars, state governments would be wise to approach diversion slowly.

SUMMARY

Cheyenne crime-settlement mechanisms reveal two prominent characteristics of diversion policy that make it different than the traditional policies of deterrence and rehabilitation. Diversion relies on (1) alternatives to adjudication for resolving crime problems, and (2) the resources of the community rather than established institutions of the criminal justice system. Thus, diversion is an approach in which adults accused of certain criminal offenses have their prosecution halted for a period of time based on a negotiated agreement to participate in community-based conflict resolution, counseling, or treatment programs.

Mediation, as one alternative to adjudication, has strong roots in contemporary American society. It is used to settle labor disputes, international problems, and institutional problems of criminal justice agencies. Mediation has also worked its way into the courtroom through the extensive use of plea bargaining.

Critical to the carrying out of diversion policy in contemporary society is the availability and commitment of community resources. While such alternatives to adjudication as mediation are available in our society, it is questionable whether sufficient neighborhood and community resources exist in many parts of the country to provide a strong enough foundation on which diversion programs can build.

Traditional diversion derives from the discretion possessed by patrol officers on the beat and assistant district attorneys. It refers to the informal handling of crimes involving personal disputes, health-related problems, and minor property crimes. New diversion refers to the establishment of programs with eligibility criteria for clients, a variety of methods to help them, and full-time staff positions filled by trained community residents.

The federal government has given verbal and financial support to the establishment of new diversion programs. Powerful interest groups have also lent support to diversion programs, and personnel from the criminal justice system have made sure that the emergence of new diversion offers no threat to their self-interests. In fact, diversion programs are designed to enhance personal and organizational self-interest goals associated with the courtroom.

Diversion policy is formulated to meet the public interest goals of efficiency, justice, accountability, and crime prevention. Civil libertarians have attacked diversion because it clashes with some principles of due process.

Diversion policy has led to the creation of three kinds of programs—counseling service, dispute settlement, and treatment alternatives. Implementation of these programs may become bogged down in administrative quagmires. To survive and have a chance to meet intended public interest goals, the programs' leaders must learn to adjust to the self-interest motivations of courtroom personnel, develop eligibility in communities, acquire scarce resources, and gain the cooperation of many government agencies and private community organizations.

Research efforts to test the impact of diversion programs' success in meeting public interest goals are in a crude state. Many evaluations are conducted by program staff members who lack the expertise to conduct objective assessments and who are strongly motivated to show their own programs' success. Few studies use sophisticated scientific methods of research. And criminal justice personnel and public officials who determine the fate of these programs often ignore evaluation research when they determine whether or not diversion programs should be retained. Until more reliable evidence is collected on the effectiveness of such programs, state and local governments should move slowly in institutionalizing diversion.

FOOTNOTES

[1] K. N. Llewellyn and E. A. Hoebel, *The Cheyenne Way* (Norman, Okla.: University of Oklahoma Press, 1941), pp. 12–13.

[2] Ibid., p. 190.

[3] Minnesota Department of Corrections, *Past Effort, Future Directions: Summary Report* (St. Paul, Minn.: Minnesota Department of Corrections, 1977), p. 47.

[4] For detailed definitions of adult diversion, see Raymond Nimmer, *Diversion: The Search for Alternative Forms of Prosecution* (Chicago: American Bar Foundation, 1974), p. 5; and Nora Klapmuts, "Diversion from the Justice System," in *Readings in Contemporary Criminology*, ed. Stephen Schafer (Reston, Va.: Reston Publishing, 1976), p. 222.

[5] George Barnett and David McCabe, *Mediation, Investigation and Arbitration in Industrial Disputes* (New York: Arno Press, 1971), pp. 14–16.

[6] Jerome Frank, *Courts on Trial* (Cornwall, N.Y.: Cornwall Press, 1949), p. 62.

[7] Kai Erikson, *Wayward Puritans* (New York: Wiley, 1966), pp. 9–10.

[8] Ibid.

[9] See, for example, Alan H. Altshuler, *Community Control* (New York: Pegasus, 1970).

[10] See Milton Kotler, *Neighborhood Government* (New York: Bobbs-Merrill, 1969).

[11] Peter Arnett, "South Bronx an Abandoned Battlefield," *Los Angeles Times*, July 3, 1977, p. 20.

[12] Raymond Nimmer, *Diversion: The Search for Alternative Forms of Prosecution* (Chicago: American Bar Foundation, 1974), p. 15.

[13] Ibid.

[14] Ibid., p. 42.

[15] Wallace Loh, "Pretrial Diversion from the Criminal Process," *Yale Law Journal* 83 (1974), 828.

[16] Paul Nejelski, "Diversion: The Promise and the Danger," *Crime and Delinquency* 22, no. 4 (October 1976), 393.

[17] Ibid., 404.

[18] Ibid., 395.

[19] Saleem Shah, *Diversion from the Criminal Justice System* (Rockville, Md.: National Institute of Mental Health, 1973), p. 3.

[20] President's Commission on Law Enforcement and the Administration of Justice, *The Challenge of Crime in a Free Society* (Washington, D.C.: U.S. Government Printing Office, 1967), p. 134.

[21] Roberta Rovner-Pieczenik, *Pretrial Intervention Strategies* (Lexington, Mass.: Lexington Books, 1976), p. 4.

[22] Ann M. Watkins, *Cost Analysis of Correctional Standards: Pretrial Diversion*, vol. 1 (Washington, D.C.: National Institute of Law Enforcement and Criminal Justice, 1975), pp. 3–4.

[23] Rovner-Pieczenik, op. cit., pp. 5–6.

[24] Loh, op. cit., p. 829.

[25] Ibid.

[26] Gene Blake, "Neighborhood Justice Center to Settle Disputes," *Los Angeles Times*, January 15, 1978, p. 4.

[27] David Aaronson et al., *The New Justice: Alternatives to Conventional Criminal Adjudication* (Washington, D.C.: National Institute of Law Enforcement and Criminal Justice, 1977), p. 30.

[28] See John Robertson, "Pre-Trial Diversion of Drug Offenders: A Statutory Approach," *Boston University Law Review* 52 (1972), 335–71.

[29] Norval Morris, *The Future of Imprisonment* (Chicago: University of Chicago Press, 1974), p. 10.

[30] Nimmer, op. cit., p. 81.

[31] Ibid., pp. 48–49.

[32] Andrew T. Scull, *Decarceration: Community Treatment and the Deviant* (Englewood Cliffs, N.J.: Prentice-Hall, 1977), p. 2.

[33] Ibid., pp. 145–47.

[34] Aaronson et al., op. cit., p. 25.

[35] Ibid., p. 27.

[36] Klapmuts, op. cit., p. 226.

[37] Nimmer, op. cit., pp. 43–91.

[38] A third classification system using a two-dimensional approach (stage of the criminal justice process and institutional source) is developed by Aaronson et al., op. cit., pp. 15–21.

[39] For further information, see Vera Institute of Justice, *The Manhattan Court Employment Project: Final Report* (New York: Vera Institute of Justice, 1972).

[40] See, for example, Robert Steadman, ed. *The Police and the Community* (Baltimore: Johns Hopkins University Press, 1972); and Raymond Parness, "Police Discretion and Diversion of Incidents of Intra-Family Violence," *Law and Contemporary Problems* 36 (Autumn 1971), 539–65.

[41] See Malcolm Bard, *Training Police as Specialists in Family Crisis Interventions* (Washington, D.C.: Law Enforcement Assistance Administration, 1970).

[42] Parness, op. cit., p. 551.

[43] Ibid.

[44] Bard, op. cit.

[45] Robertson, op. cit., p. 340.

[46] Ibid., p. 355.

[47] Ibid., p. 359.

[48] Loh, op. cit., p. 835.

[49] Robertson, op. cit., pp. 348–49.

[50] Ibid., p. 359.

[51] Loh, op. cit., pp. 847–48.

[52] Franklin Zimring, "Measuring the Impact of Pretrial Diversion from the Criminal Process," *University of Chicago Law Review* 41 (1973–1974), 225.

[53] Ibid., p. 235.

[54] Ibid., p. 236.

[55] Loh, op. cit., p. 849.

[56] See for example, Watkins, op. cit., pp. 19–22.

[57] Rovner-Pieczenik, op. cit., pp. 71–72.

[58] Ibid., p. 99.

BIBLIOGRAPHY

Aaronson, David, et al. *The New Justice: Alternatives to Conventional Adjudication*. Washington, D.C.: National Institute of Law Enforcement and Criminal Justice, 1977.

Keating, Michael, Jr. "Arbitration of Inmate Grievances." *The Arbitration Journal."* 30, no. 1 *(March 1975)*, 177–90.

Klapmuts, Nora. "Diversion from the Justice System." In *Readings in Contemporary Criminology*, edited by Stephen Schafer. Reston Va.: Reston Publishing, 1976.

Llewellyn, K. N., and Hoebel, E. A. *The Cheyenne Way*. Norman, Okla.: University of Oklahoma Press, 1941.

Loh, Wallace. "Pretrial Diversion from the Criminal Process." *Yale Law Journal* 83 (1974), 827–55.

Nejelski, Paul. "Diversion: The Promise and the Danger." *Crime and Delinquency* 22, no. 4 (October 1976), 393–410.

Nimmer, Raymond. *Diversion: The Search for Alternative Forms of Prosecution*. Chicago: American Bar Foundation, 1974.

Robertson, John. "Pre-Trial Diversion of Drug Offenders: A Statutory Approach." *Boston University Law Review* 52 (1972), 335–71.

Rovner-Pieczenik, Roberta. *Pretrial Intervention Strategies*. Lexington, Mass.: Lexington Books, 1976.

Scull, Andrew T. *Decarceration: Community Treatment and the Deviant*. Englewood Cliffs, N.J.: Prentice-Hall, 1977.

Zimring, Franklin. "Measuring the Impact of Pretrial Diversion from the Criminal Process." *University of Chicago Law Review* 41 (1973–1974), 224–42.

ASSESSING AND IMPROVING CRIMINAL JUSTICE POLICY

Ideally, before a business firm brings out a new product, it engages in market research to determine how well the product will be received. Then the firm promotes the good heavily, and, if it is an efficient company, it continuously evaluates feedback about its new offering.

Not all business firms do this, but in an ideally competitive economic market, those that do not will not survive. Thus, there is a built-in incentive in the private enterprise system to force continuous evaluation of business policies.

No analogous incentive exists in the public sector. Government agencies that do not evaluate their programs do not disappear as a result. So, very few public agencies evaluate what they do. Their activities are primarily the outcome of various pressures applied during the formation and implementation of policy rather than the result of a formal evaluation to see whether they are effective and efficient. This is why so little is known about the impact of policies discussed in Part III.

Because of political efforts to reduce government spending, this situation is changing. Increasingly, legislation at the federal, state, and even the local level requires that public programs be evaluated. No systematic means of making such evaluations has yet been discovered. But the pressure to have public agencies evaluate their programs is likely to persist. The public wants to be sure that its taxes are being spent properly.

One of the first requirements for good evaluation is to define quantitatively the goals and objectives of criminal justice policy. The measurement process for doing this is a complicated one. Chapter 13 describes this process, including the conflicts among public interests, self-interests, and the scientific demands for accurate data collection and interpretation. The uses of criminal justice data are also described. Crime is the central concept that must be measured in order to perform effective evaluations of criminal justice policies. Chapter 13 discusses the advantages and pitfalls of various ways of measuring crime, including reports of crime, victimization surveys, and other sources of crime data. It also discusses how to interpret crime data and how to measure other concepts in criminal justice.

There is, of course, no ideal measure of crime or other criminal justice concepts. But assuming there were, how should we go about designing research so as to determine the extent to which these policies are or are not achieving their goals? This question is addressed in Chapter 14. The goals and objectives of evaluation as well as various types of research design are described in this chapter. Techniques for measuring program success or failure, including various statistical methods for analyzing data, are described there. Finally, even if a piece of evaluation research comes up with a clear-cut conclusion, can we expect criminal justice administrators to respond or react to the evaluation? The answer, unfortunately, is no, and Chapter 14 explores some of the reasons for this as well as the research technique called "action research," which might be used as a method to increase utilization of research results.

Evaluation, therefore, is only one—and a relatively small—factor in determining what kinds of criminal justice policies are likely to emerge in the future. Socioeconomic and political forces are likely to continue to have an impact on the future of criminal justice policy. Based in part on an analysis of current social and political conditions, Chapter 15 explores what some of these policies are likely to be.

There are ways of trying to see that criminal justice policy in the future will be better than it has been in the past, although, of course, no one can assure that bad or even disastrous policies will not be adopted. The final section of Chapter 15 discusses ways of improving criminal justice policy, based primarily on the theory of balancing individual self-interests with the public interest. Thus, we conclude our analysis of crime and criminal justice policies by returning to a discussion of the goals, human motivation, and organizational realities that ultimately shape the implementation of both established and emerging criminal justice policies.

When Richard Nixon was campaigning for the presidency in 1968, he pledged that a high priority of his administration would be a crackdown on the rampant street crime in Washington, D.C. After winning the election, his administration tried to fulfill this promise. The police force was expanded about 70 percent in two years, giving it the largest number of police per capita in the nation; a new police chief committed to crime reduction was hired; a highly refined computer system was installed; high-intensity streetlights were erected; and an elaborate program for treating narcotics addicts was developed. These and other measures, according to Nixon, would make Washington a "model city as far as law enforcement is concerned—a national laboratory."[1]

Not long after these initiatives were taken, District of Columbia police produced data purporting to show a signifi-

CHAPTER THIRTEEN

MEASURING CRIME AND OTHER CRIMINAL JUSTICE CONCEPTS

cant reversal of the rising trend in crime that had given the city the dubious reputation as the nation's crime capital. For the first time in many years a decline was noticeable in so-called index crimes—those crimes that the F.B.I. considered to be most serious (i.e., murder, rape, robbery, aggravated assault, burglary, grand larceny, and auto theft). On the whole these crimes dropped 5 percent in 1970 and 20 percent in 1971. The anticrime program was hailed a success.

However, close examination of crime-reporting practices later showed that much, if not all, of this turnabout was due to manipulation of the statistics.[2] Whether by design or unconsciously, police began to downgrade incidents—to classify them as noncriminal in nature or to designate them as less serious offenses. For the political purposes of appeasing the public and demonstrating that tax dollars were being spent effectively, fraudulent crime-accounting practices evolved.

Close inspection of the figures on larceny revealed this deception most vividly. To qualify as "grand larceny" (which is an index crime) rather than "petty larceny" (which is not), the value of stolen property must exceed $50. Figure 13-1(a) shows that in American society as a whole grand larcenies have accounted for an increasingly large proportion of all thefts—largely as a result of inflation, which has catapulted the price of many frequently stolen articles such as bicycles over the $50 mark. This national trend can be contrasted to the Washington, D.C., experience, which is shown in Figure 13-1(b). After August 1969, when the new police chief was installed, large thefts became much less common. The implication is clear: To keep crime out of the F.B.I. record books, police in Washington began underestimating the value of stolen property.

This inference was substantiated by two kinds of inquiries. A *Washington Daily News* reporter investigated various reported thefts and found that police were using the figure of $49 in describing the value of goods that were taken, while insurance companies were paying several times that amount in compensat-

493

FIGURE13-1

Percentage of All Larcenies
That Are $50 or More in Value

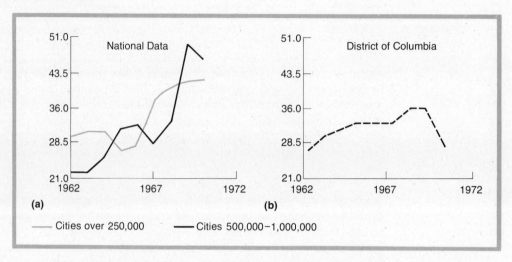

(a)

(b)

------ Cities over 250,000   ——— Cities 500,000–1,000,000

SOURCE: David Seidman and Michael Couzens, "Getting the Crime Rate Down: Political Pressure
and Crime Reporting," *Law & Society Review* 8 (Spring 1974), 470. Reprinted by permission of the
Law and Society Association.

ing the victim. The political hullabaloo engendered by this exposé resulted in an
auditing of crime statistics by a private firm, which showed that one-sixth of the
police valuations were erroneous and that most of these errors (87 percent) were
understatements of the value of the goods in question. Consequently, in the critical zone between $35 and $65 where police discretion can be decisive, the
proportion of grand larcenies to all larcenies dropped from 59 percent in 1970 to
40 percent in 1971 and 36 percent in 1972. Whether the actual number of grand
larcenies increased or decreased as a result of the "attack" on crime is problematic, but clearly the crime data were distorted to satisfy the interests of those in
power.

The moral of this story is that crime data and other criminal justice indicators must always be viewed with skepticism; facts must be separated from fiction.
Sometimes errors are willful, as apparently was the case in Washington; often
they are inadvertant. Understanding and evaluating the criminal justice system
requires improvement in the quality of information, but the measurement process is inherently imperfect.

Data collection is the process of garnering facts in a systematic way, and
measurement is the technique of making factual observations about the collected
data with some degree of precision. Data, especially quantitative data, can
enrich our knowledge of criminal justice, but they can also create false illusions.
Expressing ideas numerically sometimes gives them an aura of truthfulness that

is undeserved. Numbers have been aptly demystified in the punchline to the old joke about the three kinds of prevarications people tell: "Lies, damned lies, and statistics!"

An awareness of both the potentialities and pitfalls of observation and quantitative analyses is necessary in order to derive the benefits of a scientific approach without falling prey to the deceptions. In this chapter we shall describe some of the commonly used kinds of data in criminal justice, assessing their strengths and weaknesses. But before we discuss specific measures, it is imperative to recognize first certain underlying methodological problems in describing a social phenomenon such as crime.

Conflicting Interests and the Measurement Process

Sergeant Friday, the police detective in the television series "Dragnet," was known for repeatedly interrupting the rambling speculations and polemics of witnesses he was questioning with the deadpan comment: "Just the facts, ma'am; just the facts." This attitude reflects the scientific approach to knowledge, which makes judgments about the way the world functions on the basis of solid factual information.

Two ideals are paramount in this approach—reliability and validity.[3] Reliability refers to consistency and accuracy in measurement—the ability to discriminate finely between varying amounts of the phenomenon in question and to produce the same results repeatedly if the underlying reality remains unchanged. A yardstick is a highly reliable measure because it regularly gives the same number of feet or inches in measuring the same distance.

Rarely is such high reliability obtained in criminal justice research. For example, if fear of crime is higher in central cities than in small towns, a public opinion poll measuring people's attitudes is reliable to the extent that it captures this difference. But the poll is unreliable if it yields (as it sometimes does) wildly fluctuating results when replicated in the same geographic area or even when given more than once to the very same people (unless public anxiety changes abruptly, which is unlikely). The crux of reliability, then, is measurement that accurately reflects real differences and minimizes error.

Validity refers to the extent to which an instrument measures what we want it to measure—whether the concrete data are good indications of the abstract concepts under investigation. In studying the prevalence of injustice, data on different sentencing patterns among judges are commonly collected, but such information may in fact fail to denote whether equal justice is actually being dispensed because it ignores variations in the amount of prison time served. The latter may be more relevant in assessing whether punishments are meted out uniformly to those convicted of similar crimes. No matter how precise information is, it is misleading if it is measuring the wrong thing.

Obtaining valid results is quite problematic in most social science research.

Attempts are made to "operationalize" key concepts—to devise concrete ways (sometimes called "operational definitions") to measure theoretical notions such as intelligence, power, and neurosis as they exist in the real world. Because these concepts have very complex meanings, the techniques that are used to measure them, such as test results or responses to interviews, may be invalid.

In criminal justice research validity is an especially sticky problem. Although the penal code gives legal definitions of crime in a fairly straightforward manner, figuring out methods for determining when crimes have actually occurred is not easy. Crimes do not "announce" themselves to be automatically registered on a master scoreboard. Concepts such as deterrence and rehabilitation, which have been discussed at length in this book, are equally perplexing notions, and therefore they are not easily operationalized.

Under the best of conditions measurement can never be more than an approximation of reality. This holds true in the physical sciences and even more so in the social sciences. Even in the most carefully controlled chemistry or physics experiment in which highly tuned and calibrated instruments are used, some error in making observations is unavoidable.

For a variety of reasons the capacity for error in social research is many times greater. Human behavior is quite variable, so that describing it accurately and capturing its subleties is difficult. Frequently, observers are remote from the situations they are characterizing, and the information that they obtain is often second- or third-hand. Bias stemming from likes and dislikes can distort observations, causing researchers to see what they *want* to see rather than what exists. Mental states (like "fear") cannot be perceived directly but must be inferred from words or actions. Finally, social research is plagued by the peculiar problem of *reactivity*—the notion that people often act differently when being observed than under normal circumstances.

Whether we use interviews, government archives such as census records, or direct observations of behavior as our source of data, the potential for erroneous recording of what people say or do (let alone what they think or feel) is pervasive despite the best intentions of those collecting the data. Thus, in determining whether the police treat suspects brutally we can *ask* officers, we can *ask* suspects, we can *read* official reports, or we can *watch* actual encounters—but none of these methods guarantees that what really happens will be captured. The very same human fallibilities encountered in trying to obtain the truth about the commission of crimes (discussed in Chapter 7) are inherent obstacles to the social scientist seeking the reality of social processes.

While the nature of social inquiry and the limitations of human perceptions thus preclude the attainment of absolute truth in describing human behavior, a less ambitious and more realistic aim is feasible—"intersubjectivity."[4] We can strive to obtain data that are relatively unaffected by the idiosyncratic perspectives of the observer or the atypical reactions of those being observed. In identifying, describing, and counting events (e.g., crimes), we want to be able to say that virtually everyone with an open mind would agree that what supposedly happened actually occurred. The human element cannot be removed from the measurement process, but optimally the intrusion of highly personal factors that distort reality can be reduced or at least recognized and accounted for.

THE PUBLIC INTEREST AND DATA COLLECTION

Unfortunately, conflicting interests can frustrate the use of reliable and valid measures just as they can hamper the development of criminal justice policy. Data collection priorities often reflect the changing nature of dominant public interests.

It takes time, effort, resources, and commitment to develop sound data, and prevailing political winds often determine what kinds of information are sought. In the mid-1960s when civil rights was a dominant public concern, some intriguing efforts were made to measure the extent of police harassment of minorities—ranging from interviews of ghetto residents to "ride-alongs" with police.[5] Toward the end of that decade a series of civil disorders occurred in many cities, and urban unrest became a national preoccupation. This concern led to the formation of a "Riot Data Clearinghouse" at Brandeis University. In the 1970s street crime replaced racial discrimination and riots as the overriding issue, resulting in massive undertakings to determine the amount of crime more accurately than ever before, such as the federal government's expenditure of $53 million for a series of victimization surveys.[6] As the crime-conscious 1970s gives way to the tax-conscious 1980s, the emphasis in data collection may shift again—this time in the direction of measuring the productivity and efficiency of law enforcement agencies.[7] Acquiring good data is expensive; thus, government agencies and the researchers they support are normally inclined to spend money documenting only those things the public deems worth knowing at any given point in time. Such accountability to the public is no doubt a virtue, but it can also handicap the pursuit of basic research and the gradual accumulation of knowledge in criminal justice that ultimately might be more beneficial socially than restricting research to popular issues and the dominant preoccupations of the day.

The complexity of the public interest can affect data collection in another way. Not only are there economic costs associated with careful inquiries but other values may also be at stake. When the public learned that the "Jury Project" of the University of Chicago Law School concealed microphones in real jury rooms (with the permission of the presiding judge), they reacted negatively.[8] Indeed, because such eavesdropping was thought to interfere with the integrity of jury deliberations and certainly violated jurors' expectations of confidentiality, Congress passed a law barring such attempts in the future. The sacrosanct nature of jury seclusion outweighed the need for reliable data on a very obscure aspect of the judicial process.

A particularly acute constraint on data collection in criminal justice matters is the prohibition against invasion of privacy. Concern about privacy is continuously raised in regard to the attempts of law enforcement agencies to compile "criminal histories" of arrested persons. As of 1978 the F.B.I. had such files on 816,000 people stored in its massive computers.[9] The F.B.I. also maintains data on various kinds of stolen property like automobiles and guns in its National Crime Information Center. All of its information can be retrieved almost instantaneously by any one of 7,000 computer terminals housed in various state and local police agencies around the country, and over 250,000 inquiries are made daily to the system.[10] While the F.B.I. contends that the system creates "a high risk of detection for criminals," the possibilities of transmission of wrongful, damaging information about people, of information leaks to unauthorized hands, and of misuse of the data by law enforcement agencies has caused much debate. As of 1978 Congress had refused to permit the Carter Administration to expand the operation of the system until misgivings about the threat to privacy were resolved. In fact, the Freedom of Information Act was passed, which permits citizens to find out what data about themselves have been accumulated by government agencies.

Social scientists, too, can invade privacy in their quest for data. One of the more controversial instances of such ethically questionable research was the investigation by sociologist Laud Humphreys of impersonal male homosexuality in public places—the so-called tearoom trade.[11] What Humphreys did was disguise himself as a "lookout" or "watchqueen" (a person who gets enjoyment out of

F.B.I. computers

watching homosexual acts of others). Over a period of a year he was thus able to observe hundreds of homosexual acts in 19 different washrooms of various public parks and to report them in graphic detail.

During the course of the research Humphreys was able to document a wide range of "police lawlessness"—blackmail, entrapment (the use of police decoys to solicit illegal homosexual acts), corruption of minors, and harassment of guilty parties as well as innocent bystanders.[12] But in order to disclose these important realities about criminal justice, he had to pry into the most intimate details of people's sexual activities, an aspect of life generally considered totally personal; this was a gross invasion of privacy. Whether the gains in knowledge obtained by intrusions such as Humphreys' justify the interference with individual privacy poses a profound dilemma of public choice about values—as do almost all attempts to acquire social information.

SELF-INTEREST AND DATA ACCURACY

The workings of self-interest also impinge on data collection in criminal justice. Sometimes personal ambitions inspire officials to improve the validity or reliability of the information that is generated. Legislatures trying to ingratiate themselves with tax-conscious voters may request outside agencies to monitor the performance of law enforcement agencies in order to determine if productivity can be increased and costs cut. City politicians eager to attract federal funds that may depend on the seriousness of the city's crime problem may pressure police chiefs to devise more thorough methods of recording crime. Energetic prosecutors trying to demonstrate their effectiveness have an incentive to develop sound statistics on case dispositions that can show how tough they have been. As these examples suggest, accurate data on crime and criminal justice can benefit those producing them.

On the other hand, there are many occasions when the self-interests of officials as well as private citizens can hinder attempts to get sound information. Actions are concealed, data are distorted, responses to surveys are faked, events are misinterpreted—for the purposes of self-protection and personal gain. These possibilities are clear with regard to crime reporting: Police downgrade or overlook crime (depending on the circumstances) to make the department look better; citizens fabricate crimes (e.g., auto theft) to collect insurance; the F.B.I. exaggerates crime to encourage law enforcement expenditures.

Similarly, criminal justice officialdom often balks at revealing the true nature of the system when such exposure would disclose improper, illegal, imprudent, or unconstitutional practices. The resistance of the F.B.I. to external scrutiny no doubt reflects in some part a fear that revelations will reflect poorly on some of their intelligence and harassment techniques—perhaps making individual agents vulnerable to prosecution and at the very least jeopardizing the public standing of the agency. Even when no such nefarious activities are taking place, people working in institutions of all kinds often resent the inconvenience and tension resulting from exposure to outsiders and therefore resist divulging facts about their normal operations.

Nor can we accept at face value the information that is provided. Government records sometimes contain half-truths and even bald-faced lies. It would be naive to assume, for example, that the official registers listing court-approved electronic surveillance are a full accounting of all wiretapping since many unauthorized taps are done on a sub rosa basis. Interview data, too, are often suspect. Prosecutors are reluctant to mention political motivations when asked about their criteria for dismissing cases, and prison guards certainly never admit using corporal punishment against inmates. Even actual behavior under observation can be faked for self-serving purposes. The even-tempered judge who appears perfectly neutral while in public view on the bench may be quite biased when dealing with attorneys in the privacy of his or her chambers. The point is that personal and organizational self-interests often prompt participants in the criminal justice system to suppress or falsify data about the true nature of their functioning.

To acquire genuine data about crime and criminal justice, three strategies are conceivable. First, both officials and private citizens can be encouraged by law to give honest information. Most penal codes make it a crime to report crimes that did not occur,[13] although citizens usually have no legal duty to report crimes that did occur. Likewise, regulations can require correct recordkeeping by police, prosecutors, court administrators, and corrections officials. A strong incentive to produce truthful data would exist if reprimands, firings or criminal penalties could result from falsification of documents. However, if those at the top with the responsibility to enforce such mandates also have an interest in false portrayals, they may well conspire with subordinates and cover up such malpractices.

Second, in some circumstances it is possible to ward off deception by the use of "unobtrusive measures"—means to acquire pertinent information about behavior without the knowledge of these being observed.[14] Police can be watched surreptitiously when handling demonstrations or riots, and the behavior of judges can be tracked by unannounced observers who simply appear to be spectators in the gallery. Sometimes less secretive indirect measures can be obtained unbeknownst to those under study. Examination of court records to determine the speediness of judicial dispositions is one such measure.

Inconspicuously obtained data are likely to be more truthful, but two major limitations must be noted. Such data are likely to contain much irrelevant information unrelated to the phenomena under study (e.g., the hours of court testimony during which judges may remain totally silent); this must be painstakingly sorted out. More importantly, few opportunities exist for observers to get into a position to secure relevant information about criminal justice without being noticed by insiders. Bureaucrats have an uncanny ability to sense when they are being directly watched or the fruits of their labors are being subjected to study. Moreover, they have a remarkable capacity to cope with the threats posed by such investigators by temporarily altering their behavior or slanting the data they generate.

Consequently, a third strategy may well be the most practical one to deal with the potential of criminal justice participants for blocking inquiries or contaminating data in order to protect themselves. In evaluating criminal justice performance and policies, researchers must fight the defensiveness of officialdom and the tendency to produce only favorable data about extant programs. If careers and institutions are threatened by data showing negative results, the temptation is great to make actual failures in criminal justice look like successes by manipulating data. Therefore, at a minimum officials must be given the freedom to be honest—a guarantee that they will not be penalized for policies that fail despite their reasonable efforts to carry them out because of factors beyond their control.

In addition to removing such fears researchers can secure the trust and cooperation of criminal justice personnel by establishing a kind of partnership arrangement. We have stressed in this book that government officials need positive incentives to perform according to expectations, and in lieu of tangible monetary payoffs (which are often unfeasible) appeal to their desires for job fulfillment and power may provide that incentive. The official who has a chance to participate actively in the formulation, design, and execution of policy experiments may feel a greater commitment to the generation of valid data than the individual who feels that he or she is a pawn of the politicians, administrators, planners, and evaluators. The attempts in private industry to give ordinary workers a voice in decision making have increased morale and productivity, and the same results can be forthcoming in the public sector if lower-level personnel are involved in the policy-making and policy-evaluation process. This approach to evaluation, called "action research," is discussed fully in the next chapter, which deals with research design.

The complexity inherent in measuring *anything* is many times compounded by the conflicting interests affecting the criminal justice system. Good information is not cheap: It requires investment of scarce public resources; it can entail sacrifices of cherished values; and it can adversely affect vested interests. Just as political reality sets an upper limit on what can be achieved in the development of crime policy, so it restricts the potential for the collection of sound data. Counting crime and measuring other criminal justice concepts are very human processes that are therefore inevitably fraught with error.

Counting Crime: The Quest for the "Least Worst" Measure

If an omniscient God exists, only he (or she) can render a full and complete accounting of all crimes that are committed. Any earthly measure that we employ will miss some crimes and include some noncrimes; there is no perfectly reliable and valid way of counting crime. The reason is that several very human, discretionary processes must operate for crimes to wend their way into the tally books, and the potential for error—serious error—is present at every stage. Political sci-

Borderline crimes

entist Wesley Skogan puts this idea well: "Every [crime] statistic . . . is shaped by the process which operationally defines it, the procedures which capture it, and the organization which processes and interprets it."[15] Consequently, we must strive to find the "least worst" measure, or combination of measures, of crime—indicators that contain the least number of errors and provide the greatest degree of intersubjective agreement that they represent the "true" amount of crime.

Even the all-knowing Lord might have trouble producing an accurate enumeration of crime because a crime is a socially defined act rather than a physical event. Someone must *decide* whether a law has been violated; a violation is not always self-evident. The statute books define certain behaviors as illegal, but legal definitions are often vague and complex—giving rise to many borderline cases. If someone shoves another person to get a seat on the subway, is that an assault? Does a noisy party with stereos blaring at two o'clock in the morning constitute disturbing the peace? Is it robbery when a schoolchild approaches a younger classmate in the school yard and demands money?

The people who make these decisions, and the criteria they use, affect whether particular events are classified as crimes. The juridical approach to crime measurement requires a judicial pronouncement of guilt for an action to qualify as a crime; this narrow definition results in a low enumeration. At the other extreme is the crime-boosting perspective: Crimes are said to occur as long as people think they have been victimized. And midway between the two is the pragmatic compromise: acts are crimes when someone (a police officer? a pollster? an insurance company?) decides that evidence is sufficient to say the law has been broken.

Aside from the conceptual problem of defining crime, there are four stages of the data-gathering process at which mistakes and omissions can occur. To be

502

included in crime statistics, a crime must be detected, communicated, classified, and recorded. Many actual crimes (about which even legalistic quibblers could have no doubts) never appear in crime data because they are filtered out somewhere along the path from the commission of the crime to its recognition by some authority; this "fade-out" deflates crime figures. On the other hand, crime is inflated when alleged crimes manage to survive all stages even though they do not really qualify as such. What we are seeking are crime data that include as many "real" crimes as possible but exclude most noncrimes—in short, a relatively accurate, objective measure of crime. We can assess the commonly used kinds of crime data against this criterion.

REPORTED CRIME

The most extensive data on crime are police reports. Virtually every government body with law enforcement responsibilities keeps a running inventory of crimes that come to their attention as a result of victim complaints or direct police observations. Since 1929 most police departments have sent these data to the F.B.I., which annually aggregates and summarizes the information in the *Uni-*

FIGURE 13-2

Crime and Population, 1966–1971:
Percent Change over 1966

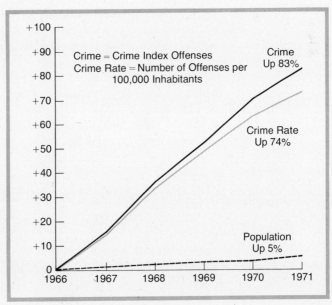

SOURCE: U.S. Federal Bureau of Investigation, *Uniform Crime Reports for the United States—1971* (Washington, D.C.: U.S. Government Printing Office, 1972), p. 2.

form Crime Reports.[16] The seven crimes considered to be most serious are totaled to create the index of crimes mentioned previously.

These data are broken down in various ways—by individual cities, size of cities, states, regions, and the like. Current data are normally contrasted with those from previous years to indicate trends (as is shown in Figure 13-2). Thus, the *Uniform Crime Reports* provide data on the geographic distribution of crime as well as shifts in the incidence of specific crimes.

Reported crime data have a number of advantages. They are by-products of normal police recordkeeping, so that the initial data collection entails little additional cost. Because the reported data attempt to enumerate all crimes and not just a sample of them, enough cases are obtained to permit geographic and temporal comparisons. For the researcher the ready accessibility and comprehensiveness of the *Uniform Crime Reports* makes it a convenient source of information.

What about validity? Although there are serious deficiencies in such data to be discussed below, there are also virtues. Compared to ordinary citizens the police are relatively knowledgeable about the penal code so that they are in a good position to make sophisticated decisions about whether crimes have been committed and what particular laws have been broken. Also, the investigations by police when they arrive at the scene of a crime allow them to "unfound" many crimes—to exclude them from crime records for want of any plausible evidence that a crime was in fact committed. In other words, they are in a position to provide some independent corroboration of a citizen's complaints and to eliminate those misfortunes that do not amount to crimes (e.g., the abusive landlord) or those fantasies that have no basis in fact (e.g., the imagined prowler).

On the minus side, many bona fide crimes are never reported to the police. Very little serious crime is observed by police as a result of their own patrolling, and they are almost totally dependent on victims or bystanders to become apprised of crime. Victims often fail to notify police for a variety of reasons most of which stem from self-interest—because the crime was trivial, because they think nothing can be done or will be done, because they are too embarrased (e.g., in the case of rape), out of fear of retaliation from the criminal (e.g., in wife-beatings), or simply to avoid the inconvenience. Many people find it bad enough to bear the grief of being victimized without adding to their problems by involving the police. Thus, reported crime data seriously underestimate the risk posed by crime, and according to one estimate three times as much crime occurs as appears in police reports.[17]

Another limitation of reported crime data is the vast discretion of both individual officers and police departments in recording the crime that is unfolded to them. One observational study of police investigations of citizen complaints found that whether police recorded incidents depended on many factors, including the perceived seriousness of the crime, the deference of the complainant toward the officer, and the relationship between suspects and victims.[18] Filling out forms and interrogating victims are tedious and time-consuming tasks that are especially burdensome near the end of a tour of duty, and the police sometimes overlook crimes out of personal self-interest. Thus, crime data are often reflections of a police officer's disposition and energy, which are capable of almost infinite variation and are totally *unrelated to whether crimes took place.* Years ago a British economist sized up the situation perfectly:

> Government [s] are very keen on amassing statistics. They collect them, raise them to the *n*th power, take the cube root and prepare wonderful diagrams. But you must never forget that every one of these figures comes in the first instance from the village watchman, who just puts down what he damn pleases.[19]

Patrol officers also receive cues from administrators, and the episode recounted at the beginning of this chapter reveals how the demands of officialdom can be translated into a falsification of crime data. Nor is the Washington "fudging" of data an isolated example; the same downgrading to make the police force look better has been detected in Baltimore, Philadelphia, and New York City.[20] Moreover, the message to officers can work both ways: They can find crime as well as forget crime. Thus, when Orlando Wilson was appointed as a reform police superintendent for Chicago in 1959 in the wake of a big scandal within the department (eight officers were caught burglarizing warehouses), he encouraged

THE NUMBERS GAME

[New York City] Transit Police Chief Sanford D. Garelik played a numbers game with crime statistics that misled the public into thinking subway crime went down when it actually went up.

Garelik did this by inventing a system that counted some crimes and did not include others— a statistical method unrecognized by any other law enforcement agency.

As a result, he made it appear that crime was lower than it actually was in 1977.

But last year [1978], Garelik's arbitrary methods backfired.

Using the TA [Transit Authority] chief's own unique statistics, subway crime against passengers was up a whopping 41 percent in 1978. . . .

So the TA, in an apparent attempt to paint a rosier picture, reverted back to the recognized method of compiling crime statistics which showed a much smaller increase.

Garelik's system uses a previously unheard of category called "open felony complaints."

According to Garelik, this category consists only of crimes against passengers that are not im-

mediately solved. It omits all other serious crimes— including muggings of decoy cops. . . .

Garelik's statistics showed a 16.5 percent decrease in crimes against passengers in 1977—when overall felonies actually went up by 14 percent.

In an apparent attempt to make the subways look safer, TA crime statistics that have been released for last year [1978], were based mainly on the universally recognized Total Crime Reports (TCR), which include all felonies.

The statistics showed a relatively modest increase of 16 percent for 1978 as opposed to the 41 percent increase under the system Garelik invented and used in 1977.

In computing the 1977 figures his way, Garelik went a step further and arbitrarily dropped such crimes as stolen school pass cases and unverified larcenies from the 1977 open felony figures.

Carl Pelleck, "Scandal of the Fake Figures that Hid the Soaring TA Crime Rate," *New York Post,* March 22, 1979, p. 3. Reprinted by Permission of the New York Post. © 1979, New York Post Corporation.

more extensive police reporting to show that he was an honest administrator. The result? Within two years the number of reported robberies and burglaries more than doubled, although similar cities not undergoing "reform" experienced only incremental jumps of a few percentage points.[21] The Chicago experience, which also happened in Kansas City when the highly professional Clarence Kelley was hired as commissioner, was aptly interpreted by Professor Dorothy Guyot. As she noted in her trenchant critique of reported crime data, "A change in the incentive system of a department which had been hiding crime can raise a city's official rates, more even than an invasion from the Mafia."[22]

Ironically, the more efficient a police force becomes, the more crimes they are likely to uncover. If police officers are slow in responding, the complainant may leave or the offender may depart—resulting in the labeling of the incident as unfounded.[23] In contrast, efficient forces that patrol vigilantly and arrive on the scene soon after they are dispatched find more reportable crime. This has led some police oficers to lament, "The better we get, the worse we look."

How do new administrators who have successfully motivated their officers to ferret out more crime cope with this dilemma? In many instances they soon revert to the style of their predecessors—coaxing their men to manipulate crime data, thereby impressing the voters with the success of their regimes. Reported crime can rise or fall depending on the self-interest of the politicians and the police officials appointed by them. [24] In a nutshell, severe reliability problems abound.

VICTIMIZATION SURVEYS

Partially as a response to the inadequacies of reported crime data, researchers developed victimization surveys in the mid-1960s. These are interviews with randomly selected samples of the population, usually residents or business people, inquiring whether they have been victimized in various ways. To estimate the total amount of crime, analysts multiply whatever crime is uncovered in such surveys by the denominator of the fraction of the total population that the sample represents. Suppose 20 robberies emerge from polling 2,000 people in a city of 500,000. The sample of 2,000 is $1/250$ of the total population, so that the 20 robberies are multiplied by 250 to get an estimate of the total number of robberies.

The Census Bureau has conducted such surveys in 26 of our largest cities at the behest of the Law Enforcement Assistance Administration. To ensure a long-term record of trends in victimization, the bureau created a national crime panel composed of thousands of individuals selected nationwide who are probed about their crime experiences at regular intervals, about every six months. Figure 13-3 duplicates part of the interview form that is used to probe for crimes that occurred.

The advantages of this method of tallying crime are manifold. Much crime that ordinarily goes undetected comes out because victims do not have to take any initiative when interviewers arrive at their door nor do they incur much cost

FIGURE 13-3

The National Crime Panel Questionnaire

HOUSEHOLD SCREEN QUESTIONS		
29. Now I'd like to ask some questions about crime. They refer only to the last 6 months – between _____ 1, 197___ and _____, 197___. During the last 6 months, did anyone break into or somehow illegally get into your (apartment/home), garage, or another building on your property?	☐ Yes – How many times? ☐ No	32. Did anyone take something belonging to you or to any member of this household, from a place where you or they were temporarily staying, such as a friend's or relative's home, a hotel or motel, or a vacation home?	☐ Yes – How many times? ☐ No

29. Now I'd like to ask some questions about crime. They refer only to the last 6 months – between _____ 1, 197___ and _____, 197___. During the last 6 months, did anyone break into or somehow illegally get into your (apartment/home), garage, or another building on your property? — ☐ Yes – How many times? ☐ No

30. (Other than the incident(s) just mentioned) Did you find a door jimmied, a lock forced, or any other signs of an ATTEMPTED break in? — ☐ Yes – How many times? ☐ No

31. Was anything at all stolen that is kept outside your home, or happened to be left out, such as a bicycle, a garden hose, or lawn furniture? (other than any incidents already mentioned) — ☐ Yes – How many times? ☐ No

32. Did anyone take something belonging to you or to any member of this household, from a place where you or they were temporarily staying, such as a friend's or relative's home, a hotel or motel, or a vacation home? — Yes – How many times? No

33. What was the total number of motor vehicles (cars, trucks, etc.) owned by you or any member of this household during the last 6 months? — (057) 0 ☐ None – SKIP to 36 / 1 ☐ 1 / 2 ☐ 2 / 3 ☐ 3 / 4 ☐ 4 or more

34. Did anyone steal, TRY to steal, or use (it/any of them) without permission? — ☐ Yes – How many times? ☐ No

35. Did anyone steal or TRY to steal parts attached to (it/any of them), such as a battery, hubcaps, tape-deck, etc.? — ☐ Yes – How many times? ☐ No

INDIVIDUAL SCREEN QUESTIONS	

36. The following questions refer only to things that happened to YOU during the last 6 months – between _____ 1, 197___ and _____, 197___. Did you have your (pocket picked/purse snatched)? — ☐ Yes – How many times? ☐ No

37. Did anyone take something (else) directly from you by using force, such as by a stickup, mugging or threat? — ☐ Yes – How many times? ☐ No

38. Did anyone TRY to rob you by using force or threatening to harm you? (other than any incidents already mentioned) — ☐ Yes – How many times? ☐ No

39. Did anyone beat you up, attack you or hit you with something, such as a rock or bottle? (other than any incidents already mentioned) — ☐ Yes – How many times? ☐ No

40. Were you knifed, shot at, or attacked with some other weapon by anyone at all? (other than any incidents already mentioned) — ☐ Yes – How many times? ☐ No

41. Did anyone THREATEN to beat you up or THREATEN you with a knife, gun, or some other weapon, NOT including telephone threats? (other than any incidents already mentioned) — ☐ Yes – How many times? ☐ No

42. Did anyone TRY to attack you in some other way? (other than any incidents already mentioned) — ☐ Yes – How many times? ☐ No

43. During the last 6 months, did anyone steal things that belonged to you from inside ANY car or truck, such as packages or clothing? — ☐ Yes – How many times? ☐ No

44. Was anything stolen from you while you were away from home, for instance at work, in a theater or restaurant, or while traveling? — ☐ Yes – How many times? ☐ No

45. (Other than any incidents you've already mentioned) was anything (else) at all stolen from you during the last 6 months? — ☐ Yes How many times? ☐ No

46. Did you find any evidence that someone ATTEMPTED to steal something that belonged to you? (other than any incidents already mentioned) — ☐ Yes – How many times? ☐ No

47. Did you call the police during the last 6 months to report something that happened to YOU which you thought was a crime? (Do not count any calls made to the police concerning the incidents you have just told me about.) — ☐ No – SKIP to 48 / ☐ Yes – What happened? _____ (058) ☐☐ ☐☐ ☐☐

CHECK ITEM C → Look at 47. Was HH member 12+ attacked or threatened, or was something stolen or an attempt made to steal something that belonged to him? — ☐ Yes – How many times? ☐ No

48. Did anything happen to YOU during the last 6 months which you thought was a crime, but did NOT report to the police? (other than any incidents already mentioned) — ☐ No – SKIP to Check Item E / ☐ Yes – What happened? _____ (059) ☐☐ ☐☐ ☐☐

CHECK ITEM D → Look at 48. Was HH member 12+ attacked or threatened, or was something stolen or an attempt made to steal something that belonged to him? — ☐ Yes – How many times? ☐ No

CHECK ITEM E → Do any of the screen questions contain any entries for "How many times?" — ☐ No – Interview next HH member. End interview if last respondent, and fill item 12 on cover page. / ☐ Yes – Fill Crime Incident Reports.

SOURCE: James Garofolo and Michael Hindelang, *An Introduction to the National Crime Survey* (Washington, D.C.: U.S. Government Printing Office, 1977), p. 39.

except for a few minutes time; they need only respond to the overtures of others. Consequently, between two and three times as much crime is reported in most surveys as is reported to the police. Light is shed on what has been called the "dark figure of crime."[25]

Not only does the survey reduce error resulting from victim silence, but it controls the intrusion of error generated by the data collector. Because the science of polling has now become quite advanced and survey research is constrained by an accepted set of methodological rules, the amount of suppressed information and false reporting probably remains fairly constant from survey to survey.

The reliability of properly conducted victimization surveys is fairly high, so that the data generated can be used to compare crime rates in various communi-

TABLE 13-1

Personal Crimes: Change in Victimization Rates
for Persons Age 12 and Over, by Type of Crime, 1975 and 1976
(Rate per 1,000 persons age 12 and over)

Type of Personal Crime	Rate		Percent Change 1975–1976	Standard Error[1]
	1975	1976		
Crimes of violence	32.8	32.6	−0.8	2.3
Rape	0.9	0.8	−7.7	13.5
Robbery	6.8	6.5	−4.4	5.1
Robbery and attempted robbery with injury	2.1	2.1	−1.4	9.3
From serious assault	1.3	1.0	−18.4[2]	10.5
From minor assault	0.9	1.1	+22.7	17.1
Robbery and attempted robbery without injury	4.6	4.4	−5.8	6.1
Assault	25.2	25.3	+0.4	2.7
Aggravated assault	9.6	9.9	+2.6	4.5
With injury	3.3	3.4	+4.3	7.8
Attempted assault with weapon	6.3	6.4	+1.7	5.5
Simple assault	15.6	15.4	−1.0	3.4
With injury	4.1	4.0	−2.7	6.6
Attempted assault without weapon	11.4	11.4	−0.4	4.0
Crimes of theft	96.0	96.1	+0.1	1.3
Personal larceny with contact	3.1	2.9	−6.5	7.4
Purse snatching	1.1	0.9	−20.4[2]	11.1
Pocket picking	2.0	2.0	+1.5	9.8
Personal larceny without contact	92.9	93.2	+0.3	1.4
Total population age 12 and over	169,671,000	171,901,000		

[1] The standard error is given in percentage points at the 68 percent confidence level.
[2] Statistically significant at the 90 percent confidence level.
SOURCE: U.S. Department of Justice, Law Enforcement Assistance Administration, *Criminal Victimization in the United States: A Comparison of 1975 and 1976 Findings* (Washington, D.C.: U.S. Government Printing Office, 1977), p. 25.

ties and over the course of time; we can have confidence in the changes in national crime rates depicted in Table 13-1. This is important if we are to assess the utility of alternative crime-prevention policies, which usually entails either geographic or temporal comparisons.

The crime surveys conducted by the Census Bureau are especially rigorous.[26] As part of the effort to maintain "quality control" over the data collected and a high degree of reliability, interviewers are trained thoroughly and their performance is charted carefully. They are schooled in all phases of interviewing, and their initial work is done under the watchful eye of a supervisor. Once on their own, their completed interview forms are checked constantly for incompleteness and inconsistency. To discourage dishonorable interviewers from totally manufacturing responses without ever contacting the households in their assignments and to check on the accuracy of the interviewing report, supervisory staff members contact a certain percentage of respondents presumably already interviewed and repeat many of the questions. Discrepancies are resolved and errant interviewers are sometimes dismissed. Professionalism dominates the data collection process, and reliability is probably as high as in any survey research.

Validity problems are also confronted directly in the Census surveys and handled in a sophisticated way. Rather than rely on the dubious legal knowledge of either victims or interviewers, crimes are classified by a computer programed to recognize the constituent elements of certain crimes. Interviewers ask respondents a variety of detailed factual questions about their experiences: Was there a theft? Was a weapon used? Was there an injury? Was a threat made? The computer analyzes patterns of responses and is able to detect those combinations of answers that constitute a specified crime. While the information given by respondents is certainly subject to error, its classification is done in an objective manner.

In addition to being more robust measures of crime because they cast a wider net, surveys can produce ancillary information unavailable in reported crime data. Respondents provide rich data on the losses they have sustained from crime, on the nature of offenders (if they have been directly witnessed), on the details of crimes (e.g., types of weapons used), and on the reasons for not reporting the crimes to the police. This information can be of enormous value in criminal justice planning.[27]

But the surveys are a mixed blessing; they have flaws. The first problem is cost. It is very expensive to get a sufficiently large random sample in order to justify generalizing to an entire population, and the cost of monitoring the administration of surveys in order to standardize procedures can be prohibitive.[28] Sample size is a greater problem than in an ordinary survey because some serious crimes such as rape occur relatively infrequently so that a large number of respondents is necessary to increase the likelihood that a proportionate number of victims will be included.

Another difficulty is the representativeness of the sample. Since interviews are conducted in homes, nonresident visitors who are victimized in cities are excluded altogether. Moreover, ghetto crime, and therefore total crime, is likely to be underestimated because interview refusal rates are highest in low-income minority areas where outsiders are often distrusted.[29] And males and young people, who are home less frequently, are less likely to be contacted—again contributing to underreporting of crime since they are more common targets of crime. But these sampling biases are less of a problem when the overall response rate is high as was the case in the Census Bureau's 1975 study of 13 cities, in which at least one interview was conducted with 96 percent of all the housing units that were selected.[30]

Another kind of problem is response error—the dishonesty and inaccuracy sometimes produced by the artificial nature of the survey setting. Numerous studies have demonstrated that those questioned frequently give incorrect information.[31]

The direction of error stemming from response invalidity is less clear. Sometimes out of embarrassment or forgetfulness, people fail to report crimes committed against them. Less obviously, respondents may claim they have been victimized when such is not the case as a result of incorrect interpretations of mysterious events like broken windows or misunderstandings about what constitutes crime.

Another source of error is interviewer cuing. A recent study has shown enormous variation in the amount of crime found by different interviewers, suggesting that they affect responses by the impressions they make.[32] Whether or not crimes are mentioned by respondents may well depend on the facial expressions, rephrasing of questions, and general demeanor of those asking the questions.

Unquestionably, survey data give a fuller accounting of the dimensions of the crime problem. However, such data may exaggerate the risk of crime by incorporating many minor incidents that are not all that alarming—bicycle thefts, petty skirmishes, unsuccessful lock pickings, and the like. Indeed, reporting to police is directly proportional to the damage inflicted. Only 7 percent of thefts involving less than $10 are reported; 44 percent of those engendering losses of between $50 and $99 are reported; and 73 percent of larcenies resulting in losses over $1,000 are reported. Likewise, most major assaults with weapons are reported to police, whereas police are rarely notified of attempted assaults without weapons.[33] Unreported crime is largely "small potatoes."

While surveys do produce a more exact crime count than do police reports, the relative ordering of the crime risk in different cities and communities obtained by both methods is very similar.[34] Put otherwise, the two types of data are fairly well correlated so we may be able to compare areas and eras using the *Uniform Crime Reports* even though we surely cannot use such data as the primary indicator of the actual amount of crime occurring.[35] Therefore, for the purpose of evaluating policies, where we want to know whether things have improved or worsened, reported crime data, though they are woefully incomplete and chock-full of errors, may be good enough. But one caveat is essential: Always, always investigate the "hanky-panky" factor—the potential for data manipulation by police officials.

OTHER SOURCES OF CRIME DATA

Other sources of crime data are less frequently used. However, they can be helpful in corroborating the more standard measures and in providing information on crimes not revealed through police reports or surveys.

Insurance company records can provide fairly reliable insights into changing commercial crime patterns and can also indicate trends in burglaries and auto thefts in more affluent neighborhoods where many property owners can afford insurance. Not only is it in the self-interest of insured victims to notify the insurer so they can be compensated for losses, but it is in the company's interest to investigate thoroughly the authenticity of such claims to prevent fraud and protect its investment.

Similarly, data on causes of death collected by the Center for Health Statistics of the Department of Health, Education, and Welfare provide an excellent check on the authenticity of *Uniform Crime Reports* homicide rates. The center aggregates the information provided on the death certificates by local coroners, who determine whether a killing has occurred without regard to police judgments. Figure 13-4 shows the close correspondence between the two independently derived sets of data over the years, implying that we have been able to isolate the actual number of murders committed.

Self-reports of the criminal population have been used to assess the degree of undetected crimes, such as tax evasion, and victimless crimes, such as soliciting prostitutes.[36] Neither kind of crime appears in either reported crime data or victimization survey data because in the first case the victim is so diffuse (i.e., the entire body politic), and in the second case no one is injured (except, perhaps, the criminals themselves). However, the information emerging from asking people to identify themselves as criminals is highly suspect because many offenders are afraid to reveal their crimes, even if promised anonymity, for fear of repercussions and because of guilt. Also, others, especially juveniles, may well pretend to criminality to appear manly, daring, or adventurous. But where we have *no* knowledge about the dimensions of certain kinds of crime, even such unreliable data that may give us vague inklings can be useful.

Finally, in a few instances unobtrusive measures of crime can be devised to achieve maximum reliability. This is the case with regard to certain minor traffic offenses that constantly occur in the same location. Studies of stop sign violators, in which observers planted behind parked cars inconspicuously record the proportion of cars failing to make a full stop, have shown how much of a folk crime this is; such lawbreaking is rampant.[37] The first-hand knowledge of crime gained by this method is what makes it so appealing; seeing *is* believing. Unfortunately, such an approach is applicable to few crimes; rarely are we in a position to surreptitiously watch a steady stream of crime in progress. Thus, the method is limited to the pettiest of violations and misdemeanors—smoking on elevators, littering, and the like.

Measuring crime is therefore a complex and frustrating enterprise. No method is free of severe validity and reliability problems. But while we have no

FIGURE 13-4

Rates of Homicide as Reported by the Uniform Crime Reports
and the Center for Health Statistics, 1935–1971

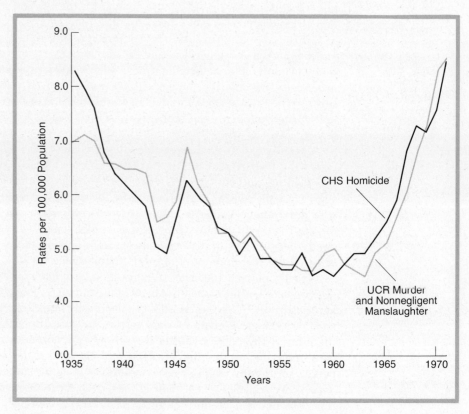

SOURCE: Reprinted with permission from *Journal of Criminal Justice* 2 (Spring 1974), Michael Hindelang, "The Uniform Crime Reports Revisited," p. 4, Pergamon Press, Ltd.

choice but to use one or more of such measures in examining the impacts of programs and policies on crime, we can be sensitive to the large degree of error inherent in those measures. The user of crime data must confront the possibility that observed differences in crime merely reflect differences in measurement procedures and adopt a tough standard in determining whether crime rates have significantly varied. So much error is inherent in crime data that modest differences ought to be dismissed out of hand.

Interpreting Crime Data

The total amount of crime in a community or nation is a rather meaningless statistic in itself. Learning that there were 420,210 reported robberies in the United States in 1976, for example, tells us no more about the dimensions of the crime problem than discovering that over 2 billion bushels of wheat were produced in the same year sheds light on farming difficulties.[38] Such "raw data" give little inkling of the crime risk to individuals, trends in crime occurrence, the harm done by crime, or the incidence of crime committed by repeaters. To make sense of crime data, we must draw on other information in order to put crime into a larger perspective. Crime data must be interpreted to be understood.

CRIME RATES

Let us suppose that in 1978, 750 rapes occurred in Los Angeles (as determined from some method of data collection) and 500 rapes were committed in San Francisco. Which city poses the greatest threat of sexual attack to women? If we answered Los Angeles because it experienced 50 percent more rapes, we would be wrong because Los Angeles has three times the population, which must be taken into account in comparing the cities. Thus, assuming the accuracy of the data, the likelihood of being raped in San Francisco is twice as great as in Los Angeles, because San Francisco, with one-third of the population, has two-thirds as many rape cases.

Just as in baseball we must consider the number of "at bats" in determining a batting average in order to assess whether one batter's 100 hits are a greater showing of competence than another batter's 75 hits, so in analyzing crime we must adjust the raw numbers of crimes by referring to some standard unit such as city population to equalize the nature of the places being compared. Crime rates do this. They express the total amount of crime for an area over a given time period (usually one year) in relation to the size of the target population. One way the crime rate is figured is by simply dividing total crime by the total population to achieve a per capita crime rate that permits cities of any size to be compared and allows fluctuations in a single area's population over time to be considered in determining trends. But to avoid the use of very small decimals, crime per capita is multiplied most commonly by a constant number to achieve the more comprehensible rate of crimes per 1,000 or 10,000 people.

Crime rates are indispensable for criminal justice research, crime assessment, and evaluation, but they can also be misleading for a number of reasons. First, using large areas as a geographic unit neglects the extreme variations between different parts of a city. For residents or workers, the average rate is of little consequence; they want to know about the problem in the area they inhabit or frequent. Parts of Staten Island in New York City have crime rates lower than the most bucolic small towns in our country; conversely, sections of small towns ("on the other side of the tracks") can compete with some of New York's worst slums in terms of crime incidence. City crime rates, and certainly state or regional rates, may well paint a crime picture with too broad a brush stroke to be meaningful.

Second, the denominator of crime rates used to derive per capita figures is sometimes inappropriate to represent adequately the probability of victimization. The rate of auto thefts is more properly based on theft incidence in relation to total cars owned rather than total population: Cities with elaborate mass-transit systems like New York have fewer cars to be stolen than cities like Los Angeles where almost everyone drives. Whereas New York City has the least number of auto thefts per 1,000 population of the nation's five largest cities, it has the most auto thefts per 1,000 owned vehicles of any of these cities; the latter rate, which deals with opportunity for theft, more convincingly measures crime risk.[39] By the same token, rapes per 1,000 females is a better rate than rapes per capita; and arson rates are more sensibly expressed as a percentage of numbers of buildings or of total property value in an area rather than of the total population base. Refining the denominator of crime rates (per *what?*) is an important methodological concern.

Finally, the presentation of crime data as crime rates can be used for political purposes—to heighten or ease people's anxiety about crime. Some biblical prophets such as Ezekiel were propagandists who used stark prose to portray the dangers that afflicted the Promised Land in 600 B.C.: "The land is full of bloody crimes, and the city is full of violence."[40]

Nowadays charts depicting crime rates can accomplish the same thing, as Figure 13-5 showing the F.B.I.'s "crime clocks" illustrates. By reporting annual crime incidence nationwide (a high figure) in terms of very small time periods (minutes and seconds), the figure conveys the impression that violent assailants and predators are constantly poised to strike at any one of us. Thus, while one reported crime occurred every 32 seconds (a scary idea), we could express the same point by saying one person out of 500 was subjected to such crime (a less frightening prospect).

The essential defect of crime clocks is that they contain only 60 minutes and 3,600 seconds, so that they cannot expand as the population does. Obviously, the more people in a country or city, the more crime that will ordinarily occur even if the proportion of criminals in the society remains constant; this simple idea is not reflected in crime clocks. Thus, crime clocks are an excellent device available to officials or candidates to inflame the public for political purposes by exaggerating the incidence of crime.

THE IMPACT OF CRIME

Another way of interpreting crime is to analyze the damage it causes. There is a wide disparity between the impact of a bicycle theft (even of a Peugeot ten-speed) and the ransacking of an apartment, let alone a brutal rape or murder. Thus, simply aggregating total crimes may be a distorted way of assessing the havoc that crime wreaks on the lives of the citizenry.

FIGURE 13-5

Crime Clocks, 1976

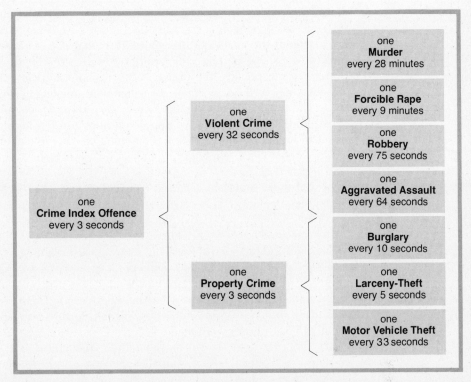

SOURCE: U.S. Federal Bureau of Investigation, *Uniform Crime Reports in the United States—1976* (Washington, D.C.: U.S. Government Printing Office, 1977), p. 6.

Two approaches have been used to measure the harm rendered by crime. One tries to convert the damages from crime into financial injuries—replacement costs of stolen property, medical bills, and lost wages. Such information is gleaned from victimization surveys and the records of crime compensation boards, which in some states reimburse certain kinds of crime victims for damages suffered. This technique, however, has several flaws that hinder valid, reliable measurement: Attaching dollars-and-cents figures to psychological injuries caused by crime, which are sometimes the greatest burdens borne by victims, is often impossible; the damage from some crimes is diffuse and indirect, as in the case of price fixing, of environmental pollution, and Medicaid fraud by doctors; and the losses stipulated by victims are sometimes inflated so they may receive more insurance benefits or greater crime compensation.

To obviate the task of measuring the seemingly immeasurable intangible losses, researchers use another measure that depends on subjective estimates of the seriousness of crime to weigh diffrent kinds of crime. Various groups are given vignettes of crimes and asked to rate their seriousness on a scale. These public assessments are then aggregated and averaged to derive a "score" for each crime. In a scheme devised by criminologists Thorsten Sellin and Marvin Wolfgang, for example, murders are worth 26 points, rape victims get 10 points, hospitalized assault victims get 7 points, while those who merely lose less than $10 only get 1 point.[41]

One of the virtues of this approach is that it takes account of moral blows dealt to the social fabric of communities as well as the physical destruction that is caused. Conceptually, the depravity of a crime and the evil intentions of the criminal may well be an important component in gauging seriousness.

The approach does entail some measurement complications, however. First, finding a representative sample of raters is a forbidding task. Second, difficult technical problems arise in combining the diverse opinions of the various crime raters. Third, applying the index on a massive basis may be cumbersome and impractical.

But these problems can be minimized or surmounted. A quite useful set of seriousness weights has been devised by a team of sociologists who presented a randomly selected set of Baltimore residents with a set of 140 cards, each of which specified a different crime.[42] The list of crimes ran the entire gamut of the penal code and included several variations of each crime (e.g., armed holdup of a taxi driver as well as armed robbery of a supermarket). Respondents were required to place each card into one of nine slots in a box—each slot representing a gradation of seriousness from "most serious" to "least serious." No attempt was made to define seriousness; this was left up to each respondent's intuition. In all, 15,521 ratings were made.

The results are shown in Table 13-2. Average weights were used to rank seriousness: Planned killing of a police officer was in first place; passing worthless checks of over $500 was in the middle; and public drunkenness received the lowest score. Given the many diverse items to be rated, a remarkable consensus among respondents emerged. Agreement among various subgroups was substantial. Whites and blacks, males and females, poorly eudcated and well educated—all had a fairly similar perspective on the crimes under consideration, which implies that generalized social norms rather than just individual sentiments were operating in the assessment of the seriousness of crime. Only a few items such as mother-son incest (no. 86) and draft resistance (no. 99) produced high variance—that is, drastic disagreements among respondents. The subjective feelings of many individuals can be measured and combined to create a relatively objective standard of seriousness. The findings in Table 13-2 provide an easily applied score sheet that can be used to convert the broad range of crimes afflicting a community into an estimate of the moral affront to society the crimes represent.

But is the work involved in utilizing such ratings justified? It turns out that the assessment of crime produced by traditional data and those resulting from weightings are very close because property offenses account for five out of six offenses and the Sellin-Wolfgang index primarily weights violent crime. Because the most common property crime, petty theft, receives only one point, a large amount of crime is being counted in the same way as if there were no weighting

TABLE 13-2

Average Seriousness Ratings of Crimes (N is at least 100)

Rank	Crime	Mean	Variance
1	Planned killing of a policeman	8.474	2.002
2	Planned killing of a person for a fee	8.406	2.749
3	Selling heroin	8.293	2.658
4	Forcible rape after breaking into a home	8.241[1]	2.266
5	Impulsive killing of a policeman	8.214	3.077
6	Planned killing of a spouse	8.113[1]	3.276
7	Planned killing of an acquaintance	8.093	3.273
8	Hijacking an airplane	8.072	2.776
9	Armed robbery of a bank	8.021	8.020
10	Selling LSD	7.949	3.048
11	Assault with a gun on a policeman	7.938	3.225
12	Kidnapping for ransom	7.930	3.844
13	Forcible rape of a stranger in a park	7.909	3.737
14	Killing someone after an argument over a business transaction	7.898	3.536
15	Assassination of a public official	7.888	5.400
16	Killing someone during a serious argument	7.867	3.663
17	Making sexual advances to young children	7.861	3.741
18	Assault with a gun on a stranger	7.847[1]	2.172
19	Impulsive killing of a spouse	7.835	3.952
20	Impulsive killing of a stranger	7.821[1]	3.429
21	Forcible rape of a neighbor	7.778	3.726
22	Impulsive killing of an acquaintance	7.717	4.205
23	Deliberately starting a fire which results in a death	7.707	4.189
24	Assault with a gun on a stranger	7.662[2]	2.976[1]
25	Manufacturing and selling drugs known to be harmful to users	7.653	3.280
26	Knowingly selling contaminated food which results in a death	7.596	5.202
27	Armed robbery of a company payroll	7.577	3.080
28	Using heroin	7.520	4.871
29	Assault with a gun on an acquaintance	7.505	3.482
30	Armed holdup of a taxi driver	7.505	3.336
31	Beating up a child	7.490	3.840
32	Armed robbery of a neighborhood druggist	7.487[1]	3.221
33	Causing auto accident death while driving when drunk	7.455	3.904
34	Selling secret documents to a foreign government	7.423[1]	5.722
35	Armed street holdup stealing $200 cash	7.414	3.633
36	Killing someone in a bar room free-for-all	7.392	4.637
37	Deliberately starting a fire in an occupied building	7.347	5.177
38	Assault with a gun on a spouse	7.323	4.650
39	Armed robbery of a supermarket	7.313	3.911
40	Assault with a gun in the course of a riot	7.245	3.218
41	Armed hijacking of a truck	7.198	3.866
42	Deserting to the enemy in time of war	7.194	4.673
43	Armed street holdup stealing $25 in cash	7.165	4.431
44	Armed robbery of an armored truck	7.163	5.210
45	Spying for a foreign government	7.135	7.024
46	Killing a pedestrian while exceeding the speed limit	7.122	3.964
47	Seduction of a minor	7.021	5.729
48	Beating up a policeman	7.020	5.734
49	Selling marijuana	6.969[1]	7.216
50	Father-daughter incest	6.959	7.112
51	Causing the death of an employee by neglecting to repair machinery	6.918	4.556
52	Breaking and entering a bank	6.908	4.641
53	Mugging and stealing $25 in cash	6.873[1]	5.305
54	Selling pep pills	6.867	5.683
55	Cashing stolen payroll checks	6.827	4.784
56	Mugging and stealing $200 cash	6.796	5.051
57	Causing the death of a tenant by neglecting to repair heating plant	6.704	6.314
58	Killing spouse's lover after catching them together	6.691	7.695
59	Blackmail	6.667	5.122
60	Advocating overthrow of the government	6.663	7.715
61	Neglecting to care for own children	6.660	6.977

TABLE 13-2 (*continued*)

Rank	Crime	Mean	Variance
62	Forcible rape of a former spouse	6.653	6.394
63	Manufacturing and selling autos known to be dangerously defective	6.604	5.968
64	Beating up a stranger	6.604	5.379
65	Using LSD	6.557	7.479
66	Driving while drunk	6.545	6.006
67	Practicing medicine without a license	6.500[1]	6.908
68	Burglary of a home stealing a color TV set	6.440[1]	5.048
69	Knowingly passing counterfeit money	6.392	5.220
70	Beating up someone in a riot	6.368	5.788
71	Performing illegal abortions	6.330	5.723
72	Passing worthless checks for more than $500	6.309	5.119
73	A public official accepting bribes in return for favors	6.240	6.467
74	Employee embezzling company funds	6.207[1]	5.030
75	Knowingly selling stolen stocks and bonds	6.138[1]	4.960
76	Refusing to obey lawful order of a policeman	6.118[1]	5.806
77	Burglary of a home stealing a portable transister radio	6.115[1]	5.871
78	Theft of a car for the purpose of resale	6.093[1]	5.085
79	Knowingly selling defective used cars as completely safe	6.093	5.023
80	Burglary of an appliance store stealing several TV sets	6.062	5.371
81	Looting goods in a riot	6.043	5.052
82	Knowingly selling stolen goods	6.021	4.463
83	Leaving the scene of an accident	5.949	6.620
84	Printing counterfeit $10 bills	5.948	6.820
85	Shoplifting a diamond ring from a jewelry store	5.939	5.466
86	Mother-son incest	5.907	9.189
87	Theft of a car for joy-riding	5.876	6.047
88	Intimidating a witness in a court case	5.853	4.850
89	Brother-sister incest	5.825	8.709
90	Knowingly selling worthless stocks as valuable investments	5.821	5.021
91	Beating up a spouse	5.796	7.051
92	Selling liquor to minors	5.789	7.572
93	Burglary of a factory stealing machine tools	5.789	5.317
94	Using stolen credit cards	5.750	5.832
95	Using pep pills	5.656	9.512
96	Joining a riot	5.656	6.750
97	Lending money at illegal interest rates	5.653	5.775
98	Knowingly buying stolen goods	5.596	5.794
99	Refusal to serve when drafted in peace time	5.535	8.863
100	Resisting arrest	5.449	6.271
101	Impersonating a policeman	5.449	7.405
102	Using false identification to obtain goods from a store	5.438	6.628
103	Bribing a public official to obtain favors	5.394	6.198
104	Passing worthless checks involving less than $100	5.339[1]	5.921
105	Desertion from military service in peace time	5.323	7.526
106	Under-reporting income on income tax return	5.305	6.321
107	Willfully neglecting to file income tax returns	5.157[1]	6.470
108	Soliciting for prostitution	5.144	7.687
109	Proposing homosexual practices to an adult	5.140	9.361
110	Overcharging on repairs to automobiles	5.135	6.455
111	Shoplifting a dress from a department store	5.070	6.308
112	Beating up an acquaintance	5.032	5.644
113	Driving while license is suspended	5.031	7.988
114	Pouring paint over someone's car	4.938	7.449
115	Shoplifting a pair of shoes from a shoe store	4.990	6.781
116	Overcharging for credit in selling goods	4.970	6.213
117	Shoplifting a carton of cigarettes from a supermarket	4.969	6.793
118	Smuggling goods to avoid paying import duties	4.918	5.618
119	Killing a suspected burglar in home	4.868[1]	8.930
120	False claims of dependents on income tax return	4.832	6.801
121	Knowingly using inaccurate scales in weighing meat for sale	4.786	5.902
122	Refusal to make essential repairs to rental property	4.781	6.678

Table 13-2 (*continued*)

Rank	Crime	Mean	Variance
123	Engaging in male homosexual acts with consenting adults	4.736	9.396
124	Engaging in female homosexual acts with consenting adults	4.729	9.042
125	Breaking a plate glass window in a shop	4.653	6.697
126	Fixing prices of a consumer product like gasoline	4.629	6.069
127	Fixing prices of machines sold to businesses	4.619	6.218
128	Selling pornographic magazines	4.526	7.826
129	Shoplifting a book in a bookstore	4.424[1]	6.551
130	Repeated refusal to obey parents	4.411	9.074
131	Joining a prohibited demonstration	4.323	6.486
132	False advertising of headache remedy	4.083	7.972
133	Refusal to pay alimony	4.063	6.670
134	Refusal to pay parking fines	3.583[1]	6.475
135	Disturbing the peace	3.779	7.174
136	Repeated truancy	3.573	7.658
137	Repeated running away from home	3.571[1]	6.342
138	Loitering in public places	3.375	8.111
139	Refusal to answer census taker	3.105	7.329
140	Being drunk in public places	2.849	6.021

NOTE: Scores have a range of 9 (most serious) to 1 (least serious).

[1] Crimes rated by all members (200) of the Baltimore sample.

[2] This offense was inadvertently repeated (see crime rank No. 18), indicating that differences in scores as much as .185 can be obtained through response unreliability.

SOURCE: Peter Rossi, Emily Waite, Christine Bose, and Richard Berk, "The Seriousness of Crimes: Normative Structure and Individual Differences," *American Sociological Review* 39 (April 1974), 228–29. Reprinted by permission of the American Sociological Association and the authors.

scheme. Indeed, a study of 3,141 counties across the country produced a very high correlation between the *Uniform Crime Reports* index crime rate, which lumps all crimes together equally, and the Sellin-Wolfgang weightings.[43] Such a close association between measures is very rare in the social sciences, strongly implying that not enough additional information is gained by using such weightings to warrant the complications and costs that they entail.

MEASURING RECIDIVISM

Sometimes knowing something about criminals is more important than knowing about the crimes themselves. For the purpose of evaluating rehabilitation and specific deterrence policies, recidivism rates must be compiled. These are indications of the percentage of offenders who repeat their crimes. One common approach is to use fingerprint data of those arrested to secure a listing from F.B.I. files of previous arrests (sometimes called "rap sheets").[44] The F.B.I. itself did this for over 200,000 persons arrested between 1970 and 1972, discovering an inordinately high recidivism rate—65 percent for all felons and as high as 77 percent for robbers and 74 percent for forgers.[45]

The approach of using F.B.I. data has two serious drawbacks—one acting as a depressant and the other as a stimulant of recidivism rates. First, previous arrest data are *not* conclusive of prior criminality because arrest is not tantamount to guilt and sometimes merely represents the suspicions (or worse, the harrassment) of police officers. Indeed, when the police discover that suspects have a previous record, they are more likely to arrest again—setting up a vicious cycle of continually increased probability of arrest.

On the other hand, when crimes are successful (more often than not), *no* indication of previous criminal behavior is apparent. The term *first offender* is often a misnomer standing for "first time caught." Skilled or lucky repeaters who get away with their crimes can foil attempts to measure recidivism and assess the extent to which the criminal justice system is a revolving door.

No very promising solution to this problem is in sight. There is simply no way of detecting all crimes committed by repeaters or anyone else. The difficulty really involves the difference between those who are *actually* guilty and those who are found to be *legally* guilty. We can roughly approximate the latter in order to calculate recidivism rates, but the former is likely to remain a mystery.

Building on an admittedly weak data base of reported or solved crime, some program evaluators have refined the techniques for measuring recidivism. One shortcoming of traditional methods of determining recidivism rates is that crime repetition is analyzed at a single point in time, so that the effectiveness of programs of different lengths intended to prevent recidivism cannot be compared. Looking at the experience of the early months of two programs is unsound because crucial long-range impacts are not disclosed. To cope with this difficulty, experts have devised mathematical equations to project the probable degree of recidivism in the future among a group of convicted criminals on the basis of past experience of others in the same group.[46]

Other experts such as Dennis Palumbo have examined the frequency of crime repetition and the length of abstinence from crime as important facets of recidivism.[47] Not only are offenders who continuously break the law greater threats to society than the occasional offender but they represent a more acute failure of the criminal justice system. The point is that crime repetition is not an either/or phenomenon. There is a vast middle ground between "going straight" and continuing a life steeped in crime. So recidivism measures that take into account the *degree* of repeating make an important contribution to criminal justice evaluation.

Operationalizing Criminal Justice Goals

Attempts have been made to operationalize other criminal justice concepts besides crime. Here we can illustrate only some of the potentialities for measurement since comprehensive coverage would be encyclopedic in length. As we shall see, the same problems that plague measurement of crime afflict other measures. Thus, skepticism is always in order when judging data-based findings.

MEASURING DUE PROCESS

As was discussed in Chapter 1, due process is a concept that represents many different protections for individuals. One facet of due process is the use of minimum necessary force by police in subduing persons they are trying to apprehend, question, or arrest. While it is fairly easy to establish gradations of police force—ranging from police brutality at one extreme to police restraint at the other—operationalizing the concept in a concrete way is no mean feat.

One approach that has been used is direct observations of police encounters with citizens. A group of 36 observers rode with patrol officers in three cities during their eight-hour tours of duty in the summer of 1966 and were able to watch and describe 5,012 police-citizen interactions involving 13,139 citizens. Carefully constructed coding categories were devised to record the exchanges: Police conduct during each transaction was labeled personal, civil, demeaning, authoritarian, or threatening and hostile. A special category was reserved for the use of excessive force, which occurred in only three interactions per thousand. The conclusion was that incivility was a far greater problem than the misuse of force.[48]

The immediate question that comes to mind is whether the measure was reactive: Did police "go easy" on civilians because their conduct was being closely scrutinized? The temptation is to answer in the affirmative, but it must be realized that the demands of the job and the instinctive tendency to handle situations routinely may well outweigh the fear of being exposed; often the police almost forget the presence of outsiders. Indeed, the following incident was recorded, suggesting that at least some officers were relatively unaffected by observers:

> The watch began rather routinely as the policemen cruised the district. Their first radio dispatch came at about 5:30 P.M. They were told to investigate two drunks in a cemetery. In arriving they found two white men "sleeping one off." Without questioning the men, the older policeman began to search one of them, ripping his shirt and hitting him in the groin with a nightstick. The younger policeman, as he searched the second, ripped away the seat of his trousers, exposing his buttocks. The policemen then prodded the men toward the cemetery fence and forced them to climb it, laughing at the plight of the drunk with the exposed buttocks. As the drunks went over the fence, one policemen shouted, "I ought to run you fuckers in!" The other remarked to the observer, "Those assholes won't be back; a bunch of shitty winos."[49]

Still, this anecdote is inconclusive. Other officers may have been on their good behavior during the study, and the very officers that manhandled the drunks might have done even worse if they were unobserved. The "guinea pig" effect is a serious threat to the reliability of the data.

Another approach that is sometimes used to measure force is to interview police. One older study (done in 1953) that promised police confidentiality elicited a finding that 67 percent felt justified in using force in situations when it was legally impermissible—for example, to deal with citizen disrespect, to obtain information from recalcitrant individuals, and to punish "hardened" criminals.[50] Police may well be more honest when talking hypothetically about what they might do than when they are being observed on the spot, but a large gap still remains between what is said and what is done. Indeed, with greater concern about brutality at the present time, the police may not be so ready to reveal their proclivity to violate regulations so openly today. Self-interest demands otherwise.

A third technique used to measure force is indirect—looking at the numbers of civilians killed at the hands of police. Thus, one study revealed that during the regime of Chicago Mayor Richard Daley (known for his "law and order" ideology), police there killed four times as many citizens per capita as their counterparts in New York, Los Angeles, or Detroit.[51] Moreover, this study and others showed that blacks were many more times as likely to be fatally shot by police as whites. While many instances can be cited in which the use of fatal force is appropriate, it is at least arguable that such comparative data reveal "over-kill"—abuse of police authority.

These data are *reliable:* A dead body is unmistakable, and in no cases did doubt arise about who did the shooting. But substantial *validity* problems remain because the meaning of the reported data is unclear. Perhaps Chicago police are just vigilant in pursuing crime and therefore become embroiled with more violent criminals. Or the greater number of black men killed may be the result of high levels of police deployment in black neighborhoods. The finding that black police officers are six times more likely than their white counterparts to kill suspects has been explained by the fact that more black police are assigned to dangerous undercover work in high-crime precincts.[52]

Alternative explanations abound, and so it would be highly presumptuous to equate civilian deaths with police impropriety. Thus, even the most accurate data can be worthless if they cannot be interpreted. Police shootings, unless placed in context, are simply too far afield from the concept of due process to be good indicators of its observance. Therefore, more direct measures such as those discussed previously give better information.

MEASURING EFFICIENCY

Efficiency is the effective utilization of resources. One aspect of this is professional performance by personnel. But measuring this quality with regard to the police is very difficult because the kinds of tasks they perform are so varied and successful execution of them is so subtle. It is hard to measure when an officer has done a good job in calming a lost child, breaking up a fight, or keeping close watch on a neighborhood trouble spot.

Thus, measures of police performance have generally been abysmal. One study trying to relate background characteristics of police to performance on the job is indicative. To obtain quantitative information, researchers used a range of variables—career advancement, receipt of awards, complaints against police, and number of days sick—on which data were readily available.[53] Examining these measures closely reveals that they hardly speak to the question of what the police do on a daily basis. The data may be reliable, and they certainly are convenient; but they are not in the least valid.

The invalid data in this study can be contrasted with the output of the Knapp Commission, which in 1970 was given the task of uncovering corruption in the New York City Police Department. The absence of corruption is an important indication of efficiency in that graft-ridden departments protect criminals instead of pursuing them. Since the mandate of the commission was to measure the amount of illegal police behavior, standard methods of data collection were of no avail; it would have been laughable to interview police to ask them if they took bribes.

What did the commission do? With the authorization of the mayor and police commissioner, undercover investigators went to places like bars where payoffs allegedly were frequent to observe police comings and goings. Informants from the underworld were paid money for their information, and some of them were electronically wired to record subsequent conversations with police. Cooperative police spied on other police. In short, the whole gamut of undercover intelligence-gathering activity was used.[54]

The result was information revealing payments of up to $80,000 to some narcotics police and lesser degrees of corruption indulged in by a "sizable majority" of the entire police force.[55] The data were not precise: They did not facilitate comparison of individual police officers or assessment of trends. But they were valid—they measured what they were supposed to measure. Sometimes researchers do better to obtain relevant data not reducible to numbers than to search out inappropriate quantitative indicators.

MEASURING THE EQUALITY OF JUSTICE

At the top of the Supreme Court building in Washington, D.C., are engraved the noble words "Equal Justice under Law." Yet a constant lament about the criminal justice system is that this ideal is far removed from reality. Many attempts to examine this alleged disparity empirically have been made, and some of these were discussed in Chapter 7.

The most direct measures of inequality of treatment are comparisons of different categories of people who are adjudicated to see if they are accorded different treatment. Do some groups—blacks, the poor, the young—fare worse than others at various stages of the criminal justice process?

An example of such research is a study of the so-called black shift among female defendants handled in District of Columbia courts.[56] Figure 13-6 shows that whites are filtered out as the process continues. At the outset 27 percent of those booked are white, but only 3 percent of those sentenced to more than three months in jail are white. This appears to be solid evidence of racial discrimination.

However, as with all such disposition data, the information given is insufficient to warrant such a negative conclusion. Figure 13-6 does not reveal the seriousness of the charges against defendants of both races, the strength of the evidence against them, and what percentage of each race had criminal records. In interpreting disposition data, researchers must introduce as many controls for legally relevant variables as possible so that we achieve crime and defendant comparability. However, this is easier said than done because many court records are woefully lacking in such relevant details. It is easier to divine injustice than to prove it.

Care must also be taken to watch for the opposite phenomenon—data which camouflage real inequality. Disparities are sometimes concealed when averages are used to compare the treatment of two groups such as blacks and whites. They may appear to be treated the same if, for example, the average length of sentence of the two groups is identical, but, in fact, deliberate discrimination occurring in both groups may offset each other.

A hypothetical example of how this can occur was nicely presented by political scientists Stuart Nagel and Marian Neef in an article appropriately entitled "Racial Disparities Which Supposedly Do Not Exist." Assume that 100 black defendants receive an average of two years imprisonment in a group of cases in-

FIGURE 13-6

Racial Disparities in Criminal Justice Dispositions of Women in the District of Columbia

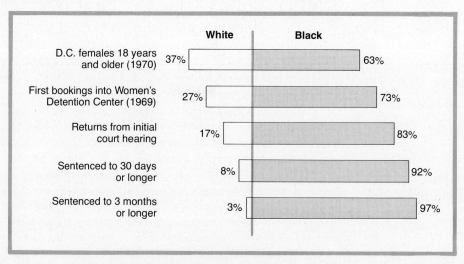

SOURCE: Stuart Adams, "The 'Black Shift' Phenomenon in Criminal Justice," *The Justice System Journal* 2 (Winter 1976), p. 185. Reprinted with permission.

volving "moderately serious" felonies and that the same average holds for 100 white defendants in a similar batch of cases. Does this mean they are being sentenced equally? No—because 50 of the blacks may have received one-year sentences for aggravated assault, which is generally an intra-race crime, while the other 50 may have gotten three-year sentences for larceny, which is more likely to have a white victim. On the other hand, all whites may have been sentenced to two years in prison regardless of whether their crimes were aggravated assault or larceny. Consequently, both blacks and whites receive equal average sentences but only because blacks are being *under*sentenced in black-on-black assaults and *over*-sentenced in black-on-white larcenies.[57]

The moral is plain: The use of averages in criminal justice research can cloak injustice. It is often necessary to break down dispositions far more closely to isolate nuances of discrimination that are concealed by the use of summary statistics.

MEASURING PUBLIC TRANQUILLITY

Public tranquillity is freedom from fear and annoyance. It is a mental phenomenon made up of feelings and perceptions. Consequently, it is best measured by surveys—asking people if they are afraid of crime. In addition, information about whether they have changed any of their behavior to protect themselves or thwart criminals is a good way of determining whether their expressed fears are related to action.

One study created a "safety scale" composed of responses to survey questions inquiring about fear of crime. The questions were as follows:

Is there any area here—that is within a mile—where you would be afraid to walk at night?

Have there been any times recently when you wanted to go out somewhere in your neighborhood, but stayed home instead because you thought it would be unsafe to go there?

Do you make sure that all of the doors in your house are locked when you leave for a few minutes?

Some people worry a great deal about having their house broken into, and other people are not as concerned. Are you very concerned, somewhat concerned, or not at all concerned about this?

How likely is it that a person walking around here at night will be held up or attacked?[58]

By combining answers, researchers can differentiate those who are very frightened, moderately so, or completely at ease. While the persistent problems of response invalidity and interviewer cuing are present, the role of self-interest as a confounding factor seems less prominent.

Some unobtrusive measures seem feasible but have never been used. Numbers of people seen on the street at night can be used to measure public tranquillity, but this may be an invalid indicator if there are other good reasons for remaining indoors, as is the case in Houston during the summer when the heat is unbearable. Other possibilities for nonreactive measurement of public tranquillity are the numbers of apartments with window bars, the number of car windows left open, and the number of bicycles left unchained. Even with regard to a psychological phenomenon like public tranquillity, actions may speak louder than words.

Conclusion

Whether we are measuring crime, due process, or any other phenomenon, skepticism about the quality of data obtained is the proper stance. Except for those relatively few instances when nonreactive measures are appropriate, the collectors of data can juggle words and behavior to distort the nature of reality. The "fudge factor"—whether premeditated or unconscious—is a constant threat to the reliability of criminal justice measurement.

In quest of the most error-free measures, there is often a trade-off between validity and reliability. To gain the precision that permits comparability and the monitoring of minute (but meaningful) changes, researchers sometimes collect data that are only tangentially related to the concepts under study. If a broad inferential leap must be taken to go from empirical measures to abstract concepts like justice or efficiency, then any findings that result are put in jeopardy.

In the search for proper measures, we must also beware of what has been called "the law of the instrument," which states, "Give a small boy a hammer and he will find that everything he encounters needs pounding."[59] Just because a measurement technique (such as the survey) has been used ad infinitum and has been refined carefully does *not* mean that it is necessarily appropriate for the purpose at hand. Many concepts in criminal justice have been dealt with primarily in a philsophic way, and only quite recently have strides been made to find ways of zeroing in on them empirically. Consequently, the wise course would seem to be the imaginative use of untried measures in addition to more orthodox approaches in order to come to grips with reality.

In order to guard against the undermining of research findings through revelations that the data on which they are based are inadequate, multiple measures of the same phenomenon are desirable. The beauty of the Kansas City preventive patrol experiment discussed in Chapter 9 is that two totally indpendent measures of crime, surveys and police reports, led to the same results. Confidence in evaluations and the credibility of research findings are vastly augmented if several indicators substantiate the claims being made.

Finally, self-interest ought to be turned on its head in the quest for good data. Currently, it is often an obstacle to sound measurement in that administrators, politicians, criminal justice personnel, and private citizens all perceive personal benefits from being dishonest. One way of changing this is to cater to people's interest in partaking in significant communal activity, and generating a crime-fighting spirit is an eminently plausible way of bringing people together. Improved morale within criminal justice agencies and greater citizen trust in government may well be the key to furnishing genuine data and reliable measurement.

SUMMARY

The acquisition of data about criminal justice can improve our understanding of how the system works, provide a better assessment of the crime problem, and contribute to the sound evaluation of policies. But social measurement is an imperfect process, and attempts to operationalize criminal justice concepts always pose validity and reliability problems. The public interest in values such as privacy can curtail the use of some strategies for gaining information, and the self-interests of officials can cause them to distort or even conceal facts. Thus, the users of criminal justice data must be wary of their accuracy.

Crime data are particularly imperiled by these problems largely because the definition of crime is fraught with ambiguity and someone must use personal judgment to decide whether a crime has occurred. Reported crime data have the virtue of being a normal by-product of police work, but they suffer from the failure of many victims to report crime and the vast discretion of officers in recording crime. While victimization surveys that poll people about their crime experiences are expensive, they do reveal more crime than police reports, and, notwithstanding problems such as inadequate sampling, interviewer cuing, and response error, they have substantial validity.

The total amount of crime detected by one or another method must be put into a frame of reference to make sense. Hence, crime rates are used to compare areas with different populations or numbers of crime targets. Other ways of interpreting crime are by measuring its economic impact on victims or weighting the seriousness of the various crimes committed. For the purpose of evaluating rehabilitation and specific deterrence policies aimed at preventing crime repetition, recidivism rates can be calculated.

Operationalizing other concepts can be an even more precarious task than measuring crime, and the danger of subjectivity is greater. In trying to secure information about due process, efficiency, justice, and public tranquillity, we must be especially alert to the conscious or unconscious deception by criminal justice officials and be cautious about attaching faulty interpretations to facts that are garnered. Facts do not speak for themselves but must be constantly evaluated for accuracy and put into proper perspective if they are not to be misleading.

FOOTNOTES

[1] Quoted in David Seidman and Michael Couzens, "Getting the Crime Rate Down: Political Pressure and Crime Reporting," *Law and Society Review* 8 (Spring 1974), 457.

[2] Ibid., 466–79.

[3] For an extended discussion of reliability and validity, see Fred Kerlinger, *Foundations of Behavioral Research* (New York: Holt, Rinehart & Winston, 1964), esp. chaps. 24 and 25.

[4] The term is that of Abraham Kaplan, *The Conduct of In-*

quiry (San Francisco: Chandler Publishing, 1964), pp. 127–28.

[5] See, for example, the President's Commission on Law Enforcement and the Administration of Justice, *Task Force Report: The Police* (Washington, D.C.: U.S. Government Printing Office, 1967), pp. 144–49.

[6] *New York Times*, September 25, 1977, p. 39.

[7] See Rodney Mabry, *An Economic Investigation of State and Local Judiciary Services* (Washington, D.C.: National Institute of Law Enforcement and Criminal Jutice, 1977).

[8] Harry Kalven and Hans Zeisel, *The American Jury* (Boston: Little, Brown, 1966), pp. vi–vii.

[9] *Law Enforcement News*, October 4, 1977, pp. 1, 11.

[10] *New York Times*, September 5, 1977, p. 6.

[11] Laud Humphreys, *Tearoom Trade: Impersonal Sex in Public Places* (Chicago: Aldine Publishing, 1970).

[12] Ibid., pp. 84–96.

[13] For example, false reporting of crimes is a misdemeanor in New York State punishable by a three-month jail sentence. New York Penal Law, Sec. 240.50.

[14] Eugene Webb, Donald Campbell, Richard Schwartz, and Lee Sechrest, *Unobtrusive Measures: Nonreactive Research in the Social Sciences* (Chicago: Rand McNally, 1966).

[15] Wesley Skogan, "Measurement Problems in Official and Survey Crime Rates," *Journal of Criminal Justice* 3 (Spring 1975), 18.

[16] For a history of the *Uniform Crime Reports*, see Michael Maltz, "Crime Statistics: A Historical Perspective," *Crime and Delinquency* 23 (January 1977), 32–40.

[17] Wesley Skogan, "Crime and Crime Rates," in *Sample Surveys of the Victims of Crime*, ed. Wesley Skogan (Cambridge, Mass.: Balinger Publishing, 1976) pp. 105–19.

[18] Donald Black, "Production of Crime Rates," *American Sociological Review* 35 (August 1970), 733–48.

[19] This remark of Sir Josiah Stamp was quoted in Gwynn Nettler, *Explaining Crime* (New York: McGraw-Hill, 1974), p. 45.

[20] For a discussion of the Philadelphia and Baltimore situations, see Seidman and Couzens, op. cit., 479–84; concerning apparent data manipulation by the New York City Transit Authority, see J. M. Chaiken, *What's Known about Deterrent Effects of Police Activities* (Santa Monica, Calif.: Rand Corporation, 1976).

[21] Dorothy Guyot, "The Uniform Crime Reports as a Clipper Ship in Competition with Steam" (Paper presented to the American Society of Criminology, 1977), pp. 3–7.

[22] Dorothy Guyot, "What Productivity? What Bargain?" *Public Administration Review* 36 (May/June 1976), 341.

[23] Michael Maltz, "Crime Statistics: A Mathematical Perspective," *Journal of Criminal Justice* 3 (1975), 179.

[24] Michael Milakovich and Kurt Weis, "Politics and Measures of Success in the War on Crime," *Crime and Delinquency* 21 (January 1975), 1–10.

[25] Albert Biderman and Albert Reiss, "On Exploring the 'Dark Figure' of Crime," *The Annals of the American Academy of Political and Social Science* 374 (November 1967), 1–15.

[26] James Garofalo and Michael Hindelang, *An Introduction to the National Crime Survey* (Washington, D.C.: U.S. Government Printing Office, 1977), pp. 15–33.

[27] Wesley Skogan, "Victimization Surveys and Criminal Justice Planning," *University of Cincinnati Law Review* 45 (1976), 167–206.

[28] See James Garofalo, *Local Victim Surveys: A Review of the Issues* (Albany, N.Y.: Criminal Justice Research Center, 1977); and James P. Levine, "On Victimization Surveys: Reply to Singer," *Criminology* 16 (May 1978), 104–107.

[29] Alan Booth, David Johnson, and Harvey Choldin, "Correlates of City Crime Rates: Victimization Surveys Versus Official Statistics," *Social Problems* 25 (December 1977), 188.

[30] Garofalo and Hindelang, op. cit., p. 21.

[31] See, for example, C. Cannell and R. Kahn, "Interviewing," in *The Handbook of Social Psychology*, vol. 2, ed. G. Lindzey and E. Aronson (Reading, Mass.: Addison-Wesley, 1968), 548.

[32] L. Bailey, T. F. Moore, and B. A. Bailar, *An Interviewer Variance Study for the Eight Impact Cities of the National Crime Survey Cities* (Washington, D.C.: U.S. Government Printing Office, 1976).

[33] Wesley Skogan, "Citizen Reporting of Crime: Some National Panel Data," *Criminology* 13 (February 1976), 545.

[34] Scott Decker, "Official Crime Rates and Vitimization Surveys: An Empirical Comparison," *Journal of Criminal Justice* 5 (1977), 47–54.

[35] See Wesley Skogan, "The Validity of Official Crime Statistics: An Emipirical Investigation," *Social Science Quarterly* 55 (June 1974), 25–38; and Michael Hindelang, "The Uniform Crime Reports Revisited," *Journal of Criminal Justice* 2 (Spring 1974), 1–17.

[36] See Gwynn Nettler, *Explaining Crime* (New York: McGraw-Hill, 1974), pp. 73–96, for a summary of such studies.

[37] See Vladimir Konecni, Ebbe Ebbesen, and Daiva Konecni, "Decision Processes and Risk Taking in Traffic: Driver Response to the Onset of the Yellow Light," *Journal of Applied Psychology* 61 (June 1976), 359–67; and Denis Ugwuegba, "The Stop Sign Is for the Other Guy; a Naturalistic Observation of Driving Behavior in Nigeria," *Journal of Applied Psychology* 62 (October 1977), 574–77.

[38] The statistics are from the Federal Bureau of Investigation, *Uniform Crime Reports for the United States—1976* (Washington, D.C.: U.S. Government Printing Office, 1977), p. 18, and the U.S. Department of Commerce, *Statistical Abstract of the United States—1977* (Washington, D.C.: U.S. Government Printing Office, 1978), p. 699.

[39] Skogan, "Victimization Surveys and Criminal Justice Planning," op. cit., 171–75.

[40] *Ezek.* 7:23.

[41] Thorsten Sellin and Marvin Wolfgang, *The Measurement of Delinquency* (New York: Wiley, 1964), p. 402.

[42] Peter Rossi, Emily Waite, Christine Bose, and Richard Berk, "The Seriousness of Crimes: Normative Structure and Individual Differences," *American Sociological Review* 39 (April 1974), 224–37.

[43] Hindelang, op. cit., 14. See also Alfred Blumstein,

"Seriousness Weights in an Index of Crime," *American Sociological Review* 39 (December 1974), 854–64.

44 See Daniel Glaser, *Routinizing Evaluation: Getting Feedback on Effectiveness of Crime and Delinquency Programs* (Rockville, Md.: National Institute of Mental Health, 1973), chap. 7.

45 U.S. Federal Bureau of Investigation, *Uniform Crime Reports for the United States—1972* (Washington, D.C.: U.S. Government Printing Office, 1973), p. 37.

46 Michael Maltz and Richard McCleary, "The Mathematics of Behavioral Change: Recidivism and Construct Validity," *Evaluation Quarterly* 1 (August 1977), 421–38.

47 Dennis Palumbo, "Evaluating the Effectiveness of Different Methods of Probation" (Unpublished paper, 1978).

48 Albert Reiss, *The Police and the Public* (New Haven, Conn.: Yale University Press, 1971), p. 142.

49 Albert Reiss, "Police Brutality—Answers to Key Questions," *Trans Action* 5 (July–August 1968), 13.

50 William Westley, "Violence and the Police," *American Journal of Sociology* 59 (July 1953), 38.

51 Ralph Knoohuizen, Richard Fahey, and Deborah Palmer, *The Police and Their Use of Fatal Force in Chicago* (Chicago: Chicago Law Enforcement Study Group, 1971).

52 John Goldkamp, "Minorities as Victims of Police Shootings: Interpretations of Racial Disproportionality and Police Use of Deadly Force," *The Justice System Journal* 2 (Winter 1976), 180.

53 Bernard Cohen and Jan Chaiken, *Police Background Characteristics and Performance* (Lexington, Mass.: Lexington Books, 1973), pp. 40–48.

54 *The Knapp Commission Report on Police Corruption* (New York: George Braziller, 1972), pp. 42–46.

55 Ibid., p. 61.

56 Stuart Adams, "The 'Black Shift' Phenomenon in Criminal Justice," *The Justice System Journal* 2 (Winter 1976), 185–94.

57 Stuart Nagel and Marian Neef, "Racial Disparities Which Supposedly Do Not Exist: Some Pitfalls in Analysis of Court Records," *Notre Dame Lawyer* 52 (October 1976), 89.

58 John Conklin, *The Impact of Crime* (New York: Macmillan, 1975), pp. 82–83.

59 Kaplan, op. cit., p. 28.

BIBLIOGRAPHY

Garofalo, James, and Hindelang, Michael. *An Introduction to the National Crime Survey.* Washington, D.C.: U.S. Government Printing Office, 1977.

Law Enforcement Assistance Administration. *Sourcebook of Criminal Justice Statistics.* Washington, D.C.: U.S. Government Printing Office, annual.

Levine, James. "The Potential for Crime Overreporting in Criminal Victimization Surveys." *Criminology* 14 (November 1976), 307–30.

Maltz, Michael. "Crime Statistics: A Historical Perspective." *Crime and Delinquency* 23 (January 1977), 32–40.

National Research Council, Panel for the Evaluation of Crime Surveys. *Surveying Crime.* Washington, D.C.: National Academy of Sciences, 1976.

President's Commission on Law Enforcement and the Administration of Justice. *Task Force Report: Crime and Its Impact—An Assessment.* Washington, D.C.: U.S. Government Printing Office, 1967.

Seidman, David, and Couzens, Michael. "Getting the Crime Rate Down: Political Pressure and Crime Reporting." *Law and Society Review* 8 (Spring 1974), 457–93.

Sellin, Thorsten, and Wolfgang, Marvin. *The Measurement of Delinquency.* New York: Wiley, 1964.

Skogan, Wesley. "Measurement Problems in Official and Survey Crime Rates." *Journal of Criminal Justice* 3 (Spring 1975), 17–31.

Skogan, Wesley, ed. *Sample Surveys of the Victims of Crime* (Cambridge, Mass.: Balinger Publishing, 1976).

U.S. Federal Bureau of Investigation. *Uniform Crime Reports for the United States* (Washington, D.C.; U.S. Government Printing Office, annual).

Webb, Eugene; Campbell, Donald; Schwartz, Richard; and Sechrest, Lee. *Unobtrusive Meaures: Nonreactive Measures in the Social Sciences.* Chicago: Rand McNally, 1966.

Beginning on October 1, 1972, and ending a year later, the Police Foundation conducted an experiment in Kansas City, Missouri, that called into serious question the traditional assumption about the routine patrol function. The assumption is that putting police out on the streets on patrol is a deterrent to crime. In the experiment three similar areas of the city were selected. In one of the three areas the number of routine patrols was quadrupled; in a second the number of patrols remained at normal level; and in the third area no routine patrols were used at all. Because the experiment was conducted for a full year in three similar areas, the researchers assumed that the differences in crime rates could be attributed strictly to the differences in patrol number. No other variables could confuse the results. Here, then, was an excellent test of the impact of patrols on crime.[1]

CHAPTER FOURTEEN

EVALUATING CRIMINAL JUSTICE POLICY

The experiment found that the three areas exhibited no differences in crime rates nor were differences found in citizen attitudes toward the police, reported victimization rates, citizen behavior, or the number of traffic accidents. With such clear and unequivocal results, we might expect that cities throughout the country would discontinue routine patrols. But they have not. Despite the clear evidence that patrols do not reduce crime, most cities continue nevertheless to use them.

Perhaps the reason why routine and somewhat intensified patrols have not been discontinued is that police administrators look upon Kansas City as a special case, or they believe that more than a single study would have to be made to justify discontinuing routine patrols. But other examples can be given to show that even clear evidence by a number of studies does not often lead to the demise of a program. As noted in Chapter 10 on rehabilitation, New York City's work release program was evaluated in 1970, 1971, 1973, 1974, and 1976 by prestigious evaluation agencies such as the New York City Rand Institute, the Urban Coalition, and the Corrections Department itself, all of which found grave deficiencies in the program and recommended changes. They were all ignored.

Many believe that something is amiss when, despite evidence that a program is not working, it is still continued anyway. What is wrong, of course, is that as rational and logical people, we expect the world of organizations to be rational and logical as well. That is why most evaluation studies are undertaken in the first place—to see if financial resources are being wasted on things that do not work. But most evaluation results are ignored. The clear evidence of a particular study seldom automatically leads to action.

The problem is not new. Over thirty years ago in a new journal devoted to trying to find ways of increasing the impact of research on policy, one of the

531

founders of the journal, Donald Krech, lamented that "our political and economic policymakers are still, too frequently, attempting to cure a tortured world by ancient rule of thumb. . . . The man of action is yet to be convinced that the social scientist has much to contribute."[2] Today the same complaint is frequently heard. Even though millions of dollars have been spent on evaluation research in all areas of public policy, most of the results are ignored.

One of the reasons evaluation research is not used in policy and program decisions is that evaluation results are only one factor to be considered in making a decision about a program. The Kansas City preventive patrol experiment, for example, touched on a very delicate political matter. The study results received a great deal of publicity and were well known by police throughout the country. But police departments still must respond to political pressures by the public, and the public wants and demands visible police patrols on the street. Police departments cannot ignore these demands, and they would have a difficult time convincing citizens that patrols do not help deter criminals.[3]

The utilization or nonutilization of evaluation research, therefore, depends not only upon the soundness of its design but also upon the appropriateness of its implementation strategy. Social scientists have long believed that their impact on policy is assured if they conduct sound scientific studies based upon good theories and methods. But unless decision makers are convinced that they should use evaluation research, no impact can be expected. There are thus two sides to evaluating criminal justice policies: (1) the design of evaluation research, and (2) the implementation of the results. We shall look at each of these in this chapter.

Designing Evaluation Research

THE GOALS AND OBJECTIVES OF EVALUATION

Because evaluation serves different purposes, no single type of evaluation research is always appropriate. The type of design used depends upon what the purposes of the evaluation are. Many classifications of research types exist.[4] We recognize six principal types:

1. Problem solving, which aims to find an answer to a problem facing an agency so that it may more efficiently allocate its resources. An example is determining how to allocate resources in a police department so as to shorten the time it takes to respond to calls for assistance.[5]
2. Exploratory research, the objective of which is to decide what the goals of a particular policy should be. An example is an examination of a piece of legislation such as the Safe Streets Act of 1968 to see what it was intended to accomplish.[6]
3. Impact research, whose purpose is to try to determine if a particular

policy or program is achieving its intended goals or objectives. An example of this is an examination of whether or not adding police officers actually reduces crime rates.[7]

4. Process research, the goal of which is to see how policy is being made, who is participating in its formulation and implementation, and whose interests are reflected in policy. The usual focus of this research is the passage and implementation of a particular piece of legislation, such as the Marijuana Tax Act of 1937.[8]

5. Muckraking research, which aims to expose wrongdoing and corruption. There are, of course, many examples of this, such as the exposure of official malfeasance and corruption.[9]

6. Radical social criticism, which attempts to stop a particular policy or program or get one adopted. An example of this is the research about political repression in the United States, particularly during the Nixon years.[10]

Not only are there different types of evaluation research, but evaluation can serve different functions as well. It can be used to improve decision making, reduce conflict within an agency, alert agencies to difficulties they do not anticipate, and convince the public that an agency is being efficient.[11] Although evaluation may serve several different functions, the term *evaluation research* normally is used for impact research. Criminologist Daniel Glaser, for example, defines it as follows: "For economic, humanitarian, scientific, and other reasons, many wish to know which of the alternative forms of organization, policy or procedure is most effective in altering a particular type of client. The effort to provide such knowledge is what is referred to . . . as 'evaluative research.' "[12] Evaluation researcher Carol Weiss agrees with Glaser's definition: "The purpose of evaluation research is to measure the effects of a program against the goals it set out to accomplish as a means of contributing to subsequent decision-making about the program and improving future programming."[13]

These definitions stress the rational and scientific aspects of evaluation research. The scientific approach to evaluation research, some believe, requires value-free detachment. Its purpose is to discover laws and the causes of crime. A value-free approach requires the researcher to accept the official legal definition of crime and work from there. Some believe that the scientific approach to evaluation runs the risk of accepting the basic assumptions that society makes about crime and criminals through its laws, and that this can have very conservative consequences. American University criminal justice professor Emilio Viano, for example, says that academic criminologists such as Glaser and Weiss hide behind the following assumptions: (1) that the causes of crime can be located by finding the factors that differentiate criminals from noncriminals: (2) that if the cause of crime can be located by studying individual offenders, then the prevention of crime can best be achieved by doing something to these same individuals rather than by changing society itself; and (3) that rational research will provide data that will help reduce crime.[14] These optimistic assumptions find support among public officials because they pose no threat to existing social institutions; Viano writes, "Train a police force more efficiently, reduce the case load of probation and parole officers, produce prediction tables, and experiment with sentencing procedures, and you have the answer to our society's crime problem."[15] Viano believes this will not happen. Instead, researchers should focus on the political forces that cause them to do the kinds of research they do.

To the more radical researcher such as Viano, on the other hand, the definition of crime is itself the problem, and the goal of research is to study changes in the laws. In their approach no dichotomy exists between criminals and noncriminals; they are interrelated. The concept of criminal pathology is purged in this view, and society itself, rather than the criminal, is the target of reform and rehabilitation.[16]

We shall return to the issue raised by the radicals later in this chapter when we discuss the problem of implementing evaluation research. Here, the position we take is that it is possible both to challenge goals and definitions of crime and at the same time to use a scientific approach to evaluation. The extreme position that research must be completely value-free and objective is not, in our view, valid. Some of the new methods of scientific research are based on subjectivity (i.e., Bayesean statistics) and probability, and scientific researchers increasingly recognize the need to infuse research with value positions, as we shall see in the rest of the chapter.

TYPES OF RESEARCH DESIGN

One type of research design dominates most of evaluation research—the classical experiment. So dominant is it that some say it is not possible to perform adequate evaluations without it.[17] But as we shall see, experiments with human subjects are seldom possible, and alternative methods must be used if evaluation is to occur.

Classical experimentation was the method used to study megavitamin therapy, the administration of massive doses of vitamins, for schizophrenics. Three times a day 265 patients were each given two tablets that contained either 500 mg. of nicotinamide or an inert substance (a placebo), the allotment being made on a random basis. Neither the staff nor the patients knew who was being given the vitamins or the placebo. Only new patients were involved in the program, and full notes on patient progress were kept for one year. At the end of that time it was found that 65 percent of those receiving nicotinamide and 72 percent of those receiving the placebo were recovered or much improved. Since more receiving the placebo than those receiving the vitamins showed improvement, researchers concluded that the megavitamin therapy does not work.[18]

The essential elements of the megavitamin experiment are the following:

1. Two groups were involved—a control group (which did not receive the vitamins) and an experimental group (which did receive the vitamins).
2. Neither the staff nor the patients knew who was receiving the vitamins.
3. The decision as to who was to be given the vitamins was made on a random basis.
4. Only newly received patients were involved in the program.

This classical experimental design is also called "control-experimental group" design. There are other forms of experimental design, such as the before-after design. If the latter had been used, the rate of recovery for a single group before they had received the vitamins would have been compared with the rate of recovery after they had received the vitamins. The before-after design is not considered as good as the control-experimental design because it does not control for possible maturation effects—the effects that occur naturally over the course of time. Thus, some individuals might have recovered from schizophrenia simply as a result of time passing. The control-experimental design takes the passage of time into account because both those who received the vitamins and those who did not have the same time experience; any improvement with time would affect both groups equally, and the effect could be canceled out.

Keeping both the staff and the clients from knowing who received the vitamins is a control instituted to eliminate the "testing effect." This effect occurs when changes in behavior are produced by the test itself. If the staff or patients had known who was receiving the vitamins, patients might have gotten better because they expected or were expected to improve—a self-fulfilling prophesy.

Patients were randomly assigned to the control or experimental group to control for all other variables that could affect the outcome except the ones being tested. If they had not been assigned at random, then the difference in the recovery rates could have been attributed to variables other than the ones being studied. For example, more younger individuals might have been assigned to the control group than the experimental group, and it might be the case that younger people recover more rapidly from schizophrenia. Finally, only new patients were involved in order to eliminate any effect from previous treatment.

When all of the conditions of good experimental design are met, the research meets all of the canons of scientific rigor, and its results are therefore far more likely to be correct. This explains why classical experimentation is preferred for evaluation research. Unfortunately, as we said before, it is seldom possible to follow classical experimental design when humans are the subjects. Both practical and ethical difficulties arise in experimenting with humans, not the least of which is the possibility that the rights and welfare of human subjects may be abused by overzealous researchers bent on making a name for themselves.

As a consequence, more and more researchers are using a quasi-experimental design. In quasi-experimental design two groups are studied that are similar in a number of ways except that one has been exposed to a particular experience that the other has not. Differences between the groups might be attributed to differences in exposure to the experience, but, as we shall see, because all other possible variables have not been controlled, the conclusions cannot be as firm as in a classical experiment. An example of this kind of research is described by criminologists Franklin Zimring and Gordon Hawkins. The two researchers wanted to determine if the death penalty effectively reduces the murder rate. They chose two neighboring states as the experimental and control groups—Indiana, which had the death penalty, and Michigan, which did not— because the two states were similar in many ways except for their stand on the death penalty. They found that the average rate of homicide per 100,000 people from 1940 and 1955 for Michigan was 3.49 and for Indiana, 3.50.[19]

The problem with their quasi-experimental approach is that the researchers could not conclude from their data that the death penalty does not deter homicide. Other factors not controlled for in the experiment could explain the homicide rates in both states. Although Indiana and Michigan are neighboring states, they are not exactly alike, and methods of law enforcement are not the same in each. Thus, factors not subject to control in the quasi-experimental approach interfere with establishing a cause-and-effect relationship.

The Zimring and Hawkins quasi-experimental design is similar to the control-experimental group design described above in the schizophrenia study. The next study we shall describe is a before-after quasi-experimental design.

In 1955, after experiencing a record high of traffic fatalities, the governor of the state of Connecticut instituted a crackdown on speeding. At the end of the year of strict enforcement of speeding laws, there were 284 traffic deaths as compared with the 324 the year before, a reduction of 12.3 percent. Did the crackdown achieve its objectives? It is not certain for the decline could be attributed to other causes in addition to or besides the crackdown on speeding.

As Figure 14-1 indicates, one possible explanation is that the death rate was on a downward trend that started before the crackdown and continued even after it ended. Another explanation is that the weather may have been better in 1955–1956 than it was in the previous year when the fatality rate took its sudden upward surge. A third alternative explanation is that the fatality rate had reached such a high point in late 1954 that it was bound to go down. And finally, a fourth rival hypothesis is that there might have been a switch in the method used to record traffic fatalities, and some of the decline might have reflected this.[20]

In contrast to the classical experimental design, quasi-experiments do not control for the effect of all other variables. A number of things might be done to

FIGURE 14-1

Connecticut Traffic Fatalities, 1951–1959

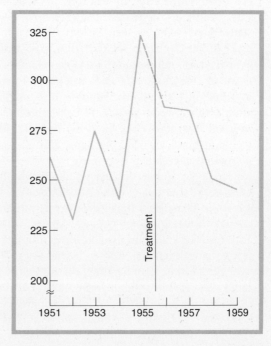

SOURCE: Donald Campbell, "Reforms as Experiments," *American Psychologist* 24, No. 4 (April 1969), 413. Copyright 1969 by the American Psychological Association. Reprinted by permission.

attempt to control for these other variables. But, in the end, researchers cannot control the possible impact of other variables, and therefore they can never be sure of how much impact the variable under study has on the outcome.

The major alternative to experimental design is cross-sectional research design. In this kind of research the analyst looks at the relationship between variables for a number of cases or individuals at a particular point in time in an attempt to see if one variable, called the "independent variable," is related to and possibly produces changes in another variable, called the "dependent variable." For example, suppose the goal is to find out what the relationship is between unemployment (the independent variable) and crime rates (the dependent variable). The unemployment and crime rates for a large sample of cities can be collected from sources such as the *Uniform Crime Reports* and the *County and City Data Book*. A statistical analysis of the two variables can be conducted to see if changes in the rate of unemployment are related to changes in crime rates.

Notice that in this research no attempt is made to establish a control and an experimental group, nor does the researcher control the time period or any other possible variable that might influence crime rates. It is possible to set up mathematical controls for some other factors that may be related to crime rates (as will be described below). But, as with quasi-experimental design, researchers can never control for all other factors that may explain the differences in crime rates, and thus, cross-sectional research designs never establish causal conclusions.[21]

In the research designs discussed thus far, changes in the relationships over time are not considered. When changes are considered, the research design is called "longitudinal." Data are plotted over the course of time. For example, as Table 14-1 shows, the number of handguns imported into the United States after 1964 showed a consistent increase until 1968 but then dropped dramatically in 1969 after the Gun Control Act of 1968 was passed. When the trend in handgun homicides for the same period is examined, a decline in the rate of increase is also shown beginning in 1969. By examining these trends, researchers can come to some conclusions about whether the availability of handguns increases the amount of handgun homicides. Franklin Zimring, who studied this question, concluded that lower levels of handgun ownership ensure against increases in handgun violence only when ownership levels are low enough to have an impact on handgun availability.[22] Longitudinal studies such as this are superior to cross-sectional studies because they focus upon changes in relationships over time rather than looking at a single instant in time. But they suffer from the same flaw as other nonexperimental research designs. For example, other reasons for a drop in the rate of increase of handgun homicides might be a change in economic conditions or changes in attitudes about the use of violence; researchers do not control for these factors in longitudinal studies unless they explicitly collect data about them. One of the principal drawbacks of longitudinal

TABLE 14-1

Handgun Imports by Year, 1964–1973

Year	Imports
1964	253,000
1965	346,906
1966	513,019
1967	747,013
1968	1,155,368
1969	349,252
1970	226,516
1971	345,557
1972	293,343
1973	309,471

SOURCE: Adapted from Franklin Zimring, "Firearms and Federal Law: The Gun Control Act of 1968," *Journal of Legal Studies* 4 (January 1975), 168. Reprinted by permission.

research is the fact that data about many variables over extended time periods are not readily available.

Evaluating Program Success or Failure

Good design is an important part of evaluation research, but it is only one question. An even more important and difficult issue is what criterion of program success or failure to use. For example, what criterion should be used to measure the success of police programs? The general goals of police are to prevent crime, maintain order, and assist citizens who are in trouble. But those goals are rather broad ones and not what would be used in evaluating police programs. We should distinguish between policy goals, which are broad and far-reaching, and program objectives, which are more specific and therefore more amenable to evaluation. Some specific objectives that are related to the achievement of the general police department goals are reducing the number of burglaries in the city, providing a sense of security in the community, participating in the prosecution of those against whom criminal charges are preferred, reducing the opportunities for people to commit crimes, and arresting individuals identified as having committed an offense. But, of course, even these objectives are rather broad, and it would be difficult to measure success or failure of programs aimed at achieving them.

Measuring achievement of the goals and objectives of an aggregate unit as large as a police department (or any other criminal justice agency) is difficult because police are supposed to accomplish a number of diverse tasks. One researcher used five separate indicators of police performance: (1) direct crime-related measures, such as the crime rate, clearance rate, and arrest rate; (2) style measures, such as the amount of specialization and professionalism; (3) input measures, such as the total level of expenditures for police and expenditures per capita; (4) direct activity measures, such as the average number of officers on duty per 1,000 residents or response time to calls for service; and (5) citizen attitude measures, such as their evaluation of the police and their perceptions of the crime trend in their city. Using these measures of police performance, the researcher investigated one city's police department and found a moderate positive relationship between the response time of a department and the clearance rate (i.e., number of crimes solved by arrest), and a positive relationship between rapid response rate and positive evaluation of police performance by citizens.[23] Thus, departments were evaluated higher by citizens if they believed crime in their neighborhood was not increasing, they had received assistance by the police, a larger number of crimes were solved by arrests by the police, and the police responded rapidly to calls for assistance.

A study such as this attempts to evaluate an entire police department, and the criteria used were developed by the evaluation researchers rather than by the department itself. Police officials themselves tend to evaluate the performance of individual officers rather than the entire department. Rules, procedures, recordkeeping, and productivity tend to be emphasized in these evaluations. Thus, the number of traffic tickets written, arrests, interrogation cards filled out, stolen cars identified, crimes cleared by arrest, percent of offenders convicted, and the value of stolen property recovered are the principal measures that are used to evaluate the performance of individual officers.

The reason why departments fall back on or use such easily counted measures is partly because such quantatative measures give the appearance of being objective and partly because it is easier to measure individual as opposed to group performance. However, some of these individual measures conflict with each other: A police officer is supposed to prevent crime by arresting offenders, but not violate the rights of the person while doing so. The appropriate use of force is one criterion that might be used to measure accomplishment of these conflicting goals. The assumption is that an officer should avoid using excess physical force in making arrests. The ratio of the number of arrests in which physical force is used to the number of arrests in which the charge of assaulting a police officer is made can be used as a way of determining if an officer is using excessive force. But the line separating justifiable use of force from excessive force is a thin one. An officer who uses escessive force in making an arrest can say that the reason why he or she did so was the the accused attacked him or her. There are times when this claim is legitimate, but, in some cases it is used as a way to cover up brutality.[24]

Even more difficult to measure and include in overall performance are the many non–law enforcement activities that an officer often performs. Performance measures should include activities such as returning a lost child, arbitrating a family dispute, or helping a young offender. In all of these activities the important dimension in police behavior is how well the officer interacts with and assists the public. But police departments are reluctant to include these activities as a part of an officer's evaluation because they do not reflect the "crime fighter" image that police prefer to promote.

The problems of measuring police performance are typical of measuring performance in all criminal justice agencies. Criminal justice agencies have multiple goals, and these goals often are ambiguous and difficult to translate into objectives that are easily measured. One solution is to use a variety of outcome measures rather than just one. For example, Gene Kassebaum, David Ward, and Daniel Wilner evaluated treatment programs in prisons by prisoners' reactions to group counseling, attitudinal changes about crime, rule breaking while in prison, technical parole violations, rearrest after release, and success or failure in obtaining employment. They found that prison treatment programs have no effect as measured by these outcomes.[25] Using multiple measures of outcomes such as these gives much more credence to evaluation research. Another example involves the evaluation of prisons. Daniel Glaser has suggested that a prison's operation can be evaluated by its escape rate, number of mass disturbances, inmates receiving disciplinary reports, proportion of prisoners completing education or vocational training programs, productivity rate of prison work farms and industries, and recidivism rates.[26] Notice that these criteria reflect the different kinds of goals of prisons—their custodial goal of ensuring that prisoners do not escape and their rehabilitation goal. Not all of these goals are equal in importance, and sometimes trade-offs must be made. Is preventing escapes more important than rehabilitation? This question must be answered for the various different indices to be added together in a single scale.

In addition, the problem of distinguishing between manifest and latent goals must be dealt with. The manifest goal of parole boards, for example, is to release those who have given sufficient evidence of being rehabilitated so that they can continue their progress outside of prison. But parole boards serve a number of latent goals as well, such as reducing disparities in sentences, supporting prison officials, maximizing public support, and balancing their budget. Some of these may be deemed more important than the manifest goals of parole boards, and none can be ignored. An evaluation study, therefore, should consider latent as well as manifest goals if it is to be successful.

Some researchers refer to the latent goals of an organization as part of its hidden agenda.[27] It is hidden, frequently, because the latent goals serve the personal objectives of the members of the organization, which may be different from and actually conflict with organizational goals. Such self-interest goals pertain to career and other personal aspirations of organizational members. Thus, a parole board member may become concerned with maximizing public support and the image of the parole board more because this will help him more than aiding officers will. As we have said throughout this book, latent self-interest goals can be made congruent with manifest public interest goals. Evaluation research can help reduce the disparity between personal and organizational goals by allowing the administrator to participate in determining the goals to be used in evaluating his or her agency.

Analyzing Data

The technical aspect of evaluation research is data analysis. The methods of analyzing data range from the simplest form of description in percentages to highly complex foms of multiple regression analysis and statistical inference. It is not possible to cover all of these methods in a book such as this. At the same time, no discussion of evaluation research can be complete without some discussion of the more important methods. This section describes some of the less complicated methods of analyzing the relationship between two variables, using actual studies in the area of criminal justice.

The goal of most analyses of the relationship between two variables is to understand how strongly they are related, whether the relationship is positive or inverse, and whether it is significantly different from chance. The shorthand term for this kind of analysis is *correlation analysis*. We shall consider several forms of correlation analysis.

Before doing that, we must first make some important distinctions. The type of correlation analysis that is possible depends upon the level of measurement of the data. Three levels of measurement—nominal, ordinal, and interval— are generally used in statistics. Nominal-scale measurement is achieved when the variables being studied can be placed into discrete categories. For example, murder, as a variable, is usually classified as a dichotomous event: One is either murdered or not murdered. This is a nominal-scale level of measurement. Of course, the law recognizes degrees of murder such as first and second-degree murder. But murder itself cannot be ranked or scaled, for one cannot be more murdered than someone else (although it is possible to rank the *way* someone is murdered, from heinous and foul to clean and simple!). An ordinal-scale measurement is achieved when a variable can be ranked as first, second, third, and so on. For example, prison rehabilitation programs might be ranked, ranging from the best (or one that has the most success), to the second best, and so on down to the least successful. An interval-scale measurement is the next level up. It is achieved when a variable cannot only be ranked but given a specific numerical value. For example, the number of robberies reported to the police is an interval-scale variable because the figure can range from none to a large number, and the distance between any two points is the same throughout the scale.

Many technical questions are associated with measurement scales that we need not go into here. The above description of the three major measurement scales is sufficient for our purpose, which is to describe the most important method of measuring correlation for each measurement level. So let us begin with the lowest form of measurement, the nominal scale.

CORRELATIONS FOR NOMINAL MEASUREMENTS

Why do some citizens hold negative attitudes toward the police? Do the police themselves help create these negative attitudes? A study by Paul E. Smith and Richard O. Hawkins of attitudes toward police in Seattle, Washington, attempted to answer these questions.[28] Their independent variable was race, which is a nominal-scale variable; the two categories for this variable are white and nonwhite. The dependent variable in the Smith and Hawkins study was attitude toward the police. If attitudes are placed into categories such as favorable and unfavorable, what level of measurement is achieved? A nominal scale. If attitudes are measured in degrees, such as most favorable, second most favorable . . . least favorable, this constitutes an ordinal scale. Smith and Hawkins measured attitudes toward police on an ordinal scale, but, since we want to illustrate how to compute a correlation for nominal scales, we will first describe how they constructed their ordinal scale and then convert it to a nominal scale.

Five statements about police fairness were used by Smith and Hawkins to measure attitudes toward police. For example, those surveyed were asked their opinion in response to a statement such as: "Police in this city usually are fair in their dealings with people." They were told to circle the number that most closely corresponded to their opinion on a five-point scale like the one below.

5	4	3	2	1

Strongly   Strongly
Disagree   Agree

The answers of a respondent to five similar statements were then summed. The most favorable attitude possible toward police was expressed by a score of 5 (the smallest number possible), and the least favorable attitude was represented by a score of 25. The surveyors were actually setting up an ordinal scale of measurement because the respondents could be ranked by degrees of favorableness toward the police, but we have changed it to a nominal scale in Table 14-2.

The Smith and Hawkins Seattle survey found that the majority of citizens—72 percent—held positive views of the police. Those questioned were asked to supply certain socioeconomic data about themselves—the independent variables that the researchers tried to correlate with attitudes. Smith and Hawkins found that education, income, occupation, and sex were not related to attitudes toward police. Only two characteristics—race and age—were related to such attitudes.

As shown in Table 14-2, nonwhites were much less favorable in their attitudes than whites. While only 45.9 percent of nonwhites held favorable attitudes, 73.5 percent of the whites did. These percentages by themselves give us some idea about the magnitude of the difference between the two groups. But we can get an even more precise measure if we correlate the two variables, race and attitude toward police, on a scale that ranges from 0 to 1, which is called a correlation coefficient. A correlation of 0 means no relationship and a correlation of 1 means a perfect relationship. Degrees of correlation are indicated by

TABLE 14-2
Race and Attitudes Toward Police

Attitude	Percent of Whites	Percent of Nonwhites
Favorable	a. 73.5	b. 45.9
Unfavorable	c. 26.5	d. 54.1
Total	100.0	100.0
N	1,322	85
Q = .53		

SOURCE: These data are adapted from Paul E. Smith and Richard O. Hawkins, "Victimization, Types of Citizen-Police Contacts, and Attitudes Toward the Police," *Law & Society Review* 8 (Fall 1973), 137–38. Reprinted by permission of the Law and Society Association.

numbers between 0 and 1, with a higher correlation coefficient indicating a stronger relationship. One measure of correlation for data measured on a nominal scale is Kendall's Q, computed by the following formula:

$$Q = \frac{ad - bc}{ad + bc}$$

The letters a, b, c, and d refer to the cells in the Table 14.2. The upper left-hand cell is a, the upper right-hand cell is b, and so on. Thus, using the data in the table, the correlation is:

$$Q = \frac{(73.5)(54.1) - (45.9)(26.5)}{(73.5)(54.1) + (45.9)(26.5)}$$

$$= \frac{3976.35 - 1216.35}{3976.35 + 1216.35}$$

$$= .53$$

The coefficient indicates a fairly strong correlation between race and attitude toward police.

The other independent variable found by Smith and Hawkins to be related to attitudes toward police is age. Younger respondents held more negative attitudes toward police than older respondents. When the researchers compared whites and nonwhites by age categories, they found some interesting relationships. Table 14-3 shows that there was a tendency for young whites to have more unfavorable attitudes toward police than older whites. Thus there was an inverse correlation between the two variables of age and attitude: The younger the white respondent, the more negative his or her attitude. But the same was

TABLE 14-3

Race, Age, and Attitude Toward Police

Attitude	Percent of Whites by Age <35	≥35	Percent of Nonwhites by Age <35	≥35
Favorable	61.3	79.0	43.8	48.6
Unfavorable	38.7	21.0	56.2	51.4
Total	100.0	100.0	100.0	100.0
	$Q = -.41$		$Q = -.09$	

SOURCE: Adapted from Paul E. Smith and Richard O. Hawkins, "Victimization, Types of Citizen-Police Contacts, and Attitudes Toward the Police," *Law & Society Review* 8 (Fall 1973), 137–38. The data have been combined to make two categories for each variable. Reprinted by permission of the Law and Society Association.

not true for blacks. No matter what the age category, blacks were equally as negative toward the police.

What are the policy implications of this analysis? Smith and Hawkins concluded that although good relations with the community are important for good police work, the police themselves often oppose community relations efforts. Do the data examined above indicate that good community relations will increase citizen reporting of crime? Negative attitudes toward the police are not related to whether one has been a victim of a crime, but they are related to fear of crime. Close personal relations with police do not affect attitudes toward police. The most important things affecting attitudes toward police, Smith and Hawkins found, are the behavior of police officers (brutality, drinking on duty, violating traffic rules), and how they handle crime reporting. Many victims (33 percent) said that police did little or nothing when they reported a crime. These findings led Smith and Hawkins to conclude that "the police are much to blame for poor police-community relations, but in ways more easily rectified than previously believed." Principally, changes in individual police behavior should be encouraged, but this will not improve the police image in minority neighborhoods. Here, "more drastic and sweeping structural changes within society as well as within the organization of the police" are required.[29]

CORRELATION AND REGRESSION ANALYSES
FOR INTERVAL MEASUREMENTS

Correlations can also be made for data measured on an interval scale. In addition, interval data can be subjected to regression analysis, which involves description of data by a mathematical equation. The mathematics needed for such analyses is complicated, and we will not actually show the computations. Instead evaluation research results will be presented using the actual data; that is, we will report the correlation and regression coefficients, without showing the methods of arriving at them. Standard statistics texts should be consulted for these methods.

Several studies using correlation and repression analyses have dealt with the question of whether adding more police deters crime. For example, economist Charles R. Wellford conducted a correlation study to see if socioeconomic factors are more important than crime control measures in reducing crime.[30] Using a sample of the 21 largest urban centers in the United States, he correlated a number of socioeconomic variables—including unemployment, percentage of owner-occupied homes, median family income, median years of school completed, percentage of homes overcrowded, and percentage of women divorced or separated—with crime rates. He then correlated violent crime rates with crime-control measures such as number of police, the ratio of civilian to uniformed police, per capita police budget, and the ratio of the police budget to the total city budget. He found that the correlation between socioeconomic variables and the violent crime rate was .77 while the correlation of crime control variables and the violent crime rate was only .24. The per capita budget for police and number of police per thousand population were not significantly correlated with the violent crime rate. To further test his hypothesis, Welford correlated the same independent variables with the percent of crimes solved by arrest (i.e., clearance rates). The average clearance rates in 1970 were .23 for total index crimes, .61 for violent crimes, and .19 for property crimes. The correlation of crime-control variables with these clearance rates was .39 for the index crimes, .38 for violent crimes, and .35 for property crimes. These are not very high correlations. Wellford concluded the following:

> The current range of police budgets and personnel does not account for much variation in crime rates . . . or clearance rates. Crime rates are largely a function of demographic and social (broadly interpreted) characteristics, and clearance of index crimes is largely a function of the nature of the crime (in particular, the identification of the offender by the victim or a witness).[31]

A number of other researchers have reached similar conclusions about the relationship between police power and crime rates. James P. Levine did a correlation analysis of crime rates and police strength.[32] He found that the cities with the greatest police force expansion from 1961 to 1971 experienced about the same average increase in their robbery and murder rates as the cities with the least police force expansion.[33] The conclusion was based on an analysis of all cities of over 500,000 population. When an individual city, such as New Orleans, was examined, Levine found that the addition of police was followed by jumps in the crime level rather than by stabilization or decline. Part of the increase might be explained by an increase in reporting that a more visible police presence may inspire. But, Levine noted, a more convincing explanation is that crime rates were accelerating prior to the addition of police, creating popular agitation for putting officers on the beat. Thus, adding police did not cause a change in the crime rate; in general, upward changes in the crime rate cause a city to increase its police force.

We can gain an even better understanding of the relationship between police strength and crime rates by looking at another study that used economic theory and regression analysis. The research done by economist Gene Swimmer used a model that assumes that the decision to commit crime is based upon more than police strength alone, but also upon gains from successful crime, the losses if apprehended and convicted, the likelihood of being convicted, and sociological or psychologically determined tastes for crime.[34] In other words, Swimmer assumed that a person will perform an act if the benefits he or she receives in doing so exceed the costs. Using a regression model that incorporated all these variables, Swimmer hypothesized that if police effectively control crime, an increase in police strength should lead to a decrease in crime rates. However, he acknowledged that at the same time an increase in crime rates could lead to greater demand for police and increased police strength. This he explained by looking at the intersection of the supply and demand for crime. The supply of crime is related to the probability of being caught, while the demand for police is related to the amount of crime. Hence, if the probability of being caught and convicted is low, crime will increase; the increase, in turn, will cause a greater demand for more police. This will raise the probability of being caught and crime will then decrease.

Swimmer hypothesized that the variables related to the *supply* of crime in a community are the expected sentence, median family income, unemployment, the teen-age schooling rate, the percentage of nonwhites in the population, and the distribution of income. The *demand* for police, on the other hand, is dependent upon crime rates, median income, per capita property tax receipts, and socioeconomic variables. Regression analysis conducted by Swimmer enabled him to test these hypotheses because, in contrast to correlation analyses, it allowed him to measure the relative impact of each variable while holding all the others constant. He found that the unemployment rate, median income, and schooling had little effect on the supply of crime. But the percentage of families with incomes of less than $3,000 and greater than $10,000 was positively related to property crime; and the proportion of nonwhites was the key variable in explaining violent crime. Turning to the demand for police, Swimmer found that the higher the income of a community, the greater the loss from property crime and the more protection demanded. Police expenditures were associated with reduced property crime, and property and violent crime were significantly related to the demands for police expenditure.

Swimmer concluded that increases in police expenditures per capita population are associated with higher probabilities of arrest and consequently lower crime rates. Simultaneously, higher crime rates are related to greater public demand for protection in the form of more police expenditures. The only way he was able to disentangle this dual relationship was through a special form of regression analysis. He could not have accomplished this through correlation analysis. The causal sequence is that changes in police strength are produced by changes in the crime rate. As the crime rate goes up, demands for more police protection are made, and more police officers are added to the force. The addition, in turn, may reduce crime, but there will be a time lag from the time police are added to the time the crime rate goes down.

TIME-SERIES ANALYSIS

In addition to correlation and regression analyses, researchers also make use of time-series analysis to evaluate the results of a policy. Time-series analysis involves plotting changes in events over the course of time and then determining if there is a trend or change in them.

The technique was used to analyze the impact of a law decriminalizing public intoxication in Washington, D.C. As we noted in Chapter 11, the law—the District of Columbia Alcoholic Rehabilitation Act—went into effect on August 1, 1968, and made public intoxication a health problem rather than a criminal offense. The act retained the police as the legal instrument for moving intoxicated persons from the streets, but they were required to take them home, to a private health facility, or to a detoxification center. The question tested by a group of researchers was whether police would continue to pick up drunks once the offense was decriminalized.[35] Figure 14-2 shows data for an eight-year period and indicates that the level of police intakes per month following decriminalization dropped significantly, and this drop could not be attributed to chance alone. Furthermore, when two other jurisdictions were compared, one where public drunkenness was not decriminalized, a similar change in police arrests could not be detected. The authors concluded that decriminalization seems to lead to neglect on the part of police of the public inebriate and that the drop in arrests could not be attributed to a decline in public intoxication.

Time-series analysis has been used to answer the issue dealt with above about whether increasing the strength of police can help reduce crime. In New York City between 1963 and 1964 the number of reported felonies in the subway system increased 52.5 percent. When a 17-year-old youth was murdered on a subway train in early 1965, the public demanded greater protection. On April 2, 1965, the city police increased the extra men on the subways by 83 percent, and the Transit Authority Police Department also increased its patrol force. Figure 14-3 shows that there was a substantial drop in total offenses after this. Felonies remained stable, but began to increase again after 1968, as did robberies. Thus the decrease was only temporary. Time-series analysis enables us to follow these

FIGURE 14-2

Monthly Police Intake for Public Intoxication, Washington, D.C., 1966–1974[1]

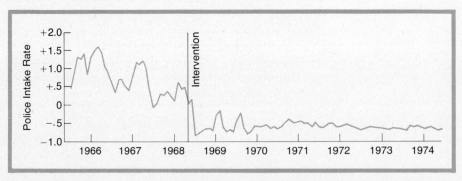

[1] The monthly intake rate at the point of intervention was designated as "0." All other intake rates were recalculated to represent a percentage increase or decrease from the point of intervention.
SOURCE: Based on official statistics of the Metropolitan Police Department, Washington, D.C., and Official Records of the D.C. Detoxification Center, as compiled by David Aaronson, C. Thomas Dienes, and Michael Musheno, "Changing the Public Drunkenness Laws: The Impact of Decriminalization," *Law & Society Review* 3 (Spring 1978), 410. Reprinted by permission of the Law and Society Association.

FIGURE 14-3

Reported Crimes in the New York Subway System, 1963–1970

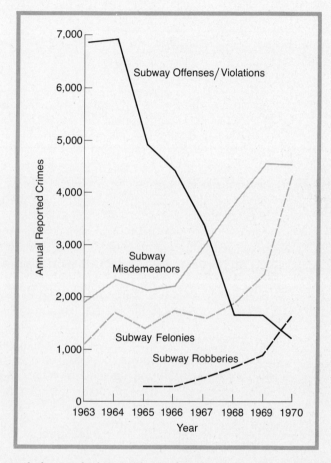

SOURCE: Jan M. Chaiken, Michael W. Lawless, and Keith Stevenson, *The Impact of Police Activity on Crime: Robberies on the New York City Subway System* (New York City Rand Institute, R-1424-NYC, January 1974), p. 14. Reprinted by permission of The Rand Corporation.

changes. The authors of the study that compiled these figures concluded: "The increased manning of the Transit Police did not keep the overall rate of serious subway crime low over the long run, although it may well be true that the rate in the late 1960s would have been even higher without the extra men."[36] The increased manning had an initial effect on subway offenses, but whether or not it was worth the increased expense depends on one's perspective. The study estimated that it cost the city $35,000 for each felony crime deterred. From a strict economic perspective one might say the benefits were not worth the cost. But politically the increased violence on the subways became a "hot potato," and no officeholder or office seeker who wanted to remain in power or win office could afford to ignore the popular demands to make the subways safe.

Evaluating Evaluation Research

Evaluation research seldom is able to reach conclusions that are as unequivocal and clear as the Kansas City patrol study cited at the beginning of this chapter. More often, the findings about the impact of a program, even when very sophisticated scientific methods are used, are usually full of qualifications and conditions. And, even when one study is conducted that seems to lead to clear conclusions, such as the Kansas City one, replications of the study in other places may turn up contrary results. For example, the police in Saginaw, Michigan, conducted a burglary reduction project to test the effect of patrol strategies. Three areas of the city that had less than 10 percent of the city's total population accounted for 25 percent of all reported burglaries. During the summer of 1977 specialized police patrols were deployed in each of these three high-crime areas.

In one area a high-visibility, uniformed tactical patrol—consisting of marked police vehicles, helicopters, and canine units—was used. The patrol was concentrated on the streets with the highest incidence of burglaries. Another area was the site for a low-visibility patrol composed of plain-clothes officers, unmarked cars, and stakeout operations. The third area combined high- and low-visibility tactics. The police department also began an antiburglary campaign, circulating information about suspects, parolees, and fences to all officers participating in the project. And it began a neighborhood watch program, which encouraged residents to watch out for each other. Finally, the courts cooperated by bringing suspects to trial with a minimum of delay. The results: Burglaries were reduced by 13 percent in the area using a low-visibility patrol, by 45 percent in the area using a high-visibility patrol, and by 65 percent in the area using the combined tactic.[37]

This project seems to have demonstrated that patrols do make a difference. But it also included an antiburglary campaign, neighborhood watch, and changes in court procedures. From a research perspective, those additional changes make it difficult to tell how much of the reduction in burglaries was due to differences in patrol tactics and how much to other factors. Thus, one can read into the project a vindication of the efficacy of patrol, but the study does not unequivocally show this.

The uncertain nature of much evaluation research is one of the reasons it tends to be ignored or used by decision makers to support the position they want to take anyway. Decision makers, it has been said, often use statistics like a drunk uses a lamppost—more for support than illumination. They frequently need unequivocal results to justify taking action, but evaluation researchers seldom can meet this need.

Implementing Evaluation Research

Problems relating to the nature and quality of the research itself can hinder implementation of evaluation research. But such research is also ignored very often because of problems associated with the researchers themselves and the practitioners who are to implement the results.[38]

In discussing the lack of influence by sociologists on the policy-making process, one scholar noted, "There is a kind of arrogance that what's good and right for academic studies is good and right for public policy studies. Our passion for multivariate analysis [a sophisticated statistical technique] may be exactly what the decision maker doesn't want."[39] In general, researchers seem to want to become more and more mathematically and methodologically elegant in order to impress colleagues and peers. Yet, practitioners need research that is relatively simple and uncomplicated so they can use it. The problem is not restricted to the United States. In a study of 120 research projects conducted for government agencies in the Netherlands, the investigators found that "for the most part . . . the higher a study's methodological standards, the less likely it was used by policymakers."[40]

Good evaluation research must therefore combine some rather paradoxical qualities if it is to be utilized effectively. It must be methodologically sound yet not too complicated or sophisticated. It must be conducted objectively yet produce results that help policy makers evaluate their decisions. In short, the virginal product of the ivory towers must be made "street wise" to be of use in the policy-making process.

It is also frequently the case that decision makers are not sure themselves of what would best help them. The program administrator's desire to reaffirm his or her position with favorable program evaluations may conflict with the social scientist's desire to acquire an objective appraisal of a program's impact. The end result may be either a research design with low scientific credibility and tainted results or a credible study that never receives a public hearing because the administrator does not like the results.

The conflict of interest between researcher and practitioner is not always an evil. As a matter of fact, it is necessary and unavoidable in the case of radical social critics because their goal is to force change in policies they oppose, and they cannot expect to get decision makers' cooperation. The conflict of interest is dysfunctional, however, for the evaluation researcher who wants to help or work cooperatively with the decision maker. But even here the decision maker may be suspicious of the researcher because of what University of Southern California professor Neely Gardner calls the "law of the other guy's thing."[41] Because the nature of the researcher's actions are unknown to the decision maker and are not completely understood, the decision maker will not trust the researcher's proposals and solutions.

Perhaps some of this fear could be overcome if practitioners were educated about the research process. As organizational development expert Ronald Lippitt suggests: "It seems clear that part of the current negative orientation toward scientific resources in mental health, education and social welfare results from a serious lack of any concrete education about the nature and utility of social research and the social scientists."[42] This "education" of decision makers might create an open and nonthreatening decision-making environment in which policy makers would welcome the additional data provided by well-designed and well-executed research. A nonthreatening environment could be facilitated by nurturing and encouraging policy makers to become involved in the evaluation process itself. The result might then be that decision makers would no longer see such research as a threat to their professional status or their self-images but rather as a tool for making better decisions.[43]

Contemporary evaluation research is concerned with results. Carol Weiss's definition of evaluation research mentioned earlier stresses that evaluation is supposed to have an effect on programs: It is intended to be used, it considers the decision maker's questions rather than the evaluator's, it is prescriptive and it takes place in an action setting. Furthermore, although it frequently involves interpersonal frictions between evaluators and practitioners, the researcher has a responsibility to the organization that funds his or her study. The point is an important one. Good evaluation research is not conducted in the sterile atmosphere of a laboratory. Researchers must establish a cooperative relationship with the program administrator to ensure access for the researcher to all relevant sources of data and to guarantee subsequent attention to the research results by the program administrator. In short, evaluators must "get their hands" dirty to be effective.

The notion that research will produce action only if the social scientist becomes engaged in the process being investigated was not articulated until psychologist Kurt Lewin became interested in the applicability of social science research to social problems. His attempt to integrate research and action into a single technique has become known throughout the literature is "action research."

While a number of researchers used the phrase "action research" in the 1940s, Kurt Lewin generally is credited with being the father of the idea. Lewin developed the approach as a way of trying to improve community race relations. He defined it as "a type of . . . comparative research of the conditions and effects of various forms of social action, and research leading to social action."[44] To Lewin action research was a continuous process involving planning, executing, reconnaissance to see what happened, then making new plans based on the reconnaissance, and so on. It consisted of three elements—action, research, and training—conceived of as parts of a triangle that should be kept together for the sake of any of its corners. Viewed somewhat as a learning process, the principal purpose of action research, according to Lewin, was to evaluate how well plans have worked so that they could be modified and tried again.

This earlier view of action research has undergone somewhat of a transformation over the past 30 years. Action research today has become a tool for dealing with or creating a specific *intra*organizational environment, an environment that promotes the self-actualization of its members. It is used to deal with the interpersonal dynamics of an organization. In this capacity, action research might help to improve employee morale, enhance individual worth, change management styles, develop in-house assessment and problem-solving capabilities, deal with resistance to change, or calm hostility within an organization. In short, action research is now thought of as a method of improving the internal climate of an organization. One of the foremost contemporary advocates of action research, Neely Gardner, expresses it this way: "Action training and research strategies bring people together rather than divide them; lead to cooperation rather than opposition; and help promote a sense of community and trust."[45] This sense of community and trust is important to the researcher–decision maker relationship. It establishes a climate in which the fruits of evaluation research are not only expected, but welcomed.

The following example illustrates how action research might work. Assume that the goal of a researcher is to evaluate a new community corrections program that is being implemented in a state. The first step in an action research project is to work with the administrators in charge of implementing the program; this involves collaborating on designing the evaluation research, collecting and analyzing the data, and writing the final report. The second step, which actually begins and takes place while the first step is being carried out, is to help the agency (in this case, a department of corrections) bring about the desired changes so that the community corrections program is successfully implemented. Several things might be done here. A newsletter can be developed by the researcher to be distributed to potential participants in various counties (i.e., judges, social service workers, probation and parole officers). The purpose of the newsletter is to make sure individuals are informed about what is happening in each county and about what steps might be taken by those interested in adopting community corrections programs. The newsletter also will stimulate interest in the program. Another thing that could be done by the action researcher is to work with corrections officials in developing a prototype model that can be used for demonstrations and to show what steps must be taken in implementing the program. The action researcher also should help the administrator develop training programs for various county officials who need to learn what community corrections entails. Such training would be directed at jail administrators and county sheriffs, probation and parole officers, social service workers, mental health and drug program workers, and county commissioners.

Conclusion

Action research, therefore, aims at the dual goals of promoting change and, at the same time, understanding something about the change process. The action researcher is both a change agent who helps bring about change and a student of change. But what happens to scientific objectivity in the process? How can the researcher who is helping to promote change step back and objectively study the change process? It is apparent that it is not possible to be value free and objective in such a situation. But, then, it is never possible to be value free and completely objective in research, even if the researcher is not following an action research perspective. The relationship between researcher and the agency that is being studied unavoidably involves ethical questions. In action research the researcher takes on the role of collaborator, not adversary, and this requires that an agreement be reached about what criteria will be used to judge a program. But it does not require that researchers "sell out" to the administrator. The researcher is obliged to bring problems to the surface and to expose wrongdoing, incompetence, and corruption if such things are found.

Action research is the best way to get access to data and inside information. Without it, the researcher may never get past the front door and thus miss important data. With it, the researcher becomes a part of the change process set in motion by a policy and thus a participant rather than an objective observer.

SUMMARY

Evaluation research has a number of different goals and objectives. The usual goal of evaluation research is to determine if a program is achieving its goals and generally uses scientific methods.

The classical method of evaluating the impact of a program (or "treatment") is experimental research design. This involves using a control and experimental group, introducing a change to the experimental group, and then trying to determine if it had an effect. Such classical experiments seldom are possible with human subjects. Quasi-experimental design is the more likely method used in criminal justice. This involves an attempt to observe events as they are occurring to determine if a particular intervention, such as a crackdown on speeders, has an effect on some dependent variable, such as the death rate. However, it is not possible to control for the possible effect of other factors and thus never possible to reach unequivocal results.

Other types of research design suffer from the same flaws. Cross-sectional research, which correlates events at a particular point in time,

is often used, but it does not enable us to reach cause-effect conclusions.

Determining what will be used as a criterion of success or failure greatly complicates the evaluation task. Among the problems encountered here are making sure the goals are explicitly stated so that they can be measured, deciding whether single individuals or entire units are to be evaluated, and deciding which of a number of goals is to be considered most important.

A number of statistical techniques can be used to analyze data collected in evaluating a program. The kind of statistical technique applicable depends upon the level of measurement that has been achieved—nominal, ordinal, or interval. In all cases, the objective generally is to determine if a correlation exists between the independent variable and the dependent variable. For example, does adding police (independent variable) reduce the crime rate (dependent variable)? A great deal of research has been conducted on this question, most of which indicates that little correlation exists.

No matter how clear the findings of evaluation research, seldom are they immediately implemented. There are two kinds of reasons. One pertains to the individuals who do the evaluating. They usually are academically trained and concerned with reaching "objective" conclusions that have theoretical rather than applied relevance. The other pertains to the administrators whose programs are being evaluated. They are often more concerned with protecting their self-interests and projecting a positive self-image than with discovering the objective truth about their programs. The conflict between administrators and academics cannot easily be be resolved, although action research is a promising way to do so.

FOOTNOTES

[1] George Kelling, et al., *The Kansas City Preventive Patrol Experiment: Summary Report* (Washington, D.C.: Police Foundation, 1974). While many reviewers of the Kansas City experiment believe that it was a good test, an excellent critique of the experiment by Richard C. Larson has pointed to rather enormous flaws in the design. See Richard C. Larson, "What Happened to Patrol Operations in Kansas City," *Evaluation* 3, nos. 1–2 (1976), 117–31.

[2] Donald Krech, "The Challenge and the Promise," *The Journal of Social Issues* 2 (1946), 2.

[3] Jeffrey Henry, Robert L. Lineberry, and Neal A. Milner, "The Policy Impact of Policy Evaluation: Some Implications of the Kansas City Patrol Experiment," in *Public Law and Public Policy*, ed. John A. Gardiner (New York: Praeger, 1977), pp. 225–39.

[4] See Martin Rein and Susan White, "Can Policy Research Help Policy?" *The Public Interest* 49 (1977), 119–36, for a different classification of types of evaluation research.

[5] Richard C. Larson, "On Quantitative Approaches to Urban Police Patrol Problems," *Journal of Research in Crime and Delinquency* 7, no. 2 (July 1970), 26–43.

[6] Malcolm Feeley, Austin Sarat, and Susan O. White, "The Role of State Planning in the Development of Criminal Justice Federalism," in *Public Law and Public Policy*, op. cit., pp. 204–23.

[7] James P. Levine, "The Ineffectiveness of Adding Police to Prevent Crime," *Public Policy* 23, no. 4 (Fall 1975), 523–45.

[8] Howard S. Becker, "The Marijuana Tax Act," in *Crime and Justice in Society*, ed. Richard Quinney (Boston: Little, Brown, 1969), pp. 98–108.

[9] See John A. Gardiner, "Wincanton: The Politics of Corruption," in *Criminal Justice, Law and Politics*, ed. George F. Cole. (North Scituate, Mass.: Duxbury, 1972), pp. 204–24.

[10] Alan Wolfe, "Political Repression and the Liberal Democratic State," in *Criminal Justice in America, A Critical Understanding*, ed. Richard Quinney (Boston: Little, Brown, 1974), pp. 49–62.

[11] Robert E. Floden and Steven S. Weiner, "Rationality to Ritual: The Multiple Roles of Evaluation in Governmental Processes," *Policy Sciences* 9 (1978), 9–18.

[12] Daniel Glaser, *Routinizing Evaluation: Getting Feedback on Effectiveness of Crime and Delinquency Programs* (Washington, D.C.: U.S. Government Printing Office, 1973), p. 2.

[13] Carol Weiss, *Evaluation Research: Methods of Assessing Program Effectiveness* (Englewood Cliffs, N.J.: Prentice-Hall, 1972), p. 4.

[14] Emilio Viano, ed., *Criminal Justice Research* (Lexington, Mass.: Lexington Books, 1975), pp. ii–xiii.

[15] Ibid., p. xiii.

[16] Tony G. Poveda and Edward Schaffer, "Positivism and Interactionism: Two Traditions of Research in Criminology," in ibid., pp. 105–22.

[17] James Wholey et al., *Federal Evaluation Policy* (Washington, D.C.: The Urban Institute, 1971), p. 109.

[18] S. D. McGrath, P. F. O'Brien, P. J. Power, and J. R. Shea, "Nicotinamide Treatment of Schizophrenia," *Schizophrenia Bulletin* 5 (Spring 1972), 74–76.

[19] Franklin E. Zimring and Gordon J. Hawkins, *Deterrence, The Legal Threat in Crime Control* (Chicago: University of Chicago Press, 1973), p. 254.

[20] This example is based on the seminal work of Donald Campbell, "Reforms as Experiments," *American Psychologist* 24, no. 4 (April 1969), 409–28.

[21] However, in recent years, a large amount of methodological research has been done to find a way to make causal inferences based on correlation and other types of statistical analysis. This literature is vast and mathematically complicated. See Hubert Blalock and Ann Blalock, *Methodology in Social Research* (New York: McGraw-Hill, 1968); and David Nachmias, *Public Policy Evaluation* (New York: St. Martin's Press, 1979).

[22] Franklin E. Zimring, "Firearms and Federal Law: The Gun Control Act of 1968," *The Journal of Legal Studies* (January 1975), 133–98.

[23] Roger Parks, "Complementary Measures of Police Performance," in *Public Policy Evaluation*, ed. Kenneth M. Dolbeare (Beverly Hills, Calif.: Sage Publications, 1975), pp. 185–219.

[24] Gary T. Marx, "Alternative Measures of Police Performance," in Emilio Viano, op. cit., pp. 105–200.

[25] Gene Kassebaum, David Ward, Daniel Wilner, *Prison Treatment and Parole Survival: An Empirical Assessment* (New York: Wiley, 1971).

[26] Glaser, op. cit., p. 5.

[27] See, for example, Weiss, op. cit., p. 28.

[28] Paul E. Smith and Richard O. Hawkins, "Victimization, Types of Citizen-Police Contacts, and Attitudes Toward the Police," *Law and Society* 8 (Fall 1973), 135–52.

[29] Ibid., p. 148.

[30] Charles R. Wellford, "Crime and the Police: A Multivariate Analysis," *Criminology* 12, no. 2 (August 1974), 195–273.

[31] Ibid., 208.

[32] James P. Levine, "The Ineffectiveness of Adding Police to Prevent Crime," *Public Policy* 23, no. 4 (Fall 1975), 523–45.

[33] Ibid., 530.

[34] Gene Swimmer, "The Relationship of Police and Crime: Some Methodological and Empirical Results," *Criminology* 12, no. 3 (November 1974), 294.

[35] David Aaronson, C. Thomas Dienes, and Michael Musheno, "Changing the Public Drunkenness Laws: The Impact of Decriminalization," *Law and Society Review*, 12, no. 3 (Spring 1978), 405–36.

[36] Jan M. Chaiken, Michael Lawless, and Keith A. Stevenson, *The Impact of Police Activity on Crime: Robberies on the New York City Subway System.* (New York City Rand Institute, R-1424-NYC, January 1974), p. 15.

[37] International City Manager's Association, *Target* 7 (February 1978), 1–2.

[38] This section draws heavily upon Dennis J. Palumbo and Paula J. Wright, "Optimizing Policy Analysis: Can Research Make a Difference in Public Policy?" (Paper presented before the Annual Meeting of the American Society of Public Administration, Phoenix, Arizona, April 10, 1978).

[39] Phillip W. Semas, "How Influential Is Sociology?" *Chronicle of Higher Education* 4 (September 19, 1977), 4.

[40] It should be noted that the opposite also occurs —research often is not scientifically sound. The Russell Sage Foundation evaluated all federally supported research for 1970 with budgets over $10,000 and found that less than 20 percent of the evaluation studies "consistently follow generally accepted procedures with respect to design, data, collection, and data analysis." See Rein and White, op. cit., 121.

[41] Neely Gardner, "The Law of the Other Guy's 'Thing,'" in *The Dallas Connection*, ed. R. A. Luke (Washington, D.C.: National Training and Development, 1974), pp. 55–83.

[42] Ronald Lippitt, "The Use of Social Research to Improve Social Practice," *American Journal of Orthopsychiatry* 35 (1965), 663–69.

[43] Gordon Lippitt, *Visualizing Change* (LaJolla, Calif.: University Associates, 1968).

[44] Kurt Lewin, "Action Research and Minority Problems," *The Journal of Social Issues* 2 (1946), 42.

[45] Neely Gardner, "Action Training & Research: Something Old and Something New," *Public Administration Review* 34 (1974), 106–115.

BIBLIOGRAPHY

Aaronson, David; Dienes, C. Thomas; and Musheno, Michael. "Changing the Public Drunkenness Laws: The Impact of Decriminalization." *Law & Society Review* 12, no. 3 (Spring 1978), 405–36.

Campbell, Donald. "Reforms as Experiments." *American Psychologist* 24, no. 4 (April 1969), 409–28.

Caro, Francis. *Readings in Evaluation Research.* New York: Russell-Sage Foundation, 1971.

Chaiken, Jan M.; Lawless, Michael; and Stevenson, Keith A. *The Impact of Police Activity on Crime: Robberies on the New York City Subway System.* New York: Rand Institute, 1974.

Chein, Isador; Cook, S. W.; and Harding, John. "The Field of Action Research." *American Psychologist* 3 (1948), 43–50.

Dolbeare, Kenneth M. *Public Policy Evaluation.* Beverly Hills, Calif: Sage Publications, 1975.

Deutsch, Morton "Field Theory in Social Psychology." In *The Handbook of Social Psychology*, vol. 1, edited by Garner Lindzey and E. Aronson. Reading, Mass.: Addison-Wesley, 1968, pp. 412–88.

Evans, J. W. "Evaluating Social Action Programs." *Social Science Quarterly* 50 (1969), 568–81.

Gardiner, John. *Public Law and Public Policy.* New York: Praeger, 1977.

Gardner, Neely "Action Training & Research: Something Old and Something New." *Public Administration Review* 34 (1974), 106–15.

Glaser, Daniel. *Routinizing Evaluation: Getting Feedback on Effectiveness of Crime and Delinquency Programs.* Washington, D.C.: U.S. Government Printing Office, 1973.

Henry, Jeffrey; Lineberry, Robert L.; and Milner, Neal A. "The Policy Impact of Policy Evaluation: Some Implications of the Kansas City Patrol Experiment." In *Public Law and Public Policy*, edited by John A. Gardiner. New York: Praeger, 1977, pp. 225–39.

Krech, Donald. "The Challenge and the Promise." *The Journal of Social Issues* 2 (1946), 1–5.

Larson, Richard C. "On Quantitative Approaches to

Urban Police Patrol Problems." *Journal of Research in Crime and Delinquency* 7, no. 2 (July 1970), 26–43.

———. "What Happened to Patrol Operations in Kansas City." *Evaluation* 3, nos. 1, 2 (1976), 117–31.

Levine, James P. "The Ineffectiveness of Adding Police to Prevent Crime." *Public Policy* 23, no. 4 (Fall 1975), 523–45.

Lewin, Kurt. "Action Research and Minority Problems." *The Journal of Social Issues* 2 (1946), 35–60.

Rein, Martin, and White, Susan. "Can Policy Research Help Policy?" *The Public Interest*, 4 (Fall 1977), 119–36.

Smith, Paul E., and Hawkins, Richard O. "Victimization, Types of Citizen-Police Contacts, and Attitudes Toward the Police." *Law & Society Review* 8 (Fall 1973), 135–49.

Swimmer, Gene. "The Relationship of Police and Crime: Some Methodological and Empirical Results." *Criminology* 12, no. 3 (November 1974), 293–314.

Viano, Emilio. *Criminal Justice Research*. Lexington, Mass.: Lexington Books, 1975.

Weiss, Carol. *Evaluation Research: Methods of Assessing Program Effectiveness*. Englewood Cliffs, N.J.: Prentice-Hall, 1972.

Wellford, Charles R. "Crime and the Police: A Multivariate Analysis." *Criminology* 12, no. 2 (August 1974), 195–273.

Wholey, James, et. al. *Federal Evaluation Policy*. Washington, D.C.: The Urban Institute, 1971.

Zimring, Franklin E. "Firearms and Federal Law: The Gun Control Act of 1968." *The Journal of Legal Studies* 4 (January 1975), 133–98.

The general topic of change is a difficult one in the social sciences. The previous chapters of this section have revealed the weaknesses of data and methodology that often prohibit experts from making accurate pronouncements about the present state of criminal justice. Making statements about future trends and needs in criminal justice is even more risky. Hindsight remains the only sure way of testing the strength of prognoses about criminal justice.

Given the public policy approach of this book, we are interested in what changes might be expected or realistically brought about in the way criminal justice policy is formulated and implemented. We make no claim to predict the future. However, by looking at emerging trends that are gaining the support of the public, politicians, and professionals in the field, we can say something about likely changes in criminal justice policy.

CHAPTER FIFTEEN

CHANGES AHEAD
Crime Policy in the Future

Also, because this book has uncovered serious problems with the implementation of criminal justice policies, we are interested in offering recommendations on how bureaucratic bottlenecks might be unclogged or by-passed. Specifically, we want to examine here how the private interests of agencies and their personnel might be better used to translate policy into effective administrative action. Too often, proposed change fails to take into account the realities of administering public policies. The prescriptions usually end by calling for the creation of a new law to solve a lingering problem. In this chapter we concentrate on how criminal justice bureaucracies might be made more effective, and therefore our suggestions should help to overcome what Richard Elmore, a public affairs professor, has called the "embarrassingly large gap between experts' recommendations and the solutions implemented by administrators."[1]

Policies on the Horizon

In Part III we analyzed four policies for coping with today's crime problem—deterrence, rehabilitation, decriminalization and legalization, and diversion. While the first two are quite orthodox approaches to fighting crime and the latter two have appeared more recently, all of these strategies represent established policies being tried in contemporary American society. As Part III has shown, however, none of the approaches has been overwhelmingly successful.

Simultaneously, additional policies are the subject of much discussion, and some have even been enacted by legislatures. In this section we describe two such strategies that are gaining momentum as we move into the 1980s—incapacitation of criminals and citizen crime proofing. While the two emerging policies have historical precedents, we can do little more than provide an overview of these strategies because they are just beginning to be implemented and studied by researchers.

Before exploring them, we should mention that because policies emerge from the political process, they can come and go with the political climate of the times. As Chapter 2 pointed out, deliberations on how to cope with crime are partly designed to serve the self-interests of politicians and to quell citizens' perceptions of crime.

In the 1960s social welfare was supported by many as the best approach for controlling crime. It was promoted during an era of great social unrest in which basic American values (e.g., capitalism) were broadly questioned and at a time when spending public funds was a much less heated political issue. The premise of social welfare policy was that defective environments caused crime. The "fountainheads of crime" were said to be slums, racism, poverty, disease, bad housing, and other social ills.[2] Accordingly, improving the quality of life for the disadvantaged was the key to reducing crime.

To deal with crime, some experts said that this country needed a massive program of social reconstruction to give more people a chance to achieve success here. This was the gist of the famous *Report of the Commission on Civil Disorders* (or, more familiarly, the Kerner Commission) of the late 1960s, which attributed the urban riots of that decade to the miserable conditions in which minorities were living. The commission's report included recommendations for more jobs, higher income, better education, decent housing, and adequate recreational opportunities for those who were economically deprived so that they could become less dependent on crime to satisfy their needs and less hostile to the entire society.

There are two basic reasons why this crime-prevention strategy seems outmoded today. First, it assumes that we know how to improve the standard of living of the poor; in fact, our knowledge of how to do this is quite deficient. Second, even if effective policies could be devised and tested, American society is today unwilling to pay the price necessary to implement them. Whether the answer lies in better schools, welfare reform, or slum clearance, a substantial commitment of national resources would be necessary. One way or another, either the government's spending priorities would have to be rearranged or taxes would need to be raised to secure the revenues for such programs.

Other strategies seem more feasible in today's political climate. Incapacitation and crime proofing are two policies "on the horizon." Whether they can deliver what they promise is an important question.

INCAPACITATION

In the early seventeenth century, the British initiated a crime-fighting strategy that used their settlements outside Europe as a dumping ground for hardened convicts. The first law incorporating this "new" strategy required the following:

If any of the said Rogues shall appear to be dangerous . . . or othewyse be such as will not be reformed, that in every such case it shall and may be lawfull to commit that rogue to the House of Correccion . . . there to remain until the next Quarter Sessions . . . and then such of the Rogues so committed as . . . shalbe thought fitt not to be delivered, shall . . . be banyshed out of this Realme and all the domyn-ions thereof . . . and shall be conveied unto such partes beyond the seas as shalbe at any tyme hereafter for that purpose assigned by the Privie Counsell . . . And if any such Rogue so banyshed as aforesaid shall returne agayne into any part of the Realme . . . without lawfull Lycence or Warrant so to do, that in every such case the offense shalbe Fellony and the Party offending therein Suffer Death as in case of Felony.[3]

Between 1787 and 1857 the British continued this policy and transported approximately 135,000 convicts to Australia under the provisions of such laws. Once there,

the prisoners would injure and mutilate themselves—as for instance by putting lime in their eyes—to get in the hospital. . . . Likewise, at each and all of the penal set-tlements, the prisoners committed desperate assaults, often upon each other by pre-arrangement, "from absolute weariness of their lives," in order to get away from those dreadful places, if only as witnesses, or even as persons accused of murder.[4]

As with the penal colonies depicted above, incapacitation involves prevent-ing offenders from repeating their crimes through physical isolation. Prisons, to an extent, are places that can achieve the goal of removing criminals from society and depriving them of opportunities to commit crimes, at least against law-abid-ing citizens.

It is sometimes difficult to differentiate the strategy of incapacitation from the movement toward fixed-term sentences—a policy designed both to assure equal treatment among those convicted of crimes and to provide the certainty of punishment that is needed to make deterrence effective.[5] However, as political scientist James Q. Wilson confesses, fixed-term sentencing policy is also de-signed simply to take hardened criminals out of circulation.

A sober view of man requires a modest definition of progress. A 20-percent reduc-tion in robbery would still leave us with the highest robbery rate of almost any Western nation but would prevent about 60,000 robberies a year. A small gain for society, a large one for the would-be victims. Yet a 20-percent reduction is unlikely if we concentrate our efforts on dealing with the causes of crime or even if we con-centrate on improving police efficiency. But were we to devote those resources to a strategy that is well within our abilities—to incapacitating a larger fraction of the convicted serious robbers—then not only is a 20-percent reduction possible, even larger ones are conceivable.[6]

But is incapacitation as simple to implement in contemporary society as Wilson implies?

Arizona is one of five states that has enacted fixed-term sentencing legislation. An Arizona prosecutor, Rudy Gerber, has shown that the new criminal code will put many more people in prison for much longer time spans than the old code, with its provisions for indeterminate sentencing.[7] As Table 15-1 shows, Arizona's new code will produce longer prison sentences for individuals who are convicted of offenses ranging from drug use to murder. (Of course, even with the new code the courts will continue to find discretionary opportunities for reducing the number of defendants they must process.)

As the code neared its implementation date (November 1978), Arizona's policy makers began to question whether the state could afford an incapacitation strategy. Because of federal court intervention in behalf of inmates already held in Arizona's prisons, the state was forced to allocate $300 million in 1978 to provide humane facilities for the current inmate population. With the new code expected to increase the convict population by 40 percent in ten years, consultants for the state estimated that this policy change would cost taxpayers more than $1 billion over the next decade.[8] These projections dampened the earlier enthusiasm for this legislation by the state senate. An influential senator serving on the

TABLE 15-1

Comparative Sentences: Arizona's Old and New Criminal Codes

First Offense Being Punished	Number at Prison as of 8/31/77	Average Maximum Years Imposed (1976)	Average Time Served Now (1976)	Presumptive Sentence Under New Code	Years Before Parole Eligibility Under New Code
Murder	} 393	life	6 yrs.	10½ yrs.	10½ yrs.
Negligent manslaughter		2.0	1 yr., 9 mo. (1975 data)	4 yrs.	2 yrs.
Robbery with gun	217	11.9	4 yrs., 1 mo. (1973 data)	10½ yrs.	7 yrs.
Aggravated assault with injury	183	12.5	2 yrs., 2 mo.	7½ yrs.	5 yrs.
Robbery without gun	292	5.7	4 yrs., 5 mo. (1973 data)	4 yrs.	2 yrs.
Burglary (second degree)	506	5.4	1 yr., 7 mo.	5 yrs.	2½ yrs.
Rape (without injury)	178	26.3	3 yrs., 3 mo.	7 yrs.	3½ yrs.
Theft over $1 thousand	153	5.2	1 yr., 10 mo.	5 yrs.	2½ yrs.
Theft of motor vehicle (value over $1 thousand)	32	3.9	1 yr., 4 mo.	5 yrs.	2½ yrs.
Other sex crimes (child molestation)	68	14.1	3 yrs., 3 mo.	7 yrs.	7 yrs.
Dangerous drugs	474	8.5	1 yr., 6 mo.	2 yrs.	1 yr.
Forgery fraud	126	4.5	1 yr., 8 mo.	4 yrs.	2 yrs.

SOURCE: Rudolph J. Gerber, "Sentencing Policies in the New Criminal Code," *Arizona Bar Journal* 13 (December 1977), 34. Reprinted by permission.

Senate's Judiciary Committee stated: "There is substantial sentiment within the Senate that if we cannot find agreement on enough measures to ameliorate the impact of the new code . . . [then we should] postpone the effective date of the code for another year . . ."[9] The legislature did enact new measures to offset the impact of the new code, including the expansion of diversion programs, and therefore, they implemented the new code as scheduled.

In general, however, advocates of incapacitation have ignored the potential costs of resurrecting this strategy in the twentieth century. While officials of the British and French empires could simply export criminals to the Caribbean, the Georgia colony, or Australia and confine them in work camps, American policy makers must fund the construction of expensive "brick and mortar" facilities and pay for their staffing.

Also, Arizona was not the only state affected by the federal courts' new requirement that correctional institutions provide more humane facilities than in the past for the confinement of inmates.[10] In general, then, prisons of the future are likely to be even more costly.

However, if citizens were willing to bear the costs, incapacitation might produce a reduction in crime. At the very least the rate of recidivism, however it is determined, would be cut. Some experts have examined the previous records of convicted felons to determine how many crimes would have been prevented if the felons had been imprisoned after the first or second charged offense. One estimate suggests that 90 percent of "safety crimes" (which include violent crimes plus burglary) are committed by repeaters who carry out between 6 and 14 crimes per year and are caught only once.[11] But others contend that career criminals strike much less frequently.[12]

While incapacitation of criminals would reduce crime, experts do not agree on the exact rate of decrease. The reason is that researchers use different kinds of data and diverse methods of statistical analysis. Thus, two advocates of mandatory five-year sentences for convicted violent criminals and three-year sentences for burglars who are caught and convicted claim that the effect of removing these criminals from society would bring about a significant reduction in serious crimes.[13] Other researchers have arrived at very pessimistic findings. One projection shows that no more than 4 percent of violent crimes would be averted by mandatory five-year sentences.[14] Another concludes that increasing the average time served by 50 percent, from two to three years, would decrease crime by only .6 percent to 4 percent.[15] Still another study of incapacitation claims that doubling the number of juveniles incarcerated would prevent just 1 to 4 percent of all major crimes.[16]

Since the costs of imprisonment are so great, it is essential that these contradictory findings be reconciled and more reliable estimates of the benefits from such policies be obtained. Given the current state of knowledge about the possible impact of incapacitation, evaluation of this policy is impossible. Until more reliable data are provided, the debate about incapacitation is likely to be based more on political ideology and emotional pleas than on sound evidence.

CITIZEN CRIME PROOFING

Chapter 5 revealed that crime prevention became the primary responsibility of the police only in the twentieth century. Few experts argue for shifting this responsibility back to the community, but citizens are increasingly being viewed as a critical resource for reducing crime. The use of prevention measures that make it difficult for criminals to commit crimes, sometimes called "crime proofing," is another trend in the attempt to reduce crime. In *The Impact of Crime*, sociologist John Conklin has divided potential citizen crime-proofing strategies into individual and collective actions.[17]

INDIVIDUAL EFFORTS   Many precautions associated with property crimes can easily be taken at all times. Locking cars and homes, shopping accompanied by friends, and riding subway cars that are heavily occupied are only a few ways that citizens can insulate themselves against crimes without excessively inhibiting their mobility. In the student ghetto surrounding one major university, undercover police attempting to catch a rapist were appalled to discover that students routinely left windows open in large apartment complexes so that neighbors could circulate among apartments without the need for keys. Too many Americans make themselves easy victims through neglect. Clearly, the

Drawing by C.E.M.
© 1976 The New Yorker Magazine, Inc.

police can do little to control property crimes where residents neglect to protect themselves.

Further, why do individual citizens who witness a crime being committed not play an active role in coming to the aid of a victim? In his study of the responses of bystanders to crime, Conklin attempted to determine what general factors inhibit citizens from coming to the aid of crime victims. In addition to discussing the role that fear of getting hurt plays in such situations, he found that American legal policy and the lack of systematic government rewards for safe bystander activity significantly inhibit citizen involvement.[18] While the laws in France and Germany, for example, include sanctions (i.e., fines and jail sentences) for bystanders who fail to help a crime victim, our legal system has no such penalties. Also, Conklin found that other countries offer compensation to rescuers if they suffer injuries; but most of our state governments lack systematic policies for compensating injured rescuers.

Even when there is clearly no threat of physical harm, a study revealed that many bystanders fail to report shoplifting they observe because they fear being sued by the offender.[19] In short, government policies rarely offer incentives to the self-interested motivation of potential Good Samaritans.

A law that would require witnesses to call the police could potentially increase Good Samaritan behavior without threatening the lives of citizens. However, such a policy would be hard to enforce. For example, how would prosecutors prove that a nonresponsive witness knew of an emergency and failed to take action?[20] A more realistic policy would be establishment of programs aimed at educating citizens in ways to reduce their own potential of being victims and to show them how they might safely aid victims of crimes in progress. Several police departments have already developed special units that teach citizens about techniques in crime proofing.

Nonetheless, the problem today is one of too little action by individual citizens to cope with crime. We have become overly reliant on public agencies to handle our crime worries. The emergence of citizen crime-proofing measures is a potential signal of community reinvolvement to protect property and, more broadly, one effort to stem the nation's heavy dependency on public service bureaucracies to solve our social problems. Many of the policies discussed in Part III required additional government personnel and more expenditures, putting another drain on public budgets. Crime proofing has the virtue of putting the onus and costs of crime prevention on the individual. So, it is consistent with the prevailing sentiment in favor of keeping taxes down.

COLLECTIVE ACTIONS For two months of 1968, 12 local merchants of West Hollywood, Florida, nightly patrolled the streets in prowl cars, armed with shotguns.[21] They felt the Broward County sheriff was incapable of protecting their shops and stores.

In the South Bronx during 1976, residents of the Bronxdale Housing Project operated a tenant patrol, monitoring the security of their building during peak-crime periods.[22] Their intent was to serve as extra eyes and ears for officers of the New York Housing Authority Police who were assigned to their public housing project.

Although collective citizen action against crime has deep historical roots, it offers significantly more dangers than does individual involvement. As exemplified by the West Hollywood case above, it can evolve into vigilantism, or organized, extralegal movements of citizens who take the law into their own hands.[23] Perceptions of vigilante actions often evolve from romantic portrayals of citizens banding together to tame the Wild West. In *The Vigilantes of Montana*, historian Thomas Dimsdale offers a description of the vigilante movements in the mid-1800s that illustrates this:

> The face of society was changed, as if by magic; for the Vigilantes, holding in one hand the invisible yet effectual shield of protection, and in the other, the swift descending and inevitable sword of retribution, struck from his nerveless grasp the weapon of the assassin; commanded the brawler to cease from strife; warned the thief to steal no more; bade the good citizen take courage; and compelled the ruffians and marauders who had so long maintained the "reign of terror" in Montana, to fly the Territory, or meet the just rewards of their crimes.[24]

Closer examination of vigilantism indicates that it dealt with different law enforcement problems than those that exist in contemporary America. A century ago outlaws flocked to frontier areas in order to take advantage of social disorganization. Law enforcement was grossly inadequate because the emerging towns often lacked fiscal resources to support sheriffs or constables in their pursuit of criminals. Transportation and communication networks were undependable for tracking down criminals. Jails were either nonexistent or too flimsy to prevent escapes on a routine basis. Finally, juries often failed to convict known criminals through fear or a variety of other factors.[25] Vigilante movements provided solutions to these problems.

While many vigilante movements served to protect law-abiding citizens during unstable periods, others deteriorated into "mobocracy" that could not be stopped once the groups had served their legitimate usefulness. The potential of mob rule raises a critical question about collective group action: What collective activities offer both the potential of crime prevention and the retention of the rule of law? In *The Impact of Crime* Conklin differentiates between adversarial groups, which operate without the cooperation of law enforcement agencies, and supplemental groups, which provide the police with extra eyes and ears. Like the tenant patrol mentioned above, these supplemental groups communicate directly with the police, serve to report unusual behavior to law enforcement officers, and generally provide a community with saturated patrol.[26]

Almost no reliable evaluation research has been carried out to test whether these collective groups directly contribute to a reduction of crime where they operate. Conklin implies that these patrols do "enhance self-esteem" among members and lower the fear of crime among citizens in the neighborhood.[27] He also speculates that because there are many organizing and operating problems

A vigilante group that patrols the subways in New York City

associated with sustaining civilian patrols, they will work only in homogeneous communities that have a history of organized citizen activity.[28] Finally, researchers think that these patrols will work most effectively in well-defined settings, such as housing projects. All of these propositions require further inquiry.

Perhaps, the most effective and least oppressive forms of collective action are those in which government agencies require users of public services to aid in crime proofing. For example, in New York City buses were major targets of robbers until the Transit Authority imposed a system of exact fares. Bus robberies occurred at a yearly rate of 235 for three years preceding the implementation of the exact-fare system, but they fell to a yearly average of eight for the four years after the program went into operation.[29] Similarly, the Chicago Transit Authority reported a decline in bus robberies after involving citizens in crime proofing through an exact-fare program.[30] However, unless coordinated with other public service agencies, these efforts may lead to crime displacement in which thieves simply shift their efforts to more vulnerable targets (e.g., taxicabs). Little is known to date about the displacement effect of collective crime proofing efforts.

POLICY SOURCES AND GOALS

As emerging policies crime proofing and incapacitation are quite different in the way they are evolving from the policy-making process. As pointed out in Chapter 4, most policies are formulated by legislative or judicial bodies. In this sense incapacitation is a typical policy because it is originating in revisions of state criminal codes. As more legislatures revise their states' criminal codes to emphasize determinate rather than indeterminate sentencing, the roots of incapacitation become more deeply implanted throughout the country.

On the other hand, crime proofing is a grass-roots policy that shows the potential of local communities to shape their own response to crime in contemporary American society. It is emerging little by little at the local level rather than the state or national levels as communities and local law enforcement agencies seek to involve their citizens in crime problems. The impact of crime proofing in meeting its intended goals will be extremely difficult to assess because there are already so many varieties of this emerging strategy. Incapacitation will be easier to evaluate because policy analysts will be able to study changes in crime rates over time as determinate and mandatory sentencing policies are implemented on a comprehensive basis.

While the discussion above has emphasized the public interest goal of crime prevention, we should also note that each of these emerging policies, like the more established ones, is intended to meet other goals outlined in Chapter 1. For example, incapacitation represents a shift in this society's definition of justice from mercy and the weighing of an individual's circumstances to equality and retribution. One reason that incapacitation measures are gaining strong political support in legislative bodies throughout the country is that they appeal to both liberals and conservatives. Liberals support mandatory and determinate sentencing because they want individuals to receive like punishments for like crimes. It is a buffer against class and racial discrimination. Conservatives who adovcate "law and order" embrace mandatory sentencing because it increases the likelihood of confining repeat offenders and stings recidivists more acutely than indeterminate sentencing, which emphasizes rehabilitation.

Crime proofing helps achieve the goal of efficiency because it stresses encouraging voluntary efforts of citizens rather than increasing the size of criminal justice agencies to attack crime problems. It also reflects a desire to increase accountability by expanding the opportunity for direct citizen participation in local criminal justice policies.

Prescriptions for Better Policy

Whether we are talking about an emerging or a more established policy, no single strategy can be applied to the entire spectrum of criminal behavior. As legislatures weigh the introduction of a crime-fighting policy, they must assess what criminal subpopulation they most want to influence.

RECONSIDERING LAW ENFORCEMENT PRIORITIES

In Chapter 3 we identified the range of criminal activities and suggested some dimensions that might be weighed in determining what criminal activities should receive top consideration from policy makers and criminal justice agencies. Our survey of established and emerging policies shows a strong emphasis on violent criminals and occasional property criminals. Technological innovations and private security efforts, on the other hand, have increased our ability to better cope with such professional criminals as check forgers and safecrackers.

However, too little expert research, legislative deliberation, and agency attention have been devoted to white-collar criminals. In Chapter 3 we outlined the range of white-collar crime activity that experts know about. It is likely that our review understresses the breadth of such crime because so little is known about how it ultimately affects our individual lives or our national economy.

Certainly, the 1980s should be a decade of increased public policy concern about the reach of white-collar crime. However, legislators have a strong self-interest in shying away from the development of policies to attack these crimes. The 1970s have shown that white-collar criminals command such financial resources that they can easily corrupt public officials with direct bribes, material "gifts," and campaign support. Moreover, repeated scandals have implicated many legislators themselves directly in criminal activity, so that they often have very clear self-interests to protect in not going after white-collar crime.

BALANCING PUBLIC INTEREST GOALS

Policy makers need to develop crime-fighting strategies that assure a balanced attack against the full range of serious criminal activity, but they must also construct public policies so as to strike a balance between two critical public policy goals—due process and crime prevention.[31] Striking the right balance is one of the most important policy problems for criminal justice. If either of the two goals emerges to dominate totally the underlying philosophy of our criminal justice system, we should become alarmed. We can point to an historical incident when crime prevention was overzealously pursued to exemplify this potential danger.

The 1968 Democratic National Convention was held in Chicago during a period of broad social unrest. Many cities had experienced severe riots earlier that year sparked by the assassination of Martin Luther King Jr. The Democratic party was in turmoil as a result of the Vietnam war—as was much of the rest of the country.

Approximately 5,000 antiwar demonstrators had come to Chicago to express their dissent against the Johnson Administration's policies in Vietnam. According to the report of the official government inquiry into the events surrounding the convention, although revolutionaries were present, "the vast majority of the demonstrators were intent on expressing by peaceful means their dissent either from society generally or from the administration's policies in Vietnam."[32]

Richard Daley, mayor of Chicago at that time, had indicated his distaste for the demonstrators and vowed to maintain order in the streets of his city. He reinforced his determination by greatly restricting demonstration permits, assuring massive police presence wherever demonstrators gathered, and calling up National Guardsmen, who were armed with heavy weapons. After several minor verbal and physical confrontations between the police and the demonstrators that resulted in some routine arrests, the police unleashed their obvious anger toward the demonstrators without the due-process constraints they normally abide by in handling such incidents. As recorded in a report submitted to the National Commission on the Causes and Prevention of Violence, the results were shocking:

> [The] violence was made all the more shocking by the fact that it was often inflicted upon persons who had broken no law, disobeyed no order, made no threat. These included peaceful demonstrators, onlookers, and large numbers of residents who were simply passing through, or happened to live in, the areas where confrontations were occurring.
>
> Newsmen and photographers were singled out for assault, and their equipment deliberately damaged. Fundamental police training was ignored; and officers, when on the scene, were often unable to control their men. As one police officer put it: "What happened didn't have anything to do with police work."[33]

Chicago, 1968: The excesses of crime prevention

Although much more difficult to illustrate dramatically, excessive emphasis on due-process requirements can leave the police handcuffed in their pursuit of certain criminals. For example, law enforcement officials argue that it is difficult to bring charges against organized criminals and white-collar criminals because police agencies are legally restricted in their ability to use sophisticated eavesdropping equipment to uncover the activities of such individuals. Some experts have also argued that extremely strict court-imposed standards are causing the police to expand their use of informants.

Excessive concern for defendants' rights can make arrests and convictions very difficult. Constitutional rights can become devices cynically used by professional criminals to shield themselves from law enforcement authorities; the apparent invulnerability of many organized-crime figures attests to this. Due process, an important goal, must be tempered by the society's need to protect itself.

PUTTING SELF-INTEREST TO WORK

Throughout the book we have revealed ways in which criminal justice agencies and their street-level personnel misuse discretion and consequently thwart the implementation of public policies. At the same time we have pointed out how these same institutions and their personnel creatively use discretion to adapt to street-level and community realities without destroying the intent of the law.

Even with the growth of such policies as diversion and crime proofing, which directly involve citizens in criminal justice, our communities will continue to rely largely on criminal justice agencies and professionals to carry out crime-fighting efforts. Therefore, we must learn how to improve the use of discretion and channel it toward intended goals.

To do this a higher priority should be given to organizational changes that make public-service bureaucracies and their personnel more humane and more sensitive than in the past in order to better meet the basic goals of American criminal justice. Our primary suggestions for improving the implementation of criminal justice policies are similar to ideas for improving bureaucratic behavior called "organizational development."[34] This model for improving the implementation of policies attempts to provide answers to the question, "How is it possible to create an organization in which the individuals may obtain optimum expression and, simultaneously, in which the organization itself may obtain optimum satisfaction of its demands?"[35] Before providing some examples of how this might be done in criminal justice, we review two suggested methods for improving organizational decision making in criminal justice (i.e., judicialization and rule making) that are in our estimate unlikely by themselves to produce desired results.

In *Justice by Consent*, legal scholar Arthur Rosett and sociologist Donald Cressey assert general support for the retention of plea bargaining, which they see as having the potential to balance considerations of individual offenders' characteristics with the need to protect society against crime.[36] In suggesting ways to improve the inner workings of plea bargaining, they strongly condemn proposals that concentrate solely on reforming the procedure of plea bargaining. They label such tinkering with plea bargaining "judicialization":

> These proposals proceed on the assumption that a crucial fault with existing practice is the irregular, informal and invisible status of guilty plea negotiations. The aim is to move the guilty plea into the courtroom. The assumption is that if the process is subjected to procedural restraints, made visible to all, and made a regular and binding part of the court process, its vices can be controlled or eliminated.
>
> • • •
>
> It is time to recognize that problems of justice cannot be solved merely by imposing an adversary system model on every facet of the criminal justice system. Judicialization cannot eliminate the causes of police unfairness or probation officers' incompetence. It cannot make prison officers less interested in expediency and more concerned with fairness. The judicial call for adversary resistance to officials ignores the causes of the conduct that is to be resisted.[37]

Policy makers have become hooked on judicialization, or imposing the adversary system model, as a way to solve policy-implementation problems. Rosett and Cressey point out that judicialization will increase formalization and costs without checking the abuses of poor discretionary decision making on the part of court personnel. Discretion exists because criminal justice personnel need discretion; therefore, if rules are imposed at one stage of the criminal justice process to squeeze out discretion, it will merely show up in another.[38] Moreover, legal processes often fail to achieve the goals of justice and due process that they are intended to secure.

To solve many of the abuses associated with another point of discretion, street discretion, legal scholar Kenneth Culp Davis suggests rule making, or the development by police commanders of rules to guide enforcement activities that take place at the street level.[39] Because the legislature fails to designate which criminal laws should receive primary attention by the police and because many actual enforcement practices are developed ad hoc by patrol officers on the beat, Davis argues that police headquarters should step in to make clear what criminal laws should receive highest attention and how street officers are to carry out these laws.

Like the judicialization reform of plea bargaining, administrative rule making ignores the human qualities of public service bureaucracies and their employees. Davis grants that patrol officers would need to retain some flexibility in interpreting these rules, but basically he assumes that mechanical procedural techniques can solve the abuses of discretion. In fact, the police already operate under the guidance of many rules. They carry loose-leaf notebooks that are filled with reams of police orders from headquarters that tell officers what they are to do for hundreds of police tasks. However, these rules are frequently kept in the trunk of the patrol car or used merely as a serving tray for balancing a cup of hot coffee.

BROADENING INVOLVEMENT   In *The Semi-Sovereign People* political scientist E. E. Schattschneider argues that one way to change the direction of public policy is to expand the scope of conflict or increase the number of involved parties so as to assure that a broader range of interests are heard in the political arena.[40] For example, in the 1960s and early 1970s ecologists decided to organize as interest groups to inject their views into legislative deliberations over pollution. Since the emergence of these interest groups, legislators have felt a need to weigh the arguments of both industrialists and ecologists in deciding which government actions are needed to regulate the quality of the nation's water and air.

Like legislative bodies public service bureaucracies are political arenas where much is decided about public policy. However, with the professionalization of the nation's police departments, courts, and correctional institutions, these criminal justice bureaucracies are closed political arenas, with decision making almost completely controlled by the personnel of the respective agencies. Recently, researchers and policy makers alike have suggested that citizens critically influenced by the decisions of these bureaucracies (e.g., victims) should play clearly defined roles in the criminal justice process.

For example, to improve plea bargaining, Rosett and Cressey call for shaking up the courtroom bureaucracy by: (1) eliminating "zone defense," or the structured use of a different public defender at every stage of the court process; (2) including the defendant in deliberations among the judge, prosecutor, and public defender over a plea settlement; and (3) giving the victim a place in the process.[41]

This latter proposal, injecting the rights of the victim into the courtroom process, has significant potential because it appeals to the self-interests of both

---

ONE MAN'S CRUSADE

There was very little enforcement in the United States of either state or federal obscenity statutes during the first 70 years of the 19th Century. This situation changed significantly after 1868, largely as the result of the efforts of Anthony Comstock. In 1868, the New York legislature, at the urging of Protestant leaders in New York City and the Young Men's Christian Association, enacted legislation prohibiting the dissemination of obscene literature. Comstock, a grocery-store clerk by profession, began on his own initiative, to investigate violations of the 1868 Act by local retail dealers and to report to prosecutors. Comstock then joined efforts with the Y.M.C.A. to work for national obscenity legislation to reach publishers as well as local dealers. They formed the Committee for the Suppression of Vice, with Comstock as chief Washington lobbyist. In 1873, Congress responded to these efforts by broadening the 1865 federal mail act to essentially its present form. Comstock was made special agent of the Post Office in charge of enforcing the federal law and he vigorously pursued these duties.

The report of the Commission on Obscenity and Pornography (1970), p. 301.

courtroom professionals, who need victims as cooperative witnesses, and victims, who want to see offenders fully prosecuted. As we will see below, some states are experimenting with victim-witness programs, which offer specific inducements to both parties.

Until recently, victims have been a neglected class of citizens. J. L. Barkas, a criminal justice lecturer, points to five basic avenues of recourse available to crime victims today: (1) private insurance policies, (2) civil action against offenders, (3) restitution programs, (4) compensation programs, and (5) victim-witness programs.[42] Insurance and civil actions against offenders are options that have been available to individuals for a considerable period of time. However, these avenues seem less than ideal for working-class and poor victims.

Barkas points to several deficiencies of these private solutions. Many victims of violent crimes are too poor to purchase medical insurance policies; and those who can afford such policies find that private insurance programs are mostly designed to aid victims of accidents rather than victims of crimes.[43] Civil actions are equally ineffective for a number of reasons: Many citizens are unaware of this option; offenders "are judgement-proof, too poor to pay any damages"; and victims fear retaliation by offenders and often cannot afford to retain an attorney.[44]

To overcome the drawbacks of these private options, local and state governments have initiated restitution and compensation programs on an experimental basis. Minnesota's restitution program is typical, with its focus on property crimes:

> The offender and victim sign a legal agreement in which they state the amount of compensation to be paid. As soon as the agreement is signed, the offender is paroled from prison. He takes a job arranged by the program and repays the victim at the same time that he works at becoming financially independent. The paroled offenders live in a minimum-security facility until they have completed their payments. Violent criminals or those with more than three felony convictions are ineligible for the program.[45]

Interestingly, this is a return to the policy of the medieval period, when, prior to the development of criminal law, the only requirement placed on those who did harm to others was to repay the victim. But restitution programs have some serious flaws because the offender might not be caught or, if caught, might be unwilling to particpate in a program.

A few states have initiated victim compensation programs that award minimal financial benefits directly from state revenue to citizens or their families who have been injured as a result of a violent personal crime (e.g., rape), a robbery, or an assault. Victim compensation programs do not depend on the actions of the offender or those of the police in catching the offender. Citizens file claims and a review board investigates cases to determine both the reliability and merit of requests for assistance.[46] While these programs demonstrate the states' compassion for victims, they do little to influence crime-prevention efforts or improve the implementation of criminal justice policy. Also, they are highly susceptible to those who fabricate injuries or even the crimes themselves.

Of the various experimental local and state programs, the ones that seem to have the greatest potential for both aiding victims and improving the administration of justice are victim-witness programs. Often administered in prosecutors' offices, these programs attempt to both provide social services to victims and inform them of their role in the court process as potential witnesses.[47] The programs both educate victims about the actual workings of the muncipal courtroom and put them in contact with social service agencies to determine what benefits they are eligible for as victims and citizens. Courtroom personnel have grown too accustomed to using victims of crimes as witnesses without giving much attention to their individual plights. As a result many cases are dismissed because victims decide not to testify against offenders, often because they fear retribution by the offender.

Such programs should meet with little resistence by courtroom personnel because they accomodate the self-interest of both attorneys and judges by improving the likelihood of witness cooperation. Victims stand to benefit from such programs because personnel are assigned to ensure that citizens will be protected against intimidation by the offender and to determine victim eligibility for any social services provided by the state (see Figure 15-1).[48]

INCENTIVES FOR CHANGE As described in Chapter 1, criminal justice personnel are motivated by a number of personal aspirations, including economic gain and job security. However, supervisors of criminal justice personnel have neglected to determine what specific work incentives are available that appeal to these critical personal motivations.[49]

A group of researchers examined work incentives in a study of police discretion and the handling of public inebriates.[50] The researchers studied localities that had either diverted public drunks or decriminalized public drunkenness; the police, however, were still required to pick up drunks and deliver them to public health facilities.

In some jurisdictions the police stopped picking up drunks, so the point of diversion was defeated. The reason? The officers received no credit from their supervisors for delivering a drunk to a public health facility.[51] However, in other jurisdictions the program worked because supervisors allowed the same credit for taking drunk to a public health facility as they did for making a misdemeanor arrest.[52] Thus, with this incentive, there was no reason for police not to pick up drunks; and their own self-interests in security, promotion, and higher pay were satisfied.

This is just one example of incentives available to criminal justice policy makers to achieve the aim of public policies. Too often, though, supervisors simply issue a memorandum on the change and expect that this communication will shift street-level performance in the desired direction. Such supervisory laziness could be replaced by the creative use of incentives that recognize workers' self-interest drives. In his article on using financial bonuses to improve the quality of

FIGURE 15-1

Victims' Counterpart of the Miranda Warning

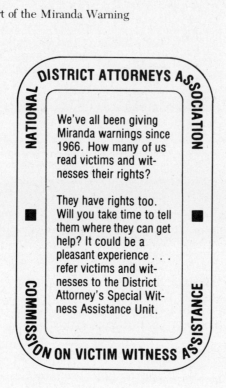

NATIONAL DISTRICT ATTORNEYS ASSOCIATION COMMISSION ON VICTIM WITNESS ASSISTANCE

We've all been giving Miranda warnings since 1966. How many of us read victims and witnesses their rights?

They have rights too. Will you take time to tell them where they can get help? It could be a pleasant experience . . . refer victims and witnesses to the District Attorney's Special Witness Assistance Unit.

You have the right as a crime victim or witness:

- to be free from intimidation;
- to be told about compensation available to victims for their injuries;
- to be told about social service agencies which can help you;
- to be assisted by your criminal justice agency.

Your **District Attorney** operates a special **Witness Assistance Unit.** If you need help, call:

914-682-2827

SOURCE: Courtesy of the Office of the Westchester County (N.Y.) District Attorney.

police work, political scientist James P. Levine argues that if some resources were set aside in the budgets of our criminal justice programs to reward those who comply with new directives, "massive policy failures might be lessened."[53]

Unfortunately, the potential for using financial bonuses to reward street-level personnel has greatly eroded as a realistic option during the inflation-plagued 1970s. It is most unlikely that political leaders could lend support to giving criminal justice agencies special funds for inducing better performance of their personnel. Citizens would no doubt wonder why decent salaries and pride in one's work were not sufficient incentives to assure proper use of discretion. Thus, alternative incentives must be sought.

SELF-ACTUALIZATION   Many workers in public service agencies get very little self-satisfaction from their jobs. Psychologist Rollo May argues that emptiness and boredom represent states of mind for many workers in modern society, and he illustrates this by describing the following, rather bizarre case:

A bus driver in the Bronx simply drove away in his empty bus one day and was picked up by police several days later in Florida. He explained that, having gotten tired of driving the same route every day, he had decided to go away on a trip. While he was being brought back it was clear from the papers that the bus company was having a hard time deciding whether or how he should be punished. By the time he arrived in the Bronx he was a "cause célèbre," and a crowd of people who apparently had never personally known the errant bus driver [was] on hand to welcome him. When it was announced that the company had decided not to turn him over for legal punishment but to give him his job back again if he would promise to make no more jaunts, there was literal as well as figurative cheering in the Bronx.[54]

Much of the work of criminal justice personnel is also boring and frustrating. Public defenders are often a part of "zone defense" processing of accused persons in which they work only on a particular stage of a case. Patrol officers are removed from the scene of a serious crime as soon as investigators from a special squad arrive on the scene. Judges, too, have often complained of monotony. This was very well expressed by a New York judge who resigned his judgeship and gave up his $49,000 salary with the following comment: "It was like being a third base umpire in a no hit game. You have got to be there for the two balls that go down the third baseline and need a decision."[55]

Psychologist Abraham Maslow reports that human beings have personal needs to gain self-fulfillment, or self-actualization.[56] According to Maslow, the seeds of creative endeavors are contained in the drive for self-fulfillment. Today, many people turn to hobbies and recreation instead of work to gain such fulfillment.

While public service bureaucracies often fulfill individuals needs for security and belongingness, they do very little to enhance self-actualization. Training and administrative efforts are needed that at least provide the opportunities for professionals to meet these needs while on the job.

Fortunately, training techniques are emerging that attack institutional and street-level frustration and attempt to improve essential job skills (e.g., verbal communication). Psychologist Kenn Rogers identifies a range of techniques that are now available to criminal justice agencies, including the so-called Tavistock Model.[57] A criminal justice professor, Ronald Weiner, describes an application of the Tavistock Model to police training. The objective is to learn about fear and points of frustration as well as to enhance communication skills through participation in group sessions. Weiner recommends the following in order to teach police about race relations:

[Police] must have opportunities to conceptualize and experience the meaning of behavior expressed by individuals from different sociocultural backgrounds. This does not mean merely giving them a course in race relations. These are men of action who desire a sense of excitement and challenge that requires a learning model which will allow them to participate actively in the learning process.[58]

While these techniques are finding their way into training and university educational programs, we know almost nothing about their actual impact on the administration of public policy. They do, however, seem to offer avenues for putting self-interest to work for the public good.

The self-esteem of individuals can be enhanced by giving them a feeling that they are doing important work. Work itself can be restructured so that criminal justice personnel participate in decisions, even to the point of defining the nature of their jobs. Employees who feel they are doing something important, who are part of a professional enterprise, are more likely to do their jobs well than those who are supervised by strict and unrealistic rules and regulations. In short, professionalism is achieved only through internal motivations and commitments.

Conclusion

Nearly all of the reforms proposed here to improve crime policy pose threats to some vested interests in the criminal justice system. For example, the inclusion of the defendant in plea-bargaining deliberations could potentially retard the speed with which courtroom personnel can now dispense with cases. Also, such a reform implies that we cannot simply rely on the professional integrity of attorneys to provide "justice" to defendants. Given these slaps at organizational self-interests and personal self-interests, we would expect resistance to almost any bureaucratic reforms that threaten doing business as usual in the criminal justice system.

How do we realistically expect these reforms to be successfully implemented? All reforms require bold leadership in which some individuals demonstrate the skill, sensitivity, and personal motivation to put the public interest in front of narrow self-interest. Certainly, we can find evidence of such leadership in the criminal justice system.

Tom O. Murton was hired in 1967 to "clean up" the Arkansas correctional system. Within a very short time, he gained leadership over the Tucker Farm Prison and acquired strong support from its inmate population. To turn around the environment of the prison, he ended corruption that benefited local town residents and inmate guards; stopped the use of torture as a means of maintaining control over inmates; and openly revealed the depth of past atrocities, including the apparent murder and secret burial of uncooperative inmates.[59]

This example of bold leadership also reveals the potential costs of promoting organizational change. After national media attention became focused on the Arkansas prison system as a result of Murton's actions, he was fired by then Governor Winthrop Rockefeller. In *Accomplices to the Crime* Tom Murton describes his interpretation of leadership and reform:

The model of reform viewed from the perspective of time can be represented as a spiral. At the low point there is a scandal which sparks a demand for drastic reform measures. The reforms are implemented. The curve of progress arcs upward toward the apex of achievement.

Just short of consolidating the gains, the reformer is removed. The process is reversed and the arc curves downward until it approaches the point of origin.

The linear difference between the beginning point of the spiral and the new low indicates the net gain (or loss) that has been accomplished. The reformer must be willing to scale a mountain of obstacles and fall short of the pinnacle of "success" to attain the foothills of reform.[60]

Making reform efforts last requires that leaders gain the support both of important clienteles within their organization and groups outside of the organization that can influence a leader's reform efforts.[61] Thus, for example, prison reform requires the cooperation of inmates as well as staff members within the institution. In addition, a leader must gain the endorsement of some important political officials (e.g., the governor and key legislative leaders). The extent to which leaders can acquire broad-based internal and external support for their reforms determines how much change will be retained and made a lasting component of the criminal justice system. Ultimately, then, an effective leader uses the "power of persuasion" to mobilize groups to look a bit beyond the status quo and recognize that they can gain something by supporting a particular reform.

SUMMARY

Because public policies emerge from the political process, they can come and go with the political climate of the times. Only ten years ago rehabilitation was advocated by experts and politicians alike as the best approach for controlling crime. Today incapacitation and citizen crime proofing are two policies on the horizon.

Incapacitation, the removal of criminals from society to deprive them of crime opportunities against law-abiding citizens, grew in the 1970s with the movement toward mandatory minimum sentences. Prisons rather than penal colonies (which were used in the past) are being designated as places that can achieve these modest goals.

Advocates of incapacitation have ignored its high costs. Proponents of resurrecting incapacitation fail to recognize that the colonial powers had an economic reason for promoting the confinement of criminals in the New World. Another drawback of incapacitation is that its reintroduction will increase the size of correctional bureaucracies at a time when they are unable to handle current inmate populations.

If the public were willing to bear the costs and if correctional agencies could improve their efficiency, incapacitation could undoubtedly produce a reduction in crime. Experts are in disagreement over how much of a reduction could be achieved, however.

Crime proofing, increasing the use of citizens as critical resources for reducing crime, can be divided into individual and collective actions. Individual efforts include improvement of the habits of people so as to lower their potential for being victims of crime. Incentives are also needed to aid victims of crime. Citizens are reluctant to come to the aid of victims not only because they fear reprisal but because they perceive no legal or personal incentives for taking such a risk.

Collective actions include citizens' serving as extra eyes and ears of the police as well as vigilante activity. Vigilantism—the organized, extralegal movement of citizens to take the law into their own hands—has a long history in the United States. Most of the conditions that led to its emergence in the frontier era no longer exist in today's society. While many vigilante movements served to protect law-abiding citizens during unstable periods, others deteriorated into "mobocracy" that could not be stopped.

No reliable evaluations have been completed of contemporary, supplemental citizen groups that serve as extra eyes and ears for the police. Perhaps the most effective and least oppressive forms of collective action are those in which government agencies require users of public services to aid in crime proofing. An example of such collective action is the exact fare system for buses.

No single policy can be applied to the entire spectrum of criminal behavior. Especially lacking at the present are policies that attack white-collar criminals. Just as policy makers need to develop crime-fighting strategies to assure a balanced attack against the full range of serious criminal activity, they must also construct public policies so as to strike a balance between two public policy goals—due process and crime prevention.

Our communities will continue to rely largely on criminal justice agencies and professionals to carry out crime-fighting efforts. Therefore, we must better learn how to control discretion and channel it to meet intended goals. Judicialization and rule making are approaches that are unlikely to improve discretionary behavior because they ignore the human and political aspects of administering criminal justice. Injecting alternative self-interests into bureaucracies, developing incentives for change, and promoting opportunities for self-actualization offer some possible avenues for improving the administration of the criminal justice system. In addition any efforts to improve the operation of criminal justice agencies will require creative leadership.

FOOTNOTES

[1] Richard F. Elmore, "Organizational Models of Social Program Implementation," *Public Policy* 26 (Spring 1978), 189.

[2] Ramsey Clark, *Crime in America* (New York: Pocket Books, 1971), p. 5.

[3] Quoted in Harry Elmer Barnes, *The Story of Punishment* (Montclair, N.J.: Patterson Smith, 1972), p. 69.

[4] Ibid., p. 79.

[5] For further discussion of fixed-form sentencing, see David Fogel, *We Are the Living Proof* (Cincinnati, Ohio: W. H. Anderson, 1975).

[6] James Q. Wilson, "Lock 'Em Up," in *Crime and Justice in America*, Jerome Skolnick (Del Mar, Calif.: Publisher's Inc., 1977), p. 8.

[7] Rudy J. Gerber, "Sentencing Policies in the New Criminal Code," *Arizona Bar Journal* 13 (December, 1977), 28–37.

[8] Greg O'Brien, "Report Warns Con Population Will Sky-Rocket," *Arizona Republic*, December 13, 1977, p. A1.

[9] Quoted in Joel Nilsson, "Panel to Begin Criminal-Code Talks This Week," *Arizona Republic*, May 15, 1978, p. A1.

[10] For an overview of correctional case law, see Robert Carter, Richard McGee, and E. Kim Nelson, *Corrections in America* (N.Y.: Lippincott, 1975), pp. 328–46.

[11] Shlomo Shinnar and Reuel Shinnar, "The Effects of the Criminal Justice System on the Control of Crime: A Quantitative Approach," *Law and Society Review* 9 (Summer 1975), 581–611.

[12] Stephan Van Dine, Simon Dintz, and John Conrad, "The Incapacitation of the Dangerous Offender: A Statistical Experiment," *Journal of Research in Crime and Delinquency* 14 (January 1977), 22–34.

[13] Shinnar and Shinnar, op. cit., 608–11.

[14] Van Dine, Dintz, and Conrad, op. cit.

[15] David Greenberg, "The Incapacitative Effect of Imprisonment: Some Estimates," *Law and Society Review* 9 (Summer 1975), 541–80.

[16] Steven Clarke, "Getting 'Em Out of Circulation: Does Incarceration of Juvenile Offenders Reduce Crime?" *Journal of Criminal Law and Criminology* 65 (December 1974), 528–35.

[17] John Conklin, *The Impact of Crime* (New York: Macmillan, 1975), pp. 185–247.

[18] Ibid., pp. 217–18.

[19] Donald Hartmann et al., "Rates of Bystander Observation and Reporting of Contrived Shoplifting Incidents," *Criminology* 10 (November 1972), 247–67.

[20] Conklin, op. cit., p. 220.

[21] Richard Maxwell Brown, "The American Vigilante Tradition," in *The History of Violence in America*, eds. Hugh Graham and Ted Gurr (New York: Praeger, 1969), p. 205.

[22] Michael Musheno, James Levine, and Dennis Palumbo, "Television Surveillance and Crime Prevention: Evaluating an Attempt to Create Defensible Space in Public Housing," *Social Science Quarterly* 58 (March 1978), 647–56.

[23] Brown, op. cit., p. 154.

[24] Thomas J. Dimsdale, *The Vigilantes of Montana* (Norman, Okla.: University of Oklahoma Press, 1953), p. 15.

[25] Brown, op. cit., p. 178.

[26] Conklin, op. cit., pp. 197, 203.

[27] Ibid., p. 209.

[28] Ibid., p. 208.

[29] Memorandum from Leonard Ingalls, director of Public Information, New York City Transit Authority, February 23, 1973.

[30] Memorandum from C. W. Baxa, director of Public Information, Chicago Transit Authority, February 13, 1973.

[31] See Herbert Packer, *The Limits of the Criminal Sanction* (Stanford, Calif.: Stanford University Press, 1968), pp. 149–204.

[32] Daniel Walker, *Rights in Conflict* (New York: Dutton, 1968), p. 4.

[33] Ibid., p. 1.

[34] See Richard Elmore, op. cit., 209–17; Chris Argyris, *Integrating the Individual and the Organization* (New York: Wiley, 1964); and Warren Bennis, *Organization Development: Its Nature, Origins and Prospects* (Reading, Mass.: Addison-Wesley, 1969).

[35] Chris Argyris, "The Individual and Organization: Some Problems of Mutual Adjustment," *Administrative Science Quarterly* 2 (June 1957), 24.

[36] Arthur Rosett and Donald R. Cressey, *Justice by Consent* (New York: Lippincott, 1976).

[37] Ibid., pp. 168–69.

[38] Ibid., p. 170.

[39] Kenneth Culp Davis, *Police Discretion* (St. Paul, Minn.: West Publishing, 1975).

[40] E. E. Schattschneider, *The Semi-Sovereign People* (New York: Holt, Rinehart & Winston, 1960).

[41] Rosett and Cressey, op. cit., pp. 173–74.

[42] J. L. Barkas, *Victims* (New York: Scribner's, 1978), pp. 168–204.

[42] Ibid., pp. 178–79.

[44] Ibid., pp. 179–82.

[45] Ibid., p. 183.

[46] Ibid., pp. 184–91.

[47] Donald MacNamara and John J. Sullivan, "Composition, Restitution, Compensation: Making the Victims Whole," *The Urban Review* 6 (1973), 21–25.

[48] Barkas, op. cit., pp. 198–99.

[49] See James Levine, Michael Musheno, and Dennis Palumbo, "The Limits of Rational Choice Theory in Choosing Criminal Justice Policy," in *Policy Studies and the Social Sciences*, ed. Stuart Nagel (Lexington, Mass.: D.C. Heath, 1975), pp. 89–104; Michael Musheno, Dennis Palumbo, and James Levine, "Evaluating Alternatives in Criminal Justice: a Policy-Impact Model," *Crime and Delinquency* 22 (July 1976), 265–80; and Dennis Palumbo, James Levine, and Michael Musheno, "Individual Group and Social Rationality in Controlling Crime," in *Modeling in the Criminal Justice System*, ed. Stuart Nagel (Beverly Hills, Calif.: Sage Publications, 1977), pp. 73–88.

[50] David Aaronson, C. Thomas Dienes, and Michael Musheno, "Improving Police Discretion Rationality in Handling Public Inebriates," Part I, *Administrative Law Review* 29, no. 4 (1977), 447–85; and Part II, *Administrative Law Review* 30, no. 1 (1978), 93–132.

[51] David Aaronson, C. Thomas Dienes, and Michael Musheno, "Changing the Public Drunkenness Laws: The Impact of Decriminalization," *Law and Society Review* 12 (Spring 1978), 405–36.

[52] Aaronson, Dienes, and Musheno, "Improving Police Discretion Rationality in Handling Public Inebriates," Part II, op. cit., 117–18.

[53] James P. Levine, "Implementing Legal Policies Through Operant Conditioning: The Case of Police Practices," *Law and Society Review* 5 (November 1971), 219.

[54] Rollo May, *Man's Search for Himself* (New York: W. W. Norton, 1953), pp. 21–22.

[55] Quoted in Tom Goldstein, "From Bench to Legal Aid Post," *New York Times*, June 30, 1978, p. A15.

[56] Abraham Maslow, *Motivation and Personality* (New York: Harper & Row, 1970).

[57] Kenn Rogers, "Group Processes in Police-Community Relations," *Bulletin of the Menninger Clinic* 14 (September 1972), 517.

[58] Ronald I. Weiner, "Group Relations in Criminal Justice," in *Social Work and Social Justice*, eds. Bernard Ross and Charles Shereman (Washington, D.C.: National Association of Social Workers, 1973), p. 63.

[59] Tom Murton and Joe Hyams, *Accomplices to the Crime* (New York: Grove Press, 1969), pp. 182–96.

[60] Ibid., pp. 236–37.

[61] Tom Murton, *Dilemma of Prison Reform* (New York: Holt, Rinehart & Winston, 1976), pp. 133–46.

BIBLIOGRAPHY

Argyris, Chris. *Integrating the Individual and the Organization.* New York: Wiley, 1964.

Barkas, J. L. *Victims.* New York: Scribner's, 1978.

Barnes, Harry Elmer. *The Story of Punishment.* Montclair, N.J.: Patterson Smith, 1972.

Brown, Richard Maxwell. "The American Vigilante Tradition." In *The History of Violence in America*, edited by Hugh Graham and Ted Gurr. New York: Praeger, 1969, pp. 154–217.

Conklin, John. *The Impact of Crime.* New York: Macmillan, 1975.

Elmore, Richard. "Organizational Models of Social Program Implementation." *Public Policy* 26 (Spring 1978), 185–228.

Greenberg, David. "The Incapacitation Effect of Imprisonment: Some Estimates." *Law and Society Review* 9 (Summer 1975), 541–80.

Rogers, Kenn. "Group Processes in Police-Community Relations." *Bulletin of the Menninger Clinic* 14 (September 1972), 515–34.

Schattschneider, E. E. *The Semi-Sovereign People.* New York: Holt, Rinehart & Winston, 1960.

Van Dine, Stephan; Dintz, Simon; and Conrad, John. "The Incapacitation of the Dangerous Offender: A Statistical Experiment." *Journal of Research in Crime and Delinquency* 14 (January 1977), 22–34.

Weiner, Ronald. "Group Relations in Criminal Justice." In *Social Work and Social Justice*, edited by Bernard Ross and Charles Shereman. Washington, D.C.: National Association of Social Workers, 1973, pp. 51–64.

GLOSSARY

Absolute deterrence The complete refusal to commit specific crimes out of fear of legal consequences.

Accountability The right of the public to play a major role in criminal justice decision making.

Action research Research in which those being studied participate in the design of the research.

Actual enforcement of the law Enforcing the law within the discretionary constraints imposed on police agencies and street officers.

Adjudication A method of conflict resolution, used primarily by courts, in which outcomes are determined by the use of formal hearings and the application of legal norms and procedures.

Adversary system A process of deciding legal controversies in which presumably neutral parties such as judges reach decisions after listening to two opposing sides (i.e., prosecution and defense).

Aggravated assault A physical attack on a person that results in serious bodily injury.

Analytical jurisprudence An approach to the study of law that emphasizes the use of logic in analyzing authoritative precedents and documents to determine the nature and scope of law.

Arraignment The first appearance of a defendant before a judge after arrest, at which time a plea of guilty or not guilty is made and the defendant's legal rights are stipulated.

Bail bondsmen Businesspeople who agree to post bond for some defendants to allow them to go free prior to trial, in return for a fee.

Behavior modification The attempt to rehabilitate offenders through psychological techniques and the use of drugs.

Bureaucracy A hierarchically arranged, formalized, and professionalized organization that functions on the basis of a division of labor and established rules.

Burglary The crime of breaking into a building to commit a felony, such as theft.

Cash bail A bail reform that allows defendants to post a percentage of a bond in cash, with the proviso that most of that money will be returned if they show up in court.

Celerity Swift administration of punishment following the commission of criminal acts.

Change of venue Moving the trial away from the city where the crime in question was committed in order to select a jury unbiased by pretrial publicity.

Civil law The law that deals with private wrongs as opposed to public wrongs and gives those who are injured redress against those who wronged them.

Community corrections A program for rehabilitating offenders in community programs rather than sending them to prison.

Conflict criminology A school of criminology that attempts to explain crime as a by-product of capitalism and class bias.

Control group The group of subjects in an experiment, similar in other respects to the experimental group, that is not administered the special treatment under investigation.

Correlation The statistical relationship that exists when two kinds of phenomena vary simultaneously either in the same or opposite directions.

Corruption The taking of bribes by government officials in exchange for giving special favors.

Crime Any act that lawmakers designate as subject to punishment imposed by courts.

Crime displacement The altering of the location, time, or target of crime by criminals in response to intensified law enforcement campaigns.

Crime prevention The police function of deterring people from committing crime, catching lawbreakers in the act of crime, and apprehending them after they commit crimes.

Crime proofing A grass-roots policy that attempts to reduce the opportunities for successful commission of crimes by directly involving private citizens in various self-protection programs.

Crime rates The amount of crime expressed in relation to some other factor, such as population.

Criminal law Conduct that is forbidden by government and punishable by sanctions such as fines and imprisonment.

Criminal law overreach The extension of criminal law into the domain of personal morality.

Criminology An academic field of sociology that concentrates on the study of crime and its causes.

Cross-sectional research design A type of research design in which the relationship between variables at a particular point in time is examined.

Decriminalization The legislative policy designed to limit, but not end, government prohibition of using goods and services associated with victimless crimes. Sanctions are reduced from prison sentences to fines.

Defense lawyer An attorney who represents those accused of crimes.

Dependent variable A variable phenomenon whose magnitude must be explained by other factors.

Deterrence The use of threat of punishment to prevent illegal behavior.

Differential association The theory that crime is learned and passed on to individuals through their interaction with peers who come from a crime subculture.

Discretion The ability of government officials to use personal judgment in decision making and to decide which policies to enforce.

Diversion A policy in which adults accused of certain criminal offenses have their prosecution halted for a period of time based on a negotiated agreement to participate in community-based conflict-resolution, counseling, or treatment programs.

Due process Fair and civilized treatment by government authorities of people accused of crimes.

Dynamite charge Lectures that are given by judges to juries having trouble reaching agreement on verdicts, and that urge the minority to listen carefully to the majority (also called an "Allen" charge).

Efficiency The effective use of resources by government agencies so that waste is minimized.

Elites The community notables or powerful persons who can influence the formulation and implementation of public policy.

Evaluation research Measuring the effect of a program against the goals it is supposed to accomplish.

Exclusionary rule The constitutional rule forbidding the use of illegally seized evidence in court.

Experimental group The group of subjects in an experiment that is administered some special treatment whose effects are being measured.

Experimental research design A research method that determines the impact of a variable by exposing a randomly selected group of subjects to some treatment and comparing that group after treatment to a similar group not given the treatment.

False positive An inaccurate prediction by law enforcement authorities that an individual will commit a crime in the future.

Felony A serious crime that carries a penalty of one or more years of incarceration.

Fixed-term sentence A system of sentencing that specifies the punishments for various crimes and that does not allow a judge to change them.

Full enforcement of the law Enforcement of all criminal laws within the bounds of due process.

General deterrence The restraining effect of punishing offenders who are caught on the total population of potential offenders.

Grand jury A group of citizens (usually 23 in number) that investigates wrongdoing and that, in some states, after hearing evidence submitted by the prosecutor, decides by majority vote whether to indict defendants.

Halfway house A place where released prisoners may live as they adjust to outside life.

Hearsay evidence Second-hand evidence, normally not admissible in court, of what other people who are not present in court have said.

Homicide Murdering a person with premeditation and malice aforethought.

Hung jury A jury that is unable to reach agreement about whether a defendant is guilty or innocent—an outcome that allows prosecutors to retry the case if they choose.

Incapacitation An emerging criminal justice policy whose aim is to remove criminals from society and deprive them of opportunities for crime (usually accomplished through the imposition of mandatory minimum sentences).

Incentives Inducements, such as money, sometimes used to prompt conformity to policy.

Independent variable A changeable phenomenon that may have various impacts on other phenomena. The presence or absence of a criminal justice program may for some purposes be viewed as an independent variable.

Indeterminate sentence An open-ended prison sentence, such as from one to five years, that gives prison authorities the right to determine the amount of time actually served within the prescribed limits.

In forma pauperis A special process that allows poor people who have been convicted of crimes to appeal to the United States Supreme Court without having to use all the formalities normally required.

In loco parentis The idea that juvenile courts should have enormous leeway in disposing of juvenile defendants because they are acting in the place of parents.

Instructions to the jury The judge's explanation to a jury of what the law requires to find a defendant guilty.

Interval scale A measurement scale in which events are given precise numerical values.

Judicialization Reform proposals to improve the implementation of public policy that concentrate solely on adjusting and formalizing procedures.

Jurisdiction The type or range of a court's authority.

Justice Giving criminals the punishment they deserve, on the basis of principles of equality, retribution, and mercy.

Legalization The legislative policy that ends criminal sanctions for certain victimless crimes (e.g., gambling) but uses a regulative approach to discourage and channel the public's use of certain goods and services.

Longitudinal research design A type of research design that examines changes in a variable over the course of time.

Manslaughter Unintentional homicide caused by recklessness or committed during a fit of emotion.

Marginal deterrence The difference between the deterrent efficacy of two alternative policies.

Mediation One alternative to adjudication that attempts to resolve conflicts cooperatively by involving the accused, the victim, and the community.

Miranda warning The constitutional requirement that those arrested be advised of their rights before being questioned.

Misdemeanor A minor crime that usually carries a penalty of less than a year of incarceration.

Moral enterpreneurs Religious and moral groups that use their political influence to lobby for the enactment or retention of victimless crime statutes.

Natural law Fundamental moral principles that some philosophers of law contend must be the basis for legal regulation.

New diversion A type of diversion policy that establishes programs with definite eligibility criteria for clients, a variety of ways to help them, and full-time staff positions filled by trained community residents and professionals.

No true bill The decision of grand juries not to indict a defendant brought before them by the prosecutor.

Nolle prosequi The decision of prosecutors to dismiss charges against defendants, often abbreviated nol. pros. (literally, "being unwilling to prosecute").

Nominal scale A measurement scale in which events are simply classified into discrete categories, such as the presence or absence of some characteristic.

Operationalization The devising of concrete ways (sometimes called "operational definitions") to measure theoretical concepts.

Opportunity costs The alternative programs and policies that could be instituted through use of government funds if established practices had not been chosen.

Order maintenance The police task of keeping the peace in a community.

Ordinal scale A measurement scale in which events are ranked in order of relative value without regard for the absolute amount of the quantity in question.

Overcharging The practice of some prosecutors of instituting more serious charges against defendants than are warranted by the evidence (also called "overfiling").

Parole Release of convicts from prison under supervision of a court officer prior to the serving of the entire sentence.

Partial deterrence Reducing the intensity or boldness of criminal activity to ward off the chance of punishment (also called "restrictive deterrence").

Peremptory challenge In criminal cases, the right of both the prosecution and the defense to eliminate a specified number of prospective

jurors without giving any reasons whatsoever.

Persistent offender A criminal who commits crimes to support his or her own high living and who rationally plans crime.

Personal bond A form of bail that allows defendants to pay nothing prior to their release but makes them liable for a certain amount of money if they do not show up in court.

Petit jury A group of lay people, from 6 to 12 in number, supposedly a cross-section of the population, that decides the guilt or innocence of defendants who choose a jury trial.

P.I.N.S. An acronym for "persons in need of supervision," that covers the broad range of conditions under which juvenile courts are empowered to deal with so-called unruly youngsters.

Plea bargaining The negotiating process between the prosecution and the defense in criminal cases, whereby defendants are allowed to plead guilty to lesser charges in return for dismissal of more serious ones.

Police atomization Dispersal of police power as a result of federalism and localism.

Police brutality Police breaches of due process guarantees by the physical abuse of citizens without legitimate cause.

Policy analysis The development and application of empirical models and social science methods to assess the effectiveness of crime-fighting strategies.

Political culture Community sentiments shaping law enforcement practices that evolve from public opinion, the socioeconomic makeup of the community, the history of law enforcement standards, and the concerns of local elites.

Predatory crime Crime in which a specific victim is involved and the criminal is seeking personal gain.

Preliminary hearings Pretrial hearings in which judges determine whether sufficient evidence ("probable cause") exists to justify a full trial.

Presentence report A report by a probation officer made prior to sentencing that diagnoses offenders, predicts their chance of being rehabilitated, and assesses the danger they pose to society.

Presumptive sentencing Legislative policy that gives judges strict guidelines for sentencing.

Preventive detention The right of courts to deny bail altogether if they think defendants pose a danger to society.

Preventive patrol The use of cruising police patrols to frighten potential criminals and thus keep them from carrying out crimes.

Probation A sentence whereby an offender is not incarcerated but required to follow certain rules and report regularly to a court officer.

Productivity Obtaining the highest possible performance by a government agency at the lowest possible cost.

Professional criminal One who engages in crime as a full-time occupation.

Professionalism Performing one's job with skill and expertise, free of political pressures.

Prosecutor An attorney who represents the government in criminal cases (also called "district attorney").

Public defender A lawyer hired by the government to represent poor defendants who cannot afford to hire their own lawyers.

Public order victimless crimes Morality crimes that are traditionally associated with public tranquillity problems (e.g., public drunkenness).

Public policy The programs, regulations, and other actions of government intended to accomplish certain goals.

Public tranquillity A peaceful environment that is free of fear and provocations.

Quasi-experimental research design A research design that examines differences in the natural course of events to determine relationships among variables.

Reactivity The notion that people often act differently when being observed or studied from the way they act under normal circumstances.

Recidivism The commission of additional crimes or the breaking of rules after an individual has been caught, arrested, and punished.

Recidivism rates Measures of the frequency with which various categories of criminals repeat their crimes.

Recusation The judges' practice of removing themselves from cases in which they are related to any of the parties or in which they have some special personal interest.

Regression analysis A statistical technique for determining how two variables are related that attempts to describe their relationship by a straight or curved line such that the amount of one variable can be predicted from the amount of the other.

Rehabilitation Restoration of a person to a state of mental and moral health through treatment and training, so that the person no longer commits crimes.

Release on recognizance The practice of releasing some defendants thought to be reliable prior to trial, simply on the basis of their promise to appear in court when scheduled.

Reliability The consistency and accuracy of a measure.

Reported crime Crime that comes to the attention of police.

Retribution Inflicting punishment on criminals to make them pay for their crimes.

Robbery The crime of taking money or goods by force or the threat of force.

Rule of law The principle that conduct is to be regulated according to fixed legal standards rather than by varying human judgments.

Saturation policing Use of massive police presence in a particular setting to try to deter crime.

Self-actualization The desire for self-fulfillment, to develop one's innate capabilities to their fullest.

Self-incrimination Testifying against oneself in a way that implicates the person testifying in a crime. The Constitution prohibits law enforcement authorities from forcing people to incriminate themselves.

Self-interest The wide-ranging set of personal needs, desires, and aspirations that motivate human behavior.

Sociological jurisprudence A philosophy of law that analyzes the impact of society on law and law on society.

Sociopathy A personality disorder found in some criminals, in which an individual displays unfavorable attitudes toward authority, negativism toward others, and suspicion.

Specific deterrence The extent to which punishment prevents those experiencing it from repeating their crimes in the future.

Stare decisis The principle that judges should be bound by precedents established in previous similar cases when they decide cases at hand (literally, "to stand by things that have been settled").

Surety bond A form of bail that allows defendants to post a certain amount of money or buy a bond from a bail bondsman to win their release prior to trial.

Territoriality The interest of organizations in protecting themselves from attempts of other organizations to invade their area of responsibility.

Time-series analysis The statistical techniques of examining changes in the magnitude of a phenomenon over time.

Total enforcement of the law Enforcing all criminal laws with unobstructed vigor and without concern for human rights.

Traditional diversion Informal settlement of crimes involving personal disputes, health-related problems, and minor property infractions. Patrol officers and assistant district attorneys use their discretion to handle the difficulties without use of legal sanctions.

Transactional immunity The promise given to witnesses by prosecutors that they will not be prosecuted for crimes that they discuss when testifying.

Trusty system The system of maintaining order in prisons by giving trusted inmates authority over other prisoners.

Type 1 error The error that occurs when a parole board releases an offender who subsequently relapses into crime.

Type 2 error The error that occurs when a parole board fails to release an offender who actually would not relapse into crime.

Uniform Crime Reports The F.B.I. summaries and nationwide totals of the reported crime figures submitted by local police departments.

United States attorney A prosecutor for the federal government.

Unobtrusive measures The acquisition of information about human behavior without the knowledge of the people under investigation.

Use immunity The promise given to witnesses by prosecutors that their testimony will not be used against them in court.

Validity The extent to which an instrument or technique measures what it is supposed to measure.

Venire The pool of jurors, ordinarily selected from voter registration lists, out of which particular juries are selected.

Victim-witness programs Programs that provide services to victims and witnesses in an attempt to get them to cooperate with law enforcement authorities.

Victimization surveys Surveys of samples of the population that ask respondents whether and how they have been victimized by crime.

Victimless crimes Criminal acts in which an assailant-victim relationship is more difficult to identify than in murder, robbery, theft, or most other common criminal actions. Such crimes usually are characterized by the exchange of sought-after goods (e.g., drugs) or services (e.g., gambling) by consenting adults rather than by one individual's seizure of another's property or injury to another's body. (Also called "morality crimes" or "folk crimes.")

Vigilantism Extralegal groups of citizens who take the law into their own hands and mete out punishment to presumed offenders.

Voir dire The interrogation of prospective jurors by judges or lawyers to determine whether they are biased and should therefore be eliminated by the judge from the jury.

White-collar crime Violation of legal codes in the course of activity in a legitimate occupation.

Work release A rehabilitation program that permits a prisoner to leave prison each day to go to a job.

INDEX

Note: Page numbers in italics refer to tables, figures, or illustrations